**PEARSON**  ALWAYS LEARNING

# The Prentice Hall Custom Program for CIS

## Heald Computer Applications 100: 2010 Update Supplemental Chapters

Custom Edition

**Heald**
COLLEGE
EST. 1863

Taken from:

*GO! with Microsoft® Outlook 2010 Comprehensive*
by Shelley Gaskin, Alicia Vargas, and Nancy Graviett

*GO! Getting Started with Microsoft® Windows® 7*
by Shelley Gaskin and Robert L. Ferrett

*GO! Getting Started with Basic Computer Concepts*
by Shelley Gaskin and Victor Giol

*GO! Getting Started with Internet Explorer 8*
by Shelley Gaskin and Rebecca Lawson

ISBN 10: 1-256-50837-3
ISBN 13: 978-1-256-50837-3

# Contents

Taken from: *GO! Getting Started with Microsoft® Windows® 7* by Shelley Gaskin and Robert L. Ferrett.

# Outlook 2010: Common Features

## Chapter 1 Introduction to Outlook 2010 and E-mail ......................................... 105

## Chapter 5    Organizing and Managing Outlook Information and Notes ..... 317

## Glossary ..... 365

Taken from: *GO! with Microsoft® Outlook 2010 Comprehensive* by Shelley Gaskin, Alicia Vargas, and Nancy Graviett.

# Basic Computer Concepts

Taken from: *GO! Getting Started with Basic Computer Concepts* by Shelley
Gaskin and Victor Giol.

# Internet Explorer 8

Taken from: *GO! Getting Started with Internet Explorer 8* by Shelley Gaskin and Rebecca Lawson.

# Getting Started with Windows 7

## OUTCOMES

At the end of this chapter, you will be able to:

## OBJECTIVES

Mastering these objectives will enable you to:

### PROJECT 1A
Familiarize Yourself with Windows 7.

1. Get Started with Windows 7 (p. 3)
2. Use the Start Menu and Manage Windows (p. 13)
3. Resize, Move, and Scroll Windows (p. 21)

### PROJECT 1B
Manage Files and Folders.

4. Create, Move, and Rename Folders (p. 29)
5. Copy, Move, Rename, and Delete Files (p. 35)
6. Find Files and Folders (p. 43)

Dmitriy Shironosov/Shutterstock

## In This Chapter

Windows 7 is the software that coordinates the activities of your computer's hardware. Windows 7 controls how your screen is displayed, how you open and close programs, and the start-up, shut-down, and navigation procedures for your computer. It is useful to become familiar with the basic features of the Microsoft Windows operating system, especially working with the Start button and the taskbar; opening, closing, moving, and resizing windows; and finding, saving, and managing files and folders.

# Project 1A Familiarize Yourself with Windows 7

## Project Activities

In Activities 1.01 through 1.09, you will explore the Windows 7 screen and practice navigating Windows 7. You will open, close, resize, and move windows, and you will open several windows at one time. The screens that you will be working with will look similar to those in Figure 1.1.

## Project Files

For Project 1A, you will need the following files:

No files are needed for this project

You will save your documents as

Lastname_Firstname_1A_Taskbar (not submitted)
Lastname_Firstname_1A_Windows (not submitted)
Lastname_Firstname_1A_WordPad

## Project Results

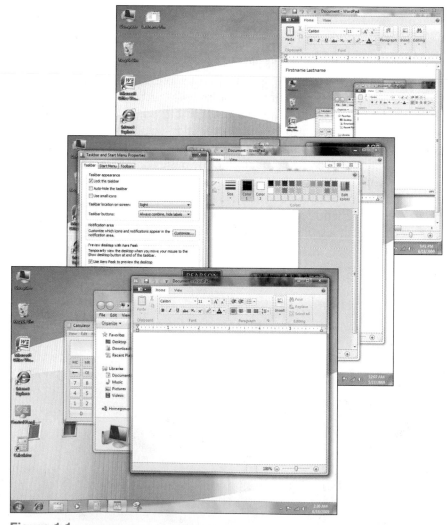

Figure 1.1

# Objective 1 | Get Started with Windows 7

Windows 7 is an *operating system*—software that controls the *hardware* attached to your computer, including its memory, disk drive space, attached devices such as printers and scanners, and the central processing unit. Windows 7 and earlier versions of Windows are similar; they use a *graphical user interface (GUI)*. A GUI uses graphics or pictures to represent commands and actions and lets you see document formatting on the screen as it will look when printed on paper. *Windows*, when spelled with a capital *W*, refers to the operating system that runs your computer.

Starting Windows is an automatic procedure; you turn on your computer, and after a few moments, the version of Windows installed on your computer displays. Some computers require that you log in, and some do not. Windows 7 is available in several versions: Starter, Home Premium, Professional, and Ultimate. For large institutions, there is also an Enterprise edition. For most tasks, the Home Premium, Professional, and Ultimate editions work the same. The Starter edition is typically used only on small notebook computers.

---

**Alert! | Does your screen differ?**

This chapter uses Windows 7 Ultimate edition, and there may be some differences in the look of this edition and the other editions. More importantly, the look of the screen will depend largely on the setting options that have been selected for your computer, the shape of your monitor, and on the type of hardware installed in your computer—especially the video card and memory.

---

## Activity 1.01 | Exploring the Windows 7 Desktop

In this activity, you will examine the different components of the Windows 7 desktop.

**1** Turn on your computer and wait for the Windows program to display, or follow the log-on instructions required for the computer you are using. For example, you might have to click a name on a Welcome screen, or enter a user ID or password. If this is your home computer and you are the only user, it is likely that you need do nothing except wait for a few moments.

> The Windows *desktop*, which is the working area of the Windows 7 screen, displays. The screen look will vary, depending on which version of Windows you are using and what you have on your own desktop.

**2** Compare your Windows desktop with Figure 1.2 and then take a moment to study the Windows elements identified in the table in Figure 1.3. Your icons may vary.

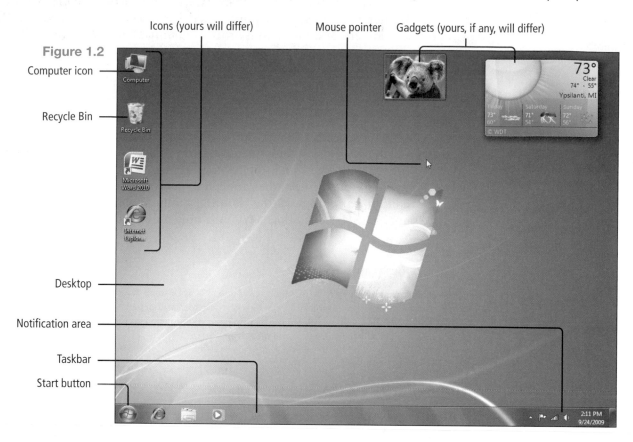

Figure 1.2

Figure 1.3

## Windows Screen Elements

| Screen Element | Description |
|---|---|
| Command bar | A toolbar that offers easy access to settings or features. |
| Computer icon | An icon that represents the computer on which you are working, and that provides access to the drives, folders, and files on your computer. |
| Desktop | The working area of the Windows 7 screen, consisting of program icons, a taskbar, gadgets (optional), and a Start button. |
| Gadgets | Small dynamic programs that run on the desktop, such as a clock, a stock market ticker, or a weather forecast. |
| Icon | A graphic representation of an object that you can select and open, such as a drive, a disk, a folder, a document, or a program. |
| Mouse pointer | The arrow, I-beam, or other symbol that moves when you move the mouse or other pointing device, and that indicates a location or position on your screen—also called the *pointer*. |
| Notification area | The area on the right side of the taskbar, formerly called the *system tray* or *status area*, where the clock and system notifications display. These notifications keep you informed about active processes. |
| Recycle Bin | A temporary storage area for files that you have deleted from hard drives. Files can be either recovered or permanently removed from the Recycle Bin. |
| Start button | The button on the left side of the taskbar that is used to start programs, change system settings, find Windows help, search for programs or documents, or shut down the computer. |
| Taskbar | Displays the Start button and icons for any open programs. The taskbar also displays shortcut buttons for other programs. |

**3** On the left side of the taskbar, *click*—press the left mouse button one time—the **Windows Explorer** button. Compare your screen with Figure 1.4, and then take a moment to study the *Windows Explorer* window elements in the table in Figure 1.5. *Windows Explorer* is a program used to create and manage folders, and to copy, move, sort, and delete files. If the Windows Explorer button does not display on your taskbar, click the Start button, click All Programs, click Accessories, and then click Windows Explorer. If the Menu bar does not display, on the Toolbar, click the Organize button, point to Layout, and then click Menu bar.

The Windows Explorer window displays. When you click the Windows Explorer button, the window opens with *Libraries* selected in the Navigation pane and displayed in the file list. A *window*—spelled with a lowercase *w*—is a rectangular box that displays information or a program. When a window is open, the name of the window is sometimes displayed in the title bar.

---

**Alert! | Does your screen differ?**

Because the configuration of your Windows Explorer window depends on how it was last used, your window may not display all of the elements shown in Figure 1.4, in particular the Menu bar, Details pane, Navigation pane, and Search pane. A Preview pane may display on the right side of the window, and the window may cover the entire screen.

---

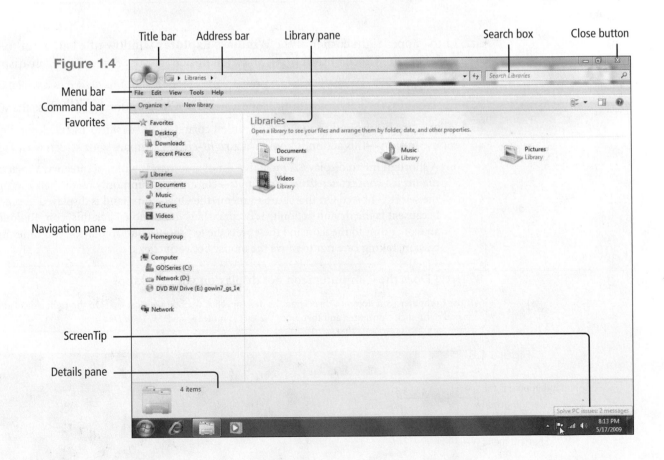

Figure 1.4

## Parts of a Window

| Screen Element | Description |
|---|---|
| Address bar | A toolbar that displays the organizational path to the active file, folder, or window. |
| Close button | A button in a title bar that closes a window or a Program |
| Details pane | Displays details about the drive, folder, or file selected in the file list. |
| Favorites | The upper part of the Navigation pane that displays favorite destinations associated with the current user. |
| File list | Displays the contents of the current folder or library. |
| Library pane | Displays above the file list when a Library is selected in the Navigation pane. |
| Menu bar | The bar near the top of a window that lists the names of menu categories. |
| Navigation pane | The pane on the left side of the Windows Explorer window that contains personal Favorites, Libraries, access to personal files and folders, and other items. |
| ScreenTip | A small box, activated by pointing to a button or other screen object, that displays the name of or further information about the screen element. |
| Search box | A box in which you type a search word or phrase. |
| Title bar | The area at the top of a window that includes the Minimize, Maximize, and Close buttons. The title bar also often contains the name of the program and the name of the open document. |
| Toolbar | A row of buttons that activates commands with a single click of the left mouse button. |

Figure 1.5

**4** In the upper right corner of the **Windows Explorer** window title bar, point to, but do not click, the **Close** button ![](close button), and then notice that the ScreenTip *Close* displays.

> A *ScreenTip* is a small note that provides information about or describes a screen element.

**5** Click—press the left mouse button one time—the **Close** button ![](close button) to close the window.

**6** Point to the **Computer** icon in the upper left corner of the desktop and click the right mouse button—this action is known as a *right-click*. Compare your screen with Figure 1.6.

> A shortcut menu displays. A *menu* is a list of commands within a category. *Shortcut menus* list *context-sensitive commands*—commands commonly used when working with the selected object. On this shortcut menu, the Open command is displayed in bold because it is the default action that occurs when you double-click this icon. To *double-click* an icon, point to the icon and then press the left mouse button quickly two times in succession, taking care not to move the mouse between clicks.

> **Alert! | Does the Computer icon not display on your desktop?**
>
> If the Computer icon does not display on the desktop, click the Start button . On the right side of the Start menu, right-click Computer, and then from the shortcut menu, click *Show on Desktop*.

Figure 1.6

Command in bold is the default action

Shortcut menu

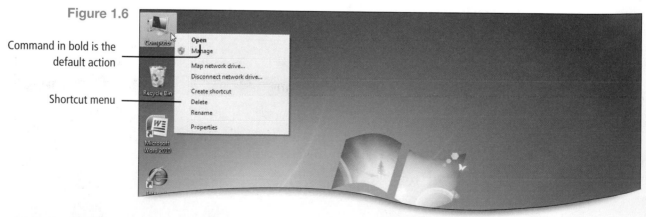

**7** From the displayed shortcut menu, point to **Open** to select the command, and then click one time. Compare your screen with Figure 1.7.

The Windows Explorer window displays, but this time the pane on the right is a file list, not a Libraries pane. The *file list* displays the contents of the item selected in the Navigation pane; in this case, the fixed and removable drives attached to the computer. A *drive* is an area of storage that is formatted with the Windows file system, and that has a drive letter such as C, D, E, and so on. The main drive inside your computer is referred to as the *hard drive*—there may be more than one hard drive in a computer. Also, network drives may display here.

Figure 1.7

Fixed local drives

Removable drives

File list

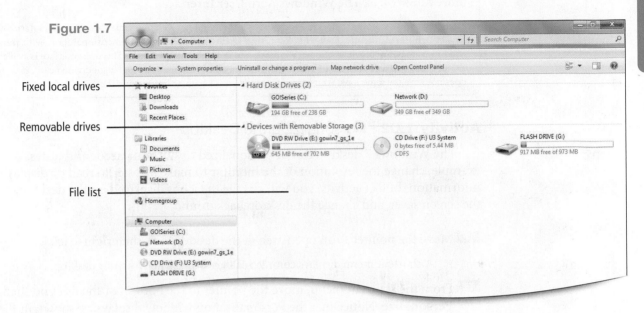

**8** Near the top of the **file list**, point to and then click the disk drive labeled (**C:**), and then notice the **Details** pane. Compare your screen with Figure 1.8.

Figure 1.8

Drive C: selected

Details of drive C: (your
drive name may vary)

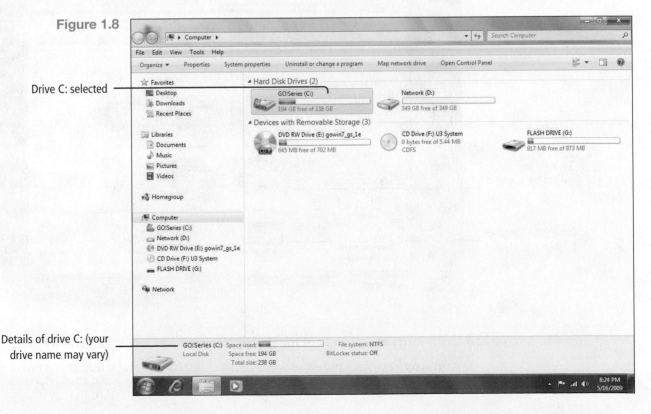

> **Alert! | Is your Details pane missing?**
>
> Recall that the configuration of your Windows Explorer window may vary, depending on how it was last configured. If your Details pane does not display, in the Command bar, click Organize, point to Layout, and then click *Details pane*.

**9** In the **Windows Explorer** window title bar, click the **Close** button .

> **More Knowledge | The Windows Aero User Interface**
>
> The screen you see in the figures in this book uses the Windows Aero user interface. *Windows Aero*—which is an acronym for *A*uthentic, *E*nergetic, *R*eflective, *O*pen—features a three-dimensional look, with transparent window frames, live previews of open windows, and multiple color schemes. This user interface is available with all but the most basic versions of Windows 7, but requires extra memory and a good video card. If your screen does not have the same look, your computer may not be capable of displaying the Aero interface.

## Activity 1.02 | Personalizing the Desktop

The Windows 7 desktop can be personalized to suit your needs and tastes. You can, for example, change the resolution of the monitor to make it easier to read or display more information. In this activity, you will change the icons displayed on the desktop, change the screen saver, and change the desktop background.

**1** Move the pointer to an open area of the desktop, and then right-click.

A shortcut menu displays commands that are available for your desktop.

**2** From the shortcut menu, move the pointer to the bottom of the list, and then click **Personalize**. Notice that the Personalization window displays, as shown in Figure 1.9.

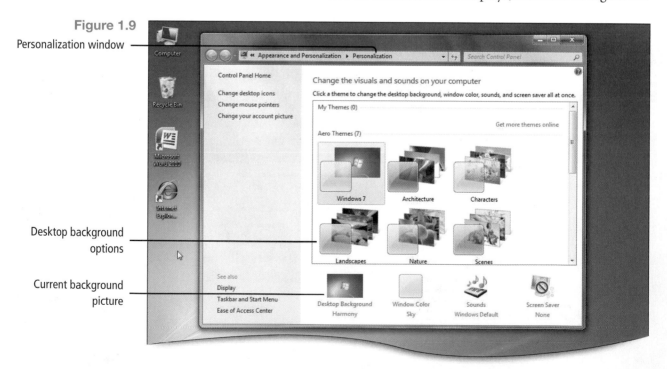

Figure 1.9
Personalization window
Desktop background options
Current background picture

**3** In the lower right corner of the **Personalization** window, click **Screen Saver**.

A *screen saver* is a picture or animation that displays on your screen after a preset period of computer inactivity.

**4** In the **Screen Saver Settings** dialog box, click the **Screen saver box arrow**. From the displayed list, click **Ribbons**, and then compare your screen with Figure 1.10.

A *dialog box* is a box that asks you to make a decision about an individual object or topic. The Ribbons screen saver is selected, and a preview displays near the top of the dialog box. The default length of inactivity to trigger the screen saver is 1 minute.

Figure 1.10

Preview of Ribbons screen saver

Screen saver box arrow

Selected screen saver

Period of inactivity before screen saver displays

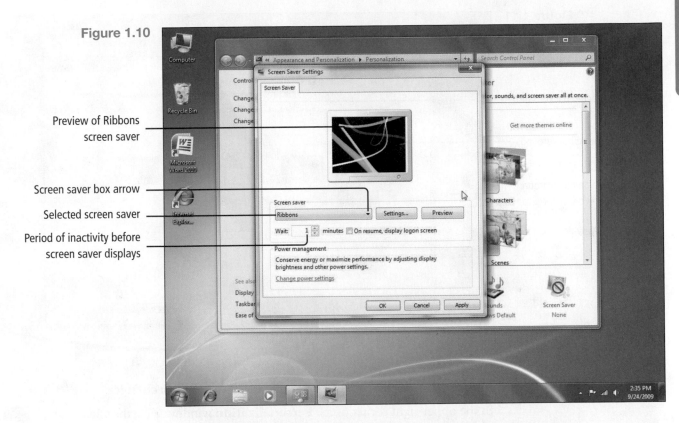

**5** In the **Screen Saver Settings** dialog box, click the **Preview** button to preview a full-screen version of the screen saver. When you are through, move the mouse to turn off the full-screen screen saver preview. If you want to turn on the screen saver, click **OK**; otherwise, click **Cancel**.

**6** In the left panel of the **Personalization** window, click **Change desktop icons**.

**7** At the top of the **Desktop Icon Settings** dialog box, select—click to add a check mark to—the **Control Panel** check box. Click **OK** to save your changes and close the Desktop Icon Settings dialog box. Notice that a Control Panel icon is added to the left side of the desktop.

**8** At the bottom of the **Personalization** window, click **Desktop Background**. Click the **up arrow** ▲ at the top of the scroll bar several times to move to the top of the backgrounds list. Under **Architecture**, click the third picture—the picture of the white building. The new background previews on the screen, as shown in Figure 1.11.

The *desktop background* is the picture, pattern, or color that displays on the desktop.

Figure 1.11

Selected background

Architecture backgrounds

Selected background previewed on the desktop

New desktop icon

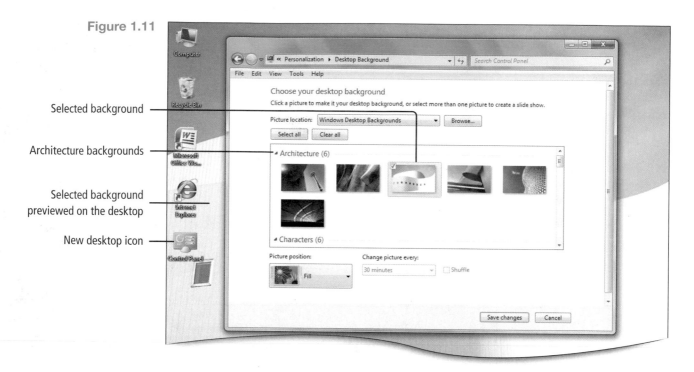

**9** At the bottom of the **Personalization** window, click **Save changes**.

**10** In the upper right corner of the **Personalization** window, click the **Close** button ▣, and then compare your screen with Figure 1.12.

Figure 1.12

New background applied to desktop

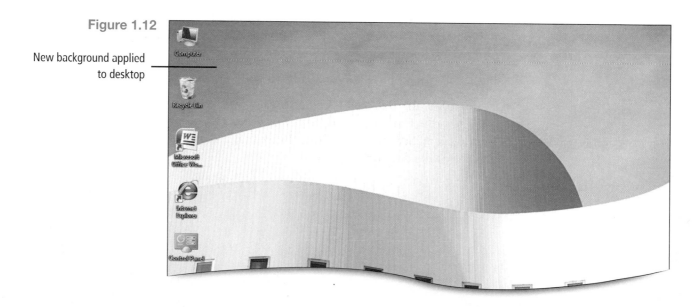

## Activity 1.03 | Adding and Removing Gadgets

*Gadgets* are used to display dynamic programs such as a currency converter, a calendar, a stock market ticker, or a clock. You can move the gadgets anywhere on the screen, and you can modify or resize most of them.

**1** In an open area of the desktop, right-click to display a shortcut menu. On the shortcut menu, click **Gadgets**. Compare your screen with Figure 1.13.

Figure 1.13

Gadgets available on your computer ————

Online link to other gadgets ————

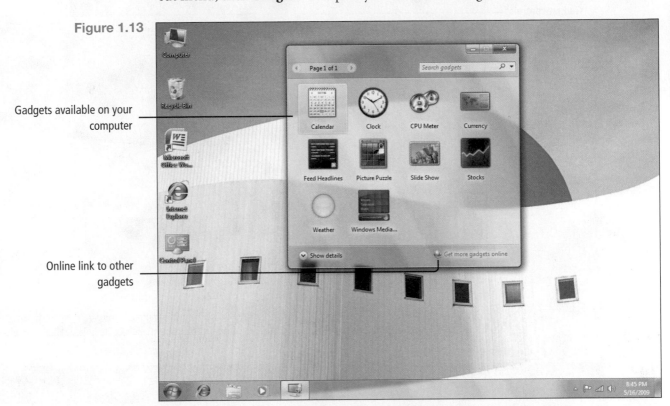

**2** In the **Gadgets** window, double-click the **Weather** gadget. In the upper right corner of the **Gadgets** dialog box, click the **Close** button .

> **Alert! | Are there already gadgets on your desktop?**
>
> Your desktop may contain one or more gadgets, including a Weather gadget. In fact, you can have more than one of the same gadgets on the desktop at a time. For example, if you are interested in the weather in two different locations, you can add two weather gadgets to the desktop and keep an eye on two locations at one time.

**3** Point to the **Weather** gadget. Notice that a four-button tool set, called the *gadget controls*, displays on the right, as shown in Figure 1.14. Take a moment to study the functions of the buttons, as shown in the table in Figure 1.15.

Figure 1.14

Weather gadget ——

Gadget controls ——

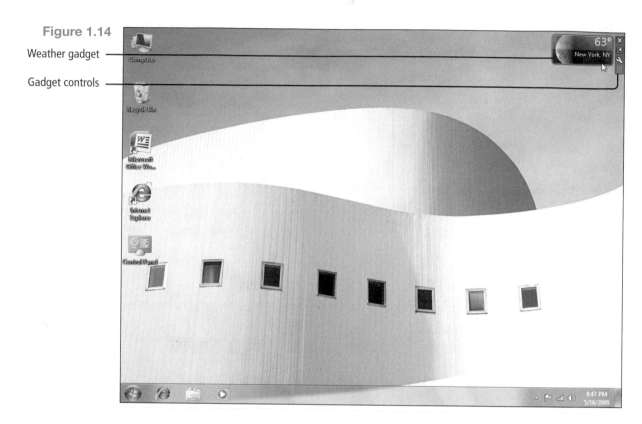

## Gadget Controls

| Button Name | Button | Description |
|---|---|---|
| Close | ☒ | Closes the gadget. |
| Larger size | ◪ | Increases the size of the gadget; occupies the same position as the Smaller size button. |
| Smaller size | ◪ | Decreases the size of the gadget; occupies the same position as the Larger size button. |
| Options | ⚲ | Displays different settings for each gadget. |
| Drag gadget | ▦ | Used to move the gadget anywhere on the desktop. |

Figure 1.15

**4** Point to the **Weather** gadget, click the **Larger size** button ⬜, and then click the **Options** button 🔍. In the **Select current location** box, type **Madison, Wisconsin** and then press Enter. Click **OK**, and then compare your screen with Figure 1.16.

**Figure 1.16**

Weather gadget enlarged

Selected city

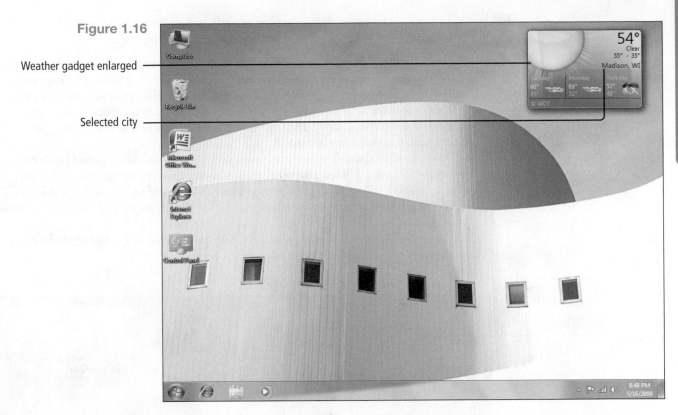

**5** In an open area of the desktop, right-click to display a shortcut menu. On the shortcut menu, click **Gadgets**. In the **Gadgets** window, double-click the **Slide Show** gadget, and then double-click the **Slide Show** gadget again. In the upper right corner of the **Gadgets** dialog box, click the **Close** button 🔳.

Two additional gadgets are added to the desktop.

**6** Point to either of the **Slide Show** gadgets, and then in the gadget controls, click the **Close** button ❌ to remove the gadget from the desktop.

**7** Point to the remaining **Slide Show** gadget, point to the **Drag gadget** button ▦, and then drag the gadget near the upper edge of the desktop. Notice that as you move near the top of the desktop, the gadget snaps into position, slightly below the top of the desktop.

## Objective 2 | Use the Start Menu and Manage Windows

Some programs and documents are available from the desktop. For most things, however, you will turn to the Start menu. The *Start menu* gives you access to all of the programs on your computer, and also enables you to change the way Windows operates, to access and configure your network, and to get help and support when it is needed. After you have opened several programs, you can rearrange and resize the program windows to fit your needs.

## Activity 1.04 | Using the Start Menu

In this activity, you will use the Start menu to open a program, and also to open the Windows Explorer window.

**Another Way**

Press the Start button on your keyboard—a key with the Windows logo, often found to the left of the spacebar.

**1** In the lower left corner of the screen, on the left end of the taskbar, point to and then click the **Start** button. Compare your screen with Figure 1.17.

The left side of the Start menu contains four areas. At the bottom is the Search box, which enables you to search for files or programs. Above the Search box is the *All Programs* command, which takes you to a list of all of the programs you can access on the computer. *All Programs* displays an arrow, which indicates that a submenu is available for a command. A *submenu* is a second-level menu; the arrow indicates that more items can be found related to the menu command.

Above *All Programs* is an area that contains the most recently opened programs. On the upper left is the *pinned programs area*—an area reserved for programs that you want to display permanently, although you can also remove programs from this area. To remove a program from the pinned list, right-click the program, and then click *Remove from this list*.

On the top of the right side are links to your personal folders, while the bottom sections give you access to computer management features.

Figure 1.17

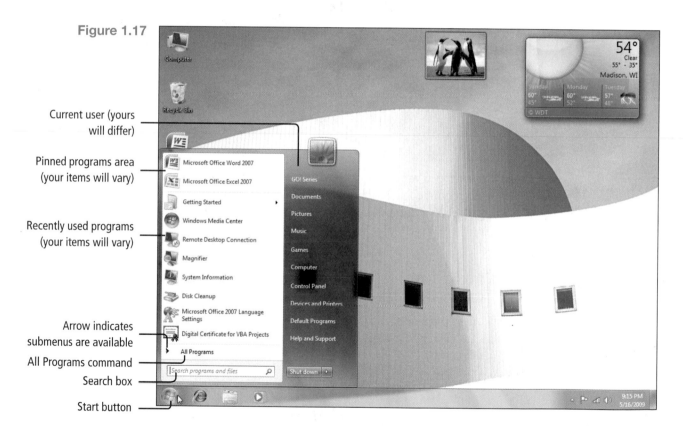

Current user (yours will differ)

Pinned programs area (your items will vary)

Recently used programs (your items will vary)

Arrow indicates submenus are available

All Programs command

Search box

Start button

---

**Alert! | Is your taskbar hidden?**

Some computers are set up to hide the taskbar when it is not in use. This adds more workspace to the desktop, and is particularly useful on portable computers with small screens. When the taskbar is hidden, move the pointer to the bottom of the screen, and it will display. However, in this chapter, it is assumed that the taskbar is displayed at all times.

To keep the taskbar displayed on your screen, find an open area on the taskbar, right-click, and then from the shortcut menu, click Properties. In the Taskbar and Start Menu Properties dialog box, on the Taskbar tab, locate the *Auto-hide the taskbar* check box. If the taskbar is hidden, there will be a check mark in the check box. To remove the Auto-hide feature, click the check box one time to clear—remove—the check mark.

**2** From the **Start** menu, point to, but do not click, the **All Programs** command. Compare your screen with Figure 1.18.

The All Programs submenu displays—displaying a portion of the contents found within All Programs—and the *All Programs* command changes to a *Back* command. Your menu will differ from the one shown in Figure 1.18 because your computer will have different programs installed. Folders in the menu contain more programs or more folders or some of each.

Figure 1.18

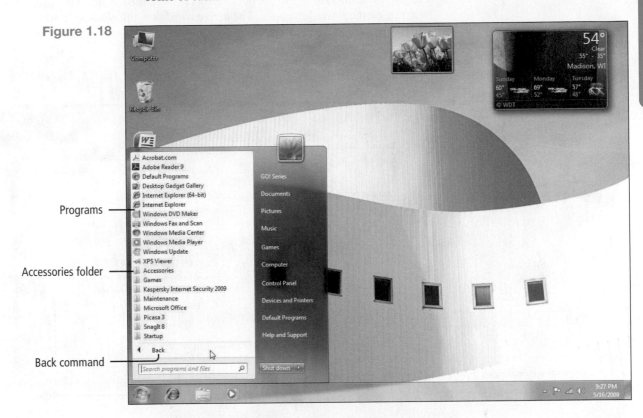

Programs

Accessories folder

Back command

**3** Click the **Accessories** folder, and then from the displayed list, click **Calculator**. Notice that the *window name*—*Calculator*—displays in the title bar.

The Calculator window opens, and the Start menu closes. You can access the Accessories programs from the Start menu and use them while you are using other programs. For example, you might want to make a quick calculation while you are typing a document in Microsoft Word. You can open the calculator, make the calculation, and then place the result in your Word document without closing Word.

**4** Click the **Start** button again, and near the middle of the right side of the **Start menu**, click **Computer**. If the Windows Explorer window fills the entire screen, near the right side of the title bar, click the Restore Down button . Compare your screen with Figure 1.19.

> The Windows Explorer window opens, but the Calculator window is either partially or completely hidden, as shown in Figure 1.19. The buttons in the taskbar, however, indicate that two programs are open. The buttons that are outlined indicate the programs that have one or more windows open. The *active window*—the window in which the pointer movements, commands, or text entry occur when two or more windows are open—displays a darker title bar.

Figure 1.19

Darker title bar indicates the active window

Window name in title bar

Computer window hides most of the Calculator window

Calculator window button

Computer window button

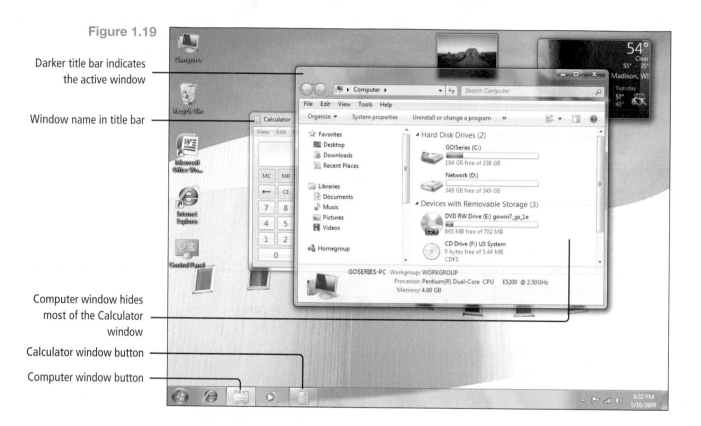

**5** Click the **Start** button , and then click in the **Search programs and files** box. Type **wordpad** and press Enter. If the WordPad window fills the entire screen, near the right side of the title bar, click the Restore Down button .

> If you type a program name into the Start menu Search box, the program will open, which enables you to quickly open programs rather than try to find them. *WordPad* is a simple word processing program that comes with Windows 7.

### Activity 1.05 | Adding Shortcuts to the Start Menu, Desktop, and Taskbar

There are programs that you will seldom use, and there are programs that you will use all the time. To make frequently used programs easily and quickly available, you can pin a shortcut to the program in the Start menu *pinned programs area*, or you can add a shortcut icon to the desktop or pin the program to the taskbar.

**1** Click the **Start** button , point to **All Programs**, click **Accessories**, and then right-click **Calculator**.

**2** From the displayed shortcut menu, click **Pin to Start Menu**. At the bottom of the **Start menu**, click the **Back** button, and notice that *Calculator* has been added to the pinned programs area, as shown in Figure 1.20.

Figure 1.20

Calculator program pinned to Start menu

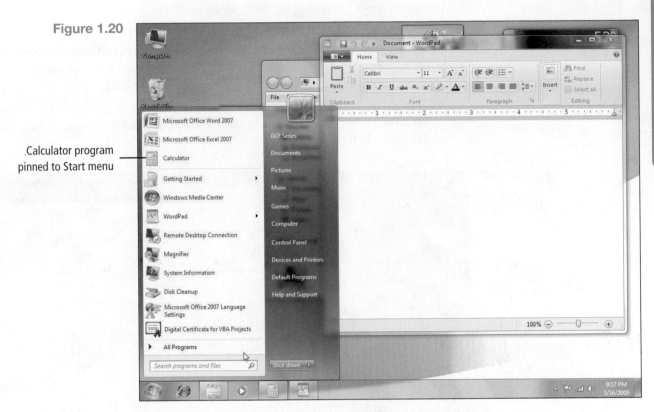

**3** Click the **Start** button , point to **All Programs**, if necessary click **Accessories**, right-click **Calculator**, and then point to—but do not click—**Send to**. Notice the available commands on the *Send to* list, as shown in Figure 1.21.

Figure 1.21

Shortcut menu

*Send to* command

Desktop (create shortcut) command

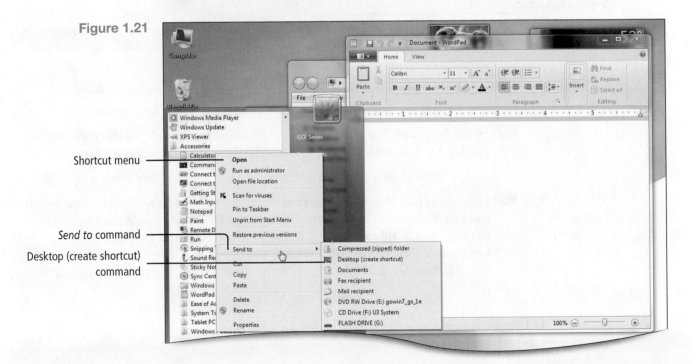

**4** From the displayed shortcut menu, click **Desktop (create shortcut)**, and then click in any open area of the desktop.

A Calculator icon is placed on the desktop. The shortcut icon has a small blue arrow in the lower left corner. Depending on the windows you have open, and the number of icons on your desktop, your Calculator shortcut icon may be hidden.

**5** Click the **Start** button ⊕, point to **All Programs**, if necessary click **Accessories**, right-click **Snipping Tool**, and then click **Pin to Taskbar**. Click in an open area on the desktop, and then compare your screen with Figure 1.22.

You can use *Snipping Tool* to capture a screen shot, or *snip*, of the entire screen or of any object on your screen, and then make notes on, save, or share the image. You will use this tool throughout this chapter.

Figure 1.22

Calculator shortcut icon added to the desktop

Snipping Tool added to taskbar

**6** On the taskbar, click the **Snipping Tool** button ✂.

The Snipping Tool window displays, and the rest of the screen appears faded.

**7** In the **Snipping Tool** window, click the arrow to the right of the **New** button to display a list of potential snips. From the list, click **Full-screen Snip**.

The entire screen is captured, and displays in the Snipping Tool window.

**8** Near the top of the **Snipping Tool** window, click the **Save Snip** button 💾. In the **Save As** dialog box, in the left column, click **Desktop** to save the snip to the desktop. In the **File name** box, using your own last and first names, type **Lastname_Firstname_1A_Taskbar** Use the underscore between words—hold down (Shift) and press the dash (-) button to the right of the numbers near the top of the keyboard. Click in the **Save as type** box, and then from the menu, click **JPEG file**. Compare your screen with Figure 1.23.

Figure 1.23

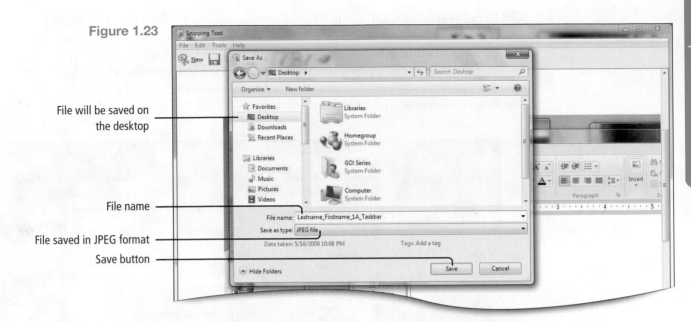

File will be saved on the desktop

File name

File saved in JPEG format

Save button

> ⑨ At the bottom of the **Save As** dialog box, click **Save** to save the snip on the desktop.

> ⑩ In the upper right corner of the **Snipping Tool** window, click the **Close** button. Notice that your file displays as an icon on the desktop.

## Activity 1.06 | Minimizing, Maximizing, and Restoring a Window

You can *maximize* a window, which enlarges the window to occupy the entire screen, and you can *restore* a window, which reduces the window to the size it was before being maximized. You can also *minimize* a window, which reduces the window to a button on the taskbar, removing it from the screen entirely without actually closing it. When you need to view the window again, you can click the taskbar button to bring it back into view.

> ① Click anywhere in the **WordPad** window to make it the active window, and then examine the three buttons in the upper right corner of the window. The left button is the **Minimize** button, the middle button is the **Maximize** button, and the right button is the **Close** button.

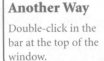

**Another Way**

Double-click in the bar at the top of the window.

> ② In the **WordPad** window, click the **Maximize** button. Notice that the window expands to cover the entire screen, and the Maximize button changes to a Restore Down button, as shown in Figure 1.24.

Figure 1.24

Maximize button changes to Restore Down button

**Another Way**

Double-click in the title bar at the top of the window.

➌ In the **WordPad** window, click the **Restore Down** button 🔲. Notice that the window resumes its former shape, size, and location.

➍ In the **WordPad** window, click the **Minimize** button 🔲. In the taskbar, click the **Calculator** button to make it the active window, and then in the **Calculator** window, click the **Minimize** button 🔲 to display the Windows Explorer window. Notice that the Windows Explorer window now displays as the active window. Notice also that the two programs that you minimized are not closed—their buttons are still outlined on the taskbar, as shown in Figure 1.25.

Figure 1.25

WordPad window minimized to taskbar

Calculator window minimized to taskbar

➎ In the taskbar, click the **Calculator** button to restore the Calculator window. Then, click the **WordPad** button to restore the WordPad window.

---

**More Knowledge** | Keeping More Than One Program Window Open at a Time

The ability to keep more than one window open at a time will become more useful as you become more familiar with Microsoft Office. For example, if you want to take information from two word processing documents to create a third document, you can open all three documents and use the taskbar to move among them, copying and pasting text from one document to another. Or, you could copy a chart from Excel and paste it into Word or take a table of data and paste it into PowerPoint. You can even have the same document open in two windows.

---

## Activity 1.07 | Hiding and Displaying Windows

There is a shortcut that enables you to temporarily hide all open windows and view the desktop, and also a way to display just one window and hide the rest.

**1** Move the pointer to the lower-right corner of the desktop to point to the **Show desktop** button. Notice that all open windows become transparent to give you a *peek* at the desktop—all desktop items display, as shown in Figure 1.26.

This only works if the Aero interface is turned on.

Figure 1.26

Outlines of transparent windows

Show desktop button

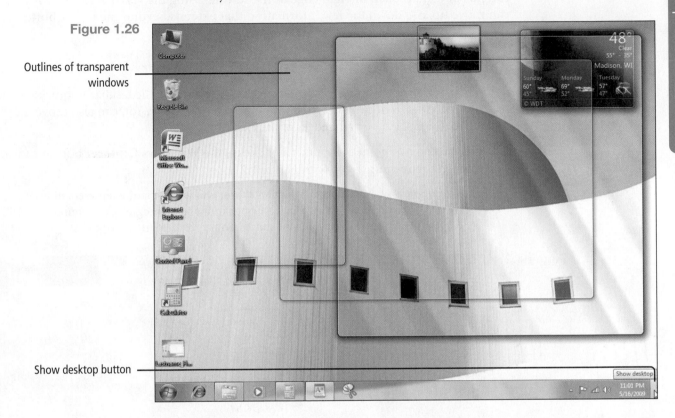

**2** Move the pointer away from the **Show desktop** button and notice that the windows display again.

**3** Point to the **Show desktop** button, but this time click the button. Notice that all open windows are hidden, and no outlines display.

**4** Click the **Show desktop** button again to display all open windows.

**5** In the taskbar, locate and click the **Calculator** button to make the Calculator the active window. Notice that the background of the Calculator icon on the taskbar is brighter than the icons for the other open windows.

**6** Point to the **Calculator** title bar, hold down the left mouse button, and then *shake*—move the window back and forth quickly—the window.

All windows except the shaken window are hidden.

**7** Shake the **Calculator** window again to display all of the open windows.

## Objective 3 | Resize, Move, and Scroll Windows

When a window opens on your screen, it generally opens in the same size and shape as it was when last used. If you are using more than one window at a time, you can increase or decrease the size of a window, or move a window so that you can see the information you need.

As you work within a program, the information you create will likely grow larger than the screen can display. When the information in a window extends beyond the right or lower edges of the window, scroll bars display at the bottom and right. Using the *horizontal scroll bar*, you can move left and right to view information that extends beyond the left or right edge of the screen. Using the *vertical scroll bar*, you can move up and down to view information that extends beyond the top or bottom of the screen.

### Activity 1.08 | Customizing and Using the Taskbar

When you have a number of windows open, you can use the taskbar to quickly review the contents of each document to determine which one to use. You can also move the taskbar to the top, left, or right edges of the desktop.

**1** On the taskbar, point to—but do not click—the **Windows Explorer** button , and then compare your screen with Figure 1.27.

> A thumbnail of the window displays. A *thumbnail* is a miniature representation of a window or a file. If two documents are open in the same program, two thumbnails will display. The Aero interface must be turned on for this feature to work.

Figure 1.27

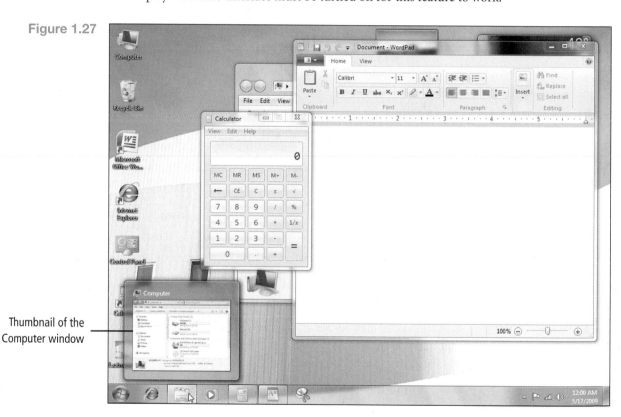

Thumbnail of the Computer window

**2** On the taskbar, point to—but do not click—the **Calculator** button. Move the pointer and point to the **WordPad** button.

**3** Click the **Start** button , point to **All Programs**, click **Accessories**, and then click **Paint**.

> If the Paint window is maximized, click the Restore Down button .

> *Paint* is a simple drawing program that comes with Windows 7. Four programs are now open, and there are icons on the taskbar for other unopened programs, such as Snipping Tool.

**4** Hold down the ⌨Alt⌨ key, and then press the ⌨Tab⌨ key. Compare your screen with Figure 1.28.

> The screen displays thumbnails of the windows that are open, including the desktop; if the Aero interface is not turned on, only the program icons display.

**Figure 1.28**

⌨Alt⌨ + ⌨Tab⌨ enables you to move between open windows

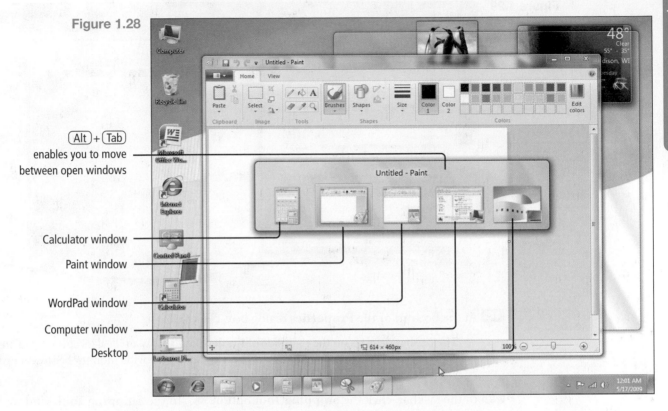

Calculator window

Paint window

WordPad window

Computer window

Desktop

**5** Continue to hold down ⌨Alt⌨, but press ⌨Tab⌨ several times. Notice that the selected window moves from left to right in the list of thumbnails.

> When you release the ⌨Alt⌨ key, the window in the active thumbnail becomes the active window on the desktop.

**6** Move to the **Calculator** window, and then release the ⌨Alt⌨ button.

**7** On the taskbar, point to the **Windows Explorer** window, and then right-click.

> A *jump list* displays frequent destinations you might want to jump to from the Windows Explorer window. If you display a jump list for a program such as a word processor or a spreadsheet, a list of recently edited files also displays, enabling you to quickly open any desired files.

**8** Right-click an open area of the taskbar, and then from the shortcut menu, click **Properties**.

**9** In the **Properties** dialog box, be sure the Taskbar tab is selected. Under **Taskbar appearance**, click the **Taskbar location on screen arrow**, and then click **Right**. Compare your screen with Figure 1.29.

Figure 1.29

Taskbar tab

Screen location of the taskbar

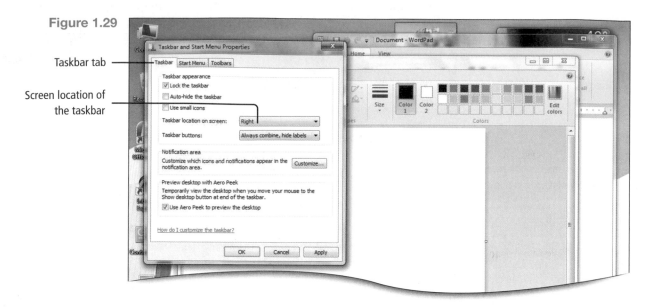

**10** At the bottom of the **Properties** dialog box, click **OK**.

> The taskbar displays on the right side of the desktop. This is an ideal location if you are using a widescreen monitor or a portable computer with a wide monitor because it gives you more vertical space on the screen for your documents.

**11** In the taskbar, click the **Snipping Tool** button 🖈. In the **Snipping Tool** window, click the arrow to the right of the **New** button to display a list of potential snips. From the list, click **Full-screen Snip**.

**12** Near the top of the **Snipping Tool** window, click the **Save Snip** button 🖫. In the **Save As** dialog box, in the left column, click **Desktop**. In the **File name** box, using your own last and first names, type **Lastname_Firstname_1A_Windows** Click in the **Save as type** box and be sure **JPEG file** is selected.

**13** At the bottom of the **Save As** dialog box, click **Save** to save the snip on the desktop.

**14** In the upper right corner of the **Snipping Tool** window, click the **Close** button [✕]. Notice that your file displays as an icon on the desktop.

**15** Use the procedure you practiced in Steps 8 through 10 to return the taskbar to the bottom of the desktop.

## Activity 1.09 | Resizing, Moving, Scrolling, and Closing Windows

In the following activity, you will resize and move the Windows Explorer window. You will also use the vertical scroll bar in the window to view information that does not fit in the window.

**1** On the right end of the taskbar, click the **Show desktop** button to hide all of the windows.

**2** On the taskbar, click the **Windows Explorer** button 📁 to display the Windows Explorer window.

**3** Move the pointer to the lower right corner of the window to display the diagonal resize pointer, 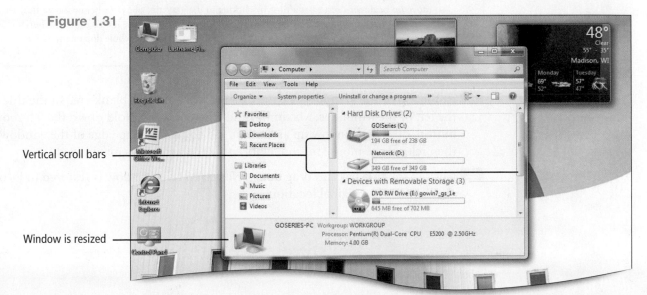 and then compare your screen with Figure 1.30.

When the mouse pointer is in this shape, you can use it to change the size and shape of a window.

**Figure 1.30**

Diagonal resize pointer ——

Show desktop button ——

**4** Hold down the left mouse button, **drag**—move the mouse while holding down the left mouse button and then release at the appropriate time—diagonally up and to the left until you see a scroll bar at the right side of the window, and then release the mouse button. Adjust as necessary so that the Windows Explorer window is the approximate size of the one shown in Figure 1.31.

Notice that a vertical scroll bar displays on the right side of the window, and another one displays on the right side of the Navigation pane. A scroll bar is added to the window whenever the window contains more than it can display.

**Figure 1.31**

Vertical scroll bars ——

Window is resized ——

**5** In the **Windows Explorer** window **file list**, at the bottom of the vertical scroll bar, point to the **down arrow** ▼ and click two times. Notice that information at the bottom of the window scrolls up so that you can see the information that was not visible before, as shown in Figure 1.32.

Figure 1.32

Vertical scroll bar up arrow

Scroll box

Vertical scroll bar down arrow

**6** On the same scroll bar, point to the **up arrow** ▲, and then click and hold down the left mouse button.

> The window scrolls to the top of the file list. You can click and hold down the left mouse button on the up or down scroll arrows to scroll rapidly through a long list of information.

**7** Point to the scroll box, and then drag it downward.

> The *scroll box* displays within the vertical and horizontal scroll bars and provides a visual indication of your location within the information displayed. It can also be used with the mouse to reposition the information on the screen. Moving the scroll box gives you more control as you scroll because you can see the information as it moves up or down in the window.

---

**Note** | Moving a Screen at a Time

You can move up or down a screen at a time by clicking in the gray area above or below the vertical scroll box. You can also move left or right a screen at a time by clicking in the area to the left or right of a horizontal scroll box. The size of the scroll box indicates the relative size of the display to the whole document. If the scroll box is small, it means that the display is a small portion of the entire document.

---

**8** At the top of the **Windows Explorer** window, point to a blank area in the title bar to the left of the Minimize, Maximize, and Close buttons. Hold down the left mouse button, drag the window up as far as it will go past the top edge of the window, and then release the mouse button. Notice that the window is maximized.

**9** Click in the title bar and drag down. Notice that the window is restored to its original size, but not its original location.

**10** In the **Windows Explorer** window title bar, click the **Close** button ![x]. In the taskbar, right-click the **Paint** button ![paint], and then click **Close window**. Use the same technique to close the **Calculator** window ![calc].

**11** In the taskbar, click the **WordPad** button to display the WordPad window. Using the title bar, drag the WordPad window to the right edge of the desktop until it changes shape to occupy the right half of the desktop, and then release the mouse button.

> You can use this method to open two windows side by side if you drag a second window to the left border.

**12** Click in the WordPad window, type your first and last names, and then press ⏎. Locate the **Lastname_Firstname_1A_Taskbar** icon on the desktop—you may have to click the two snip files to find the correct file.

**13** Drag the **Lastname_Firstname_1A_Taskbar** file to the line below your name in the WordPad document, and then release the mouse button. Compare your screen with Figure 1.33.

> The contents of the file you dragged are pasted into the WordPad document.

**Figure 1.33**

Your name ————

File dragged into WordPad document ————

File icon ————

**14** Drag the **Lastname_Firstname_1A_Windows** file to the line below the figure you just inserted into the WordPad document. In the WordPad title bar, click the **Save** button ![save].

**15** In the **Save As** dialog box, in the **Navigation** pane, click **Desktop**. In the **File name** box, type **Lastname_Firstname_1A_WordPad** and then click **Save**.

**16** If you are to print your document, hold down Ctrl and then press P to display the Print dialog box. Be sure the correct printer is selected, and then click **Print**. If you are to submit this document electronically, follow your instructor's directions.

**17 Close** ![x] the WordPad window.

**End You have completed Project 1A** ————

# Project 1B Manage Files and Folders

## Project Activities

In Activities 1.10 through 1.18 you will create folders, and then copy, move, rename, and delete files and folders. You will add tags to files and use the Windows 7 search features to search for files. Your screens will look similar to those in Figure 1.34.

## Project Files

For Project 1B, you will need the following files:

36 sample files, and two folders containing 14 additional files

You will save your documents as:

Lastname_Firstname_1B_Renamed_Folder
Lastname_Firstname_1B_Compressed_Folder
Lastname_Firstname_1B_Search_Folder

## Project Results

Figure 1.34

# Objective 4 | Create, Move, and Rename Folders

Information that you create in a computer program is stored in the computer's memory, which is a temporary storage location. This data will be lost if the computer is turned off. To keep the information you create, you must save it as a file on one of the drives available to you. For example, a five-page term paper that you create in a word processing program such as Microsoft Word, when saved, is a *file*. Files can be stored directly on a drive, but more commonly are stored in a folder on the drive. A *folder* is a container for programs and files, represented on the screen by a picture of a common paper file folder.

Use folders to organize your files so that you can easily locate them for later use. Folders and files must be created and stored on one of the drives attached to your computer. Your available drives fall into three categories: 1) the nonremovable hard drive, also called the *local disk*, inside the computer; 2) removable drives that you insert into the computer, such as a flash drive, an external hard drive, or a writable CD or DVD; or 3) a shared network drive connected to your computer through a computer network, such as the network at your college.

## Activity 1.10 | Opening and Navigating Windows Explorer

Windows Explorer is a program that enables you to create and manage folders, and copy, move, sort, and delete files. In the following activity, you will create a folder on one of the three types of drives available to you—the local disk (hard drive), a removable drive (USB flash drive, an external hard drive, or some other type of removable drive), or a network drive. If you are using a computer in a college lab, you may have space assigned to you on a shared network drive. You can create these folders on any drive that is available to you. For the rest of this chapter, a flash drive will be used.

**1** On the taskbar, click the **Windows Explorer** button ▢. If this button is not available, click the **Start** button ◉, point to All Programs, click Accessories, and then click Windows Explorer.

> The Windows Explorer window opens, with the Navigation pane displayed on the left, and the Libraries pane displayed on the right. You may also see a Details pane just above the taskbar and a Preview pane on the right side of the window.

---

**More Knowledge | Using Libraries**

*Libraries* are folders used to sort files with similar content. By default, Windows 7 sets up four libraries: Documents, Music, Pictures, and Videos. Each of these libraries is assigned two folders—a user folder and a public folder. For example, the Documents library contains the My Documents subfolder for the current user, along with the Public Documents subfolder on the hard disk, which contains files that can be shared with all users. If you have other fixed drives on your computer, or permanent network drives, you can add other folders to a library so that all files of a similar type can be accessed quickly using the library.

---

**Another Way**

On the right side of the title bar, click the Maximize button ▢.

**2** If the window is not maximized, drag the title bar to the top of the screen.

**3** On the Command bar, click the **Organize** button, and then point to **Layout**. If the Details pane does not display at the bottom of your window, click Details Pane. If the Navigation pane does not display on the left side of your window, repeat the procedure and click Navigation Pane. Compare your screen with Figure 1.35.

Figure 1.35

Organize button ——

Libraries pane ——

Navigation pane ——

Details pane ——

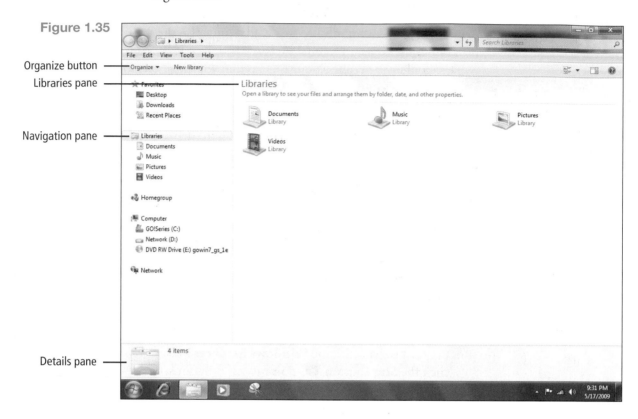

**4** In the **Navigation** pane, if necessary scroll down, and then click **Computer**.

The file list displays a list of hard drives, removable storage devices, network drives, and other devices connected to the computer.

**5** In the **Navigation** pane, if necessary, to the left of **Computer**, click the open arrow ▷. Notice that the arrow changes to a filled arrow pointing downward at an angle ◢.

The open arrow indicates that there are other folders and drives to be displayed. When you click the open arrow, the next level of folders and drives displays. The list of drives in the Navigation pane matches the list of drives in the file list.

**6** Insert your USB flash drive or other removable drive. If an AutoPlay dialog box displays asking what you want Windows to do, click the Close button. In the **Navigation** pane, under **Computer**, click your removable drive—for this chapter, the removable drive name will be FLASH DRIVE (G:); yours will be different.

**7** Compare your screen with Figure 1.36. Notice that the file list in the figure is empty; your storage device or drive may already contain files and folders.

Figure 1.36

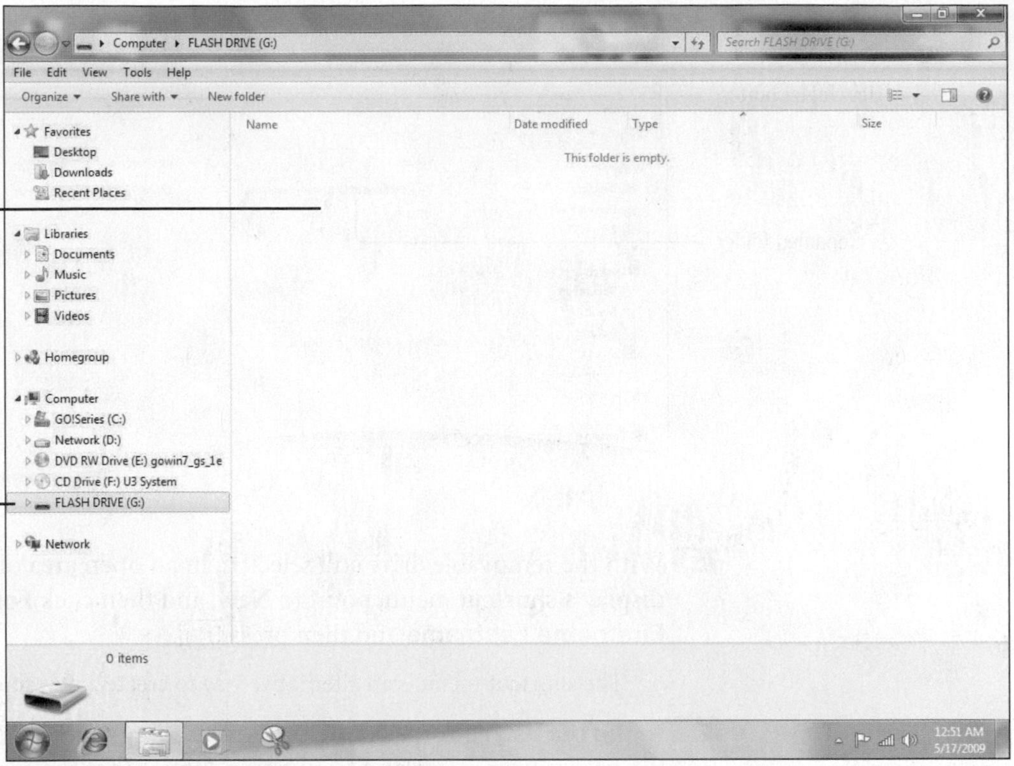

File list is empty; yours may have files and folders

Flash drive (your drive name and letter will vary)

---

> **More Knowledge | Computer Storage Devices**
>
> The hard drive (local disk) is usually identified on your computer by the notation C: (and sometimes D:, E:, and so on for additional drives). *Flash drives*—also known as *USB drives* or *thumb drives*—are small storage devices that plug into a computer's Universal Serial Bus (USB) port, which provides a connection between a computer and a peripheral device such as a printer, a mouse, a keyboard, or a USB drive.
>
> You may also have access to files on another type of storage device, a *CD*—Compact Disc, or a *DVD*—Digital Video (or Versatile) Disc. CD and DVD drives are optical storage devices that come in two formats—read-only and read-write. If you are using files stored on a read-only CD or a DVD disc, you will need to open a file from the disc, and then save it to a writable drive, or copy a file to another disk and then open it.

## Activity 1.11 | Creating a New Folder

It is always a good idea to create a new folder when you have a new category of files to store. You do not need to create a new folder for each type of file, however. You can store many different kinds of files in the same folder.

**Another Way**

If you accidentally press Enter before you have a chance to name the folder, you can still rename it. Right-click the folder, click Rename from the shortcut menu, type a new name, and then press Enter.

**1** With the flash drive selected, in the Command bar, click the **New folder** button.

A new folder—named *New folder*—is created with the name of the folder displayed in the *edit mode*. Edit mode enables you to change the name of a file or folder, and works the same in all Windows programs.

**2** With *New Folder* selected, substitute your name where indicated, and type **Pictures of Firstname Lastname** and then press ⏎. Click anywhere in the blank area of the file list to deselect the new folder and compare your screen with Figure 1.37.

Figure 1.37

New folder button

Renamed folder

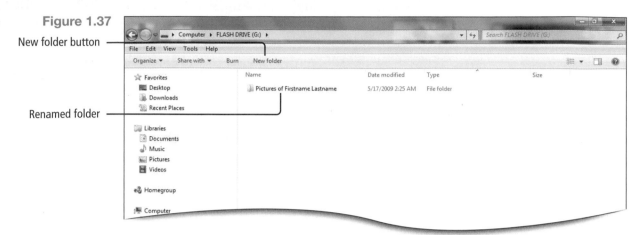

**3** With the removable drive still selected, in an open area of the **file list**, right-click to display a shortcut menu, point to **New**, and then click **Folder**. Type **Documents of Firstname Lastname** and then press ⏎.

The shortcut menu is an alternative way to create a new folder.

**4** In the **file list**, click the **Name** column heading several times to sort the folders and file names from *a* to *z* and from *z* to *a*. Notice that the arrow in the Name column heading points up when the folders are displayed in *ascending order* (*a* to *z*), and points down when the folders are displayed in *descending order* (*z* to *a*). Stop when the folders are sorted in descending alphabetical order—from *z* to *a*.

**5** In the **file list**, move the pointer to the line at the right of the **Name** column heading to display the resize pointer ⟷, as shown in Figure 1.38. Drag the resize pointer ⟷ to the right or left to make the column slightly wider than the longest folder name.

Figure 1.38

*Name* column heading with arrow indicating sort order

Folders in descending alphabetical order

Resize pointer

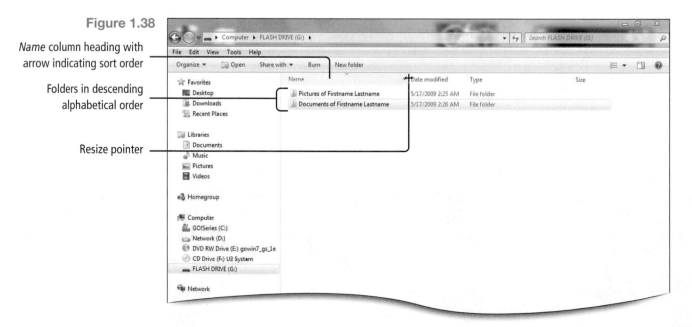

## Activity 1.12 | Moving and Renaming Folders

Your student files and folders for this book are stored on a CD or another location chosen by your instructor. You can move the folders, including the files in the folders, from another location to your flash drive or other storage device.

**1** Navigate to the location where your student files for this book are stored. They may be stored on a CD, in a course management system, on a hard drive, or on a shared network drive. In this chapter, the data CD is used.

**2** In the **Navigation** pane, on the data CD, click the open arrow ▷ to display the folder on the disc. Click the **01_student_data_files** folder, and then compare your screen with Figure 1.39. If your files and folders do not display the way they display in the figure, on the Command bar, to the right of the *Change your view* button, click the *More options* arrow, and then click Details.

There are two folders and a number of files in this folder. The total number of files and folders is displayed in the Details pane at the bottom of the screen. There are more files in the two folders, but they are not included in the totals in the Details pane—only the files and the folders currently displayed in the file list are counted.

**Figure 1.39**

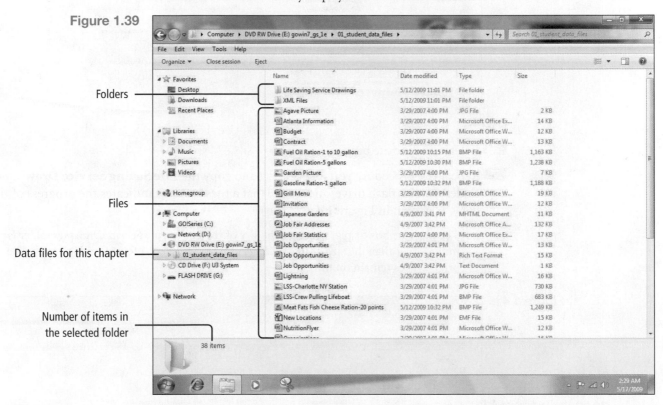

Folders

Files

Data files for this chapter

Number of items in the selected folder

**3** In the **file list**, move the pointer to the right border of the **Name** column heading to display the ⬌ pointer. Double-click to resize the border to the widest folder or file name. Repeat this procedure to display the full **Date modified** and **Type** column contents.

> **Note** | Changing the Columns that Display in the File List
>
> If one or more of the columns displayed in Figure 1.39 do not display, right-click anywhere in the file list column titles, and then click the desired column.

**4** In the **Navigation** pane, if necessary, click the open arrow ▷ to the left of your flash drive. Be sure your student files and folders from the data CD still display in the file list.

**5** Near the top of the **file list**, locate the **XML Files** folder. Click on the folder, hold the mouse button down, and drag the folder to the **Navigation** pane directly on top of your storage drive, as shown in Figure 1.40. Notice that a folder displays attached to the pointer, and a ScreenTip says *Copy to FLASH DRIVE (G:)*—your folder or drive name will vary.

Figure 1.40

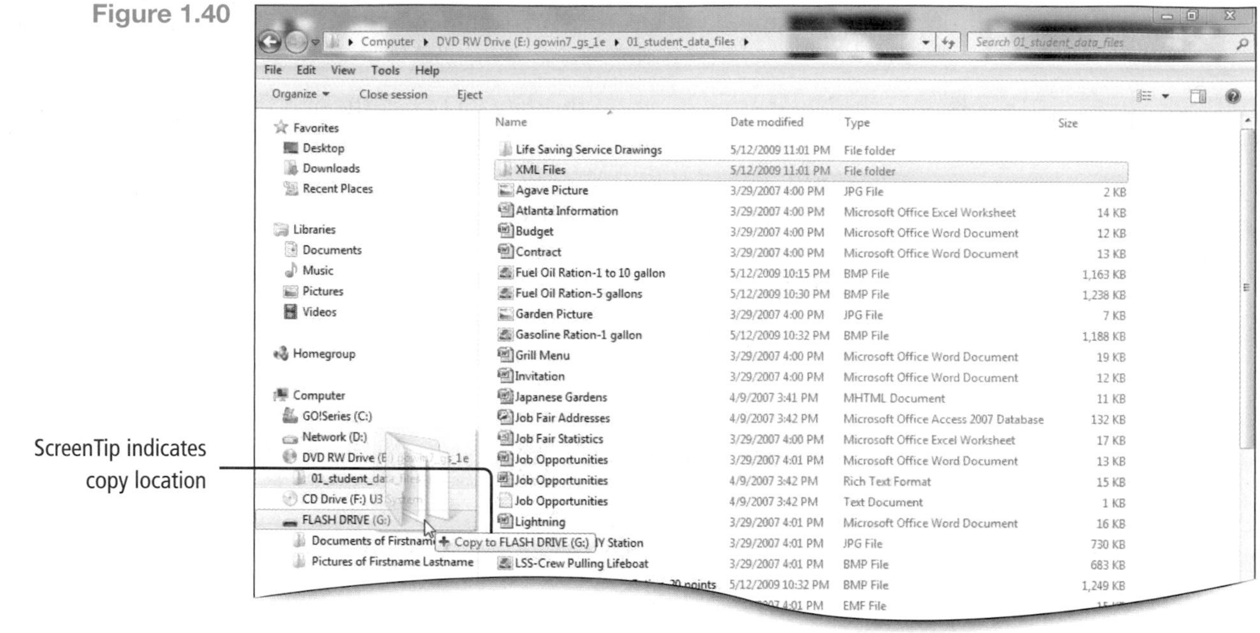

ScreenTip indicates copy location

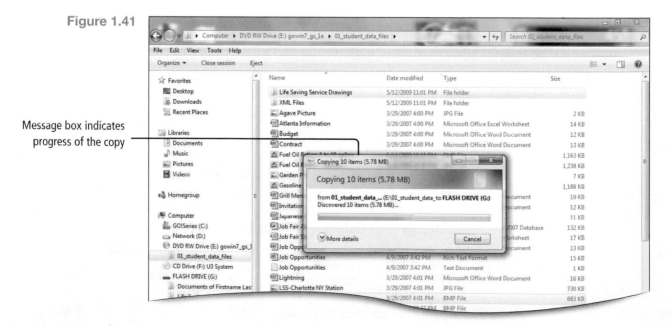

**6** Release the mouse button.

**7** Repeat the procedure you just practiced to copy the **Life Saving Service Drawings** folder to your flash drive, and notice that a message box indicates the progress of the copy, as shown in Figure 1.41.

The message box displays because the size of the *Life Saving Service Drawings* folder is much larger than the size of the *XML Files* folder and takes a few seconds to copy. The original files remain on the CD.

Figure 1.41

Message box indicates progress of the copy

**8** In the **Navigation** pane, click the flash drive or other device where you are storing your files and folders. In the **file list**, right-click the **Life Saving Service Drawings** folder, and then from the displayed shortcut menu, click **Rename**.

**9** With the folder name in edit mode, type **LSS Drawings** and then press Enter.

> The folder name is changed. When text is selected, typing replaces all of the selected text.

**10** Use the skills you practiced earlier to create a **Full-screen Snip**. Click the **Save Snip** 🖫 button. In the **Save As** dialog box, in the left pane, scroll down to display the **Computer** drives. Click your flash drive, and then in the Command bar, click the **New folder** button. Name the new folder **Windows Chapter 1** Press Enter, and then press Enter again to open the new folder. In the **File name** box, type **Lastname_Firstname_1B_Renamed_Folder** Click **Save**, and then **Close** ✕ the Snipping Tool window.

## Objective 5 | Copy, Move, Rename, and Delete Files

Copying files from one folder to another is a frequent data management task. For example, you might want to make a backup copy of important information, copy a file from a CD to a local disk, or copy information from your local disk drive to a removable drive. Copying files works the same regardless of the type of drive.

Performing other operations on files, such as deleting them or moving them, also works the same regardless of the type of drive. As you accumulate files, you will likely need to delete some to reduce clutter on your hard drive. You might also want to move documents into other folders on another drive to *archive* them—place them somewhere for long-term storage. Finally, you may want to change the names of file to make the names more descriptive. All of these tasks are functions of your Windows 7 operating system.

### Activity 1.13 | Copying Files

**1** In the **Navigation** pane, under **Computer**, scroll to the location where your student data files for this book are stored. Locate and click the folder named **01_student_data_files** to display the files and folders in the folder.

**2** In the **Navigation** pane, scroll as necessary to display your flash drive or other storage device. Be sure your student data files and folders still display in the file list.

**3** Near the middle of the **file list**, locate the **Garden Picture** file, and then drag it to your storage device. Recall that dragging also includes releasing the mouse button at the destination location.

> When you drag a file or folder from one device to another, it is copied, which means that the original file remains on the original drive and a copy of the file is placed on the new drive. If you drag a file or folder to another place (such as a folder) on the same drive—for example, from one folder to another—the file or folder is moved and no longer resides in the original location.

**4** Locate the **Grill Menu** file, right-click the file, and then click **Copy**.

> This creates a copy of the Grill Menu file and places it in a temporary storage area called the *Clipboard*. Files in the Clipboard can be placed in other folders using the Paste command.

**5** In the **Navigation** pane, click your storage device. In the **file list**, right-click in an open area, and then from the shortcut menu, click **Paste**. Notice that the file is copied to the open folder.

**6** Click the **Name** column heading as necessary to sort the folders in ascending order—the arrow in the column heading should be pointing up. Compare your screen with Figure 1.42.

> The file list should display five folders—the three that you created and the two that you copied. In addition, the two files that you copied should display below the folders. When you sort a folder in ascending order, the folders always display first.

Figure 1.42

Folders display first

Folders and files sorted in alphabetical order by Name

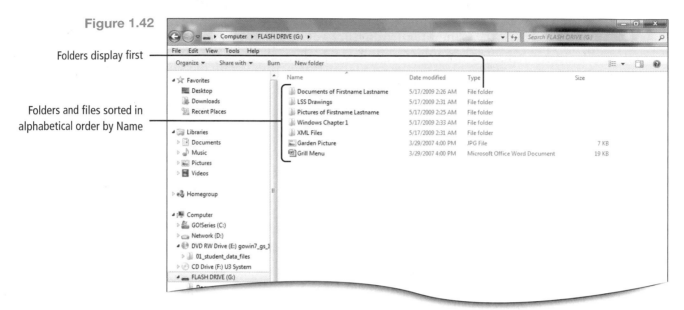

**7** Display the files and folders in the **01_student_data_files** folder again. Click the **Atlanta Information** file, hold down Shift, and then click the **Fuel Oil Ration-1 to 10 gallon** file.

> By holding down the Shift key, you select the two files you click and all of the files in between.

**8** In the **Navigation** pane, scroll as necessary to display your storage area. Drag the selected files to your storage area.

**9** Click the **Agave Picture** file, hold down Ctrl, and then click the **Fuel Oil Ration-5 gallons** file, and then the **Gasoline Ration-1 gallon** file. Notice that by using the Control key, you can select several files that are not next to each other, as shown in Figure 1.43.

Figure 1.43

Selected files

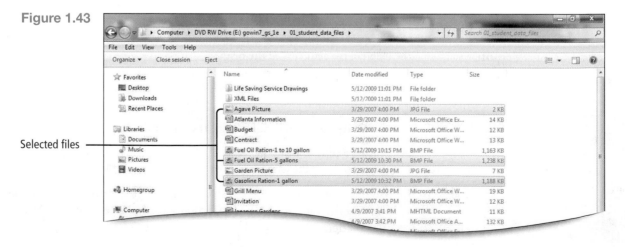

**10** Drag the selected files to your storage area.

**11** In the **file list**, click the **Invitation** file, and then use the vertical scroll bar to scroll to the bottom of the file list. Hold down $\boxed{\text{Shift}}$, and then click the **Volunteers** file. In the Detail area, notice that the number of files displays, as shown in Figure 1.44. If the total size of the files does not display, in the Details pane, click Show more details.

Figure 1.44

Selected files —

Click to show more details —

*Show more details* command

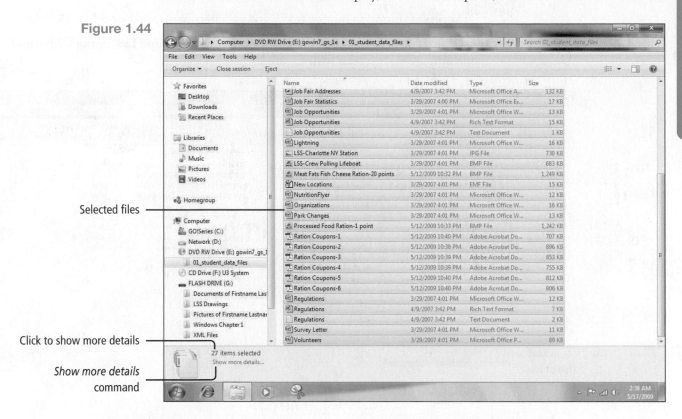

**12** Drag the selected files to your storage area.

> **More Knowledge | File Extensions**
>
> The files you see may display three or four letters following the file name, such as *.docx*. These are **file extensions**, and most files have these extensions—although they may or may not display on your system. Files created by Microsoft Office programs have a standard set of extensions that identify the type of program used to create the file. For example, Microsoft Word documents end in *.doc* or *.docx*, Excel worksheets end in *.xls* or *.xlsx*, PowerPoint presentations end with *.ppt* or *pptx*, and so on. The default setting in Windows 7 is to hide the file extensions.

## Activity 1.14 | Moving, Renaming, and Deleting Files

In the following activity, you will move files from one location on your removable drive to another location on the same drive. You will also rename and delete files.

**1** In the **Navigation** pane, scroll as necessary and then click on your flash drive or other storage device.

Your storage device should display five folders at the top, and a total of 36 files in the drive—41 objects, as displayed in the Details pane.

**2** In the **file list**, click the **Type** column header to sort the files by file type. Move the pointer to the right border of the **Type** column heading to display the ⟷ pointer. Double-click to resize the border to the widest file type.

**3** In the **file list**, use the wheel in the middle of your mouse, or the vertical scroll bar, to scroll down until you can see all of the **Microsoft Office Word Document** files.

**4** Click the **Budget** file, hold down ⇧Shift, and then click the **Survey Letter** file to select all of the Word documents. Drag the selected files to the **Documents of Firstname Lastname** folder.

The files are moved to the new folder, and no longer display in their original location.

**5** In the **Navigation** pane, click the **Documents of Firstname Lastname** folder, and then compare your screen with Figure 1.45.

Figure 1.45

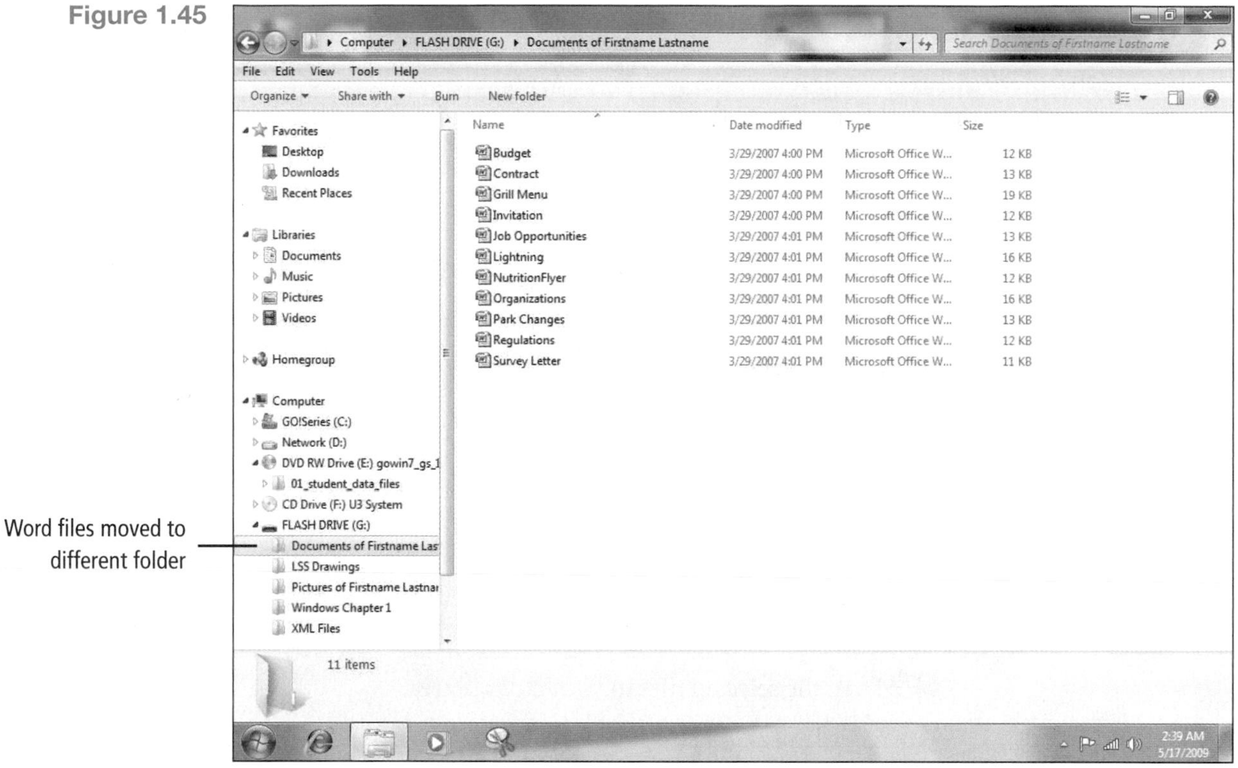

Word files moved to different folder

**6** In the **Navigation** pane, click on your flash drive or other storage device. Using the technique you just practiced, select the three **JPG Images**, and then drag them to the **Pictures of Firstname Lastname** folder.

---

**Alert! | What if your file types differ?**

Files can be associated with several different programs, and will display a different file type in the Type column. For example, the three files labeled JPG in Figure 1.46 could be called JPEG files on your computer.

---

**7** Select the six **BMP Files** and drag them to the **Pictures of Firstname Lastname** folder. If you do not see files labeled *BMP File*, select the six files beginning with *Fuel Oil Ration-1 to 10 gallon* and ending with *Processed Food Ration-1 point*.

**8** In the **Navigation** pane, click the **Pictures of Firstname Lastname** folder, and then compare your screen with Figure 1.46.

Figure 1.46

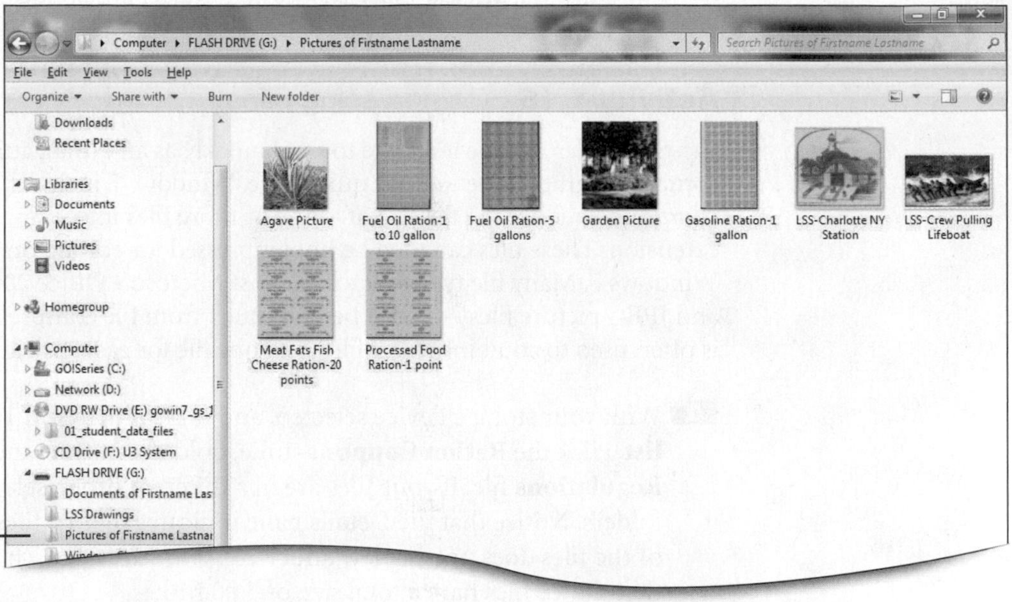

Picture files moved to new folder

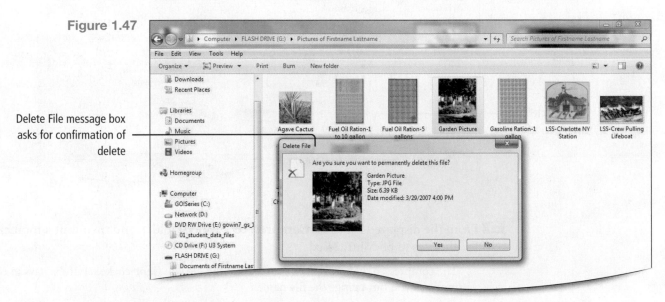

**9** If thumbnails do not display for the files, on the Command bar, to the right of the **Change your view** button, click the **More options arrow**, and then click **Large Icons**.

**10** In the **file list**, right-click the **Agave Picture** file, and then click **Rename**. Type **Agave Cactus** and then press Enter.

**11** In the **file list**, right-click the **Garden Picture** file, and then click **Delete**. The **Delete File** message box displays, as shown in Figure 1.47.

Figure 1.47

Delete File message box asks for confirmation of delete

**Another Way**

In the Navigation pane, click your flash drive or other storage location name.

**12** In the **Delete File** message box, click **Yes** to send the file to the Recycle Bin.

**13** In the upper left corner of the window, click the **Back** button ⬅ to move back to your main storage area.

**14** In the **file list**, right-click the **XML Files** folder, and then click **Delete**. In the displayed **Delete Folder** message box, click **Yes**.

When you delete a folder, all files in the folder are also deleted.

## Activity 1.15 | Compressing Files

Some files may be too large to send quickly as an e-mail attachment. For example, files containing graphics tend to be quite large. Windows 7 includes a feature with which you can *compress*—reduce the file size of—one or more files into a single file that uses a *.zip* file extension. These files can then be uncompressed for editing on any other computer running Windows 7. Many file types—such as most Microsoft Office 2007 files, Adobe Acrobat files, and JPEG picture files—do not benefit much from file compression. However, compression is often used to combine many files into one file for easy distribution.

**1** With your storage device selected, and four folders and 16 files displayed in the **file list**, click the **Ration Coupons-1** file, hold down ⟨Shift⟩, and then click the second **Regulations** file. If your files are in a different order, select all 16 files, but not the folders. Notice that the Details pane indicates that 16 files are selected. If the total size of the files does not display, under *16 items selected*, click *Show more details*. Notice that the 16 files have a total size of 5.00 MB.

**2** In the **file list**, right-click any of the selected files, and then from the displayed shortcut menu, point to **Send to**. Compare your screen with Figure 1.48.

Figure 1.48

*Compressed (zipped) folder* command

Selected files

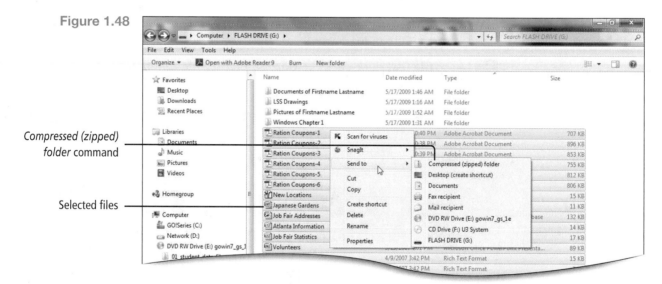

**3** From the displayed list, click **Compressed (zipped)** folder, and then wait a moment for the files to be compressed.

The compressed folder displays the name of the file you right-clicked, but displays in edit mode so you can change the file name.

---

**Note** | To Work with Third-Party Zip Programs

If you are using a third-party zip program, such as WinZip™ or PKZIP™, you will need to use that program to complete this task—the procedure listed below will not work.

---

**4** With the compressed folder name still in edit mode, type **Files of Firstname Lastname** and then press Enter. Notice that the compressed folder size is approximately 4.9 MB, which is not a great space savings. Compare your screen with Figure 1.49.

Figure 1.49

Compressed folder

File size reduced slightly

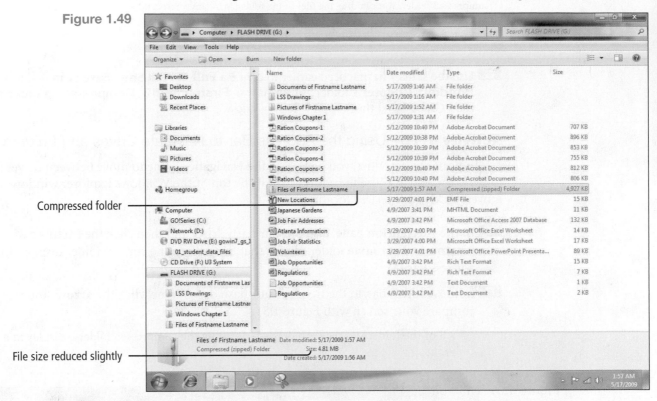

**5** In the **file list**, double-click the **Files of Firstname Lastname** compressed folder. Compare your screen with Figure 1.50.

The files in the compressed folder are listed, along with their original sizes and their compressed sizes. The percent of space saved is indicated for each file. Some of the files show very little space savings, while in others the space saved is considerable. To extract the files from the compressed folder, you would click the *Extract all files* button on the Command bar. You can also open the files directly from the compressed folder.

Figure 1.50

Original file size

Extract all files button

Compressed file size

Files in compressed folder

Percent of space saved

Compressed folder

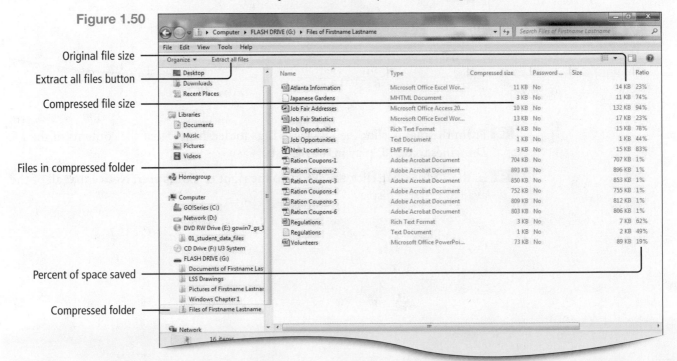

> **More Knowledge** | Adding More Items to a Compressed Folder
>
> You can add more files to an existing compressed folder by dragging files and dropping them on the compressed folder. You can drag the files to the folder from anywhere, and you can also drag folders into a compressed folder.

**6** Use the skills you practiced earlier to create a **Full-screen Snip**. **Save Snip** 🖫 to your **Windows Chapter 1** folder as **Lastname_Firstname_1B_Compressed_Folder** and then **Close** ✖ the Snipping Tool window.

## Activity 1.16 | Using the Address Bar to Navigate Drives and Folders

In previous activities, you have used the Navigation pane to move between drives and folders. You can also use the address bar at the top of the Windows Explorer window to move quickly to a desired location.

**1** In the **Navigation** pane, display your flash drive, and then click the **Pictures of Firstname Lastname** folder. Notice that the path to the current folder displays in the address bar.

**2** In the Address bar, to the right of your flash drive name, click the **arrow**, and then compare your screen with Figure 1.51.

All of the folders on the flash drive—including the compressed folder—display in a menu.

Figure 1.51

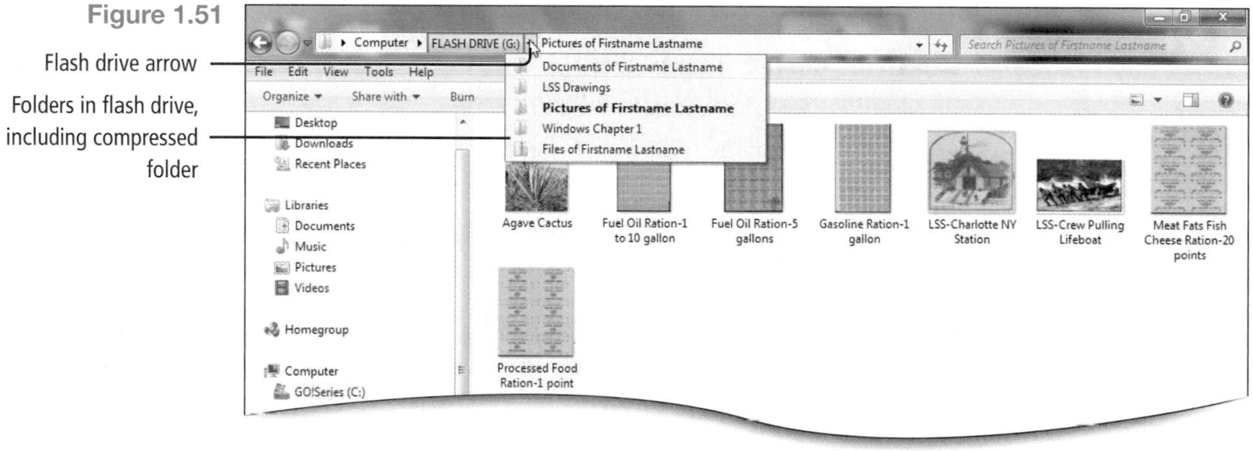

Flash drive arrow

Folders in flash drive, including compressed folder

**3** From the menu, click the **LSS Drawings** folder. Notice that the contents of the *LSS Drawings* folder display in the file list.

**4** In the address bar, click the **arrow** to the right of **Computer**. Notice that all of the available drives display.

**5** To the left of **Computer**, click the **arrow**, and then compare your screen with Figure 1.52.

The top-level items in the Navigation pane display in a menu, along with commands for the Control Panel and the Recycle Bin.

**Figure 1.52**

Top-level items in Navigation pane

Opens the Control Panel

Opens the Recycle Bin

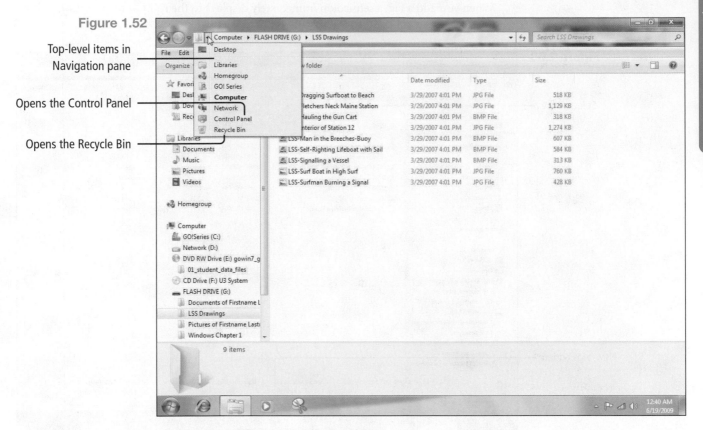

**6** Click anywhere in the **file list** to close the menu.

## Objective 6 | Find Files and Folders

As you use a computer, you will likely accumulate a large number of files and folders. It's easy to forget where you stored a file, or what you named it. Windows 7 provides several search functions with which you can find files and folders. You can also add tags to files. *Tags* are custom file properties that help you find and organize your files. Tags are part of a file's *metadata*—items that record and display information about a file, such as a title, a rating, the file name, and the file size.

### Activity 1.17 | Adding Descriptions and Tags to Files

**1** Be sure your storage device is selected, with the contents of the **LSS Drawings** folder displayed in the file list. Also be sure the **Details** pane is open at the bottom of the window.

**2** Click the first file in the **file list—LSS-Dragging Surfboat to Beach**. Move the pointer to the line at the top of the **Details** pane to display the pointer, and then drag the top of the Details pane to display three lines of details.

**3** In the **Details** pane, click in the **Tags** box—to the right of the word *Tags*. Type **LSS** and then press →. Type **LSS Boat** and then press →. Type **Surfboat** and then compare your screen with Figure 1.53. Notice on the left side of the Details pane that the file type for this file is JPG—one of a number of image file types.

> When you add a tag, a semicolon immediately displays to the right of the insertion point. Semicolons separate multiple tags.

Figure 1.53

Selected file ——

New tags added ——

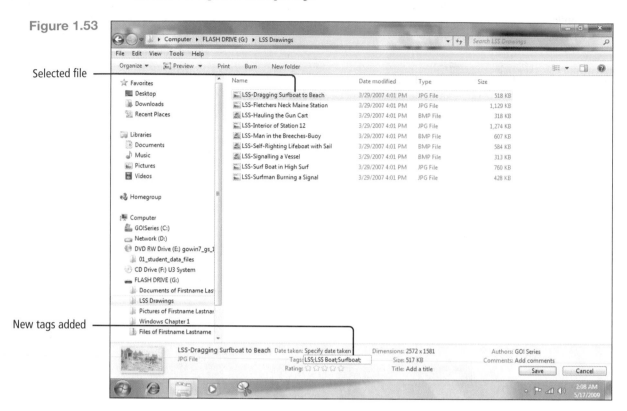

**4** Press Enter to confirm the tags. Using the procedure you just practiced, add the same three tags to the **LSS-Surf Boat in High Surf** file. Notice on the left side of the Details pane that the file type for this file is JPG or JPEG.

**5** Click the **LSS-Self-Righting Lifeboat with Sail** file. Notice that there is no place to add a tag.

> This image is a bitmap image, which does not support tags. Most Microsoft Office 2007 and 2010 default file formats support tags, as do many other file formats.

**6** In the **Navigation** pane, click the **Pictures of Firstname Lastname** folder, and then click the file **LSS-Charlotte NY Station**. Add the following tags: **LSS** and **LSS Boat** and **LSS Boat Ramp** and then press Enter.

**7** In the **Details** pane, click the **Title** box, type **Life Saving Station at Charlotte, NY** and then press Enter.

**8** In the **file list**, right-click the **LSS-Charlotte NY Station** file, and then from the shortcut menu, click **Properties**. In the **Properties** dialog box, click the **Details tab**.

> The items you entered in the Details pane display, and there are several other categories of tags that you can add, including a rating of the picture or document.

**9** In the **Properties** dialog box, under **Description**, click the fourth **Rating** star from the left. Under **Origin**, click the **Copyright** box, type **Public Domain** and then compare your screen with Figure 1.54.

**Figure 1.54**

Selected file

Rating tag

Copyright box

Title added

New tags added

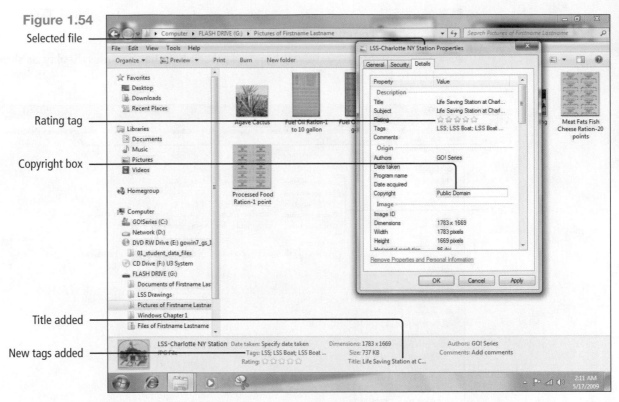

**10** At the bottom of the **Properties** dialog box, click **OK**.

## Activity 1.18 | Finding Files and Folders and Creating a Search Folder

**1** In the **Navigation** pane, click your storage location name. Be sure your storage device is selected, and four folders, one compressed folder, and 16 files display in the file list.

**2** Near the upper right corner of the window, click in the **Search** box, type **J** and then in the **file list**, examine the results of your search, as shown in Figure 1.55. If your search results do not display in the list format, to the right of the *Change your view* button ▣ ▾, click the *More options* arrow, and then click Details.

> The program found all files and folders with words that begin with the letter *J*, along with all file types (file extensions) with words that begin with the letter *J*—in this case, all JPEG image files. Your files may display in a different order.

**Figure 1.55**

Letter to search for

File types beginning with the letter *J*

Files beginning with the letter *J*

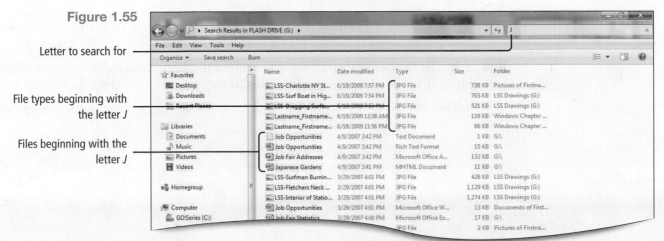

**3** With the letter *J* already in the **Search** box, type the letter **P** and examine the search results. Notice that the only files, folders, or file types in your storage device that begin with the letters *JP* are the JPEG image files.

**4** Press (Bksp), and notice that the search results again display all files, folders, and file types that contain the letter *J*.

**5** Now type **ob** to complete the word *Job*. Notice that five files display, as shown in Figure 1.56.

Figure 1.56

Search term ——

Files that begin with *Job* ——

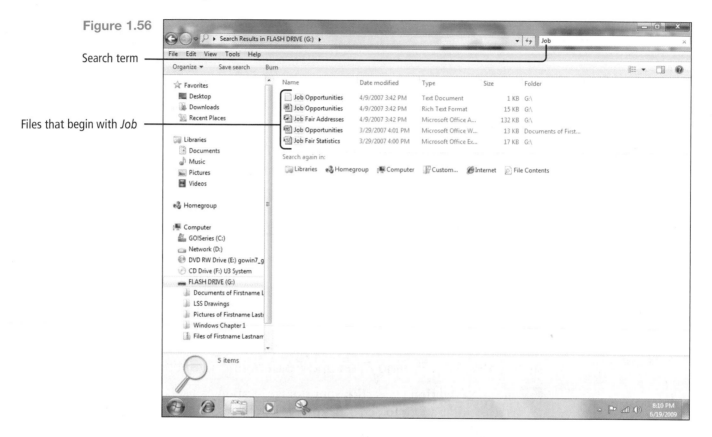

**6** Press (Bksp) three times, type **LSS** and then notice that files and folders from various locations display in the file list.

**7** Press (Spacebar), type **boat** and then notice that only one file or folder meets this search condition, even though you added *LSS Boat* as a tag to several files. Also notice that the file that was found had both search words, but they do not have to be next to each other.

> When you enter a word or phrase in the Search pane, only the file names, folder names, and file types are searched.

**8** In the **file list**, below the displayed file, notice the search alternatives that are available. Under **Search again in**, click **File Contents**. Notice that three files display.

> The *File Contents* search extends the search to include tags, text that is a portion of a file name, or text inside the file.

**9** On the Command bar, click the **Save search** button. In the displayed **Save As** dialog box, click **Save**. Compare your screen with Figure 1.57.

A *search folder* is saved on your computer under **Favorites**—not on your removable storage device. A search folder retains all of the search conditions you specified during your search, and recreates the search every time you click the search folder. As you add more pictures with the *LSS Boat* tag to your removable storage device, the search folder will find them. It is important to remember that the search folder will only search the location you specified—it will not search the rest of the computer.

**Figure 1.57**

New search folder ⎯⎯

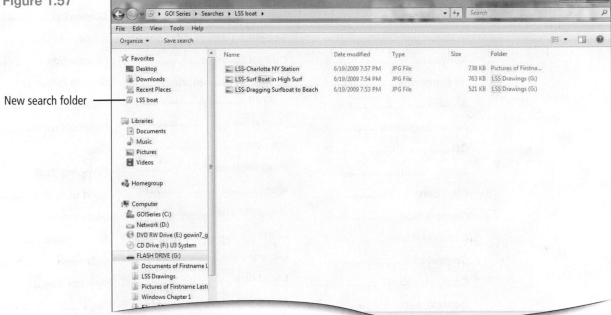

**10** Use the skills you practiced earlier to create a **Full-screen Snip**. Save ⊟ the snip to your **Windows Chapter 1** folder as **Lastname_Firstname_1B_Search_Folder** and submit all three file snips from Project 1B as directed. If you are directed to print the files, use the skills practiced in Activity 1.9 to create a WordPad document, add your name, drag the three snip files from this project, and then print the document. It is not necessary to save the WordPad file once you have printed it.

**11** In the title bar, click the **Close** ⊠ button to close the Windows Explorer window. Select and **Delete** the files and shortcuts you saved on the desktop, and then **Close** ⊠ the gadgets that you added to the desktop.

---

**More Knowledge | Using Wildcards in Searches**

When you are searching for a particular type of file, you can specify the extension by using a wildcard, followed by the extension. A *wildcard* takes the place of one or more characters in a search. For example, if you wanted to search for all of your Excel 2007 files in the My Documents folder, select the folder, and then type *.xlsx in the Search box. All files with the *.xlsx* extension will display. If you want to display all of your Excel files, including older versions (with the *.xls* extension), type *.xls. This search will locate all *.xls* and *.xlsx* files. Similarly, you can search for all files beginning with *Fun* by typing *Fun\**, which will return all files with those first three letters, including *Fundamentals of Business* and *Fun with Trombones*.

---

 **You have completed Project 1B** ⎯⎯⎯⎯⎯⎯⎯⎯⎯⎯⎯⎯⎯⎯⎯

## Summary

Windows 7 is a robust operating system that enables you to easily locate information and programs. It enables you to create, rename, move, copy, and delete files and folders. You can add key words and other information to the files to make searching easier and more accurate.

## Key Terms

Active window ................16
Address bar ......................6
Aero...................................8
All Programs....................14
Archive ...........................35
Ascending order.............32
CD ...................................31
Click .................................5
Clipboard ........................35
Close button.....................6
Command bar ...................4
Compress ........................40
Computer icon ..................4
Context-sensitive
   command ......................6
Descending order............32
Desktop.............................3
Desktop background ......10
Details pane .....................6
Dialog box.........................9
Double-click .....................6
Drag................................25
Drive .................................7
DVD .................................31
Edit mode .......................31
Favorites...........................6
File...................................29
File extension .................37
File list..............................7
Flash drive......................31

Folder .............................29
Gadget.............................11
Gadget controls .............12
Graphical user interface
   (GUI)..............................7
Hard drive .........................7
Hardware ..........................3
Horizontal scroll bar ......22
Icon ..................................4
Jump list .........................23
Libraries ...........................5
Library pane .....................6
Local disk .......................29
Maximize.........................19
Menu .................................6
Menu bar...........................6
Metadata.........................43
Minimize .........................19
Mouse pointer .................4
Navigation pane ..............6
Notification area..............4
Operating system.............3
Paint ...............................22
Peek.................................21
Pinned programs area ....14
Pointer...............................4
Recycle Bin.......................4
Restore ...........................19
Right-click ........................6
Screen saver.....................8

ScreenTip ..........................6
Scroll box ........................26
Search box ........................6
Search folder ..................47
Shake...............................21
Shortcut menu ..................6
Snip .................................18
Snipping Tool ..................18
Start button ......................4
Start menu ......................13
Status area ........................4
Submenu..........................14
System tray........................4
Tags .................................43
Taskbar .............................4
Thumb drive ....................31
Thumbnail .......................22
Title bar.............................6
Toolbar ..............................6
USB drive ........................31
Vertical scroll bar ...........22
Wildcard ..........................47
Window .............................5
Window name..................15
Windows ...........................3
Windows Aero ..................8
Windows Explorer ............5
WordPad ..........................16

## Screen ID

Identify each element of the screen by matching callout numbers shown in Figure 1.58 to a corresponding description.

**Figure 1.58**

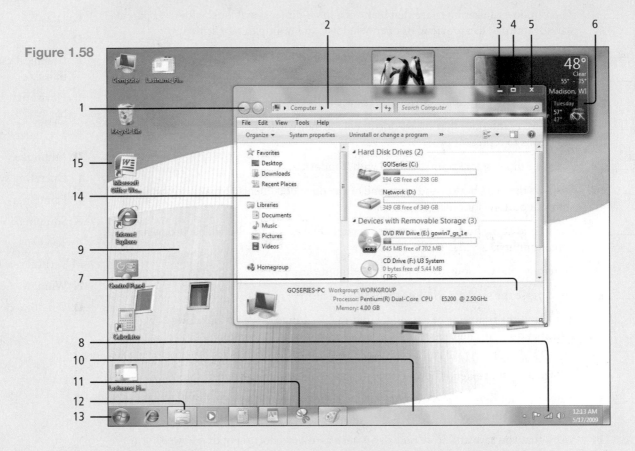

_____ A. Address bar

_____ B. Back button

_____ C. Close button

_____ D. Desktop

_____ E. Details pane

_____ F. Gadget

_____ G. Icon

_____ H. Maximize button

_____ I. Minimize button

_____ J. Navigation pane

_____ K. Notification area

_____ L. Snipping Tool button

_____ M. Start button

_____ N. Taskbar

_____ O. Windows Explorer button

## Matching

Match each term in the second column with its correct definition in the first column. Write the letter of the term on the blank line in front of the correct definition.

_____ 1. The Windows 7 user interface that features a three-dimensional look, with transparent window frames, live previews of open windows, and multiple color schemes.

_____ 2. A program that captures a screen or part of a screen.

_____ 3. Displays information about the drive, folder, or file selected in the file list.

_____ 4. A set of instructions that coordinates the activities of your computer.

_____ 5. A computer interface that shows documents as they will look in their final form and uses icons to represent programs.

_____ 6. A simple drawing program included with Windows 7.

_____ 7. Displays the Start button and the name of any open documents; it may also display shortcut buttons for other programs.

_____ 8. Command at the bottom of the Start menu that takes you to all available programs on your computer.

_____ 9. To remove the window from the screen without closing it.

_____ 10. To increase the size of a window to fill the screen.

_____ 11. The bar at the right side of a window that enables you to move up and down to view information that extends beyond the top and bottom of the screen.

_____ 12. The bar at the bottom of a window that enables you to move left and right to view information that extends beyond the left and right edges of the screen.

_____ 13. Move the mouse pointer while holding down the left mouse button, and then release at the appropriate time.

_____ 14. Work that you save and store on a drive, such as a Word document or a PowerPoint presentation.

_____ 15. A program that enables you to create and manage folders, and copy, move, sort, and delete files.

**A** All Programs

**B** Details pane

**C** Drag

**D** File

**E** Graphical user interface

**F** Horizontal scroll bar

**G** Maximize

**H** Minimize

**I** Operating system

**J** Paint

**K** Snipping Tool

**L** Taskbar

**M** Vertical scroll bar

**N** Windows Aero

**O** Windows Explorer

## Multiple Choice

Circle the correct answer.

1. In the Windows Explorer window, this pane displays Favorites, Libraries, Computer, and Network information.
   a. Preview           b. Navigation           c. Details

2. The working area of the Windows 7 screen—consisting of program icons, a taskbar, a Start button, and gadgets—is the:
   a. desktop           b. window               c. Notification area

3. The arrow, I-beam, or other symbol that shows the location or position of the mouse on your screen is the mouse:
   a. button            b. cursor               c. pointer

4. The area on the right side of the taskbar that keeps you informed about processes that are occurring in the background, such as antivirus software, network connections, and other utility programs, is the:
   a. Quick Launch toolbar   b. Notification area   c. program icon

5. Custom file properties such as names, places, and descriptions that are added to files are called:
   a. jump lists        b. details              c. metadata

6. You can activate this by pointing to an object and clicking the right mouse button.
   a. active window     b. shortcut menu        c. gadget

7. When you create a new folder, the folder name displays:
   a. in edit mode      b. in the Details pane   c. on the desktop

8. When you create a search folder, it displays in the Navigation pane under this category:
   a. Favorites         b. Computer             c. Libraries

9. A dynamic program—such as a clock, a stock market ticker, or a weather window—that displays on the desktop is a:
   a. gadget            b. tag                  c. snip

10. The three or four characters to the right of the period in a file name is called:
    a. metadata         b. a wildcard           c. a file extension

# Content-Based Assessments

## Skills Review | Project 1C Using Windows 7

Apply a combination of the 1A and 1B skills.

In the following Skills Review, you will copy files from your student data disk to a flash drive, create and rename folders, and move files. You will also add tags to files and search for files using the Search box. Your completed documents will look similar to the ones shown in Figure 1.59.

### Project Files

For Project 1C, you will need the following files:

36 sample files, and two folders containing 14 additional files

You will save your documents as:

Lastname_Firstname_1C_Screen_Saver
Lastname_Firstname_1C_Desktop
Lastname_Firstname_1C_Folders
Lastname_Firstname_1C_Tags

### Project Results

Figure 1.59

(Project 1C Using Windows 7 continues on the next page)

# Content-Based Assessments

## Skills Review | Project 1C Using Windows 7 (continued)

**1** Turn on your computer and if necessary follow the log-on instructions required for the computer you are using.

**2** Move the pointer to an open area of the desktop, and then right-click. From the shortcut menu, move the pointer to the bottom of the list, and then click **Personalize**. At the bottom of the **Personalization** window, click the **Screen Saver** button. Click the **Screen saver box arrow**, and then from the displayed list, click **Bubbles**.

**3** If the **Snipping Tool** does not display on your taskbar, click the **Start** button, point to **All Programs**, click **Accessories**, right-click **Snipping Tool**, and then click **Pin to Taskbar**. On the taskbar, click the **Snipping Tool** button. In the **Snipping Tool** window, click the arrow to the right of the **New** button, and then click **Full-screen Snip**.

**4** In the **Snipping Tool** window, click the **Save Snip** button. In the **Save As** dialog box, in the left pane, scroll down to display the **Computer** drives. Click your flash drive, and then in the Command bar, click the **New folder** button. Name the new folder **Windows Project C** Press Enter, and then press Enter again to open the new folder. In the **File name** box, type **Lastname_Firstname_1C_Screen_Saver** Be sure the **Save as type** box displays *JPEG file*. Click **Save**, and then **Close** the Snipping Tool window.

**5** If you want to use the Bubbles screen saver, at the bottom of the Screen Saver Settings dialog box, click OK; otherwise, click Cancel.

**6** At the bottom of the **Personalization** window, click **Desktop Background**. Use the vertical scroll bar to display the **United States** desktop backgrounds, and then click the picture of the **stone arch**. Click **Save changes** to apply the new background, and then **Close** the Personalization window.

**7** Click the **Start** button, point to **All Programs**, and then click **Accessories**. Right-click **WordPad**, point to **Send to**, click **Desktop (create shortcut)**, and then click in any open area of the desktop.

**8** In an open area of the desktop, right-click to display a shortcut menu, and then click **Gadgets**. Double-click the **Clock** gadget, double-click the **Stocks** gadget, and then double-click the **CPU Meter** gadget. **Close** the Gadgets window. Point to the **CPU Usage** gadget, and then click the **Larger size** button. Drag the **CPU Usage** gadget to the top of the desktop.

**9** Use the skills you practiced to create a **Full-screen Snip** of the desktop, **Save** it in the **Windows Project C** folder as **Lastname_Firstname_1C_Desktop** and then **Close** the Snipping Tool window.

**10** On the taskbar, click the **Windows Explorer** button. If this button is not available, click the Start button, point to All Programs, click Accessories, and then click Windows Explorer. Insert your student data CD. In the **Windows Explorer** window, in the **Navigation** pane, click the drive that contains your student data files. To the left of the drive name, click the open arrow to display the **01_student_data_files** folder, and then click that folder to display the folders and files in the file list.

**11** In the **Navigation** pane, in the drive that contains your student files, be sure the folders display. In the **file list**, drag the **XML Files** folder to the **Windows Project C** folder on your flash drive.

**12** At the top of the **file list**, click the **Type** column heading. Widen the **Type** column so you can see all of the file types. Click the first **Adobe Acrobat** document—*Ration Coupons-1*—, hold down Shift, and then click the last **Adobe Acrobat** document—*Ration Coupons-6*. Drag the selected files to the **Windows Project C** folder on your flash drive. Then, select all of the files with a **Type** that begins *Microsoft Office*. Drag these 15 files to the **Windows Project C** folder on your flash drive.

**13** In the **Navigation** pane, locate your flash drive, and then click the **Windows Project C** folder. On the Command bar click the **New Folder** button, and then name the folder **Adobe Acrobat Files** Select the six **Adobe Acrobat Files** and drag them to the folder you just created. In the **Navigation** pane, expand the **Windows Project C** folder, and then click the **Windows Project C** folder to display the folder contents.

**14** In the **file list**, right-click the file **Volunteers**, and then click **Rename**. Rename the file **Job Fair Volunteers** In the same list of files, right-click the **Lightning** file, and then from the shortcut menu, click **Delete**. In the message box, click **Yes**.

**15** At the top of the **file list**, click the **Name** column heading as necessary to display the folders and files in ascending (*a* to *z*) order. Use the skills you practiced to create a **Full-screen Snip** of the Windows Explorer window, **Save** it in the **Windows Project C** folder as

(Project 1C Using Windows 7 continues on the next page)

# Content-Based Assessments

**Lastname_Firstname_1C_Folders** and then **Close** the Snipping Tool window.

 In the **file list**, click the **Job Fair Statistics** file. In the **Details** pane, click to the right of **Tags**. In the **Tags** box, type **Atlanta** press →, and then type **Job Fair** Add the same tags to the **Atlanta Information** file.

**17** In the **Search** box, type **Atlanta** and then press Enter. In the **file list**, click **File Contents** to include files with the word *Atlanta* in the files or in the file tags. If necessary, change the display to Details. Use the skills you practiced to create a **Full-screen Snip** of the Windows Explorer window, **Save** it in the **Windows Project C**

folder as **Lastname_Firstname_1C_Tags** and then **Close** the Snipping Tool window.

**18** Submit all four snips as directed. If you are directed to print the files, use the skills practiced in Activity 1.9 to create a WordPad document, add your name, drag the four snip files from this project, and then print the document. It is not necessary to save the WordPad file once you have printed it.

**19** Remove all desktop and taskbar shortcuts that you created in this project, and then **Close** all three gadgets that you added.

**End** **You have completed Project 1C** _____

# Glossary

**Active window** The window in which the mouse pointer's movements commands, or text entry occur when two or more windows are open.

**Address bar** A toolbar that displays the organizational path to the active file, folder, or window.

**Aero** See Windows Aero.

**All Programs** Command at the bottom of the Start menu that takes you to all available programs on your computer.

**Archive** To back up files and store them somewhere other than the main hard drive.

**Ascending order** Files or folders listed from *a* to *z* when sorted.

**Background** See Desktop background.

**CD** A compact disc—an optical storage device used to store data and which can be read-only or read-write.

**Click** To press the left mouse button one time.

**Clipboard** A temporary storage area in Windows that stores the most recently copied item.

**Close button** A shortcut button in a title bar that closes a window or a program.

**Command bar** The area at the top of a window that displays commands relevant to the open window.

**Compress** Reduce the size of a file or combine several files into one.

**Computer icon** An icon that represents the computer on which you are working, and that provides access to the drives, folders, and files on your computer.

**Content pane** Displays files and folders stored in the selected disk drive or folder in the Navigation pane.

**Context-sensitive command** A command associated with activities in which you are engaged; often activated by right-clicking a screen item.

**Descending order** Files or folders listed from *z* to *a* when sorted.

**Desktop** The working area of the Windows 7 screen, consisting of program icons, a taskbar, a sidebar, and a Start button.

**Desktop background** The picture, pattern, or color that displays on the desktop.

**Details pane** Displays details about the drive, folder, or file selected in the Content pane.

**Dialog box** A box that asks you to make a decision about an individual object or topic. Dialog boxes do not have Minimize buttons.

**Double-click** Press the left mouse button two times in rapid succession, using caution not to move the mouse.

**Drag** Move the mouse pointer while holding down the left mouse button, and then release at the appropriate time.

**Drive** An area of storage that is formatted with the Windows file system and that has a drive letter such as C.

**DVD** A digital video (or versatile) disc—an optical storage device used to store data, and which can be read-only or read-write.

**Edit mode** A Windows mode that enables you to change the name of a file or folder, and works the same in all Windows applications.

**Favorites** The top part of the Navigation pane that displays favorite destinations associated with the current user.

**File** Work that you save and store on a drive, such as a Word document or a PowerPoint presentation.

**File extension** The three or four characters to the right of the period in a file name. Extensions tell the computer the program to use to open the file. File extensions can be displayed or hidden.

**File list** Displays the contents of the current folder or library.

**Flash drive** A small storage device that plugs into a computer USB port; also called a thumb drive or a USB drive.

**Folder** Storage area, represented on the screen by a picture of a paper file folder, used to store files or other folders.

**Gadget** A dynamic program—such as a clock, a stock market ticker, or a weather window—that displays on the desktop, usually in the Windows Sidebar.

**Gadget controls** A set of tools that includes a Drag gadget button in the shape of 12 small dots, an Options button in the shape of a wrench, a Larger/Smaller size button, and a Close button.

**Graphical user interface (GUI)** A computer interface that shows documents as they will look in their final form and uses icons to represent programs.

**Hard drive** A large disk drive inside your computer, also referred to as a Local Disk.

**Hardware** The computer memory, disk drive space, attached devices such as printers and scanners, and the central processing unit (CPU).

**Horizontal scroll bar** The bar at the bottom of a window that enables you to move left and right to view information that extends beyond the left and right edges of the screen.

**Icon** A graphic representation; often a small image on a button that enables you to run a program or program function.

**Jump list** A shortcut menu from an icon on the taskbar that displays frequent destinations you might want to visit from that program.

**Libraries** Folders used to sort files by file type.

**Library pane** Displays above the file list when a library is selected in the Navigation pane.

**Local disk** A large disk drive inside your computer, also referred to as a hard disk.

**Maximize** To increase the size of a window to fill the screen.

**Menu** A list of commands within a category.

**Menu bar** The bar near the top of a window that lists the names of menu categories.

**Metadata** Information about a file, such as tags, a title, a rating, the file name, and the file size.

**Minimize** To remove the window from the screen without closing it. Minimized windows can be reopened by clicking the associated button in the taskbar.

**Mouse pointer** The arrow, I-beam, or other symbol that shows the location or position of the mouse on your screen. Also called the pointer.

**Navigation pane** The pane on the left side of the Computer or Windows Explorer window that contains Favorites, Libraries, access to personal files and folders, and other items.

**Notification area**  Area on the right side of the taskbar that keeps you informed about processes that are occurring in the background, such as antivirus software, network connections, and other utility programs. It also displays the time.

**Operating system**  A set of instructions that coordinates the activities of your computer. Microsoft Windows 7 is an operating system.

**Paint**  A program included with Windows in which graphics are created or edited.

**Peek**  Use the *Show desktop* button to make the open windows transparent so you can see the desktop.

**Pinned programs area**  An area at the top of the Start menu that is reserved for programs that you want to display permanently, although you can also delete programs from this area.

**Pointer**  See mouse pointer.

**Recycle Bin**  A storage area for files that have been deleted. Files can be recovered from the Recycle bin or permanently removed.

**Restore**  Return a window to the size it was before it was maximized, using the Restore Down button.

**Right-click**  Click the right mouse button to activate a shortcut menu.

**Screen saver**  A picture or animation that displays on your screen after a set period of computer inactivity.

**ScreenTip**  A small box, activated by holding the pointer over a button or other screen object, that displays the name of a screen element.

**Scroll box**  The box in the vertical and horizontal scroll bars that can be dragged to reposition the document on the screen. The size of the scroll box also indicates the relative size of the document.

**Search box**  A box in which you type a search word or phrase.

**Search folder**  Retains all of the search conditions you specified during your search, and recreates the search every time you click the search folder.

**Shake**  Use the title bar to move a window back and forth quickly to hide all other open windows.

**Shortcut menu**  A menu activated by placing the pointer over an object and clicking the right mouse button.

**Snip**  A screen or part of a screen captured using the Snipping Tool.

**Snipping tool**  A program used to capture a screen or part of a screen.

**Start button**  The button on the left side of the taskbar that is used to start programs, change system settings, find Windows help, or shut down the computer.

**Start menu**  A menu that enables you to access the programs on your computer, and also enables you to change the way Windows operates, to access and configure your network, and to get help and support when it is needed.

**Status area**  Another name for the notification area on the right side of the taskbar.

**Submenu**  A second-level menu activated by selecting a menu option.

**System tray**  Another name for the notification area on the right side of the taskbar.

**Tags**  Custom file properties such as names, places, and descriptions that are added to files to enable you to categorize and find files more quickly.

**Taskbar**  Displays the Start button and the name of any open documents. The taskbar also displays shortcut buttons for other programs.

**Thumb drive**  A small storage device that plugs into a computer USB port; also called a USB drive or a flash drive.

**Thumbnail**  A miniature representation of the contents of a window or file.

**Title bar**  Displays the program icon, the name of the document, and the name of the program. The Minimize, Maximize/Restore Down, and Close buttons are grouped on the right side of the title bar.

**USB drive**  A small storage device that plugs into a computer USB port; also called a thumb drive or a flash drive.

**Vertical scroll bar**  The bar at the right side of a window that enables you to move up and down to view information that extends beyond the top and bottom of the screen.

**Wildcard**  A character, such as an asterisk, that can be used to match any number of characters in a file search.

**Window**  A box that displays information or a program, such as a letter, Excel, or a calculator. Windows usually consist of title bars, toolbars, menu bars, and status bars. A window will always have a Minimize button.

**Window name**  The name that displays in a window's title bar.

**Windows**  An operating system that coordinates the activities of a computer.

**Windows Aero**  The Windows user interface that features a three-dimensional look, with transparent window frames, live previews of open windows, and multiple color schemes. Aero is an acronym for **A**uthentic, **E**nergetic, **R**eflective, **O**pen.

**Windows Explorer**  A program that enables you to create and manage folders, and manage copy, move, sort, and delete files.

**WordPad**  A simple word processing program that comes with Windows 7.

# Using the Common Features of Microsoft Office 2010

## OUTCOMES
At the end of this chapter you will be able to:

## OBJECTIVES
Mastering these objectives will enable you to:

### PROJECT 1A
Create, save, and print a Microsoft Office 2010 file.

1. Use Windows Explorer to Locate Files and Folders (p. 59)
2. Locate and Start a Microsoft Office 2010 Program (p. 62)
3. Enter and Edit Text in an Office 2010 Program (p. 65)
4. Perform Commands from a Dialog Box (p. 67)
5. Create a Folder, Save a File, and Close a Program (p. 69)
6. Add Document Properties and Print a File (p. 74)

### PROJECT 1B
Use the Ribbon and dialog boxes to perform common commands in a Microsoft Office 2010 file.

7. Open an Existing File and Save It with a New Name (p. 78)
8. Explore Options for an Application (p. 81)
9. Perform Commands from the Ribbon (p. 82)
10. Apply Formatting in Office Programs (p. 88)
11. Use the Microsoft Office 2010 Help System (p. 99)
12. Compress Files (p. 100)

olly/Shutterstock

## In This Chapter

In this chapter, you will use Windows Explorer to navigate the Windows folder structure, create a folder, and save files in Microsoft Office 2010 programs. You will also practice using the features of Microsoft Office 2010 that are common across the major programs that comprise the Microsoft Office 2010 suite. These common features include creating, saving, and printing files.

Common features also include the new Paste Preview and Microsoft Office Backstage view. You will apply formatting, perform commands, and compress files. You will see that creating professional-quality documents is easy and quick in Microsoft Office 2010, and that finding your way around is fast and efficient.

The projects in this chapter relate to **Oceana Palm Grill**, which is a chain of 25 casual, full-service restaurants based in Austin, Texas. The Oceana Palm Grill owners plan an aggressive expansion program. To expand by 15 additional restaurants in North Carolina and Florida by 2018, the company must attract new investors, develop new menus, and recruit new employees, all while adhering to the company's quality guidelines and maintaining its reputation for excellent service. To succeed, the company plans to build on its past success and maintain its quality elements.

# **Project 1A** PowerPoint File

## Project Activities

In Activities 1.01 through 1.06, you will create a PowerPoint file, save it in a folder that you create by using Windows Explorer, and then print the file or submit it electronically as directed by your instructor. Your completed PowerPoint slide will look similar to Figure 1.1.

## Project Files

For Project 1A, you will need the following file:

New blank PowerPoint presentation

You will save your file as:

Lastname_Firstname_1A_Menu_Plan

## Project Results

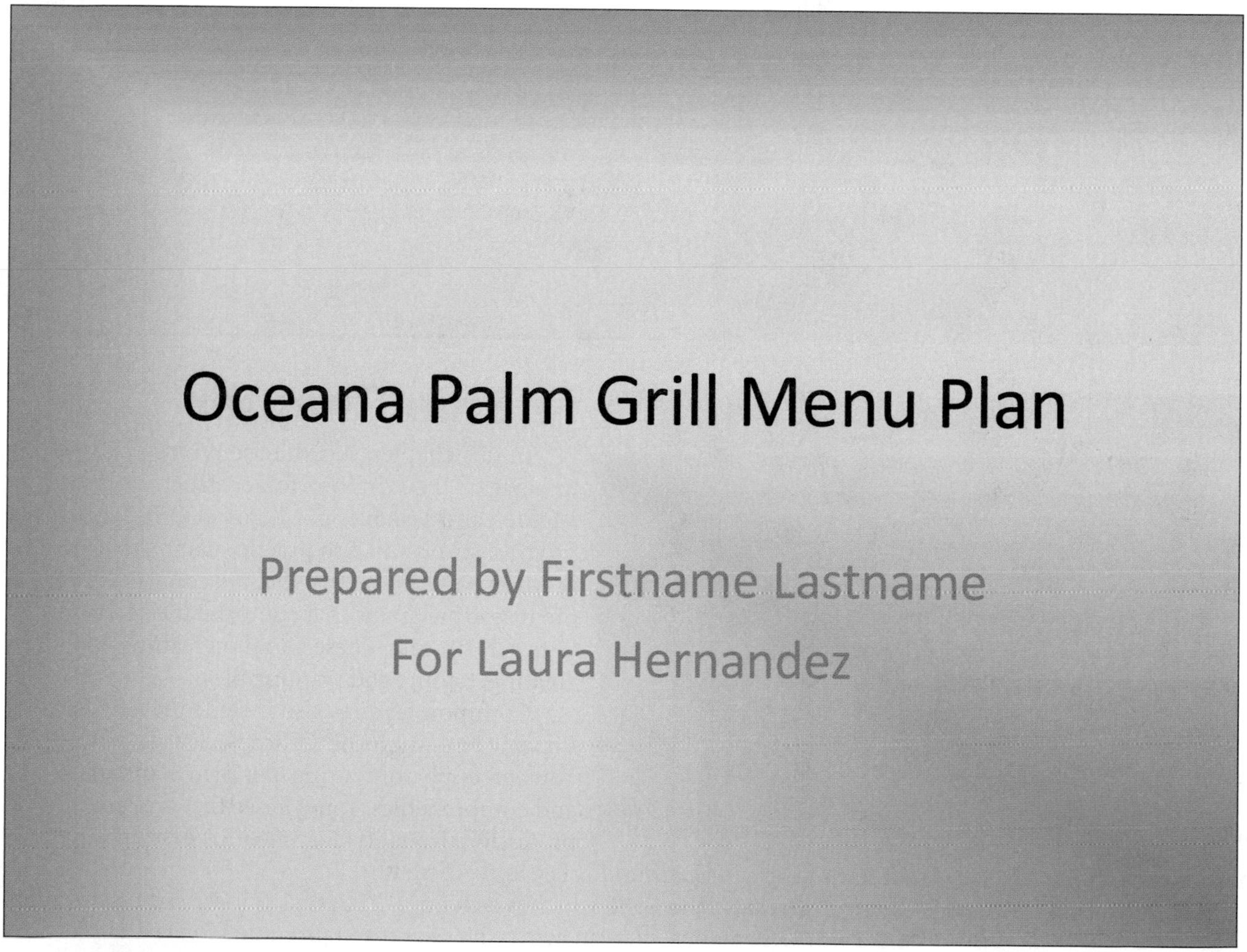
Oceana Palm Grill Menu Plan
Prepared by Firstname Lastname
For Laura Hernandez

**Figure 1.1**
Project 1A Menu Plan

# Objective 1 | Use Windows Explorer to Locate Files and Folders

A *file* is a collection of information stored on a computer under a single name, for example, a Word document or a PowerPoint presentation. Every file is stored in a *folder*—a container in which you store files—or a *subfolder*, which is a folder within a folder. Your Windows operating system stores and organizes your files and folders, which is a primary task of an operating system.

You *navigate*—explore within the organizing structure of Windows—to create, save, and find your files and folders by using the *Windows Explorer* program. Windows Explorer displays the files and folders on your computer, and is at work anytime you are viewing the contents of files and folders in a *window*. A window is a rectangular area on a computer screen in which programs and content appear; a window can be moved, resized, minimized, or closed.

## Activity 1.01 | Using Windows Explorer to Locate Files and Folders

**1** Turn on your computer and display the Windows *desktop*—the opening screen in Windows that simulates your work area.

> **Note | Comparing Your Screen with the Figures in This Textbook**
>
> Your screen will match the figures shown in this textbook if you set your screen resolution to 1024 × 768. At other resolutions, your screen will closely resemble, but not match, the figures shown. To view your screen's resolution, on the Windows 7 desktop, right-click in a blank area, and then click Screen resolution. In Windows Vista, right-click a blank area, click Personalize, and then click Display Settings. In Windows XP, right-click the desktop, click Properties, and then click the Settings tab.

**2** In your CD/DVD tray, insert the **Student CD** that accompanies this textbook. Wait a few moments for an **AutoPlay** window to display. Compare your screen with Figure 1.2.

> *AutoPlay* is a Windows feature that lets you choose which program to use to start different kinds of media, such as music CDs, or CDs and DVDs containing photos; it displays when you plug in or insert media or storage devices.

> **Note | If You Do Not Have the Student CD**
>
> If you do not have the Student CD, consult the inside back flap of this textbook for instructions on how to download the files from the Pearson Web site.

**Figure 1.2**

AutoPlay window

Close button

Windows desktop (yours may vary in color and arrangement)

**3** In the upper right corner of the **AutoPlay** window, move your mouse over—*point to*—the **Close** button ![X button], and then *click*—press the left button on your mouse pointing device one time.

**4** On the left side of the **Windows taskbar**, click the **Start** button ![Start] to display the **Start menu**. Compare your screen with Figure 1.3.

> The *Windows taskbar* is the area along the lower edge of the desktop that contains the *Start button* and an area to display buttons for open programs. The Start button displays the *Start menu*, which provides a list of choices and is the main gateway to your computer's programs, folders, and settings.

Figure 1.3

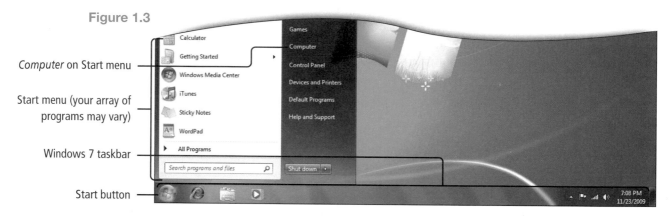

*Computer* on Start menu

Start menu (your array of programs may vary)

Windows 7 taskbar

Start button

**5** On the right side of the **Start menu**, click **Computer** to see the disk drives and other hardware connected to your computer. Compare your screen with Figure 1.4, and then take a moment to study the table in Figure 1.5.

> The *folder window* for *Computer* displays. A folder window displays the contents of the current folder, *library*, or device, and contains helpful parts so that you can navigate within Windows.

> In Windows 7, a library is a collection of items, such as files and folders, assembled from *various locations*; the locations might be on your computer, an external hard drive, removable media, or someone else's computer.

> The difference between a folder and a library is that a library can include files stored in *different locations*—any disk drive, folder, or other place that you can store files and folders.

Figure 1.4

Back and Forward

Address bar

File list

Navigation pane

Folder window toolbar

Views button

Search box

Preview pane button

Details pane

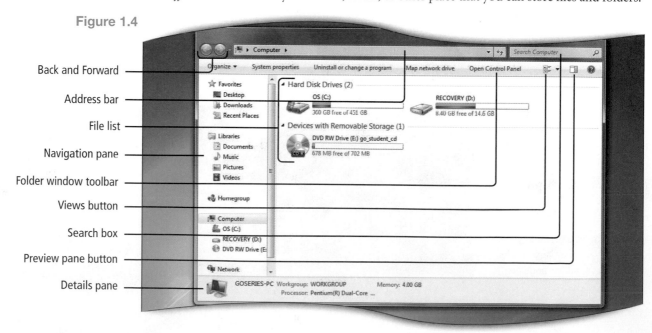

| Window Part | Use to: |
|---|---|
| Address bar | Navigate to a different folder or library, or go back to a previous one. |
| Back and Forward buttons | Navigate to other folders or libraries you have already opened without closing the current window. These buttons work in conjunction with the address bar; that is, after you use the address bar to change folders, you can use the Back button to return to the previous folder. |
| Details pane | Display the most common file properties—information about a file, such as the author, the date you last changed the file, and any descriptive *tags*, which are custom file properties that you create to help find and organize your files. |
| File list | Display the contents of the current folder or library. In Computer, the file list displays the disk drives. |
| Folder window for *Computer* | Display the contents of the current folder, library, or device. The Folder window contains helpful features so that you can navigate within Windows. |
| Folder window toolbar | Perform common tasks, such as changing the view of your files and folders or burning files to a CD. The buttons available change to display only relevant tasks. |
| Navigation pane | Navigate to, open, and display favorites, libraries, folders, saved searches, and an expandable list of drives. |
| Preview pane button | Display (if you have chosen to open this pane) the contents of most files without opening them in a program. To open the preview pane, click the Preview pane button on the toolbar to turn it on and off. |
| Search box | Look for an item in the current folder or library by typing a word or phrase in the search box. |
| Views button | Choose how to view the contents of the current location. |

Figure 1.5

**6** On the toolbar of the **Computer** folder window, click the **Views button arrow** ⬛ᵛ—the small arrow to the right of the Views button—to display a list of views that you can apply to the file list. If necessary, on the list, click **Tiles**.

The Views button is a *split button*; clicking the main part of the button performs a *command* and clicking the arrow opens a menu or list. A command is an instruction to a computer program that causes an action to be carried out.

When you open a folder or a library, you can change how the files display in the file list. For example, you might prefer to see large or small *icons*—pictures that represent a program, a file, a folder, or some other object—or an arrangement that lets you see various types of information about each file. Each time you click the Views button, the window changes, cycling through several views—additional view options are available by clicking the Views button arrow.

**Another Way**

Point to the CD/DVD drive, right-click, and then click Open.

**7** In the **file list**, under **Devices with Removable Storage**, point to your **CD/DVD Drive**, and then *double-click*—click the left mouse button two times in rapid succession—to display the list of folders on the CD. Compare your screen with Figure 1.6.

When double-clicking, keep your hand steady between clicks; this is more important than the speed of the two clicks.

Figure 1.6

Views button indicates
Details view

List of folders on the
CD in Details view

Views button arrow

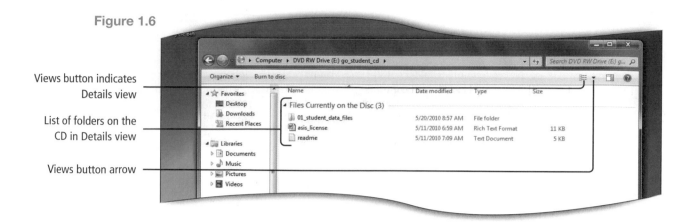

**8** In the **file list**, point to the folder **01_student_data_files** and double-click to display the list of subfolders in the folder. Double-click to open the folder **01_common_features**. Compare your screen with Figure 1.7.

The Student Resource CD includes files that you will use to complete the projects in this textbook. If you prefer, you can also copy the **01_student_data_files** folder to a location on your computer's hard drive or to a removable device such as a *USB flash drive*, which is a small storage device that plugs into a computer USB port. Your instructor might direct you to other locations where these files are located; for example, on your learning management system.

Figure 1.7

Address bar displays
sequence of folders

One folder in the
*01_common_features*
folder

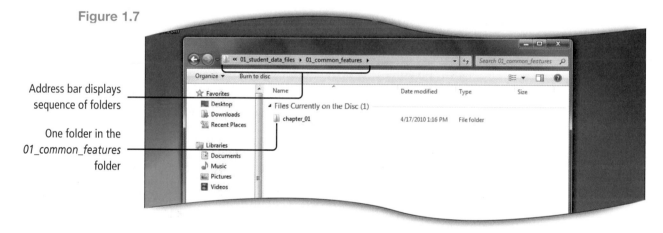

**9** In the upper right corner of the **Computer** window, click the **Close** [X] button to redisplay your desktop.

## Objective 2 | Locate and Start a Microsoft Office 2010 Program

*Microsoft Office 2010* includes programs, servers, and services for individuals, small organizations, and large enterprises. A *program*, also referred to as an *application*, is a set of instructions used by a computer to perform a task, such as word processing or accounting.

### Activity 1.02 | Locating and Starting a Microsoft Office 2010 Program

**1** On the **Windows taskbar**, click the **Start** button [start] to display the **Start** menu.

**2** From the displayed **Start** menu, locate the group of **Microsoft Office 2010** programs on your computer—the Office program icons from which you can start the program may be located on your Start menu, in a Microsoft Office folder on the **All Programs** list, on your desktop, or any combination of these locations; the location will vary depending on how your computer is configured.

> *All Programs* is an area of the Start menu that displays all the available programs on your computer system.

**3** Examine Figure 1.8, and notice the programs that are included in the Microsoft Office Professional Plus 2010 group of programs. (Your group of programs may vary.)

> *Microsoft Word* is a word processing program, with which you create and share documents by using its writing tools.

> *Microsoft Excel* is a spreadsheet program, with which you calculate and analyze numbers and create charts.

> *Microsoft Access* is a database program, with which you can collect, track, and report data.

> *Microsoft PowerPoint* is a presentation program, with which you can communicate information with high-impact graphics and video.

> Additional popular Office programs include *Microsoft Outlook* to manage e-mail and organizational activities, *Microsoft Publisher* to create desktop publishing documents such as brochures, and *Microsoft OneNote* to manage notes that you make at meetings or in classes and to share notes with others on the Web.

> The Professional Plus version of Office 2010 also includes *Microsoft SharePoint Workspace* to share information with others in a team environment and *Microsoft InfoPath Designer and Filler* to create forms and gather data.

Figure 1.8

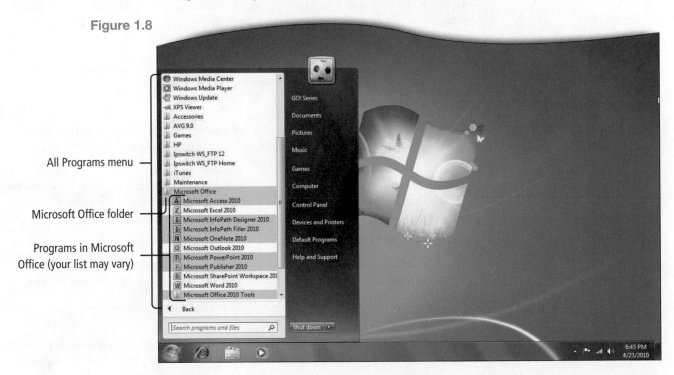

All Programs menu

Microsoft Office folder

Programs in Microsoft Office (your list may vary)

**4** Click to open the program **Microsoft PowerPoint 2010**. Compare your screen with Figure 1.9, and then take a moment to study the description of these screen elements in the table in Figure 1.10.

Figure 1.9

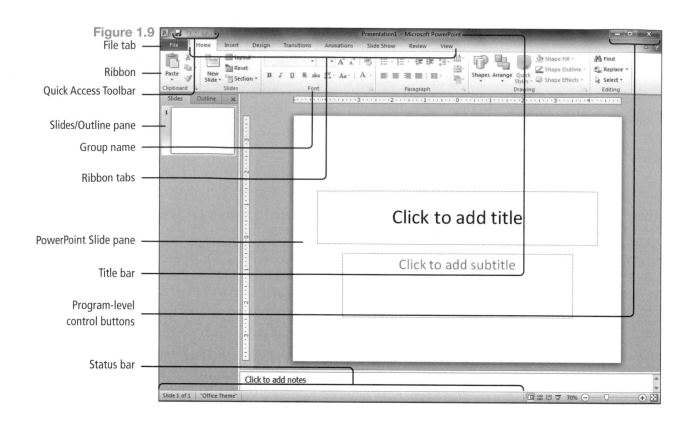

| Screen Element | Description |
|---|---|
| File tab | Displays Microsoft Office Backstage view, which is a centralized space for all of your file management tasks such as opening, saving, printing, publishing, or sharing a file—all the things you can do *with* a file. |
| Group names | Indicate the name of the groups of related commands on the displayed tab. |
| PowerPoint Slide pane | Displays a large image of the active slide in the PowerPoint program. |
| Program-level control buttons | Minimizes, restores, or closes the program window. |
| Quick Access Toolbar | Displays buttons to perform frequently used commands and resources with a single click. The default commands include Save, Undo, and Redo. You can add and delete buttons to customize the Quick Access Toolbar for your convenience. |
| Ribbon | Displays a group of task-oriented tabs that contain the commands, styles, and resources you need to work in an Office 2010 program. The look of your Ribbon depends on your screen resolution. A high resolution will display more individual items and button names on the Ribbon. |
| Ribbon tabs | Display the names of the task-oriented tabs relevant to the open program. |
| Slides/Outline pane | Displays either thumbnails of the slides in a PowerPoint presentation (Slides tab) or the outline of the presentation's content (Outline tab). In each Office 2010 program, different panes display in different ways to assist you. |
| Status bar | Displays file information on the left and View and Zoom on the right. |
| Title bar | Displays the name of the file and the name of the program. The program window control buttons—Minimize, Maximize/Restore Down, and Close—are grouped on the right side of the title bar. |

Figure 1.10

## Objective 3 | Enter and Edit Text in an Office 2010 Program

All of the programs in Office 2010 require some typed text. Your keyboard is still the primary method of entering information into your computer. Techniques to *edit*—make changes to—text are similar among all of the Office 2010 programs.

### Activity 1.03 | Entering and Editing Text in an Office 2010 Program

**1** In the middle of the PowerPoint Slide pane, point to the text *Click to add title* to display the ⎉ pointer, and then click one time.

The *insertion point*—a blinking vertical line that indicates where text or graphics will be inserted—displays.

In Office 2010 programs, the mouse *pointer*—any symbol that displays on your screen in response to moving your mouse device—displays in different shapes depending on the task you are performing and the area of the screen to which you are pointing.

**2** Type **Oceana Grille Info** and notice how the insertion point moves to the right as you type. Point slightly to the right of the letter *e* in *Grille* and click to place the insertion point there. Compare your screen with Figure 1.11.

Figure 1.11

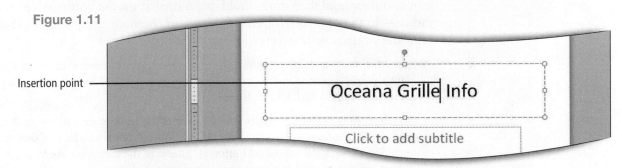

Insertion point

**3** On your keyboard, locate and press the ⎵Backspace⎵ key to delete the letter *e*.

Pressing ⎵Backspace⎵ removes a character to the left of the insertion point.

**4** Point slightly to the left of the *I* in *Info* and click one time to place the insertion point there. Type **Menu** and then press ⎵Spacebar⎵ one time. Compare your screen with Figure 1.12.

By *default*, when you type text in an Office program, existing text moves to the right to make space for new typing. Default refers to the current selection or setting that is automatically used by a program unless you specify otherwise.

Figure 1.12

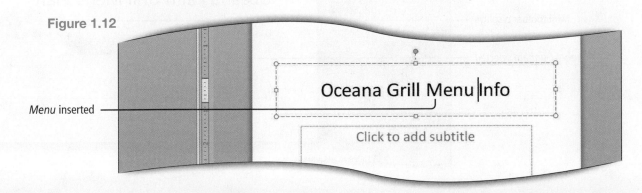

*Menu* inserted

**5** Press `Del` four times to delete *Info* and then type **Plan**

> Pressing `Del` removes—deletes—a character to the right of the insertion point.

**6** With your insertion point blinking after the word *Plan*, on your keyboard, hold down the `Ctrl` key. While holding down `Ctrl`, press `←` three times to move the insertion point to the beginning of the word *Grill*.

> This is a **keyboard shortcut**—a key or combination of keys that performs a task that would otherwise require a mouse. This keyboard shortcut moves the insertion point to the beginning of the previous word.

> A keyboard shortcut is commonly indicated as `Ctrl` + `←` (or some other combination of keys) to indicate that you hold down the first key while pressing the second key. A keyboard shortcut can also include three keys, in which case you hold down the first two and then press the third. For example, `Ctrl` + `Shift` + `←` selects one word to the left.

**7** With the insertion point blinking at the beginning of the word *Grill*, type **Palm** and press `Spacebar`.

**8** Click anywhere in the text *Click to add subtitle*. With the insertion point blinking, type the following and include the spelling error: **Prepered by Annabel Dunham**

**9** With your mouse, point slightly to the left of the *A* in *Annabel*, hold down the left mouse button, and then **drag**—hold down the left mouse button while moving your mouse—to the right to select the text *Annabel Dunham*, and then release the mouse button. Compare your screen with Figure 1.13.

> The **Mini toolbar** displays commands that are commonly used with the selected object, which places common commands close to your pointer. When you move the pointer away from the Mini toolbar, it fades from view.

> To **select** refers to highlighting, by dragging with your mouse, areas of text or data or graphics so that the selection can be edited, formatted, copied, or moved. The action of dragging includes releasing the left mouse button at the end of the area you want to select. The Office programs recognize a selected area as one unit, to which you can make changes. Selecting text may require some practice. If you are not satisfied with your result, click anywhere outside of the selection, and then begin again.

**Figure 1.13**

Mini toolbar displays

*Annabel Dunham* selected

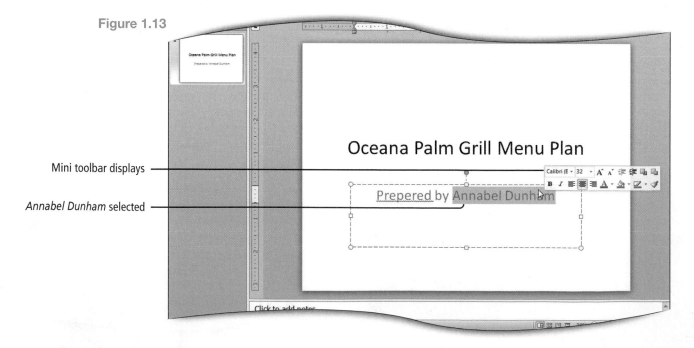

**10** With the text *Annabel Dunham* selected, type your own firstname and lastname.

In any Windows-based program, such as the Microsoft Office 2010 programs, selected text is deleted and then replaced when you begin to type new text. You will save time by developing good techniques to select and then edit or replace selected text, which is easier than pressing the [Del] key numerous times to delete text that you do not want.

**11** Notice that the misspelled word *Prepered* displays with a wavy red underline; additionally, all or part of your name might display with a wavy red underline.

Office 2010 has a dictionary of words against which all entered text is checked. In Word and PowerPoint, words that are *not* in the dictionary display a wavy red line, indicating a possible misspelled word or a proper name or an unusual word—none of which are in the Office 2010 dictionary.

In Excel and Access, you can initiate a check of the spelling, but wavy red underlines do not display.

**12** Point to *Prepered* and then ***right-click***—click your right mouse button one time.

The Mini toolbar and a ***shortcut menu*** display. A shortcut menu displays commands and options relevant to the selected text or object—known as ***context-sensitive commands*** because they relate to the item you right-clicked.

Here, the shortcut menu displays commands related to the misspelled word. You can click the suggested correct spelling *Prepared*, click Ignore All to ignore the misspelling, add the word to the Office dictionary, or click Spelling to display a ***dialog box***. A dialog box is a small window that contains options for completing a task. Whenever you see a command followed by an ***ellipsis*** (…), which is a set of three dots indicating incompleteness, clicking the command will always display a dialog box.

**13** On the displayed shortcut menu, click **Prepared** to correct the misspelled word. If necessary, point to any parts of your name that display a wavy red underline, right-click, and then on the shortcut menu, click Ignore All so that Office will no longer mark your name with a wavy underline in this file.

---

**More Knowledge | Adding to the Office Dictionary**

The main dictionary contains the most common words, but does not include all proper names, technical terms, or acronyms. You can add words, acronyms, and proper names to the Office dictionary by clicking Add to Dictionary when they are flagged, and you might want to do so for your own name and other proper names and terms that you type often.

---

## Objective 4 | Perform Commands from a Dialog Box

In a dialog box, you make decisions about an individual object or topic. A dialog box also offers a way to adjust a number of settings at one time.

### Activity 1.04 | Performing Commands from a Dialog Box

**1** Point anywhere in the blank area above the title *Oceana Palm Grill Menu Plan* to display the ▱ pointer.

**2** Right-click to display a shortcut menu. Notice the command *Format Background* followed by an ellipsis (...). Compare your screen with Figure 1.14.

Recall that a command followed by an ellipsis indicates that a dialog box will display if you click the command.

Figure 1.14

Shortcut menu ———

Ellipsis following command ———

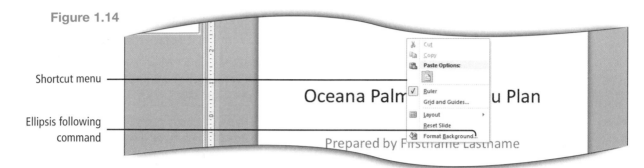

**3** Click **Format Background** to display the **Format Background** dialog box, and then compare your screen with Figure 1.15.

Figure 1.15

Fill selected ———

Format Background dialog box ———

Options related to the background fill ———

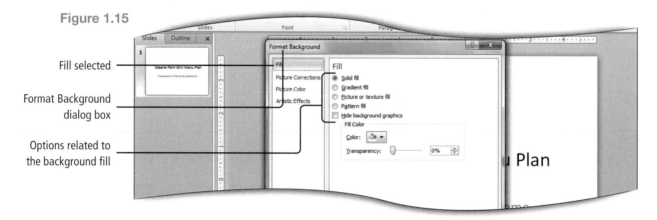

**4** On the left, if necessary, click **Fill** to display the **Fill** options.

*Fill* is the inside color of an object. Here, the dialog box displays the option group names on the left; some dialog boxes provide a set of tabs across the top from which you can display different sets of options.

**5** On the right, under **Fill**, click the **Gradient fill** option button.

The dialog box displays additional settings related to the gradient fill option. An *option button* is a round button that enables you to make one choice among two or more options. In a gradient fill, one color fades into another.

**6** Click the **Preset colors arrow**—the arrow in the box to the right of the text *Preset colors*—and then in the gallery, in the second row, point to the fifth fill color to display the ScreenTip *Fog*.

A *gallery* is an Office feature that displays a list of potential results. A *ScreenTip* displays useful information about mouse actions, such as pointing to screen elements or dragging.

**7** Click **Fog**, and then notice that the fill color is applied to your slide. Click the **Type arrow**, and then click **Rectangular** to change the pattern of the fill color. Compare your screen with Figure 1.16.

Figure 1.16

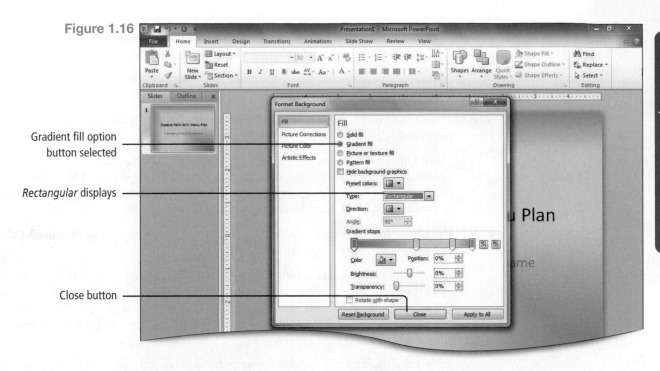

Gradient fill option button selected

*Rectangular* displays

Close button

**8** At the bottom of the dialog box, click **Close**.

> As you progress in your study of Microsoft Office, you will practice using many dialog boxes and applying dramatic effects such as this to your Word documents, Excel spreadsheets, Access databases, and PowerPoint slides.

## Objective 5 | Create a Folder, Save a File, and Close a Program

A *location* is any disk drive, folder, or other place in which you can store files and folders. Where you store your files depends on how and where you use your data. For example, for your classes, you might decide to store primarily on a removable USB flash drive so that you can carry your files to different locations and access your files on different computers.

If you do most of your work on a single computer, for example your home desktop system or your laptop computer that you take with you to school or work, store your files in one of the Libraries—Documents, Music, Pictures, or Videos—provided by your Windows operating system.

Although the Windows operating system helps you to create and maintain a logical folder structure, take the time to name your files and folders in a consistent manner.

### Activity 1.05 | Creating a Folder, Saving a File, and Closing a Program

A PowerPoint presentation is an example of a file. Office 2010 programs use a common dialog box provided by the Windows operating system to assist you in saving files. In this activity, you will create a folder on a USB flash drive in which to store files. If you prefer to store on your hard drive, you can use similar steps to store files in your My Documents folder in your Documents library.

**1** Insert a USB flash drive into your computer, and if necessary, **Close** ⊠ the **AutoPlay** dialog box. If you are not using a USB flash drive, go to Step 2.

> As the first step in saving a file, determine where you want to save the file, and if necessary, insert a storage device.

**2** At the top of your screen, in the title bar, notice that *Presentation1 – Microsoft PowerPoint* displays.

> Most Office 2010 programs open with a new unsaved file with a default name— *Presentation1*, *Document1*, and so on. As you create your file, your work is temporarily stored in the computer's memory until you initiate a Save command, at which time you must choose a file name and location in which to save your file.

**3** In the upper left corner of your screen, click the **File tab** to display **Microsoft Office Backstage** view. Compare your screen with Figure 1.17.

> Microsoft Office ***Backstage view*** is a centralized space for tasks related to *file* management; that is why the tab is labeled *File*. File management tasks include, for example, opening, saving, printing, publishing, or sharing a file. The ***Backstage tabs***—*Info*, *Recent*, *New*, *Print*, *Save & Send*, and *Help*—display along the left side. The tabs group file-related tasks together.

> Above the Backstage tabs, ***Quick Commands***—*Save*, *Save As*, *Open*, and *Close*—display for quick access to these commands. When you click any of these commands, Backstage view closes and either a dialog box displays or the active file closes.

> Here, the ***Info tab*** displays information—*info*—about the current file. In the center panel, various file management tasks are available in groups. For example, if you click the Protect Presentation button, a list of options that you can set for this file that relate to who can open or edit the presentation displays.

> On the Info tab, in the right panel, you can also examine the ***document properties***. Document properties, also known as ***metadata***, are details about a file that describe or identify it, such as the title, author name, subject, and keywords that identify the document's topic or contents. On the Info page, a thumbnail image of the current file displays in the upper right corner, which you can click to close Backstage view and return to the document.

---

**More Knowledge | Deciding Where to Store Your Files**

Where should you store your files? In the libraries created by Windows 7 (Documents, Pictures, and so on)? On a removable device like a flash drive or external hard drive? In Windows 7, it is easy to find your files, especially if you use the libraries. Regardless of where you save a file, Windows 7 will make it easy to find the file again, even if you are not certain where it might be.

In Windows 7, storing all of your files within a library makes sense. If you perform most of your work on your desktop system or your laptop that travels with you, you can store your files in the libraries created by Windows 7 for your user account—Documents, Pictures, Music, and so on. Within these libraries, you can create folders and subfolders to organize your data. These libraries are a good choice for storing your files because:

- From the Windows Explorer button on the taskbar, your libraries are always just one click away.
- The libraries are designed for their contents; for example, the Pictures folder displays small images of your digital photos.
- You can add new locations to a library; for example, an external hard drive, or a network drive. Locations added to a library behave just like they are on your hard drive.
- Other users of your computer cannot access your libraries.
- The libraries are the default location for opening and saving files within an application, so you will find that you can open and save files with fewer navigation clicks.

---

Figure 1.17

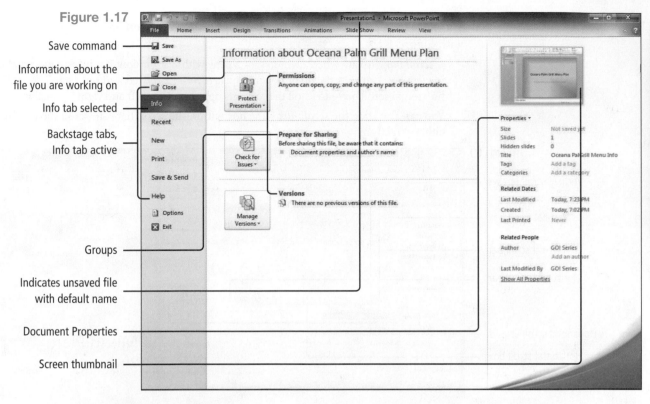

Save command

Information about the file you are working on

Info tab selected

Backstage tabs, Info tab active

Groups

Indicates unsaved file with default name

Document Properties

Screen thumbnail

**4** Above the **Backstage tabs**, click **Save** to display the **Save As** dialog box.

Backstage view closes and the Save As dialog box, which includes a folder window and an area at the bottom to name the file and set the file type, displays.

When you are saving something for the first time, for example a new PowerPoint presentation, the Save and Save As commands are identical. That is, the Save As dialog box will display if you click Save or if you click Save As.

> **Note** | Saving Your File
>
> After you have named a file and saved it in your desired location, the Save command saves any changes you make to the file without displaying any dialog box. The Save As command will display the Save As dialog box and let you name and save a new file based on the current one—in a location that you choose. After you name and save the new document, the original document closes, and the new document—based on the original one—displays.

**5** In the **Save As** dialog box, on the left, locate the **navigation pane**; compare your screen with Figure 1.18.

By default, the Save command opens the Documents library unless your default file location has been changed.

Figure 1.18

Save As dialog box
Address bar

Default save location

Navigation pane

File list (yours will vary)

File name box

Save as type defaults to *PowerPoint Presentation*

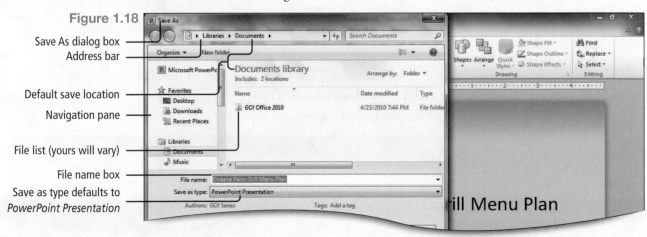

**6** On the right side of the **navigation pane**, point to the **scroll bar**. Compare your screen with Figure 1.19.

> A *scroll bar* displays when a window, or a pane within a window, has information that is not in view. You can click the up or down scroll arrows—or the left and right scroll arrows in a horizontal scroll bar—to scroll the contents up or down or left and right in small increments.
>
> You can also drag the *scroll box*—the box within the scroll bar—to scroll the window in either direction.

Figure 1.19

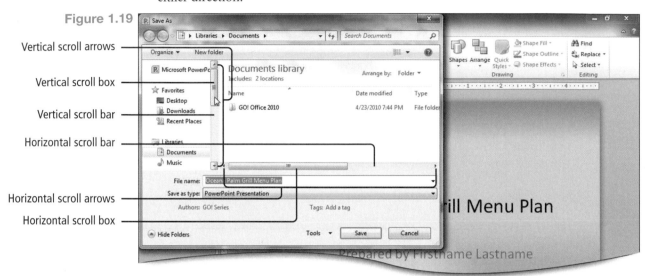

Vertical scroll arrows
Vertical scroll box
Vertical scroll bar
Horizontal scroll bar
Horizontal scroll arrows
Horizontal scroll box

**7** Click the **down scroll arrow** as necessary so that you can view the lower portion of the **navigation pane**, and then click the icon for your USB flash drive. Compare your screen with Figure 1.20. (If you prefer to store on your computer's hard drive instead of a USB flash drive, in the navigation pane, click Documents.)

Figure 1.20

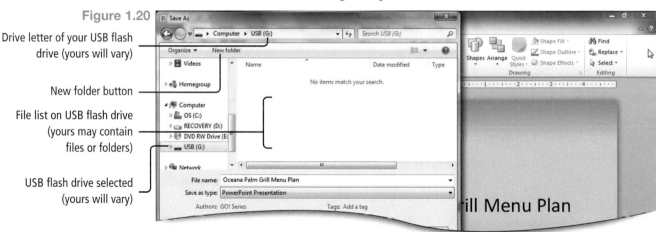

Drive letter of your USB flash drive (yours will vary)
New folder button
File list on USB flash drive (yours may contain files or folders)
USB flash drive selected (yours will vary)

**8** On the toolbar, click the **New folder** button.

> In the file list, a new folder is created, and the text *New folder* is selected.

**9** Type **Common Features Chapter 1** and press Enter. Compare your screen with Figure 1.21.

> In Windows-based programs, the Enter key confirms an action.

Figure 1.21

New folder

**10** In the **file list**, double-click the name of your new folder to open it and display its name in the **address bar**.

**11** In the lower portion of the dialog box, click in the **File name** box to select the existing text. Notice that Office inserts the text at the beginning of the presentation as a suggested file name.

**12** On your keyboard, locate the ⌐ key. Notice that the Shift of this key produces the underscore character. With the text still selected, type **Lastname_Firstname_1A_ Menu_Plan** Compare your screen with Figure 1.22.

> You can use spaces in file names, however some individuals prefer not to use spaces. Some programs, especially when transferring files over the Internet, may not work well with spaces in file names. In general, however, unless you encounter a problem, it is OK to use spaces. In this textbook, underscores are used instead of spaces in file names.

Figure 1.22

File name box indicates your file name

Save as type box indicates *PowerPoint Presentation*

Save button

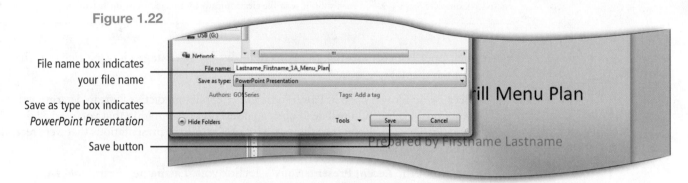

**13** In the lower right corner, click **Save**; or press Enter. See Figure 1.23.

> Your new file name displays in the title bar, indicating that the file has been saved to a location that you have specified.

Figure 1.23

File name in title bar

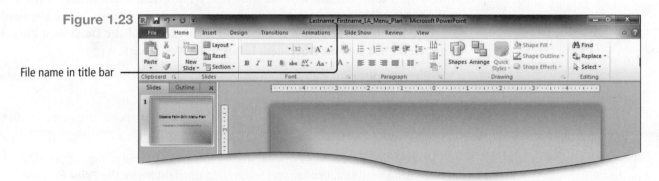

**14** In the text that begins *Prepared by*, click to position the insertion point at the end of your name, and then press Enter to move to a new line. Type **For Laura Hernandez**

**15** Click the **File tab** to display **Backstage** view. At the top of the center panel, notice that the path where your file is stored displays. Above the Backstage tabs, click **Close** to close the file. In the message box, click **Save** to save the changes you made and close the file. Leave PowerPoint open.

> PowerPoint displays a message asking if you want to save the changes you have made. Because you have made additional changes to the file since your last Save operation, an Office program will always prompt you to save so that you do not lose any new data.

## Objective 6 | Add Document Properties and Print a File

The process of printing a file is similar in all of the Office applications. There are differences in the types of options you can select. For example, in PowerPoint, you have the option of printing the full slide, with each slide printing on a full sheet of paper, or of printing handouts with small pictures of slides on a page.

### Activity 1.06 | Adding Document Properties and Printing a File

> **Alert! | Are You Printing or Submitting Your Files Electronically?**
>
> If you are submitting your files electronically only, or have no printer attached, you can still complete this activity. Complete Steps 1-9, and then submit your file electronically as directed by your instructor.

**1** In the upper left corner, click the **File tab** to display **Backstage** view. Notice that the **Recent tab** displays.

Because no file was open in PowerPoint, Office applies predictive logic to determine that your most likely action will be to open a PowerPoint presentation that you worked on recently. Thus, the Recent tab displays a list of PowerPoint presentations that were recently open on your system.

**2** At the top of the **Recent Presentations** list, click your **Lastname_Firstname_1A_ Menu_Plan** file to open it.

**3** Click the **File tab** to redisplay **Backstage** view. On the right, under the screen thumbnail, click **Properties**, and then click **Show Document Panel**. In the **Author** box, delete the existing text, and then type your firstname and lastname. Notice that in PowerPoint, some variation of the slide title is automatically inserted in the Title box. In the **Subject** box, type your Course name and section number. In the **Keywords** box, type **menu plan** and then in the upper right corner of the **Document Properties** panel, click the **Close the Document Information Panel** button ☒ .

Adding properties to your documents will make them easier to search for in systems such as Microsoft SharePoint.

**Another Way**

Press Ctrl + P or Ctrl + F2 to display the Print tab in Backstage view.

**4** Redisplay **Backstage** view, and then click the **Print tab**. Compare your screen with Figure 1.24.

On the Print tab in Backstage view, in the center panel, three groups of printing-related tasks display—Print, Printer, and Settings. In the right panel, the *Print Preview* displays, which is a view of a document as it will appear on the paper when you print it.

At the bottom of the Print Preview area, on the left, the number of pages and arrows with which you can move among the pages in Print Preview display. On the right, *Zoom* settings enable you to shrink or enlarge the Print Preview. Zoom is the action of increasing or decreasing the viewing area of the screen.

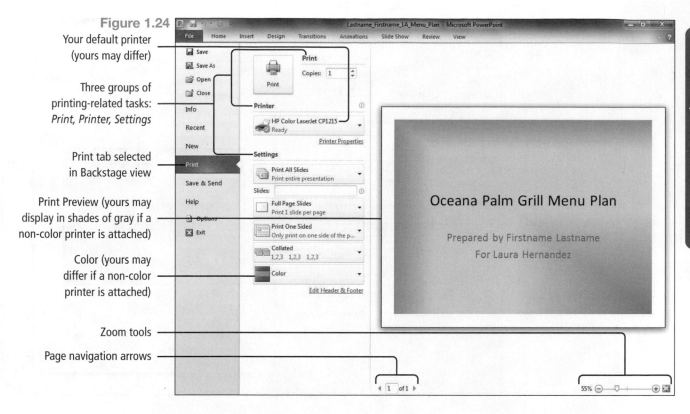

Figure 1.24

Your default printer
(yours may differ)

Three groups of
printing-related tasks:
*Print, Printer, Settings*

Print tab selected
in Backstage view

Print Preview (yours may
display in shades of gray if a
non-color printer is attached)

Color (yours may
differ if a non-color
printer is attached)

Zoom tools

Page navigation arrows

**5** Locate the **Settings group**, and notice that the default setting is to **Print All Slides** and to print **Full Page Slides**—each slide on a full sheet of paper.

**6** Point to **Full Page Slides**, notice that the button glows orange, and then click the button to display a gallery of print arrangements. Compare your screen with Figure 1.25.

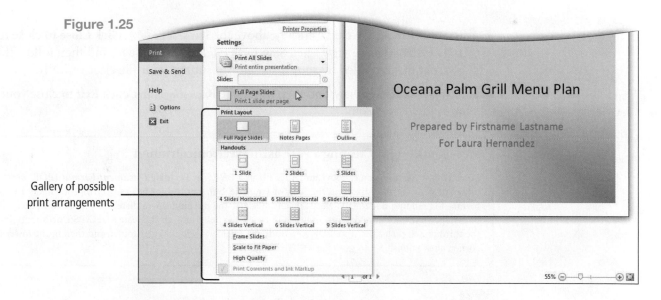

Figure 1.25

Gallery of possible
print arrangements

**7** In the displayed gallery, under **Handouts**, click **1 Slide**, and then compare your screen with Figure 1.26.

The Print Preview changes to show how your slide will print on the paper in this arrangement.

**Figure 1.26**

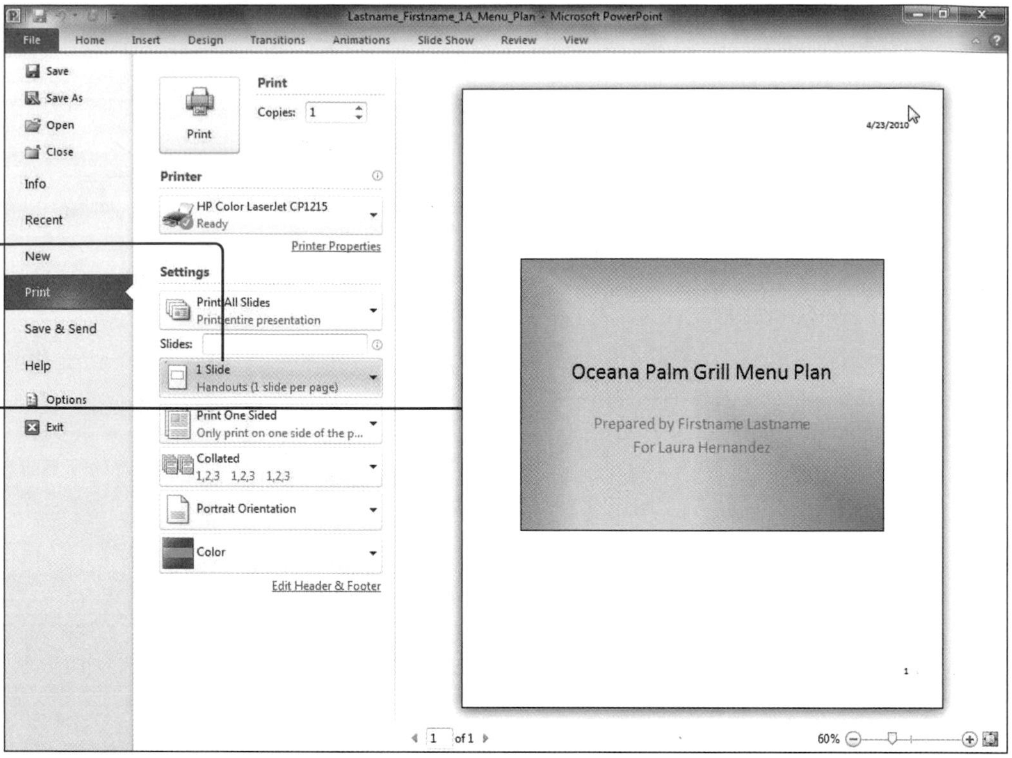

*Handouts* selected

Print Preview displays
the 1 slide printed as
handouts setting

**8** To submit your file electronically, skip this step and move to Step 9. To print your slide, be sure your system is connected to a printer, and then in the **Print group**, click the **Print** button. On the Quick Access Toolbar, click **Save** 🖫, and then move to Step 10.

> The handout will print on your default printer—on a black and white printer, the colors will print in shades of gray. Backstage view closes and your file redisplays in the PowerPoint window.

**9** To submit your file electronically, above the **Backstage tabs**, click **Close** to close the file and close **Backstage** view, click **Save** in the displayed message, and then follow the instructions provided by your instructor to submit your file electronically.

**Another Way**

In the upper right corner of your PowerPoint window, click the red Close button.

**10** Display **Backstage** view, and then below the **Backstage tabs**, click **Exit** to close your file and close PowerPoint.

---

**More Knowledge** | **Creating a PDF as an Electronic Printout**

From Backstage view, you can save an Office file as a *PDF file*. *Portable Document Format* (PDF) creates an image of your file that preserves the look of your file, but that cannot be easily changed. This is a popular format for sending documents electronically, because the document will display on most computers. From Backstage view, click Save & Send, and then in the File Types group, click Create PDF/XPS Document. Then in the third panel, click the Create PDF/XPS button, navigate to your chapter folder, and then in the lower right corner, click Publish.

---

**End** **You have completed Project 1A**

# Project 1B Word File

## Project Activities

In Activities 1.07 through 1.16, you will open, edit, save, and then compress a Word file. Your completed document will look similar to Figure 1.27.

## Project Files

For Project 1B, you will need the following file:

cf01B_Cheese_Promotion

You will save your Word document as:

Lastname_Firstname_1B_Cheese_Promotion

## Project Results

### Memo

**TO:**        Laura Mabry Hernandez, General Manager

**FROM:**    Donna Jackson, Executive Chef

**DATE:**      December 17, 2014

**SUBJECT:**    Cheese Specials on Tuesdays

*To increase restaurant traffic between 4:00 p.m. and 6:00 p.m., I am proposing a trial cheese event in one of the restaurants, probably Orlando. I would like to try a weekly event on Tuesday evenings where the focus is on a good selection of cheese.*

I envision two possibilities: a selection of cheese plates or a cheese bar—or both. The cheeses would have to be matched with compatible fruit and bread or crackers. They could be used as appetizers, or for desserts, as is common in Europe. The cheese plates should be varied and diverse, using a mixture of hard and soft, sharp and mild, unusual and familiar.

I am excited about this new promotion. If done properly, I think it could increase restaurant traffic in the hours when individuals want to relax with a small snack instead of a heavy dinner.

The promotion will require that our employees become familiar with the types and characteristics of both foreign and domestic cheeses. Let's meet to discuss the details and the training requirements, and to create a flyer that begins something like this:

### Oceana Palm Grill Tuesday Cheese Tastings

Lastname_Firstname_1B_Cheese_Promotion

**Figure 1.27**
Project 1B Cheese Promotion

## Objective 7 | Open an Existing File and Save It with a New Name

In any Office program, use the Open command to display the *Open dialog box*, from which you can navigate to and then open an existing file that was created in that same program.

The Open dialog box, along with the Save and Save As dialog boxes, are referred to as *common dialog boxes*. These dialog boxes, which are provided by the Windows programming interface, display in all of the Office programs in the same manner. Thus, the Open, Save, and Save As dialog boxes will all look and perform the same in each Office program.

### Activity 1.07 | Opening an Existing File and Saving it with a New Name

In this activity, you will display the Open dialog box, open an existing Word document, and then save it in your storage location with a new name.

**1** Determine the location of the student data files that accompany this textbook, and be sure you can access these files.

> For example:
>
> If you are accessing the files from the Student CD that came with this textbook, insert the CD now.
>
> If you copied the files from the Student CD or from the Pearson Web site to a USB flash drive that you are using for this course, insert the flash drive in your computer now.
>
> If you copied the files to the hard drive of your computer, for example in your Documents library, be sure you can locate the files on the hard drive.

**2** Determine the location of your **Common Features Chapter 1** folder you created in Activity 1.05, in which you will store your work from this chapter, and then be sure you can access that folder.

> For example:
>
> If you created your chapter folder on a USB flash drive, insert the flash drive in your computer now. This can be the same flash drive where you have stored the student data files; just be sure to use the chapter folder you created.
>
> If you created your chapter folder in the Documents library on your computer, be sure you can locate the folder. Otherwise, create a new folder at the computer at which you are working, or on a USB flash drive.

**3** Using the technique you practiced in Activity 1.02, locate and then start the **Microsoft Word 2010** program on your system.

**Another Way**

In the Word (or other program) window, press Ctrl + F12 to display the Open dialog box.

**4** On the Ribbon, click the **File tab** to display **Backstage** view, and then click **Open** to display the **Open** dialog box.

**5** In the **navigation pane** on the left, use the scroll bar to scroll as necessary, and then click the location of your student data files to display the location's contents in the **file list**. Compare your screen with Figure 1.28.

> For example:
>
> If you are accessing the files from the Student CD that came with your book, under Computer, click the CD/DVD.
>
> If you are accessing the files from a USB flash drive, under Computer, click the flash drive name.
>
> If you are accessing the files from the Documents library of your computer, under Libraries, click Documents.

**Figure 1.28**

Open dialog box

Scroll bar in
navigation pane

Navigation pane

CD/DVD selected
(or location of your
student files)

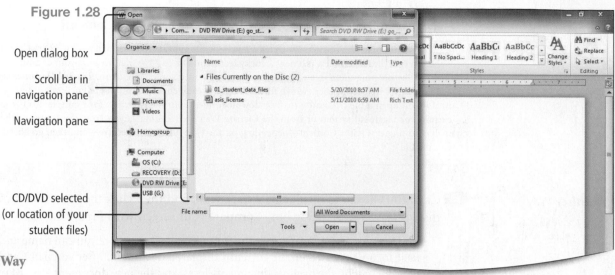

**Another Way**

Point to a folder name,
right-click, and then
from the shortcut
menu, click Open.

**6** Point to the folder **01_student_data_files** and double-click to open the folder. Point
to the subfolder **01_common_features**, double-click, and then compare your screen
with Figure 1.29.

**Figure 1.29**

File list displays
the contents of the
*01_common_features* folder

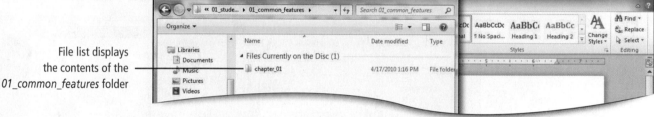

**Another Way**

Click one time to select
the file, and then press
Enter or click the Open
button in the lower
right corner of the
dialog box.

**7** In the **file list**, point to the **chapter_01** subfolder and double-click to open it. In the
**file list**, point to Word file **cf01B_Cheese_Promotion** and then double-click to open
and display the file in the Word window. On the Ribbon, on the **Home tab**, in the
**Paragraph group**, if necessary, click the **Show/Hide** button ¶ so that it is active—
glowing orange. Compare your screen with Figure 1.30.

On the title bar at the top of the screen, the file name displays. If you opened the document
from the Student CD, (*Read-Only*) will display. If you opened the document from another
source to which the files were copied, (*Read-Only*) might not display. ***Read-Only*** is a property
assigned to a file that prevents the file from being modified or deleted; it indicates that you
cannot save any changes to the displayed document unless you first save it with a new name.

**Figure 1.30**

File name displays in the
title bar (*Read-only* will
display if opened from
the CD)

Show/Hide button active

Word document displays
in the Word window

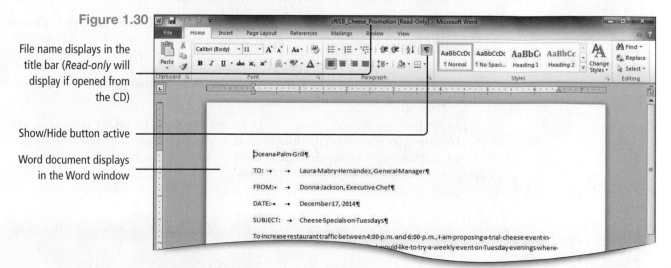

**Another Way**

Press F12 to display the Save As dialog box.

**8** Click the **File tab** to display **Backstage** view, and then click the **Save As** command to display the **Save As** dialog box. Compare your screen with Figure 1.31.

The Save As command displays the Save As dialog box where you can name and save a *new* document based on the currently displayed document. After you name and save the new document, the original document closes, and the new document—based on the original one—displays.

Figure 1.31

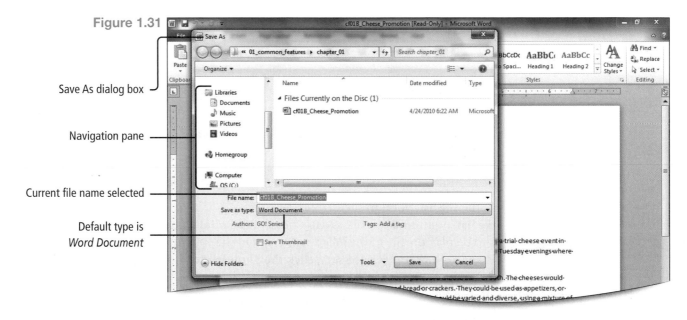

Save As dialog box

Navigation pane

Current file name selected

Default type is *Word Document*

**9** In the **navigation pane**, click the location in which you are storing your projects for this chapter—the location where you created your **Common Features Chapter 1** folder; for example, your USB flash drive or the Documents library.

**10** In the **file list**, double-click the necessary folders and subfolders until your **Common Features Chapter 1** folder displays in the **address bar**.

**11** Click in the **File name** box to select the existing file name, or drag to select the existing text, and then using your own name, type **Lastname_Firstname_1B_Cheese_Promotion** Compare your screen with Figure 1.32.

As you type, the file name from your 1A project might display briefly. Because your 1A project file is stored in this location and you began the new file name with the same text, Office predicts that you might want the same or similar file name. As you type new characters, the suggestion is removed.

Figure 1.32

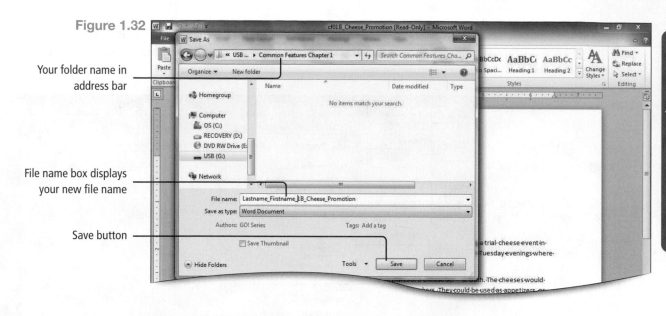

Your folder name in
address bar

File name box displays
your new file name

Save button

**12** In the lower right corner of the **Save As** dialog box, click **Save**; or press ⏎. Compare
your screen with Figure 1.33.

> The original document closes, and your new document, based on the original, displays
> with the name in the title bar.

Figure 1.33

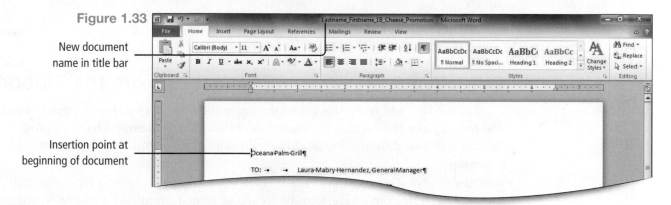

New document
name in title bar

Insertion point at
beginning of document

## Objective 8 | Explore Options for an Application

Within each Office application, you can open an *Options dialog box* where you can
select program settings and other options and preferences. For example, you can set
preferences for viewing and editing files.

### Activity 1.08 | Viewing Application Options

**1** Click the **File tab** to display **Backstage** view. Under the **Help tab**, click **Options**.

**2** In the displayed **Word Options** dialog box, on the left, click **Display**, and then on the
right, locate the information under **Always show these formatting marks on the screen**.

> When you press ⏎, Spacebar, or Tab on your keyboard, characters display to represent
> these keystrokes. These screen characters do not print, and are referred to as *formatting
> marks* or *nonprinting characters*.

**3** Under **Always show these formatting marks on the screen**, be sure the last check box, **Show all formatting marks**, is selected—select it if necessary. Compare your screen with Figure 1.34.

Figure 1.34

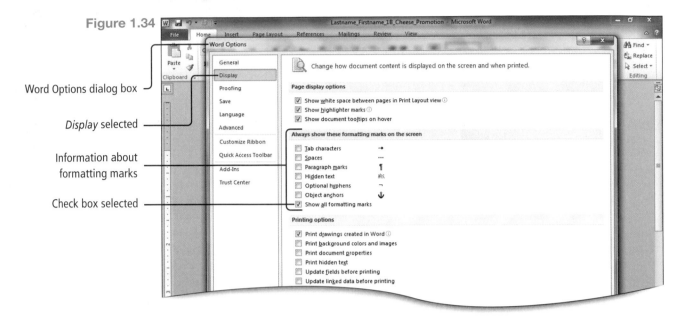

Word Options dialog box

*Display* selected

Information about formatting marks

Check box selected

**4** In the lower right corner of the dialog box, click **OK**.

# Objective 9 | Perform Commands from the Ribbon

The *Ribbon*, which displays across the top of the program window, groups commands and features in a manner that you would most logically use them. Each Office program's Ribbon is slightly different, but all contain the same three elements: *tabs*, *groups*, and *commands*.

Tabs display across the top of the Ribbon, and each tab relates to a type of activity; for example, laying out a page. Groups are sets of related commands for specific tasks. Commands—instructions to computer programs—are arranged in groups, and might display as a button, a menu, or a box in which you type information.

You can also minimize the Ribbon so only the tab names display. In the minimized Ribbon view, when you click a tab the Ribbon expands to show the groups and commands, and then when you click a command, the Ribbon returns to its minimized view. Most Office users, however, prefer to leave the complete Ribbon in view at all times.

## Activity 1.09 | Performing Commands from the Ribbon

**1** Take a moment to examine the document on your screen.

This document is a memo from the Executive Chef to the General Manager regarding a new restaurant promotion.

**2** On the Ribbon, click the **View tab**. In the **Show group**, if necessary, click to place a check mark in the **Ruler** check box, and then compare your screen with Figure 1.35.

> When working in Word, display the rulers so that you can see how margin settings affect your document and how text aligns. Additionally, if you set a tab stop or an indent, its location is visible on the ruler.

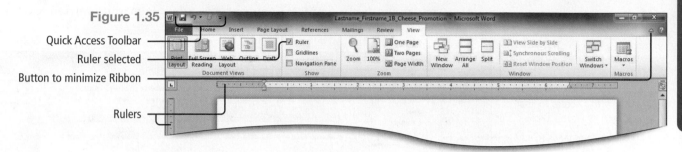

Figure 1.35

Quick Access Toolbar
Ruler selected
Button to minimize Ribbon

Rulers

**3** On the Ribbon, click the **Home tab**. In the **Paragraph group**, if necessary, click the **Show/Hide** button ¶ so that it glows orange and formatting marks display in your document. Point to the button to display information about the button, and then compare your screen with Figure 1.36.

> When the Show/Hide button is active—glowing orange—formatting marks display. Because formatting marks guide your eye in a document—like a map and road signs guide you along a highway—these marks will display throughout this instruction. Many expert Word users keep these marks displayed while creating documents.

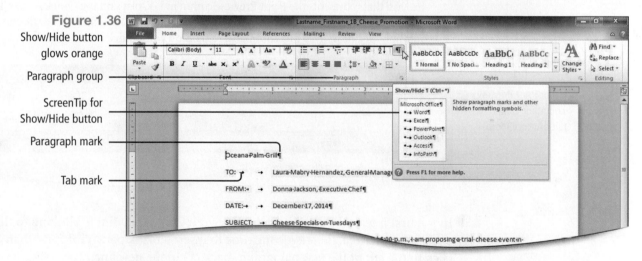

Figure 1.36
Show/Hide button glows orange
Paragraph group

ScreenTip for Show/Hide button
Paragraph mark

Tab mark

**4** In the upper left corner of your screen, above the Ribbon, locate the **Quick Access Toolbar**.

> The *Quick Access Toolbar* contains commands that you use frequently. By default, only the commands Save, Undo, and Redo display, but you can add and delete commands to suit your needs. Possibly the computer at which you are working already has additional commands added to the Quick Access Toolbar.

**5** At the end of the Quick Access Toolbar, click the **Customize Quick Access Toolbar** button ▾.

**6** Compare your screen with Figure 1.37.

> A list of commands that Office users commonly add to their Quick Access Toolbar displays, including *Open*, *E-mail*, and *Print Preview and Print*. Commands already on the Quick Access Toolbar display a check mark. Commands that you add to the Quick Access Toolbar are always just one click away.
>
> Here you can also display the More Commands dialog box, from which you can select any command from any tab to add to the Quick Access Toolbar.

Figure 1.37

Customize Quick Access Toolbar

Popular commands to add

Existing commands checked

Displays *More Commands* dialog box

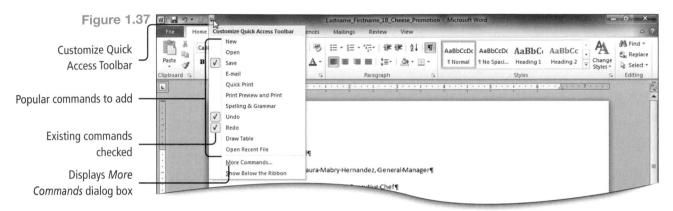

**Another Way**

Right-click any command on the Ribbon, and then on the shortcut menu, click Add to Quick Access Toolbar.

**7** On the displayed list, click **Print Preview and Print**, and then notice that the icon is added to the **Quick Access Toolbar**. Compare your screen with Figure 1.38.

> The icon that represents the Print Preview command displays on the Quick Access Toolbar. Because this is a command that you will use frequently while building Office documents, you might decide to have this command remain on your Quick Access Toolbar.

Figure 1.38

Icon for Print Preview command added to Quick Access Toolbar

**8** In the first line of the document, be sure your insertion point is blinking to the left of the *O* in *Oceana*. Press Enter one time to insert a blank paragraph, and then click to the left of the new paragraph mark (¶) in the new line.

> The *paragraph symbol* is a formatting mark that displays each time you press Enter.

**9** On the Ribbon, click the **Insert tab**. In the **Illustrations group**, point to the **Clip Art** button to display its ScreenTip.

> Many buttons on the Ribbon have this type of *enhanced ScreenTip*, which displays more descriptive text than a normal ScreenTip.

**10** Click the **Clip Art** button.

> The Clip Art *task pane* displays. A task pane is a window within a Microsoft Office application that enables you to enter options for completing a command.

**11** In the **Clip Art** task pane, click in the **Search for** box, delete any existing text, and then type **cheese grapes** Under **Results should be:**, click the arrow at the right, if necessary click to *clear* the check mark for **All media types** so that no check boxes are selected, and then click the check box for **Illustrations**. Compare your screen with Figure 1.39.

Figure 1.39

Search term

Blank paragraph

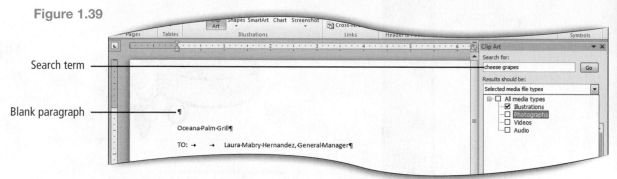

**12** Click the **Results should be arrow** again to close the list, and then if necessary, click to place a check mark in the **Include Office.com content** check box.

By selecting this check box, the search for clip art images will include those from Microsoft's online collections of clip art at www.office.com.

**13** At the top of the **Clip Art** task pane, click **Go**. Wait a moment for clips to display, and then locate the clip indicated in Figure 1.40.

Figure 1.40

Check box selected

Locate this image

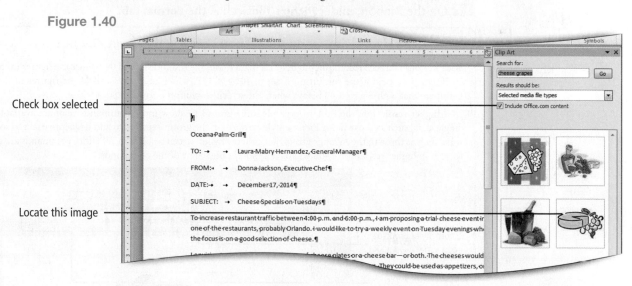

**14** Click the image indicated in Figure 1.40 one time to insert it at the insertion point, and then in the upper right corner of the **Clip Art** task pane, click the **Close** button.

> **Alert! | If You Cannot Locate the Image**
>
> If the image shown in Figure 1.40 is unavailable, select a different cheese image that is appropriate.

**15** With the image selected—surrounded by a border—on the Ribbon, click the **Home tab**, and then in the **Paragraph group**, click the **Center** button. Click anywhere outside of the bordered picture to *deselect*—cancel the selection. Compare your screen with Figure 1.41.

**Figure 1.41**

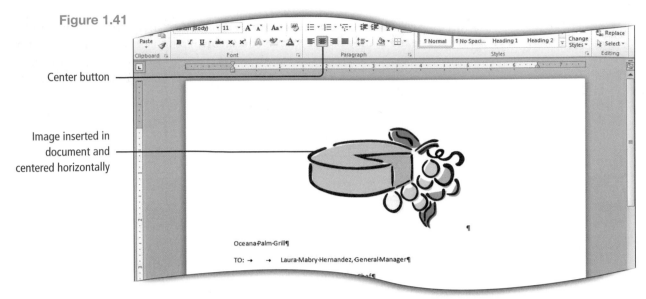

Center button

Image inserted in
document and
centered horizontally

Oceana·Palm·Grill¶

TO: → → Laura·Mabry·Hernandez,·General·Manager¶

---

**16** Point to the inserted clip art image, and then watch the last tab of the Ribbon as you click the image one time to select it.

> The *Picture Tools* display and an additional tab—the *Format* tab—is added to the Ribbon. The Ribbon adapts to your work and will display additional tabs—referred to as *contextual tabs*—when you need them.

**17** On the Ribbon, under **Picture Tools**, click the **Format tab**.

---

**Alert! | The Size of Groups on the Ribbon Varies with Screen Resolution**

Your monitor's screen resolution might be set higher than the resolution used to capture the figures in this book. In Figure 1.42 below, the resolution is set to 1024 × 768, which is used for all of the figures in this book. Compare that with Figure 1.43 below, where the screen resolution is set to 1280 × 1024.

At a higher resolution, the Ribbon expands some groups to show more commands than are available with a single click, such as those in the Picture Styles group. Or, the group expands to add descriptive text to some buttons, such as those in the Arrange group. Regardless of your screen resolution, all Office commands are available to you. In higher resolutions, you will have a more robust view of the commands.

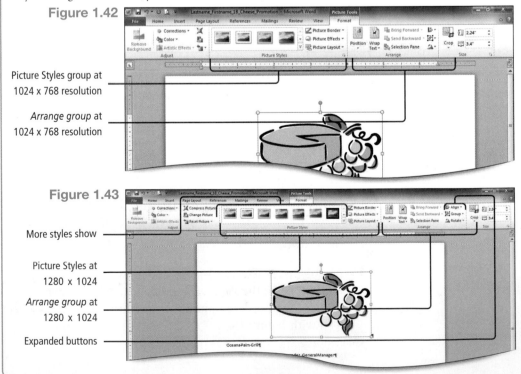

**Figure 1.42**

Picture Styles group at
1024 x 768 resolution

*Arrange group* at
1024 x 768 resolution

**Figure 1.43**

More styles show

Picture Styles at
1280 x 1024

*Arrange group* at
1280 x 1024

Expanded buttons

---

**18** In the **Picture Styles group**, point to the first style to display the ScreenTip *Simple Frame, White*, and notice that the image displays with a white frame.

**19** Watch the image as you point to the second picture style, and then to the third, and then to the fourth.

This is *Live Preview*, a technology that shows the result of applying an editing or formatting change as you point to possible results—*before* you actually apply it.

**20** In the **Picture Styles group**, click the fourth style—**Drop Shadow Rectangle**—and then click anywhere outside of the image to deselect it. Notice that the Picture Tools no longer display on the Ribbon. Compare your screen with Figure 1.44.

Contextual tabs display only when you need them.

Figure 1.44

Picture Tools no longer display on the Ribbon

*Drop Shadow Rectangle* picture style applied to image

**21** In the upper left corner of your screen, on the Quick Access Toolbar, click the **Save** button to save the changes you have made.

### Activity 1.10 | Minimizing and Using the Keyboard to Control the Ribbon

Instead of a mouse, some individuals prefer to navigate the Ribbon by using keys on the keyboard. You can activate keyboard control of the Ribbon by pressing the Alt key. You can also minimize the Ribbon to maximize your available screen space.

**1** On your keyboard, press the Alt key, and then on the Ribbon, notice that small labels display. Press N to activate the commands on the **Insert tab**, and then compare your screen with Figure 1.45.

Each label represents a *KeyTip*—an indication of the key that you can press to activate the command. For example, on the Insert tab, you can press F to activate the Clip Art task pane.

Figure 1.45

KeyTips indicate that keyboard control of the Ribbon is active

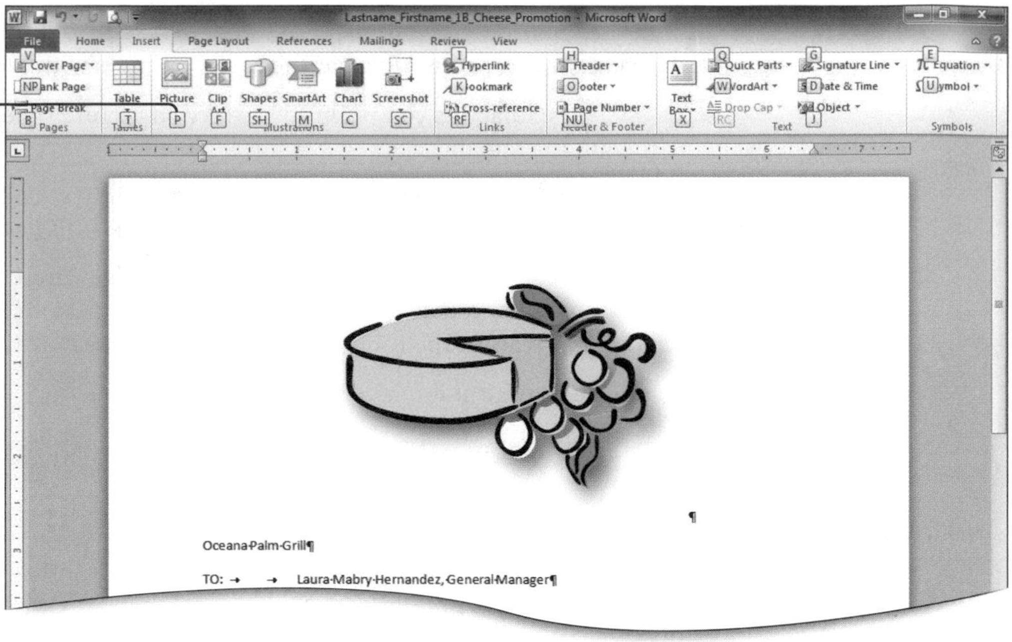


**2** Press Esc to redisplay the KeyTips for the tabs. Then, press Alt again to turn off keyboard control of the Ribbon.

**3** Point to any tab on the Ribbon and right-click to display a shortcut menu.

Here you can choose to display the Quick Access Toolbar below the Ribbon or minimize the Ribbon to maximize screen space. You can also customize the Ribbon by adding, removing, renaming, or reordering tabs, groups, and commands on the Ribbon, although this is not recommended until you become an expert Office user.

> **Another Way**
>
> Double-click the active tab; or, click the Minimize the Ribbon button at the right end of the Ribbon.

**4** Click **Minimize the Ribbon**. Notice that only the Ribbon tabs display. Click the **Home tab** to display the commands. Click anywhere in the document, and notice that the Ribbon reverts to its minimized view.

> **Another Way**
>
> Double-click any tab to redisplay the full Ribbon.

**5** Right-click any Ribbon tab, and then click **Minimize the Ribbon** again to turn the minimize feature off.

Most expert Office users prefer to have the full Ribbon display at all times.

**6** Point to any tab on the Ribbon, and then on your mouse device, roll the mouse wheel. Notice that different tabs become active as your roll the mouse wheel.

You can make a tab active by using this technique, instead of clicking the tab.

## Objective 10 | Apply Formatting in Office Programs

***Formatting*** is the process of establishing the overall appearance of text, graphics, and pages in an Office file—for example, in a Word document.

### Activity 1.11 | Formatting and Viewing Pages

In this activity, you will practice common formatting techniques used in Office applications.

**1** On the Ribbon, click the **Insert tab**, and then in the **Header & Footer group**, click the **Footer** button.

**Another Way**

On the Design tab, in the Insert group, click Quick Parts, click Field, and then under Field names, click FileName.

**2** At the top of the displayed gallery, under **Built-In**, click **Blank**. At the bottom of your document, with *Type text* highlighted in blue, using your own name type the file name of this document **Lastname_Firstname_1B_Cheese_Promotion** and then compare your screen with Figure 1.46.

Header & Footer Tools are added to the Ribbon. A *footer* is a reserved area for text or graphics that displays at the bottom of each page in a document. Likewise, a *header* is a reserved area for text or graphics that displays at the top of each page in a document. When the footer (or header) area is active, the document area is inactive (dimmed).

Figure 1.46

*Design* tab added

Header & Footer Tools active

Document area inactive (dimmed) when footer area is active

*Close Header and Footer* button

Your file name

Footer area displays

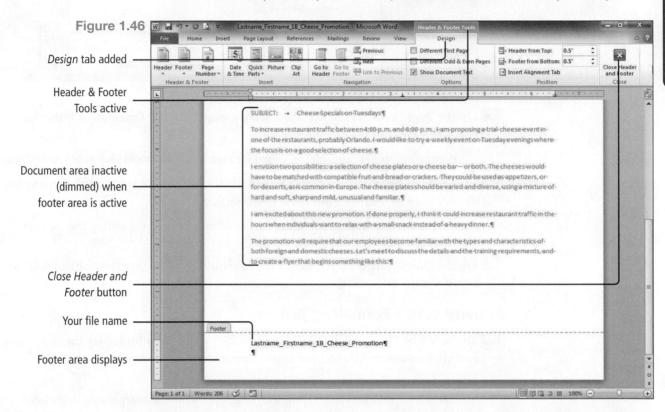

**3** On the Ribbon, on the **Design tab**, in the **Close group**, click the **Close Header and Footer** button.

**4** On the Ribbon, click the **Page Layout tab**. In the **Page Setup group**, click the **Orientation** button, and notice that two orientations display—*Portrait* and *Landscape*. Click **Landscape**.

In *portrait orientation*, the paper is taller than it is wide. In *landscape orientation*, the paper is wider than it is tall.

**5** In the lower right corner of the screen, locate the **Zoom control** buttons.

To *zoom* means to increase or decrease the viewing area. You can zoom in to look closely at a section of a document, and then zoom out to see an entire page on the screen. You can also zoom to view multiple pages on the screen.

**6** Drag the **Zoom slider** to the left until you have zoomed to approximately *60%*. Compare your screen with Figure 1.47.

Figure 1.47

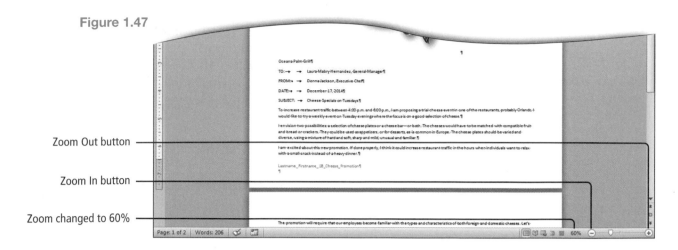

Zoom Out button

Zoom In button

Zoom changed to 60%

**7** On the **Page Layout tab**, in the **Page Setup group**, click the **Orientation** button, and then click **Portrait**.

Portrait orientation is commonly used for business documents such as letters and memos.

**8** In the lower right corner of your screen, click the **Zoom In** button ⊕ as many times as necessary to return to the **100%** zoom setting.

Use the zoom feature to adjust the view of your document for editing and for your viewing comfort.

**9** On the Quick Access Toolbar, click the **Save** button 🖫 to save the changes you have made to your document.

## Activity 1.12 | Formatting Text

**1** To the left of *Oceana Palm Grill*, point in the margin area to display the 🖈 pointer and click one time to select the entire paragraph. Compare your screen with Figure 1.48.

Use this technique to select complete paragraphs from the margin area. Additionally, with this technique you can drag downward to select multiple-line paragraphs—which is faster and more efficient than dragging through text.

Figure 1.48

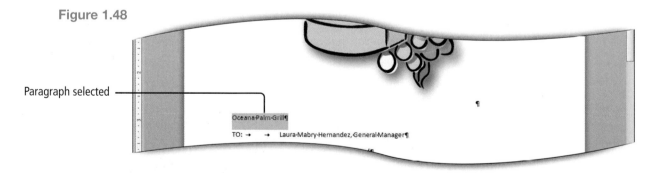

Paragraph selected

**2** On the Ribbon, click the **Home tab**, and then in the **Paragraph group**, click the **Center** button ☰ to center the paragraph.

*Alignment* refers to the placement of paragraph text relative to the left and right margins. *Center alignment* refers to text that is centered horizontally between the left and right margins. You can also align text at the left margin, which is the default alignment for text in Word, or at the right margin.

**3** On the **Home tab**, in the **Font group**, click the **Font button arrow** Calibri (Body) ▾ . At the top of the list, point to **Cambria**, and as you do so, notice that the selected text previews in the Cambria font.

> A *font* is a set of characters with the same design and shape. The default font in a Word document is Calibri, which is a ***sans serif*** font—a font design with no lines or extensions on the ends of characters.
>
> The Cambria font is a ***serif*** font—a font design that includes small line extensions on the ends of the letters to guide the eye in reading from left to right.
>
> The list of fonts displays as a gallery showing potential results. For example, in the Font gallery, you can see the actual design and format of each font as it would look if applied to text.

**4** Point to several other fonts and observe the effect on the selected text. Then, at the top of the **Font** gallery, under **Theme Fonts**, click **Cambria**.

> A *theme* is a predesigned set of colors, fonts, lines, and fill effects that look good together and that can be applied to your entire document or to specific items.
>
> A theme combines two sets of fonts—one for text and one for headings. In the default Office theme, Cambria is the suggested font for headings.

**5** With the paragraph *Oceana Palm Grill* still selected, on the **Home tab**, in the **Font group**, click the **Font Size button arrow** 11 ▾ , point to **36**, and then notice how Live Preview displays the text in the font size to which you are pointing. Compare your screen with Figure 1.49.

Figure 1.49

Font Size button

Font button

Font Size list

Pointing to 36 pt font size

*Oceana Palm Grill* centered, Cambria font applied

**6** On the displayed list of font sizes, click **20**.

> Fonts are measured in ***points***, with one point equal to 1/72 of an inch. A higher point size indicates a larger font size. Headings and titles are often formatted by using a larger font size. The word *point* is abbreviated as ***pt***.

**7** With *Oceana Palm Grill* still selected, on the **Home tab**, in the **Font group**, click the **Font Color button arrow** A ▾ . Under **Theme Colors**, in the seventh column, click the last color—**Olive Green, Accent 3, Darker 50%**. Click anywhere to deselect the text.

**8** To the left of *TO:*, point in the left margin area to display the 🔾 pointer, hold down the left mouse button, and then drag down to select the four memo headings. Compare your screen with Figure 1.50.

> Use this technique to select complete paragraphs from the margin area—dragging downward to select multiple-line paragraphs—which is faster and more efficient than dragging through text.

**Figure 1.50**

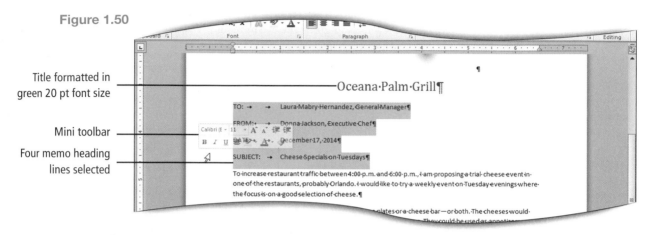

Title formatted in green 20 pt font size

Mini toolbar

Four memo heading lines selected

**9** With the four paragraphs selected, on the Mini toolbar, click the **Font Color** button 🔠, which now displays a dark green bar instead of a red bar.

> The font color button retains its most recently used color—Olive Green, Accent 3, Darker 50%. As you progress in your study of Microsoft Office, you will use other buttons that behave in this manner; that is, they retain their most recently used format.

> The purpose of the Mini toolbar is to place commonly used commands close to text or objects that you select. By selecting a command on the Mini toolbar, you reduce the distance that you must move your mouse to access a command.

**10** Click anywhere in the paragraph that begins *To increase*, and then ***triple-click***—click the left mouse button three times—to select the entire paragraph. If the entire paragraph is not selected, click in the paragraph and begin again.

**11** With the entire paragraph selected, on the Mini toolbar, click the **Font Color button arrow** 🔠, and then under **Theme Colors**, in the sixth column, click the first color— **Red, Accent 2**.

> It is convenient to have commonly used commands display on the Mini toolbar so that you do not have to move your mouse to the top of the screen to access the command from the Ribbon.

**12** Select the text *TO:* and then on the displayed Mini toolbar, click the **Bold** button **B** and the **Italic** button *I*.

> ***Font styles*** include bold, italic, and underline. Font styles emphasize text and are a visual cue to draw the reader's eye to important text.

**13** On the displayed Mini toolbar, click the **Italic** button *I* again to turn off the Italic formatting. Notice that the Italic button no longer glows orange.

> A button that behaves in this manner is referred to as a ***toggle button***, which means it can be turned on by clicking it once, and then turned off by clicking it again.

**14** With *TO:* still selected, on the Mini toolbar, click the **Format Painter** button ✄. Then, move your mouse under the word *Laura*, and notice the 🅰I mouse pointer. Compare your screen with Figure 1.51.

> You can use the *Format Painter* to copy the formatting of specific text or of a paragraph and then apply it in other locations in your document.

> The pointer takes the shape of a paintbrush, and contains the formatting information from the paragraph where the insertion point is positioned. Information about the Format Painter and how to turn it off displays in the status bar.

Figure 1.51

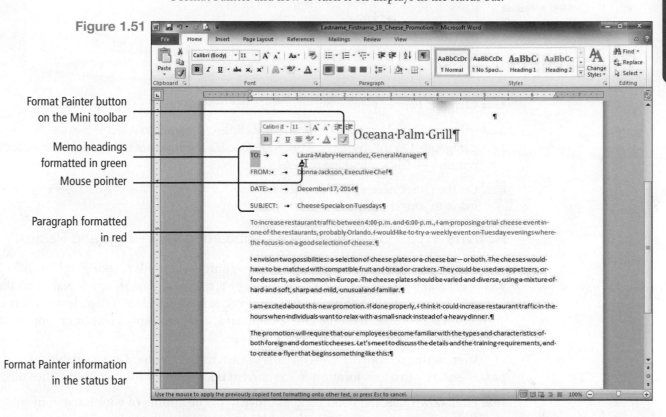

Format Painter button on the Mini toolbar

Memo headings formatted in green

Mouse pointer

Paragraph formatted in red

Format Painter information in the status bar

**15** With the 🅰I pointer, drag to select the text *FROM:* and notice that the Bold formatting is applied. Then, point to the selected text *FROM:* and on the Mini toolbar, *double-click* the **Format Painter** button ✄.

**16** Select the text *DATE:* to copy the Bold formatting, and notice that the pointer retains the 🅰I shape.

> When you *double-click* the Format Painter button, the Format Painter feature remains active until you either click the Format Painter button again, or press `Esc` to cancel it—as indicated on the status bar.

**17** With Format Painter still active, select the text *SUBJECT:*, and then on the Ribbon, on the **Home tab**, in the **Clipboard group**, notice that the **Format Painter** button ✄ is glowing orange, indicating that it is active. Compare your screen with Figure 1.52.

Figure 1.52

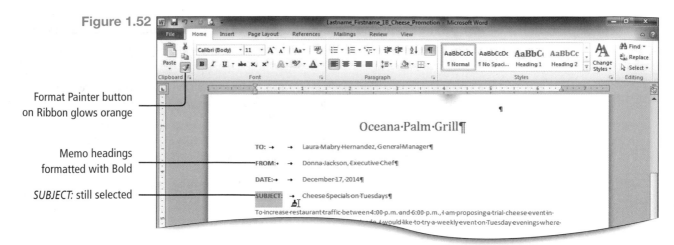

Format Painter button on Ribbon glows orange

Memo headings formatted with Bold

*SUBJECT:* still selected

**18** Click the **Format Painter** button ✐ on the Ribbon to turn the command off.

**19** In the paragraph that begins *To increase*, triple-click again to select the entire paragraph. On the displayed Mini toolbar, click the **Bold** button B and the **Italic** button I. Click anywhere to deselect.

**20** On the Quick Access Toolbar, click the **Save** button 🖫 to save the changes you have made to your document.

## Activity 1.13 | Using the Office Clipboard to Cut, Copy, and Paste

The **Office Clipboard** is a temporary storage area that holds text or graphics that you select and then cut or copy. When you **copy** text or graphics, a copy is placed on the Office Clipboard and the original text or graphic remains in place. When you **cut** text or graphics, a copy is placed on the Office Clipboard, and the original text or graphic is removed—cut—from the document.

After cutting or copying, the contents of the Office Clipboard are available for you to **paste**—insert—in a new location in the current document, or into another Office file.

**1** Hold down Ctrl and press Home to move to the beginning of your document, and then take a moment to study the table in Figure 1.53, which describes similar keyboard shortcuts with which you can navigate quickly in a document.

| To Move | Press |
| --- | --- |
| To the beginning of a document | Ctrl + Home |
| To the end of a document | Ctrl + End |
| To the beginning of a line | Home |
| To the end of a line | End |
| To the beginning of the previous word | Ctrl + ← |
| To the beginning of the next word | Ctrl + → |
| To the beginning of the current word (if insertion point is in the middle of a word) | Ctrl + ← |
| To the beginning of a paragraph | Ctrl + ↑ |
| To the beginning of the next paragraph | Ctrl + ↓ |
| To the beginning of the current paragraph (if insertion point is in the middle of a paragraph) | Ctrl + ↑ |
| Up one screen | PgUp |
| Down one screen | PageDown |

Figure 1.53

**Another Way**

Right-click the selection, and then click Copy on the shortcut menu; or, use the keyboard shortcut Ctrl + C.

**2** To the left of *Oceana Palm Grill*, point in the left margin area to display the ⟋ pointer, and then click one time to select the entire paragraph. On the **Home tab**, in the **Clipboard group**, click the **Copy** button ⬚.

Because anything that you select and then copy—or cut—is placed on the Office Clipboard, the Copy command and the Cut command display in the Clipboard group of commands on the Ribbon.

There is no visible indication that your copied selection has been placed on the Office Clipboard.

**3** On the **Home tab**, in the **Clipboard group**, to the right of the group name *Clipboard*, click the **Dialog Box Launcher** button ⬚, and then compare your screen with Figure 1.54.

The Clipboard task pane displays with your copied text. In any Ribbon group, the ***Dialog Box Launcher*** displays either a dialog box or a task pane related to the group of commands.

It is not necessary to display the Office Clipboard in this manner, although sometimes it is useful to do so. The Office Clipboard can hold 24 items.

Figure 1.54

Copy button

Dialog Box Launcher in Clipboard group

Clipboard task pane displays

Selected text on the Office Clipboard

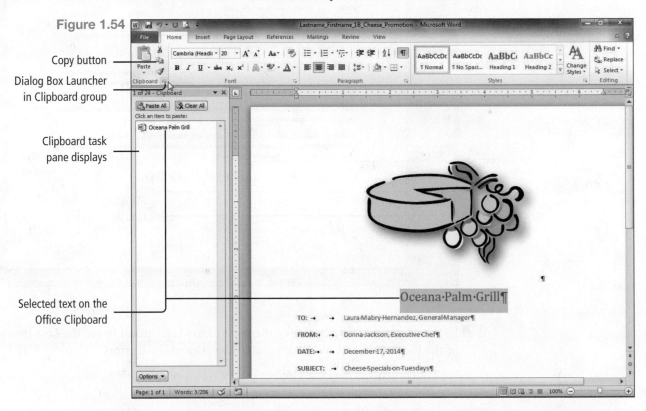

**4** In the upper right corner of the **Clipboard** task pane, click the **Close** button ✖.

**Another Way**

Right-click, on the shortcut menu under Paste Options, click the desired option button.

**5** Press Ctrl + End to move to the end of your document. Press Enter one time to create a new blank paragraph. On the **Home tab**, in the **Clipboard group**, point to the **Paste** button, and then click the *upper* portion of this split button.

The Paste command pastes the most recently copied item on the Office Clipboard at the insertion point location. If you click the lower portion of the Paste button, a gallery of Paste Options displays.

**6** Click the **Paste Options** button 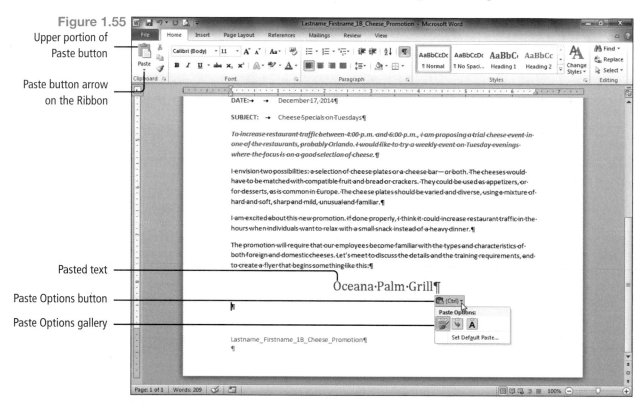 that displays below the pasted text as shown in Figure 1.55.

> Here you can view and apply various formatting options for pasting your copied or cut text. Typically you will click Paste on the Ribbon and paste the item in its original format. If you want some other format for the pasted item, you can do so from the *Paste Options gallery*.
>
> The Paste Options gallery provides a Live Preview of the various options for changing the format of the pasted item with a single click. The Paste Options gallery is available in three places: on the Ribbon by clicking the lower portion of the Paste button—the Paste button arrow; from the Paste Options button that displays below the pasted item following the paste operation; or, on the shortcut menu if you right-click the pasted item.

**Figure 1.55**
Upper portion of Paste button
Paste button arrow on the Ribbon
Pasted text
Paste Options button
Paste Options gallery

**7** In the displayed **Paste Options** gallery, *point* to each option to see the Live Preview of the format that would be applied if you clicked the button.

> The contents of the Paste Options gallery are contextual; that is, they change based on what you copied and where you are pasting.

**8** Press Esc to close the gallery; the button will remain displayed until you take some other screen action.

**9** Press Ctrl + Home to move to the top of the document, and then click the **cheese image** one time to select it. While pointing to the selected image, right-click, and then on the shortcut menu, click **Cut**.

> Recall that the Cut command cuts—removes—the selection from the document and places it on the Office Clipboard.

**Another Way**

On the Home tab, in the Clipboard group, click the Cut button; or, use the keyboard shortcut Ctrl + X.

**10** Press [Del] one time to remove the blank paragraph from the top of the document, and then press [Ctrl] + [End] to move to the end of the document.

**11** With the insertion point blinking in the blank paragraph at the end of the document, right-click, and notice that the **Paste Options** gallery displays on the shortcut menu. Compare your screen with Figure 1.56.

Figure 1.56

Paste Options on shortcut menu

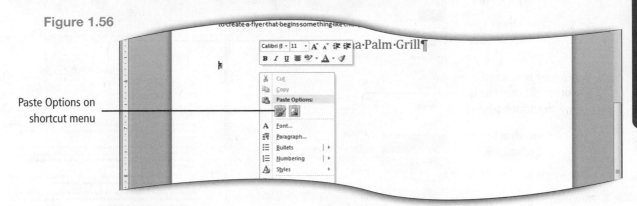

**12** On the shortcut menu, under **Paste Options**, click the first button—**Keep Source Formatting** .

**13** Click the picture to select it. On the **Home tab**, in the **Paragraph group**, click the **Center** button .

**14** Above the cheese picture, click to position the insertion point at the end of the word *Grill*, press [Spacebar] one time, and then type **Tuesday Cheese Tastings** Compare your screen with Figure 1.57.

Figure 1.57

Heading

Picture inserted and centered

## Activity 1.14 | Viewing Print Preview and Printing a Word Document

**1** Press [Ctrl] + [Home] to move to the top of your document. Select the text *Oceana Palm Grill*, and then replace the selected text by typing **Memo**

**2** Display **Backstage** view, on the right, click **Properties**, and then click **Show Document Panel**. Replace the existing author name with your first and last name. In the **Subject** box, type your course name and section number, and then in the **Keywords** box, type **cheese promotion** and then **Close** the **Document Information Panel**.

**Another Way**

Press [Ctrl] + [F2] to
display Print Preview.

**3** On the Quick Access Toolbar, click **Save** 💾 to save the changes you have made to your document.

**4** On the Quick Access Toolbar, click the **Print Preview** button 🔍 that you added. Compare your screen with Figure 1.58.

**Figure 1.58**

*Memo* typed

If no printer is attached to
your system, OneNote is
the default printer

Print tab active in
Backstage view

Print Preview (if you have a
non-color printer as your default
printer, the preview may display
in shades of gray)

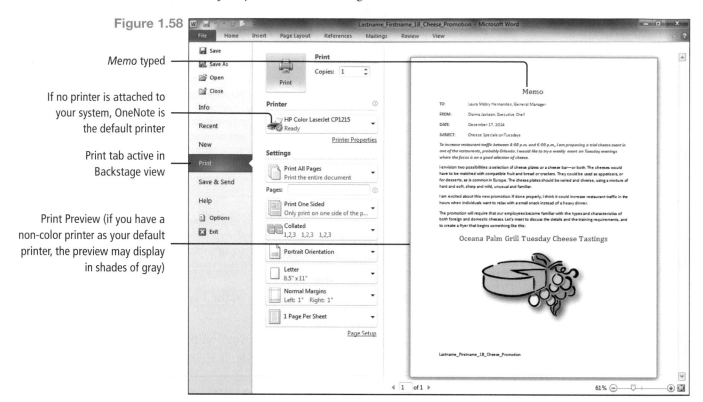

**5** Examine the **Print Preview**. Under **Settings**, notice that in **Backstage** view, several of the same commands that are available on the Page Layout tab of the Ribbon also display.

> For convenience, common adjustments to Page Layout display here, so that you can make last-minute adjustments without closing Backstage view.

**6** If you need to make any corrections, click the Home tab to return to the document and make any necessary changes.

> It is good practice to examine the Print Preview before printing or submitting your work electronically. Then, make any necessary corrections, re-save, and redisplay Print Preview.

**7** If you are directed to do so, click Print to print the document; or, above the Info tab, click Close, and then submit your file electronically according to the directions provided by your instructor.

> If you click the Print button, Backstage view closes and the Word window redisplays.

**8** On the Quick Access Toolbar, point to the **Print Preview icon** 🔍 you placed there, right-click, and then click **Remove from Quick Access Toolbar**.

> If you are working on your own computer and you want to do so, you can leave the icon on the toolbar; in a lab setting, you should return the software to its original settings.

**9** At the right end of the title bar, click the program **Close** button [x] .

**10** If a message displays asking if you want the text on the Clipboard to be available after you quit Word, click **No**.

This message most often displays if you have copied some type of image to the Clipboard. If you click Yes, the items on the Clipboard will remain for you to use.

## Objective 11 | Use the Microsoft Office 2010 Help System

Within each Office program, the Help feature provides information about all of the program's features and displays step-by-step instructions for performing many tasks.

### Activity 1.15 | Using the Microsoft Office 2010 Help System in Excel

In this activity, you will use the Microsoft Help feature to find information about formatting numbers in Excel.

**Another Way**

Press [F1] to display Help.

**1** Start the **Microsoft Excel 2010** program. In the upper right corner of your screen, click the **Microsoft Excel Help** button [?] .

**2** In the **Excel Help** window, click in the white box in upper left corner, type **formatting numbers** and then click **Search** or press [Enter].

**3** On the list of results, click **Display numbers as currency**. Compare your screen with Figure 1.59.

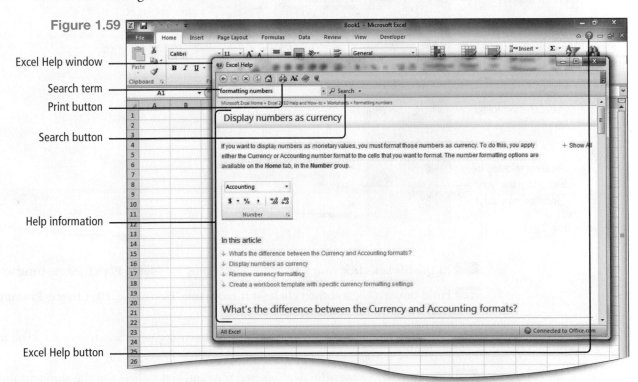

Figure 1.59

Excel Help window

Search term

Print button

Search button

Help information

Excel Help button

**4** If you want to do so, on the toolbar at the top of the **Excel Help** window, click the Print [🖶] button to print a copy of this information for your reference.

**5** On the title bar of the Excel Help window, click the **Close** button ![x]. On the right side of the Microsoft Excel title bar, click the **Close** button ![x] to close Excel.

# Objective 12 | Compress Files

A *compressed file* is a file that has been reduced in size. Compressed files take up less storage space and can be transferred to other computers faster than uncompressed files. You can also combine a group of files into one compressed folder, which makes it easier to share a group of files.

## Activity 1.16 | Compressing Files

In this activity, you will combine the two files you created in this chapter into one compressed file.

**1** On the Windows taskbar, click the **Start** button ![start], and then on the right, click **Computer**.

**2** On the left, in the **navigation pane**, click the location of your two files from this chapter—your USB flash drive or other location—and display the folder window for your **Common Features Chapter 1** folder. Compare your screen with Figure 1.60.

Figure 1.60

Address bar displays path ——

Your chapter files in file list (your name displays) ——

Folder window for your chapter folder ——

Location selected in navigation pane (your location may vary) ——

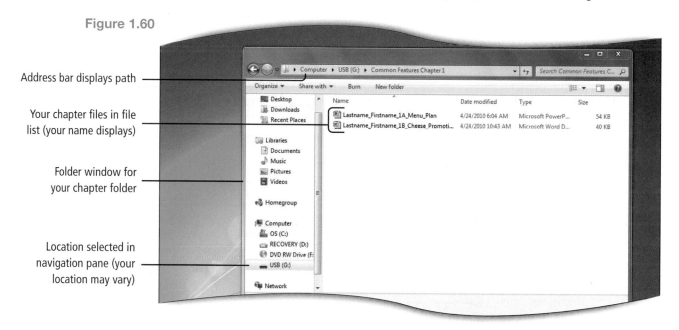

**3** In the **file list**, click your **Lastname_Firstname_1A_Menu_Plan** file one time to select it.

**4** Hold down Ctrl, and then click your **Lastname_Firstname_1B_Cheese_Promotion** file to select both files. Release Ctrl.

In any Windows-based program, holding down Ctrl while selecting enables you to select multiple items.

**5** Point anywhere over the two selected files and right-click. On the shortcut menu, point to **Send to**, and then compare your screen with Figure 1.61.

Figure 1.61

Two files selected ————

Send to submenu ————

Shortcut menu
(yours may vary) ————

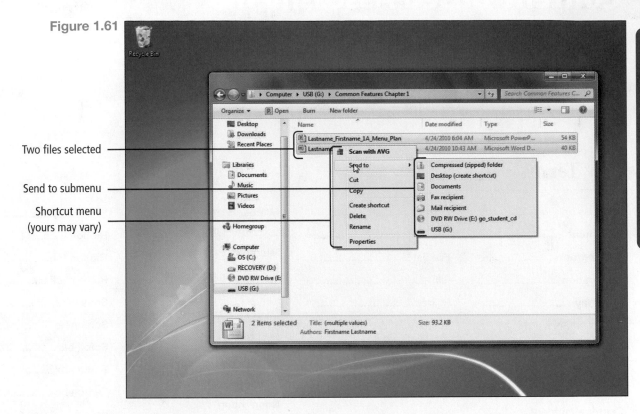

6 On the shortcut submenu, click **Compressed (zipped) folder**.

> Windows creates a compressed folder containing a *copy* of each of the selected files. The folder name is the name of the file or folder to which you were pointing, and is selected—highlighted in blue—so that you can rename it.

7 Using your own name, type **Lastname_Firstname_Common_Features_Ch1** and press (Enter).

> The compressed folder is now ready to attach to an e-mail or share in some other electronic format.

8 **Close** [ X ] the folder window. If directed to do so by your instructor, submit your compressed folder electronically.

---

**More Knowledge | Extracting Compressed Files**

*Extract* means to decompress, or pull out, files from a compressed form. When you extract a file, an uncompressed copy is placed in the folder that you specify. The original file remains in the compressed folder.

---

**End You have completed Project 1B** ————————————

# Content-Based Assessments

## Summary

In this chapter, you used Windows Explorer to navigate the Windows file structure. You also used features that are common across the Microsoft Office 2010 programs.

## Key Terms

# Content-Based Assessments

## Matching

Match each term in the second column with its correct definition in the first column by writing the letter of the term on the blank line in front of the correct definition.

_____ 1. A collection of information stored on a computer under a single name.

_____ 2. A container in which you store files.

_____ 3. A folder within a folder.

_____ 4. The program that displays the files and folders on your computer.

_____ 5. The Windows menu that is the main gateway to your computer.

_____ 6. In Windows 7, a window that displays the contents of the current folder, library, or device, and contains helpful parts so that you can navigate.

_____ 7. In Windows, a collection of items, such as files and folders, assembled from various locations that might be on your computer.

_____ 8. The bar at the top of a folder window with which you can navigate to a different folder or library, or go back to a previous one.

_____ 9. An instruction to a computer program that carries out an action.

_____ 10. Small pictures that represent a program, a file, a folder, or an object.

_____ 11. A set of instructions that a computer uses to perform a specific task.

_____ 12. A spreadsheet program used to calculate numbers and create charts.

_____ 13. The user interface that groups commands on tabs at the top of the program window.

_____ 14. A bar at the top of the program window displaying the current file and program name.

_____ 15. One or more keys pressed to perform a task that would otherwise require a mouse.

**A** Address bar

**B** Command

**C** File

**D** Folder

**E** Folder window

**F** Icons

**G** Keyboard shortcut

**H** Library

**I** Microsoft Excel

**J** Program

**K** Ribbon

**L** Start menu

**M** Subfolder

**N** Title bar

**O** Windows Explorer

## Multiple Choice

Circle the correct answer.

1. A small toolbar with frequently used commands that displays when selecting text or objects is the:
   **A.** Quick Access Toolbar     **B.** Mini toolbar     **C.** Document toolbar

2. In Office 2010, a centralized space for file management tasks is:
   **A.** a task pane     **B.** a dialog box     **C.** Backstage view

3. The commands Save, Save As, Open, and Close in Backstage view are located:
   **A.** above the Backstage tabs     **B.** below the Backstage tabs     **C.** under the screen thumbnail

4. The tab in Backstage view that displays information about the current file is the:
   **A.** Recent tab     **B.** Info tab     **C.** Options tab

5. Details about a file, including the title, author name, subject, and keywords are known as:
   **A.** document properties     **B.** formatting marks     **C.** KeyTips

6. An Office feature that displays a list of potential results is:
   **A.** Live Preview     **B.** a contextual tab     **C.** a gallery

**7.** A type of formatting emphasis applied to text such as bold, italic, and underline, is called:

**A.** a font style        **B.** a KeyTip        **C.** a tag

**8.** A technology showing the result of applying formatting as you point to possible results is called:

**A.** Live Preview        **B.** Backstage view        **C.** gallery view

**9.** A temporary storage area that holds text or graphics that you select and then cut or copy is the:

**A.** paste options gallery        **B.** ribbon        **C.** Office clipboard

**10.** A file that has been reduced in size is:

**A.** a compressed file        **B.** an extracted file        **C.** a PDF file

# Introduction to Outlook 2010 and E-mail

## OUTCOMES

At the end of this chapter you will be able to:

### PROJECT 1A
Read and respond to e-mail using Outlook 2010.

## OBJECTIVES

Mastering these objectives will enable you to:

1. Start and Navigate Outlook (p. 107)
2. Compose and Send E-mail (p. 118)
3. Read and Respond to E-mail Messages (p. 124)
4. Use Mail Options and Signatures (p. 133)
5. Manage E-mail (p. 143)
6. Use Outlook Help and Close Outlook (p. 152)

©iStockphoto/track5

## In This Chapter

One of the most common uses of the personal computer is to send and receive e-mail. E-mail is a convenient way to communicate with coworkers, business contacts, friends, and family members. Outlook combines all the features of a personal information manager with e-mail capabilities in one program that you can use with other programs within Microsoft Office.

Outlook's e-mail features enable you to send, receive, and forward e-mail messages. With optional features, you can personalize and prioritize sent messages and received messages. After you have started using e-mail on a regular basis, you will need to manage your e-mail by deleting messages you no longer need, sorting your messages, and performing other tasks that will keep your Inbox organized.

In this chapter, you will become familiar with Outlook and practice using Outlook's e-mail capabilities. You will practice sending and replying to e-mail messages, creating signatures, using the mail options, and managing e-mail messages.

**Lake Michigan City College** is located along the lakefront of Chicago—one of the country's most exciting cities. The college serves its large and diverse student body and makes positive contributions to the community through relevant curricula, partnerships with businesses and nonprofit organizations, and learning experiences that allow students to be full participants in the global community. The college offers three associate degrees in 20 academic areas, adult education programs, and continuing education offerings on campus, at satellite locations, and online.

# Project 1A E-mail Inbox

In Activities 1.01 through 1.26, you will start Microsoft Office Outlook 2010 and become familiar with the components of Outlook. Then you will compose, send, read, and respond to e-mail messages for Darron Jacobsen, Vice President of Administrative Affairs at Lake Michigan City College. You will use various Outlook options and manage his Inbox. The messages you send, reply to, and forward will be stored in your Outbox rather than being sent to actual recipients. You will also print a forwarded message. Upon completion, your Inbox, Outbox, and one of the printed messages will look similar to the ones shown in Figure 1.1.

## Project Files

For Project 1A, you will need the following files:

> New blank message form
> o01A_College_Inbox
> o01A_Proposed_Schedule

You will print or create a PDF for three files with the following footers:

> Lastname_Firstname_1A_College_Inbox
> Lastname_Firstname_1A_College_Outbox
> Lastname_Firstname_1A_College_Message

## Project Results

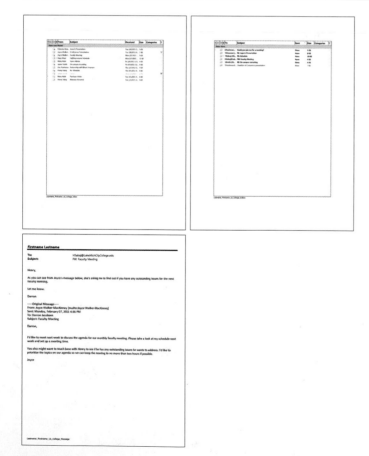

**Figure 1.1**
Project 1A E-mail Inbox

# Objective 1 | Start and Navigate Outlook

Microsoft Outlook 2010 has two functions: It is an e-mail program, and it is a *personal information manager*. Among other things, a personal information manager enables you to store information about your contacts in electronic form. *Contacts* are the names of your friends, family members, coworkers, customers, suppliers, or other individuals with whom you communicate. By using a personal information manager, you can also keep track of your daily schedule, tasks to complete, and other information. Thus, Outlook's major parts include Mail for e-mail and Calendar, Contacts, and Tasks for personal information management.

Your e-mail and personal information in Outlook is stored in folders, and there are separate folders for each of Outlook's components. For example, e-mail is stored in a folder named *Inbox*. Outlook presents information in *views*, which are ways to look at similar information in different formats and arrangements. Mail, Contacts, Calendar, and Tasks all have different views.

> **Alert! | Starting Project 1A**
>
> Because Outlook stores information on the hard drive of the computer at which you are working, it is recommended that you schedule enough time to complete this project in one working session, unless you are working on a computer that is used only by you. Allow approximately one to two hours for Project 1A.

## Activity 1.01 | Creating a User Account in Windows 7

A *user account* is a collection of information that tells Windows 7 what files and folders the account holder can access, what changes the account holder can make to the computer system, and what the account holder's personal preferences are. Each person accesses his or her user account with a user name and password, and each user has his or her own desktop, files, and folders. Although it is not required that you create a new and separate Windows 7 user account to complete the activities in this textbook, it is recommended that you do so to ensure that your screens will match the figures in the textbook and so that you do not delete any of your own personal information.

> **Alert! | Creating a Windows 7 Account**
>
> It is *strongly recommended* that you create a new user account in Windows 7 as described in the following steps to complete this instruction. Doing so will ensure that your own e-mail is not mixed in with this instruction. You can complete this activity if you are logged on as an administrator account, or if you know the administrator password. Some Windows 7 features are available only to users who are logged on with an administrator account; for example, only an administrator can add new user accounts or delete user accounts. If you are logged on with administrator rights, you can complete the steps in this activity. If you are in a classroom or computer lab, check with your instructor for permission to create an account.

**1** From the **Start** menu ⊕, display **Control Panel**, and then under **User Accounts and Family Safety** (or User Accounts), click **Add or remove user accounts**—enter the password if prompted.

**2** In the lower portion of the screen, click **Create a new account**.

The Create New Account window displays. Here you create the name for the new user account. The new user account name will display on the Windows 7 welcome screen. It will also display in the Start menu when this account holder is logged on. The default user account type is a standard user, as indicated by the selected option button.

**3** In the **New account name** box, using a form of your own name that is *not* the user name on your own computer, type **Firstname Lastname** and then compare your screen with Figure 1.2.

Figure 1.2

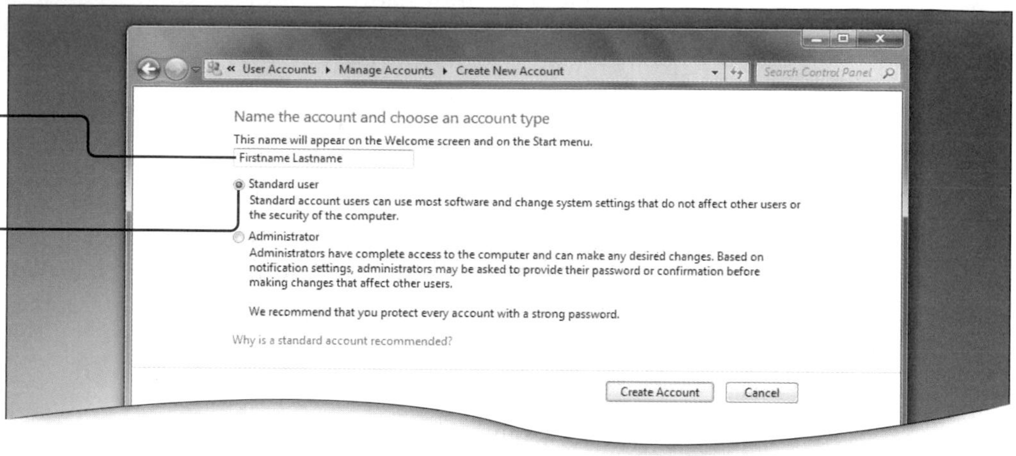

Your name, something different from the user name on your own computer

Standard user option button

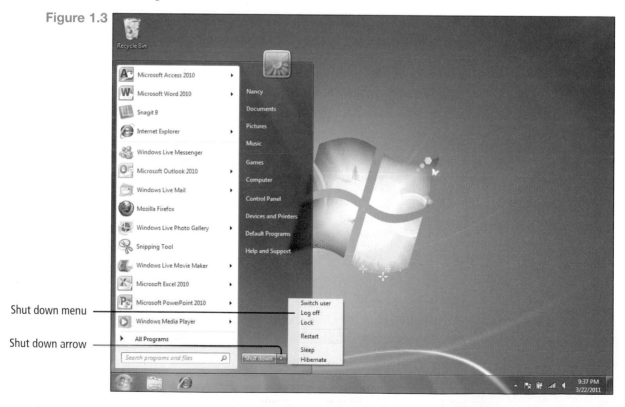

**4** In the lower right corner, click the **Create Account** button, and then **Close** the **Manage Accounts** window.

Windows 7 creates the new standard user account and applies one of the pictures. You may not see the user pictures if you are logged on as a standard user and accessed this screen by typing the administrator password.

**5** On the **Start** menu, point to the **Shut down arrow**, and then compare your screen with Figure 1.3.

Figure 1.3

Shut down menu

Shut down arrow

**6** On the **Shut down** menu, click **Switch user**. Wait a moment for the Welcome screen to display, and then notice the new account with the name you typed. Notice also that the account you used to create your new account is indicated as *Logged on*.

**7** Click your new user name to begin using your account.

> Recall that each user account has its own desktop and set of personal folders. When a new account user logs on the first time, Windows displays *Preparing your desktop*.

## Activity 1.02 | Creating an Account in Outlook

Outlook uses an e-mail *profile* to identify which e-mail account you use and where the related data is stored. When Outlook is initially configured, a single profile is created. You might choose to create separate profiles to keep your work data and personal information separate.

**1** On the **Windows taskbar**, click the **Start** button 🌐 to display the **Start** menu. Locate and open the program **Microsoft Outlook 2010**.

> The Microsoft Outlook 2010 Startup Wizard displays to configure Outlook 2010 in your new account.

---

**Alert! | Did Microsoft Outlook open without displaying the Startup Wizard?**

If Microsoft Outlook was previously configured on your system or if you were unable to create the user account in Activity 1.01, Outlook will open without displaying the Startup Wizard. To create the user account, click the File tab to display Backstage view, and then on the Info tab, under Account Information, click Add Account to open the Add New Account dialog box. Then, continue with Step 3 through Step 8.

---

**2** In the **Microsoft Outlook 2010 Startup** dialog box, click **Next** two times.

> The Add New Account dialog box displays for you to create your e-mail account to complete the activities in this textbook.

**3** In the **Add New Account** dialog box, in the **Your Name** box, using your own name, type **Firstname Lastname** In the **E-mail Address** box, using your own first and last name, type **Firstname_Lastname@GOMAIL.com**

---

**Note | GOMAIL.com and PHMAIL.com are fictitious domains**

GOMAIL.com and PHMAIL.com are fictitious domains used only for this instruction.

---

**4** In the **Add New Account** dialog box, in the lower left corner, click the **Manually configure server settings or additional server types** option button, and then compare your screen with Figure 1.4.

Figure 1.4

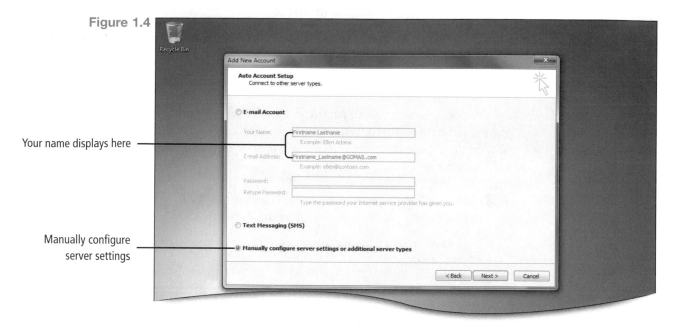

Your name displays here

Manually configure server settings

**5** Click **Next** two times. If necessary set the **Account Type** to POP3. In the **Incoming mail server** box, type **GOMAIL.com** and for the **Outgoing mail server (SMTP)** box, type **PHMAIL.com** Under **Logon Information**, in the **User Name** box, type your **Firstname_Lastname** and in the **Password** box, type **123456**

**6** Click to *clear* the check box to the left of **Test Account Settings by clicking the Next button**, and then compare your screen with Figure 1.5.

Figure 1.5

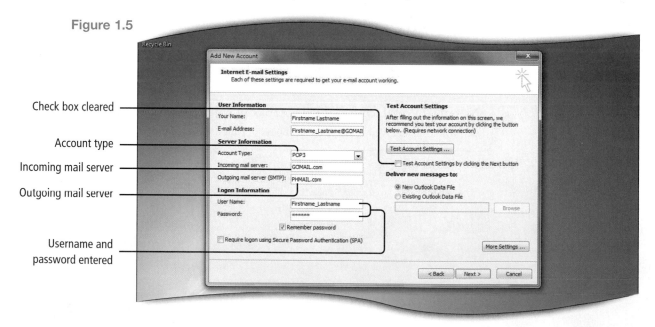

Check box cleared

Account type

Incoming mail server

Outgoing mail server

Username and password entered

**7** Click **Next**. In the screen indicating *Congratulations!* click **Finish** to return to **Outlook**.

**8** Click **OK** to close the **User Name** dialog box. If a **Microsoft Hotmail Connector** dialog box is displayed, click **No**. If the Welcome to Microsoft Office dialog box displays, click Use Recommended Settings, and then click OK. If a User Account Control box displays, click Yes.

Outlook configures your account, and the Outlook window is displayed.

---

**Note** | Firstname Lastname User Account

Use your Firstname Lastname user account when completing projects in this textbook. If you use a different computer each time you begin a project, you should refer back to Activities 1.01 and 1.02 to create the Firstname Lastname user account and to configure Outlook with your Firstname_Lastname@GOMAIL.com account.

---

## Activity 1.03 | Exploring the Outlook Window

**1** Compare your screen with Figure 1.6, and then take a moment to study the description of the screen elements in the table in Figure 1.7.

Your Outlook screen might differ from the one shown in Figure 1.6. The appearance of the opening screen depends on settings that were established when Outlook was installed on the computer you are using. A Send/Receive error may display at the bottom of your Outlook window as a result of the fictitious e-mail address used.

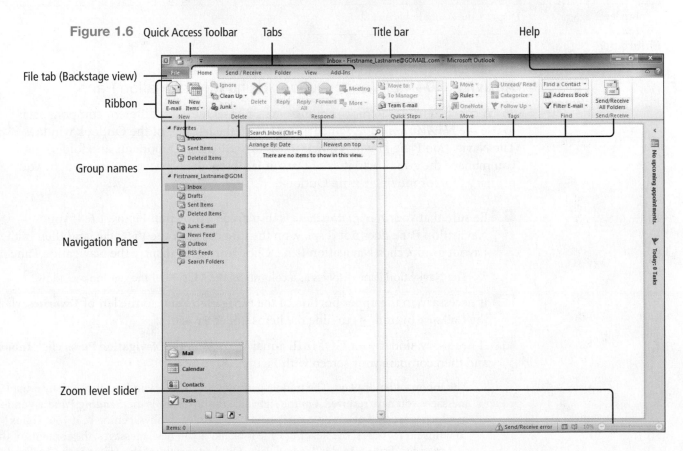

Figure 1.6

## Microsoft Outlook Screen Elements

| Screen Element | Description |
| --- | --- |
| Navigation Pane | Displays a list of shortcuts to Outlook's components and folders. |
| Title bar | Displays the name of the program and the program window control buttons—Minimize, Maximize/Restore Down, and Close. |
| File tab | Displays Microsoft Office Backstage view, a centralized space for all of your file management tasks such as opening, saving, or printing—all the things you can do *with* a file. |
| Ribbon | Displays a group of task-oriented tabs that contain the commands, styles, and resources you need to work in Outlook. The look of your Ribbon depends on your screen resolution. A high resolution will display more individual items and button names on the Ribbon. |
| Tabs | Displays the names of tasks relevant to the open program. |
| Group names | Indicate the names of the groups of related commands on the displayed tab. |
| Help button | Displays the Microsoft Outlook Help system. |
| Quick Access Toolbar | Displays buttons to perform frequently used commands with a single click. The default commands include Send/Receive and Undo. You can add and delete buttons to customize the Quick Access Toolbar for your convenience. |
| Zoom level | Displays the Zoom levels on a slider. |

Figure 1.7

### Activity 1.04 | Exploring Outlook Using the Navigation Pane

A convenient way to move among—navigate—Outlook's different components is to use the *Navigation Pane*, which is located on the left side of the Outlook window. The Navigation Pane provides quick access to Outlook's components and folders. As you manage the e-mail activities of Darron Jacobsen, the Navigation Pane will be your primary tool for moving within Outlook.

**1** Be sure that your **Navigation Pane** is displayed as shown in Figure 1.6. If your Navigation Pane does not display, on the Ribbon, click the View tab, and then in the Layout group, click Navigation Pane. Click Normal to display the Navigation Pane.

The Navigation Pane displays as a column on the left side of the Outlook window.

**2** If necessary, in the upper portion of the **Navigation Pane**, to the left of **Favorites**, click the **Collapse** button ◢ to hide the items under **Favorites**.

**3** If necessary, under your GOMAIL e-mail address in the **Navigation Pane**, click **Inbox**, and then compare your screen with Figure 1.8.

The Inbox folder displays. The middle pane of the Outlook window displays any e-mail messages you have received. On the right side of the screen is the *Reading Pane*, a window in which you can preview an e-mail message without actually opening it. If your Inbox contains no messages, the Reading Pane is blank. If you have messages, the contents of the first message displays in the Reading Pane. On the far right of the screen is the *To-Do Bar*, which when expanded provides a consolidated view of appointments, tasks, and e-mail messages that have been flagged for follow-up. It enables you to set your priorities for the day. In the figure, the To-Do Bar is collapsed.

Figure 1.8

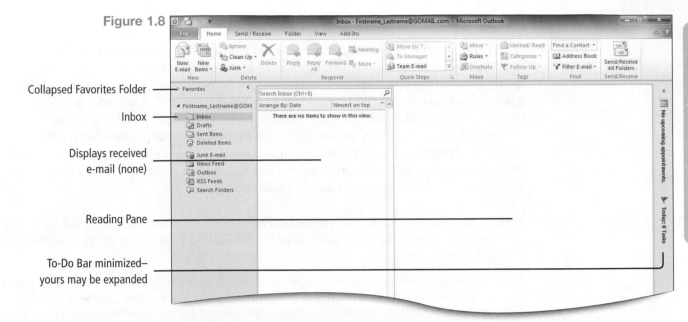

**Collapsed Favorites Folder** ——

**Inbox** ——

**Displays received e-mail (none)** ——

**Reading Pane** ——

**To-Do Bar minimized— yours may be expanded** ——

---

**Alert! | Does your screen differ?**

Depending on the configuration of Outlook on your system, your Reading Pane and To-Do Bar may not display. To display the Reading Pane, from the View tab, in the Layout group, click the Reading Pane button, and then click Right. To hide the To-Do Bar, from the View tab, in the Layout group, click the To-Do Bar button, and then click Minimized.

---

**4** In the lower portion of the **Navigation Pane**, click the **Calendar** button 📅 to display the **Calendar** folder.

> The right portion of the Outlook window displays the calendar for the current day, and the Navigation Pane displays calendar-related information. In this manner, each of Outlook's folder views displays different information.

**5** In the lower portion of the **Navigation Pane**, click the **Contacts** button 📇 to display the **Contacts** folder.

> Depending on whether contacts have been created, contact names may or may not display in the middle pane of the Outlook window.

**6** In the **Navigation Pane**, click the **Tasks** button ☑ to display the **Tasks** folder.

> The To-Do List shows any pending tasks. If no tasks have been created, the list is blank. The Reading Pane may or may not be visible.

**7** In the lower portion of the **Navigation Pane**, locate the three small buttons that have *icons*—graphic representations of objects you can select and open. Point to each one to display its *ScreenTip*—a small box that displays the name of a screen element— and then click the **Notes** button 📝 to display the Notes folder.

> Use the Notes component to keep track of information you might use later, such as directions or a question you have for someone.

**8** In the lower portion of the **Navigation Pane**, click the **Mail** button 📧 to return to the Inbox.

## Activity 1.05 | Exploring Outlook Using the Folder List

Outlook uses folders to organize information. Individual folders store *items*. An item is an element of information in Outlook, such as a message, a contact name, a task, or an appointment. The most used folders are listed at the top of the Navigation Pane—**Inbox**, **Drafts**, **Sent Items**, and **Deleted Items**. These are followed by additional storage folders listed in alphabetical order. Data in your Outlook folders is stored in a data file that uses the .pst file extension. If you are working in an *Exchange Server environment*, a special shared environment set up by your system administrator, your Outlook information is probably stored in an Exchange Server mailbox rather than a local .pst file. In either case, you can use the folder list to navigate in Outlook.

**1** In the lower portion of the **Navigation Pane**, click the **Folder List** button ⬚ to display the **Folder List** in the upper portion of the **Navigation Pane**. Compare your screen with Figure 1.9.

The right portion of the Outlook window continues to display the Inbox folder; the upper portion of the Navigation Pane displays the folder list. Folders shown in the Navigation Pane may contain more folders than can fit in the All Folders pane. If necessary, you can scroll down the pane to view the additional folders. *Scrolling* is the action of moving a pane or window vertically (up or down) or horizontally (side to side) to bring unseen areas into view.

Figure 1.9

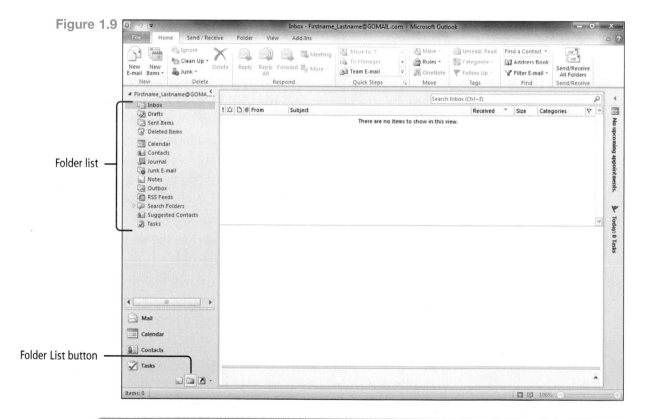

Folder list

Folder List button

---

**Alert! | Does your screen differ?**

Depending on the configuration of Outlook on your system, the Folder List shown in the Navigation Pane might differ from the one shown in Figure 1.9. No scroll bar displays if the folder list fits within the boundaries of the pane.

**2** In the **Navigation Pane**, click the **Journal** folder to display its contents. If a Microsoft Outlook dialog box prompts you to turn on automatic journaling, click **No**. Compare your screen with Figure 1.10.

> You can use the Folder List to display folders that do not have buttons on the Navigation Pane. The *Journal* folder provides a timeline of your activities and interactions. Like a personal journal, it is a record of your day-to-day events.

Figure 1.10

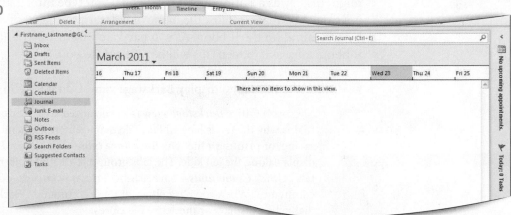

**3** In the lower portion of the **Navigation Pane**, click the **Mail** button 📧 to display the **Inbox** folder.

> Outlook hides the folders in the Folder List that are not associated with the Mail feature when you click the Mail button in the Navigation Pane.

---

**More Knowledge | Servers and Exchange Server Accounts**

Your e-mail account may be a Microsoft Exchange Server account. Exchange Server is an e-mail–based communications server for businesses and organizations. A *server* is a computer or device on a network that handles shared network resources. Microsoft Exchange Server functions as a mail server for a business or organization. In an Exchange Server environment, Outlook functions as a client of the server. A *client* is a program that runs on a personal computer and relies on the server to perform some of its operations. A few Outlook features require an Exchange Server e-mail account. Home users typically do not have Exchange Server accounts. Most home users of Outlook have a *POP3* e-mail account with an Internet service provider. POP3 is a protocol that provides a simple, standardized way for users to access mailboxes and download messages to their computers.

If you have a free Hotmail or Windows Live e-mail account, you can download Outlook Connector to use Outlook to manage and view your e-mail. This gives you the advantages of using Outlook 2010 to compose and filter messages, as well as use other features that you would not otherwise be able to access.

You can configure Outlook to use either POP3 or IMAP to access your Google Gmail account. Log into your Gmail account through your Web browser, click Help, and then click either the POP or IMAP links under Other Ways to Access Gmail. Follow the instructions there. If you use Google Apps, you can use Outlook to manage all of your Google Apps mail, calendar events, and contacts from within Outlook—provided you have either a paid or an education account.

---

## Activity 1.06 | Identifying and Displaying Ribbons and ScreenTips

Outlook commands are displayed using a **Ribbon**, which displays across the top of the program window. The Ribbon contains three elements: tabs, groups, and commands to group commands and features in a manner that you would most logically use them.

**Tabs** display across the top of the Ribbon, and each tab relates to a type of activity; for example, sending and receiving. **Groups** are sets of related commands for specific tasks. **Commands**—instructions to computer programs—are arranged in groups, and might display as a button or a box in which you type information. Recall that a ScreenTip is a small box that contains the name or a descriptive label of a screen element, such as a button found on the Ribbon. As you navigate within Darron Jacobsen's Inbox, the Ribbon, tabs, and ScreenTips will be available to you.

**1** Click the **File tab** to display **Backstage** view. Compare your screen with Figure 1.11.

Microsoft Office **Backstage view** is a centralized space for tasks related to *file management*; that is why the tab is labeled *File*. File management tasks include, for example, opening, saving, or printing a file. The **Backstage tabs**—*Info, Open, Print, Help,* and *Options*— display along the left side. The tabs group file-related tasks together. Above the Backstage tabs, **Quick Commands**—*Save As,* and *Save Attachments*—display for quick access to these commands. When you click either of these commands, Backstage view closes and either a dialog box displays or the active file closes.

Here, the **Info tab** displays information—*info*—about the current account. On the Info page, a thumbnail image of the current window displays in the upper right corner, which you can click to close **Backstage** view and return to Outlook.

Figure 1.11

**2** Click the **Print tab**. Compare your screen with Figure 1.12.

In Backstage view, on the Print tab, in the center panel, three groups of printing-related tasks display—Print, Printer, and Settings. In the right panel, the **Print Preview** displays, which is a view of a screen or message as it will appear on the paper when you print it.

At the bottom of the Print Preview area, on the left, the number of pages and arrows with which you can move among the pages in Print Preview display. On the right, buttons enable you to modify the Print Preview.

**Figure 1.12**

Print Preview

Page information

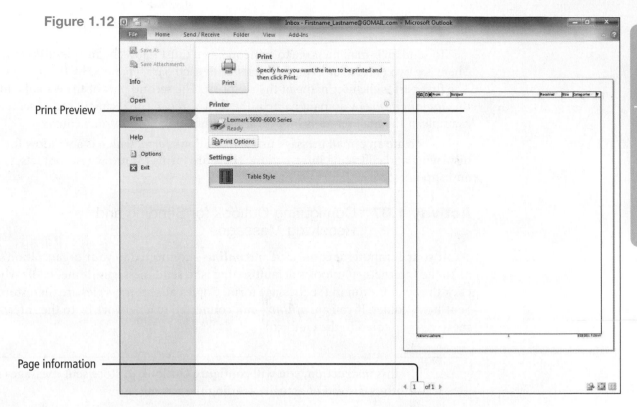

> 3 On the **Ribbon,** click the **Home tab** to close **Backstage** view without performing any commands.

> 4 On the **Home tab**, in the **New group**, *point* to the **New E-mail** button. Compare your screen with Figure 1.13.

> When you position the pointer over a button, Outlook highlights the button and displays a ScreenTip that describes the button, in this case—*New Item*.

**Figure 1.13**

New E-mail button

ScreenTip

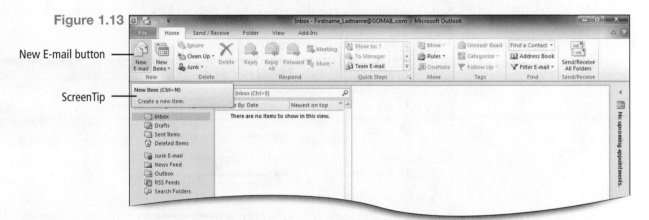

> 5 Point to other buttons on the **Home tab**, observing the ScreenTip for each button.

> Shaded or gray buttons indicate that the command represented by the button is not currently available.

## Objective 2 | Compose and Send E-mail

To send an e-mail message to someone, you must know the recipient's e-mail address. There are two parts to an e-mail address, with each part separated by the *at sign* (@). The first part is the user name of the recipient. The second part of the e-mail address is the *domain name*. A domain name is the host name of the recipient's mail server. For example, if the mail server is MSN Hotmail, the domain is hotmail.com.

You create an e-mail message using an Outlook *form*, which is a window for displaying and collecting information. There are forms for messages, contacts, tasks, and appointments.

### Activity 1.07 | Configuring Outlook for Sending and Receiving Messages

If your computer is connected and *online*—connected to your organization's network or to the Internet—Outlook's default setting is to send messages immediately when you click the Send button in the Message form. Copies of sent messages are then stored in the Sent Items folder. If you are *offline*—not connected to a network or to the Internet—messages are stored in the Outbox.

> **Alert!** | In this instruction, you will configure Outlook to store sent messages in the Outbox instead of actually sending the messages.
>
> In this activity, you will configure Outlook to store all your sent messages in the Outbox instead of actually sending the messages from your GOMAIL account. You will be handling the e-mail activities of Darron Jacobsen. You can create and send his messages even if your computer is not actually connected and online.

**1** Click the **File tab** to display **Backstage** view, and then click **Options**. In the **Outlook Options** dialog box, on the left, click **Advanced**.

**2** Scroll down to the section **Send and receive**, click to *clear* the check mark from the **Send immediately when connected** check box, and then compare your screen with Figure 1.14.

Figure 1.14

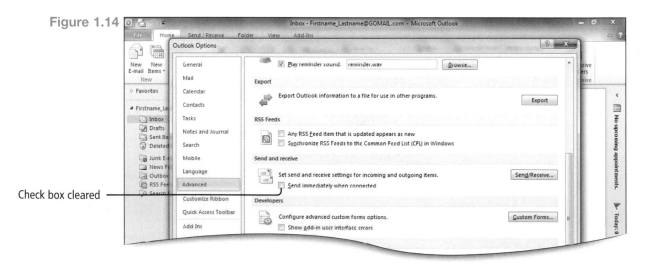

Check box cleared

**3** To the right, click the **Send/Receive** button.

**4** In the **Send/Receive Groups** dialog box, under **Setting for group "All Accounts"**, click to *clear* the **Include this group in send/receive (F9)** check box, and then click to *clear* the **Schedule an automatic send/receive every** check box.

**5** Under **When Outlook is Offline**, click to *clear* the **Include this group in send/receive (F9)** check box.

**6** Click the **Close** button, and then in the **Outlook Options** dialog box, click **OK** to close the dialog box.

### Activity 1.08 | Creating a New E-mail Message

You can use two *editors*—programs with which you can create or make changes to existing files—to create and view messages in Outlook. These are the Outlook editor and the Microsoft Word editor. The default e-mail editor is the Microsoft Word editor, with which you can use many Word features when creating your messages, for example, the spelling checker, tables, and bullets and numbering. In this activity, you will create a message for Darron Jacobsen using the Word editor and send it to one of his colleagues at Lake Michigan City College.

**1** If necessary, in the **Navigation Pane**, under your GOMAIL e-mail address, click **Inbox**. On the **Home tab**, in the **New group**, click the **New E-mail** button, and then compare your screen with Figure 1.15.

The top of the form displays a Ribbon with commands organized by groups and tabs based on particular activities, such as setting message options or formatting text.

**Figure 1.15**

Message tab

Format Text tab

Ribbon

Message area

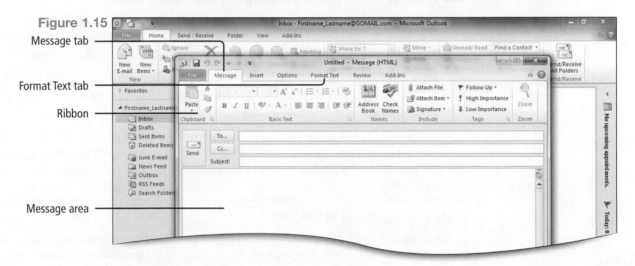

### Alert! | Does your Ribbon look different?

The size of the Outlook window determines how much information appears with each command on the Ribbon. Users with larger screen resolutions will notice both icons and words for all commands, while those with small screens may see only the icons for certain commands.

**2** Click the **Format Text tab** and locate the **Format group**. Notice the **HTML** button is selected. Compare your screen with Figure 1.16.

The default message format in Outlook is *HTML*, which allows your message to include numbering, bullets, lines, backgrounds, HTML styles, and multimedia features that can be viewed in a Web browser. *Rich Text* format can include character and paragraph formatting and embedded graphics. *Plain Text* allows no special formatting.

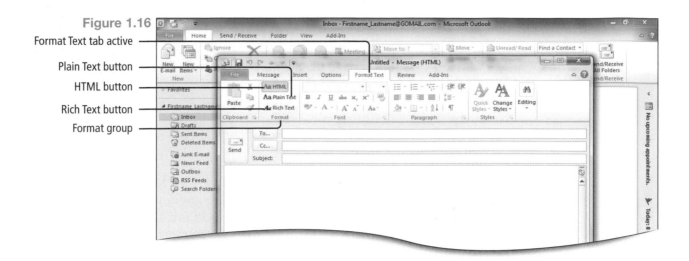

Figure 1.16

**Format Text tab active**
**Plain Text button**
**HTML button**
**Rich Text button**
**Format group**

**3** In the **Format group**, click the **Plain Text** button.

Use Plain Text if you are certain that the recipient of your message has an e-mail program that can only read messages written in Plain Text. When you send an HTML message to a recipient who cannot receive HTML, the message will be converted to Plain Text.

**4** In the **To** box, type **LHuelsman@LakeMichCityCollege.edu**

This is the e-mail address of the recipient. Notice the *syntax*—the way in which the parts of the e-mail address are put together. The user name is to the left of the @ symbol, and the domain name is on the right. If another student has used this computer, you may see Ms. Huelsman's e-mail address display in blue.

**5** In the **Cc** box, click to place the insertion point, and then type **HSabaj@LakeMichCityCollege.edu**

This sends a *courtesy copy*, or *carbon copy*, of the message to the address specified in the Cc box. In both the To and the Cc boxes, you can enter multiple addresses, separating each address with a semicolon. Send a courtesy copy to others who need to see the message.

---

**More Knowledge** | **Carbon Copies**

Old fashioned carbon paper is rarely used anymore, but the term carbon copy has remained. Sometimes Cc is referred to as a courtesy copy. Sometimes people will just say "I cc'd (pronounced see-seed) you on an e-mail."

---

**6** Press ⟨Tab⟩ two times to bypass the **Subject** box and move the insertion point to the message area. You will add the subject later.

You can move the insertion point from one box to another either by clicking in the box or by pressing ⟨Tab⟩.

---

**Note** | **Underlined E-mail Addresses**

Outlook may display an underlined e-mail address after you type it in the box. Outlook remembers previously typed addresses, and this change in its appearance shows that this address has been used before, either by you or a previous user. Your system may also be set to automatically underline all e-mail addresses that use correct syntax.

---

**7** On the Message form title bar, click the **Maximize** button ▣ to enlarge the viewing area of the form. You can type the text of your message without enlarging the viewing area of the Message form, but it is easier to see your text as you type it when the form is maximized.

**8** With the insertion point in the message area of the Message form, type **Hi Lisa,** and then press [Enter] two times.

> This is the beginning of your message. It is considered good etiquette to address the recipient(s) by name and add an appropriate salutation. Keep your messages short and to the point. It is usually helpful to the recipient if you restrict your message to only one topic. If you have another topic to discuss, send another e-mail message.

**9** Type **I just received confirmation from the Chamber of Commerce; they would like to have you speak at their next monthly meeting. Let's arrange a time for us to meet and discuss your presentation. I'd like Henry to meet with us as well.**

> As you type, the insertion point moves left to right. When it reaches the right margin, Outlook determines whether the next word will fit within the established margin. If the word does not fit, the insertion point moves the whole word down to the next line. This feature is called *wordwrap*.

**10** Press [Enter] two times and type **You might want to look at Joyce's presentation from last month when she spoke at the Illinois Special Needs Teachers Conference. Mary has a copy of it, if you don't have one.**

> To leave a single blank line between paragraphs, press [Enter] two times. Keep paragraphs short and single-spaced with a double-space between them. Do not indent the first line of paragraphs, and press [Spacebar] only one time following the punctuation at the end of a sentence.

**11** Press [Enter] **two** times, type **Darron** and then click somewhere in the text of the message.

> Darron is flagged with a wavy red line, indicating that it is not in Word's dictionary. Proper names are often not in Word's dictionary; however, this is the correct spelling of Mr. Jacobsen's name.

**12** Point to *Darron* and right-click, and then click **Ignore**. Review the message to check for errors, and then take a moment to study the keystrokes for moving the insertion point as described in the table in Figure 1.17.

> Always double-check the addresses of your recipients. Address errors result in either the return of the message or delivery to the wrong person. Edit and proofread your messages carefully. Messages containing errors in style, grammar, punctuation, and keyboarding reflect poorly on you, the sender. E-mail messages may use a more casual tone than if the message was sent in a formal business letter. However, as in any business communication, keep the tone of your message courteous and professional.

| Keystrokes for Moving the Insertion Point in a Message | |
|---|---|
| **Keystrokes** | **Result** |
| Ctrl + End | Moves to the end of the message |
| Ctrl + Home | Moves to the beginning of the message |
| End | Moves to the end of the line |
| Home | Moves to the beginning of the line |
| PgUp | Moves up one window |
| PgDn | Moves down one window |
| ↑ | Moves up one line |
| ↓ | Moves down one line |

Figure 1.17

**13** Press Ctrl + Home to move your insertion point to the beginning of the message, and then compare your screen with Figure 1.18.

Figure 1.18

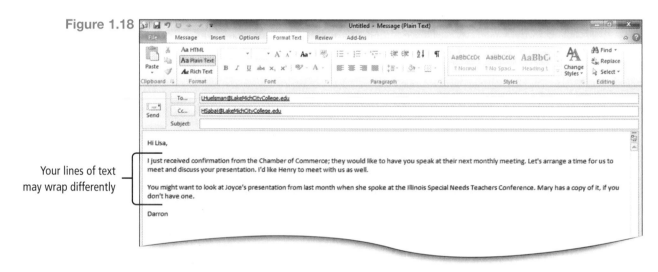

Your lines of text may wrap differently

**14** On the Message form title bar, click the **Restore Down** button ⬜ to restore the Message form to its original size.

### Activity 1.09 | Sending a Message and Checking the Outbox

Recall that for purposes of this instruction, and because you are working with fictitious e-mail addresses, you configured Outlook to store all your sent messages in the Outbox. This allows you to send Darron Jacobsen's messages even if your computer is not actually online. When opening a message, you can either double-click it or you can right-click—the action of clicking the right mouse button—and then click Open. Right-clicking displays a shortcut menu—a list of context-related commands.

**1** In the message header, to the left of **To**, click the **Send** button. Compare your screen with Figure 1.19.

> A dialog box displays to remind you that a subject was not included for the message. A subject makes it easier for people who receive your e-mail messages to quickly know the contents of your message. Always include a brief, meaningful subject for your messages.

Figure 1.19

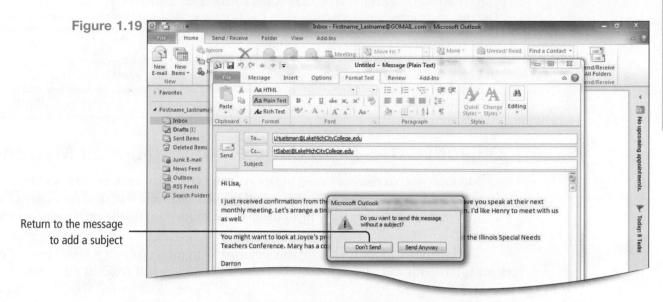

Return to the message to add a subject

**2** In the **Microsoft Outlook** dialog box, click **Don't Send**. In the **Subject box**, type **Chamber of Commerce presentation** Click **Send**.

> The message is sent to the Outbox folder, and the Message form closes.

**3** In the **Navigation Pane** under your account, locate and then click the **Outbox** folder. Compare your screen with Figure 1.20.

> The contents of the Outbox folder display. When the Outbox folder contains unsent messages, the folder name is displayed in bold followed by the number of items in brackets.

Figure 1.20

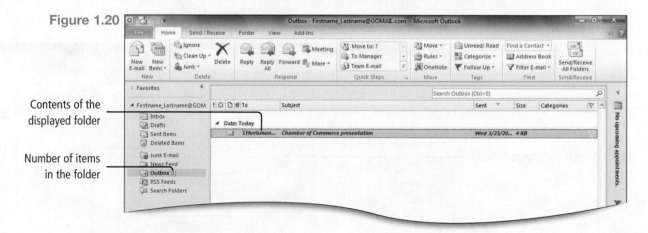

Contents of the displayed folder

Number of items in the folder

**4** In the **Outbox**, double-click the *LHuelsman* message to open it. This message has not been sent.

**5** Close [×] the message form.

Outlook receives messages sent to you many times a day. This may occur at automatic intervals, or manually, when you click the Send/Receive All Folders button on the Send/Receive tab in the Send & Receive group. When you click the Send/Receive All Folders button, Outlook checks for any received messages and places them in your Inbox. It also sends any messages in your Outbox and places a copy of the sent message in the Sent Items folder. Recall that Outlook normally sends messages as soon as you click the Send button in the Message form, but for purposes of the instruction in this textbook, you have configured Outlook to place your sent messages in the Outbox instead. If you click the Send/Receive All Folders button while not actually online, Outlook attempts to send the message and will display an error message.

By default, automatic send/receive is disabled. To set Outlook to receive your messages automatically, display the Send/Receive tab, and in the Send & Receive group, click the Send/Receive Groups button. Then click Define Send/Receive Groups. Select appropriate options and adjust the time to indicate how you would like Send/Receive to occur. Close the dialog box.

## Objective 3 | Read and Respond to E-mail Messages

Messages you receive are stored in Outlook's Inbox folder. Each message displays the name of the message sender, the subject, and the date and time sent. You can respond to a received message by either replying to the message or forwarding the message to another individual.

In Activities 1.10 through 1.15, you will work with messages that you will import into your Inbox. This will enable you to work with different types of received messages.

### Activity 1.10 | Importing Messages to the Inbox

Importing data into your Inbox involves the same steps, regardless of whether you are importing the data into the Personal Folders or into an Exchange Server mailbox. In this activity, you will import Darron Jacobsen's received messages into your Inbox.

**1** In the **Navigation Pane**, under your **GOMAIL account**, click **Inbox**.

**2** From the **Backstage** view, click **Open**, and then click **Import**. Compare your screen with Figure 1.21.

The Import and Export Wizard dialog box displays. A *wizard* is a tool that walks you through a process in a step-by-step manner.

Figure 1.21

Import and Export Wizard ———

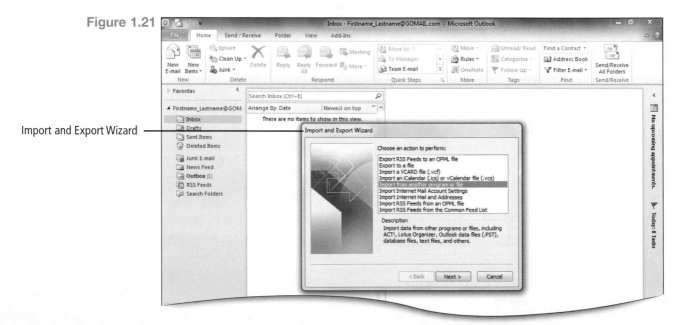

**3** In the **Import and Export Wizard** dialog box, under **Choose an action to perform**, click **Import from another program or file**, and then click **Next**.

**4** In the **Import a File** dialog box, under **Select file type to import from**, click **Outlook Data File (.pst)**, and then click **Next**. In the displayed **Import Outlook Data File** dialog box, click **Browse**.

**5** In the displayed **Open Outlook Data Files** dialog box, navigate to the location where the student files that accompany this textbook are stored. Locate **o01A_College_Inbox**, and click one time to select it. Then, in the lower right corner of the **Open Outlook Data Files** dialog box, click **Open**.

> The Open Outlook Data Files dialog box closes, and the path and file name display in the File to import box.

**6** Click **Next** and compare your screen with Figure 1.22.

> The Import Outlook Data File dialog box displays the folder structure for the file you are going to import.

Figure 1.22

**7** Under **Select the folder to import from**, click **Inbox**, and then click the **Import items into the current folder** option button.

**8** Click **Finish**. If a Translation Warning dialog box displays, click OK. Compare your screen with Figure 1.23.

Figure 1.23

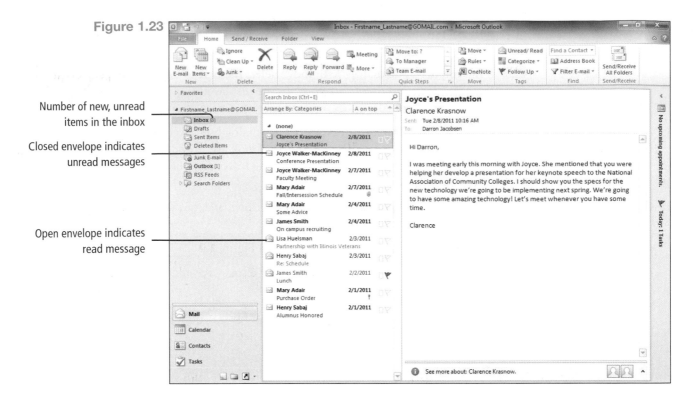

Number of new, unread items in the inbox

Closed envelope indicates unread messages

Open envelope indicates read message

## Activity 1.11 | Opening, Navigating, and Closing an E-mail Message

You can read messages in two ways. You can read the text of shorter messages in the Reading Pane without opening the message. When the Reading Pane is not displayed or the text of the message is too long to fit in the Reading Pane, you can open the message. In this activity, you will view Darron Jacobsen's messages in several ways.

**1** Look at the **Inbox**, and take a moment to study the messages shown in Figure 1.23.

In the Navigation Pane, the number in parentheses to the right of Inbox displays the number of unread messages. The Inbox pane lists the *message header* for each message. Message headers include basic information about an e-mail message such as the sender's name, the date sent, and the subject. The message header for an e-mail that has not yet been read or opened is displayed in bold, and the icon at the left shows a closed envelope. After a message has been read, the bold is removed, and the icon changes to an open envelope.

**2** Locate the second message in the **Inbox**, which is from Joyce Walker-MacKinney and has as its subject **Conference Presentation**. Click it one time to display it in the Reading Pane.

After you view a message in the Reading Pane, Outlook considers its status as read after you move to another message. The first message indicates that you have read it—the bold has been removed and the icon has changed. The Conference presentation message is too long to display entirely in the Reading Pane; however, you can scroll down to view the remainder of the message. Or, you may prefer to open the message to read it.

**3** Double-click the **Conference Presentation** message to open it. Alternatively, press Ctrl + O. Compare your screen with Figure 1.24.

The Message form displays the message. The area above the text of the message contains the message header information, which includes the sender's name and the date of the message. On the left side of the Message form title bar, the Quick Access Toolbar is displayed. This allows you to perform frequently used commands such as saving an item, viewing a previous item, or viewing the next item. In the center of the Message form title bar, the subject of the message appears.

**Figure 1.24**

Message form Quick Access toolbar

Previous Item button

Next Item button

Message header information

Scroll box

Down scroll arrow

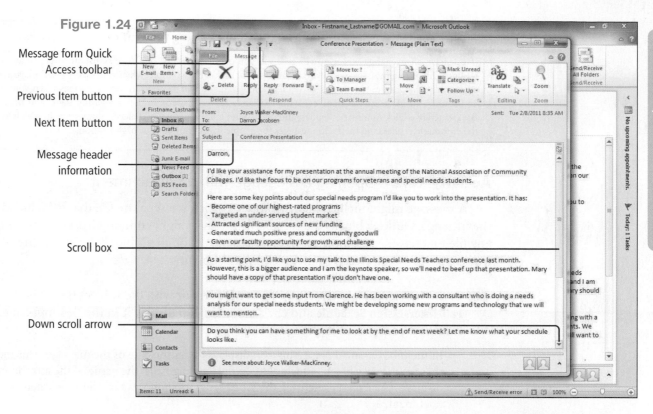

**4** In the vertical scroll bar of the Message form, click the **down scroll arrow** or drag the scroll box down until the lower portion of the message displays.

**5** On the Message form title bar, click the **Close** button ⊠.

**6** Locate the third message in the **Inbox**, which is the message from *Joyce Walker-MacKinney* with the subject heading **Faculty Meeting**, and then double-click the message to open it.

**7** If necessary, on the Message form title bar, click the **Restore Down** button 🗗 so the message does not fill the screen.

**8** In the **Message form**, on the Quick Access Toolbar, click the **Previous Item** button 🔼.

The message is closed, and the Message form displays the previous message in your Inbox, which is the message from *Joyce Walker-MacKinney* with the subject **Conference Presentation**.

**9** On the Quick Access Toolbar, click the **Next** button 🔽.

**10** Click the **Next Item** button 🔽 again.

The displayed message is closed, and the next message in your Inbox displays. You can view all the messages in your Inbox in the Message form by using this toolbar button. When you do so, the current message is closed, and the next message in the list displays.

**11** Use the **Next Item** button 🔽 to view the remaining messages in your Inbox. The last message is from Henry Sabaj and has the subject heading **Alumnus Honored**.

**12** **Close** ⊠ the Message form, and notice that no unread items remain in the Inbox; rather, all display an open envelope icon indicating they have been read.

> **More Knowledge** | Creating Automatic Replies Using the Out of Office Assistant
>
> If you have an Exchange Server e-mail account, you can use the Out of Office Assistant to create automatic replies to incoming messages when you are not in your office. For example, when you are on vacation, you might want to use this feature to let message senders know that you will respond to their messages when you return. To use the Out of Office Assistant, click the Exchange Server Mailbox in the Navigation Pane, and then from Backstage view, click Automatic Replies, and select Send automatic replies. Select a time range in which to send the automatic replies, and then add messages for people in and out of your organization.

### Activity 1.12 | Opening a Message with an Attachment

A message might include an **attachment**, which is a separate file that is included with the message. Outlook blocks the receipt of files that might contain viruses. For example, any file that has the file name extension of *.bat*, *.vbs*, or *.exe* is blocked. One of the messages Darron has received includes an attachment.

**1** In the **Inbox**, locate the message from *Mary Adair* with the subject heading **Fall/Intersession Schedule** and click it one time to display it in the Reading Pane. Compare your screen with Figure 1.25.

> In the Inbox, a small paper clip icon displays under the date of the message. This indicates that the message has an attachment. In the Reading Pane, the name of the attachment file displays. The icon representing the Word program indicates that the attachment is a Word document.

Figure 1.25

Attached file

Word icon

Paper clip icon

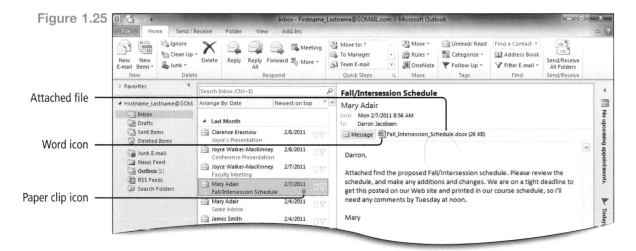

**2** Double-click to open the **Fall/Intersession Schedule** message.

> The message displays in the Message form. The attachment file name displays in the message header.

**3** Double-click the **Word icon** in the attachment file name to open the attachment. Alternatively, right-click the attachment, and then click Open. If the Opening Mail Attachment dialog box appears, click Open.

> The Opening Mail Attachment dialog box may display. Outlook displays this dialog box to remind you that attachments might contain viruses. You have the choice of opening an attachment or saving it as a file. You should not open an attachment unless it is from a known source. Your system may include an antivirus program that scans attachments, but unless you are certain that this is the case, it is safer to save the attachment as a file and scan it with an antivirus program before opening it.

**4** If Microsoft Word displays the document in Protected View, click **Enable Editing**.

> Microsoft Word starts the Word program and displays the attached file, which is a Word document. Note that an attachment is part of an e-mail message unless you save it separately. You can save an attachment separately by right-clicking the Word icon in the attachment file name and then clicking Save As. You will not save this attachment separately.

**5** In the **Microsoft Word** title bar, click the **Close** button ☒ to close the attachment.

**6** Close ☒ the message.

## Activity 1.13 | Replying to an E-mail Message

You can reply to an e-mail message from the Inbox or while viewing it in the Message form. When replying from the Inbox, the Reply button is available on the Home tab in the Respond group. When viewing the message form, a Reply button is located on the Message tab in the Respond group. Recall that you configured Outlook to place your sent messages in the Outbox. In this activity, you will send a reply to one of the messages that Darron Jacobsen received.

**1** In the **Inbox**, select the message from *James Smith* that has the subject **On campus recruiting** to display it in the Reading Pane. Then, on the **Home tab**, in the **Respond group**, click the **Reply** button. Compare your screen with Figure 1.26.

> You do not have to open a message to reply to it—selecting and displaying it in the Reading Pane is sufficient to create a reply. A Message form displays. Outlook adds the prefix *RE:* to the subject and title of the message. *RE:* is commonly used to mean *in regard to* or *regarding*. The text of the original message is included in the message area of the form, and Outlook places the sender's e-mail address in the To box.

Figure 1.26

RE: Indicates that this message is a reply

Original message text

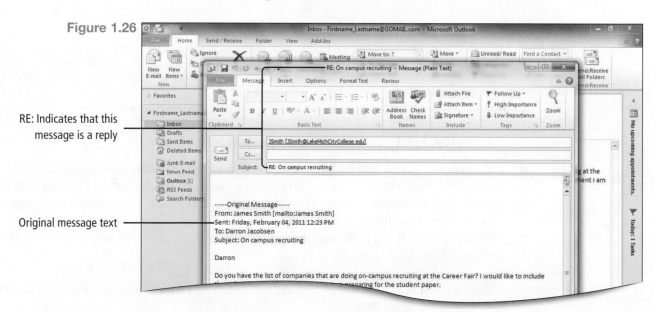

**2** With the insertion point at the top of the message area, type **Jim,** and press ⏎ two times. Type **I will have the list ready for you by the end of the day.** Press ⏎ two times, and type **Darron**

> A message reply is typed above the original message so that the recipient does not have to scroll down to see your reply.

**3** On the Message form, click the **Send** button.

> The message is sent to the Outbox, and the Message form closes.

**4** In the **Inbox**, locate and, if necessary, select the *James Smith*, **On campus recruiting** message, and then compare your screen with Figure 1.27.

> The arrow on the message in the Inbox shows that you have replied to the message. In the Reading Pane, a banner indicates the date and time that you replied to the message.

**Figure 1.27**

Banner indicates when the reply was sent (your dates will differ)

Icon with purple arrow indicates that a reply has been sent

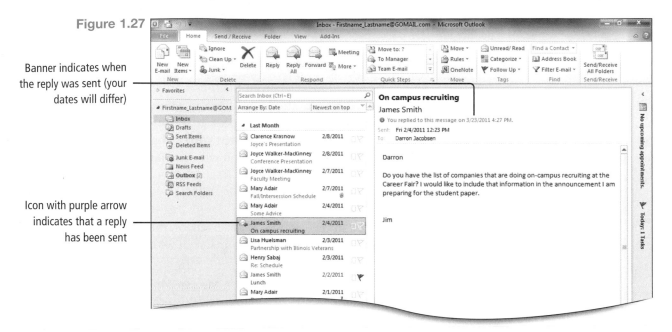

---

**More Knowledge | Replying to Multiple Recipients**

When you receive a message that has been sent to a group of individuals including you, you can use the Reply All button to send your reply to everyone who received the original message. Be sure that everyone who received the message needs to receive the reply before using the Reply All button. To reply only to the sender of the original message, use the Reply button as you did in this activity.

---

## Activity 1.14 | Forwarding an E-mail Message

You can forward an e-mail message you receive to someone else—commonly referred to as a *third party*. This is called *forwarding*. However, do not forward messages to others unless you are sure the sender of the original message would approve of forwarding the message. You can forward a message from the Inbox or while viewing the opened message. Darron Jacobscn has received a message that he wants to forward to a third party, Henry Sabaj at Lake Michigan City College.

**1** In the **Inbox**, click the *Joyce Walker-MacKinney* **Faculty Meeting** message to display it in the Reading Pane.

**2** On the **Home tab**, in the **Respond group**, click the **Forward** button.

> You do not have to open a message to forward it. A Message form displays. Outlook adds the prefix FW: to the subject and title of the message. The text of the original message is included in the message area of the form.

**3** In the **To** box, type the first letter of the recipient's address, which is **h** and then compare your screen with Figure 1.28.

> Under the To box, Outlook displays the address *HSabaj@LakeMichCityCollege.edu*. This is an example of Outlook's **AutoComplete** feature; Outlook remembers addresses you have typed previously. If more than one address begins with the first character you type, Outlook displays all suggested addresses. You may continue typing the address if you do not want to use any of the displayed addresses.

**Figure 1.28**

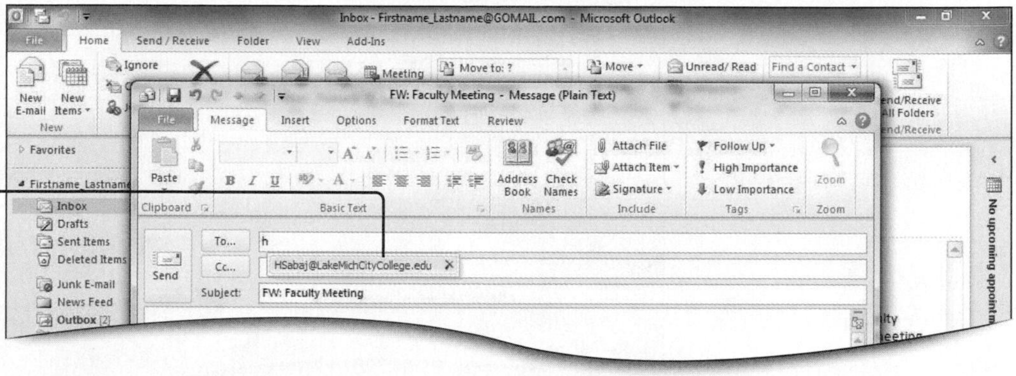

AutoComplete suggests address (one or more may display)

**4** Point to *Henry Sabaj's* address and click one time, or, if his address is highlighted, press [Enter] to accept the suggested address. Then, click to place the insertion point at the top of the message area, type **Henry,** and press [Enter] two times.

**5** Type **As you can see from Joyce's message below, she's asked me to find out if you have any outstanding issues for the next faculty meeting.** Press [Enter] two times, and type **Let me know.**

**6** Press [Enter] two times and type **Darron** Then, on the **Message form**, click the **Send** button.

> The message is sent to the Outbox, and the Message form closes. The blue arrow on the message in the Inbox shows you have forwarded the message. In the Reading Pane, a banner indicates the date and time that you forwarded the message. Notice that the icons for the forwarded and replied messages are different and that they match the respective buttons on the Ribbon.

## Activity 1.15 | Sending a Message with an Attachment

You can attach one or more files to any message you send. When you reply to a message, you may prefer not to include some of, or the entire, previous message. You can delete portions of text by *selecting text* and pressing [Del]. Selecting text refers to highlighting areas of the text by dragging with the mouse.

**1** In the **Inbox**, click the *Henry Sabaj* **RE: Schedule** message to display it in the Reading Pane, and then, on the **Home tab**, in the **Respond group**, click the **Reply** button.

**2** **Maximize** 🔲 the viewing area, if necessary, and then click to place the insertion point at the beginning of the second instance of the line *Original Message*. Drag downward to the lower portion of the message area to select the lower portion of the text, as shown in Figure 1.29.

**Figure 1.29**

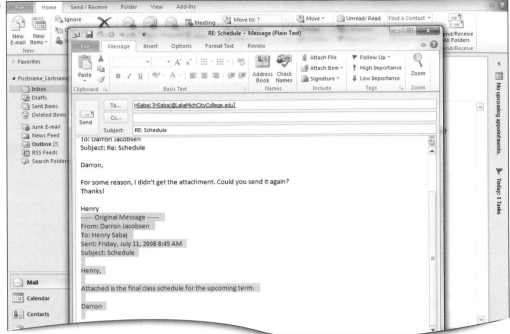

**3** Press `Del` to delete the selected text. Press `Ctrl` + `Home` to place the insertion point at the top of the message area. Type **Henry,** and then press `Enter` two times.

**4** Type **Here it is again.** Press `Enter` two times and then type **Darron** On the **Message tab**, in the **Include group**, click the **Attach File** button.

> The Insert File dialog box displays a list of the drives and folders available on your system.

**5** Navigate to the location where the student files that accompany this textbook are stored. Locate and click the Word file **o01A_Proposed_Schedule**. Then, in the lower right corner of the **Insert File** dialog box, click **Insert**.

> The Insert File dialog box closes, and the Message form redisplays. Outlook attaches the document to the message. The Word icon and the name of the attached file display in the Attached box.

> If you decide later you do not want to attach the file to the message, you can click the attachment icon and press `Del`.

**6** If necessary, on the Message title bar, click the **Restore Down** button 🗗 so the message does not fill the screen, and compare your screen with Figure 1.30.

**Figure 1.30**

Outlook | Chapter 1

Message window restored to its original size

File attached

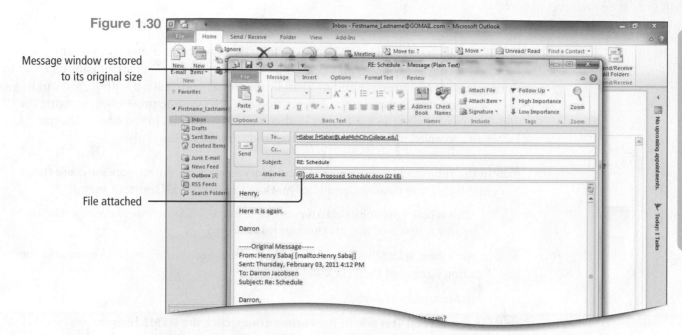

## Note | Deleting Original Text in Messages

Many Outlook users prefer not to include the original text of a message when they reply to or forward a message, especially when the original text is lengthy or contains multiple responses. You can manually delete the original text of a message. You can also have Outlook delete the original text of messages automatically. To automatically delete original text, display the Backstage view, click Options, and then click Mail. Scroll down to display the Replies and forwards section, and you can choose how you want Outlook to handle original text for replies and forwarded messages.

**7** Click **Send**.

The message is sent to the Outbox, and the Message form closes. The Inbox and the Reading Pane indicate that you have replied to the message.

## More Knowledge | Resending and Recalling Messages

You may need to resend or recall a sent message if the message was not received by the recipient or the sent message contained an error you would like to correct. If you use an Exchange Server e-mail account, you can recall a sent message as long as the message recipient is logged on and has not read the message. To resend or recall a message, display the Sent Items folder and open the message you want to resend or recall. On the Message tab, in the Move group, click the Actions button, and then click Resend This Message or Recall This Message. When you recall a message, Outlook will tell you whether the recall succeeds or fails. You can also replace a recalled message with a new one.

# Objective 4 | Use Mail Options and Signatures

Outlook has options that you can apply to messages. For example, you can mark a message to remind yourself or the message recipient to take follow-up action. You can check the spelling of messages you compose. A message can be marked for sensitivity or importance. *Sensitivity* refers to a security label applied to messages that should not be read by others because of the message content—for example, information about employee salaries. *Importance* refers to marks that are applied to messages based on the urgency of the message—for example, information that should be read immediately or information that can be read later.

You can create *signatures* for your messages. A signature is a block of text that is added at the end of your message and can be inserted manually or automatically. A signature commonly includes your name, title, address, and phone number. It might also include a paragraph informing a recipient how to reach you or respond to your message.

## Activity 1.16 | Marking Messages and Formatting Text

Marking messages unread is one way to draw attention to a message within your Inbox. Marking a message with a flag—referred to as *flagging*—gives you another way to draw attention to a message and to include additional information with it. You can flag both sent and received messages. *Formatting text* refers to the process of changing the appearance of the text in a message. In this activity, you will reply to one of Darron Jacobsen's received messages, adding a flag and formatting the reply.

**1** In the **Inbox**, select the message from *Mary Adair* with the subject **Purchase Order**. Right-click the message, and click **Mark as Unread** on the shortcut menu.

> This is how a previously read message can be reverted to an unread message. Notice the sender is now bold and the envelope icon is closed.

**2** In the **Inbox**, select the **Joyce's presentation** message from *Clarence Krasnow* in the Reading Pane, and then click **Reply**.

> A Message form displays.

**3** On the **Format Text tab**, in the **Format group**, click the **HTML** button.

> Because the text is in HTML format, you can apply formatting to the text.

**4** With the insertion point at the top of the message area, type **Clarence,** and then press Enter two times. Type **This sounds like a great idea. Let's meet at 3:00 tomorrow in my office. I will put it on my schedule.** Press Enter two times, and then type **Let me know if this is OK with you.** Press Enter two times, and then type **Darron**

**Another Way**

On the Message tab in the Basic Text group, click the Italic button to apply the italic style to the selected text. In the Basic Text group, click the Font Size button arrow, and then click 12 to increase the font size.

**5** Select the sentence *Let me know if this is OK with you.* On the **Format Text tab**, in the **Font Group**, click the **Italic** button $I$ to apply italic to the selected text. Click the **Font Size button arrow** 11, and then click **12** to increase the font size. Click anywhere in the message to cancel the text selection. If **Darron** has a red wavy underline, right-click on **Darron**, and then click **Ignore**. Compare your screen with Figure 1.31.

**Figure 1.31**

Font Size button arrow
Italic button
Font group
Formatted text

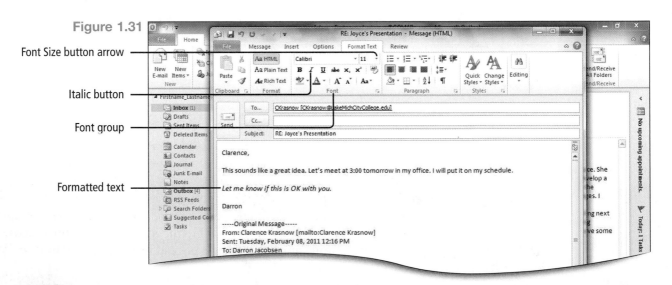

**6** On the **Message tab**, in the **Tags group**, click the **Follow Up** button, and then click **Add Reminder**. Compare your screen with Figure 1.32.

Figure 1.32

Follow up Custom dialog box (your dates will differ)

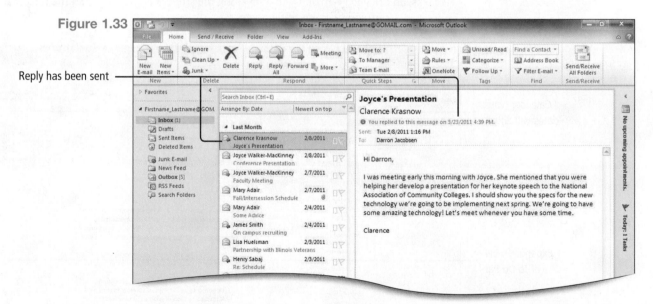

**7** In the **Custom** dialog box, under **Flag for Me**, click the **Flag to: arrow** to view a predefined list of requested actions you can add to the message. From the **Flag to** list, click **Reply**.

You can use any of the predefined messages. Notice that you can also specify a date and time. If the message recipient uses Outlook, a reminder will display on the recipient's system at the appropriate time.

**8** At the lower portion of the **Custom** dialog box, click **OK**, and then, on the Message form, click the **Send** button. Compare your screen with Figure 1.33.

The message is sent to the Outbox, and the Message form closes. Both the Inbox and the Reading Pane indicate that you have replied to the message.

Figure 1.33

Reply has been sent

**9** In the **Inbox**, select the message from *James Smith* with the subject **Lunch**. Notice that a red flag displays to the right of the date.

This is how a flagged message appears to you, the recipient. At the top of the Reading Pane, a banner indicates Follow up.

**10** Select the message from *Joyce Walker-MacKinney* with the subject **Conference Presentation**. On the **Home tab**, in the **Tags group**, click the **Follow Up** button, and then click the **Tomorrow** flag.

> The message displays a flag. You can choose from a variety of flags to call attention to messages you have received, as described in the table in Figure 1.34.

| Outlook Message Flags | | |
|---|---|---|
| **Flag** | **Start Date** | **Due Date** |
| Today | Current date | Current date |
| Tomorrow | Current date plus one day | Current date plus one day |
| This Week | Current date plus two days, but no later than the last work day of this week | Last work day of this week |
| Next Week | First work day of next week | Last work day of next week |
| No Date | No date | No date |
| Custom | Choose a custom date if desired | Choose a custom date if desired |

**Figure 1.34**

**11** At the extreme right of the Outlook window, on the **To-Do Bar**, if necessary, click the **Expand the To-Do Bar** button ☑. Compare your screen with Figure 1.35.

> The subject names for flagged e-mail messages are listed at the bottom of the To-Do Bar. Recall that the To-Do Bar is designed to give you a consolidated view for appointments, tasks, and flagged e-mail. Double-clicking the subject name will open the related e-mail, regardless of your current folder view.

Figure 1.35

Calendar (your dates will differ)

Expanded view of To-Do Bar

Flagged e-mail messages display (yours may differ)

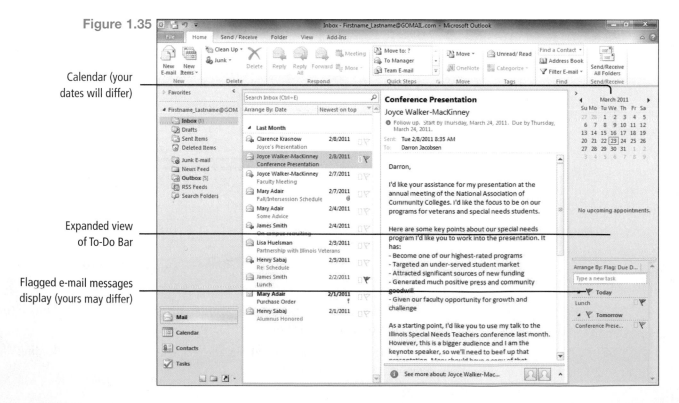

**12** On the **To-Do Bar**, click the **Minimize the To-Do Bar** button >.

**13** On the **Folder tab**, in the **New group**, click **New Search Folder**. Compare your screen with Figure 1.36.

> A Search Folder is a virtual folder that allows you to view all e-mail items that match specific conditions. For example, the *Unread Mail* folder allows you to view all unread messages, regardless of where the messages may be located.

Figure 1.36

New Search Folder dialog box

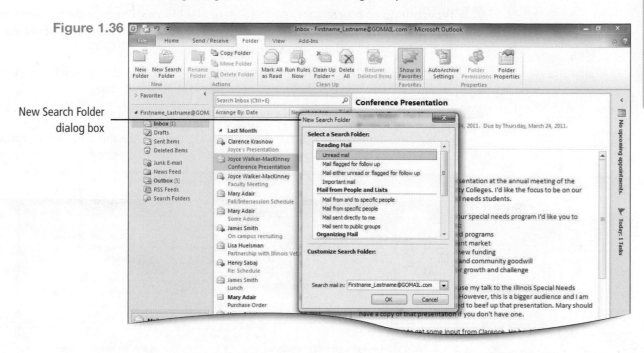

**14** Under **Reading Mail**, click **Unread mail**, and then click **OK**.

> Notice the Search Folder named *Unread Mail* is now active in the Navigation Pane and the message from Mary Adair is displayed in the Reading Pane.

**15** Click the **Inbox** folder, and notice all messages have been read.

> Because the message from Mary Adair was displayed in the Reading Pane, it is now considered read.

## Activity 1.17 | Using the Spelling Checker

Outlook's automatic spelling and grammar checker is active when Outlook is installed. Outlook indicates a misspelled word by underlining it with a wavy red line. To manually check the spelling of a word that has a wavy red line in a message, point to the word and right-click. In this activity, you will send a new message for Darron Jacobsen to one of his colleagues and use the spelling checker to correct spelling errors.

**1** On the **Home tab**, click the **New E-Mail** button to display a new, blank Message form. In the **To** box, type **LHuelsman@LakeMichCityCollege.edu** As you type, if the e-mail address displays as a ScreenTip, indicating that Outlook remembers it, you can press [Enter] to have the AutoComplete feature fill in the address for you.

**2** Press Tab two times to move the insertion point to the **Subject** box, and then type **Could you join me for a meeting?** Press Tab one time to place the insertion point in the message area.

> Recall that it is a good e-mail practice to create a subject that is brief and informative for recipients when they view your message in a list of other received messages.

**3** In the message area, type **Lisa,** and then press Enter two times.

**4** Type, but do not correct any spelling errors, as follows: **I'm arranging a meeting with the Illanois Veterans Association to discuss our partnerchip program. Could you join me?** Press Enter two times and type **Darron**

> If you typed *Illanois*, Outlook indicates this word as misspelled by underlining it with a wavy red line. You can also have Outlook find the correct spelling.

**5** Point to the word **Illanois** and right-click. Compare your screen with Figure 1.37.

> A shortcut menu displays near the pointer. At the top of the shortcut menu, Outlook suggests a correct spelling of the word. If there is more than one possible correct spelling, the shortcut menu displays multiple choices.

Figure 1.37

Misspelled word

Suggested spelling of the word

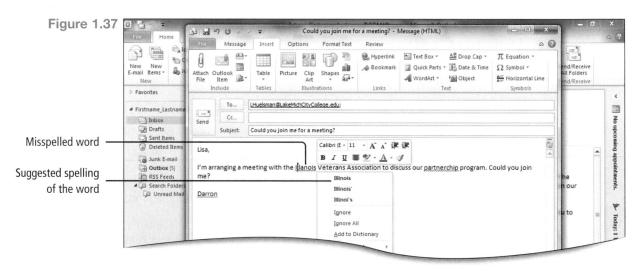

**6** From the shortcut menu, click **Illinois** to correct the spelling.

**7** Point to the word **partnerchip** and right-click to display the shortcut menu. At the top of the shortcut menu, click **partnership**.

**8** Point to the name **Darron** at the end of the message and right-click.

> A shortcut menu displays. There are multiple spellings of this name. However, the name as it is typed is correct. Using the shortcut menu command, you can add the word to the dictionary so it will not appear as misspelled again.

**9** Click **Ignore** to close the shortcut menu without adding Darron to the dictionary.

---

**More Knowledge | Checking the Spelling of an Entire Message**

To check spelling in the entire message at one time, click the Review tab. In the Proofing group, click the Spelling & Grammar button. The Spelling and Grammar dialog box displays the first misspelled word and displays suggested corrections. You can proceed through the entire message, correcting each misspelled word.

---

## Activity 1.18 | Modifying Message Settings and Delivery Options

Recall that setting message importance and message sensitivity are options that you can use with messages. You can also set various *message delivery options* that are applied at the time a message is delivered. One of the messages you will send for Darron Jacobsen is of a personal nature, and he also wants to know when the recipient has actually read it.

**1** With Darron's message to Lisa still displayed, on the **Message tab**, in the **Tags group**, click the **High Importance** button.

The orange color and line border around the button on the Ribbon indicate that the *Importance: High* status is active.

**2** On the **Options tab**, in the **More Options group**, click the **More Options** dialog box launcher, and then compare your screen with Figure 1.38.

**Figure 1.38**

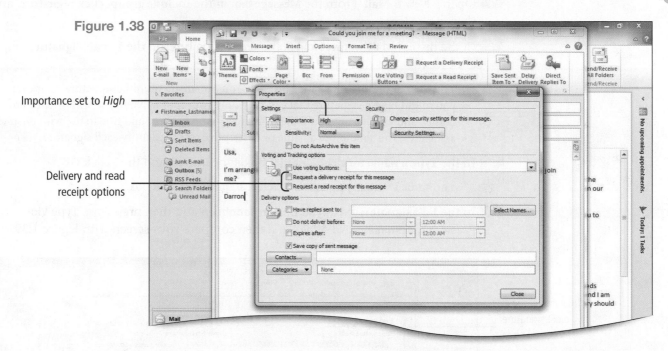

Importance set to *High*

Delivery and read receipt options

**3** In the displayed **Properties** dialog box, notice that under **Settings**, **Importance** is set to **High**. Click the **Sensitivity** arrow, and then click **Personal**.

It is good practice to use discretion when discussing confidential or personal information in your e-mail messages. Recall that the privacy of your e-mail messages cannot be guaranteed.

**4** Under **Voting and Tracking options**, click to select the **Request a read receipt for this message** check box.

By selecting this option, you will be notified when the recipient reads this message.

> **More Knowledge** | Delivery and Read Receipts
>
> To request delivery receipts for messages you send to others, you must be using Microsoft Exchange Server as your mail service. To request a read receipt for messages you send to others, you can use either Microsoft Exchange Server or Internet Mail as your mail service.

**5** In the lower right corner of the **Properties** dialog box, click **Close**, and then **Send** the message.

**6** Be sure the **Inbox** folder is displayed, and then locate and select the message from *Mary Adair* with the subject **Purchase Order** to display it in the Reading Pane.

> When Mary sent this message, she applied the *Importance: High* setting. In the Inbox folder list, an Importance icon displays under the date, and a banner displays at the top of the message in the Reading Pane.

### Activity 1.19 | Creating and Adding Signatures for Messages

Recall that an e-mail signature is a block of text that can be automatically added to the end of your messages. It is common to include your name, title, address, or phone number in a signature. It can also include a picture. In this activity, you will create a signature for Darron Jacobsen and add it to a new message.

**1** Open a **New E-Mail.** From the **Message tab**, in the **Include group**, click **Signature**, and then click **Signatures**.

**2** In the displayed **Signatures and Stationery** dialog box, on the **E-mail Signature tab**, click **New**.

> The **New Signature** dialog box displays. You can create multiple signatures. For example, you might have a signature that contains only your first name to use with friends and family, and another signature that contains your full name and title to use with business associates. You should use a name or descriptive text to identify each signature.

**3** In the **Type a name for this signature** box, type **Darron** and then click **OK**.

> The name Darron appears in the **Select signature to edit** box.

**4** In the **Edit signature** box, type **Darron Jacobsen** and then press Enter. Type **Vice President, Administrative Affairs** and then compare your screen with Figure 1.39.

Figure 1.39

Select signature to edit box

New Messages arrow

Edit signature box

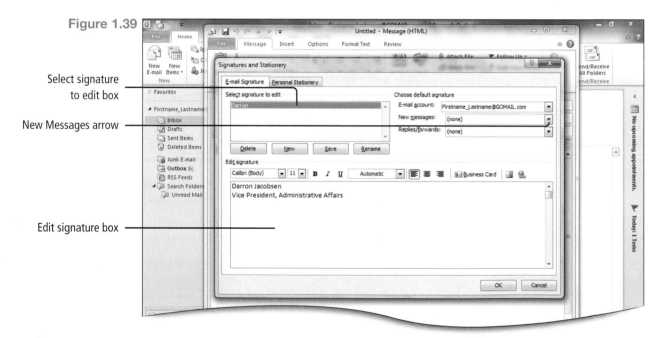

**5** Under **Choose default signature**, verify that your *GOMAIL.com* e-mail address displays in the **E-mail account** box. To indicate when you want to use the new signature, click the **New messages arrow**. From the displayed list, click **Darron**, and then click **OK** to close the **Signatures and Stationery** dialog box.

> The new signature will be applied only to new messages. Replied messages and forwarded messages normally will not display your signature. An option in the Signatures and Stationery dialog box enables you to apply a signature to replies and forwards if you want to do so.

---

**Note** | Applying Your Signature Settings

The signature you just created will not appear in the currently open message; it must be inserted into that message. If you open a New e-mail message, the signature will display.

---

**6** Close ☒ the Message form. Click the **New E-mail** button and notice that Outlook adds the signature text to the message area of the Message form.

> You add text to the message above the signature as you would with any message. New messages are created in HTML format. You can change the format to Plain Text for the message.

**7** On the **Format Text tab**, in the **Format group**, click the **Plain Text** button, and then compare your screen with Figure 1.40.

> The Microsoft Outlook Compatibility Checker dialog box displays indicating that the signature text will be reformatted as Plain Text.

Figure 1.40

Warning message

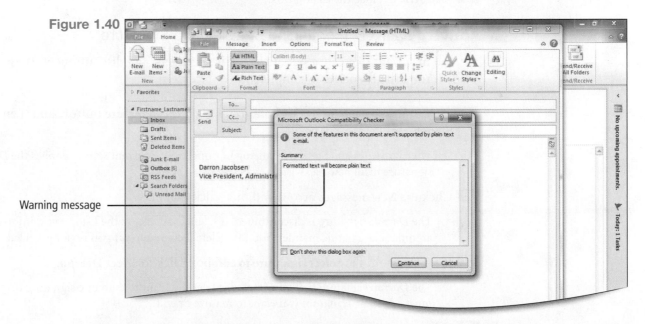

**8** In the **Microsoft Outlook Compatibility Checker** dialog box, click **Continue**.

> The signature is reformatted as Plain Text.

## Activity 1.20 | Editing a Signature

You can make changes to signatures you have created. In this activity, you will add the organization name and telephone number to Darron's signature.

**1** On the **Message tab**, in the **Include group**, click the **Signature** button, and then click **Signatures**.

The Signatures and Stationery dialog box displays. Under Select signature to edit, the signature named Darron that you created in the previous activity is selected.

**2** In the **Edit signature** box, click to place the insertion point at the end of the word Affairs and press Enter. Type **Lake Michigan City College** and then press Enter. Type **(312) 555-0134** Compare your screen with Figure 1.41.

Figure 1.41

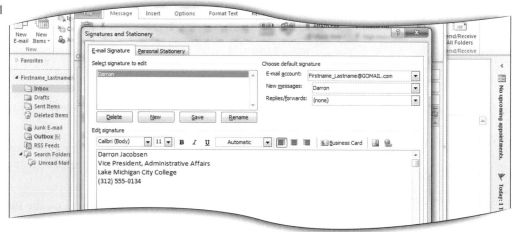

**3** Click **OK** to close the dialog box.

## Activity 1.21 | Discontinuing or Deleting a Signature

You may want to create a signature, use it selectively, and discontinue it when it is not needed. You can also delete it completely.

**1** On the **Message tab**, in the **Include group**, click the **Signature** button, and then click **Signatures**.

The Signatures and Stationery dialog box opens. The current setting applies the *Darron* signature to all new messages.

**2** Click the **New messages** arrow, and then click **(none)**.

The *Darron* signature is discontinued. It is still available on the list if you want to renew its automatic use in this manner. You can delete it completely if you no longer need it.

**3** If necessary, in the **Select signature to edit** box, click to select **Darron**.

The *Darron* signature that you created is selected. If more than one signature displays, you must select the signature you want to remove or edit.

**4** Below the **Select signature to edit** box, click **Delete**, and then compare your screen with Figure 1.42.

A warning message asks you whether you are sure you want to delete the signature.

Figure 1.42

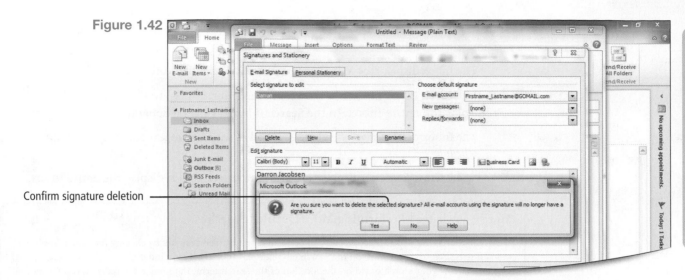

Confirm signature deletion

**5** In the **Microsoft Outlook** dialog box, click **Yes** to delete the signature. Click **OK** to close the **Signatures and Stationery** dialog box.

**6** **Close** ☒ the Message form, and then click **No** when asked whether you want to save the message.

## Objective 5 | Manage E-mail

After you have started receiving a large number of e-mail messages, you will need to manage the contents of your Inbox and other mail folders. Outlook has tools that you can use to find a specific e-mail message quickly. You can sort and organize your mail folders, and you can print your e-mail messages.

### Activity 1.22 | Finding E-mail Messages

Outlook provides an Instant Search feature that is a fast way to find your information, no matter where it is located. Instant Search will display results immediately, as you are typing your search criteria. You can search for all messages from one person. You can also search for the occurrence of a specific word or phrase in all your messages. In this activity, you will search Darron's Inbox folder for messages containing a specific phrase.

**1** Be sure the **Inbox** folder is displayed. At the top of the **Inbox pane**, locate the **Search Inbox** box, and then place your insertion point in the **Search Inbox** box, as shown in Figure 1.43.

Figure 1.43

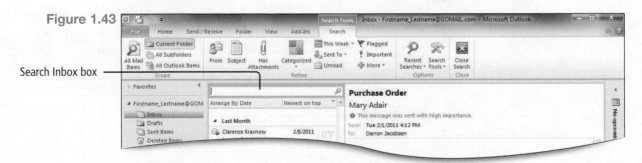

Search Inbox box

**2** In the **Search Inbox** box, type **veterans** Do not be concerned if displayed messages change as you type.

> The Inbox displays two e-mail messages that contain the word veterans.

**3** In the **Search Inbox** box, click the **Close Search** button $\boxed{\times}$ to clear the search and redisplay the entire Inbox. In the **Search Inbox** box, type **schedule**

> The Inbox displays five e-mail messages, all of which have text that contains the word *schedule*.

**4** Click the **Close Search** button $\boxed{\times}$ to clear the search and redisplay the entire Inbox.

---

**More Knowledge | Performing More Detailed Searches**

When the Search Inbox box is active, you can perform more detailed searches by clicking the Search Tools button and selecting Advanced Find on the Search tab to display the Advanced Find dialog box. In this dialog box, you can narrow your search based on the location of the search term, the sender, the receiver, or in a specific time frame. For example, you might want to search for messages sent to or received from a specific person or for messages sent during a specific time period.

---

## Activity 1.23 | Sorting Inbox Messages

Sometimes you will want to sort your messages. For example, you may want to see all the messages you received on a specific date or all the messages you received from a specific person. As you will see while working with Darron's Inbox, different arrangements offer a more visually oriented way to work with messages.

**1** On the **View tab**, in the **Layout group**, click the **Reading Pane** button, and then click **Bottom**. Compare your screen with Figure 1.44.

> The Reading Pane displays in the lower portion of the Outlook window. When the Reading Pane is turned off or is displayed in the lower portion of the Outlook window, you can see the message *column headings* in the message list. The column headings identify the message *fields*, which are categories of information within an item, such as the subject of a message or the date and time received. Depending upon your Outlook settings, the messages may display differently than the figure.

Figure 1.44

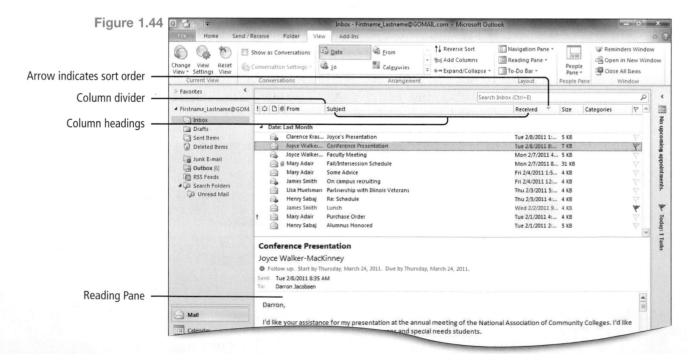

Arrow indicates sort order

Column divider

Column headings

Reading Pane

> **More Knowledge | Resizing Inbox Column Widths**
>
> When the Reading Pane is displayed in the lower portion of the Outlook screen or is turned off, you can resize the column widths for the Inbox. Point to the divider that separates the message column headers and drag it left or right to decrease or increase the width of the column, respectively.

**2** Point to the column heading **Subject**, and notice the ScreenTip *Sort by: Subject*.

Use the column headings to sort your messages. The column heading used by default to sort Inbox messages is the *Received* field, with the most recent messages displayed first. The leftmost column headings are icons for sorting by Importance, by Reminder, by Icon, or by Attachment.

**3** In the **Inbox**, click the **From** column heading, and notice that a pale upward-pointing arrow displays to the right of *From*.

The Inbox messages are sorted alphabetically by the sender's first name. The up arrow in the From header indicates that this is ascending order—from A to Z.

**4** In the **Inbox**, click the **From** column heading again to change the sort order to descending—from Z to A.

The downward-pointing arrow in the From header indicates that the sort order is descending.

**5** In the **Inbox**, drag the **scroll box** up and notice that the messages are grouped by the person they are from.

**6** In the **Inbox**, click the **Received** column heading to restore sorting by the date and time received.

Recall that received messages flow into your Inbox by the date and time received, which is the default sort order.

**7** On the **View tab**, in the **Arrangement group**, click the **More** button ⬇, and then click the **Flag: Due Date** button. Compare your screen with Figure 1.45.

The Inbox messages are arranged by due dates, with messages that do not contain a due date displayed at the top of the list.

Figure 1.45

Messages arranged
by Flag: Due Date

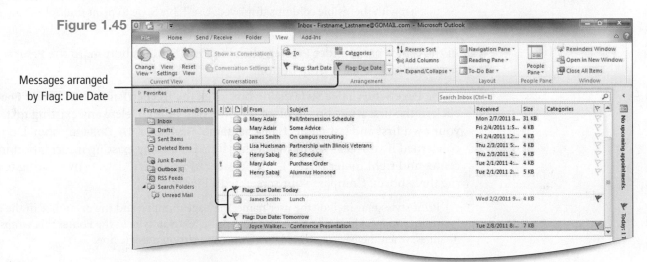

**8** On the **View tab**, in the **Arrangement group**, click the **More** button ⬇, and then click the **Attachments** button.

The Inbox messages are arranged so that messages that include an attachment are displayed before those that do not. You may need to scroll up to view the message with an attachment.

**9** In the **Inbox**, click the **Received** column heading to restore sorting by the date and time received.

**10** On the **View tab**, in the **Layout group**, click the **Reading Pane** button, and then click **Right** to display the Reading Pane in its default position.

---

**More Knowledge** | **Managing Conversations**

A *Conversation* is a chain of e-mail messages that all have the same subject. If a conversation no longer applies to you, you can click Ignore in the Delete group on the Home tab. That moves all future messages in the conversation directly to your Deleted folder. On the Home tab, in the Delete group, click Clean Up Conversation to delete previous messages when a reply includes the earlier message. These features are useful when a conversation includes many recipients and many messages back and forth.

---

## Activity 1.24 | Printing or Capturing Outlook Data

Recall that Outlook organizes its information in folders. To print information in Outlook, each folder type has one or more predefined print styles associated with it. A *print style* is a combination of paper and page settings that determines the way items print. For the Inbox folder, there are two predefined print styles—Table Style and Memo Style. You can also customize a combination of paper and page settings for a unique print style. In this activity, you will print Darron's Inbox, Outbox, and one of his sent messages.

You can also capture Outlook data electronically in OneNote, which is a Microsoft Office application with which you can create a digital notebook. For example, you can move a copy of a message directly into a OneNote notebook. In this activity, you will use OneNote to capture a screen instead of printing.

**1** Be sure your **Inbox** folder is displayed so that the contents of the Inbox display in the center pane, and if necessary, select the first message in the list. From **Backstage** view, click **Print**. Under **Settings**, click **Table Style**. In the right panel, a **Preview** image of what your printed document will look like displays.

> To print a folder list, use the *Table Style*. Table Style prints selected items or all the items in a list with the visible columns displayed. Use Table Style to print multiple items, such as the contents of the Inbox.

**2** In the center pane, under **Printer**, click the **Print Options** button. In the **Print style** section, click the **Page Setup** button.

**3** In the **Page Setup: Table Style** dialog box, click the **Header/Footer tab**. Under **Footer**, click in the first white box to place the insertion point. Delete any existing text. Using your own first and last name, type **Lastname_Firstname_1A_College_Inbox** Do not be concerned if your text wraps to another line. Delete any existing information in the center and right footer boxes. Under **Header**, if necessary, delete any existing text in the three boxes. Compare your screen with Figure 1.46.

> Print styles may include the user name, the page number, and the print date in the footer, or they may include other information. If the text you type in the Footer box wraps to two lines, when the page is printed, the footer appears on a single line.

Figure 1.46

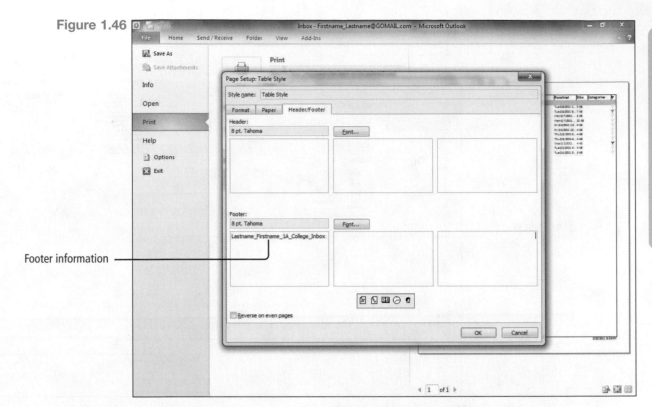

Footer information

---

**Alert! | Does your screen show a different header or footer?**

Outlook remembers previously entered headers and footers. The boxes for this information in the Page Setup dialog box may indicate a previous user's name or some other information. You can enter new information in these boxes and Outlook will retain this information for the next header or footer you print in this print style.

---

**4** In the **Page Setup: Table Style** dialog box, click the **Paper tab**. Under **Orientation**, click **Portrait** if this option is not already selected. Click **OK** to close the dialog box.

Here you can also control the margins and paper size of your documents.

**5** At the bottom of the **Print** dialog box, click **Preview**. Compare your screen with Figure 1.47.

In the right pane, the Inbox list displays as it will appear when printed.

**Figure 1.47**

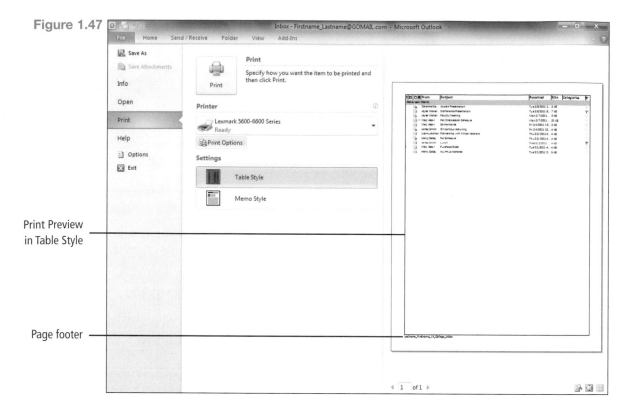

Print Preview in Table Style

Page footer

6. Point to the lower portion of the document, and click one time to enlarge the lower portion of the preview.

    The lower portion of the document is enlarged and easier to read. The pointer changes to a magnifying glass with a minus sign in it.

7. Click one time anywhere in the document to return the view to its previous magnification.

8. If your instructor has requested paper printouts for your work in this chapter, click the Print button. To create an electronic PDF, complete Steps 9–14.

    Note: If you have never opened Microsoft OneNote 2010, which is a Microsoft Office program, within the account that you are currently using, open it now, choose "On my computer," click Continue, and then close OneNote. It is necessary to activate OneNote in this manner.

9. In the center panel, click the **Printer arrow**, on the list click **Send To OneNote 2010**, and then at the top of the panel, click the large **Print** button.

10. In the **Select Location in OneNote** dialog box, under **All Notebooks**, click **Unfiled Notes**. Click **OK**.

11. In the **OneNote** window, click the **File tab**, click **Save As**, and then on the right, click **PDF (*.pdf)**. Then in the lower right corner, click the **Save As** button.

12. In the **Save As** dialog box, navigate to the location where you will store your projects for this chapter, create a new folder named **Outlook Chapter 1**, and then open the folder.

13. As the **File name**, using your own name, type **Lastname_Firstname_1A_College_Inbox** and then click **Save**.

14. **Close** the **OneNote** window.

    Your PDF will include a beginning blank page with the current date.

**15** In the **Navigation Pane**, click **Outbox** to display the Outbox folder. Click the first message in the Outbox one time to select it. Press and hold down Shift, and then click the last message in the Outbox.

> All the Outbox messages are selected. Use this technique to select a group of items in any Windows-based program, such as Outlook.

---

**More Knowledge | Selecting Nonadjacent Items**

In any Windows-based program, to select nonadjacent items, press and hold down Ctrl, and then click the individual items.

---

**16** From **Backstage** view, click **Print**. In the center pane, under **Settings**, click **Table Style**, and then click the **Print Options** button. In the **Print style** section, click the **Page Setup** button.

**17** In the **Page Setup: Table Style** dialog box, click the **Header/Footer tab**. Under **Footer**, delete the existing information in the left box. Using your own name, type **Lastname_Firstname_1A_College_Outbox** Click **OK**.

**18** To print on paper, in the **Print** dialog box, click the **Print** button. To create an electronic printout, in the **Print** dialog box, click the **Preview** button, and then follow the procedure you used in Steps 9–14, and name the file **Lastname_Firstname_1A_College_Outbox**

> Your Outlook data output—paper or PDF—is in the Table Style.

**19** In the **Outbox**, click to select the message from *Henry Sabaj* with the subject **FW: Faculty Meeting**. Recall that the FW: prefix indicates that this is a forwarded message.

**20** From **Backstage** view, click **Print** and notice that *Memo Style* is selected.

> *Memo style* is the default print setting and prints the text of the selected items one at a time. Use Memo Style to print individual items, such as an entire e-mail message.

---

**Note | Account Names in Your Outlook Printouts or PDFs**

Depending on the print style you use, your printout may include the name associated with the e-mail account that you are using on your computer. In the Memo Style print style, it displays in bold just above the header. It may be different from your own name.

---

**21** In the center pane, click the **Print Options** button. In the **Print style** section, click the **Page Setup** button. On the **Header/Footer tab**. under **Footer**, delete any existing information in the three boxes. In the left box, using your own first and last name, type **Lastname_Firstname_1A_College_Message** Click **OK**.

**22** As directed by your instructor, submit your paper printouts or submit your PDFs electronically.

## Activity 1.25 | Deleting Messages

After you read and reply to a message, it is good practice to either delete it or store it in another folder for future reference. Doing so keeps your Inbox clear of messages that you have already handled. When you delete a message in your Inbox folder, Outbox folder, or any other mail folder, it is placed in the Deleted Items folder. Items remain in this folder until you delete them from this folder, at which time they are permanently deleted. You can see that this is helpful in case you delete a message by mistake; you can still retrieve it from the Deleted Items folder until that folder is emptied. Periodically empty the Deleted Items folder to conserve your disk space. You can delete messages in a variety of ways—from the Ribbon, from the keyboard, and from a menu.

**1** Display your **Inbox** folder, and then select the message from *Mary Adair* with the subject **Some Advice**.

**2** On the **Home tab**, in the **Delete group**, click the **Delete** button to move the message to the **Deleted Items** folder.

**3** Be sure the message from *James Smith* with the subject **On campus recruiting** is selected. Press Ctrl and click the message from *James Smith* with the subject **Lunch**. Compare your screen with Figure 1.48.

> Use this technique to select nonadjacent (not next to each other) items in any Windows-based program.

Figure 1.48

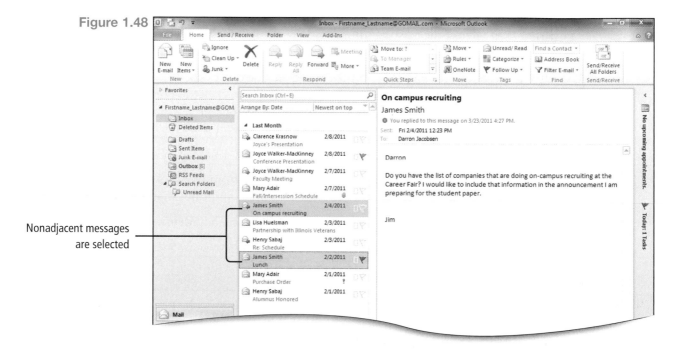

Nonadjacent messages are selected

**4** Press Del to delete the selected messages.

**5** In the **Inbox**, click the first message, hold down Shift and click the last message to select the remaining messages.

**6** Right-click on any of the selected messages to display a shortcut menu. From the displayed menu, click **Delete**.

> The selected messages are deleted, and the Inbox is empty. Use any of these techniques to delete messages.

**7** Display the **Outbox** folder. Using the technique you just practiced, select all the messages and then delete them.

**8** Display the **Deleted Items** folder. To the left of each item, notice the icons, which indicate the type of Outlook item, such as a received message or a message you forwarded. Compare your screen with Figure 1.49.

Figure 1.49

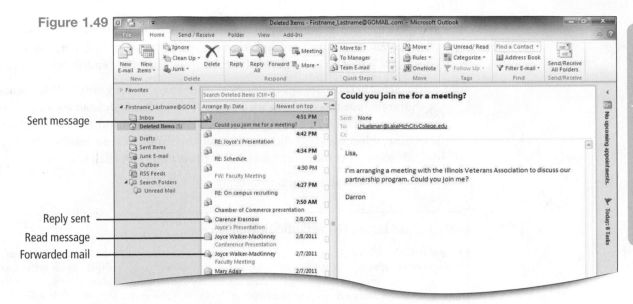

Sent message

Reply sent
Read message
Forwarded mail

**9** In the **Navigation Pane**, right-click the **Deleted Items** folder, and then from the shortcut menu click **Empty Folder**. Compare your screen with Figure 1.50.

> Outlook displays a warning box indicating that you are permanently deleting the selected items.

Figure 1.50

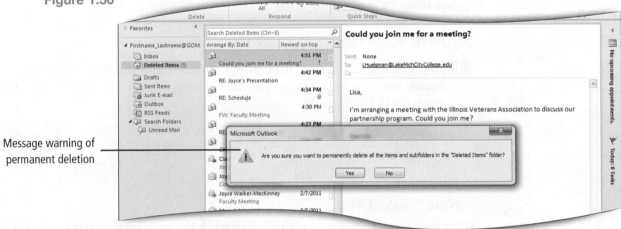

Message warning of
permanent deletion

**10** In the **Microsoft Outlook** dialog box, click **Yes** to permanently delete the items and empty the folder.

**11** In the **Folder List**, click **Inbox** to display the Inbox folder. In **Backstage** view, on the **Print tab**, under **Printer**, click **Print Options**. In the **Print** dialog box, under **Print Style**, click **Define Styles** to display the **Define Print Styles** dialog box.

> Recall that Outlook remembers header and footer information. You can restore the print style you used to its default setting.

**12** In the **Define Print Styles** dialog box, click **Table Style**, click **Reset**, and then click **OK**.

**13** In the **Define Print Styles** dialog box, click **Memo Style**, click **Reset**, and then click **OK**. **Close** the dialog box.

**14** In the **Print** dialog box, click **Cancel**.

**15** With **Backstage** view still displayed, click **Options**. In the **Outlook Options** dialog box, click **Advanced**. Under **Send and receive**, click the **Send immediately when connected** check box. Then, to the right of the check box, click the **Send/Receive** button.

**16** In the **Send/Receive Groups** dialog box, under **Setting for group "All Accounts"**, select both the **Include this group in send/receive (F9)** and **Schedule an automatic send/receive every** check boxes if this is a default setting on your computer. Under **When Outlook is Offline**, select the check box for **Include this group in send/receive (F9)** if this is a default setting on your computer. Click **Close** and then click **OK**.

Outlook's default setting is restored.

---

**More Knowledge | Using Outlook Web Access**

If you have an Exchange Server e-mail account, you may be able to use Outlook Web Access. This feature enables you to access your Microsoft Exchange Server mailbox from any computer that has an Internet connection, using your Web browser. Outlook Web Access is a useful program for individuals who work in different computer environments, such as Apple Macintosh or UNIX. It is also useful for individuals who require remote access. Outlook Web Access is usually set up by a network administrator or Internet service provider. You must have an Exchange Server e-mail account to use Outlook Web Access.

---

## Objective 6 | Use Outlook Help and Close Outlook

As you work with Outlook, you can get assistance by using the Help feature. You can ask questions, and Outlook Help will provide you with information and step-by-step instructions for performing tasks.

### Activity 1.26 | Using Outlook Help

**1** At the upper right side of the Outlook window, click the **Help** button ⑦. In the **Search box**, type **How do I open an attachment?** and then press [Enter]. Compare your screen with Figure 1.51.

The Outlook Help dialog box displays a list of related Help topics with hyperlinks in blue text. Clicking these hyperlinks displays additional information about the topic. Your display may look different.

---

**Note | Outlook Help**

You must be connected online to access the online help. Somewhat more limited help is available if you are not online.

---

Figure 1.51

Search box

Search results
(yours may differ)

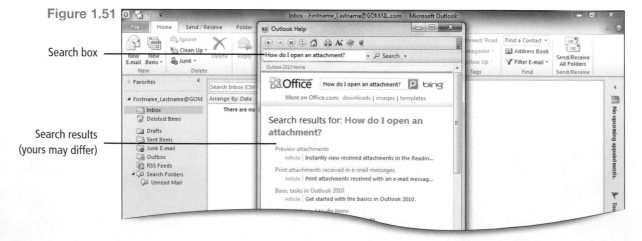

**2** In the **Results** list, locate and then click **Preview attachments**.

General information related to viewing an attachment without opening it is displayed in the Outlook Help window. Included in the article are hyperlinks for additional information.

**3** In the **Outlook Help** dialog box, click the **Close** button ☒.

**4** From **Backstage** view, click **Exit** to close Outlook. Alternatively, click the **Close** button ☒ on the Outlook title bar.

**End** **You have completed Project 1A**

# Content-Based Assessments

## Summary

Microsoft Outlook 2010 is a personal information manager and an e-mail program. Use Outlook to manage your schedule, store information about your contacts, keep track of tasks you need to complete, and send and receive e-mail messages.

## Key Terms

## Matching

Match each term in the second column with its correct definition in the first column by writing the letter of the term on the blank line in front of the correct definition.

_____ 1. A program that enables you to store information about your contacts and tasks in electronic form.

_____ 2. A collection of information that tells Windows 7 what files and folders the user can access, what changes he or she can make to the computer system, and what his or her personal preferences are.

_____ 3. Located on the left side of the Outlook screen, a pane containing buttons and smaller panes that provides quick access to Outlook's components and folders.

_____ 4. Typically located on the right side of the Outlook screen, a pane that lets you read an e-mail item without actually opening it.

_____ 5. An Outlook feature that provides a consolidated view of appointments, tasks, and e-mails that have been flagged for follow-up.

_____ 6. A copy of an e-mail message sent to one or more individuals who need to see the message.

_____ 7. A separate file included with a message, such as a Word document or an Excel spreadsheet.

_____ 8. The action of sending an e-mail message that you receive to someone else; FW: displays to indicate this action.

**A** Attachment

**B** Courtesy copy

**C** Field

**D** Forwarding

**E** Importance

**F** Memo Style

**G** Message delivery options

**H** Navigation Pane

**I** Personal information manager

**J** Reading Pane

**K** Sensitivity

**L** Signature

**M** Table Style

**N** To-Do Bar

**O** User account

_____ 9. A security label that can be applied to messages that should not be read by others because of the message content, for example, information about employee salaries.

_____ 10. Marks that can be applied to a message to indicate its urgency, for example, information that should be read immediately or that can be read later.

_____ 11. A block of text that is added, manually or automatically, at the end of your message that commonly includes your name, title, address, and phone number.

_____ 12. The print option used to print multiple items in a list, for example, the contents of your Inbox.

_____ 13. Options that you can apply to messages, such as the time a message is sent or the address to use for replies.

_____ 14. A category of information within an Outlook item, such as the subject of a message or the date and time received.

_____ 15. The print option used to print an individual message.

## Multiple Choice

Circle the correct answer.

1. The folder in which e-mail is stored.
   A. Contacts        B. Inbox        C. Journal

2. The term used to describe ways to look at similar Outlook information in different formats and arrangements.
   A. Views        B. Panes        C. Folder lists

3. An element of information in Outlook, such as a message, a contact name, a task, or an appointment.
   A. Item        B. Field        C. Article

4. A computer or device on a network that handles shared network resources.
   A. Mainframe        B. Laptop        C. Server

5. The second part of an e-mail address, which indicates the recipient's mail server.
   A. Domain name        B. Syntax        C. URL

6. An Outlook window for displaying and collecting information.
   A. Form        B. Pane        C. Journal

7. Programs with which you can create or make changes to existing files.
   A. Word processor        B. Formatters        C. Editors

8. The term used to describe the way in which the parts of an e-mail address are put together.
   A. Domain        B. Syntax        C. Function

9. The Outlook feature in which text typed in the Message form is moved from the end of one line to the beginning of the next line in order to fit within the established margins.
   A. Wrap around        B. Wordwrap        C. Return

10. A tool that walks you through a process in a step-by-step manner.
   A. Function manager        B. Wizard        C. Dialog box

# Content-Based Assessments

Apply **1A** skills from these Objectives:

1. Start and Navigate Outlook
2. Compose and Send E-mail
3. Read and Respond to E-mail Messages
4. Use Mail Options and Signatures
5. Manage E-mail
6. Use Outlook Help and Close Outlook

## Mastering Outlook | Project **1B** Enrollment Inbox

In the following Mastering Outlook project, you will send an e-mail message for James Smith, Vice President of Student Affairs at Lake Michigan City College. Your completed message will look similar to the one shown in Figure 1.52.

### Project Files

For Project 1B, you will need the following files:

o01B_Enrollments_Inbox
o01B_Enrollments_Schedule

You will print or create a PDF for three files with the following footers:

Lastname_Firstname_1B_Enrollment_Inbox
Lastname_Firstname_1B_Enrollment_Outbox
Lastname_Firstname_1B_Enrollment_Message

### Project Results

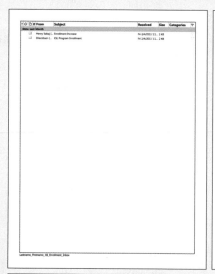

**Figure 1.52**

(Project 1B Enrollment Inbox continues on the next page)

**1** Click the **Start** button, and then point to the **Shut down button arrow**. On the **Shut down** menu, click **Switch User** to display the Windows 7 desktop. Click your **Firstname Lastname** account or the account you are using for this textbook. If the account does not exist, refer to Activities 1.01 and 1.02 to setup the Windows 7 user account and to configure Microsoft Outlook.

**2** Start **Microsoft Outlook 2010** and be sure that the **Navigation Pane** is displayed and the **To-Do Bar** is minimized.

**3** In the **Navigation Pane**, under your GOMAIL.com e-mail address, click **Inbox**.

**4** From the **Backstage** view, click **Options**. In the **Outlook Options** dialog box, on the left, click **Advanced**. Scroll down to the section **Send and receive**, *clear* the check mark from the **Send immediately when connected** check box, and then click the **Send/Receive** button. In the **Send/Receive Groups** dialog box, under **Setting for group "All Accounts"**, *clear* all check boxes. Under **When Outlook is Offline**, *clear* the two check boxes. Click the **Close** button, and then in the **Outlook Options** dialog box, click **OK** to close the dialog box.

**5** With your **Inbox** selected, click the **File tab** to display **Backstage View**, click **Open**, and then click **Import**. In the **Import and Export Wizard** dialog box, click **Import from another program or file**, and then click **Next**. Click **Outlook Data File (.pst)**, and then click **Next**. Click **Browse**, and then navigate to your student data files. Select **o01B_Enrollments_Inbox**. Click **Open**, and then click **Next**. Under **Select the folder to import from**, click **Inbox**, and then click **Import items in the current folder**. Click **Finish** to import the messages.

**6** Select the **Enrollment Increase** message from *Henry Sabaj*, and then **Reply** to the message with a **Cc** to **DJacobsen@LakeMichCityCollege.edu**

**7** Using the format that you practiced in this chapter, type the following message. Refer to Figure 1.52 for correct spacing.

**Henry, Yes, I have been hearing about this trend and have some thoughts about it. I can meet with you any day next week. Let me know what time is good for you. I am copying Darron in my reply in case he feels he should be involved in our discussion. I am also including a copy of the Winter/Spring schedule. Lisa**

**8** Correct any spelling errors that you may have made and **Ignore** the spelling error indicated for the name

*Darron*. From your student data files, attach **o01B_Enrollments_Schedule**.

**9** Mark the message with a **High Importance** tag, and then on the **Options tab**, in the **More Options group**, click the **More Options** dialog box launcher. Change the **Sensitivity** option to **Confidential**, and **Request a read receipt for this message**. Close the dialog box, and then **Send** the message.

**10** Select the **ESL Program Enrollment** message from DJacobsen. **Forward** the message to **HSabaj@LakeMichCityCollege.edu** and then format the text as **HTML**. In the message area, position the insertion point at the top of the message. Using the format that you practiced in this chapter, type the following message: **Henry, Regarding the information below from Darron, I think we should discuss this right away. Lisa**

**11** In the message that you typed, select the words *right away*, and then apply **Bold** and **Italic**. **Send** the message.

**12** With your **Inbox** folder displayed, select the message from **Henry Sabaj**. From **Backstage** view, click **Print**, and then under **Settings**, click **Table Style**. Click the **Print Options** button, and then display the **Page Setup: Table Style** dialog box. On the **Header/Footer tab**, under **Footer**, click in the first white box. Using your own first and last name, type **Lastname_Firstname_1B_ Enrollment_Inbox** Delete all other header and footer text, and then **Preview** the document. **Print** or use **OneNote** to create a PDF document and then submit the end results to your instructor as directed.

**13** In the Outlook **Navigation Pane**, click **Outbox** to display the Outbox folder, and then select the first message. Press and hold down Shift, and then click the last message in the Outbox. In **Backstage View**, on the **Print tab**, display the contents of the Outbox in **Table Style** with the **Footer Lastname_Firstname_1B_ Enrollment_Outbox** Print or use OneNote to create a PDF document and then submit the end result to your instructor as directed.

**14** In the **Outbox**, select the message from *Henry Sabaj* with the subject **RE: Enrollment Increase**. In **Backstage View**, on the **Print tab**, display the message in **Memo Style** with the **Footer Lastname_Firstname_1B_Enrollment_ Message** Print or use OneNote to create a PDF document and then submit the end result to your instructor as directed.

(Project 1B Enrollment Inbox continues on the next page)

## Mastering Outlook | Project **1B** Enrollment Inbox (continued)

**15** Select and delete the items in the **Inbox** and **Outbox** folders. Right-click the **Deleted Items** folder, and then click **Empty Folder**. In the **Microsoft Outlook** dialog box, click **Yes** to permanently delete the items and empty the folder.

**16** From **Backstage** view, click **Options**, and then click **Advanced**. Under **Send and receive**, select the **Send immediately when connected** check box. Click the **Send/Receive** button, and then in the **Send/Receive**

**Groups** dialog box, under **Setting for group "All Accounts"**, select both the **Include this group in send/receive (F9)** and **Schedule an automatic send/ receive every** check boxes. Under **When Outlook is Offline**, select the check box for **Include this group in send/receive (F9)** if this is a default setting on your computer. **Close** all dialog boxes, and then **Exit** Outlook.

**End** **You have completed Project 1B** —————————————————

# Content-Based Assessments

### Apply 1A skills from these Objectives:

1. Start and Navigate Outlook
2. Compose and Send E-mail
4. Use Mail Options and Signatures
5. Manage E-mail
6. Use Outlook Help and Close Outlook

## Mastering Outlook | Project 1C Schedule Change

In the following Mastering Outlook project, you will compose and send an e-mail message from Darron Jacobsen, Vice President, Administrative Affairs at Lake Michigan City College. The message will include a signature, an attachment, and other message options. Your completed message will look similar to the one shown in Figure 1.53.

## Project Files

For Project 1C, you will need the following files:

New blank message form
o01C_Schedule_Change

You will print or create a PDF for one file with the following footer:

Lastname_Firstname_1C_Schedule_Change

## Project Results

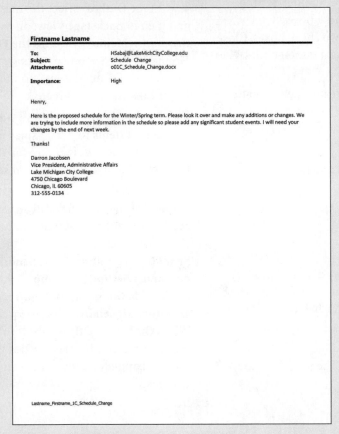

**Figure 1.53**

(Project 1C Schedule Change continues on the next page)

# Content-Based Assessments

**1** Click the **Start** button, and then point to the **Shut down button arrow**. On the **Shut down** menu, click **Switch User** to display the Windows 7 desktop. Click your **Firstname Lastname** account or the account you are using for this textbook. If the account does not exist, refer to Activities 1.01 and 1.02 to setup the Windows 7 user account and to configure Microsoft Outlook.

**2** **Start** Outlook and display the **Navigation Pane**.

**3** In the **Navigation Pane**, under your GOMail.com e-mail address, click **Inbox** and then from the **Backstage** view, display the **Outlook Options** dialog box. Click **Advanced**, and then under **Send and receive**, *clear* the check mark from the **Send immediately when connected** check box. Click the **Send/Receive** button, and then in the **Send/Receive Groups** dialog box, under **Setting for group "All Accounts"**, *clear* all check boxes. Under **When Outlook is Offline**, *clear* the two check boxes. **Close** the **Send/Receive Groups** dialog box, and then click **OK** to close the **Outlook Options** dialog box.

**4** Start a **New E-mail**, and then create a new signature using **Darron Jacobsen** as the name for the signature. The text of the Darron Jacobsen signature is as follows:

> **Darron Jacobsen**
>
> **Vice President, Administrative Affairs**
>
> **Lake Michigan City College**
>
> **4750 Chicago Boulevard**
>
> **Chicago, IL 60605**
>
> **312-555-0134**

**5** In the **Signatures and Stationery** dialog box, apply the new signature to new messages and verify that the GOMAIL E-mail account is selected. Click **OK**, and then **Close** the e-mail message.

**6** Create a **New E-mail** message to **HSabaj@LakeMichCityCollege.edu** The subject of the message is **Schedule Change**

**7** Change the message format to **Plain Text**, and then type the following message using appropriate spacing as shown in Figure 1.53. Correct spelling errors.

**Henry, Here is the proposed schedule for the Winter/Spring term. Please look it over and make any additions or changes. We are trying to include more information in the schedule so please add any significant student events. I will need your changes by the end of next week. Thanks!**

**8** Set the message to **High Importance**, and then flag the message for the recipient for **Reply**. From the student files that accompany this textbook, attach the file **o01C_Schedule_Change**, and then **Send** the message.

**9** In the **Outbox**, select the message that you created, and then in **Backstage View**, on the **Print tab**, display the message in **Memo Style** with the **Footer Lastname_Firstname_1C_Schedule_Change Print** or use **OneNote** to create a PDF document and then submit the end result to your instructor as directed.

**10** Delete the contents of the **Outbox**, and then empty the **Deleted Items** folder. Display a new message form, and then delete the signature for **Darron Jacobsen**. Close the message form without saving it.

**11** From **Backstage** view, click **Options**. In the **Outlook Options** dialog box, click **Advanced**. Under **Send and receive**, select the **Send immediately when connected** check box. Then, to the right of the check box, click the **Send/Receive** button. In the **Send/Receive Groups** dialog box, under **Setting for group "All Accounts"**, select both the **Include this group in send/receive (F9)** and **Schedule an automatic send/receive every** check boxes. Under **When Outlook is Offline**, select the check box for **Include this group in send/receive (F9)** if this is a default setting on your computer. **Close** all dialog boxes, and then **Exit** Outlook.

**End** You have completed Project **1C**

# Outcomes-Based Assessments

## Rubric

The following outcomes-based assessments are *open-ended* assessments. That is, there is no specific correct result; your result will depend on your approach to the information provided. Make *Professional Quality* your goal. Use the following scoring rubric to guide you in *how* to approach the problem and then to evaluate *how well* your approach solves the problem.

The *criteria*—Software Mastery, Content, Format and Layout, and Process—represent the knowledge and skills you have gained that you can apply to solving the problem. The *levels of performance*—Professional Quality, Approaching Professional Quality, or Needs Quality Improvement—help you and your instructor evaluate your result.

| | Your completed project is of Professional Quality if you: | Your completed project is Approaching Professional Quality if you: | Your completed project Needs Quality Improvements if you: |
|---|---|---|---|
| 1-Software Mastery | Choose and apply the most appropriate skills, tools, and features and identify efficient methods to solve the problem. | Choose and apply some appropriate skills, tools, and features, but not in the most efficient manner. | Choose inappropriate skills, tools, or features, or are inefficient in solving the problem. |
| 2-Content | Construct a solution that is clear and well organized, contains content that is accurate, appropriate to the audience and purpose, and is complete. Provide a solution that contains no errors in spelling, grammar, or style. | Construct a solution in which some components are unclear, poorly organized, inconsistent, or incomplete. Misjudge the needs of the audience. Have some errors in spelling, grammar, or style, but the errors do not detract from comprehension. | Construct a solution that is unclear, incomplete, or poorly organized; contains some inaccurate or inappropriate content; and contains many errors in spelling, grammar, or style. Do not solve the problem. |
| 3-Format and Layout | Format and arrange all elements to communicate information and ideas, clarify function, illustrate relationships, and indicate relative importance. | Apply appropriate format and layout features to some elements, but not others. Overuse features, causing minor distraction. | Apply format and layout that does not communicate information or ideas clearly. Do not use format and layout features to clarify function, illustrate relationships, or indicate relative importance. Use available features excessively, causing distraction. |
| 4-Process | Use an organized approach that integrates planning, development, self-assessment, revision, and reflection. | Demonstrate an organized approach in some areas, but not others; or, use an insufficient process of organization throughout. | Do not use an organized approach to solve the problem. |

# Outcomes-Based Assessments

## GO! Think | Project **1D** Child Center

### Project Files

For Project 1D, you will need the following file:

New blank message form

You will print one file with the following footer:

Lastname_Firstname_1D_Child_Center

Lake Michigan City College operates a fully staffed child development center for use by its students, faculty, and staff. Because of the college's large adult education program, the center is an important resource for students. The child development center falls under the control of Clarence Krasnow, Director of Resource Development. Compose an e-mail message from Krasnow to James Smith, Vice President of Student Affairs. Dr. Smith is creating an information sheet about the child development center that will be included in the student packet for incoming adult students. Mr. Krasnow's message describes the facility, staff, and hours of operation of the center.

From your Firstname Lastname account or the account you are using for this textbook, start Outlook and display the Outlook Options dialog box. Using the techniques you have practiced in this chapter, configure the Send/Receive settings so that your sent messages will be placed in the Outbox instead of the Sent Items folder. Compose a new message to James Smith, whose e-mail address is JSmith@LakeMichCityCollege .edu. Change the message format to Plain Text and type a subject for the message that defines the purpose of the message, which is a description of the child development center.

For the text of the message, write three paragraphs of general information—an introductory paragraph describing the facility, a second paragraph describing the staff, and a third paragraph that covers the hours of operation. Close the message using the name Clarence. Suggestion: To help you compose your paragraphs, visit the Web site of your college to see whether it has a child development center or go to www.pasadena.edu and click Student Services. Then click Child Development Center.

Change the message importance to high and then send the message. Display the Outbox and then display the message in Backstage view using the Memo Style print style with **Lastname_ Firstname_1D_Child_Center** as the footer. Print or use OneNote to create a PDF document and then submit the end result to your instructor as directed.

Delete the Outbox message and then empty the Deleted Items folder. Restore the Send/Receive options to their default settings. Reset the Memo Style to its default settings. Close Outlook.

**End** You have completed Project 1D

# Outcomes-Based Assessments

Apply 1A skills.

## GO! Think | Project 1E Athletic Center

### Project Files

For Project 1E, you will need the following file:

New blank message form

You will print one file with the following footer:

Lastname_Firstname_1E_Athletic_Center

James Smith, Vice President of Student Affairs at Lake Michigan City College, is preparing a brochure for incoming students that describes the college's athletic facilities. The college has recently received a very large donation from a wealthy alumnus for a new athletic center. Darron Jacobsen is responsible for facilities management. Dr. Smith has asked Mr. Jacobsen for a brief summary of the new facility. Construction has not yet begun, and the facility has yet to be named. It is expected that it will bear the name of the donor, but this is a matter of some debate and is not yet public. Compose an e-mail message from Darron Jacobsen to James Smith describing the features of the new facility.

From your Firstname Lastname account or the account you are using for this textbook, start Outlook and display the Outlook Options dialog box. Using the techniques you have practiced in this chapter, configure the Send/Receive settings so that your sent messages will be placed in the Outbox instead of the Sent Items folder. Compose a new message to James Smith, whose e-mail address is JSmith@LakeMichCityCollege.edu. Change the message format to Plain Text and type a subject for the message that defines the purpose of the message, which is a description of the new athletic center.

For the text of the message, type three paragraphs—an introductory paragraph describing the facility, a second paragraph describing the expected start and completion dates of construction, and a third paragraph that discusses how the college has not made a decision yet on the name of the facility. Close the message using the name Darron. Suggestion: Conduct an Internet search using www.google.com and the search term construction+ athletic center to find some information for your paragraphs.

Change the message sensitivity to confidential and importance to high. Send the message, and then display the Outbox. Display the message using the Memo Style print style, and insert the footer **Lastname_Firstname_1E_Athletic_Center** Print or use OneNote to create a PDF document and then submit the end result to your instructor as directed.

Delete the contents of the Outbox and the Deleted Items folder. Restore the Send/Receive options to their default settings, and reset the print style you used when you printed your message. Close Outlook.

**End You have completed Project 1E**

# Working with Contacts and Tasks

©iStockphoto/sparky2000

# In This Chapter

The Contacts component of Outlook is a tool for storing information—for example, addresses, phone numbers, e-mail addresses, and so on—about individuals, organizations, and businesses with whom you communicate. The Contacts folder displays a list of these individuals and organizations. Used in conjunction with Outlook's Mail, Calendar, and Tasks components, you can click a button to have Outlook use contact information to address an e-mail message, send a task request, or send a meeting invitation.

In addition to helping you manage your contacts, Outlook helps you to monitor personal or work-related activities that you want to track until they are completed.

**Desert Park, Arizona**, is a thriving city with a population of just under one million in an ideal location serving major markets in the western United States and Mexico. Desert Park's temperate year-round climate attracts both visitors and businesses, making it one of the most popular vacation destinations in the world. The city expects long-term growth and has plenty of space for expansion. Most of the undeveloped land already has a modern infrastructure and assured water supply in place.

# Project 2A Contacts List

## Project Activities

In Activities 2.01 through 2.19, you will create a Contacts list for Linda Hobson, who is the publicist for Mayor David Parker. The list will contain the names of members of the city government of Desert Park, Arizona. You will use the Contacts list to send e-mail, create lists of contacts, and track the activities of specific contacts. You will sort, change the views, and organize your Contacts list in various ways. On completion, you will share a contact via e-mail and have a number of contacts in your Contacts list, similar to the individual contact and Contacts list shown in Figure 2.1.

## Project Files

For Project 2A, you will need the following files:

> New blank contact form
> New blank contact group form
> o02A_Mayor's_Contacts

You will print or create a PDF for two files with the following footers:

> Lastname_Firstname_2A_Assistant's_Contact
> Lastname_Firstname_2A_Mayor's_Office

You will save your file as:

> Lastname_Firstname_2A_Contact_Card.jpg

## Project Results

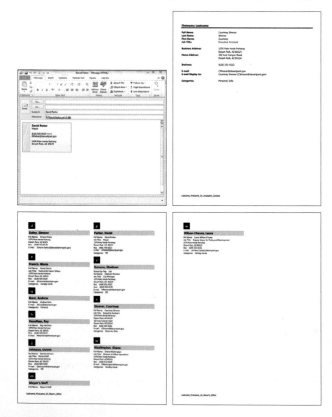

**Figure 2.1**
Project 2A Contacts List

# Objective 1 | Create Contacts

A *contact* is a person or organization about whom you can save information such as street and e-mail addresses, telephone and fax numbers, birthdays, and pictures. The *Contacts* component of Outlook is your e-mail address book for storing information about people, organizations, and businesses with whom you communicate.

The default location for Outlook's Contacts information is the *Contacts folder*. To create, edit, or display the contents of your Contacts list, you must display this folder. Build your Contacts list by entering your contact information one person, one company, or one organization at a time, adding as much or as little information about the contact as you want.

---

**Alert! | Starting Project 2A**

Because Outlook stores information on the hard drive of the computer at which you are working, it is recommended that you complete Project 2A in one working session. If possible, use the same computer that you used when you created the Windows 7 user account in Chapter 1. If you cannot use the same computer or if the Windows 7 user account that you created in Chapter 1 was deleted, refer to Chapter 1, Activities 1.01 and 1.02 to set up the Windows 7 user account and to configure Microsoft Outlook 2010. Allow approximately one to one and a half hours to complete Project 2A.

---

## Activity 2.01 | Exploring Contacts

As you manage the contacts for the members of the Desert Park city government, you will use the Navigation Pane to navigate within Outlook.

**1** Click the **Start** button, and then point to the **Shut down button arrow**. On the **Shut down** menu, click **Switch user** to display the **Windows 7** desktop. Click your **Firstname Lastname** account. If the account does not exist, refer to the Alert at the beginning of this Activity to set up the account.

**2** **Start** Outlook. From the **View tab**, in the **Layout group**, click the **Navigation Pane** button, and then click **Normal** to display the Navigation Pane. If necessary, Minimize the To-Do-Bar. At the bottom of the **Navigation Pane**, click the **Folder List** button 📁. Under your **Firstname_Lastname account**, click **Inbox**. If any existing messages display in the folder select the messages, and then on the Home tab, in the Delete group, click the Delete button.

**3** In the lower section of the **Navigation Pane**, click the **Contacts** button. If any existing contacts display in the **Contacts** folder, select the contacts, and then on the Home tab, in the Delete group, click the Delete button. Compare your screen with Figure 2.2.

On the Home tab, you can control how your Contacts list is displayed. The default view is Business Card. Recall that views provide different ways to display information.

Figure 2.2

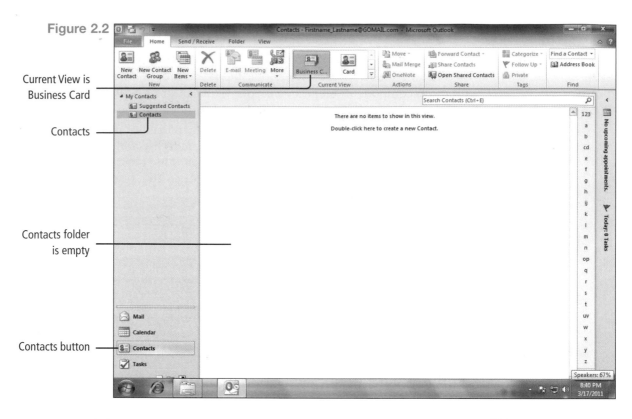

Current View is
Business Card

Contacts

Contacts folder
is empty

Contacts button

**4** At the bottom of the **Navigation Pane**, click the **Folder List** button ⬜. Notice that in the **Navigation Pane**, below your **Firstname_Lastname account**, the **Contacts** folder is selected.

## Activity 2.02 | Importing Contacts into Your Contacts Folder

In this activity, you will *import* contacts into your Contacts folder. To import means to bring the information into Outlook from another program in which the information already exists. The imported contacts contain information about various members of the Desert Park city government.

**1** From **Backstage** view, click **Open**, and then click **Import**. In the **Import and Export Wizard** dialog box, under **Choose an action to perform**, click **Import from another program or file**, and then click **Next**.

**2** In the **Import a File** dialog box, under **Select file type to import from**, click **Outlook Data File (.pst)**. Click **Next**.

**3** In the **Import Outlook Data File** dialog box, click the **Browse** button. In the **Open Outlook Data Files** dialog box, navigate to the location where the student files for this textbook are stored. Locate **o02A_Mayor's_Contacts**, click one time to select it, and then click **Open**.

**4** In the **Import Outlook Data File** dialog box, click **Next**, and then compare your screen with Figure 2.3.

The Import Outlook Data File dialog box displays the folder structure for the file you are about to import.

Figure 2.3

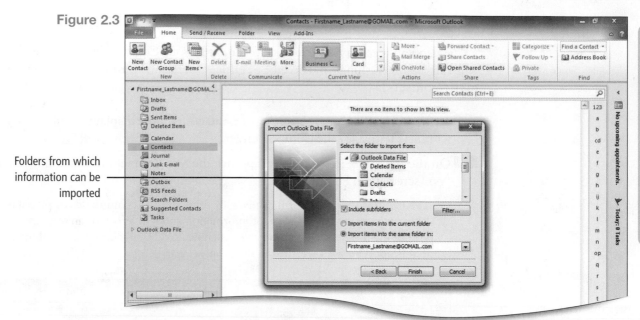

Folders from which information can be imported

**5** In the **Import Outlook Data File** dialog box, click **Finish**, and then compare your screen with Figure 2.4. If necessary, on the Home tab, in the Current View group, click Business Card to display the contacts in the Business Card view.

Five contacts are imported into your Contacts folder. One unread item is imported into your Inbox. Depending upon your screen resolution, your layout may differ.

**Figure 2.4**

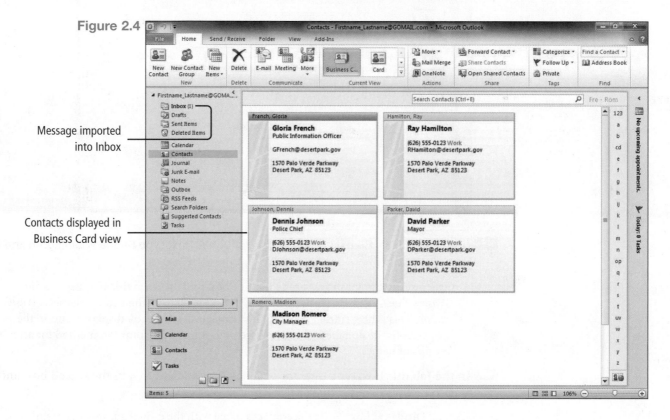

Message imported into Inbox

Contacts displayed in Business Card view

## Activity 2.03 | Creating Contacts

When you create a new contact, you add it to your Contacts list. In this activity, you will add Shane Washington, Director of Office Operations for the mayor of Desert Park, to the Contacts list.

**1** In the **Navigation Pane**, be sure your **Contacts** folder is displayed. If necessary, click Contacts to display the Contacts folder.

**2** On the **Home tab**, in the **New group**, click the **New Contact** button, and then compare your screen with Figure 2.5.

The Untitled – Contact form displays. By using different commands displayed on the Ribbon, you can store a variety of information about a person or an organization. A blank area of the form, called the *Notes area*, can be used for any information about the contact that is not otherwise specified in the form.

Figure 2.5

Untitled – Contact form

Notes area

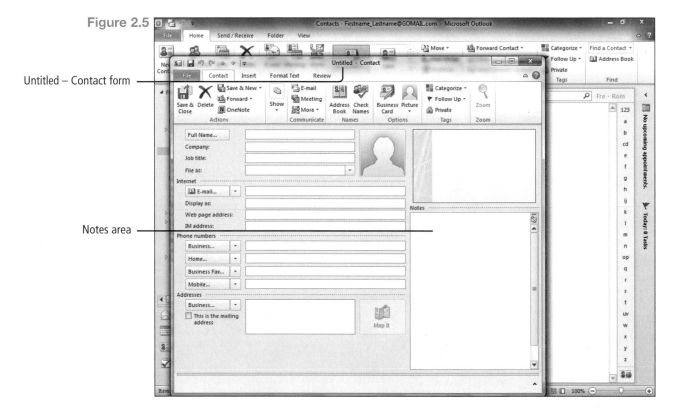

**3** In the **Untitled – Contact** form, in the **Full Name** box, type **Shane Washington** and then press Tab two times.

The insertion point moves to the Job title box, and the form title bar displays *Shane Washington – Contact*. Notice that the *File as* box displays the contact name as *Washington, Shane*. This is how it will appear in the Contacts list. Outlook displays items in the Contacts list in alphabetical order based on last names, a common method for arranging groups of names.

**4** In the **Job title** box, type **Director of Office Operations** Click in the **E-mail** box, and then type **SWashington@desertpark.gov** Press Tab.

The Display as box shows the contact's name with the e-mail address in parentheses. When you use the contact's address in an e-mail message, this is how Outlook will display the address. Sometimes a contact's e-mail address may be completely unrelated to the person's actual name. When viewing e-mail messages, this feature helps you recall the person associated with the e-mail address.

**5** Under **Phone numbers**, in the **Business** box, type **626-555-0129** and then press `Tab`. If a Location Information dialog box displays, select your country or region, type your area code, and click OK two times. Compare your screen with Figure 2.6.

Figure 2.6

Contact's name

Contact's e-mail address displays in parentheses

Parentheses added to phone number

---

**More Knowledge** | Verifying and Adding Information to Names, Internet, Phone Numbers, and Addresses

The Contact form contains the Full Name command button and command buttons under Internet, Phone numbers, and Addresses. These command buttons display dialog boxes that enable you to add more information to a name, Internet information, phone number, or address. For example, the Full Name command button displays the Check Full Name dialog box, in which you can add a prefix such as Dr. or Ms. to the contact's name. These dialog boxes also verify the accuracy of the information. Outlook displays these boxes automatically if a name, phone number, address, or Internet address is incomplete or unclear.

---

**6** Under **Addresses**, click in the **Business** box, and then type **1570 Palo Verde Parkway** Press `Enter`, and then type **Desert Park, AZ 85123**

**7** On the **Contact tab**, in the **Actions group**, click the **Save & Close** button. Compare your screen with Figure 2.7.

Outlook saves the new contact and the Contacts folder displays in Business Card view. The new contact displays at the end of the alphabetized list of contacts.

**Figure 2.7**

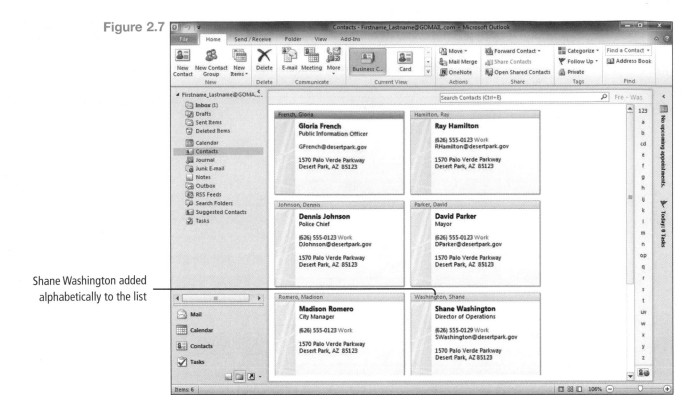

Shane Washington added alphabetically to the list

**Another Way**

Press Ctrl + N to display a new Contact form.

**8** On the **Home tab**, in the **New group**, click the **New Contact** button.

**9** In the **Untitled – Contact** form, use the technique you just practiced to add the following new contact, using **Business** for the phone number and address information.

**Laura Wilson-Chavez**

**Deputy Mayor for Policy and Development**

**LWilsonChavez@desertpark.gov**

**626-555-0131**

**1570 Palo Verde Parkway**

**Desert Park, AZ 85123**

**10** On the Ribbon in the **Actions** group, click the **Save & New** button.

Outlook saves the new contact and displays a new, blank Contact form. When you enter multiple new contacts, you can use this button to save a new contact and then display another blank form.

**11** Add the following new contact, using Business for the phone number and address information:

**Courtney Shrever**

**Executive Assistant**

**CShrever@desertpark.gov**

**626-555-0132**

**1570 Palo Verde Parkway**

**Desert Park, AZ 85123**

**12** On the **Courtney Shrever – Contact** form, under **Addresses**, click the **Business arrow**, and then click **Home**. Compare your screen with Figure 2.8.

The adjacent box clears and changes to Home. You can store multiple addresses for a contact.

Figure 2.8

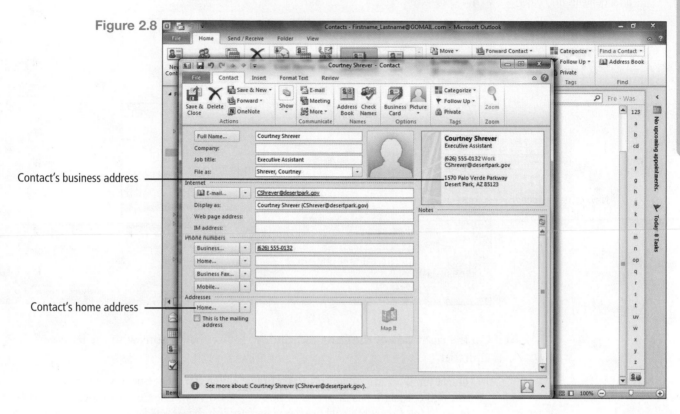

Contact's business address ——

Contact's home address ——

**13** Type the following home address information for the contact:

**322 Lost Canyon Road**

**Desert Park, AZ 85124**

**14** On the Ribbon, click the **Save & Close** button. Scroll to the bottom of the business card list, and then compare your Contacts list with the one displayed in Figure 2.9.

The new contacts are added to the Contacts list. Depending on your screen layout, the contacts may not all display.

**Figure 2.9**

Contact Index (your letter arrangements may differ)

New contacts added

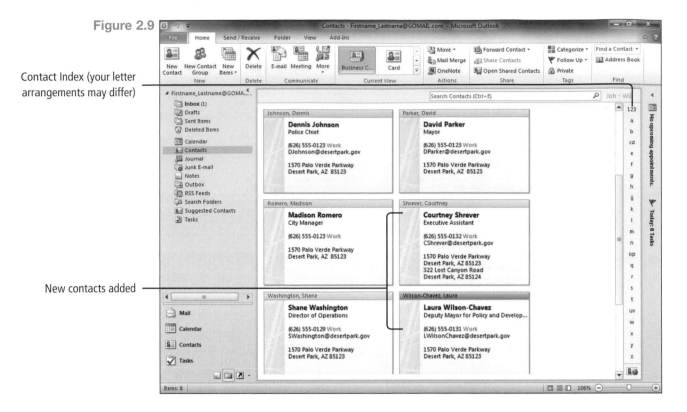

**15** On the right side of the Outlook window, locate the buttons with the letters of the alphabet.

> The lettered buttons form a *Contact Index*, which is a set of buttons used to move through contact items displayed in Business Card view. The Contact Index moves the focus to the first contact whose name begins with the selected character. In a large Contacts list, you can use the buttons on the Contact Index to quickly display a specific section of the list. Depending on the size of your monitor and screen resolution, instead of single letters, the letters may be grouped in pairs.

**16** Scroll up in the **Contacts** list, and then click **Ray Hamilton** to select this contact. In the **Contact Index**, click **r**—or **qr** if your display shows pairs of letters—and then notice that the business card for *Madison Romero* is selected, as indicated by the orange bar at the top of the business card. Then in the **Contact Index**, click **f**—or **ef** if your display shows pairs of letters—and notice that the business card for *Gloria French* is highlighted—currently no contact last names begin with the letter *e*.

> Although this is a fairly short list of contacts, you can see that with a very long list, it is convenient to use the Contact Index to jump to a specific section of the list.

---

**More Knowledge | Creating Contacts with the Same Address**

If you have several contacts from the same company or contacts that use the same address and phone number, you can use the information from an existing contact for the new entry. Open an existing contact that contains the same information as the contact you want to add. On the Contact tab, in the Actions group, click the Save & New button arrow, and then click Contact from the Same Company. Outlook displays the Contact form with the phone number, address, and company name (if any) already completed. You need only add the new name and e-mail address, and adjust other information as necessary.

---

# Objective 2 | Use Contacts with E-mail

When viewing your Contacts list, you can send an e-mail message to one of your contacts without switching to the Inbox folder. Conversely, you can use the information in an e-mail message received to create a new entry in your Contacts list using the sender's e-mail address. In this manner, Outlook is designed to make it easy to enter new contacts without switching to different folders and without extra typing on your part.

## Activity 2.04 | Sending an E-mail Message to a Contact

You can send an e-mail message to a contact either from the Contacts list or while viewing the contact information in the Contact form. You can also use the Contacts list to address messages in the Message form. In this activity, you will practice sending e-mail messages to contacts using both techniques.

**1** In the **Contacts** list, click the **Ray Hamilton** contact one time to select it.

**2** On the **Home tab**, in the **Communicate group**, click the **E-mail** button.

A blank Untitled – Message form displays. The *To* box displays the e-mail address taken from the e-mail information for the selected contact. This requires fewer steps than switching to the Mail component and starting a new message.

**3** On the **Message** form title bar, click the **Close** button ☒. In the **Microsoft Outlook** dialog box, click **No** to close the Message form without sending a message or saving a draft of the message.

The Contacts folder displays.

**4** In the **Contacts** list, right-click the **Gloria French** contact, and then point to **Create**. Compare your screen with Figure 2.10.

A shortcut menu displays from which you can choose to send an e-mail.

**Figure 2.10**

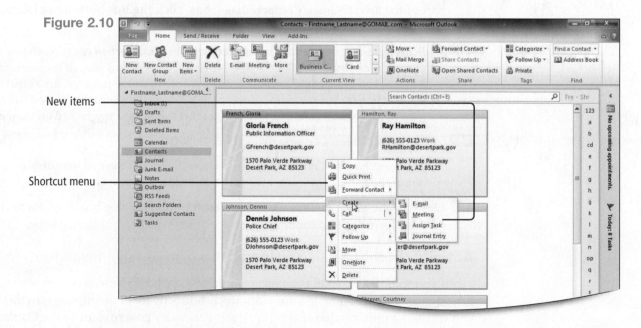

New items

Shortcut menu

**5** Click anywhere outside the shortcut menu to close it.

**6** In the **Navigation Pane**, click the **Mail** button. Click the **New E-mail** button to display a blank Untitled – Message form.

**7** In the **Message** form, point to, and then click the word **To**. Compare your screen with Figure 2.11.

> The Select Names: Contacts dialog box displays all entries in your Contacts list that contain e-mail addresses.

**Figure 2.11**

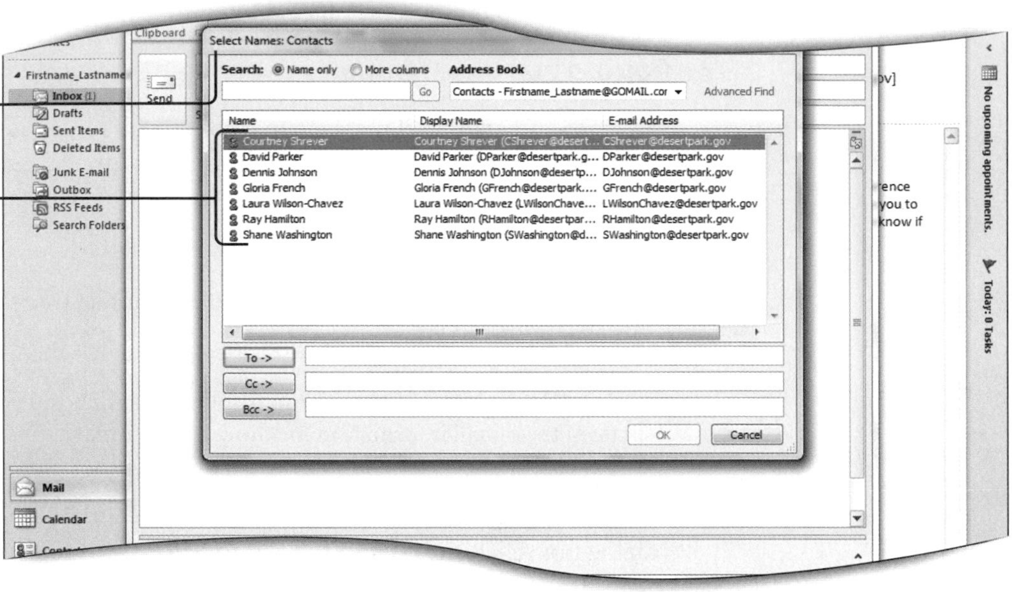

Select Names: Contacts dialog box

Names of contacts with e-mail addresses

**8** In the **Select Names: Contacts** dialog box, click **Ray Hamilton** one time to select the contact. In the lower part of the **Select Names: Contacts** dialog box, click the **To** button.

> Ray Hamilton's name and e-mail address display in the To box.

**9** In the **Select Names: Contacts** dialog box, click **David Parker**, and then in the lower part of the **Select Names: Contacts** dialog box, click the **Bcc** button to place his name in the Bcc box.

> *Bcc* is an abbreviation for *blind courtesy copy*, or *blind carbon copy*. When you add a message recipient in the Bcc box, the Bcc recipient receives a copy of the message, but the Bcc recipient's name is not visible to other recipients of the message. Recall that Cc is an abbreviation for courtesy copy. If you place a name in this box, that person will receive a copy of the message, and everyone will see that this person was copied on the message.

**10** In the **Select Names: Contacts** dialog box, click **OK**.

> The Select Names: Contacts dialog box closes. Ray Hamilton's address displays in the To box of the Message form, and David Parker's address appears in the Bcc box.

**11** **Close** ⊠ the Message form. In the **Microsoft Outlook** dialog box, click **No** to close the Message form without sending a message or saving a draft of the message.

## Activity 2.05 | Creating a Contact from an E-mail Message

If you receive an e-mail message from someone whose name is not on your Contacts list, you can add the name to your Contacts list directly from the message. In this activity, you will add another individual from Desert Park's city government to the Contacts list.

**1** In the **Navigation Pane**, click **Mail**, and be sure that the Inbox displays.

> The Inbox contains a message from Simone Daley. This message was imported into your Inbox when you imported the contacts into your Contacts folder. There is no listing in your Contacts for Simone.

**2** In the **Reading Pane**, under the *Press Conference* message title, point to **Simone Daley's** e-mail address, and right click. On the displayed shortcut menu, click **Add to Outlook Contacts**, and then compare your screen with Figure 2.12.

A Contact form displays with Simone's name in the title bar, and the form displays the name and e-mail address of the new contact. Your Contact form may be maximized.

Figure 2.12

Contact's name in title bar ⟶

Name and e-mail address ⟶

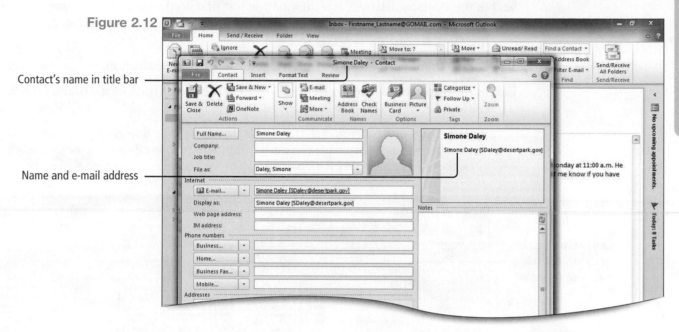

**3** Complete the form by typing the following business contact information:

**626-555-0128**

**1570 Palo Verde Parkway**

**Desert Park, AZ 85123**

**4** Click **Save & Close** to add the new contact and redisplay the Inbox.

**5** In the **Reading Pane**, right-click the e-mail address of **Simone Daley** to display the shortcut menu again, and then notice the *Look Up Outlook Contact* command.

If you receive a message from someone already on your Contacts list, you can use this command to display his or her contact information. If you wish to contact an individual immediately by phone, the contact's phone number is readily available.

**6** Click anywhere outside the shortcut menu to close it.

## Objective 3 | Edit Contacts

When information about a specific contact changes, you can easily add details, change addresses and phone numbers, or add a flag for follow-up to remind you of something related to the contact.

### Activity 2.06 | Editing a Contact

It is common to create a contact and then add additional information as it becomes available. Two members of Desert Park's government are new in their positions. In this activity, you will edit the existing entries by adding additional information.

**1** In the **Navigation Pane**, display the **Contacts**. Double-click the **Madison Romero** contact to open the Contact form.

**2** In the **E-mail** box, type **MRomero@desertpark.gov** and then **Save & Close** the form.

The new information is added to the contact, and the Contacts list displays.

**3** In the **Contacts** list, use the technique you just practiced to open the Contact form for **Gloria French**. Under **Phone numbers**, in the **Business** box, type **626-555-0123** and then **Save & Close** the form.

**4** On the **Home tab**, in the **Current View group**, click the **Card** button.

**5** In the displayed **Contacts** list, click the phone number portion of the **Gloria French** contact, and then compare your screen with Figure 2.13.

Depending on where you clicked, a blinking insertion point displays in the phone number, which indicates that you can edit the phone number directly in the Contacts list without actually opening the Contact form.

Figure 2.13

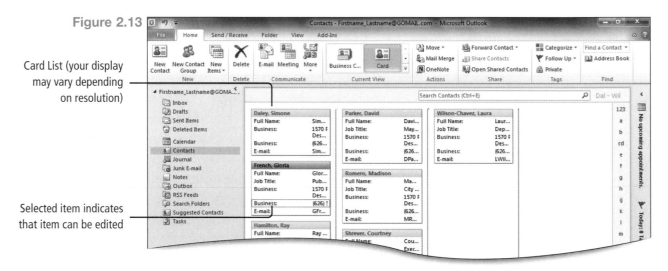

Card List (your display may vary depending on resolution)

Selected item indicates that item can be edited

**6** Click the mouse button or use the directional arrow keys on your keyboard to move the insertion point to the end of the phone number. If the entire phone number does not display, using the directional arrow keys will enable you to continue moving the insertion point to the end of the phone number. Press Backspace and then type **8** so that the phone number displays as 626-555-0128. Click any blank area in the Contacts list to complete the editing for the Gloria French contact.

**7** On the **Home tab**, in the **Current View group**, click the **Business Card** button.

Recall that *Business Card* view is the default view for the Contact list.

## Activity 2.07 | Adding Detail to a Contact

In addition to addresses and phone numbers, you can store additional details about a contact, for example, the contact's assistant or birthday. You can flag a contact to remind yourself of a follow-up action, for example, to remind yourself to call a contact for a dinner meeting. In this activity, you will add details to the contact information for Desert Park's City Manager, Madison Romero.

**1** From the **Contacts** list, open the contact form for **Madison Romero**. If necessary, **Maximize** ▣ the Contact form. Under **Phone numbers**, click the **Business** arrow, and then click **Assistant**.

The contact form provides space for four phone numbers, which are set to the defaults *Business*, *Home*, *Business Fax*, and *Mobile*. You can click the arrow to select other options, such as Assistant, and then insert appropriate phone numbers.

**2** In the **Assistant box**, type **626-555-0132**

**3** On the **Contact tab**, in the **Show group**, click the **Details** button. In the **Assistant's name** box, type **Courtney Shrever**

**4** On the **Contact tab**, in the **Tags group**, click the **Follow Up** button, and then click **Custom**.

The *Custom* dialog box displays. If you want, for example, to be reminded to call Madison Romero on a specific day, you can set a date, and Outlook will display a reminder when the date arrives.

**5** In the **Custom** dialog box, click the **Flag to arrow**, and then click **Call**. Click the **Due date arrow**, and then compare your screen with Figure 2.14.

Figure 2.14

Click arrows to scroll forward and backward through the months

Custom dialog box

Flag as a reminder

Calendar displays current date (your date will differ)

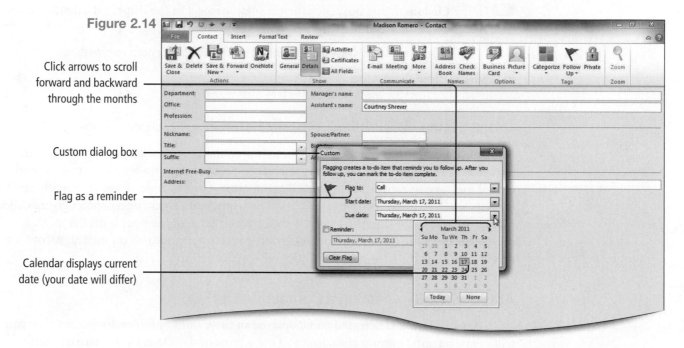

**6** On the calendar, next to the month name, click the **right arrow** once, advancing the calendar to the next month. Click **21**. Select the **Reminder** check box, and then click the **time arrow**. Scroll as necessary, and then click **8:00 AM**. Click **OK**.

The Custom dialog box closes. Outlook will display a reminder when the date arrives.

**7** On the **Contact tab**, in the **Show group**, click the **General** button, and then compare your screen with Figure 2.15.

The Contact form displays a follow-up banner under the Ribbon.

Figure 2.15

Banner indicates
follow up information
(your dates will differ)

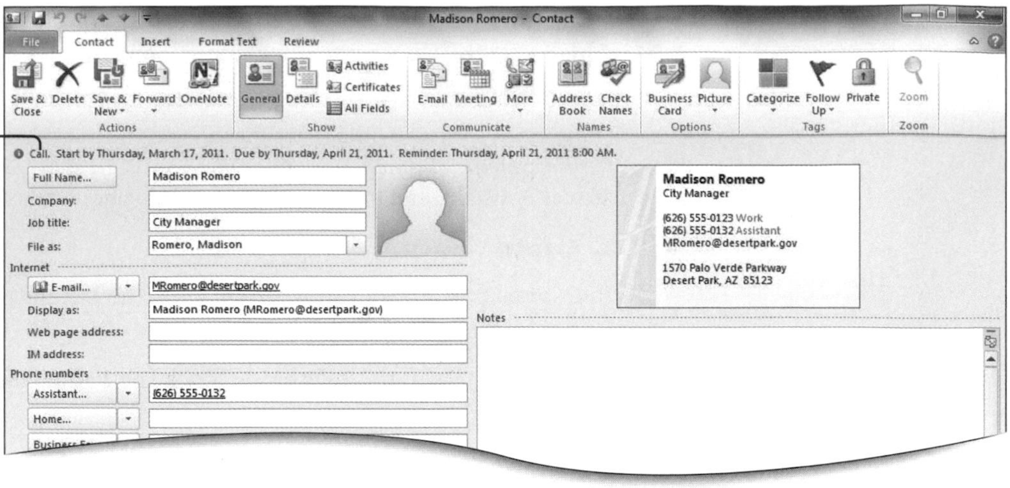

**8** In the **Tags group**, click the **Follow Up** button, and then click **Custom**.

In the *Custom* dialog box you can also remove reminders.

**9** In the **Custom** dialog box, click the **Due date arrow**. On the displayed calendar, click **None**. Clear the **Reminder** check box, and then click **OK**.

The contact still shows a Call banner, but the reminder has been removed.

**10** **Save & Close** the contact.

## Objective 4 | Manage Contact Groups

You can develop contact groups from your contacts. A ***contact group*** is a collection of contacts to whom you send e-mail messages. A contact group is an easy way to send an e-mail message to a group of people all at one time. For example, if you frequently send messages to a group of people on a marketing team, you can create a contact group called *Marketing* and include in the list the e-mail addresses of all the people on the team. A message sent to the *Marketing* contact group goes to every address on the list. A contact group can be included as members of other contact groups.

### Activity 2.08 | Creating a Contact Group

Contact groups are created and displayed in the Contacts folder. In this activity, you will create a contact group containing all the names of the Desert Park mayor's staff.

**Another Way**

To create a New Contact Group, you can use the keyboard shortcut Ctrl + Shift + L, or you can right-click a blank area of the Contacts list, and then on the shortcut menu, click New Contact Group.

**1** Be sure the **Contacts** list is displayed, and then, on the **Home tab**, in the **New group**, click **New Contact Group**.

**2** In the **Untitled - Contact Group** form, in the **Name** box, type **Mayor's Staff**

This is the name of the contact group as it will display in your Contacts list. This is also the name you will use to address e-mail messages to all the members in the list.

**3** On the **Contact Group tab**, in the **Members group**, click the **Add Members** button, and then click **From Outlook Contacts**.

The Select Members: Contacts dialog box displays with the first member of the list selected. The dialog box displays only names from your Contacts list that have e-mail addresses.

**4** At the bottom of the dialog box, click **Members**.

Outlook adds the first name in the list, *Courtney Shrever*, to the contact group.

**5** Under **Name**, click **Laura Wilson-Chavez**, and then click **Members** to add her to the contact group.

**6** Select **Shane Washington**, hold down Ctrl, and then click **Simone Daley** and **Madison Romero** so that all three are selected. Then click **Members** to add the three contacts to the contact group. Compare your screen with Figure 2.16.

Figure 2.16

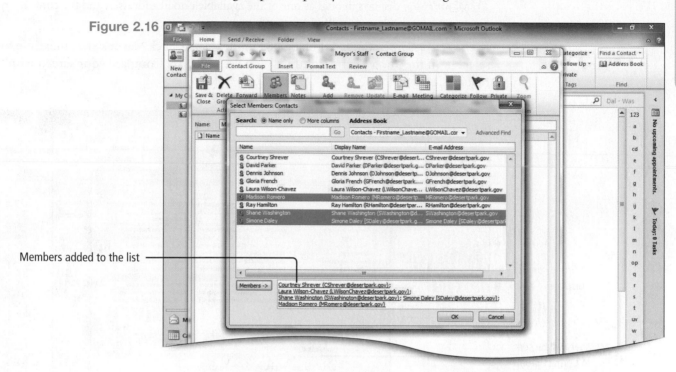

Members added to the list

**7** At the bottom of the **Select Members: Contacts** dialog box, click **OK**. On the **Contact Group** form, click the **Save & Close** button, and then compare your screen with Figure 2.17.

The Contacts list redisplays, and the contact group displays as an entry in the Contacts list. The word *Group* below the name indicates that this is a contact group.

Figure 2.17

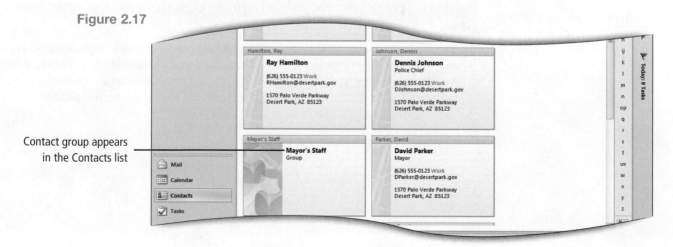

Contact group appears in the Contacts list

## Activity 2.09 | Using a Contact Group

After you create a contact group, you can use it like any other e-mail address. Every name in the list will receive the message you send. In this activity, you will practice addressing a message to the members of the Mayor's Staff by using a contact group.

**1** On the **Home tab**, click the **New Items button**, and then click **E-Mail Message**. In the **Untitled – Message** form, click **To**.

*Mayor's Staff* displays in bold as one of the available e-mail addresses, and the contact group icon displays in front of the group name.

**2** In the **Select Names: Contacts** dialog box, under **Name**, click **Mayor's Staff** one time to select it. In the lower portion of the dialog box, click **To**. Compare your screen with Figure 2.18.

Figure 2.18

Group contact displays in bold

Message will be sent to Contact group

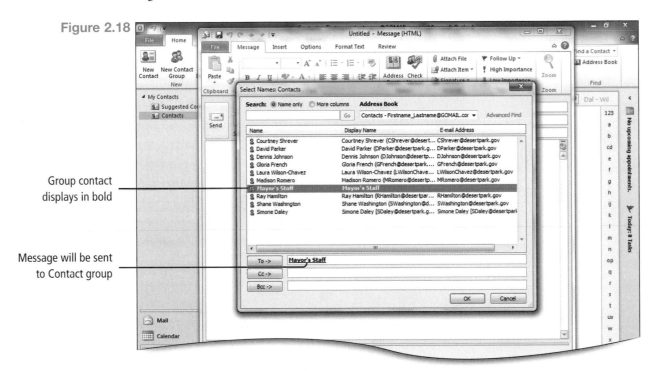

**3** Click **OK**, and in the box to the left of *Mayor's Staff*, notice the small plus (+) sign. Position the pointer over the plus (+) sign and click. Compare your screen with Figure 2.19.

The *Expand List* dialog box displays. You can use this dialog box to replace the *Mayor's Staff* contact group name in the To box with the actual e-mail addresses contained in the list. Use this feature to add or remove a specific name in the list as a recipient of the message. You cannot collapse the list in this message once it has been expanded.

Figure 2.19

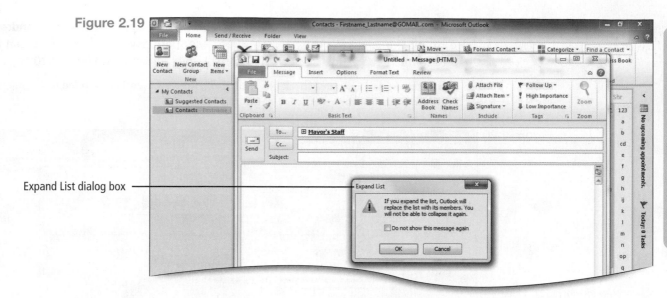

Expand List dialog box

**4** In the **Expand List** dialog box, read the information, and then click **Cancel** to close the dialog box without expanding the list.

**5** In the **To** box, position the pointer over the text *Mayor's Staff*, and then double-click.

The Mayor's Staff Contact Card displays, listing the members of the contact group. Using this technique you can confirm the names in a contact group before you send the message.

**6** Close ✕ the **Contact Card**, and then **Close** ✕ the **Message** form. In the **Microsoft Outlook** dialog box, click **No** to close without sending the message or saving a draft of the message.

## Activity 2.10 | Modifying a Contact Group

To keep a contact group up to date, you can add or remove names. In this activity, you will update the contact group you created for the Mayor's staff.

**1** With the **Contacts** list displayed, double-click the **Mayor's Staff** contact to open it. On the **Contact Group tab**, in the **Members group**, click **Add Members**, and then click **From Outlook Contacts**.

The *Select Members: Contacts* dialog box displays. Recall that the names that display represent all the contacts with e-mail addresses in your Contacts list, including the names that are already members of the *Mayor's Staff* contact group.

**2** In the **Select Members: Contacts** dialog box, click **Gloria French**, and then click **Members**. Click **OK** and notice that *Gloria French* is added to the list.

**3** In the **Contact Group** form, under **Name**, click **Simone Daley**. On the **Contact Group tab**, in the **Members group**, click **Remove Member** to remove her from the contact group.

**4** On the **Contact Group tab**, in the **Members group**, click **Add Members**, and then click **New E-Mail Contact**.

The *Add New Member* dialog box displays. Use this option if you want to add a name that is not on your Contacts list to the contact group.

**5** In the displayed **Add New Member** dialog box, in the **Display Name** box, type **Andrew Gore** In the E-mail address box, type **AGore@desertpark.gov**, and then notice that the *Add to Contacts* check box is selected. Compare your screen with Figure 2.20.

> When the Add to Contacts check box is selected, the new member is added to Contacts in addition to the Mayor's Staff contact group.

Figure 2.20

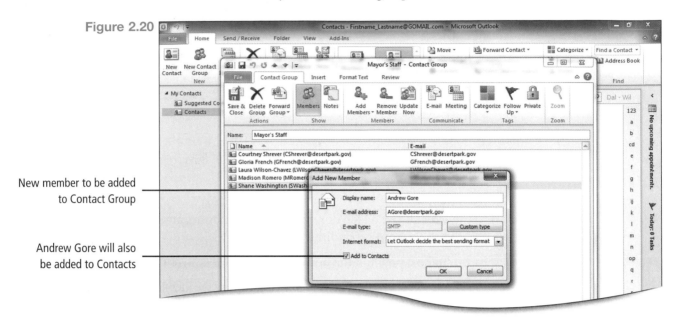

New member to be added to Contact Group

Andrew Gore will also be added to Contacts

**6** Click **OK**, and then **Save & Close** the contact group.

---

**More Knowledge** | **Using the Update Now Option**

If you change e-mail addresses in your Contacts list, you can instruct Outlook to update the contact group to which those contacts belong. To do so, open the Contact Group form, and on the Contact Group tab, in the Members group, click Update Now. Outlook will scan your Contacts list and make necessary changes to the contact group.

---

# Objective 5 | Organize Contacts

In a short Contacts list, it is easy to find the information you need. As the number of contacts increases, Outlook has tools to assist you in finding a contact if you are unsure of a name, company, or some other detail relating to the contact. You can assign contacts to *categories*, which are colors, with optional words or phrases, applied to Outlook items for the purpose of finding, sorting, filtering, or grouping them. You can also apply various views to the Contacts folder.

## Activity 2.11 | Creating Categories in Outlook

To further organize your contacts, you can assign them to categories. By default, categories in Outlook are named by color, but you can assign a descriptive name, such as *Customers* or *Family*, to each color category. In this activity, you will assign descriptive names to color categories.

**1** With the **Contacts** list displayed, on the **Home tab**, in the **Tags group**, click the **Categorize** button, and then click **All Categories**.

> The *Color Categories* dialog box displays, in which you can rename an existing color category or create a new one.

**2** In the **Color Categories** dialog box, select the text **Red Category**, and then click the **Rename** button. Compare your screen with Figure 2.21.

> Notice the box containing the Red Category is now active, so you can type a more descriptive name.

Figure 2.21

Color Categories dialog box

Rename button

Red Category selected

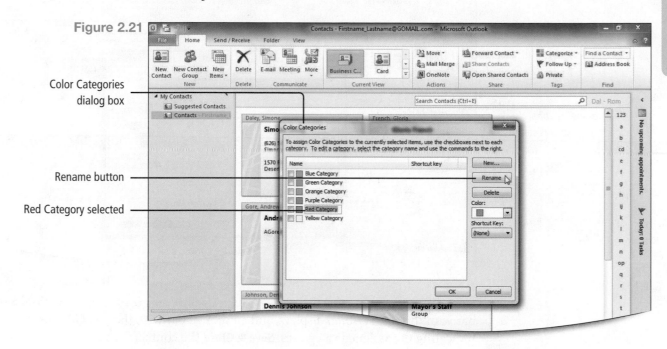

**3** In the box with **Red Category** selected, type **Personal** and then press Enter.

**4** In the **Color Categories** dialog box, select the text **Purple Category**, click **Rename**, and then type **VIP** and press Enter.

**5** Using the technique you just practiced, rename the **Green Category** as **Holiday Cards** and the **Orange Category** as **Gifts** If any check boxes are selected, click the check box to clear the check mark.

> Four color categories are renamed with descriptive words and no check boxes are selected.

**6** Click **OK** to close the **Color Categories** dialog box.

## Activity 2.12 | Assigning Contacts to Categories

Outlook provides the option to assign categories to a contact or any other Outlook item. Assign categories to a contact in the Contact form or by using a shortcut menu in the Contacts list. In this activity, you will assign the Desert Park city employees to different categories.

**1** With the **Contacts** list displayed, open **Courtney Shrever's** contact form, and if necessary, **Maximize** ▢ the form. On the **Contact tab**, in the **Tags group**, click **Categorize**, and then click **All Categories**.

**2** In the displayed **Color Categories** dialog box, select the **Gifts** and **Personal** check boxes, and then compare your screen with Figure 2.22.

The Gifts category is a useful way to group individuals for whom you regularly buy birthday or holiday gifts. The Personal category is a good way to separate family and friends from work-related contacts in your Contacts list.

Figure 2.22

Categorize button —

*Gifts* and *Personal* check boxes selected

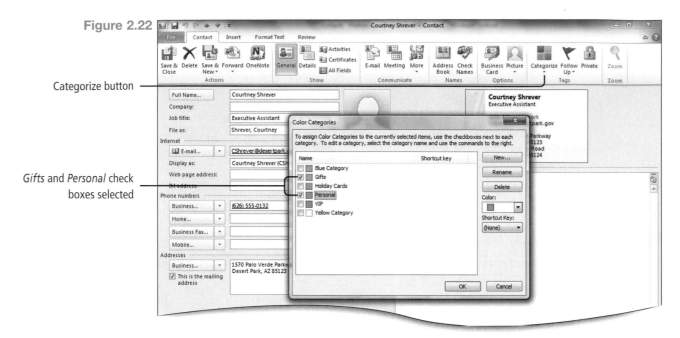

**3** Click **OK**, and then notice that above Courtney Shrever's contact information, a red bar with the text *Personal* displays, and an orange bar with the text *Gifts* displays, indicating the assigned categories. **Save & Close** the contact form.

**4** In the **Contacts** list, point to **Andrew Gore**, right-click, and then on the displayed shortcut menu, point to **Categorize**. Click **Personal** to assign a category to the contact.

**5** In the **Contacts** list, select **Dennis Johnson**. Hold down Ctrl, and then scrolling as necessary, click **David Parker** and **Madison Romero**. Release Ctrl.

Three contacts are selected. Use this technique to select two or more contacts and perform an action on all of them at one time; for example, assigning all the selected contacts to a category.

**6** Right-click any of the three selected contacts, and then on the shortcut menu, point to **Categorize**, and then click **VIP**.

All three contacts are assigned to the *VIP*—Very Important Person—category.

**7** Click the **Laura Wilson-Chavez** card and notice that the other three contacts are deselected. Then, using the technique you just practiced to select multiple contacts, select **Laura Wilson-Chavez**, **Shane Washington**, and **Gloria French**. Use the shortcut menu to assign the **Holiday Cards** category.

The three contacts are assigned to the Holiday Cards category.

## Activity 2.13 | Changing the View of the Contacts List

In this activity, you will change the view and display the Desert Park Contacts list in a different arrangement.

**1** On the **Home tab**, in the **Current View group**, click the **Card** button.

> The Contacts list displays in Card view. In this view, the categories you assigned to contacts are displayed at the bottom of each card.

**2** Point to the vertical dividing line between the first and second columns so that the pointer displays as a **Horizontal resize pointer** ⊹ as shown in Figure 2.23.

Figure 2.23

Horizontal resize pointer ——

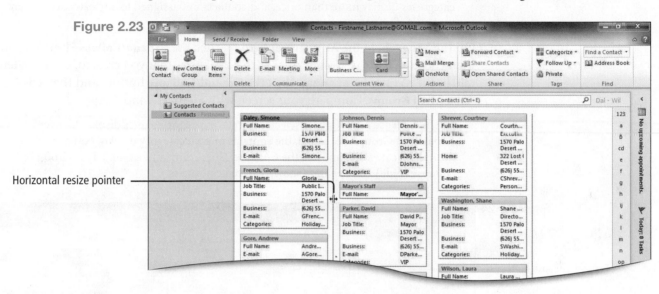

**3** With the ⊹ pointer displayed, double-click.

> The three columns are widened to fit the screen and more of the address card information is visible. Outlook retains the width you apply to the columns until you change them to a different width. If you need to view more contact information for any contact, drag the column divider to the right to widen a specific column.

**4** At the bottom of the screen, drag the horizontal scroll box to view the rightmost column, and then press F.

> The entry for *Gloria French* is selected. Using this technique, you can jump to different areas of the Contacts list by typing letters on the keyboard.

**5** Point to the vertical dividing line between columns one and two, and then drag the column divider to the left to return the columns to their approximate original width.

## Activity 2.14 | Sorting the Contacts List by Category and Field

Some views display items in a table—an arrangement of information with a separate row for each item and a separate column for each *field*. A field is an element of information within an Outlook item, such as a company name or state. You can use the column headings to sort by fields. You can also sort the Contacts list by Category, provided that you have assigned categories to your contacts in the manner you did for your Desert Park Contacts list.

**1** On the **Home tab**, in the **Current View group**, click the **More** button ⊽ and then click the **List** button.

The Contacts list displays in list or tabular view. In this view, column headings define each field.

**2** On the **View tab**, in the **Arrangement group**, click the **Categories** button.

In the category arrangement, the category groups may be collapsed or expanded. When the category groups are collapsed, the contacts assigned to each category are hidden. When the category groups are expanded, the contacts assigned to each category are shown. The default view is expanded. Contacts assigned to multiple categories display more than once, and contacts not assigned to any category display under the first category group—*(none)*.

**3** On the **View tab**, in the **Arrangement group**, click the **Expand/Collapse** button, and then click **Collapse All Groups** to view the categories that you created. On the **View tab**, in the **Arrangement group**, click the **Expand/Collapse** button, and then click **Expand All Groups**. Compare your screen with Figure 2.24.

When Collapse All Groups is selected, only the category names display. Conversely, when Expand All Groups is selected, the contacts in each category display. You can select individual categories and use the Collapse This Group and Expand This Group options to *collapse* (hide) and *expand* (show) selected categories.

Figure 2.24

Expand/Collapse button

Uncategorized contacts display first

Contacts displayed by Category assigned

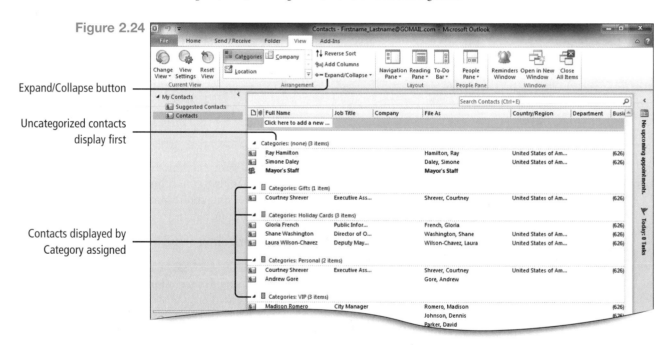

**4** Next to the **Categories: (none)** heading, click the **Collapse** button ▲ .

Outlook uses collapse buttons to display or hide groups of items, such as categories. The items in the Contacts list having no category assignments are collapsed (hidden), and the Collapse button changes to the Expand button.

**5** Next to the **Categories: (none)** heading, click the **Expand** button ▷ to show the items.

**6** In the column heading row, click **Job Title**, and then notice the upward pointing arrow next to the column heading, indicating that the field has been sorted from *A to Z*.

**7** In the column heading row, click **Job Title** again, and then notice the downward-pointing arrow next to the column heading, indicating that the list sort order is changed to descending, *Z to A*.

**8** In the column heading row, click **Full Name**, and then compare your screen with Figure 2.25.

The Contacts list is arranged alphabetically by first name. In a large Contact list, this view is a convenient way to quickly locate a contact.

**Figure 2.25**

Contact list sorted by Full name

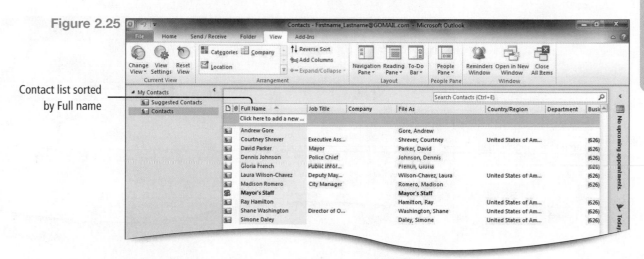

**9** On the **Home tab,** in the **Current View group**, click the **More** button ⊤, and then click **Business Card** to restore the Contacts list to its default view.

## Activity 2.15 | Searching for Contacts

In this activity, you will use the Find a Contact box and the Search Contacts box to locate specific contacts in the Desert Park Contacts list.

**1** Change the **Current View** to **Card**. On the **Home tab**, in the **Find group**, click in the **Find a Contact** box, and then type **Washington** Press Enter, and then compare your screen with Figure 2.26.

Outlook searches the Contacts folder and then locates and displays Shane Washington's contact form. Use the Find a Contact box to perform searches using a contact's name, company, or e-mail address.

**Figure 2.26**

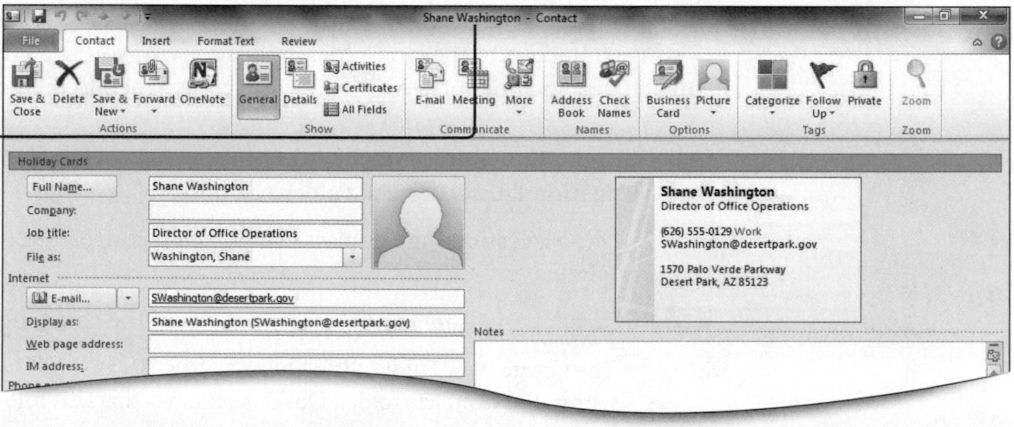

Search displays Shane Washington Contact form

**2** **Close** ☒ the **Contact** form. In the **Find a Contact** box, type **Courtney** and then press ⏎. **Close** ☒ Courtney Shrever's **Contact** form.

**3** At the top of the **Contacts** list, click in the **Search Contacts** box. Type **Lost Canyon Road** and then compare your screen with Figure 2.27.

> Outlook displays the Contact card containing this address, and the search term—the address—is highlighted. When you use the Search Contacts box to find a contact, Outlook performs a search on the current folder, using *any* information about the contact.

Figure 2.27

Search term

Search terms highlighted

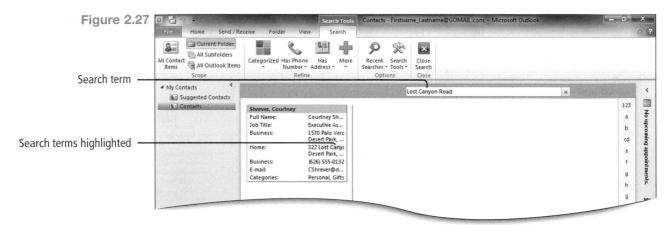

**4** On the **Search tab**, in the **Close group**, click the **Close Search** button to display the entire Contacts list. Change the **Current View** to **Business Card** to restore the Contacts list to its default view.

> The Contacts list displays in Business Card view. Depending on the size of your screen, one or more entries in the Contacts list might move out of view. Use the scroll bar to adjust the viewing area.

## Objective 6 | Manage Contacts

As your Contacts list grows, you can manage it in other ways. You can create subfolders within the Contacts folder; for example, a folder for personal contacts and a folder for work-related contacts. You can also share a contact's information in a special file format, delete contacts from your Contacts list, and print information stored in your Contacts list.

### Activity 2.16 | Creating a Personal Folder for Contacts

When you create a separate folder within your Contacts folder, it displays as a subfolder. You can create contacts that are stored only in this folder. You can also copy and move existing contacts into the new folder. In this activity, you will create a folder for Personal contacts and include the Desert Park contacts assigned to the Personal category in that folder.

**1** With the **Contacts** list displayed in **Business Card** view, at the bottom of the **Navigation Pane**, click the **Folder List** button 🗀.

> The Navigation Pane displays Outlook's folder structure, and the Contacts folder is selected.

**2** Right-click the **Contacts** folder, and then on the shortcut menu, click **New Folder**.

> The Create New Folder dialog box displays. Because you are creating this as a subfolder within the Contacts folder, Outlook assumes that this folder will contain contact information.

**3** In the **Create New Folder** dialog box, in the **Name** box, type **Personal Contacts** and then click **OK**. In the **Folder List**, under the **Contacts** folder, verify that the **Personal Contacts** folder displays. If it does not display, to the left of the Contacts folder, click the Expand button ▷. Compare your screen with Figure 2.28.

Outlook creates a folder called Personal Contacts and displays it as a subfolder of the Contacts folder.

Figure 2.28

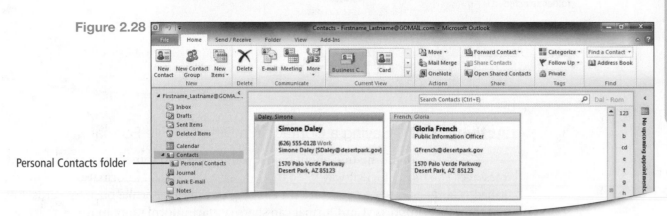

Personal Contacts folder

**4** In the **Navigation Pane**, to the left of the Contacts folder, click the **Collapse** button ◢.

The Personal Contacts folder is hidden.

**5** In the lower part of the **Navigation Pane**, click the **Contacts** button.

The Personal Contacts folder displays under My Contacts. An additional folder— Suggested Contacts—may display. The **Suggested Contacts folder** displays e-mail addresses for people who have emailed you or whom you have e-mailed that are not in your Contacts list. All the items in your Contacts list are contained in the Contacts folder.

**6** In the **Navigation Pane**, under **My Contacts**, click **Personal Contacts**.

The Contacts list in this folder is empty, and contacts created while this folder is displayed are stored here. You can also copy and move existing contacts from your Contacts folder into this folder.

**7** In the **Navigation Pane**, under **My Contacts**, click **Contacts** to display your existing Contacts list.

**8** In the **Contacts** list, click one time to select **Andrew Gore**. On the **Home tab**, in the **Actions group**, click the **Move** button, and then click **Copy to Folder**.

The Copy Items dialog box displays. The *Personal Contacts* folder is selected as the target folder—the folder to which you will copy the selected contact.

**9** Click **OK**.

Outlook copies Andrew Gore's contact information to the Personal Contacts folder.

**10** In the **Navigation Pane**, under **My Contacts**, click **Personal Contacts**, and then compare your screen with Figure 2.29.

The Personal Contacts folder displays a copy of Andrew Gore's contact information.

Figure 2.29

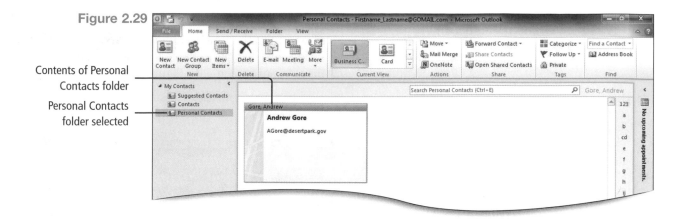

Contents of Personal
Contacts folder

Personal Contacts
folder selected

## Activity 2.17 | Saving a Contact in a Different File Format

You can send information about one of your contacts to someone else in an e-mail message. The most efficient way to do this is to save the contact information in a file format called *vCard*—an Internet standard for creating and sharing virtual business cards. Any program that supports vCard format can share contact information. In this activity, you will save one of the Desert Park contacts as a vCard.

**1** In the **Navigation Pane**, under **My Contacts**, click **Contacts** to display your primary **Contacts** list.

**2** Click the **David Parker** contact card. On the **Home tab**, in the **Share group**, click the **Forward Contact** button, and then click **As a Business Card**.

**3** In the displayed **Message form**, notice that an attachment displays, the file **David Parker.vcf**. Compare your screen with Figure 2.30.

The attachment contains the contact information for David Parker. The recipient of the message will receive this attachment with the message. When the recipient opens the attachment, Outlook will display David Parker's contact form, which can be saved in the recipient's own Contacts list.

Figure 2.30

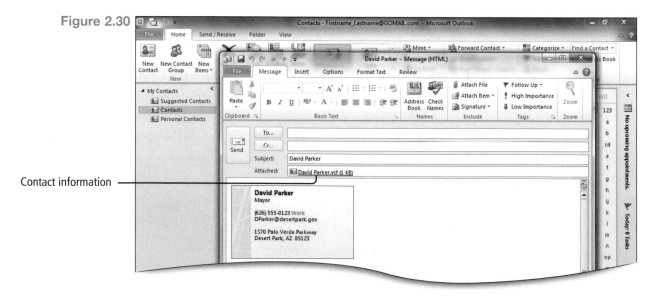

Contact information

**4** Display the **Start** menu 🌐, and then click **All Programs**. Locate and then click the **Accessories** folder. Click **Snipping Tool**. In the **Snipping Tool** dialog box, click the **New arrow**, and then click **Window Snip**. Click anywhere in the window to capture it, and then click the **Save Snip** button 🖫. Navigate to the location where you are storing your files, click in the **File name** box, and then, using your own name, type **Lastname_Firstname_2A_Contact_Card** Click the **Save as type arrow**, and then click **JPEG file**. Click **Save**, and then **Close** ⊠ the **Snipping Tool** window. Submit the end result to your instructor as directed.

> The *Snipping Tool* is a Windows 7 application with which you can capture all or part of a screen. The captured item is called a *snip*; it can be annotated using the tools provided, copied to a document or e-mail, or saved as an image file of varying file types.

**5** **Close** ⊠ the Message form without sending or saving the message as a Draft.

---

**More Knowledge | Attaching Your vCard in a Signature**

You can include a vCard with your own contact information in any e-mail messages you send by adding it to your signature. Recall that a signature is a block of text that is added at the end of your message. To include your vCard, create a new contact for yourself in your Contacts list. Create or edit your signature, and in the Signatures and Stationery dialog box, in the Edit Signature section, click Business Card (vCard). In the Insert Business Card dialog box, select your name in your Contacts list. Click OK two times to close all dialog boxes. When you create a new message, your vCard file is entered in the Attached box. It is good practice to delete the vCard attachment if the message recipient already has your information so you do not add unnecessary attachments to the messages you send.

---

## Activity 2.18 | Printing Contacts

You can print the information for a single contact, a list of selected contacts, or a list of all the contacts. In this activity, you will print information for one of the Desert Park contacts, and then you will print the entire Desert Park Contacts list.

**1** With your primary **Contacts** list displayed, click the **Courtney Shrever** contact card. From **Backstage** view, click **Print**. Under **Settings**, click the choices to view the available print styles.

> Each print style arranges the contact information in a different format. The right pane displays a preview of how the contact information will display when it is printed.

**2** Under **Settings**, click **Card Style** to preview the business card view. Scroll as necessary to view each page.

> The preview displays the entire Contacts list in the Card Style. In its default setting, the Card Style includes a *blank form* page, which is a lined page added to the printout that you can use to manually list new contacts if you choose.

**3** Under **Settings**, click **Phone Directory Style** and compare your screen with Figure 2.31.

> This print style displays only the contact names and the phone numbers for the entire Contacts list.

Figure 2.31

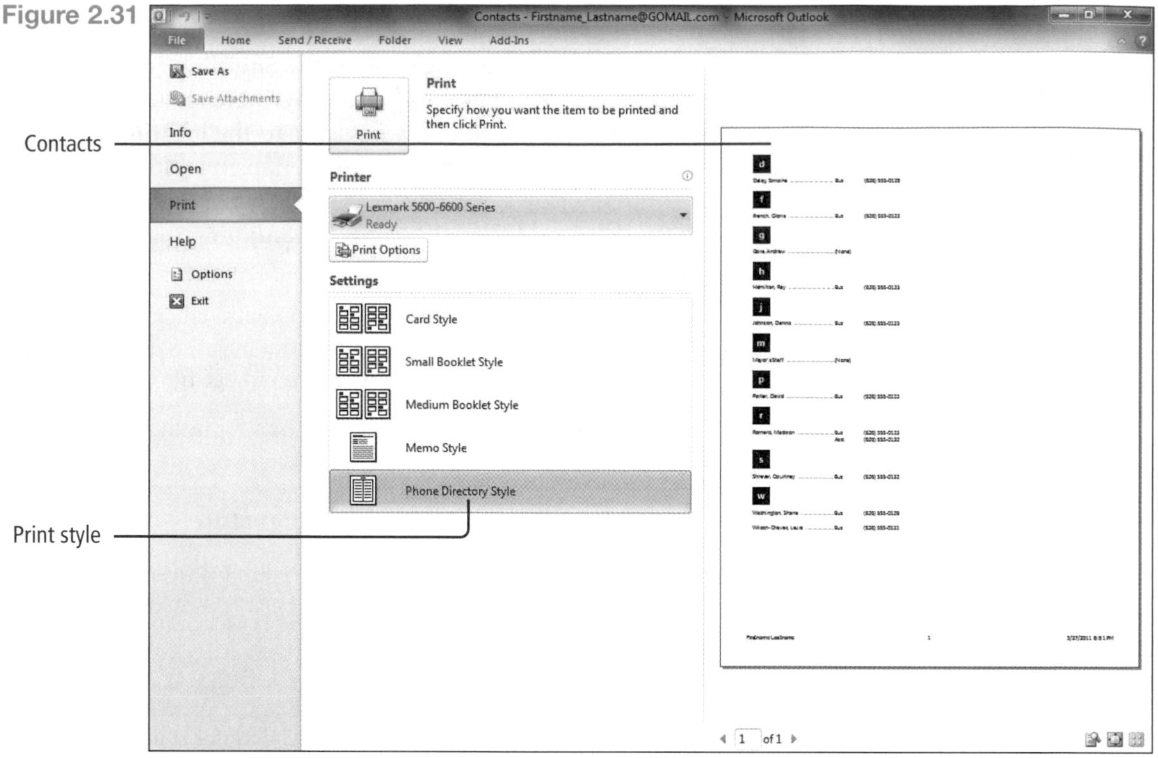

Contacts

Print style

**4** Under **Settings**, click **Memo Style**.

Memo Style prints a single contact. You can also use Memo Style to print multiple Contacts.

**5** Under **Printer**, click **Print Options**. In the **Print** dialog box, click the **Page Setup** button.

**6** Click the **Header/Footer tab**, and delete any existing header or footer information, including dates and page numbers. In the left footer box, using your own name, type **Lastname_Firstname_2A_Assistant's_Contact** Click **OK** to redisplay the **Print** dialog box.

**7** In the **Print** dialog box, click **Preview** to preview the printed document. Click **Print** to print the Contact in Memo Style or use **OneNote** to create a PDF document as instructed in Chapter 1, Activity 1.24. Submit the end result to your instructor as directed.

**8** On the **Home tab**, change the **Current View** to **Card**.

When printing your contacts, display the contacts as you want them to be printed. This view will print detailed contact information.

**9** From the **Backstage** view, click **Print**. Under **Settings**, click **Card Style**.

**10** Under **Printer**, click **Print Options**. In the **Print** dialog box, click the **Page Setup** button. Click the **Header/Footer tab**. Delete any existing header or footer information. In the left footer box, type **Lastname_Firstname_2A_Mayor's_Office** Click the **Format tab**, and then compare your screen with Figure 2.32.

**Figure 2.32**

Page Setup: Card Style dialog box

Number of blank forms that will display at end of printout (your number may vary)

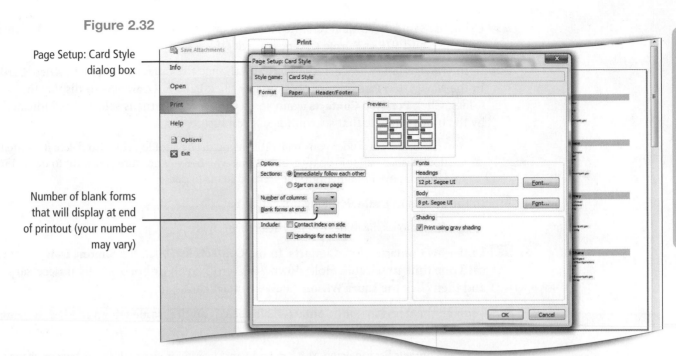

**11** Under **Options**, click the down arrow next to **Blank forms at end**, and then click **None**. Click **OK**.

> Recall that the Card Style print style includes a blank form page by default; the blank form at the end of this printout will be excluded. If this page has been previously excluded, Outlook will retain this setting.

**12** In the **Print** dialog box, click **Preview** to preview the printed document. Scroll to view all pages of the preview. Click **Print** or use **OneNote** to create a PDF document. Submit the end result to your instructor as directed.

---

**More Knowledge | Print a Group of Contacts**

If you want to print more than one contact on your Contacts list but not all of them, select the first contact you want to print. Then hold down Ctrl on the keyboard and click each of the additional contacts you want to include in the printout. In the Print dialog box, under Print range, click the Only selected items option button. Use the Phone Directory Style, the Memo Style, or the Card Style as the print style.

---

## Activity 2.19 | Deleting Contacts and Restoring Default Settings

In a manner similar to messages and other Outlook items, you can delete contacts. When you delete a contact in your Contacts folder or any other contact folder, it moves to the Deleted Items folder. Items remain in this folder until you empty the Deleted Items folder, at which time they are permanently deleted. You can also restore the default settings for print style headers and footers, and change the categories to their original names.

**1** Select any contact. On the **Home tab**, in the **Tags group**, click the **Categorize** button, and then click **All Categories**.

**2** In the **Color Categories** dialog box, select **Gifts**, click **Rename**, and then type **Orange Category** and press Enter.

> Outlook retains the most recent name change, so renaming is required to restore the category to its original, default name. You must rename the categories prior to deleting all contacts, messages, or tasks.

**3** Using the same technique, rename **Holiday Cards** as **Green Category**, **Personal** as **Red Category**, and **VIP** as **Purple Category** Click **OK**.

**4** In the **Navigation Pane**, click **Contacts** and change the **Current View** to **Business Card**. In the **Navigation Pane**, under **My Contacts**, click **Personal Contacts** to display the folder. Click **Personal Contacts** again so that the folder name is selected as indicated by the blue rectangle that surrounds it. Press Del.

> You can delete any folder you create. When you delete a folder, you also delete its contents. Outlook displays an information box asking whether you are sure you want to delete the folder and move its contents to the Deleted Items folder.

**5** In the **Microsoft Outlook** dialog box, click **Yes**.

> Outlook moves the folder to the Deleted Items folder.

**6** Under **My Contacts**, click **Contacts**. In the **Contacts** list, click the **Simone Daley** contact card one time to select it. Hold down Shift, scroll down or horizontally if necessary, and then click the **Laura Wilson-Chavez** contact card.

**7** With all the items in your **Contacts** list selected, on the **Home tab**, in the **Delete group**, click the **Delete** button.

> The Contacts list is deleted. You can undo any deletion if you make a mistake or change your mind.

**8** In the **Navigation Pane**, click the **Folder List** button 🗔. To the left of the **Deleted Items** folder, click the **Expand** button ▷ to display the subfolders in the **Deleted Items** folder. Click the **Personal Contacts** folder, and compare your screen with Figure 2.33.

> The Deleted Items folder displays the deleted subfolder *Personal Contacts*.

Figure 2.33

Personal Contacts folder in Deleted Items

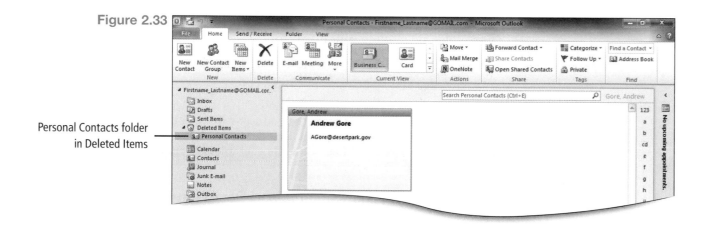

**9** Right-click the **Personal Contacts** folder, and from the displayed shortcut menu, click **Delete Folder**.

> Outlook displays a Microsoft Outlook box, warning you that you are permanently deleting the Personal Contacts folder.

**10** In the **Microsoft Outlook** box, click **Yes**. Compare your screen with Figure 2.34.

> The Personal Contacts subfolder is deleted, and the Deleted Items folder displays. The first item in the folder is displayed in the Reading Pane. Your list of deleted items may display in a different order than that shown in the Figure.

**Figure 2.34**

First item appears in
Reading Pane
(yours may differ)

Deleted Items folder
selected

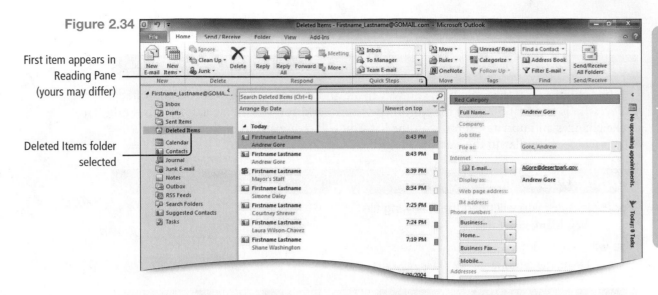

**11** In the **Folder List**, right-click the **Deleted Items** folder, and then click **Empty Folder**. Alternatively, use any method that you have practiced to select all the items in the Deleted Items folder, and then click the Delete button ☒. In the **Microsoft Outlook** box, click **Yes**.

The Deleted Items folder is emptied.

**12** In the **Folder List**, click **Inbox** to display the Inbox folder. Click the message from **Simone Daley**, and then **Delete** the message using any technique you have practiced.

**13** In the **Folder List**, click the **Deleted Items** folder to select it. Delete the item in this folder using any technique you have practiced.

**14** In the **Folder List**, click **Contacts** to display the Contacts folder. In **Backstage** view, on the **Print tab**, under **Printer**, click **Print Options**. In the **Print** dialog box, under **Print Style**, click **Define Styles** to display the **Define Print Styles** dialog box.

Recall that Outlook remembers header and footer information. You can restore the print style you used to its default setting.

**15** In the **Define Print Styles** dialog box, click **Memo Style**, click **Reset**, and then click **OK**.

**16** In the **Define Print Styles** dialog box, click **Card Style**, click **Reset**, and then click **OK**. **Close** the dialog box.

**17** In the **Print** dialog box, click **Cancel**, and then **Close** ☒ Outlook.

---

**End**  **You have completed Project 2A**

# Project 2B To-Do List

## Project Activities

In Activities 2.20 through 2.25, you will create and manage a To-Do list for Simone Daley, who is Chief of Staff for the Mayor of Desert Park. You will create a To-Do list and make changes and updates to tasks on the list. You will create a snip of the To-Do list, which will look similar to the one shown in Figure 2.35.

## Project Files

For Project 2B, you will need the following file:

New blank task form

You will save your file as:

Lastname_Firstname_2B_Task_List.jpg

## Project Results

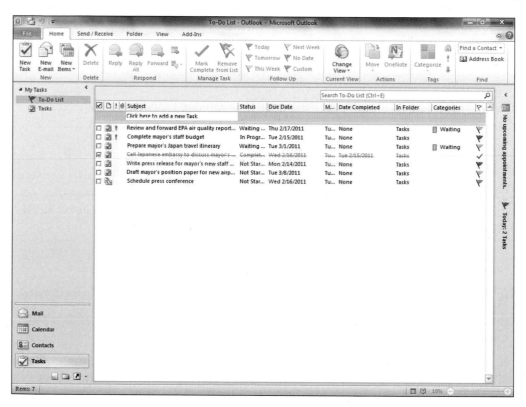

**Figure 2.35**
Project 2B To-Do List

# Objective 7 | Create and Update Tasks

In Outlook, a *task* is a personal or work-related activity that you want to keep track of until it is complete. For example, writing a report, creating a memo, making a sales call, and organizing a staff meeting are all tasks. Use Outlook's Tasks folder to create and manage a list of tasks, create one-time tasks or *recurring tasks*, and set reminders for tasks. A recurring task occurs repeatedly, for example, a weekly staff meeting or a monthly haircut.

Task items are added to the To-Do List as you create them, and some tasks take longer to complete than others. You can organize your To-Do List in multiple ways, for example, by due dates, by category, and by status. Updates to tasks, such as completing the task, modifying its due date, or changing the task to a recurring task, can be made directly on the To-Do List.

---

**Alert! | Starting Project 2B**

Because Outlook stores information on the hard drive of the computer at which you are working, it is recommended that you complete Project 2B in one working session. If possible, use the same computer that you used when you created the Windows 7 user account in Chapter 1. If you cannot use the same computer or if the Windows 7 user account that you created in Chapter 1 was deleted, refer to Chapter 1, Activities 1.01 and 1.02 to set up the Windows 7 user account and to configure Microsoft Outlook 2010. Allow approximately 45 minutes to one hour to complete Project 2B.

---

## Activity 2.20 | Creating Tasks

You can create a new task by using a Task form or by entering a new task directly in the To-Do List. In this activity, you will create tasks for Simone Daley, who is the mayor's Chief of Staff.

**1** Click the **Start** button, and then point to the **Shut down button arrow**. On the **Shut down** menu, click **Switch user** to display the **Windows 7** desktop. Click your **Firstname Lastname** account. If the account does not exist, refer to the Alert at the beginning of this Activity to set up the account.

**2** **Start** Outlook. In the **Navigation Pane**, click the **Tasks** button to display the Tasks folder. On the **View tab**, in the **Current View group**, click the **Change View** button, and then click **Simple List**. If the Tasks folder is not empty, select and delete any existing tasks. Compare your screen with Figure 2.36.

The To-Do List displays in Simple List view. The To-Do List is used to display tasks, as well as other items—for example, a message that has been flagged for follow-up. Notice in the Navigation Pane, under My Tasks, that To-Do List is selected. This is the default format to view tasks. In Simple List view, individual task items are displayed in a table with column headings for seven fields: Icon, Complete, Task Subject, Due Date, Categories, In Folder, and Flag Status, which are summarized in the table in Figure 2.37.

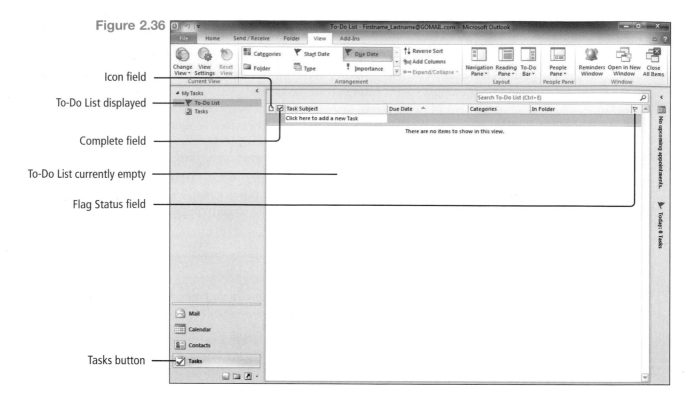

Figure 2.36

Icon field

To-Do List displayed

Complete field

To-Do List currently empty

Flag Status field

Tasks button

**3** Move the pointer over the six column headings in the **To-Do List** and observe the ScreenTip for each heading. Each of the fields is described in the table in Figure 2.37.

The ScreenTips for each column heading are prefixed with Sort by. Use the column headings to sort the To-Do List by icon type, the completed status, the task subject, the due date, category, in folder, or the flag status.

## To-Do List Column Headings

| To-Do List Column Heading Screen Tip | Sort Purpose |
|---|---|
| Sort by: Icon | Sorts the To-Do List by task type. The column displays an icon—a small graphic representation of an item type. There are four different types of tasks, each with a distinctive icon. The four task types include a task that you own, a recurring task, a task you assigned to someone else, and a task assigned to you by someone else. |
| Sort by: Complete | Sorts the To-Do List by task status. An empty box indicates that a task is not complete. A check mark indicates that a task is complete. |
| Sort by: Task Subject | Sorts the To-Do List alphabetically by the Subject name of the task. |
| Sort by: Due Date | Sorts the To-Do List in chronological order by task due date. |
| Sort by: Categories | Sorts the To-Do List by the category assigned to the task. |
| Sort by: In Folder | Sorts the To-Do List by the folder in which the task is stored. |
| Sort by: Flag Status | Sorts the To-Do List by the flag status of the task. |

Figure 2.37

> **Alert! | To-Do List versus Tasks Option**
>
> The To-Do List displays any Outlook item—such as an appointment, an e-mail message, or a task—that requires follow-up. In the *My Tasks* pane, using the default *To-Do List* option, rather than Tasks, displays all to-do items. You will work in the default view in this project.

**4** On the **Home tab**, in the **New group**, click the **New Task** button. In the **Untitled – Task** form, in the **Subject** box, type **Prepare mayor's Japan travel itinerary**

**5** Click the **Due date arrow**. On the displayed calendar, click a date **ten** *business days*— days that are not Saturday, Sunday, or a holiday—from today's date.

**6** On the **Task tab**, in the **Actions group**, click the **Save & Close** button, and notice that the **To-Do List** displays the new task.

> Recall that there are four types of tasks, each represented by an icon. The icon assigned to this task represents a task that you own. Notice the flag for this task has a custom status because you specified a particular date.

**7** Using the technique you just practiced, open a **New Task**, and as the **Subject** type **Review and forward EPA air quality report for city to mayor** Click the **Due date arrow**, and then click a date **two** business days from today's date.

**8** In the **Task** form, locate, but *do not* select the **Reminder** check box.

> You can set a date and time to be reminded of a task. The reminder is a small dialog box that appears in the middle of the Outlook screen. You can be working in any Outlook folder when a reminder displays. By default Outlook does not display a reminder—the check box is clear. If you want to use the Reminder feature, you can click in the Reminder check box, and then select the date and time of day when you would like to be reminded of the task.

**9** In the **Task** form, click the **Priority arrow**, and then click **High**. In the *task body*—the blank area in the lower half of the form in which you can add information not otherwise specified in the form—type **David needs this before the weekly press conference** and then compare your screen with Figure 2.38.

Figure 2.38

Priority set to High

Due date (your date will differ)

Reminder check box

Task body

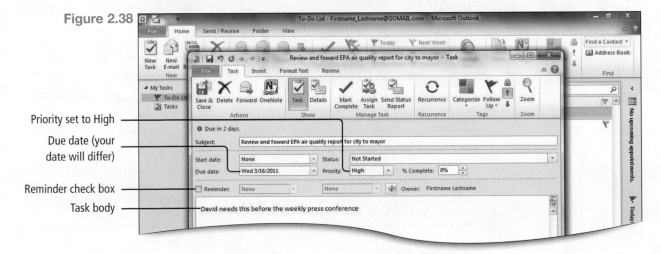

**10** **Save & Close** the task. In the **To-Do List** under the column headings, click in the **Click here to add a new Task** box, and then type **Call Japanese embassy to discuss mayor's trip** Press Tab , and in the **Due Date box**, type **Tomorrow** and then press Enter .

> The task is added to the list. Notice that the insertion point is still located in the *Click here to add a new Task* box, and the text no longer displays. Use this box to quickly create a new task with only a subject and due date. You can see that you can use natural language phrases such as *Tomorrow* to specify dates, and then Outlook converts the phrases to actual dates. *Natural language* is a language spoken or written by humans, as opposed to a computer programming language. Other examples of natural language phrases that Outlook can convert to actual dates include *next Tuesday* or *two weeks from today*.

**11** In the **Click here to add a new Task** box, type **Complete staff budget** Press Tab , in the **Due Date** box, type **One week from today** and then press Enter .

---

**Note** | Natural Language and Nonbusiness Days

When Outlook converts natural language into actual dates, it makes no distinction between business days and nonbusiness days. For example, if the current day of the week is Sunday, and you type *one week from today*, Outlook will use the calendar date of the next Sunday.

---

**12** In the **Click here to add a new Task** box, type **Write press release for mayor's new staff appointments** Press Tab to make the **Due Date** box active, type **Tomorrow** and then press Enter .

**13** In the **Click here to add a new Task** box, type **Draft mayor's position paper for new airport development** Press Tab to make the **Due Date** box active, type **Three weeks from today** and then press Enter . Compare your screen with Figure 2.39.

Figure 2.39

Your dates will differ

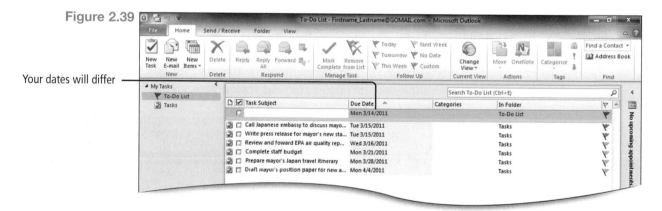

---

**More Knowledge** | Creating a Personal Folder for Tasks

In the same manner as you create folders to organize your contacts, you can create a subfolder within the Tasks folder for tasks. This is useful if you want to separate your work-related tasks from your personal tasks. To create a subfolder, right-click the Tasks folder, and select New Folder from the shortcut menu. Type a name for your folder, and then click OK.

---

## Activity 2.21 | Changing and Updating Tasks

You can make changes to a task in the To-Do List or on the Task form. In this activity, you will add more details to Simone Daley's tasks.

**1** In the **To-Do List**, click anywhere in the words *Complete staff budget* to select the task, and then click again to activate the insertion point.

**2** Position the insertion point so that it displays just before the word *staff*. Type **mayor's** and then press [Spacebar].

Use this technique to edit both the Subject text and the Due Date directly in the To-Do List.

**3** In the **Write press release for mayor's new staff appointments** task, click the **Due Date** box. Change the date to two days *prior* to the current date. Press [Enter] or click in a blank area of the **To-Do List**, and then compare your screen with Figure 2.40.

You cannot change a due date to occur before the date when the task was created—today's date. Outlook displays the message box and sounds a tone if your computer's sound is enabled.

Figure 2.40

Microsoft Outlook message box regarding due date

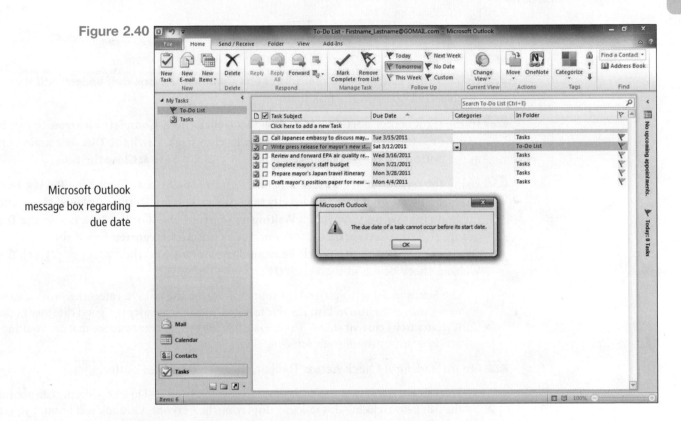

**4** Click **OK** to close the message box.

Notice that the task is still selected. Outlook will not allow you to create contradictory dates for tasks.

**5** Double-click the **Write press release for mayor's new staff appointments** task to open the **Task** form. Click the **Start date arrow**, and then select a date two days *prior* to today's date. Click the **Due date arrow** and then if necessary, select a date one day prior to today's date. **Save & Close** the task, and then compare your screen with Figure 2.41.

This task is displayed in red because it is now overdue. Notice that the To-Do Bar indicates that there is one task due today.

**Figure 2.41**

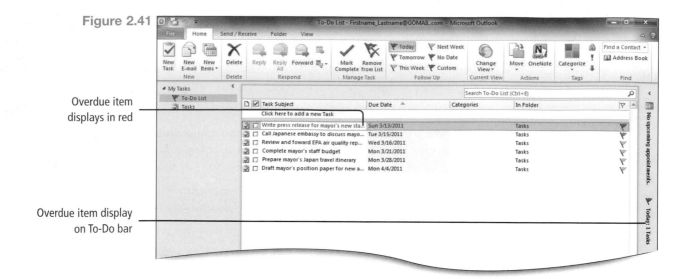

Overdue item displays in red

Overdue item display on To-Do bar

---

**6** In the **To-Do List**, point to the subject text **Complete mayor's staff budget**, and then double-click to open the task form.

**7** In the right center portion of the **Task form**, click the **% Complete up arrow** to display **25%**. Click the **Priority arrow**, and set the level to **High**. Click the **Due date arrow**, and at the bottom of the displayed calendar, click **Today**. **Save & Close** the task.

**8** Using the technique you just practiced, from the **To-Do List**, display the **Review and forward EPA air quality report for city to mayor** task form. In the displayed form, click the **Status arrow**, and then click **Waiting on someone else**. On the **Task tab**, in the **Tags group**, click the **Categorize** button, and then click **All Categories**. Select the text **Orange Category** and then click **Rename**. Type **Waiting** and then press Enter. Click the **Waiting** check box, and then click **OK**.

> Use Status to show the progress of your tasks. Assigning tasks to categories provides a way to organize your To-Do List. For this task, the Waiting category is a good category because it relates to its current status. Thus, you could sort your tasks by those that are awaiting action or information from someone else.

**9** On the *Task form* Quick Access Toolbar, click the **Next Item** button 🔽.

> You can use this button to display the next item in your To-Do List without redisplaying the list. Before closing this task and displaying the next one, Outlook will prompt you to save the changes you have made in the current task.

**10** In the **Microsoft Outlook** dialog box, click **Yes** to save the changes and display the next task in the list, which is the **Prepare mayor's Japan travel itinerary** task.

**11** In the displayed **Task** form, use the techniques you have practiced to change the **Status** to **Waiting on someone else** and the **% Complete** to **50%**. **Categorize** the task by assigning it to the **Waiting** category. In the comments area of the Task form, type **Waiting to hear from Governor's chief of staff** and then **Save & Close** the task.

**12** In the **To-Do List**, locate the **Call Japanese embassy to discuss mayor's trip** task, and in the second column of the table, click in the check box to indicate that the task has been completed. Compare your screen with Figure 2.42.

> The task is marked as complete, and a line is drawn through the task.

Figure 2.42

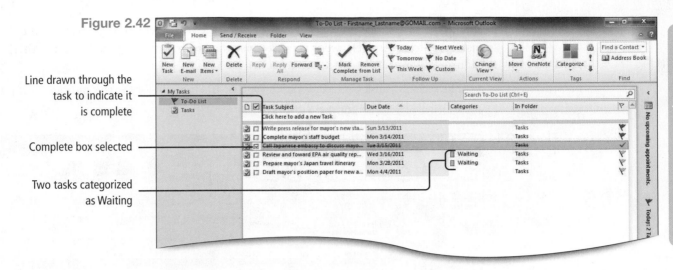

Line drawn through the task to indicate it is complete

Complete box selected

Two tasks categorized as Waiting

## Activity 2.22 | Creating a Recurring Task

Recall that a recurring task is one that occurs frequently on a regular schedule, such as preparing a weekly status report or attending a monthly staff meeting. In this activity, you will make one of Simone Daley's tasks recurring.

**1** On the **Home tab**, in the **New group**, click the **New Task** button, and then in the **Subject** box type **Schedule press conference**

**2** On the **Task tab**, in the **Recurrence group**, click the **Recurrence** button.

Here you define when and how frequently the task will recur. For example, a task can recur every day, every week, every month, or every year. Additionally, you can define a range of time for the task to recur, for example, a weekly meeting for the period January through June.

**3** In the **Task Recurrence** dialog box, click **Weekly** if it is not already selected, and then select the **Wednesday** check box if it is not already selected. Clear any other check boxes, and then compare your screen with Figure 2.43.

Figure 2.43

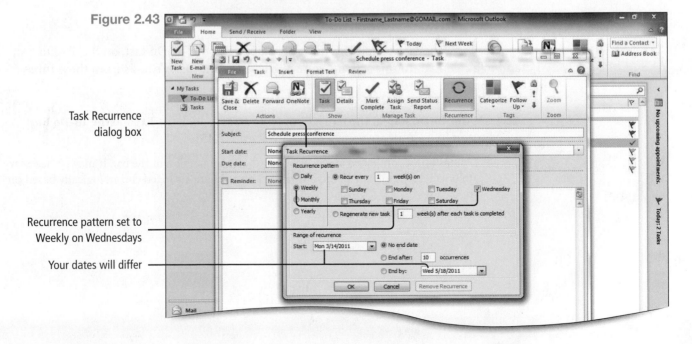

Task Recurrence dialog box

Recurrence pattern set to Weekly on Wednesdays

Your dates will differ

**4** Click **OK**, and notice the banner at the top of the form, which indicates that the task is set to recur every week. **Save & Close** the task. Compare your screen with Figure 2.44.

The recurring task is added to the To-Do List and the icon for the task indicates that it is a recurring task. Your tasks may display in a different order.

Figure 2.44

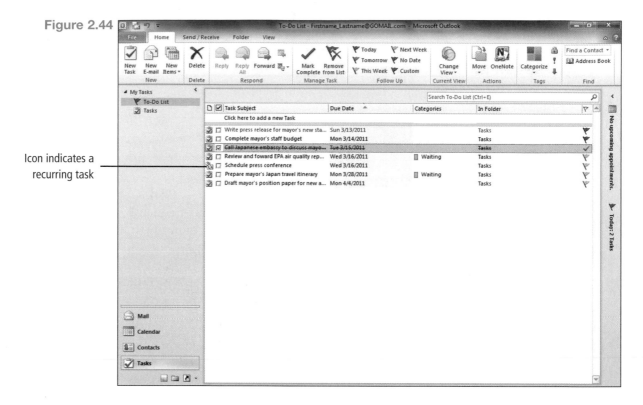

Icon indicates a
recurring task

## Objective 8 | Manage Tasks

Various tools and views are available to help you manage a large and complex To-Do List. You can also sort the To-Do List by priority, due date, or status.

### Activity 2.23 | Viewing Tasks

Tasks can be viewed in three different places—in the To-Do List, on the To-Do Bar, and in a calendar. In this activity, you will view Simone Daley's tasks from these three locations.

**1** On the **To-Do Bar**, at the far right of your screen, click the **Expand the To-Do Bar** button. Compare your screen with Figure 2.45.

All tasks not completed are displayed in the lower portion of the bar. It may be necessary to scroll down to view all of your tasks. The tasks are arranged chronologically based on due date.

**Figure 2.45**

Expanded To-Do bar

Your dates will differ

Scroll to see additional tasks

Tasks grouped by due dates

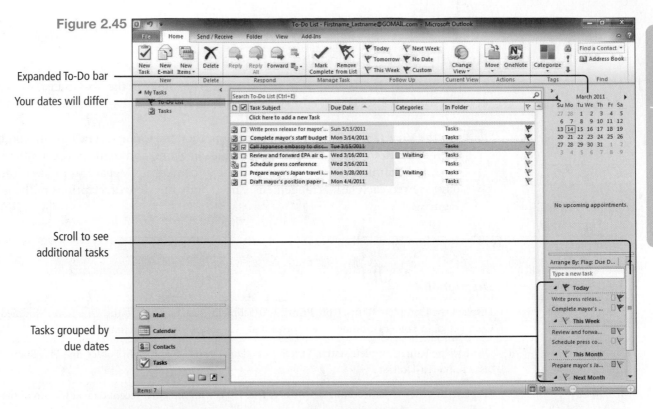

**2** On the **To-Do Bar**, click the **Minimize the To-Do Bar** button.

**3** In the lower part of the **Navigation Pane**, click the **Calendar** button, and then on the **Home tab**, in the **Arrange group**, click the **Day** button. Compare your screen with Figure 2.46.

> The Calendar displays the current date. At the bottom of the screen, notice the Tasks section, showing the overdue task, the task due today, and the task that was completed today. The recurring task may display in the list, depending on the current day of the week.

**Figure 2.46**

Calendar displays current date – your date will differ

Tasks section

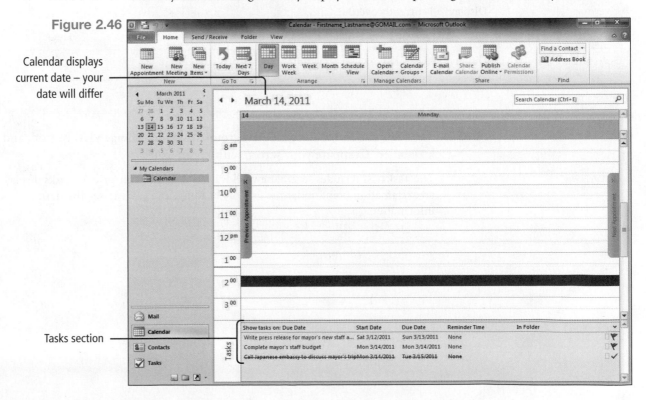

**4** In the **Navigation Pane**, click the **Tasks** button to display the **To-Do List**.

## Activity 2.24 | Sorting the To-Do List

You can sort the To-Do List from the column headings in the To-Do List. In this activity, you will display different views of Simone Daley's To-Do List.

**1** On the **View tab**, in the **Current View group**, click the **Change View** button, and then click **Prioritized**. Click the **Change View** button again, and then choose a different view and examine the arrangement of the information. Repeat this process until you have viewed each task arrangement. Then, study the view descriptions in the table in Figure 2.47.

| To-Do List Views | |
|---|---|
| **To-Do List View** | **Description** |
| Detailed | Displays the Complete status, Icon, Priority, Attachment, Task Subject, Status, Due Date, Modified, Date Completed, In Folder (location), Categories, and Flag Status for all tasks in the To-Do List. |
| Simple List | Displays the Icon, Complete status, Task Subject, Due Date, Categories, In Folder, and Flag Status for all tasks in the To-Do List. |
| To-Do List | Displays all active tasks according to the task Due Date, with the most recent date at the top of the list. To-Do List is the default view. |
| Prioritized | Displays all tasks by Priority level and then by Category. |
| Active | Displays all tasks not marked Completed or 100% Complete. |
| Completed | Displays tasks marked Completed. |
| Today | Displays the tasks due today and any overdue tasks. |
| Next 7 Days | Displays all tasks due within the next seven days. |
| Overdue | Displays all currently overdue tasks. |
| Assigned | Displays tasks you have assigned to others. |
| Server Tasks | Displays tasks stored on a server running Microsoft Sharepoint. |

**Figure 2.47**

**2** On the **View tab**, in the **Current View group**, click the **Change View** button, and then click **Detailed**. Compare your screen with Figure 2.48.

The Tasks list includes several new fields in its display. High-priority tasks display an exclamation point under the Priority heading, and you can see the status information.

Figure 2.48

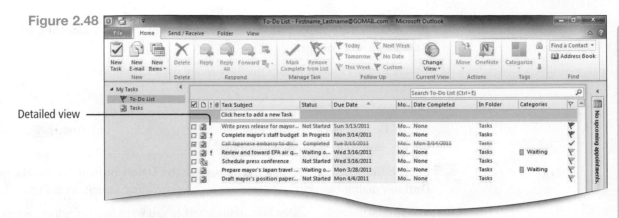

Detailed view

**3** In the column headings area of the **To-Do List**, click the **Due Date** heading, and observe the small, shaded arrow next to the heading name.

The To-Do List is sorted by Due Date. When the arrow is pointing up, the tasks are sorted in ascending order—tasks closest in time to the current date are listed first, and the overdue task is listed first. When the arrow is pointing down, the tasks are sorted in descending order. This arrow displays in other sorted column headings and works the same way in all cases.

**4** Click the **Due Date** column heading several times to observe the change in sort order and the direction of the shaded arrow. After you have observed the sort order, click the **Due Date** column heading as necessary so that the arrow is pointing up and the list is sorted by Due Date in ascending order.

**5** In the **To-Do List**, click the **Priority** column heading—the column with the exclamation point—to sort the list by priority.

**6** Display the **Start** menu 🏁, and then click **All Programs**. Locate and then click the **Accessories** folder. Click **Snipping Tool**. In the **Snipping Tool** dialog box, click the **New arrow**, and then click **Window Snip**. Click anywhere in the window to capture it, and then click the **Save Snip** button 💾. Navigate to the location where you are storing your files, click in the **File name** box, and then, using your own name, type **Lastname_Firstname_2B_Task_List** Click the **Save as type arrow**, and then click **JPEG file**. Click **Save**, and then **Close** ⊠ the **Snipping Tool** window. Submit the end result to your instructor as directed.

> **More Knowledge** | Printing a Task List or Individual Task
>
> You can use Backstage view to print your task list. To print information about an individual task, select the task before displaying the Backstage view, and then changing settings as necessary.

## Activity 2.25 | Deleting Tasks and Restoring Default Settings

After you complete a task, you may want to delete it from your To-Do List. When you delete a task in your To-Do List, it moves to the Deleted Items folder and remains there, along with other deleted items, until the Deleted Items folder is emptied. After an item is deleted from the Deleted Items folder, it is permanently deleted. In this activity, you will delete Simone Daley's tasks.

**1** In the **To-Do List**, select any task. On the **Home tab**, in the **Tags group**, click the **Categorize** button, and then click **All Categories**.

**2** In the **Color Categories** dialog box, select **Waiting**, click **Rename**, and then type **Orange Category** and press Enter.

Recall that Outlook retains the most recent name change, so renaming is required to restore the category to its default name.

**3** Click **OK** to close the dialog box, and then change the **Current View** to **Simple List**. In the **To-Do List**, click the first task one time to select it, hold down Shift, and then click the last task to select all the tasks in the list.

**4** On the **Home tab**, in the **Delete group**, click the **Delete** button. In the **Microsoft Outlook** dialog box, click **OK** and then compare your screen with Figure 2.49.

Outlook displays a dialog box asking whether you want to delete all occurrences of the *Schedule press conference* task. Recall that this is a recurring task with no end date.

Figure 2.49

Simple List view

Microsoft Outlook dialog box regarding the recurring task

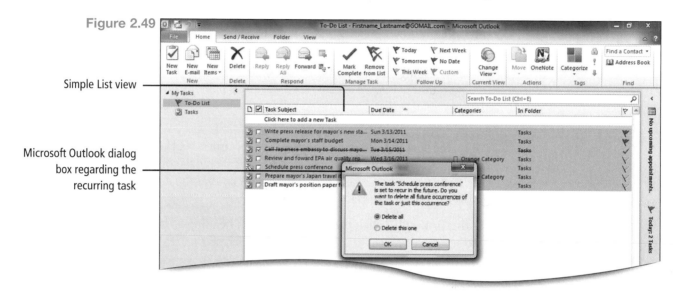

**5** In the **Microsoft Outlook** dialog box, verify that the **Delete all** option is selected and then click **OK** to delete all future occurrences of the task. Display the **Folder List** 📁, right-click the **Deleted Items** folder, and then click **Empty Folder**.

Outlook displays a warning box indicating that you are permanently deleting the selected items.

**6** In the **Microsoft Outlook** dialog box, click **Yes**.

The items are permanently deleted and the Deleted Items folder is empty.

**7** **Close** ☒ Outlook.

**End** You have completed Project 2B

# Content-Based Assessments

## Summary

Use Outlook to store information about your contacts and keep track of tasks you need to complete. In this chapter, you practiced creating a Contacts list, used the Contacts list to address e-mail messages, and added new contacts to the Contacts list from received messages. You also edited contacts, added details to contacts, and linked contacts with one another. You created, used, and modified a contact group. To organize the Contacts list, you assigned contacts to categories, sorted the Contacts list in different ways with different views, created a separate folder for contacts, and then printed and deleted items in the Contacts list. You created a To-Do List, updated tasks, created a recurring task, sorted tasks, and printed and deleted tasks.

## Key Terms

## Matching

Match each term in the second column with its correct definition in the first column. Write the letter of the term on the blank line in front of the correct definition.

_____ 1. Individuals, organizations, or companies with whom you communicate.

_____ 2. The command that brings information into Outlook from another program in which the information already exists.

_____ 3. A set of lettered buttons on the right side of the screen with which you can move through contact items displayed in Business Card view.

_____ 4. A blank area of a contact form that can be used for any information about the contact that is not otherwise specified in the form.

_____ 5. An e-mail feature in which you can have a copy of the message sent to a recipient, but the recipient's name is not visible to other recipients of the message.

_____ 6. A collection of contacts to whom you send e-mail messages.

_____ 7. Colors with optional words or phrases applied to Outlook items for the purpose of finding, sorting, filtering, or grouping them.

_____ 8. An abbreviation for Very Important Person.

_____ 9. An element of information within an item, such as a company name or state.

**A** Blind courtesy copy

**B** Categories

**C** Collapse

**D** Contact group

**E** Contact Index

**F** Contacts

**G** Expand

**H** Field

**I** Import

**J** Natural language

**K** Notes area

**L** Recurring task

**M** Task

**N** vCard

**O** VIP

_____ 10. The action of showing information by clicking a symbol.

_____ 11. The action of hiding information by clicking a symbol.

_____ 12. The Internet standard for creating and sharing virtual business cards.

_____ 13. A personal or work-related activity that you want to keep track of until it is complete.

_____ 14. A task that occurs repeatedly, for example, a weekly meeting.

_____ 15. A language written or spoken by humans, as opposed to a computer programming language.

## Multiple Choice

Circle the correct answer.

1. A person or organization, inside or outside your own organization, about whom you can save information, such as street and e-mail addresses, telephone and fax numbers, Web page addresses, birthdays, and pictures.
   **A.** Associate        **B.** Contact        **C.** Friend

2. The default location for Outlook's contact information.
   **A.** Contacts folder        **B.** Inbox        **C.** Outbox

3. An abbreviation for blind courtesy copy.
   **A.** Bcy        **B.** Blc        **C.** Bcc

4. The folder in which contact groups are created and displayed.
   **A.** Contacts        **B.** Inbox        **C.** Mail

5. In a Message form, the word that you can click to display the Contacts list and find the e-mail address of a contact.
   **A.** Subject        **B.** From        **C.** To

6. When displaying an Inbox message in the Reading Pane, the part of a message that you can right-click to add the sender's name and e-mail address to your Contacts.
   **A.** Date        **B.** Subject        **C.** E-mail address

7. A Windows 7 application with which you can capture all or part of a screen.
   **A.** Accessories        **B.** Calculator        **C.** Snipping Tool

8. An item captured with the Snipping Tool.
   **A.** Snip        **B.** Picture        **C.** Clip Art

9. A lined page added to the Card Style printout that you can use to manually list new contacts.
   **A.** Contact list        **B.** Blank form        **C.** Table form

10. Days that are not Saturdays, Sundays, or holidays.
    **A.** Business days        **B.** Work days        **C.** Employment days

# Content-Based Assessments

Apply **2A** skills from these Objectives:

1. Create Contacts
3. Edit Contacts
4. Manage Contact Groups
5. Organize Contacts
6. Manage Contacts

## Mastering Outlook | Project **2C** Executive Assistant

In the following Mastering Outlook project, you will work with the Contacts list for Courtney Shrever, the Executive Assistant for Desert Park's Mayor, David Parker. Ms. Shrever will be editing contacts, organizing her Contacts list, and creating a contact group for the mayor's staff. Your completed Contacts list will look similar to the one shown in Figure 2.50.

### Project Files

For Project 2C, you will need the following files:

> New blank contact form
> New blank contact group form
> o02C_Executive_Assistant_Contacts

You will save your file as:

> Lastname_Firstname_2C_Contact_Group.jpg

You will print or create a PDF for one file with the following footer:

> Lastname_Firstname_2C_Executive_Assistant_Contacts

### Project Results

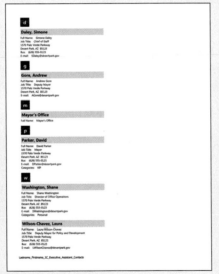

**Figure 2.50**

(Project 2C Executive Assistant continues on the next page)

# Content-Based Assessments

**1** Click the **Start** button, and then point to the **Shut down button arrow**. On the **Shut down** menu, click **Switch user** to display the Windows 7 desktop. Click your **Firstname Lastname** account. If the account does not exist, refer to Chapter 1, Activities 1.01 and 1.02 to set up the Windows 7 user account and to configure Microsoft Outlook.

**2** **Start** Outlook and be sure the **Navigation Pane** is displayed. In the **Navigation Pane**, click the **Contacts** folder. In **Backstage** view, click **Open**, and then click **Import**. In the **Import and Export Wizard** dialog box, under **Choose an action to perform**, click **Import from another program or file**, and then click **Next**. In the **Import a File** dialog box, under **Select file type to import from**, scroll down as necessary, and then click **Outlook Data File (.pst)**. Click **Next**.

**3** In the **Import Outlook Data File** dialog box, click **Browse**, and then navigate to the location where the student files for this textbook are stored. Locate **o02C_Executive_Assistant_Contacts**, and click one time to select it. Click **Open**.

**4** In the **Import Outlook Data File** dialog box, click **Next**. Under **Select the folder to import from**, select the **Contact** folder, and then click **Finish** to import the contacts and display the contacts in Business Card view.

**5** Double-click the **Shane Washington** contact to open it. In the **Contact** form, in the **E-mail** box, type **SWashington@desertpark.gov** In the **Tags group**, click **Categorize**, and then click **All Categories**. In the **Color Categories** dialog box, rename the **Blue Category** as **Personal** and then assign the **Personal** category to **Shane Washington**. **Save & Close** the form.

**6** On the **Home tab**, in the **New group**, click **New Contact Group**. In the **Contact Group** form, in the **Name** box, type **Mayor's Office** In the **Members** group, click **Add Members**, and then click **From Outlook Contacts**. Add **Laura Wilson-Chavez**, **Shane Washington** and **Simone Daley** as **Members**. Click **OK**, and then **Save & Close** the contact group.

**7** From the **Contacts** list, open the **David Parker** contact. Display the **Color Categories** dialog box, rename the **Purple Category** as **VIP** and then assign the **VIP** category to David Parker. **Save & Close** the form.

**8** On the **Home tab**, change the **Current View** to **Card**. In **Backstage** view, display the **Print tab**, and then select **Card Style**. Click **Print Options**, and then display the **Page Setup: Card Style** dialog box. With the **Format tab** displayed, under **Options**, change the **Blank forms at end** to **None**.

**9** Click the **Header/Footer tab**, and delete any header or footer information. In the left **Footer** box, using your own name, type **Lastname_Firstname_2C_Executive_Assistant_Contacts** Click **OK**, and then **Preview** the document. **Print** or use **OneNote** to create a PDF document and then submit the end result to your instructor as directed.

**10** Open the **Mayor's Office** contact group, and then **Maximize** the Contact Group window. From the **Start** menu, display the **Snipping Tool**, and then create a **New Window Snip**. Save the file as a **JPEG file** with the name **Lastname_Firstname_2C_Contact_Group** and then **Close** the Contact Group.

**11** If necessary, display the **Contacts** list, and then select any contact. Display the **Color Categories** dialog box, select **Personal,** click **Rename**, and then type **Blue Category**. Rename **VIP** as **Purple Category** and then click **OK**.

**12** In the **Contacts** list, click the first contact one time to select it without opening it. Hold down Shift and then click the last contact in the Contacts list. **Delete** the contacts.

**13** In the **Navigation Pane**, click the **Folder List** button, and then in the **Folder List**, right-click the **Deleted Items** folder. Click **Empty Folder**, and then click **Yes**.

**14** Display the **Contacts** folder, and then in **Backstage** view, on the **Print tab**, click **Print Options** and click **Define Styles** to display the **Define Print Styles** dialog box. Reset the **Card Style** print style and then **Close** the dialog box. **Cancel** the **Print** dialog box. **Close** Outlook.

**End** You have completed Project 2C

# Content-Based Assessments

Apply **2A** and **2B** skills from these Objectives:

**1** Create Contacts

**5** Organize Contacts

**6** Manage Contacts

**7** Create and Update Tasks

**8** Manage Tasks

## Mastering Outlook | Project **2D** Holiday Party

In the following Mastering Outlook project, you will develop a To-Do List and Contacts list for Courtney Shrever, who has been asked by the Desert Park Mayor, David Parker, to organize a holiday party for his office and other members of city government. Your completed To-Do List and Contacts list will look similar to the ones shown in Figure 2.51.

### Project Files

For Project 2D, you will need the following files:

> New blank contact form
> New blank task form

You will print or create a PDF for two files with the following footers:

> Lastname_Firstname_2D_Party_Suppliers
> Lastname_Firstname_2D_Holiday_Party_List

### Project Results

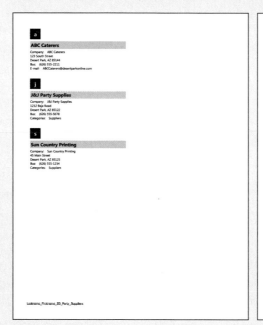

**Figure 2.51**

(Project 2D Holiday Party continues on the next page)

# Content-Based Assessments

## Mastering Outlook | Project **2D** Holiday Party (continued)

**1** Click the **Start** button, and then point to the **Shut down button arrow**. On the **Shut down** menu, click **Switch user** to display the Windows 7 desktop. Click your **Firstname Lastname** account. If the account does not exist, refer to Chapter 1, Activities 1.01 and 1.02 to set up the Windows 7 user account and to configure Microsoft Outlook.

**2** **Start** Outlook, display the **Navigation Pane**, click the **Contacts** button, and then open a new **Contact** form. As the **Company** name, type **ABC Caterers** Type the following information for the new contact, using **Business** for the address and phone information:

> ABCCaterers@desertparkonline.com
>
> 626-555-2211
>
> 123 South Street
>
> Desert Park, AZ 85144

**3** Click **Save & New**, and then, in the **Untitled – Contact** form, type the following information in the appropriate boxes for the following company:

> Sun Country Printing
>
> 626-555-1234
>
> 45 Main Street
>
> Desert Park, AZ 85123

**4** Display the **Color Categories** dialog box, rename the **Green Category** as **Suppliers** and then assign this category to Sun Country Printing contact. **Save & Close** the contact. Open a new contact, and add the following company:

> J&J Party Supplies
>
> 626-555-5678
>
> 1212 Baja Road
>
> Desert Park, AZ 85122

**5** Assign this contact to the **Suppliers** category, and then **Save & Close** the form. On the **Home tab**, change the **Current View** to **Card**. In **Backstage** view, display the **Print tab**, and then select **Card Style**. Display the **Print Options**, and then click **Page Setup**. In the **Page Setup: Card Style** dialog box, change the **Blank forms at end** to **None**. On the **Header/Footer tab**, delete any existing header or footer information, and in the left **Footer** box, type **Lastname_Firstname_2D_Party_Suppliers** Preview the document. **Print** or use **OneNote** to create a PDF document, and then submit the end result to your instructor as directed.

**6** Display your contacts in **Business Card** view, and then display the **Tasks** folder. Click the **New Task** button, and then in the **Subject** box, type **Find party location** Set the **Due date** as one week from the current

date. Set the **Priority** to **High**, and then if necessary, clear the Reminder check box. Display the **Color Categories** dialog box, rename the **Red Category** as **Holiday,** and then assign this category to the task. **Save & Close** the task.

**7** On the **View tab**, in the **Current View group**, click the **Change View** button, and then click **Simple List**. Under the column headings, click in the **Click here to add a new Task** box, and then type **Ask Shane about other caterers** In the **Due Date** box, type **Tomorrow** and then press Enter.

**8** Using one of the techniques that you practiced, create a new task with the **Subject Send printer invitation text** In the **Due Date** box, type **Today** and then press Enter. Create another new task with the **Subject Get head count, call party suppliers** In the **Due Date** box, type **One week from today** and then press Enter.

**9** Double-click the **Get head count** task to open its form. Display the **Color Categories** dialog box, rename the **Yellow Category** as **Phone Calls,** and assign this category to the task. Change the **% Complete** to **50%**, and then **Save & Close** the form.

**10** Select the **Find party location** task, and then mark it as **Complete**.

**11** Change the **Current View** to **Detailed**. From the **Priority** column heading, sort the **Tasks** list with the highest priority tasks first.

**12** From the **Backstage** view **Print tab**, display the **Page Setup: Table Style** dialog box. Delete any header or footer information. In the left **Footer** box, type **Lastname_Firstname_2D_Holiday_Party_List** and then **Preview** the document. **Print** or use **OneNote** to create a PDF document, and then submit the end result to your instructor as directed.

**13** In the **To-Do List**, select any task. Display the **Color Categories** dialog box, select **Suppliers**, click **Rename**, and then type **Green Category**. Rename **Holiday** as **Red Category**, and **Phone Calls** as **Yellow Category Close** the dialog box.

**14** Delete the contents of the **Tasks** folder. Then display the **Contacts** folder, and delete the contacts that you created.

**15** In the **Navigation Pane**, click the **Folder List** button. Empty the **Deleted Items** folder. Display the **Contacts** folder, and then in **Backstage** view, **Reset** the **Card Style** print style and then **Close** the dialog box. **Cancel** the **Print** dialog box. Display the **Tasks** folder, and then **Reset** the **Table Style** print style. **Close** the dialog box, **Cancel** the **Print** dialog box, and then **Close** Outlook.

**End You have completed Project 2D**

Apply **2A** skills from these Objectives:

■ Create Contacts

■ Use Contacts with E-mail

■ Edit Contacts

■ Manage Contacts

## Mastering Outlook | Project **2E** Computer Network

In the following Mastering Outlook project, you will create contacts and send an e-mail message for Shane Washington, the Director of Office Operations in the mayor's office. Shane is directing an upgrade of the office computer network and will be creating contacts for the consultants implementing the project. Your completed Contacts list and message will look similar to the ones shown in Figure 2.52.

### Project Files

For Project 2E, you will need the following files:

New blank contact form
New blank message form

You will print or create a PDF for two files with the following footers:

Lastname_Firstname_2E_Computer_Network_Proposal
Lastname_Firstname_2E_Computer_Network_Contact

### Project Results

**Figure 2.52**

(Project 2E Computer Network continues on the next page)

# Content-Based Assessments

**1** Log in to your Windows 7 **Firstname Lastname** account, or if necessary, create the account according to the instructions in Chapter 1, Activities 1.01 and 1.02.

**2** **Start** Outlook. In **Backstage** view, display the **Outlook Options** dialog box, and then click **Advanced**. Under **Send and receive**, *clear* the **Send immediately when connected** check box. To the immediate right, click the **Send/Receive** button. In the **Send/Receive Groups** dialog box, under **Setting for group "All Accounts"** and **When Outlook is Offline**, *clear* all five check boxes. Click **Close**, and then click **OK**.

**3** Create the following contact:

Jason Moran

Park Associates Network Solutions, Inc.

JMoran@parkassociates.com

626-555-3434

333 Rio Grande Avenue

Desert Park, AZ 95123

**4** **Save & Close** the contact. In the **Contacts** list, right-click the **Jason Moran** contact. On the displayed shortcut menu, point to **Create**, and then click **E-mail**.

**5** In the **Message** form, change the **Message format** to **Plain Text**. As the **Subject**, type **Your proposal** In the message area, using the format you have practiced for composing e-mail messages, type the following message. If you are unsure of the format, refer to Figure 2.52.

Jason, I received your proposal for upgrading our network. I will be reviewing the specifications and the budget. I have some questions about the timing that we need to discuss. Shane

**6** **Send** the e-mail, and then display the **Folder List** and click **Outbox**. Select the **Jason Moran** message, and then set the **Print Options** to print the message in **Memo Style**. Delete any header or footer information, and then, in the left **Footer** box, type **Lastname_Firstname_2E_Computer_Network_Proposal Preview** the document. **Print** or use **OneNote** to create a PDF document, and then submit the end result to your instructor as directed.

**7** Delete the contents of the **Outbox**. Display the **Contacts** folder, and open the **Contact** form for **Jason Moran**. Move the insertion point to the postal code. Change the postal code from **95123** to **85123 Save & Close** the form.

**8** In **Backstage** view, set the **Print Options** to **Memo Style** and then in the **Page Setup: Memo Style** dialog box, delete any header or footer information. In the left **Footer** box, type **Lastname_Firstname_2E_Computer_Network_Contact Preview** the document. **Print** or use **OneNote** to create a PDF document, and then submit the end result to your instructor as directed.

**9** Display the **Contacts** folder, and then display the **Define Print Styles** dialog box. **Reset** the **Card Style** print style, and then **Close** the dialog box. In the **Contacts** list, delete the contact. Then, empty the **Deleted Items** folder.

**10** From the **Backstage** view, click **Options**. In the **Advanced tab**, reset the default **Send and receive** options. Close all dialog boxes, and then **Close** Outlook.

**End** You have completed Project 2E

# Content-Based Assessments

Apply **2A** and **2B** skills from these Objectives:

**1** Create Contacts

**3** Edit Contacts

**4** Manage Contact Groups

**5** Organize Contacts

**6** Manage Contacts

**7** Create and Update Tasks

**8** Manage Tasks

## Mastering Outlook | Project **2F** Job Fair

In the following Mastering Outlook project, you will create contacts and a contact group for Gloria French, who is the Public Information Officer for the city of Desert Park. Ms. French is organizing a job fair for city agencies and departments using both internal and external personnel. Your completed Contacts list will look similar to the one shown in Figure 2.53.

### Project Files

For Project 2F, you will need the following files:

> New blank contact group form
> New blank task form
> o02F_Job_Fair_Contacts

You will print or create a PDF for three files with the following footers:

> Lastname_Firstname_2F_Job_Fair
> Lastname_Firstname_2F_Job_Fair_Managers
> Lastname_Firstname_2F_Job_Fair_Tasks

### Project Results

**Figure 2.53**

(Project 2F Job Fair continues on the next page)

# Content-Based Assessments

## Mastering Outlook | Project 2F Job Fair (continued)

**1** Log in to your Windows 7 **Firstname Lastname** account, or if necessary, create the account according to the instructions in Chapter 1, Activities 1.01 and 1.02.

**2** **Start** Outlook and display the **Contacts** folder. Display the **Import and Export Wizard** dialog box, and import the **Outlook Data File (.pst)** from your student files—**o02F_Job_Fair_Contacts**. When prompted to **Select the folder to import from**, click **Contacts**, and then click **Import items into the current folder**. Click **Finish**.

**3** Create a **New Contact Group**, and name it **Job Fair Hiring Managers** Add the following members from your contact list to the contact group: **Ray Hamilton, Madison Romero, Simone Daley**, and **Shane Washington**.

**4** In the **Contact Group** form, display the **Color Categories** dialog box, rename **Orange Category** as **Goals/Objectives** and then apply the **Goals/Objectives** category to the contact group. **Save & Close** the contact group.

**5** If necessary, display the **Contacts** folder, select **Ray Hamilton**, hold down Ctrl, and then select **Madison Romero, Simone Daley**, and **Shane Washington**. Assign the **Goals/Objectives** category. The individual contacts and the contact group are assigned to the category Ms. French is using for her job fair activities.

**6** In the **Contacts** list, select **Job Fair Hiring Managers**. In **Backstage** view, from the **Print tab**, display the **Page Setup: Memo Style** dialog box. Delete any header or footer information, and then, in the left **Footer** box, type **Lastname_Firstname_2F_Job_Fair_Managers** Preview the document. **Print** or use **OneNote** to create a PDF document, and then submit the end result to your instructor as directed.

**7** On the **Home tab**, change the **Current View** to **Card**. From **Backstage** view, display the **Page Setup: Card Style**

dialog box. Set **Blank forms at end** to **None**. Delete any header or footer information. In the left **Footer** box, type **Lastname_Firstname_2F_Job_Fair** Preview the document. **Print** or use **OneNote** to create a PDF document, and then submit the end result to your instructor as directed.

**8** In the **Contacts** list, select any contact. Display the **Color Categories** dialog box, select **Goals/Objectives**, click **Rename**, and then type **Orange Category** Click **OK**.

**9** Change to **Business Card** view. Delete all the items in the **Contacts** list. Display the **Define Print Styles** dialog box, and then **Reset** the **Card Style** and **Memo Style** print styles.

**10** In the **Navigation Pane**, click **Tasks**, and then create a **New Task**. As the **Subject** type **Finalize exhibitor list** Click the **Due date arrow**, and then click a date **two** business days from today's date. Change the **Priority** to **High** and then **Save & Close** the task.

**11** Add a **New Task**, and then as the **Subject**, type **Contact rental company regarding setup** Change the **Due Date** to **three weeks from today**. Add a **New Task**, and then as the **Subject** type **Write press release for job fair** Change the **Due date** to **Tomorrow** and set the **Priority** to **High** and the **% Complete** to **25%**. **Save & Close** the task. In the **To-Do List**, mark the **Finalize exhibitor list** task item as **Complete**.

**12** Change the **Current View** to **Detailed**, and then in **Backstage** view, click the **Print tab**. Display the **Page Setup: Table Style** dialog box. Delete all **Header/Footer** text, and then in the left **Footer** box, type **Lastname_Firstname_2F_Job_Fair_Tasks** Display the **Preview** of the document, and then submit the end result to your instructor as directed.

**13** Reset the **Print Styles** that you used, delete all tasks, and then empty the **Deleted Items** folder. **Close** Outlook.

**End** You have completed Project 2F

# Outcomes-Based Assessments

## Rubric

The following outcomes-based assessments are *open-ended* assessments. That is, there is no specific correct result; your result will depend on your approach to the information provided. Make *Professional Quality* your goal. Use the following scoring rubric to guide you in *how* to approach the problem and then to evaluate *how well* your approach solves the problem.

The *criteria*—Software Mastery, Content, Format and Layout, and Process—represent the knowledge and skills you have gained that you can apply to solving the problem. The *levels of performance*—Professional Quality, Approaching Professional Quality, or Needs Quality Improvement—help you and your instructor evaluate your result.

| | Your completed project is of Professional Quality if you: | Your completed project is Approaching Professional Quality if you: | Your completed project Needs Quality Improvements if you: |
|---|---|---|---|
| **1-Software Mastery** | Choose and apply the most appropriate skills, tools, and features and identify efficient methods to solve the problem. | Choose and apply some appropriate skills, tools, and features, but not in the most efficient manner. | Choose inappropriate skills, tools, or features, or are inefficient in solving the problem. |
| **2-Content** | Construct a solution that is clear and well organized, contains content that is accurate, appropriate to the audience and purpose, and is complete. Provide a solution that contains no errors in spelling, grammar, or style. | Construct a solution in which some components are unclear, poorly organized, inconsistent, or incomplete. Misjudge the needs of the audience. Have some errors in spelling, grammar, or style, but the errors do not detract from comprehension. | Construct a solution that is unclear, incomplete, or poorly organized; contains some inaccurate or inappropriate content; and contains many errors in spelling, grammar, or style. Do not solve the problem. |
| **3-Format and Layout** | Format and arrange all elements to communicate information and ideas, clarify function, illustrate relationships, and indicate relative importance. | Apply appropriate format and layout features to some elements, but not others. Overuse features, causing minor distraction. | Apply format and layout that does not communicate information or ideas clearly. Do not use format and layout features to clarify function, illustrate relationships, or indicate relative importance. Use available features excessively, causing distraction. |
| **4-Process** | Use an organized approach that integrates planning, development, self-assessment, revision, and reflection. | Demonstrate an organized approach in some areas, but not others; or, use an insufficient process of organization throughout. | Do not use an organized approach to solve the problem. |

# Outcomes-Based Assessments

Apply a combination of the **2A** and **2B** skills.

## GO! Think | Project **2G** Recreation Center

### Project Files

For Project 2G, you will need the following files:

> New blank contact group form
> o02G_Recreation_Center_Contacts
> New blank message form
> New blank task form

You will print or create a PDF for three files with the following footers:

> Lastname_Firstname_2G_Recreation_Center_Message
> Lastname_Firstname_2G_Recreation_Center_Contacts
> Lastname_Firstname_2G_Recreation_Center_Tasks

Desert Park, Arizona is opening a new downtown recreation center. Ray Hamilton, Desert Park's Director of Fine Arts and Parks, is coordinating the opening with other departments in the city government. You will manage his Contacts list and tasks for this project. You will import contacts, send an e-mail message to a contact, create a contact group, and create a To-Do List.

Start Outlook using your Firstname Lastname account. Configure the Send/Receive settings to place your e-mail messages in the Outbox instead of the Sent Items folder. Using the techniques you have practiced in this chapter, import o02G_Recreation_Center_Contacts into your Contacts folder. Using the Gloria French contact, create a new e-mail message to her, using a Plain Text message format. Type a subject for the message that briefly defines the purpose of the message, which is a request for assistance in publicizing the opening of the new recreation center.

For the text of the message, type a salutation of Gloria, followed by two paragraphs—an introductory paragraph describing the facility, and a second paragraph asking her for her help in publicizing the opening. End the text of the message with the name Ray, and then send the message. Display the Outbox and print the message in Memo Style with **Lastname_Firstname_2G_Recreation_Center_Message** as a left footer. Submit the end result to your instructor as directed.

Create a contact group with three names from the Contacts list. Display the Contacts list in a view that shows the contacts' details. Print the Contacts list in Card Style with **Lastname_Firstname_2G_Recreation_Center_Contacts** as a left footer. Submit the end result to your instructor as directed. Display the Contacts list in its default view.

Create a To-Do List with four tasks relating to the opening of the recreation center. Give all the tasks a due date within the next two weeks. Print the To-Do List in Table Style with **Lastname_Firstname_2G_Recreation_Center_Tasks** as a left footer. Submit the end result to your instructor as directed. Delete the contents of the Task folder, the Contacts folder, the Outbox folder, and the Deleted Items folder. Restore the Send/Receive options to their default settings. Reset the print styles used.

**End** **You have completed Project 2G** ————————————————

# Outcomes-Based Assessments

Apply a combination of the **2A** and **2B** skills.

## GO! Think | Project **2H** Visitor Center

### Project Files

For Project 2H, you will need the following file:

New blank contact form
New blank contact group form
New blank task form

You will print or create a PDF for two files with the following footers:

Lastname_Firstname_2H_Visitor_Center_Contacts
Lastname_Firstname_2H_Visitor_Center_Tasks

Gloria French, the Director of Public Information for the city of Desert Park, has hired consultants to assist in the remodeling of the city's Visitor Center. You will manage her Contacts list for the project and create two tasks. You will create new contacts and a contact group and organize the Contacts list.

Create three new contacts. Each of the three contacts works for the Desert Park design consulting firm of Oasis Designs, Inc. Create a Desert Park address for the company. All three contacts may have the same address and phone numbers. Create e-mail addresses for each contact using their first initial and last name followed by @oasisdesigns.com. Assign all three Oasis Designs contacts to a category, and rename that category with a more descriptive name. Create a contact group with the three contacts from Oasis Designs, Inc. Print the Contacts list in Card Style with no blank forms at the end and with a left footer **Lastname_Firstname_2H_Visitor_Center_Contacts** Submit the end result to your instructor as directed.

Create two tasks related to the remodeling of the Visitor Center. Set one task as a High priority, choose a due date, and mark the task as complete. For the second task, choose a due date and set the status as Waiting on someone else. Assign both tasks to a category named Visitor Center. Print the task list in Table Style with the left footer **Lastname_Firstname_2H_Visitor_Center_Tasks** Submit the end result to your instructor as directed.

Restore categories to their default color names. Delete the contents of the Contacts folder, the Tasks list, and the Deleted Items folder. Reset the print styles used.

**End** **You have completed Project 2H** ——————————————

# Using the Calendar

## OUTCOMES

At the end of this chapter you will be able to:

### PROJECT 3A
### Manage your work day.

## OBJECTIVES

Mastering these objectives will enable you to:

© iStockphoto/joe_potato

## In This Chapter

The Calendar is Outlook's tool for storing information about your schedule. Many people's workdays consist of meetings, appointments, and events. Each day can be divided into blocks of time, with different time slots reserved for activities. For each activity, you can record when, where, why, and with whom the activity occurs.

If your schedule contains many activities, keeping track of everything is a critical task. You may find that your job and your coworkers depend on your being organized and efficient in managing your schedule. Using Outlook's Calendar, you can schedule appointments, events, and meetings. You can use it to quickly and easily see the activities you have scheduled for the day, the week, the month, or longer. Used in conjunction with Outlook's other components, the Calendar can help you stay organized and productive.

About two-and-a-half hours outside Washington, D.C., the **Jefferson Inn** is located in Charlottesville, Virginia. The Inn's proximity to Washington, D.C. and Richmond, Virginia, makes it a popular weekend getaway for locals and a convenient base for out-of-town vacationers. The Inn offers 12 rooms, all individually decorated. A fresh country breakfast and afternoon tea are provided each day. Meeting rooms offering the latest high-tech amenities, such as high-speed Internet connections, have made the Inn an increasingly popular location for day-long corporate meetings and events.

# Project 3A Appointment Calendar

In Activities 3.01 through 3.17, you will create calendar entries related to activities and out-of-town trips for Carmen Jeffries, one of the co-owners of the Jefferson Inn. You will add appointments to her calendar. Some appointments will be recurring, and some will include reminders. You will make changes to scheduled appointments, moving them to different times or different days. You will work with events, scheduling annual events and multiple-day events. You will organize the calendar in different ways, using colors, fonts, and categories to differentiate calendar items. Upon completion, your calendar, for several time periods, will look similar to the ones shown in Figure 3.1.

## Project Files

For Project 3A, you will need the following files:

New blank Appointment form
New blank Event form

You will save your files as:

Lastname_Firstname_3A_Daily_Calendar.jpg
Lastname_Firstname_3A_Recurring_Appointment.jpg
Lastname_Firstname_3A_Edited_Appointment.jpg
Lastname_Firstname_3A_Weekly_Calendar.jpg
Lastname_Firstname_3A_Schedule_View.jpg
Lastname_Firstname_3A_Trifold_View.jpg

You will print or create a PDF for two files with the following footers:

Lastname_Firstname_3A_Weekly_Plans
Lastname_Firstname_3A_Breakfast_Meeting

## Project Results

**Figure 3.1**
Project 3A Appointment Calendar

# Objective 1 | Navigate the Calendar

The ***Calendar*** component of Outlook stores your schedule and calendar-related information. The default location for Outlook's calendar information is the Calendar folder. To add an item to your calendar, display the folder by clicking the Calendar button in the Navigation Pane or by clicking the Calendar folder in the folder list. You can also create other calendar folders as subfolders of the Calendar folder in the folder list.

---

**Alert!** | **Starting Project 3A**

Because Outlook stores information on the hard drive of the computer at which you are working, it is recommended that you complete Project 3A in one working session. Allow approximately two hours. If possible, use the same computer that you used when you created the Windows 7 user account in previous chapters. If you cannot use the same computer or if the Windows 7 user account that you previously created was deleted, refer to Chapter 1, Activities 1.01 and 1.02 to setup the Windows 7 user account and to configure Microsoft Outlook 2010.

---

## Activity 3.01 | Exploring the Calendar

In this activity, you will use the Navigation Pane and the Date Navigator to explore the calendar. These are the main tools you will use to manage the calendar activities of Carmen Jeffries, one of the co-owners of the Jefferson Inn.

**1** Click the **Start** button, and then point to the **Shut down button arrow**. On the **Shut down menu**, click **Switch user** to display the **Windows 7** desktop. Click the user account you created in Chapter 1. If the account does not exist, refer to the Alert at the beginning of this Activity to set up the account.

**2** Start **Outlook**. If the Navigation Pane is not displayed, on the View tab, in the Layout group, click the Navigation Pane button, and then click Normal. At the bottom of the **Navigation Pane**, click the **Calendar** button. Compare your screen with Figure 3.2.

On the right side of the screen is the ***appointment area***, a one-day view of the current day's calendar entries. An ***appointment*** is a calendar activity occurring at a specific time and day that does not require inviting people or reservations. The ***Time Bar*** displays one-hour time increments. The upper pane of the Navigation Pane is the ***Date Navigator***, a monthly view of the calendar used to display specific days in a month. The highlighted date in the Date Navigator and at the top of the appointment area is the date that you are viewing, which is, by default, the current date. On each side of the appointment area are buttons, Previous Appointment and Next Appointment, which allow quick movement to one's previous appointment or next appointment, respectively. Below the appointment area is the Task pane, a pane that can be used to schedule tasks or display tasks currently due, depending on screen resolution.

**Figure 3.2**

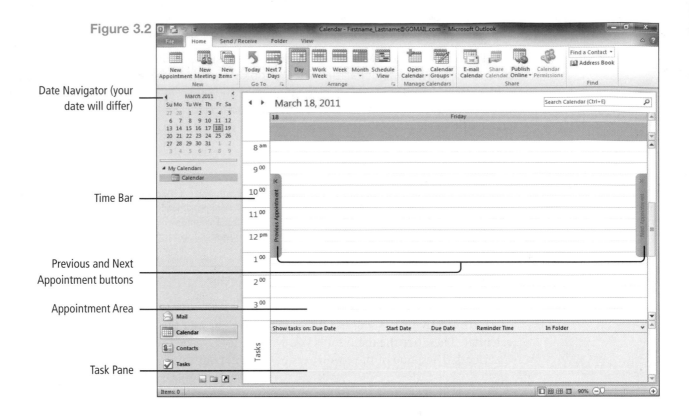

Date Navigator (your date will differ)

Time Bar

Previous and Next Appointment buttons

Appointment Area

Task Pane

---

**Alert! | Does your screen differ?**

The time range for your appointment area may differ from Figure 3.2. Larger computer screens and screens with a higher resolution may display a much larger time span. Your Date Navigator may also display two or three months instead of one. Clicking the arrows to move forward and backward in the Date Navigator displays different months based on what you click.

---

**3** In the **Navigation Pane**, in the **Date Navigator**, click a different day of the month.

The date displayed in the appointment area changes to the day of the month you selected in the Date Navigator. In the Date Navigator, the current date remains outlined in red, and the selected date is highlighted.

**4** In the **Date Navigator**, click the **left arrow** next to the month name.

The Date Navigator displays the past month. The appointment area adjusts to the same day in the past month.

**5** In the **Date Navigator**, click the **right arrow** several times, moving forward in the calendar two or three months.

The Date Navigator displays future months, and the appointment area adjusts to the same day in the future month.

**6** On the **Home tab**, in the **Arrange group**, click the **Week** button, and then click the **Work Week** button.

The *Work Week view* option shows only the weekdays, Monday through Friday, instead of the full seven-day week that is displayed in the *Week view*.

**7** On the **Home tab**, in the **Arrange group**, click the arrow below the **Month** button. This view provides three levels of detail: *Low*, *Medium*, and *High*.

A *Low* level of detail only displays all day events in the monthly view. A *Medium* level of detail displays lines on the calendar where appointments are set for the month. If a *High* level of detail is displayed, then a number of appointments can be viewed on the monthly calendar. The number of appointments may be restricted depending on screen resolution.

**8** On the **Home tab**, in the **Go To group**, click the **Today** button to return to the current day, and then in the **Arrange group**, click the **Day** button to return to Day view.

**9** In the appointment area, click a different time in the calendar grid, and then notice that the **Time Bar** displays an orange line across the current time. Compare your screen with Figure 3.3.

Use the scroll bar to adjust the times displayed in the appointment area.

Figure 3.3

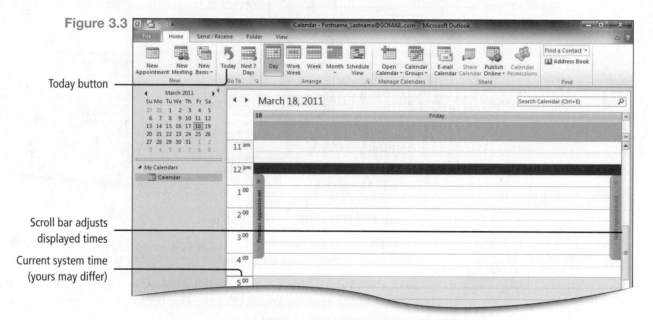

Today button

Scroll bar adjusts
displayed times

Current system time
(yours may differ)

**10** In the appointment area, drag the **scroll box** up and down to display different times of day.

Outlook displays the normal workday hours by default, but you can schedule and view appointments in any time period.

## Activity 3.02 | Creating a Personal Calendar Folder

You can create subfolders within the Calendar folder for separate calendar activities. For example, a separate calendar can be maintained for shared spaces, such as a conference room, or for separating personal calendar items and work-related calendar items. Creating a personal calendar can be especially useful in organizations where business calendars are shared, and you want to keep your personal activities private. In this activity, you will create a separate subfolder for personal calendar items and name the subfolder *Personal Calendar*. You will use this for personal calendar items you create for Carmen Jeffries.

**1** In the lower right area of the **Navigation Pane**, click the **Folder List** button ▦ to display the folder list in the middle portion of the **Navigation Pane**. On the **Folder tab**, in the **New group**, click the **New Calendar** button.

Another Way

**Another Way**
To display a new calendar, right-click *Calendar* in the Navigation Pane, and then click New Calendar

**2** In the displayed **Create New Folder** dialog box, in the **Name** box, type **Personal Calendar** and then compare your screen with Figure 3.4.

The *Folder contains* box shows that this folder will contain Calendar Items. Outlook applies this setting because you are creating this as a subfolder in the Calendar folder.

Figure 3.4

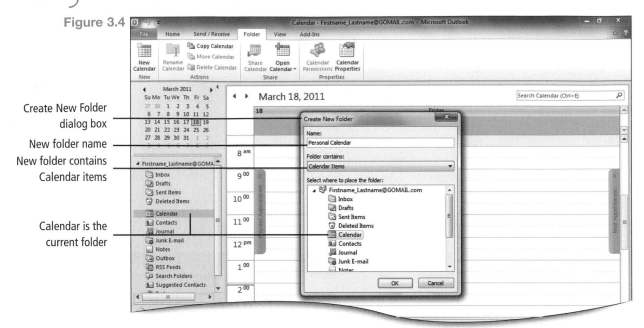

Create New Folder dialog box

New folder name

New folder contains Calendar items

Calendar is the current folder

**3** In the **Create New Folder** dialog box, click **OK**.

Outlook creates a folder named *Personal Calendar*. The collapse button next to the Calendar folder indicates that the new folder is a subfolder of the Calendar folder.

**4** In the **Navigation Pane** folder list, click **Personal Calendar**, and then, if necessary, on the Home tab, in the Arrange group, click the Day button to return to Day view. Compare your screen with Figure 3.5.

The Personal Calendar becomes the current folder. Outlook changes the color scheme for the Personal Calendar appointment area to distinguish it from other Calendar folders.

Figure 3.5

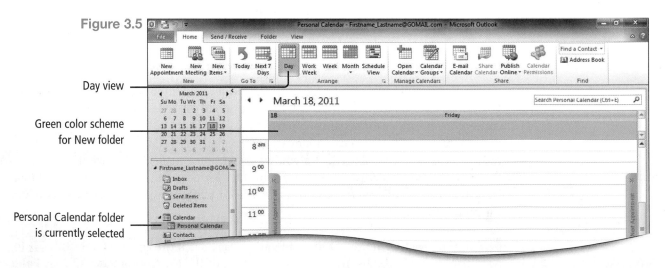

Day view

Green color scheme for New folder

Personal Calendar folder is currently selected

**5** In the **Navigation Pane** folder list, click the **Calendar** folder.

The Calendar folder becomes the current folder, and the color of the appointment area reminds you that this is the default calendar.

**6** In the lower part of the **Navigation Pane**, click the **Calendar** button.

The Navigation Pane switches to a two-pane view above the buttons. Under *My Calendars* two entries display: *Calendar* and *Personal Calendar*. The currently selected folder is the *Calendar* folder.

**7** In the **Navigation Pane**, under **My Calendars**, click the **Personal Calendar** check box, and then compare your screen with Figure 3.6.

The appointment area splits into two sections, showing both the *Calendar* and *Personal Calendar* folders. If you use more than one calendar, you can display both at the same time.

**Figure 3.6**

Personal Calendar displays on the right

Default Calendar displays on the left

Both calendars selected

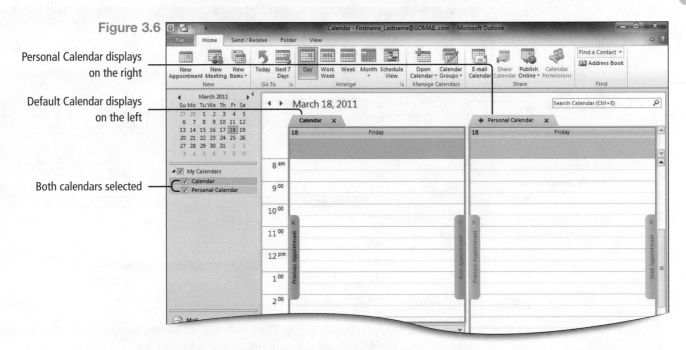

**8** In the **Navigation Pane**, clear the **Calendar** check box to display only the Personal Calendar.

## Objective 2 | Schedule Appointments

Recall that an appointment occurs at a specific time and day and does not require inviting other people or reserving a room or equipment. For example, meeting with a coworker or supervisor could be considered an appointment. Some appointments are *recurring appointments*, meaning that they occur regularly on specific dates and times and at specific intervals and have associated reminders, such as a weekly staff meeting. Outlook uses the term *meeting* to refer to a calendar activity that requires inviting other people, reserving a room, or ordering equipment. As you progress in your study of Outlook, you will practice scheduling meetings.

## Activity 3.03 | Adding Appointments in the Appointment Area

You can create a new appointment directly in the calendar by typing it in a blank time slot in the appointment area. In this activity, you will schedule appointments in the Personal Calendar for Carmen Jeffries, Jefferson Inn co-owner.

**1** In the **Date Navigator**, click the **right arrow** one time, advancing the calendar to the next month. Click the **Monday** of the first full week of the displayed month.

> The selected date displays at the top of the appointment area.

**2** In the appointment area, click the **11:00 am** time slot, type **Weekly meeting with Bradley** and notice that as you type, the time slot displays green shading surrounded by a black border. Compare your screen with Figure 3.7.

Figure 3.7

Currently selected day (your date will differ)

Personal Calendar is the current calendar

Time slot displays with green shading, black border displays as you type

**3** Click any other time slot in the appointment area.

> The appointment is scheduled from 11:00 to 11:30. When you use this method to enter an appointment, the default appointment timeframe is 30 minutes.

**4** In the appointment area, click the **12:30** pm time slot—that is, the lower half of the 12:00 pm time slot—to enter an appointment on the half hour.

**5** Type **Lunch with Marty** Click any other time slot in the appointment area, and then compare your screen with Figure 3.8.

> The appointment is scheduled from 12:30 to 1:00. Notice that the day number of a date in the Date Navigator changes to bold when an appointment is scheduled on that day.

Figure 3.8

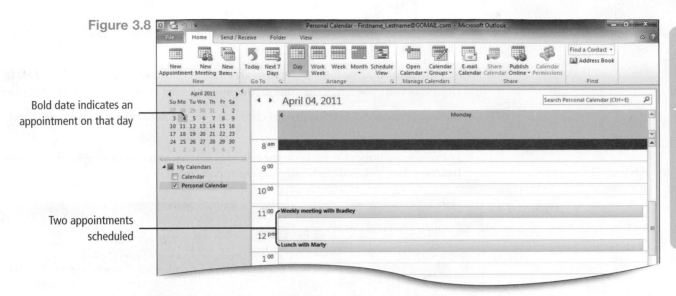

Bold date indicates an
appointment on that day

Two appointments
scheduled

## Activity 3.04 | Adding Appointments by Using the Appointment Form

In addition to typing directly into the appointment area, you can use an Appointment form to create new appointments. By using an Appointment form, you can enter more detailed information about an appointment. In this activity, you will schedule appointments for Carmen Jeffries using the Appointment form.

**1** On the **Home tab**, in the **New group**, click the **New Appointment** button, and then compare your screen with Figure 3.9.

The Untitled - Appointment form displays. You can store a variety of information about an appointment, including its subject, location, starting time, and ending time. Notice that the starting and ending times for the new appointment default to the time you clicked in the appointment area. A *comments area* in the lower half of the form enables you to enter information about the appointment not otherwise specified in the form.

Figure 3.9

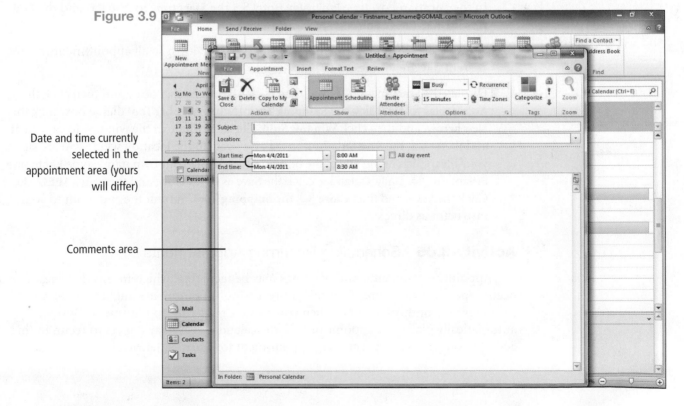

Date and time currently
selected in the
appointment area (yours
will differ)

Comments area

2 As the **Subject** of the appointment, type **Meet with Dominique** In the **Location** box, type **My office**

3 In the right **Start time** box, click the **time arrow**, and then locate and click **9:00 AM**. In the right **End time** box, click the **time arrow**, and then locate and click **10:00 AM (1 hour)**.

4 On the Ribbon, in the **Actions group**, click the **Save & Close** button, and then compare your screen with Figure 3.10.

The new appointment is added to the calendar. The appointment occupies the 9:00 to 10:00 am time slot, and the location of the appointment displays below the subject.

Figure 3.10

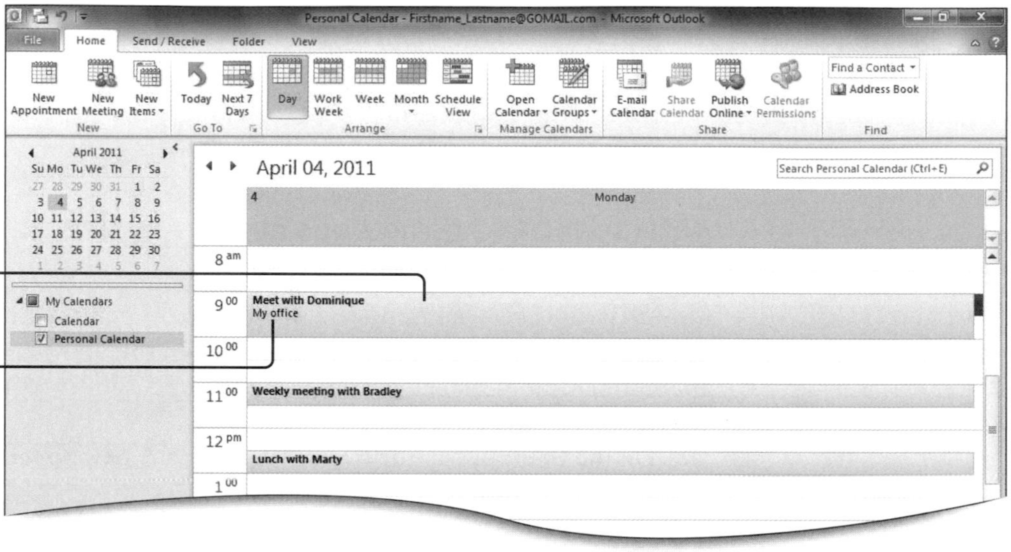


One hour appointment scheduled

Appointment location displays below subject

**Another Way**

To display an Appointment form, press Ctrl + N, or, right-click on a time slot, and then click New Appointment.

5 On the **Home tab**, in the **New group**, click the **New Appointment** button.

6 In the **Appointment** form, in the **Subject** box, type **Chamber of Commerce Orientation** In the **Location** box, type **Wellesley Hotel** Set the **Start time** to **2:30 PM** and the **End time** to **4:30 PM (2 hours)**.

7 **Save & Close** the appointment. If necessary, scroll down so all appointments for the current day are visible.

8 Display the **Start** menu, and then click **All Programs**. Locate and then click the **Accessories** folder. Click the **Snipping Tool**. In the **Snipping Tool** dialog box, click the **New arrow**, and then click **Window Snip**. Click anywhere in the window to capture it, and then click the **Save Snip** button. Navigate to the location where you are storing your files. Click in the **File name** box, and then using your own name, type **Lastname_Firstname 3A_Daily_Calendar** Click the **Save as type arrow**, and then click **JPEG file**. Click the **Save**, and then **Close** the **Snipping Tool**. Submit the end result to your instructor as directed.

## Activity 3.05 | Scheduling Recurring Appointments

Appointments, events, and meetings may be recurring, which means that these items occur repeatedly over time. Examples of recurring appointments might be weekly staff meetings or monthly haircuts. When you create a recurring appointment, Outlook automatically places the appointment in the calendar every day it is set to recur. In this activity, you will create a recurring appointment for Carmen Jeffries.

**1** In the **Date Navigator**, click the **Tuesday** of the week in which you are scheduling appointments, and then, on the **Home tab**, in the **New group**, click the **New Appointment** button to display a blank Appointment form. Alternatively, double-click a blank time slot in the appointment area.

**2** In the **Subject** box, type **Travel & Lodging Technology Seminar** and in the **Location** box, type **Richmond** Set the **Start time** for **9:00 AM** and the **End time** for **12:00 PM** (**3 hours**).

> **Another Way**
>
> To create a new, recurring appointment, right-click any blank time slot in the appointment area and, from the displayed shortcut menu, click New Recurring Appointment.

**3** On the Ribbon, in the **Options group**, click the **Recurrence** button.

> The Appointment Recurrence dialog box displays. You can set the *recurrence pattern*—the frequency—of an appointment, which may be daily, weekly, monthly, or yearly. You can also set the *range of recurrence*, which is the date of the final occurrence of the appointment based on its end date or the number of times an appointment occurs.

**4** In the **Appointment Recurrence** dialog box, under **Recurrence pattern**, select **Weekly**. In the box to the right of **Recur every**, type **2** and then select the **Tuesday** check box if it is not already selected. Under **Range of recurrence**, click to select the **End after** option, and then press [Tab] so that the number in the **occurrences** box is selected. Type **3** and then compare your screen with Figure 3.11.

> The recurrence is set for every two weeks, for three occurrences.

**Figure 3.11**

Appointment Recurrence dialog box

Recurrence patterns sets frequency of appointment

Range of recurrence sets the end of the recurring appointment

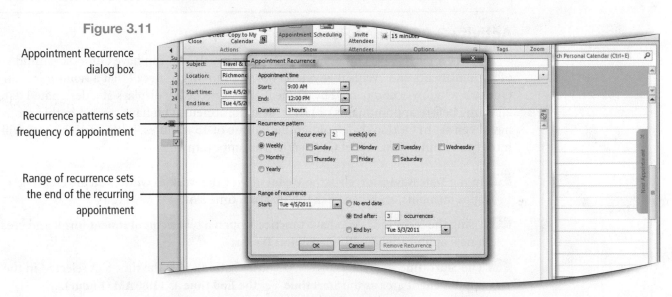

**5** Click **OK** to redisplay the Appointment form.

> The Start time and End time boxes have been replaced by Recurrence information. The appointment is set to repeat every two weeks.

**6** Display the **Start** menu ⊙, and open the **Snipping Tool**. Click the **New arrow**, and then click **Window Snip**. Click in the appointment window to capture it, and then click the **Save Snip** button 🔲. Navigate to your storage device. Click in the **File name** box, and then using your own name, type **Lastname_Firstname_3A_Recurring_ Appointment** Click the **Save as type arrow**, and then click **JPEG file**. Click **Save**. **Close** ⊠ the **Snipping Tool**. Submit the end result to your instructor as directed.

**7** **Save & Close** the appointment, and then compare your screen with Figure 3.12.

> The new appointment is added to the calendar. The recurrence icon in the lower right corner of the appointment in the calendar indicates that this is a recurring appointment. The Date Navigator for the day displays in bold, indicating that this date has an appointment scheduled. The days on which the appointment repeats also display in bold.

Figure 3.12

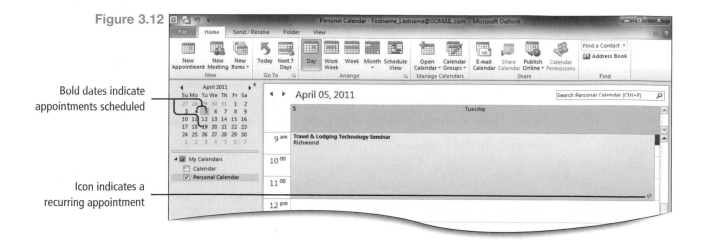

Bold dates indicate appointments scheduled

Icon indicates a recurring appointment

> **More Knowledge | Removing or Changing Appointment Recurrence**
>
> If you need to change or remove an appointment's recurrence information, open the appointment by double-clicking one of its occurrences in the appointment area. Select *Open the series* and then click OK. In the Appointment form, click the Recurrence button to display the Appointment Recurrence dialog box. Change the recurrence pattern or the range of recurrence. Click Remove Recurrence to remove all the recurrence information.

## Activity 3.06 | Using Reminders

Just as you can have Outlook remind you of a task, you can have Outlook remind you of appointments and events that you do not want to forget. Recall that a **reminder** is an Outlook window accompanied by a tone that automatically displays at a designated date and time before appointments or tasks. All appointments you have created in this project have been set to Outlook's default reminder time of 15 minutes. In this activity, you will modify a reminder for one of Carmen Jeffries' appointments.

**1** In the **Date Navigator**, click the **Wednesday** of the week in which you are creating appointments, and then click the **10:00 am** time slot.

**2** Using the techniques you have practiced, open a blank **Appointment** form, and create a new appointment with the **Subject Dentist**

**3** The Start time is already correct, because Outlook uses the time slot selected in the appointment area as the **Start time**. Set the **End time** as **11:00 AM (1 hour)**.

**4** On the **Appointment tab**, in the **Options group**, click the **Reminder arrow** 🔔, and then click **30 minutes**. Compare your screen with Figure 3.13.

Figure 3.13

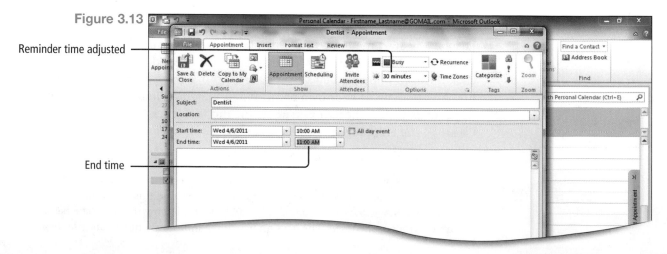

Reminder time adjusted

End time

**5** **Save & Close** the appointment.

The new appointment is added to the calendar.

---

**More Knowledge | Default Reminder Setting**

When you are working in the Calendar folder, the Reminder box is automatically set to 15 minutes for all new appointments, including appointments you type directly in the appointment area. You can change this default setting. From the Backstage view, click Options. On the left side, click Calendar, and then under Calendar options, clear the Default reminders check box so that reminders are not automatically created. You can also modify the default time with the Default reminders check box selected.

---

## Objective 3 | Edit Appointments

After you schedule an appointment, you may need to change the time, location, or other details. You can edit appointments similarly to any other Outlook item. One way to change an appointment's date or time is by dragging it to a new location. You can also open calendar items and edit them directly in the Appointment form.

### Activity 3.07 | Editing an Appointment in the Appointment Area

In this activity, you will change some of the appointments in Carmen Jeffries' calendar.

**1** In the **Date Navigator**, click the **Monday** of the week in which you are working. Click the **2:00 pm** time slot. On the right side of the appointment area, click the **down scroll arrow** until the **Meet with Dominique** appointment moves out of the viewing area, as shown in Figure 3.14.

Depending on the size of your screen and the screen resolution, some appointments may not appear in your viewing area. If that is the case, at the top right of the appointment area, a small gray arrow displays above 10:00 am in the appointment area, indicating that an appointment is scheduled that does not appear in the viewing area. When you point to the arrow it changes to yellow and a ScreenTip appears: *Click for more appointments.* A similar arrow will display at the bottom of the appointment area when later appointments are not visible in the viewing area.

Figure 3.14

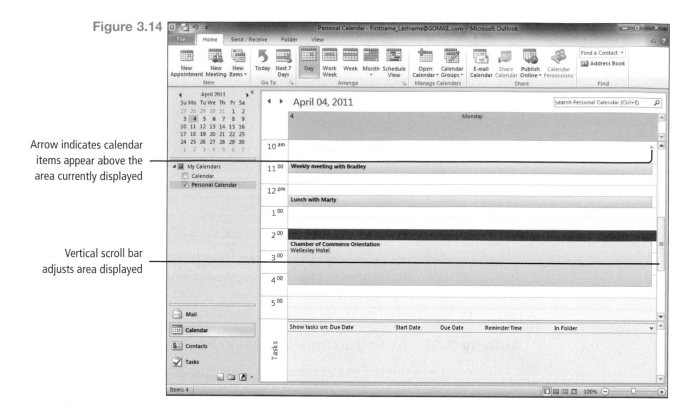

Arrow indicates calendar items appear above the area currently displayed

Vertical scroll bar adjusts area displayed

**2** Click the **up scroll arrow** until the **Chamber of Commerce Orientation** appointment moves out of the viewing area, if possible.

Depending on the size and resolution of your screen, at the bottom right of the appointment area, the gray arrow displays to indicate that some appointments are out of view.

**3** Click the **down scroll arrow** until your viewing area contains the appointment times beginning at 8:00 am. In the appointment area, click the **Lunch with Marty** appointment to select it.

The appointment is outlined by a ***black border***, which is the indication that an appointment is selected.

**4** Point to the top border so that the vertical resize pointer ⬍ displays, and then compare your screen with Figure 3.15.

You can increase or decrease the specified time of an appointment by dragging the upper and lower borders.

Figure 3.15

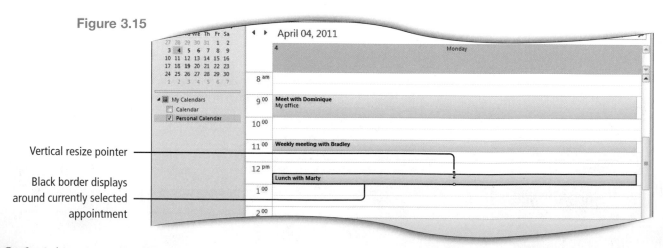

Vertical resize pointer

Black border displays around currently selected appointment

**5** With the vertical resize pointer displayed, drag the upper border of the selected appointment up to **12:00 pm**, and then release the mouse button.

The appointment is now scheduled to last from 12:00 to 1:00 pm.

**6** Click the **Meet with Dominique** appointment one time to select it. To edit this appointment, click at the beginning of the subject text.

The blinking insertion point indicates that the subject can be edited. Although the Location displays below the Subject, it cannot be modified. You can change the Location of an appointment only when editing it in the Appointment form.

**7** Press ⌈Del⌉ until all the existing text of the subject is deleted, and then type **Dominique's performance review** Press ⌈Enter⌉, or click a blank time slot in the appointment area to end the editing of the appointment.

## Activity 3.08 | Moving Appointments

In this activity, you will move some of Carmen Jeffries' appointments to different dates and times.

**1** In the **Monday** of the week in which you are working, click the **Weekly meeting with Bradley** appointment to select it.

**2** Point to the selected appointment, hold down the left mouse button, and then drag the appointment down so that the Move pointer ⌈image⌉ displays with the appointment attached, as shown in Figure 3.16.

You can drag an appointment to a new day or time.

Figure 3.16

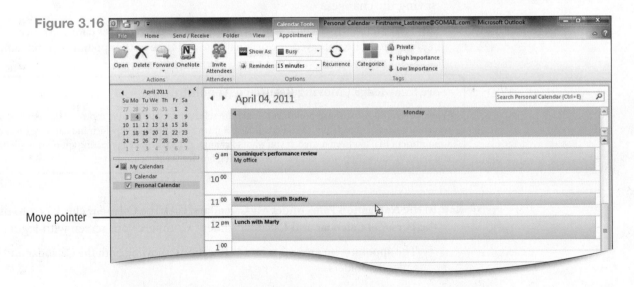

Move pointer

**3** Drag the appointment to the **1:30 pm** time slot, and then release the mouse button.

The *Weekly meeting with Bradley* appointment is scheduled for 1:30 to 2:00.

**4** Click the **Weekly meeting with Bradley** appointment again. Drag the selected appointment to the **Date Navigator**, and position the insertion point over the **Wednesday** of the week in which you are working. Release the mouse button.

The calendar displays Wednesday of that week, with the *Weekly meeting with Bradley* appointment scheduled for 1:30 to 2:00 pm on that day. When you move an appointment to a different day, Outlook uses the same time slot of the new day. If the time slot is already occupied by another appointment, Outlook displays the two appointments side by side in the calendar.

**5** In the **Date Navigator**, click the **Monday** of the week in which you are working, and then double-click the **Chamber of Commerce Orientation** appointment to open the Appointment form.

**6** In the left **Start time** box, click the **date arrow**. Click the **right arrow** beside the month name to advance the calendar one month ahead of the month in which you are working, and then compare your screen with Figure 3.17.

Figure 3.17

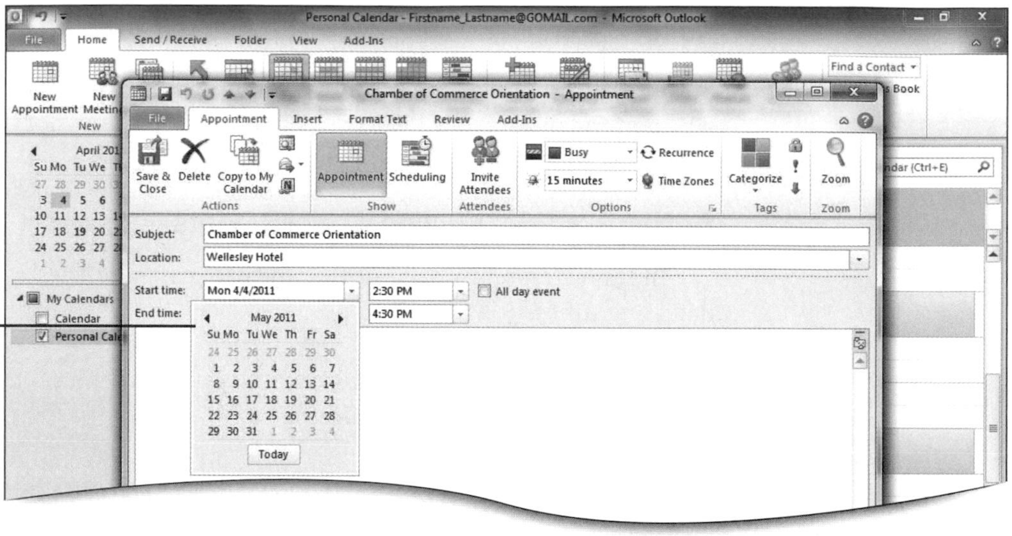

Calendar displays the month following the one in which you are working (your dates will vary)

**7** In the next month, click the first **Monday. Close** ⊠ the Appointment form without saving the changes.

You can use the calendar to drag an appointment to another date. In this case, because the changes were not saved, the original date and time of the appointment remain.

---

**More Knowledge** | **Moving Recurring Appointments**

When you move recurring appointments, only the selected appointment is moved. The item will still show a recurrence icon next to it, but the icon will have a line drawn through it, which indicates that it is a recurring appointment that has been moved. If you want to change all instances of a recurring appointment's date or time, you must open the Appointment Recurrence dialog box for the appointment.

---

**8** In the **Navigation Pane**, under **My Calendars**, click the **Calendar** check box to display both the **Personal Calendar** and **Calendar** folders. Compare your screen with Figure 3.18.

The appointment area splits into two sections, showing both the Calendar and Personal Calendar folders.

Figure 3.18

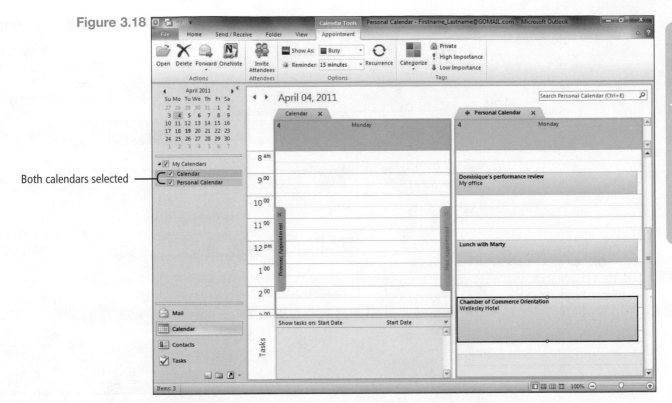

Both calendars selected

**9** Click the **Chamber of Commerce Orientation** appointment to select it, and then drag the appointment from the **Personal Calendar** folder to the same day and time in the **Calendar** folder.

> Notice that after the drag operation is complete, the appointment is copied from its *Personal Calendar* location and appears in the *Calendar* folder in the 2:30 pm time slot.

**10** In the **Personal Calendar** folder, click the **Chamber of Commerce Orientation** appointment to select it. On the **Appointment tab**, in the **Actions group**, click the **Delete** button.

> The appointment is removed from the Personal Calendar folder.

**11** On the **View tab**, in the **Arrangement group**, click the **Overlay** button, and then compare your screen to Figure 3.19.

> The *Personal Calendar* displays on top of the *Calendar*, with all appointments visible. You can use *Overlay mode* to display multiple calendars in an overlapping view. Using this mode enables you to view conflicts and free time.

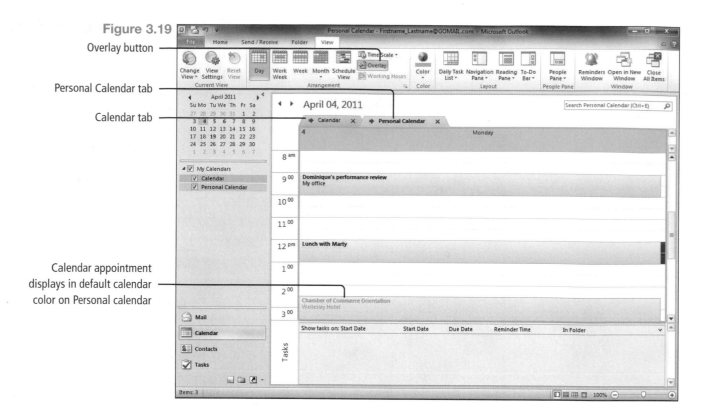

Figure 3.19

Overlay button

Personal Calendar tab

Calendar tab

Calendar appointment
displays in default calendar
color on Personal calendar

**12** On the **View tab**, in the **Arrangement group**, click the **Overlay** button to return to the previous view.

> The Overlay button is a *toggle* button—the same button is used to turn the feature on and off.

**13** In the **Navigation Pane**, under **My Calendars**, clear the **Calendar** check box to display only the **Personal Calendar** folder.

> **More Knowledge** | Using Calendar Groups
>
> If you have a group of calendars that you look at together, you can create a Calendar Group to see the combined schedules at once, as long as you are using an Exchange server account. This is helpful when planning appointments or activities with coworkers, family, or even a physical space such as a conference room. To create a Calendar Group, from the Home tab, in the Manage Calendars group, click Calendar Groups, and then click Create New Calendar Group. Once you give the group a name, you can choose contacts to add to the group. You can also view the group of calendars in Outlook and then save them as a Calendar Group.

## Activity 3.09 | Opening an Appointment

You can edit an existing appointment by opening it and changing the information in the Appointment form. In this activity, you will open several of Carmen Jeffries' appointments and make changes.

**1** In the **Date Navigator**, click the **Wednesday** of the week in which you have been working, and then click the **Dentist** appointment to select it. On the **Appointment tab**, in the **Actions group**, click the **Open** button.

**2** Change the **Start time** to **9:00 AM**, and notice that the **End time** changes to **10:00 AM**.

**3** On the **Appointment tab**, in the **Options group**, click the **Reminder arrow** 🔔 and then select **1 hour**.

**4** In the comments area of the **Appointment** form, type **Remember to get directions to the new office location** and then compare your screen with Figure 3.20.

Use the comments area of the form to record details about an appointment.

Figure 3.20

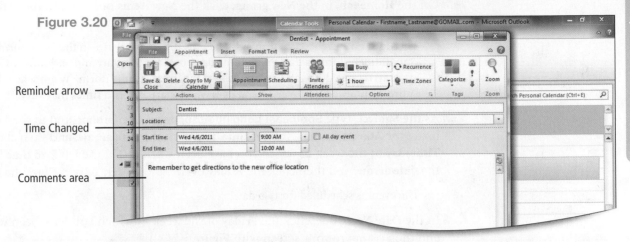

Reminder arrow

Time Changed

Comments area

**5** **Save & Close** the appointment. Double-click the **Weekly meeting with Bradley** appointment to open the Appointment form.

**6** In the **Appointment** form, change the **End time** to **2:30 PM (1 hour)**, and notice that the **Start time** did not change.

**7** Click the **Location arrow**, and then click **My office**.

Outlook remembers locations you type in the Locations box after you have entered them once. Instead of typing a previously used location, you can click the Location box arrow to display the list of past locations, and then select the one you need.

**8** In the comments area of the **Appointment** form, type **Print out next month's conference schedule for his review**

**9** Click the **Start** button, and open the **Snipping Tool**. Click the **New arrow**, and then click **Window Snip**. Click in the window to capture it, and then click the **Save Snip** button 🖫. Navigate to your storage device. Click in the **File name** box, and then using your own name, type **Lastname_Firstname_3A_Edited_Appointment** Click the **Save as type arrow**, and then click **JPEG file**. Click **Save** and then **Close** ☒ the **Snipping Tool**. Submit the end result to your instructor as directed.

**10** **Save & Close** the appointment.

---

**More Knowledge | Opening Multiple Appointments at Once**

You can open more than one appointment at a time. Select the first appointment, press Ctrl, and then select the additional appointments you want to open. After selecting all the appointments, right-click any selected appointment. From the displayed shortcut menu, click Open. An Appointment form for each selected appointment displays. You can then make changes to each appointment. For example, you might do this if you wanted to remove the Reminder for all the selected appointments.

---

## Objective 4 | Work with Events

Outlook defines any calendar activity that lasts 24 hours or longer as an ***event***. Rather than displaying as blocks of time in your calendar, events are indicated by a banner across the top of the appointment area on days in which they occur. For example, attending a conference for one or more days is indicated as an event in Outlook.

## Activity 3.10 | Scheduling Events

In this activity, you will schedule some events for Carmen Jeffries.

**1** On the **Home tab**, in the **New group**, click the **New Items** button, and then click **All Day Event**.

The Untitled - Event form displays. The only difference between the Event form and the Appointment form is that the time-of-day boxes for the start and end times of an event are grayed out. Although you can change the times, events normally are scheduled for an entire 24-hour day, or over several days where start and end times may vary.

**2** As the **Subject**, type **Southeast Lodging Association Conference** and in the **Location** box, type **Atlanta** In the left **Start time** box, click the **date arrow**, and then click the **Thursday** of the week in which you have been working. In the left **End time** box, click the **date arrow**, and then click the **Friday** of the same week. **Save & Close** the event.

The event is scheduled for two days.

**3** In the **Date Navigator**, click the **Friday** of the week in which you have been working, and then compare your screen with Figure 3.21.

The banner across the top of the calendar displays the event information. Notice in the Date Navigator that the two days of the event are *not* shown in bold. Outlook still considers these days as free because no specific time slots are occupied.

Figure 3.21

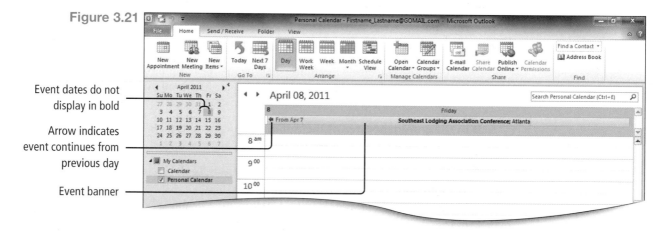

Event dates do not display in bold

Arrow indicates event continues from previous day

Event banner

**4** With **Friday** still displayed in the calendar, create a **New Appointment** using the techniques you have practiced. For the **Subject**, type **Breakfast at the conference with John McCarthy & Sonia Friedman** In the **Location** box, type **TBA** The **Start time** is **8:30 AM**, and the **End time** is **9:30 AM**.

*TBA* is a common abbreviation for To Be Arranged or To Be Announced.

**5** In the comments area of the appointment form, type **Call Sonia and John at hotel to arrange location Save & Close** the appointment.

The calendar redisplays. You can schedule appointments at the same time as events.

**6** Double-click the event banner to display the event form. In the comments area of the **Event** form, type **Breakfast with John McCarthy and Sonia Friedman on Friday morning Save & Close** the event.

> **More Knowledge | Converting Appointments and Events**
>
> You can change appointments into events and events into appointments. On both the Appointment form and the Event form, you can select or clear the All day event check box to convert the activity. The start times are added to an event to make it an appointment, the banner is then removed, and the activity displays in the specified time slot. When you convert an appointment to an event, the times are removed and only the dates remain; a banner displays in the calendar.

## Activity 3.11 | Scheduling an Annual Event

An *annual event* is a recurring event that happens once each year. Birthdays, anniversaries, or holidays are examples of annual events.

**1** In the **Date Navigator**, click the **Tuesday** in the week in which you have been working. On the **Home tab**, in the **New group**, click the **New Items** button, and then click **All Day Event**.

**2** In the **Subject** box, type **Elaine's birthday** On the **Event tab**, in the **Options group**, click the **Recurrence** button.

**3** In the displayed **Appointment Recurrence** dialog box, under **Recurrence pattern**, click **Yearly**. Compare your screen with Figure 3.22.

The default setting for the Range of recurrence is for the event to start on the currently selected day in the Date Navigator, and to never end—*No end date* is selected.

**Figure 3.22**

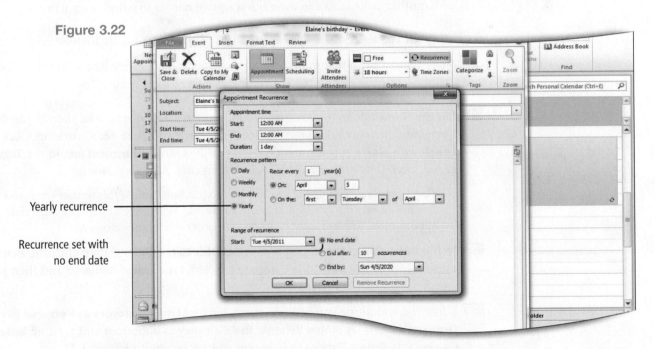

Yearly recurrence

Recurrence set with no end date

**4** Click **OK**, and then **Save & Close** the event.

A banner for the birthday displays in the calendar. A recurrence icon indicates that it is a recurring event. The event is set to display on this date with no end date.

**5** On the **Home tab**, in the **Arrange group**, click the **Work Week** button to display Monday-Friday of the week you have been working in.

**6** Click the **Start** button, and then open the **Snipping Tool**. Click the **New arrow**, and then click **Window Snip**. Click in the window to capture it, and then click the **Save Snip** button 🔲. Navigate to your storage device. Click in the **File name** box, and then using your own name, type **Lastname_Firstname_3A_Weekly_Calendar** Click the **Save as type arrow**, and then click **JPEG file**. Click **Save**, and then **Close** ❎ the **Snipping Tool**. Submit the end result to your instructor as directed.

> **More Knowledge** | **Displaying Holidays**
>
> To display holidays in the calendar, from Backstage view, click Options, and then on the left side of the Outlook Options dialog box, click Calendar. Under Calendar options, click the Add Holidays button. Select the check box next to each country/region whose holidays you want to add to your calendar, and then click OK. By default, your own country/region is automatically selected. In the Microsoft Outlook dialog box, click OK when notified that the holidays were added to your Calendar. Click OK to close the Options dialog box.

## Objective 5 | Organize and Customize the Calendar

Outlook provides a variety of useful ways to organize your calendar activities. Similar to other Outlook items, you can assign color categories to calendar activities. For example, must-attend appointments can be assigned one color, while personal activities can be assigned another color. You can assign descriptive names to color categories.

### Activity 3.12 | Assigning Descriptive Names to Categories

Recall that you can rename color categories with descriptive labels. In this activity you will assign descriptive names to particular color categories.

**1** On the **Home tab**, in the **Arrange group**, click the **Day** button, and then in the **Date Navigator**, click on **Monday** of the week in which you have been working. Click the **Lunch with Marty** appointment to select it. On the **Appointment tab**, in the **Tags group**, click the **Categorize** button, and then click **All Categories**.

> The *Color Categories* dialog box displays. Recall, you can use this option when you want to rename an existing category or create a new one. When working in Calendar view, an appointment or event must be selected in order to rename categories.

**2** In the **Color Categories** dialog box, select **Blue Category**, and then click the **Rename** button. In the box with **Blue Category** selected, type **Travel Required** and then press [Enter].

**3** Using the technique you just practiced, rename **Green Category** as **Personal** Rename **Orange Category** as **Status** Rename **Red Category** as **Important** and rename **Yellow Category** as **Time & Expenses** Compare your screen with Figure 3.23.

Figure 3.23

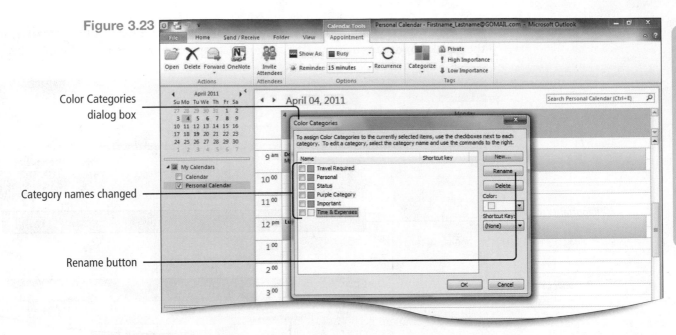

Color Categories dialog box

Category names changed

Rename button

**4** Click **OK** to close the **Color Categories** dialog box.

---

**More Knowledge | Adding Descriptive Names without Color**

You can create new categories that do not use color. In the Color Categories dialog box, click the New button. In the Add New Category dialog box, in the Name box, type a descriptive name. Click the Color box arrow and click None. Click OK two times to close the dialog boxes.

---

## Activity 3.13 | Assigning Categories to Appointments

Calendar entries can be assigned to categories in the Appointment or Event forms or by using the shortcut menu. Carmen Jeffries organizes her calendar items using categories. In the following activity, you will assign categories to activities in her calendar.

**1** Open the **Lunch with Marty** appointment. On the **Appointment tab**, in the **Tags group**, click **Categorize**, and then click **Personal**. Compare your screen with Figure 3.24.

The appointment is assigned to the Personal category.

Figure 3.24

*Personal* category assigned

**2** **Save & Close** the appointment.

**3** Right-click the **Dominique's performance review** appointment, point to **Categorize**, and then click **Important** to assign this category. Compare your screen with Figure 3.25.

Figure 3.25

*Important* category assigned

*Personal* category assigned

**4** In the **Date Navigator**, click the **Tuesday** of the week in which you have been working, and then select the **Travel & Lodging Technology Seminar** appointment. On the **Appointment Series tab**, in the **Tags group**, click **Categorize**, and then click the **Time & Expenses** category.

> Carmen Jeffries assigns the Time & Expenses category to appointments in which she will be incurring business expenses such as travel and meals. She finds that this helps her keep track of expenses for her monthly expense reports.

**5** In the **Date Navigator**, click the **Wednesday** of the week in which you have been working. Assign the **Dentist** appointment to the **Personal** category. Assign the **Weekly meeting with Bradley** to the **Status** category.

**6** In the **Date Navigator**, click the **Friday** of the week in which you have been working. Click the **Southeast Lodging Association Conference** banner one time to select it. Hold down Ctrl and click the **Breakfast at the conference with John McCarthy and Sonia Friedman** appointment.

> This technique selects both calendar items. As in other areas of Outlook, you can assign multiple items to categories at one time. You can also assign events to categories.

**7** Right-click either selected item, point to **Categorize**, and then click the **Time & Expenses** category to assign both items to this category at one time.

> The calendar items for the week are assigned to various categories. Category assignments are useful when displaying the calendar in different views.

**8** Select only the **Southeast Lodging Association Conference** banner and assign the **Travel Required** category.

> When an appointment or event is assigned to a second category, the first category displays as a colored square on the right side of the appointment or event.

**9** In the **Date Navigator**, click the **Monday** of the week in which you have been working. Open the **Dominique's performance review** appointment and assign the **Status** category.

> When an appointment or event is assigned to a second category, each of the categories is displayed in the banner in the Appointment form.

**10** **Save & Close** the appointment.

**11** In the **Date Navigator**, click the **Tuesday** of the week in which you have been working. Select the **Travel & Lodging Seminar** appointment and assign the **Travel Required** category.

### Activity 3.14 | Changing the Calendar View

Outlook has a number of views you can use to organize your calendar and display its various periods of time. In this activity, you will change the views of Carmen Jeffries' calendar.

**1** In the **Date Navigator**, click any day of the week in which you have been creating appointments, if one is not already displayed.

**2** On the **Home tab**, in the **Arrange group**, click the **Work Week** button, and compare your screen with Figure 3.26.

> In Work Week view, the Personal Calendar folder displays Monday through Friday of the selected week. In the Date Navigator, the work week is highlighted to display your work week at a glance. The color coding of appointments is especially effective in this view. Some appointment descriptions may be too long to fully display, depending on the size of your screen and its resolution.

Figure 3.26

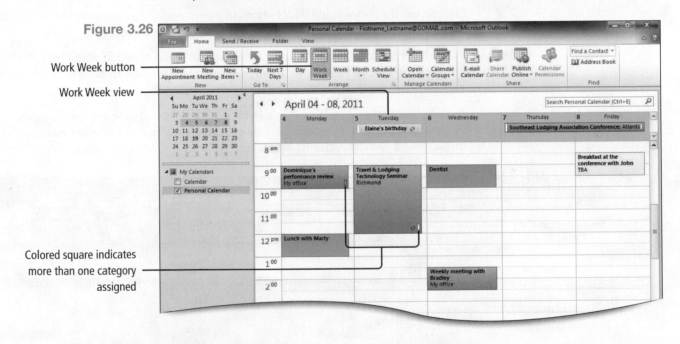

Work Week button

Work Week view

Colored square indicates more than one category assigned

**3** In the **Friday** column, point to the **Breakfast at the conference with John McCarthy & Sonia Friedman** appointment, if its description is truncated.

> Calendar items, whose full descriptions are not visible in the appointment area, display the time, subject, and location information as a ScreenTip. You also can view all the details of an appointment by opening it.

**4** On the **Home tab**, in the **Arrange group**, click the **Week** button.

> The calendar displays in *full week view*, which arranges the calendar in a weekly, seven-day view. In the Date Navigator, the entire week is highlighted, indicating that the entire week is displayed in the appointment area. Some of the appointment descriptions may also be truncated in this view, depending on your screen size and resolution.

**5** In the **Friday** frame, point to the **Breakfast at the conference with John McCarthy & Sonia Friedman** appointment to display the ScreenTip for this appointment. Compare your screen with Figure 3.27.

Figure 3.27

Forward button

Back button

ScreenTip displays date, time, and location for truncated appointment

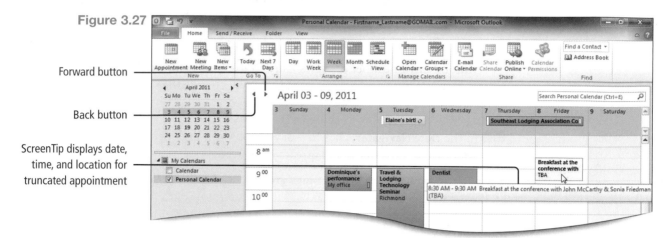

**6** Locate the **Forward** and **Back** buttons to the left of the Date in the appointment area. Click the **Forward** button [▶] one time to display the next week of the month.

You can use the Forward and Back buttons to move forward and backward by week in this view. Notice that the Date Navigator changes the highlighted week.

**7** Click the **Back** button [◀] one time to redisplay the week in which you have been working. On the **Home tab**, in the **Arrange group**, click the **Month** button to display the calendar in Month view. Compare your screen with Figure 3.28.

By default, the Month displays in High Detail view. High Detail view displays calendar events and appointments including the subject. Medium Detail view displays events with the subject and shows appointments only as colored bars. Low Detail view displays events only.

Figure 3.28

Your dates will differ

*High* detail displayed in Month view

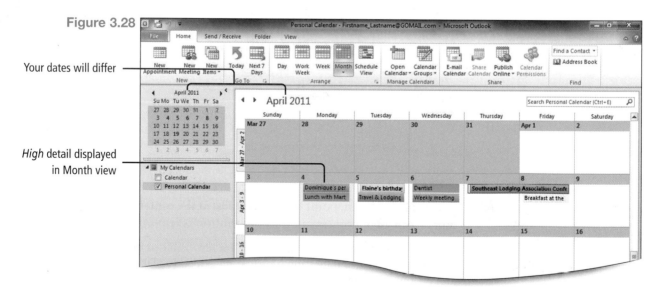

**8** In the **scroll bar**, drag the **scroll box** down to move forward in the calendar.

Notice as you drag the scroll box, Outlook displays a ScreenTip that identifies the week of the month. This ScreenTip is useful when you want to jump ahead or back in the calendar by many weeks or months.

**9** Drag the **scroll box** up so that the ScreenTip shows the same week in which you have been working.

**10** In the **Date Navigator**, click the **Monday** in the week in which you have been working. The Calendar is restored to Day view, the default view. In the **Navigation Pane**, under **My Calendars**, click **Calendar** to display it with your Personal Calendar.

**11** On the **Home tab**, in the **Arrange group**, click the **Schedule View** button. Drag the horizontal scroll bar to the right until you can see the **Chamber of Commerce Orientation** in the **Calendar** and the two appointments—**Dominique's performance review** and **Lunch with Marty** in the **Personal Calendar**.

The current day displays in *Schedule View*, which arranges the calendar horizontally on a time line. It is helpful to use this view when comparing multiple calendars to find available meeting times.

**12** Open the **Snipping Tool**. Click the **New arrow**, and then click **Window Snip**. Click in the window to capture it, and then click the **Save Snip** button. Navigate to your storage device. Click in the **File name** box, and then using your own name, type **Lastname_Firstname_3A_Schedule_View** Click the **Save as type arrow**, and then click **JPEG file**. Click **Save** and then **Close** the **Snipping Tool**. Submit the end result to your instructor as directed.

**13** In the **Navigation Pane**, under **My Calendars**, clear the **Calendar** check box to display only the **Personal Calendar** folder.

**14** On the **View tab**, in the **Layout group**, click **Reading Pane**, and then click **Right**.

The Reading Pane displays to the right of the calendar. The Reading Pane enables you to view details of an appointment without opening it.

**15** Display the **Wednesday** of the week in which you are working, and then click the **Dentist** appointment to select it. Point to the border between the Reading Pane and the calendar until the pane resize pointer displays, and then compare your screen with Figure 3.29.

The Dentist Appointment form displays in the Reading Pane. You can increase the size of the Reading Pane by dragging the left border if necessary.

Figure 3.29

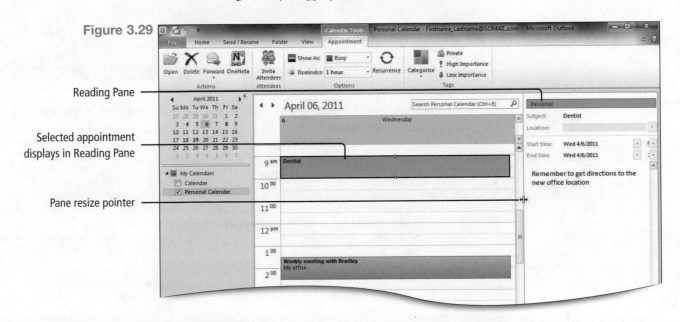

Reading Pane

Selected appointment displays in Reading Pane

Pane resize pointer

**16** To widen the **Reading Pane**, point to the left border of the **Reading Pane** until the pane resize pointer 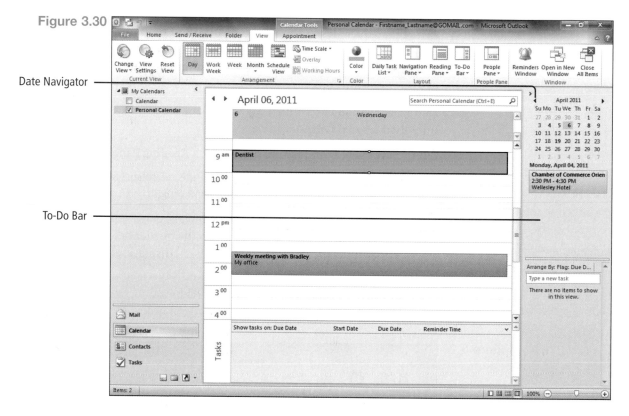 displays, drag the border to the left, releasing the mouse button when most of the Reading Pane information is visible.

**17** Restore the **Reading Pane** to its default width by dragging the left border to the right to its original location. On the **View tab**, in the **Layout group**, click **Reading Pane**, and then click **Off**.

**18** On the **View tab**, in the **Layout group**, click **To-Do Bar**, and then click **Normal**. Compare your screen with Figure 3.30.

> Outlook rearranges the calendar screen. The right side of the screen displays the To-Do Bar. Note that the Date Navigator is contained in the To-Do Bar, and is no longer displayed on the left side of your screen. Recall that the To-Do bar is used to display current tasks and appointments located in the current folder. If holidays are being displayed in the calendar, they will also display in the To-Do bar.

**Figure 3.30**

Date Navigator ——

To-Do Bar ——

**19** On the **View tab**, in the **Layout group**, click **To-Do Bar**, and then click **Off** to turn off the display of the To-Do Bar and restore the calendar to its default view.

---

**Note** | Default Setting for the To-Do Bar

By default, when viewing the Calendar folder, the To-Do Bar is not displayed. Calendar view includes the Date Navigator on the left and the Task pane below the appointment area, which displays all currently due tasks. Therefore, there is really no need to have the To-Do Bar displayed.

---

# Objective 6 | Manage a Calendar

From time to time, you will find it useful to print portions of your calendar. The procedures for printing a calendar and setting print options are similar to printing from other areas of Outlook. And, as with other Outlook folders, you may need to delete calendar items from time to time to keep it up to date.

### Activity 3.15 | Configuring and Viewing Calendar Print Options

Depending on what you want to print in your calendar, Outlook has a variety of print styles. You can print a range of hours, a day, a week, or a month. You can also print an individual appointment or event. In this activity, you will set up the print options for Carmen Jeffries' calendar.

**1** In the **Date Navigator**, click the **Wednesday** in the week in which you have been entering appointments.

**2** From the **Backstage view**, click the **Print tab**, and then, under **Settings**, the selected style is displayed in the Preview pane.

Each print style arranges calendar information in a different format. You can preview how the information will display when you print it.

**3** Under **Settings**, click **Weekly Agenda Style**, and then compare your screen with Figure 3.31.

The *Weekly Agenda Style* print style arranges the appointments in a table style, one cell per day, with the weekend day cells smaller than the work week.

Figure 3.31

Preview of Weekly Agenda Style (your dates will differ)

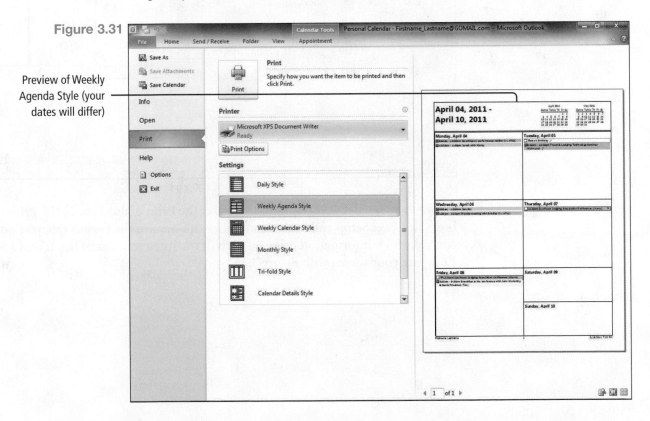

**4** In the **Print Preview area**, point to the top of the page, and click one time to increase the magnification. Use the horizontal scroll bar to view the agenda style, and then click the page one time to return to normal magnification.

**5** Under **Settings**, click **Weekly Calendar Style** to view the difference in weekly print styles.

The *Weekly Calendar Style* print style arranges the appointment frames, one column per day, similar to the Week view in the calendar.

**6** Under **Settings**, click **Monthly Style**, and then notice that the Print Preview shows how the calendar will look when this print style is used.

**7** Under **Settings**, click **Tri-fold Style**, and then compare your screen with Figure 3.32.

In the *Tri-fold Style*, the printout includes three sections. The default layout includes the Daily Calendar, the Daily Task List, and the Weekly Calendar.

Figure 3.32

Preview of Tri-fold Style
(your dates will differ)

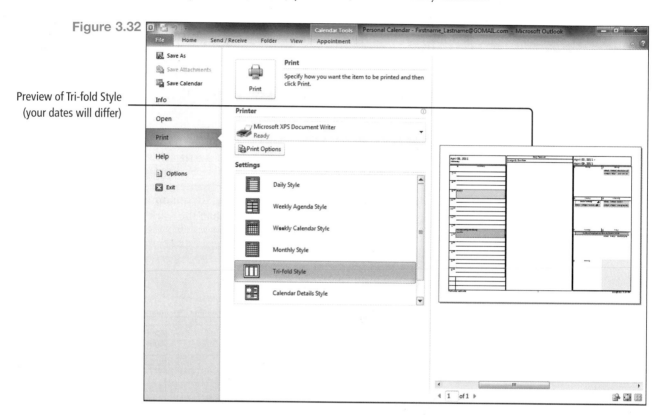

**8** Under **Printer**, click **Print Options** to display the **Print** dialog box. In the **Print** dialog box, click **Page Setup** and notice that under **Options**, on the **Format tab**, you can control which information prints in each of the three sections of the Tri-fold Style. Compare your screen with Figure 3.33.

Figure 3.33

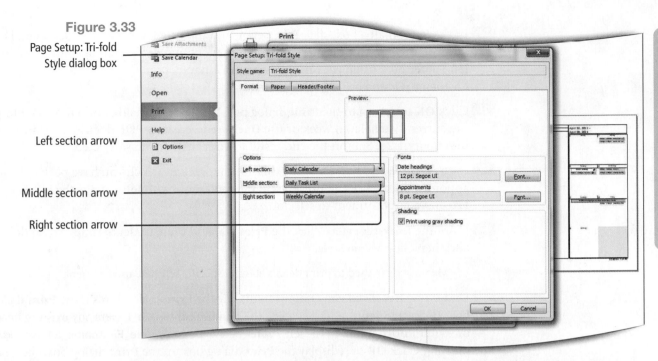

Page Setup: Tri-fold Style dialog box

Left section arrow

Middle section arrow

Right section arrow

**9** Under **Options**, click the **Middle section arrow**, and then click **Weekly Calendar**. Under **Options**, click the **Right section arrow**, and then click **Monthly Calendar**. In the **Page Setup: Tri-fold Style** dialog box, click **OK** to return to the **Print** dialog box. Click **Preview**.

In the Preview, the printout includes three sections as selected - Daily Calendar, Weekly Calendar, and Monthly Calendar.

**10** Open the **Snipping Tool**. Click the **New arrow**, and then click **Window Snip**. Click in the window to capture it, and then click the **Save Snip** button. Navigate to your storage device. Click in the **File name** box, and then using your own name, type **Lastname_Firstname_3A_Trifold_View** Click the **Save as type arrow**, and then click **JPEG file**. Click **Save** and then **Close** the **Snipping Tool**. Submit the end result to your instructor as directed.

**11** Under **Printer**, click **Print Options** to display the **Print** dialog box. In the **Print** dialog box, click **Page Setup**. Under **Options**, click the **Middle section** arrow, and click **Daily Task List**. Under **Options**, click the **Right section arrow**, and then click **Weekly Calendar**. In the **Page Setup: Tri-fold Style** dialog box, click **OK**. In the **Print** dialog box, click **Preview**.

Notice the default settings for each section have been restored. This is necessary because the Page Setup options are retained for future printing.

**12** Under **Settings**, click **Daily Style**. Preview the page, and then click the **Home tab** to redisplay the calendar.

## Activity 3.16 | Printing Calendar Information

In this activity, you will print different portions of Carmen Jeffries' calendar.

**1** Be sure that the week in which you have been working is displayed in the calendar. From the **Backstage view**, click the **Print tab**, and then, under **Settings**, click **Weekly Calendar Style**. Under **Printer**, click **Print Options** to display the **Print** dialog box.

**2** In the **Print** dialog box, click **Page Setup**, and then click the **Header/Footer tab**. Delete any existing header or footer information, including dates and page numbers. In the left **Footer** box, using your own first and last name, type
**Lastname_Firstname_3A_Weekly_Plans**

**3** Click **OK** to return to the **Print** dialog box. In the **Print** dialog box, click **Print** to print the currently displayed week or use **OneNote** to create a PDF document as instructed in Activity 1.24. Submit the end result to your instructor as directed.

**4** In the **Date Navigator**, click the **Friday** of the week in which you have been entering appointments. Click the **Breakfast at the conference with John McCarthy & Sonia Friedman** appointment to select it.

**5** From the **Backstage view**, click the **Print tab**, and then, under **Settings**, scroll down and then click **Memo Style**.

> Memo style is used to print details about a specific selected appointment.

**6** Under **Printer**, click **Print Options** to display the **Print** dialog box. In the **Print** dialog box, click **Page Setup**, and then click the **Header/Footer tab**. Delete any existing header or footer information. In the left **Footer** box, type **Lastname_Firstname_3A_Breakfast_ Meeting** Click **OK** to redisplay the **Print** dialog box. In the **Print** dialog box, click **Print** to print the currently displayed appointment or use **OneNote** to create a PDF document as instructed in Activity 1.24. Submit the end result to your instructor as directed, and then close the appointment.

## Activity 3.17 | Deleting Calendar Information

You can delete calendar information in a manner similar to any other Outlook item. In this activity, you will delete calendar items you have created for Carmen Jeffries, and then you will delete the entire calendar folder you created for her.

**1** In the **Date Navigator**, click the **Monday** of the week in which you have been entering appointments. Click the **Lunch with Marty** appointment, and then, on the **Appointment tab**, in the **Tags group**, click the **Categorize** button. Click **All Categories** to display the **Color Categories** dialog box.

**2** In the **Color Categories** dialog box, select **Travel Required**, click the **Rename** button, and type **Blue Category** Press Enter.

> Recall that Outlook retains the most recent name change, so renaming is required to restore the category to its default name.

**3** Using the same technique, rename **Personal** as **Green Category** Rename **Important** as **Red Category** Rename **Status** as **Orange Category** and rename **Time & Expenses** as **Yellow Category**. Click **OK**.

**4** Make certain the **Lunch with Marty** appointment is still selected. On the **Appointment tab**, in the **Actions group**, click the **Delete** button to delete the appointment.

**5** In the **Date Navigator**, click the **Tuesday** of the week in which you have been working. Click the **Travel & Lodging Technology Seminar** appointment to select it. Right-click the appointment, and from the displayed shortcut menu, point to **Delete**. Compare your screen with Figure 3.34.

> A submenu displays. Because this is a recurring appointment, Outlook needs to determine whether you want to delete a single occurrence or all the occurrences of the appointment.

Figure 3.34

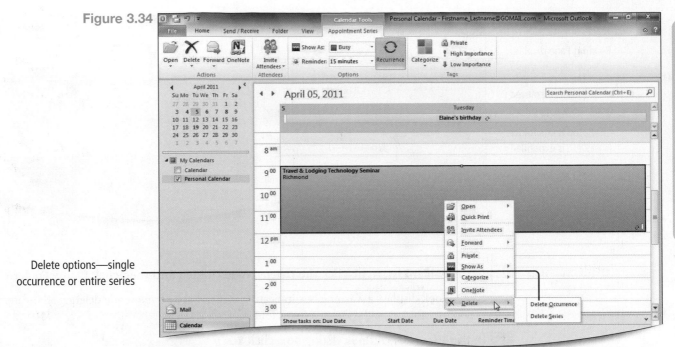

Delete options—single occurrence or entire series

**6** In the submenu, click **Delete Series**.

All occurrences of the appointment are deleted. Recurring events are deleted in the same way.

**7** At the top of the calendar, click the **Elaine's birthday** event banner, and then, on the **Appointment Series tab**, in the **Actions group**, click **Delete**. Click **Delete Series** to delete all occurrences of the event.

**8** In the **Navigation Pane**, click the **Folder List** button 🗀. In the **Folder List**, click **Personal Calendar**, so that it is selected as indicated by the blue rectangle that surrounds it. Press Del.

Outlook displays an information box asking whether you are sure you want to delete the folder and move its contents to the Deleted Items folder.

**9** In the **Microsoft Outlook** dialog box, click **Yes**.

Outlook moves the folder to the Deleted Items folder, and the Calendar folder displays.

**10** In the **Navigation Pane**, click **Deleted Items** to display the **Deleted Items** folder.

The Reading Pane displays next to the Deleted Items folder, displaying the first deleted item in the folder.

**11** In the **Folder List**, to the left of the **Deleted Items** folder, if necessary, click the **Expand** button ▷ to display the subfolders in the Deleted Items folder. Compare your screen with Figure 3.35.

**Figure 3.35**

Reading Pane displays selected appointment

Deleted items displayed (your order may differ)

Deleted Items folder is expanded

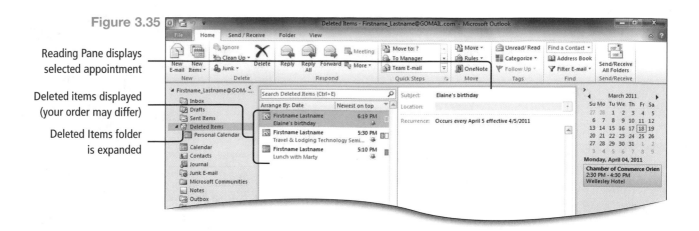

**12** In the **Folder List**, right-click the **Deleted Items** folder, and then click **Empty Folder**.

Outlook displays a warning box indicating that you are permanently deleting all the items and subfolders in the Deleted Items folder.

**13** In the **Microsoft Outlook** dialog box, click **Yes**.

The items are permanently deleted, including the Personal Calendar subfolder. The Deleted Items folder is now empty.

**14** Display the **Calendar**. On the **View tab**, in the **Current View group**, click the **Change View** button, and then click the **Active** button. Select and delete the **Chamber of Commerce** appointment, and then empty the **Deleted Items** folder.

Use the Active view to display all of your appointments, events, and meetings in a table.

**15** In the **Navigation Pane**, click the **Calendar** button. From the **Backstage view**, on the **Print tab**, under **Printer**, click **Print Options**. In the **Print** dialog box, under **Print Style**, click **Define Styles** to display the **Define Print Styles** dialog box.

Recall that Outlook remembers header and footer information. You can restore the print styles you used to their default setting.

**16** In the **Define Print Styles** dialog box, click **Weekly Calendar Style**, click **Reset**, and then click **OK**.

**17** In the **Define Print Styles** dialog box, click **Memo Style**, click **Reset**, and then click **OK**. **Close** the dialog box.

**18** In the **Print** dialog box, click **Cancel**, and then **Close** ☒ Outlook.

**End** **You have completed Project 3A** ——————————

# Content-Based Assessments

## Summary

In this chapter, you used the Outlook Calendar to manage a schedule by creating, editing, and moving appointments. You created a recurring appointment and an appointment with a reminder. You moved appointments to different times and different days of the month. You also worked with events, creating one-day events and multiple-day events. You used various ways to customize and organize your calendar activities. You assigned calendar items to categories and also assigned colors. You worked with various calendar views, and you displayed the calendar with the Reading Pane and the To-Do Bar. You printed a week of the calendar and an individual appointment. Finally, you deleted calendar items and the personal calendar folder you created at the beginning of the chapter.

## Key Terms

## Matching

Match each term in the second column with its correct definition in the first column. Write the letter of the term on the blank line in front of the correct definition.

_____ 1. The Outlook folder that contains all calendar-related items.

_____ 2. The right portion of the Calendar folder, which displays a one-day view of a day's calendar entries.

_____ 3. In the Calendar folder, the upper pane in the Navigation Pane that displays a one-month view of the calendar and is used to display specific days in a month.

_____ 4. A calendar activity occurring at a specific time and day that does not require inviting other people or reserving a room or equipment.

_____ 5. An appointment type that occurs regularly on specific dates and times and at specific intervals.

_____ 6. A calendar activity that requires inviting other people or reserving a room.

_____ 7. An Outlook window, accompanied by a tone, that displays automatically at a designated date and time before appointments or tasks.

_____ 8. The lower portion of an Appointment form enabling you to enter information not otherwise specified in the form.

_____ 9. View from which multiple calendars are displayed overlapping one another.

_____ 10. The outline around an appointment that indicates that the appointment is selected.

_____ 11. A button used to turn a feature on and off.

_____ 12. Any calendar activity that lasts 24 hours or longer.

_____ 13. A calendar view showing Monday through Friday.

**A** Appointment

**B** Appointment area

**C** Black border

**D** Calendar

**E** Comments area

**F** Date Navigator

**G** Event

**H** Meeting

**I** Overlay mode

**J** Recurring

**K** Reminder

**L** Toggle

**M** Tri-fold

**N** Week view

**O** Work Week view

_____ 14. The calendar view that displays a seven-day view in columns.

_____ 15. A calendar print style with three sections: a default layout that includes the Daily Calendar, the Daily Task List, and the Weekly Calendar.

## Multiple Choice

Circle the correct answer.

1. The area of the Outlook calendar in which the times are displayed in one-hour increments next to the appointment area.
   - **A.** Date Bar
   - **B.** Appointment Bar
   - **C.** Time Bar

2. The border that you can drag to extend the end time of an appointment.
   - **A.** Top
   - **B.** Bottom
   - **C.** Left

3. In the appointment area of the calendar, where the Location of a scheduled appointment displays.
   - **A.** Below the subject
   - **B.** Above the subject
   - **C.** To the left of the subject

4. The term that refers to the frequency of a recurring appointment, which may be daily, weekly, monthly, or yearly.
   - **A.** Recurrence pattern
   - **B.** Appointment pattern
   - **C.** Reminder pattern

5. The indicator that displays in the lower right corner of a recurring appointment or event.
   - **A.** Icon
   - **B.** Button
   - **C.** Exclamation point

6. The small, gray shape that displays when an appointment is scheduled beyond the time currently shown in the viewing area.
   - **A.** Circle
   - **B.** Square
   - **C.** Arrow

7. A calendar arrangement option in which the current day displays horizontally on a time line.
   - **A.** Schedule View
   - **B.** Week View
   - **C.** Reading View

8. A visual indicator that displays across the top of the calendar when an event is scheduled for a day.
   - **A.** Icon
   - **B.** Banner
   - **C.** Reminder

9. In the Date Navigator, the formatting applied to days on which appointments are scheduled.
   - **A.** Italic
   - **B.** Underline
   - **C.** Bold

10. A command used to assign a color category to an appointment.
    - **A.** Categorize
    - **B.** Reminder
    - **C.** Flag

# Content-Based Assessments

Apply **3A** skills from these Objectives:

1. Navigate the Calendar
2. Schedule Appointments
3. Edit Appointments
4. Work with Events
5. Organize and Customize the Calendar
6. Manage a Calendar

## Mastering Outlook | Project **3B** Wedding

In the following Mastering Outlook project, you will manage the weekly calendar activities of Dominique Amerline, the manager of Jefferson Inn. The Jefferson Inn's small size allows it to promote itself as an ideal location for wedding parties. Several times a year, especially in the late spring and early summer, the inn reserves its entire facility for weddings. Out-of-town visitors stay in the guest rooms, and the beautiful gardens serve as a backdrop for outdoor weddings. Ms. Amerline supervises these events. Your completed calendar and one appointment will look similar to the ones shown in Figure 3.36.

### Project Files

For Project 3B, you will need the following files:

New blank Appointment form
New blank Event form

You will print or create a PDF for two files with the following footers:

Lastname_Firstname_3B_Wedding_Appointment
Lastname_Firstname_3B_Wedding_Week

### Project Results

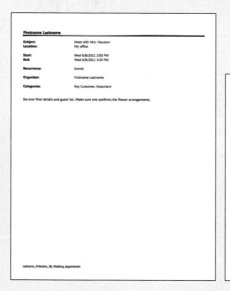

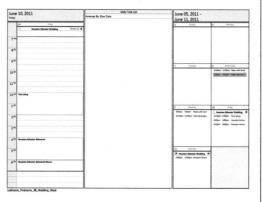

Figure 3.36

(Project 3B Wedding continues on the next page)

# Content-Based Assessments

**1** Log in to the Windows 7 user account you created in Chapter 1, or if necessary, create the account according to the instructions in Chapter 1, Activities 1.01 and 1.02.

**2** **Start** Outlook and display the **Calendar** folder. On the **View tab**, in the **Current View group**, click the **Change View** button, and then click the **Calendar** button. In the **Date Navigator**, click the right arrow next to the month name as necessary to advance the calendar to **June**. Click the **Wednesday** of the first full week. Open a **New Appointment**, and as the **Subject**, type **Meet with Bradley to discuss weekend menu** As the **Location**, type **Bradley's office** Set the **Start time** to **10:00 AM** and the **End time** to **11:00 AM**. Set the **Reminder** to **None**, and then **Save & Close** the appointment.

**3** Open another **New Appointment**. As the **Subject**, type **Meet with Mrs. Houston** and as the **Location**, type **My office** Set the **Start time** to **2:00 PM** and the **End time** to **3:30 PM**.

**4** In the comments area, type **Go over final details and guest list. Make sure she confirms the flower arrangements.** Display the **Color Categories** dialog box, and then **Rename** the **Green Category** as **Important** and the **Purple Category** as **Key Customer** Assign both categories to this appointment. Set the **Reminder** to **None** and then **Save & Close** the appointment.

**5** In the **Date Navigator**, click the **Thursday** of the same week in which you have been entering appointments. In the appointment area, click the **9:00 am** time slot and type **Meet with Carmen to discuss Houston wedding** Click the **10:30 am** time slot and type **Take beverage delivery** Open both appointments and set the **Reminder** to **None** in each Appointment form.

**6** In the **Date Navigator**, click the **Friday** of the same week in which you have been entering appointments, and then create an **All Day Event**. In the **Event** form, as the **Subject**, type **Houston-Schuster Wedding** Set the **End time** for **Sunday** so that it is a three-day event. Set the **Reminder** to **None**, and then **Save & Close** the appointment.

**7** On the **Friday** of the same week in which you have been entering appointments, click the **12:00 pm** time slot, and type **Tent setup** Drag the bottom border of the appointment to **2:00 pm**, and then create a **New Appointment**. As the **Subject**, type **Houston-Schuster Rehearsal** Set the **Start time** to **4:00 PM** and the **End time** to **6:00 PM**. Set the **Reminder** to **None**, and then **Save & Close** the appointment.

**8** Enter another **New Appointment** with the **Subject Houston-Schuster Rehearsal Dinner** Set the **Start time** at **6:00 PM** and the **End time** at **8:00 PM**. Set the **Reminder** to **None**. **Save & Close** the appointment.

**9** In the **Date Navigator**, click the **Saturday** of the same week in which you have been entering appointments. Create a **New Appointment**, and as the **Subject**, type **Houston-Schuster Wedding** Set the **Start time** to **4:00 PM** and the **End time** to **10:00 PM**. Set the **Reminder** to **None**. **Save & Close** the appointment.

**10** In the **Date Navigator**, click the **Wednesday** of the same week in which you have been working, and then select the **Meet with Mrs. Houston** appointment. In **Backstage** view, display the **Print tab**. Select **Memo Style**, and then from **Print Options**, display the **Page Setup: Memo Style** dialog box. Delete all Header and Footer text. In the left **Footer** box, type **Lastname_Firstname_3B_Wedding_Appointment** Preview the document, and then **Print** or use **OneNote** to create a PDF document and submit the end result to your instructor as directed.

**11** In the **Date Navigator**, click the **Friday** of the same week in which you have been working. In **Backstage** view, display the **Print tab**. Select **Tri-fold Style**, and then from **Print Options**, display the **Page Setup: Tri-fold Style** dialog box. Delete all Header and Footer text. In the left **Footer** box, type **Lastname_Firstname_3B_Wedding_Week** Preview the document, and then **Print** or use **OneNote** to create a PDF document and submit the end result to your instructor as directed.

**12** Select the **Houston-Schuster Wedding** event. Click the **Categorize** button, and then click **All Categories**. Rename **Important** as **Green Category** and **Key Customer** as **Purple Category** From **Backstage** view, click the **Print tab** and then from **Print Options**, display the **Define Print Styles** dialog box. **Reset** the **Tri-fold Style** and **Memo Style**. **Close** the **Define Print Styles** dialog box. **Cancel** the **Print** dialog box.

**13** On the **View tab**, in the **Current View group**, click the **Change View** button, and then click **Active**. Press [Ctrl] + [A], to select all of the appointments, and then press [Del] to delete all of the appointments. On the **View tab**, in the **Current View group**, click the **Change View** button, and then click **Calendar**.

**14** In the **Navigation Pane**, click the **Folder List** button, and then empty the **Deleted Items** folder. **Close** Outlook.

**End** **You have completed Project 3B** _____

Apply **3A** skills from
these Objectives:

■1 Navigate the
Calendar

■2 Schedule
Appointments

■3 Edit Appointments

■4 Work with Events

■5 Organize and
Customize the
Calendar

■6 Manage a Calendar

## Mastering Outlook | Project **3C** Magazine Story

In the following Mastering Outlook project, you will manage the calendar activities of Jameson Taylor, the co-owner of the Jefferson Inn. A national travel and leisure magazine is preparing a cover story on the Charlottesville area, and the Jefferson Inn will be prominently featured. The magazine is sending a writer and photographer for a two-day photo shoot. They will also use the inn as a base during their week-long stay in the Charlottesville area. One of the appointments you create and your completed calendar will look similar to the ones shown in Figure 3.37.

## Project Files

For Project 3C, you will need the following files:

> New blank Appointment form
> New blank Event form

You will print or create a PDF for two files with the following footers:

> Lastname_Firstname_3C_Magazine_Story_Week
> Lastname_Firstname_3C_Magazine_Story_Event

## Project Results

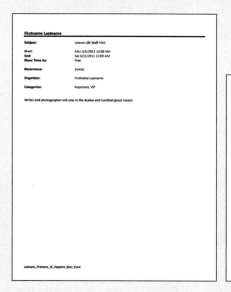
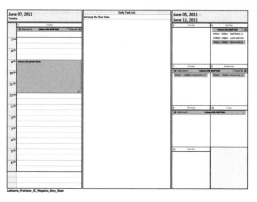

**Figure 3.37**

(Project 3C Magazine Story continues on the next page)

# Content-Based Assessments

**1** Log in to the Windows 7 user account you created in Chapter 1, or if necessary, create the account according to the instructions in Chapter 1, Activities 1.01 and 1.02. **Start** Outlook and display the **Calendar** folder. If necessary, change the view to Calendar and the Arrangement to Day.

**2** In the **Date Navigator**, click the **right arrow** to advance the calendar to **June**, and then click the **Monday** of the first full week of June. Create an **All Day Event** with the **Subject Leisure Life Staff Visit** Set the **End time** to **Friday** of the same week.

**3** Display the **Color Categories** dialog box, and then rename the **Orange Category** as **Important** and the **Purple Category** as **VIP** Assign both the **Important** and **VIP** categories to this event. Set the **Reminder** to **None**. In the comments area, type **Writer and photographer will stay in the Azalea and Cardinal guest rooms Save & Close** the appointment.

**4** In the appointment area, click the **9:00 am** time slot, and then type **Staff Meeting** Drag the bottom border down to **10:00 am**. Open the appointment, set the **Reminder** to **None**, and then make the appointment a **Weekly** recurring appointment with **No end date**. **Save & Close** the appointment.

**5** In the appointment area, click in the **12:00 pm** time slot, and type **Lunch with Carmen** Drag the bottom border down to **1:00 pm**. Set the **Reminder** to **30 minutes**.

**6** Open a new **Appointment** form. As the **Subject**, type **Dinner with Leisure Life staff** Set the **Start time** to **7:00 PM** and the **End time** to **9:00 PM**. Assign the **Important** and **VIP** categories. Set the **Reminder** to **None**. **Save & Close** the appointment.

**7** In the **Date Navigator**, click the **Tuesday** of the same week in which you are entering appointments, and then create a **New Appointment**. As the **Subject**, type **Leisure Life photo shoot** Assign the **Important** category. Set the

**Start time** to **9:00 AM** and the **End time** to **12:00 PM**. Set the **Reminder** to **None**. Display the **Appointment Recurrence** dialog box. Set the **Recurrence pattern** to **Daily** and the **Range of recurrence** to **End after 2 occurrences**. Click **OK**, and then **Save & Close** the appointment.

**8** From the **Backstage** view, click the **Print tab**, and then from the **Print Options**, display the **Page Setup: Tri-fold Style** dialog box. In the **Header/Footer tab**, delete any existing header or footer information. In the left **Footer** box, type **Lastname_Firstname_3C_Magazine_Story_Week** and then **Preview** the calendar. **Print** or use **OneNote** to create a PDF document, and then submit the end result to your instructor as directed.

**9** Click the **event banner** one time to select it. From the **Backstage view**, click the **Print tab**, and then from **Print Options**, display the **Page Setup: Memo Style** dialog box. Delete any existing header or footer information. In the left **Footer** box, type **Lastname_Firstname_3C_Magazine_Story_Event** and then **Preview** the event. **Print** or use **OneNote** to create a PDF document, and then submit the end result to your instructor as directed.

**10** Select the **event banner**, click **Categorize**, and then click **All Categories**. Rename **Important** as **Orange Category** and **VIP** as **Purple Category**. Display the **Define Print Styles** dialog box, and then **Reset** both the **Tri-fold Style** and the **Memo Style**.

**11** On the **View tab**, in the **Current View group**, click the **Change View** button, and then click **Active**. Press Ctrl + A to select all of the appointments, and then press Del to delete all of the appointments. On the **View tab**, in the **Current View group**, click the **Change View** button, and then click **Calendar**.

**12** In the **Navigation Pane**, click the **Folder List** button, and then empty the **Deleted Items** folder. **Close** Outlook.

**End You have completed Project 3C** ————————————————

# Outcomes-Based Assessments

## Rubric

The following outcomes-based assessments are *open-ended* assessments. That is, there is no specific correct result; your result will depend on your approach to the information provided. Make *Professional Quality* your goal. Use the following scoring rubric to guide you in *how* to approach the problem and then to evaluate *how well* your approach solves the problem.

The *criteria*—Software Mastery, Content, Format and Layout, and Process—represent the knowledge and skills you have gained that you can apply to solving the problem. The *levels of performance*—Professional Quality, Approaching Professional Quality, or Needs Quality Improvement—help you and your instructor evaluate your result.

| | Your completed project is of Professional Quality if you: | Your completed project is Approaching Professional Quality if you: | Your completed project Needs Quality Improvements if you: |
|---|---|---|---|
| 1-Software Mastery | Choose and apply the most appropriate skills, tools, and features and identify efficient methods to solve the problem. | Choose and apply some appropriate skills, tools, and features, but not in the most efficient manner. | Choose inappropriate skills, tools, or features, or are inefficient in solving the problem. |
| 2-Content | Construct a solution that is clear and well organized, contains content that is accurate, appropriate to the audience and purpose, and is complete. Provide a solution that contains no errors in spelling, grammar, or style. | Construct a solution in which some components are unclear, poorly organized, inconsistent, or incomplete. Misjudge the needs of the audience. Have some errors in spelling, grammar, or style, but the errors do not detract from comprehension. | Construct a solution that is unclear, incomplete, or poorly organized; contains some inaccurate or inappropriate content; and contains many errors in spelling, grammar, or style. Do not solve the problem. |
| 3-Format and Layout | Format and arrange all elements to communicate information and ideas, clarify function, illustrate relationships, and indicate relative importance. | Apply appropriate format and layout features to some elements, but not others. Overuse features, causing minor distraction. | Apply format and layout that does not communicate information or ideas clearly. Do not use format and layout features to clarify function, illustrate relationships, or indicate relative importance. Use available features excessively, causing distraction. |
| 4-Process | Use an organized approach that integrates planning, development, self-assessment, revision, and reflection. | Demonstrate an organized approach in some areas, but not others; or, use an insufficient process of organization throughout. | Do not use an organized approach to solve the problem. |

# Outcomes-Based Assessments

Apply a combination
of the **3A** skills.

## GO! Think | Project **3D** Youth Softball

### Project Files

For Project 3D, you will need the following file:

New blank Appointment form

You will print or create a PDF for one file with the following footer:

Lastname_Firstname_3D_Youth_Softball_Calendar

Jameson Taylor, the co-owner of the Jefferson Inn, is an avid softball player, and he plays regularly in an adult league. He also coaches a youth softball team, and the Jefferson Inn sponsors the team. At the end of every season, the inn hosts a barbeque for the team members. This year, his team has made the playoffs. You will manage Mr. Taylor's calendar for the week of the playoffs and the barbeque, creating appointments for the practices, games, and barbeque.

Log in to the user account you created in Chapter 1, and then start Outlook. In the Calendar, display the first full week of May to create Mr. Taylor's schedule for the week. Create a new appointment for Tuesday for Softball practice from 5:30 to 7:30 p.m. with no reminders. Create an hour-long appointment on Wednesday morning with the team's assistant coach, with a playoff-related subject. Create an appointment on Wednesday with the subject Youth softball practice from 3:30 to 5:30 p.m.

On Thursday of that same week, create an appointment for Playoffs from 3:30 to 6:00 p.m. Assign a category named Important, and make the appointment a daily recurrence, ending after two occurrences on Friday. On Thursday morning of that same week, create an hour-long appointment with the inn's chef, Bradley Matteson, with a subject related to the barbeque. On Friday, create a new appointment for the barbeque from 6:00 to 8:00 p.m.

Print or create a PDF document for the calendar for the week in Weekly Agenda Style, adding the footer **Lastname_Firstname_3D_Youth_Softball_Calendar** to the file. Submit the end result to your instructor as directed. Change the Important category to its default name. Delete the calendar entries for the week in which you have been working. Empty the contents of the Deleted Items folder, and reset the print style used.

**End** **You have completed Project 3D** ——————————————————

# Outcomes-Based Assessments

**Apply a combination of the 3A skills.**

## GO! Think | Project 3E Charity Art Show

### Project Files

For Project 3E, you will need the following files:

   New blank Appointment form
   New blank Event form

You will print or create a PDF for one file with the following footer:

   Lastname_Firstname_3E_Art_Show

A unique feature of the Jefferson Inn is its fine collection of American antiques and art. Many of America's best nineteenth-century artists are represented in the inn's collection of oil paintings and watercolors. A local charity is staging an art show, auction, and gala, and has asked the inn to donate its space for the event. The inn's collection would complement the art show and draw art lovers from around the area. In this project, you will manage the schedule of the inn's co-owner, Carmen Jeffries, during the week of the gala.

Log in to the user account you created in Chapter 1, and then start Outlook. In the Calendar, display the first full week of March to create Ms. Jeffries' schedule for the week. Create a new appointment for Tuesday with the subject Meet with gala chairwoman from 10:00 to 11:00 a.m. Create a new appointment for Wednesday with the subject Lunch with art director from 12:00 to 1:00 p.m. and set the location to Owen's Bistro.

Create a new appointment for Thursday with the subject Meet with auction master from 11:00 a.m. to 12:00 p.m. On Thursday afternoon, create a new, hour-long appointment with the inn's co-owner, Jameson Taylor, with an auction-related subject.

On Friday of that same week, create an event with the subject Charlottesville Hospice Art Show and Gala Make it a two-day event, ending on Saturday. On Friday morning, create a new, hour-long appointment with the inn's chef, Bradley Matteson, with a gala-related subject. On Friday, create a new appointment with the subject Pre-auction Showing from 5:00 to 8:00 p.m. Assign a category named Important. On Saturday of that same week, create a new appointment with the subject Auction and Dinner from 6:00 p.m. to 11:00 p.m. Assign a category named Important.

Print or create a PDF document for the calendar using the Weekly Calendar Style, adding the footer **Lastname_Firstname_3E_Art_Show** to the file. Submit the end result to your instructor as directed. Change the Important category to its default name. Delete the calendar items for Tuesday through Saturday of the week in which you have been working. Delete the contents of the Deleted Items folder, and reset the print style used.

**End** **You have completed Project 3E** ───────────

# Planning Meetings

## OUTCOMES

At the end of this chapter you will be able to:

### PROJECT 4A
Manage meetings.

## OBJECTIVES

Mastering these objectives will enable you to:

1. Publish Free/Busy Information (p. 271)
2. Schedule a Meeting (p. 278)
3. Respond to Meeting Requests (p. 289)
4. Schedule an Office Resource (p. 298)
5. Manage Meeting Information (p. 302)

© iStockphoto/livingimages

## In This Chapter

Meetings are similar to appointments in Outlook. They are stored in your Calendar folder, and they appear in your schedule resembling appointments. You create, edit, and view them like appointments. Appointments involve only your own schedule and time, but meetings involve the schedules of all meeting participants. Outlook helps you plan meetings by enabling you to share your calendar information with others. You can organize a meeting based on the participants' availability as shown in their Outlook calendars. Similarly, your calendar can be made available to others who need your participation in a meeting. You can also use Outlook to reserve resources for meetings, such as a conference room or audiovisual equipment.

**Owens Family Builders** was founded in 1968 as Owens and Sons Builders; in 1980, the name was changed to reflect the extended family that had joined the business. Today the company has more than 300 employees, including about 50 members of the Owens family. Focusing on home building, the company is known for quality construction, innovative design, and customer service. Owens Family Builders has built more than 3,000 homes in the Orlando area and has also built many schools, shopping centers, and government buildings.

# Project 4A Meeting Schedule

## Project Activities

In Activities 4.01 through 4.16, you will plan meetings for members of the management team of Owens Family Builders. You will make the calendar of Warren Owens available on the Internet, and you will schedule meetings for him. You will send meeting invitations, add and remove meeting attendees, send updates, check the response status for scheduled meetings, and cancel meetings. Warren Owens will receive invitations to attend various meetings. You will accept and decline invitations, tentatively accept invitations, and propose new meeting times. You will also book office resources and schedule a resource for a meeting. Upon completion, your screen snips, calendar, and one of your invitations will look similar to the ones shown in Figure 4.1.

## Project Files

For Project 4A, you will need the following files:

> o04A_Owens_Contacts
> o04A_Owens_Inbox
> JenniferOwens.vfb
> JohnZeidler.vfb
> JenniferOwens2014.vfb
> JohnZeidler2014.vfb

You will save your files as:

> Lastname_Firstname_4A_Schedule_Meeting.jpg
> Lastname_Firstname_4A_December_2014.jpg

You will print or create a PDF for two files with the following footers:

> Lastname_Firstname_4A_Warren's_Calendar
> Lastname_Firstname_4A_Overruns_Meeting

## Project Results

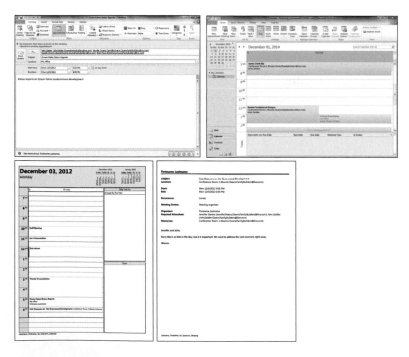

**Figure 4.1**
Project 4A Meeting Schedule

# Objective 1 | Publish Free/Busy Information

When you create an appointment in your calendar, Outlook displays one of four indicators associated with your availability for that date and time: Busy, Free, Tentative, or Out of Office. This is referred to as your *free/busy information*. Outlook's default setting for all appointments is Busy. These indicators display in your *local calendar*—the calendar stored on the hard drive of your computer. The free/busy indicators also display when others view your calendar on a shared server.

Microsoft's system for sharing Outlook information among members on a network is the *Exchange Server*—special server software for networks. In an Exchange Server environment, your free/busy schedule is shared automatically with all other users on the Exchange Server. If you want others who are not on the Exchange Server to see your free/busy schedule or you do not use an Exchange Server, you can still share your free/busy information by publishing it on any server to which you have *read/write access*—a server on which you can view and store information. For example, your company may have a server that you can use to make this information available to all your coworkers. You can configure Outlook to use such a server to show this information.

> **Alert! | Starting Project 4A**
>
> Because Outlook stores information on the hard drive of the computer at which you are working, it is recommended that you complete Project 4A in one working session using the user account you created in Chapter 1. Allow approximately one and a half to two hours to complete Project 4A. If possible, use the same computer that you used when you created the Windows 7 user account in previous chapters. If you cannot use the same computer or if the Windows 7 user account that you previously created was deleted, refer to Chapter 1, Activities 1.01 and 1.02 to setup the Windows 7 user account and to configure Microsoft Outlook 2010.

## Activity 4.01 | Exploring the Free/Busy Schedule

In this activity, you will create appointments for Warren Owens of Owens Family Builders and then explore his free/busy schedule for the day of the scheduled appointments.

**1** Click the **Start** button, and then point to the **Shut down button arrow**. On the **Shut down** menu, click **Switch user** to display the Windows 7 desktop. Click the user account you created in Chapter 1. If the account does not exist, refer to Chapter 1, Activities 1.01 and 1.02 to setup the Windows 7 user account and to configure Microsoft Outlook.

**2** **Start** Outlook and display the **Navigation Pane**. In the lower section of the **Navigation Pane**, click the **Mail** button. Under your user name account, click **Inbox**, and delete any existing messages in the **Inbox**. In the lower section of the **Navigation Pane**, click the **Contacts** button, and then delete any existing contacts.

**3** In the lower section of the **Navigation Pane**, click the **Calendar** button. In the **Date Navigator**, click the **right arrow**, and then advance the calendar to next **June** or **December**, *whichever month is closest to the current month*. Click the **first Monday** in the month. If necessary, delete any existing calendar items for that day, and then compare your screen with Figure 4.2.

Figure 4.2

December or June
displayed (your date
may differ)

First Monday of
selected month

Right arrow advances
the calendar

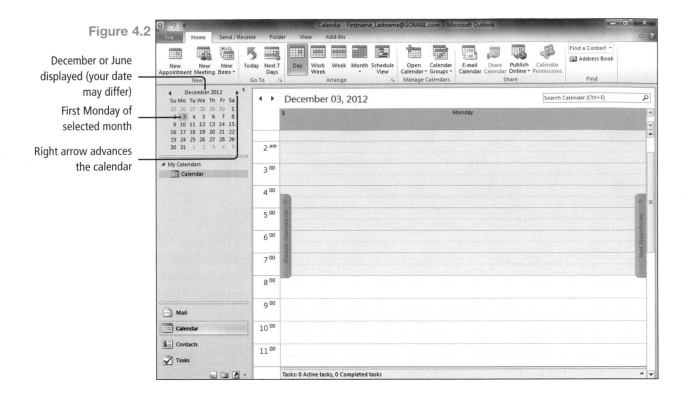

### Alert! | Is your time zone different from Eastern Time?

Meeting times for imported meeting invitations adjust to local time zones. The meetings and appointments in this chapter assume a time zone of Eastern Time (US & Canada). If this is not your time zone, for the purposes of this instruction, you will need to change your Outlook time zone. To change the time zone, from Backstage view, click Options. Click Calendar on the left, and then scroll down to the Time zones section. Click the Time zone arrow, locate and click (UTC-05:00) Eastern Time (US & Canada), and then click OK. To manually change the time on your computer, click the date in the taskbar, and then click Change date and time settings. In the Date and Time dialog box, click the Change time zone button. Click the Time zone arrow, locate and click (UTC-05:00) Eastern Time (US & Canada), and then click OK two times. If your school or network administrator does not allow you to change the computer's time or time zone, the meeting times for your imported meeting invitations will differ from those shown in this project.

**4** In the appointment area, click the **10:00 am** time slot, and type **Staff Meeting** Extend the bottom border of the appointment to **11:00 am**. In the **11:00 am** time slot, type **Joe's Presentation** In the **12:00 pm** time slot, type **Get haircut** and then extend the bottom border of this appointment to **1:00 pm**.

**5** In the **3:00 pm** time slot, type **Vendor Presentations** and extend the time to **5:00 pm**. Click any blank area of the calendar, and compare your screen with Figure 4.3.

Figure 4.3

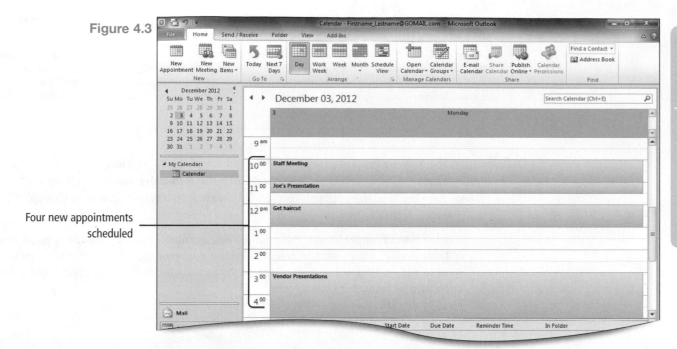

Four new appointments scheduled

6 Double-click the **Get haircut** appointment to open its appointment form, and then notice that in the **Options group**, the **Show As** box setting indicates *Busy*.

> By default, Outlook assigns the *Busy* setting to all new appointments, which indicates that you have an appointment or meeting scheduled for that time. Others on the network who can view your calendar cannot see the specific details of your appointment, but they see that your time is scheduled—you are *busy*.

7 Click the **Show As arrow** and notice that for each of the four choices, a colored or patterned box displays; for example, *Out of Office* has a purple box. Click **Out of Office**. On the **Appointment tab**, in the **Actions group**, click the **Save & Close** button, click in a blank time slot, and then compare your screen with Figure 4.4.

> The left border for the Get haircut appointment changes to purple, which indicates an *Out of Office* status. Use this setting to indicate when you are away from your office and not available for other meetings or appointments. Outlook assigns a different border color or pattern to each of the four different free/busy availability options.

Figure 4.4

Show As arrow

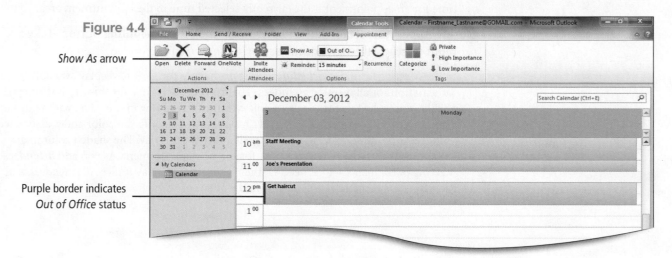

Purple border indicates *Out of Office* status

> **Note | Using the Out of Office and Busy Settings**
>
> The *Busy* and *Out of Office* settings for appointments and meetings are most meaningful when you apply them so that your coworkers can predict your availability. Use *Busy* for appointments and meetings in which you are in the building but are busy in appointments or meetings. Use *Out of Office* when you are out of the building and possibly some distance away—in other words, you are not necessarily available right after that time for another appointment or meeting.

**8** Open the **Vendor Presentations** appointment form. In the **Options group**, click the **Show As arrow**, and then click **Tentative**. Click the **Reminder arrow** and then click **None**. **Save & Close** the appointment and then click in a blank time slot. Compare your screen with Figure 4.5.

The left border for the *Vendor Presentations* appointment indicates that the appointment is *Tentative*—the appointment is scheduled but not confirmed. Use *Tentative* when you want to indicate that the specified time might be available or that your attendance at an appointment or meeting is uncertain.

Figure 4.5

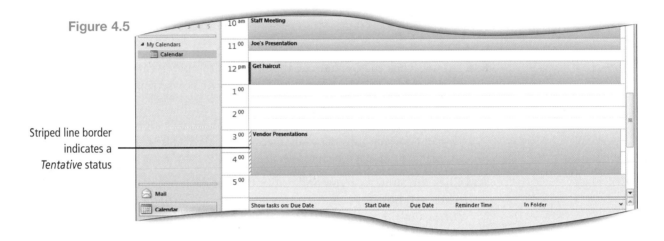

Striped line border indicates a *Tentative* status

**9** In the appointment area, click the **2:00 pm** time slot. On the **Home tab**, click the **New Appointment** button.

The Start time for the appointment is indicated as *2:00 PM*. Recall that the default Start time for an appointment is the currently selected time in the appointment area.

**10** On the **Appointment tab**, in the **Show group**, click the **Scheduling** button. Take a moment to study the parts of the screen as shown in Figure 4.6.

In the *Meeting* form, the ***Scheduling button*** changes the view to display available free/busy information for all meeting attendees. The free/busy schedule for this day is displayed as a table. Your schedule for the day displays as the second row in the table, with your name listed under *All Attendees*. Notice that Outlook uses the different color codes associated with the appointments to show your availability for this day. The shaded column at 2:00 pm is the currently selected time for the new appointment. As you add ***attendees***—meeting participants—to a meeting, their names will display under *All Attendees*, and their free/busy schedules will display in the adjacent rows.

Figure 4.6

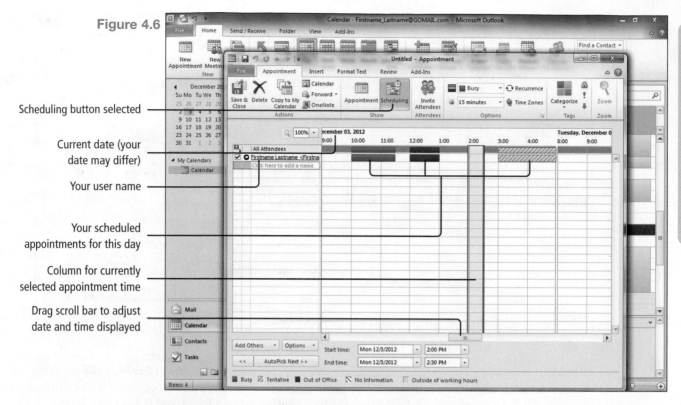

Scheduling button selected

Current date (your date may differ)

Your user name

Your scheduled appointments for this day

Column for currently selected appointment time

Drag scroll bar to adjust date and time displayed

**11** Locate the scroll bar at the bottom of the schedule, and then click the **left scroll arrow** several times to adjust the displayed time for the day.

You can use the horizontal scroll bar at the bottom of the schedule to view different days and times.

**12** Close ☒ the appointment form without saving the new appointment.

## Activity 4.02 | Publishing Your Free/Busy Information

If you work in an Exchange Server environment, your free/busy information is automatically available to anyone who uses the server and displays your calendar. If you want to make your free/busy information available to others who are not on this server or you do not use an Exchange Server, you can make this information available on any server to which you have read/write access. Thus, people who need to include you in meetings can see your availability. In this activity, you will configure Outlook to make Warren's free/busy schedule available to his coworkers at Owens Family Builders.

**1** From **Backstage** view, click **Options**. In the **Outlook Options** dialog box, on the left, click **Calendar**. Under **Calendar Options**, to the right of *Change the permissions for viewing Free/Busy information*, click the **Free/Busy Options** button. Compare your dialog box with Figure 4.7.

The Free/Busy Options dialog box displays. If you do not have an Exchange Server e-mail account, use this dialog box to specify the server that contains your calendar information. Under Options, you can specify how many months of calendar information you want to make available. The default is two months, and the information displayed from your calendar is updated every 15 minutes.

Figure 4.7

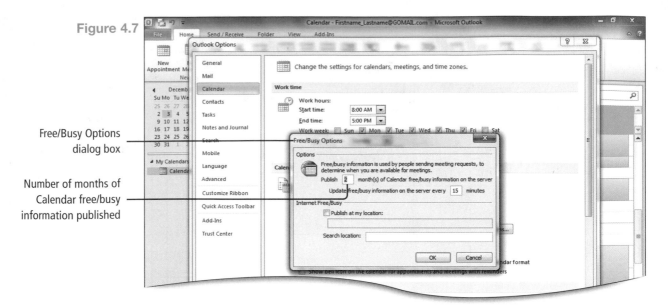

Free/Busy Options
dialog box

Number of months of
Calendar free/busy
information published

**2** In the **Free/Busy Options** dialog box, under **Internet Free/Busy**, select the **Publish at my location** check box if it is not already selected.

The text box under this option becomes available. A ***virtual free/busy file*** stores the calendar information for an individual. In this box, you specify the file that contains your calendar information. The file name is your user name, and it must include the file name extension *.vfb*—which is an abbreviation for virtual free/busy. You must also include the location of the file, which can be a local file server on your network or an address on the World Wide Web.

**3** In the **Publish at my location** text box, delete any existing text and type **file:\\g:\Schedules\WarrenOwens.vfb** Compare your dialog box with Figure 4.8.

This tells Outlook where to store Warren's free/busy information for others to use. The specified location is a server on the Owens Family Builders local area network, on drive *g* in a folder called *Schedules*. In an actual work environment, the drive letter, folder name (if any), and user name that you would specify depend on your specific work environment—in other words, your drive letter and folder would likely differ, and you would use your own name. The address must begin with the prefix *file:\\* and your file name *must* include the *.vfb* file name extension.

Figure 4.8

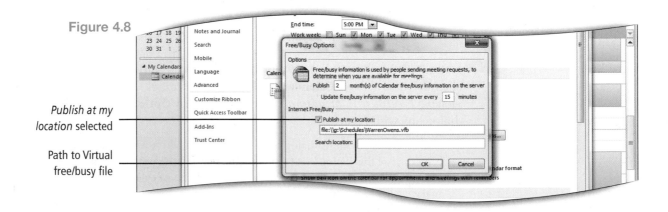

*Publish at my
location* selected

Path to Virtual
free/busy file

---

**Note** | Specifying a Location for Calendar Information

When you specify a location for your calendar information, it may be a server on your local network or an address on the Web. An example of a Web address would be *http://OwensFamilyBuilders.com/Schedules/WarrenOwens.vfb*. The address, drive, and folder location you specify depends on your particular work environment, and you would use your own user name. Your network administrator can identify the location you would use to store your calendar information if you are not working in an Exchange Server environment.

---

**4** In the **Free/Busy Options** dialog box, click **OK**. Click **OK** to close the **Outlook Options** dialog box.

Outlook will post two months of schedule information for Warren Owens every 15 minutes to the specified server. Outlook does *not* actually use the address you specified in the previous step because this is a fictional server. It is not necessary that your calendar information be available for others in this activity.

## Activity 4.03 | Accessing the Free/Busy Information of Others

You can view the free/busy schedule of other people if they publish their schedule information and you know the location and name of their free/busy file. In this activity, you will specify the location of the free/busy information for one of Warren's contacts.

**1** In the **Navigation Pane**, click the **Contacts** button. On the **Home tab**, in the **New group**, click the **New Contact** button.

**2** **Maximize** ⬜ the **Untitled - Contact** form, if necessary. Use the techniques you have practiced to add the following new contact, using **Business** for the address and phone information:

**Juan Sanchez**

**Owens Family Builders**

**JuanSanchez.OwensFamilyBuilders@live.com**

**407-555-0159**

**5000 South Orange Avenue**

**Orlando, FL 32835**

**3** On the **Contact tab**, in the **Show group**, click the **Details** button. Under **Internet Free-Busy**, in the **Address** box, type **file:\\g:\Schedules\JuanSanchez.vfb** and then compare your Contact form with Figure 4.9.

The location is a file server on the Owens Family Builders local area network, on drive *g* in a folder called *Schedules*. This contact has configured his Free/Busy Options dialog box to store his schedule information in this location using this file name. If this were an actual work environment, Warren Owens and Juan Sanchez could view each other's free/busy information.

Figure 4.9

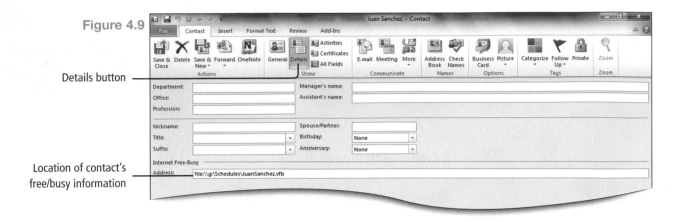

Details button

Location of contact's free/busy information

**4** On the **Contact tab**, in the **Actions group**, click the **Save & Close** button.

---

**More Knowledge** | **Performing a Search for All Contacts' Free/Busy Information**

If all your contacts use the same server to post their free/busy information, you can have Outlook perform a global search for free/busy information instead of specifying the location for each contact individually. From Backstage view, click Options, and then click Calendar. Under Calendar Options, click the Free/Busy Options button. In the Search location box, type the location for your contacts' free/busy information using the file name *%name%.vfb*. Using a Web address, an example would be *http://OwensFamilyBuilders.com/Schedules/%name%.vfb*.

---

## Objective 2 | Schedule a Meeting

Outlook uses the term *meeting* to refer to a calendar activity that requires inviting other people or reserving a room. You can schedule meetings with other Outlook users or anyone who uses an e-mail program. Meeting invitations occur as e-mail messages. Planning a meeting involves finding an available time in your schedule and inviting the meeting attendees. After you have scheduled the meeting, you can add additional attendees. You may also need to remove attendees, send updates, check the response status, or even cancel the meeting altogether.

### Activity 4.04 | Importing Contacts and Copying Pathname Information

In this activity, you will import contacts into Warren's Contacts folder. This will establish some existing contacts with which you can work. Also, you will copy the path location of your student files. A *pathname* is the sequence of the drive letter and folder names that lead to the files.

**1** Display the **Contacts** folder if it is not already displayed. From **Backstage** view, click the **Open tab**, and then click **Import** to display the **Import and Export Wizard** dialog box. Under **Choose an action to perform**, click **Import from another program or file**, and then click **Next**.

**2** In the **Import a File** dialog box, under **Select file type to import from**, click **Outlook Data File (.pst)**. Click **Next**.

**3** In the **Import Outlook Data File** dialog box, click the **Browse** button. In the **Open Outlook Data Files** dialog box, navigate to the location where the student files for this textbook are stored.

**4** At the top of the **Open Outlook Data Files** dialog box, click in a blank area of the **address bar** to select the entire path. Right-click on the selected path, and then click **Copy**. Compare your screen with Figure 4.10.

The address bar contains the path—the drive and folder location—for all of your student files.

Figure 4.10

Open Outlook Data Files dialog box

Address bar contains Pathname for this file (your drive and folder information will differ)

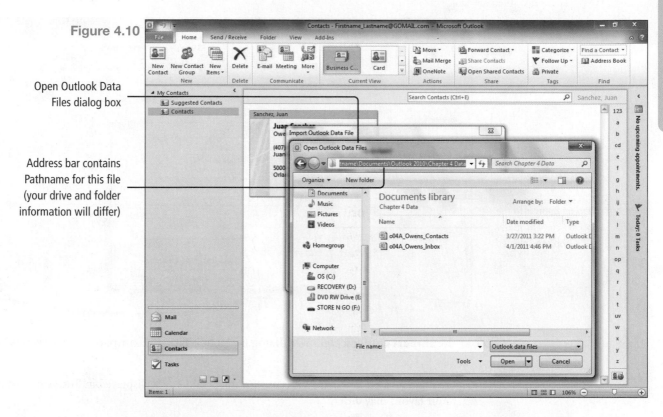

**5** In the displayed **Open Outlook Data Files** dialog box click the **o04A_Owens_Contacts** file to select it, and then, in the lower right corner of the dialog box, click **Open**. Compare your screen with Figure 4.11.

Notice that the file path and name display in the File to import box.

Figure 4.11

Path and file name

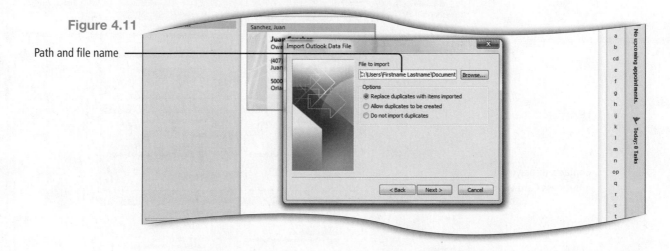

**6** In the **Import Outlook Data File** dialog box, click **Next**. Under **Select the folder to import from**, click **Contacts**, and then click **Import items into the current folder**. Compare your screen with Figure 4.12.

The Import Outlook Data File dialog box displays the folder structure for the file you are about to import.

Figure 4.12

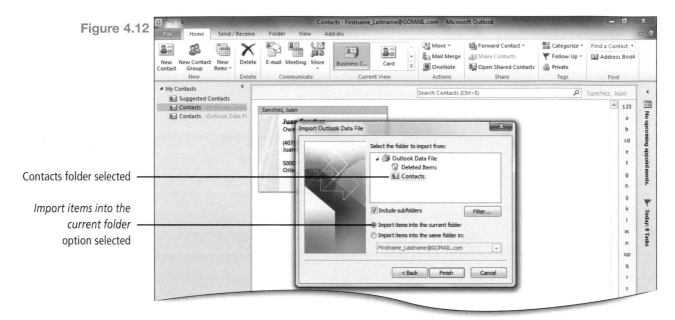

Contacts folder selected

*Import items into the current folder* option selected

**7** In the **Import Outlook Data File** dialog box, click **Finish**. Compare your screen with Figure 4.13.

The contacts are imported into your Contacts folder and displayed in Business Card view. Your layout may differ.

Figure 4.13

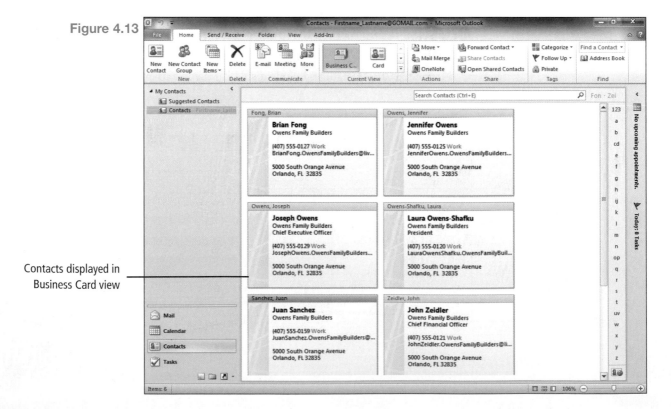

Contacts displayed in Business Card view

**8** In the **Contacts list**, double-click the **John Zeidler** contact to open it, and then on the **Contact tab**, in the **Show group**, click the **Details** button. Under **Internet Free-Busy**, in the **Address** box, delete any existing text, and then type **file:\\**

**9** With the insertion point still located in the **Address** box, right-click, and from the displayed shortcut menu, click **Paste**.

> The path to your student data files is copied from the Open Outlook Data Files dialog box and is pasted in the Address box.

**10** With the insertion point still located in the **Address** box, after the pathname information, type **\JohnZeidler.vfb** to complete the address information for this contact's free/busy file. Compare your screen with Figure 4.14.

> The address begins with the prefix *file:\\* and the file name includes the *.vfb* extension.

**Figure 4.14**

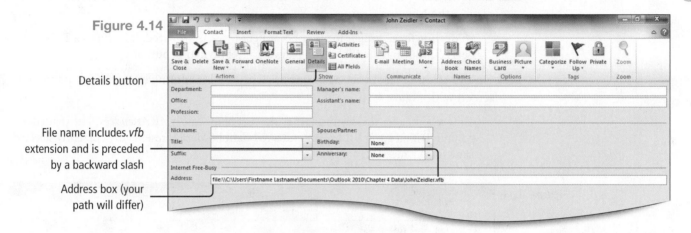

Details button

File name includes *.vfb* extension and is preceded by a backward slash

Address box (your path will differ)

---

**Alert! | Is the current year 2014 or later?**

If the current year is 2014 or later, you will need to use an alternate *.vfb* file for the John Zeidler contact. Outlook stores only three years of calendar information in the *.vfb* files, and the *JohnZeidler.vfb* file contains calendar information from 2011 through 2013. For the years 2014 through 2016, specify his file as *JohnZeidler2014.vfb* using the format described in the preceding step. Similarly, in step 12 for Jennifer Owens, if the year is 2014 or later, use *JenniferOwens2014.vfb*.

---

**11** **Save & Close** the contact.

**12** Open the **Jennifer Owens** contact and click the **Details** button. Under **Internet Free-Busy**, in the **Address** box, type **file:\\** With the insertion point still in the **Address** box, right-click, click **Paste**, and then type **\JenniferOwens.vfb Save & Close** the contact.

## Activity 4.05 | Planning a Meeting

Planning a meeting involves finding an available time in your schedule and the schedules of the meeting attendees and then inviting the attendees to the meeting. Outlook notifies meeting attendees of the meeting via e-mail, so anyone you invite to a meeting must have an e-mail address. Recall that you can configure Outlook to store all your sent messages in the Outbox. Thus, you do not have to be online to send your meeting invitations. In this activity, you will configure Outlook to place your sent messages in the Outbox, and then you will set up a meeting for Warren Owens and three of his colleagues.

**1** From **Backstage** view, click **Options**. In the **Outlook Options** dialog box, on the left, click **Advanced**.

**2** Under **Send and receive**, clear the **Send immediately when connected** check box if necessary. To the immediate right, click the **Send/Receive** button. In the **Send/Receive Groups** dialog box, under **Setting for group "All Accounts"**, *clear* the three check boxes. Under **When Outlook is Offline**, *clear* the two check boxes. Click **Close**, and then click **OK**.

**3** In the **Navigation Pane**, click the **Calendar** button. In the **Date Navigator**, click the **right arrow**, and advance the calendar to next June or December, whichever month is closest to the current month. Click the **first Monday**—the same day for which you have already scheduled appointments.

**4** Click the **2:00** pm time slot. On the **Home tab**, in the **New group**, click **New Meeting** to display the Meeting form.

> A *Meeting form*, similar to an Appointment form, is displayed. It includes a To box and a Send button, and the Ribbon displays a Cancel Invitation button.

**5** On the **Meeting tab**, in the **Show group**, click the **Scheduling** button. Compare your screen with Figure 4.15.

> Your schedule for the day displays as the first name under *All Attendees*. The shaded column with a green left border and a red right border represents the currently selected time for the meeting.

Figure 4.15

Shaded column represents currently selected time

Your schedule for the day appears first under *All Attendees*

Green border indicates start time

Red border indicates end time

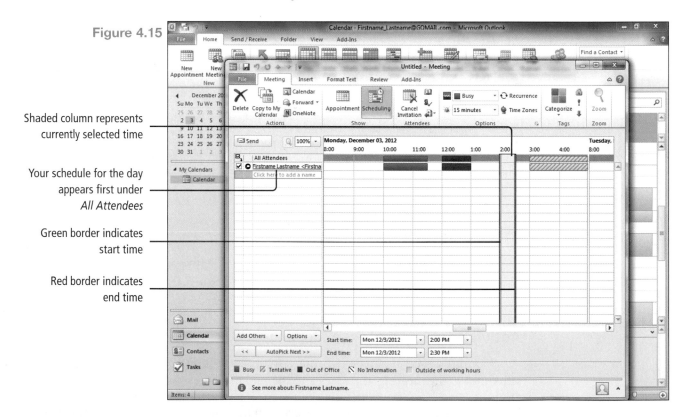

**6** In the **Untitled – Meeting** window, click different time blocks on the time grid.

> As you click various time blocks, the shaded column moves in the selected time grid. The *Meeting start time* and the *Meeting end time* boxes change as you click various time blocks.

**7** Click the time block under **1:00** so that the meeting is set to run from 1:00 PM to 1:30 PM.

You can click different time blocks to adjust the time of the meeting. You may need to change the time as you add meeting attendees and you see their availability.

**8** Click the time block between **11:30** and **12:00** so that the meeting is set to run from 11:30 AM to 12:00 PM.

This is your desired time for the meeting.

**9** In the lower left, click the **Add Others** button, click **Add from Address Book**, and then compare your screen with Figure 4.16.

The Select Attendees and Resources: Contacts dialog box displays. All the names from your Contacts list that have e-mail addresses display in this dialog box, and you can select meeting attendees from the names on this list. You can also specify attendees who are required or who are optional. *Required attendees* must be able to attend the meeting for the meeting to take place—their knowledge and association with the meeting's topic is required.

*Optional attendees* are not considered critical for the meeting; if they cannot attend, the meeting can still be held and they may or may not attend.

Figure 4.16

Select Attendees and Resources: Contacts dialog box

Names from the Contacts list that include e-mail addresses

Required attendees

Optional attendees

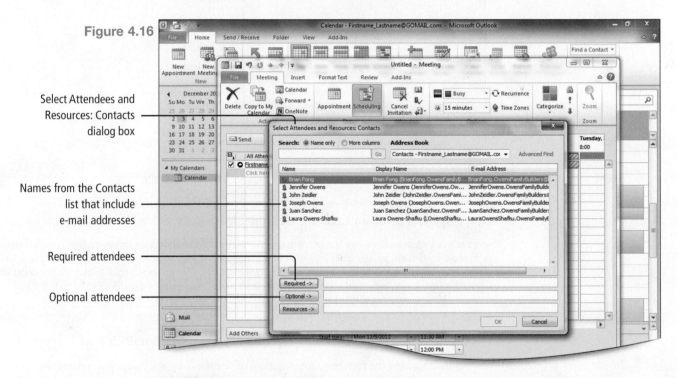

**10** In the **Select Attendees and Resources: Contacts** dialog box, under **Name**, click **John Zeidler** one time to select that name, and then click **Required** to add the name to the Required box.

**11** Select **Jennifer Owens**, and then click **Required**.

The Required box contains two names. These are the individuals who *must* be able to attend if the meeting is to take place. Outlook assumes that you, as the meeting organizer, will attend the meeting.

**12** In the **Select Attendees and Resources: Contacts** dialog box, click **OK**. If the Microsoft Office Internet Free/Busy dialog box displays, click **Cancel**. Compare your screen with Figure 4.17.

The Untitled – Meeting window redisplays and shows each attendee's free/busy information. Notice that Jennifer Owens is busy at the time of your meeting. You will need to find a different time. You can have Outlook find a time at which everyone is available.

Figure 4.17

Meeting form

Two names added to the meeting

Jennifer Owens is busy at proposed meeting time

AutoPick Next button

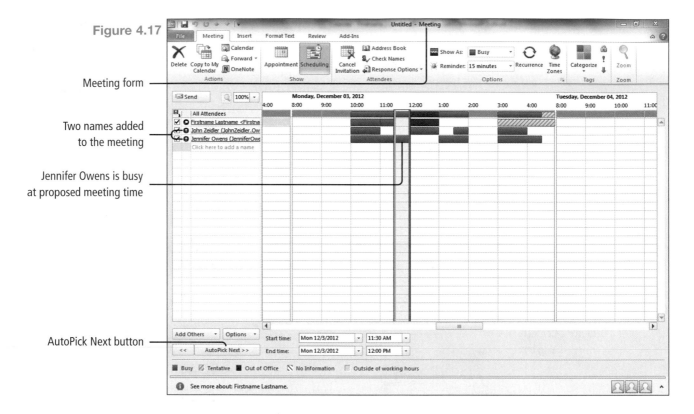

---

**Alert!** | Are you using an Exchange Server?

If you are working in an Exchange Server environment, the meeting attendees may show no free/busy information because by default, the free/busy information is stored on the Exchange Server. Although free/busy information is displayed automatically for Exchange Server users, this information may not display for the fictional users in this instruction because their information is stored with your student data files.

---

**13** At the lower left of the **Untitled – Meeting** window, click **AutoPick Next**.

Outlook scans the free/busy information of the meeting attendees and selects the first time that everyone is available, which is 2:00 to 2:30 PM. When the attendees have busy schedules, this can be a quick way to find a time for everyone to meet. Notice that the available times in the schedule are only *working hours*—8:00 a.m. until 5:00 p.m. You can schedule meetings for later in the day.

**14** In the lower portion of the **Untitled – Meeting** window, click **Options**, and then click **Show Only My Working Hours** to clear the check mark.

**15** Click the **right scroll arrow**, and click the column under **5:00**. Position the pointer on the red border of the shaded column until it changes to the **Horizontal resize pointer** ⬌ as shown in Figure 4.18.

You can drag the green (for start) and red (for end) borders of the shaded column to change the start and end times of a meeting.

Figure 4.18

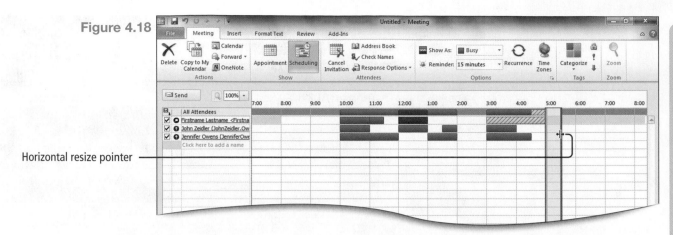

Horizontal resize pointer

**16** Drag the red border to **6:00** to make the time of the meeting **5:00 PM** to **6:00 PM**. Then, on the **Meeting tab**, in the **Show group**, click the **Appointment** button.

> The meeting form displays again. The *To* box now contains the e-mail addresses of the meeting attendees. In the meeting form you can add a Subject and other information in the same manner as you would any other e-mail message.

**17** In the **Subject** box, type **Ocean Palms Status Reports** In the **Location** box, type **My office** Click the **Reminder arrow**, and then click **None**. In the comments area, type **Status reports on Ocean Palms condominium development** Compare your screen with Figure 4.19.

> Depending on the number of attendees and the size and resolution of your screen, up and down arrows may display on the right side of the To box, indicating there are more names in the box than are visible.

Figure 4.19

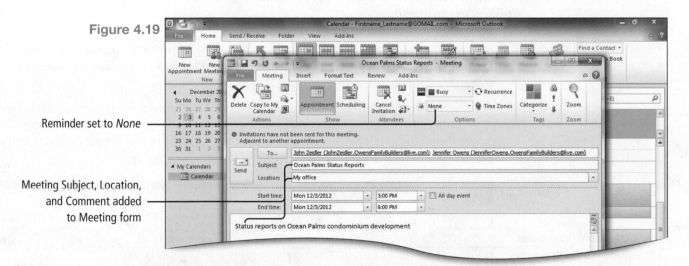

Reminder set to *None*

Meeting Subject, Location, and Comment added to Meeting form

**18** On the Meeting form, click the **Send** button. Compare your screen with Figure 4.20, scrolling if necessary.

> The invitations are sent to the Outbox, and the Meeting form closes. The meeting is added to your calendar. Notice your name is displayed as the meeting organizer. The individual who issues the meeting invitations is the ***meeting organizer***. Compare this with *Staff Meeting*, which is an appointment, not a meeting, despite its name. Because you did not invite people or reserve a room for *Staff Meeting*, it is an appointment for something you plan to do.

**Figure 4.20**

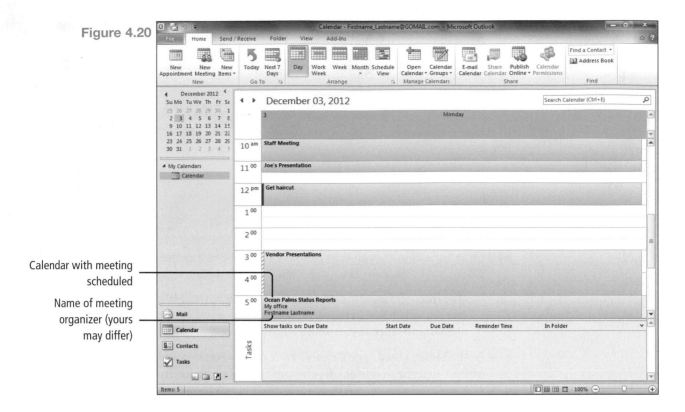

Calendar with meeting scheduled

Name of meeting organizer (yours may differ)

## Activity 4.06 | Adding Meeting Attendees

You can add more people to a scheduled meeting after you have scheduled a time and issued invitations. In this activity, you will add two more individuals at Owens Family Builders to the meeting.

**1** With your calendar still showing the first Monday in June or December, open the **Ocean Palms Status Reports** meeting. **Maximize** ▢ the Meeting form, if necessary. Compare your screen with Figure 4.21.

The Meeting form displays. A banner at the top of the form describes the responses of the meeting attendees. The banner indicates that you have not yet received any responses. The banner also reminds you that this appointment is adjacent to another appointment in the calendar.

**Figure 4.21**

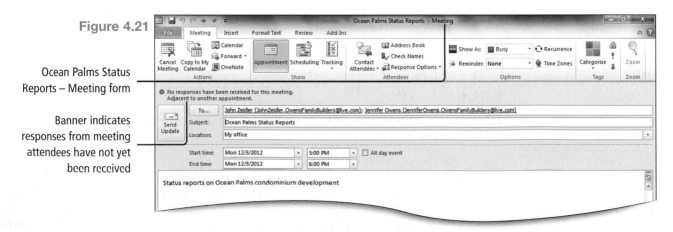

Ocean Palms Status Reports – Meeting form

Banner indicates responses from meeting attendees have not yet been received

**2** On the **Meeting tab**, in the **Attendees group**, click the **Address Book** button. In the displayed **Select Attendees and Resources: Contacts** dialog box, click **Joseph Owens**, and then in the lower left portion of the dialog box, click **Optional**.

> Joseph Owens displays in the Optional box. The attendance of an optional attendee is not critical to the meeting—the meeting can take place with or without the optional attendee.

**3** Click **Brian Fong**, and then click **Optional**. Click **OK** to close the **Select Attendees and Resources: Contacts** dialog box and redisplay the **Meeting** form.

**4** In the **Meeting form**, if not all names appear in the **To** box, click the **To down arrow** to see the two additional names you added to your meeting.

**5** On the **Meeting tab**, in the **Show group**, click the **Scheduling** button, and compare your screen with Figure 4.22.

> The schedule shows the two new names you added to the meeting. No free/busy information displays for the two new names. Joseph Owens and Brian Fong have not made their free/busy information available. The column adjacent to All Attendees shows icons indicating the type of attendee.

**Figure 4.22**
Scheduling button
Icon indicates meeting organizer
Icon indicates required attendees
Icon indicates Optional attendees
Free/busy information not available for these attendees

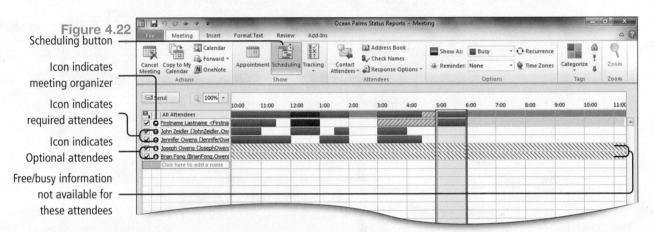

**6** To the left of each name, point to each of the icons to see the ScreenTip that describes an attendee either as Meeting Organizer, Required Attendee, or Optional Attendee.

**7** On the **Meeting tab**, in the **Show group**, click the **Appointment** button.

**8** Display the **Start** menu 🟢, and then click **All Programs**. Locate and then click the **Accessories** folder. Click the **Snipping Tool**. In the **Snipping Tool** window, click the **New arrow**, and then click **Window Snip**. Click anywhere in the window to capture it, and then click the **Save Snip** button 🖫. Navigate to the location where you are storing your files. Click in the **File name** box, and then using your own name, type **Lastname_Firstname_4A_Schedule_Meeting** Click the **Save as type arrow**, and then click **JPEG file**. Click **Save**, and then **Close** ☒ the **Snipping Tool**. Submit the end result to your instructor as directed.

**9** On the **Meeting** form, click **Send Update**.

> The Send Update to Attendees dialog box displays. You have the option of sending updates to all meeting attendees or only to those individuals you have added or deleted. If you expect to make additional changes to the individuals attending a meeting, you can wait until you have finalized the meeting to send the update to all attendees.

**10** Click **Send updates only to added or deleted attendees**, and then click **OK**.

> The Meeting form closes. Meeting invitations are sent to the two additional meeting attendees.

## Activity 4.07 | Removing Meeting Attendees

After you have organized a meeting, you may decide that one or more of the individuals you have invited do not need to attend the meeting. You can remove an attendee from a meeting. In this activity, Warren Owens, the meeting organizer, has learned that Joseph Owens will not be available for the meeting, so you will remove him from the list of meeting attendees.

**1** In the calendar, click the **Ocean Palms Status Reports** meeting. On the **Meeting tab**, in the **Attendees group**, click the **Add or Remove Attendees** button.

The Meeting form displays with the Select Attendees and Resources: Contacts dialog box overlaid on top.

**2** In the displayed **Select Attendees and Resources: Contacts** dialog box, in the **Optional** box, click **Joseph Owens**, as shown in Figure 4.23.

Figure 4.23

Select Attendees and Resources: Contacts dialog box

Joseph Owens selected in the Optional box

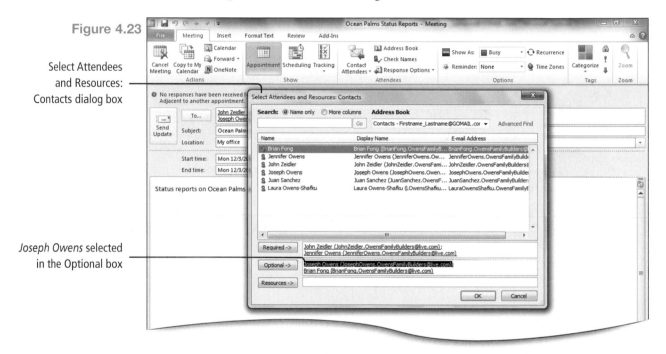

**3** Press Del, and then click **OK**. In the redisplayed **Meeting form**, if not all names appear in the **To** box, at the right edge of the **To** box, click the **To down arrow** and notice that Joseph Owens is no longer included.

**4** Click the **Send Update** button. In the **Send Update to Attendees** dialog box, click **Send updates only to added or deleted attendees**, and then click **OK**.

A meeting update is sent only to Joseph Owens, and the Meeting form closes. As the meeting organizer, you should update the meeting attendees after the list of attendees is finalized.

## Activity 4.08 | Checking the Response Status

When an invited meeting attendee responds to a meeting request, a message is returned to you indicating his or her response. You can keep track of which attendees have responded to your request in the Meeting form. In this activity, you will check and modify the response status for the meeting Warren Owens has planned.

**1** Open the **Ocean Palms Status Reports** meeting.

**2** On the **Meeting tab**, in the **Show group**, click the **Tracking** button, and then compare your screen with Figure 4.24.

> The *Tracking button* changes the view to display a list of each meeting attendee, his or her status as a required or optional attendee, and the attendee's response status. As you receive responses to the meeting invitation, Outlook updates the Response column for each meeting attendee. You can also update the responses manually. You might want to do this if a meeting attendee verbally accepts a meeting invitation.

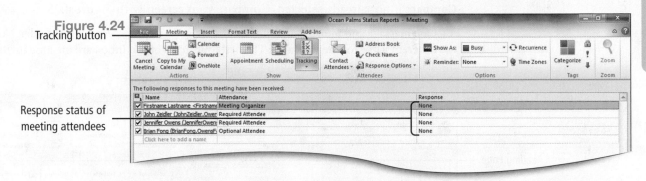

**Figure 4.24**
Tracking button

Response status of meeting attendees

**3** Under **Response**, in the row for **Brian Fong**, click **None**, and then click **Tentative**.

**4** Using the technique you just practiced, change the response statuses for **John Zeidler** and **Jennifer Owens** to **Accepted**.

> The default status of the Meeting Organizer indicates *None* because you—the meeting organizer—would not be responding to your own meeting invitation.

**5** Close ☒ the **Meeting form**. In the **Microsoft Outlook** dialog box, click **Save changes but don't send**, and then click **OK**.

## Objective 3 | Respond to Meeting Requests

When you are invited to a meeting by someone, the invitation displays in your Inbox as an e-mail message. An icon differentiates it from ordinary e-mail messages. You can reply to a meeting invitation in one of four ways: Accept, Tentative, Propose New Time, and Decline. Outlook notifies the meeting organizer of your response. If your response is Accept or Tentative, Outlook places an item in your calendar for the meeting.

### Activity 4.09 | Importing Meeting Invitations into Your Inbox Folder

In this activity, you will import e-mail messages that include meeting invitations into Warren's Inbox folder.

**1** In the **Navigation Pane**, click the **Mail** button. From **Backstage** view, click the **Open tab**, and then click **Import** to display the **Import and Export Wizard** dialog box. Under **Choose an action to perform**, click **Import from another program or file**, and then click **Next**.

**2** In the **Import a File** dialog box, under **Select file type to import from**, click **Outlook Data File (.pst)**. Click **Next**.

**3** In the **Import Outlook Data File** dialog box, click the **Browse** button. In the **Open Outlook Data Files** dialog box, navigate to the location where the student files for this textbook are stored.

**4** Locate **o04A_Owens_Inbox**, and click one time to select it. Then, in the lower right corner of the **Open Outlook Data Files** dialog box, click **Open**, and notice that the file name and path display in the **File to import** box. In the **Import Outlook Data File** dialog box, click **Next**.

**5** Under **Select the folder to import from**, scroll down and click **Inbox**, and then click **Import items into the current folder**. In the **Import Outlook Data File** dialog box, click **Finish**.

**6** On the **View tab**, in the **Current View group**, click the **Change View** arrow, and select **Compact** if not already selected. Compare your screen with Figure 4.25.

> One message and four meeting invitations are imported into your Inbox folder. Notice the different icons for the messages. The first four items in the Inbox are meeting invitations. The remaining item is an e-mail message.

Figure 4.25

Reading Pane

Meeting invitation icons

E-mail message icon

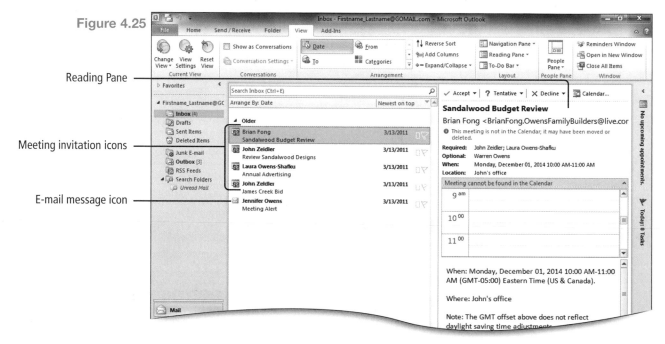

**7** Select but do not open the message from **Brian Fong**, and look at the message in the **Reading Pane**. If the **Reading Pane** is not visible, on the **View tab**, in the **Layout group**, click the **Reading Pane arrow**, and then click **Right**. Notice the commands that appear at the top of the message.

> When you view meeting invitations in the Reading Pane, the three possible responses to the meeting invitation appear as commands at the top of the message: Accept, Tentative, and Decline. Not all the commands may display in the Reading Pane in this screen position. In the message, a banner reads *Please respond* or it may indicate that there is no calendar entry for the meeting.

**8** On the **View tab**, in the **Layout group**, click the **Reading Pane arrow**, and then click **Bottom**. Compare your screen with Figure 4.26.

> With the Reading Pane displayed at the bottom of the screen, all the meeting invitation commands display at the top of the message.

**Figure 4.26**

Reading Pane positioned at the bottom

Meeting invitation responses

Message banner (yours may differ)

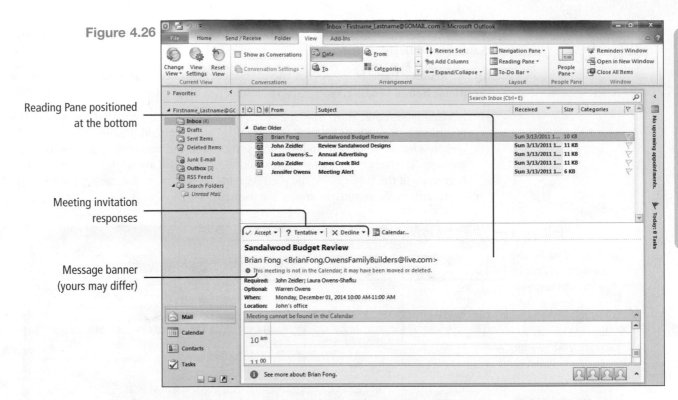

> **9** Select each of the remaining meeting invitations and take a moment to examine each one in the Reading Pane. Then, select the e-mail message from **Jennifer Owens** and notice how, in the Reading Pane, it differs from a meeting invitation.
>
> The format for all the meeting invitations is the same. Each contains the commands at the top of the Reading Pane, and each states the time, location, required attendees, and optional attendees, if any.

---

**Note** | Calendar Entries with Meeting Invitations

A meeting invitation normally arrives in your Inbox as an e-mail message. The incoming message adds a tentative appointment to your calendar for the date and time of the meeting. This calendar item is linked to the Inbox message, and it changes depending on how you respond to the invitation.

---

> **10** Select each of the meeting invitations, and look at the dates of the meetings.
>
> All the meetings occur on December 1, 2014. If the current date is later than this date, the message banner for the meeting may indicate that the meeting occurred in the past. For the purpose of this instruction, you can still respond to meeting invitations if they occurred in the past.

> **11** Compare the meeting times for the **Review Sandalwood Designs** meeting and the **Annual Advertising** meeting.
>
> There is a conflict for the two afternoon meetings. You will have to either decline one of the meetings or propose a new time.

## Activity 4.10 | Accepting and Declining Meeting Invitations

You can respond to a meeting invitation either in the Reading Pane or by opening the message and responding in the Message form. In this activity, you will accept one of the invitations for Warren Owens and decline another.

**1** With the **Inbox** still displayed, select the message from **John Zeidler (Review Sandalwood Designs)**.

**2** In the **Reading Pane**, at the top of the message, click **Accept**, and then click **Edit the Response before Sending**. Compare your screen with Figure 4.27.

> A Meeting Response form displays. When you **accept** a meeting invitation, the meeting organizer is notified in an e-mail message that you will attend the meeting. Editing the response before sending the reply enables you to add comments or questions to the reply message. The banner under the toolbar indicates *Yes, I will attend this meeting.* At the beginning of the Subject box, the prefix *Accepted* is displayed. You can type your comments in the comments area of the form.

**Figure 4.27**

Accepted: Review Sandalwood Designs – Meeting Response form displays

Banner indicates you are accepting the meeting invitation

Date, time and location of the meeting

Comments area

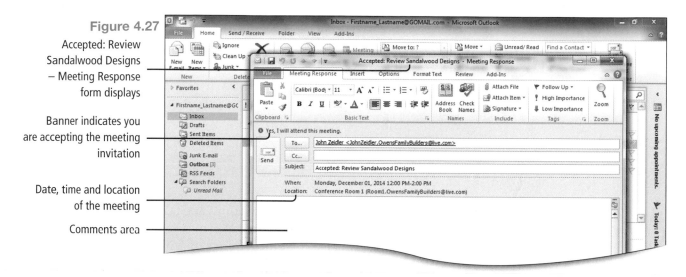

**3** Using the spacing technique you have practiced for typing messages, create the following message in the comments area: **John, Would you ask Brian to bring the Deerfield Farms designs with him? I would like to compare them to the Sandalwood designs. Warren**

**4** On the **Meeting Response** form, click the **Send** button.

> The Meeting Response form closes. The message is sent to the Outbox, and the Inbox redisplays. The John Zeidler message has been removed from your Inbox, and the accepted meeting is now a calendar entry on the date of the meeting.

**5** In the **Navigation Pane**, click the **Calendar** button. On the **Home tab**, in the **Go To group**, click the **Go To** dialog box launcher ⬚. Compare your screen with Figure 4.28.

> Recall that the Go To Date command is an alternative way to jump to dates in the calendar.

Figure 4.28

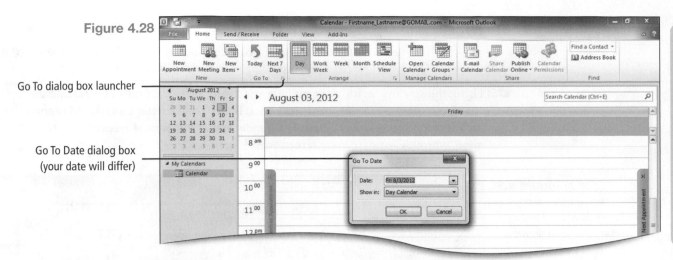

Go To dialog box launcher

Go To Date dialog box
(your date will differ)

**6** In the **Go To Date** dialog box, type **12/01/14** and then click **OK**.

The calendar for December 1, 2014 displays. Outlook has created an appointment for the time of the meeting invitation.

> **Note** | Dates for Received Meeting Invitations
>
> The dates for your accepted meetings may vary significantly from the date you have been using to schedule your own meetings. A fixed date was necessary in the received meeting invitation. Depending on the current date, these meetings may take place far in the future, or they may have occurred in the past. Outlook will enter the accepted meeting into your calendar regardless of its date.

**7** Double-click the **Review Sandalwood Designs** meeting to open the Meeting form.

The Meeting form displays. The banner indicates the date on which you accepted the invitation. The name of the meeting organizer—John Zeidler—displays at the top of the form.

**8** **Close** ☒ the **Review Sandalwood Designs - Meeting** form.

**9** In the **Navigation Pane**, click the **Mail** button, select the message from **Brian Fong**, and then, in the **Reading Pane**, notice that *Warren Owens* is an optional attendee. If he declines to attend, the meeting can still take place.

**10** Open the **Brian Fong** message. On the **Meeting** form, in the **Respond group**, click the **Decline** button, and then compare your screen with Figure 4.29.

When you *decline* a meeting invitation, there are three choices regarding the response – Edit the Response before Sending, Send the Response Now, and Do Not Send a Response. When declining a meeting, it is polite to include comments along with a response.

Figure 4.29

Decline meeting menu

**11** In the displayed shortcut menu, click **Edit the Response before Sending**.

A Meeting Response form displays. The banner indicates that you will not attend, and the prefix Declined is placed at the beginning of the Subject text.

**12** Using the spacing technique you have practiced for typing messages, create the following message in the comments area: **Brian, I really need this time to prepare for a presentation the next day. Laura can handle any of the budget questions that might arise. Warren** Compare your screen with Figure 4.30.

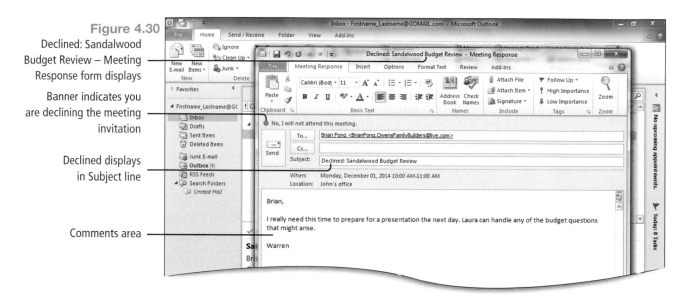

**Figure 4.30**

Declined: Sandalwood Budget Review – Meeting Response form displays

Banner indicates you are declining the meeting invitation

Declined displays in Subject line

Comments area

**13** **Send** the message.

The Meeting Response form closes. The message is sent to the Outbox, and the Inbox redisplays. The Brian Fong message has been removed from your Inbox.

## Activity 4.11 | Replying with a Tentative Status

If your schedule is especially busy, you might need to tentatively accept a meeting invitation. In this activity, you will tentatively accept one of Warren's meeting invitations.

**1** In the **Inbox**, open the **John Zeidler – James Creek Bid** message. On the **Meeting tab**, in the **Respond group**, click the **Tentative** button.

When your response to a meeting invitation is tentative, the meeting organizer is notified by an e-mail message that you might attend the meeting.

**2** From the displayed shortcut menu, click **Edit the Response before Sending**.

A Meeting Response form displays. The banner indicates *Yes, I might attend this meeting*, and the prefix *Tentative* is placed at the beginning of the Subject text.

**3** Using the proper format for typing messages, create the following message in the comments area: **John, As luck would have it, I have a 7:30 dentist appointment that morning. I should be able to reschedule it. I will let you know. Warren** Compare your screen with Figure 4.31.

Figure 4.31

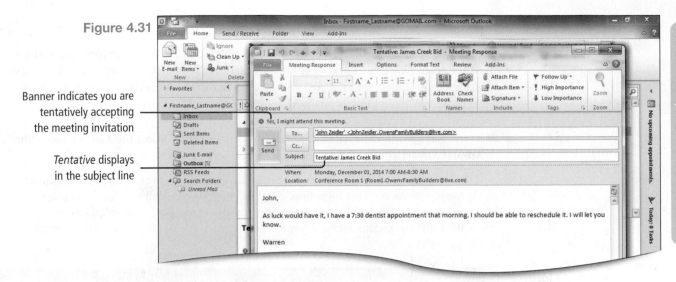

Banner indicates you are
tentatively accepting
the meeting invitation

*Tentative* displays
in the subject line

**4** **Send** the message.

The Meeting Response form closes. The message is sent to the Outbox, and the Inbox redisplays. The John Zeidler-James Creek Bid message has been removed from your Inbox. The tentatively accepted meeting is now a calendar entry on the meeting date.

**5** In the **Navigation Pane**, click the **Calendar** button. On the **Home tab**, in the **Go To group**, click the **Go To** dialog box launcher ⬚. In the **Go To Date** dialog box, type **12/01/14** and then click **OK**. If necessary, scroll up to see the 7:00 a.m. meeting, and then compare your screen with Figure 4.32.

This date now contains two confirmed meetings. Outlook has created an appointment for the time of the James Creek Bid meeting invitation. The patterned border indicates that the meeting's status is Tentative.

Figure 4.32

Patterned border
indicates the tentative
status of the meeting

Shaded text with
patterned border indicates
you have not responded
to this meeting invitation;
acceptance is tentative
by default

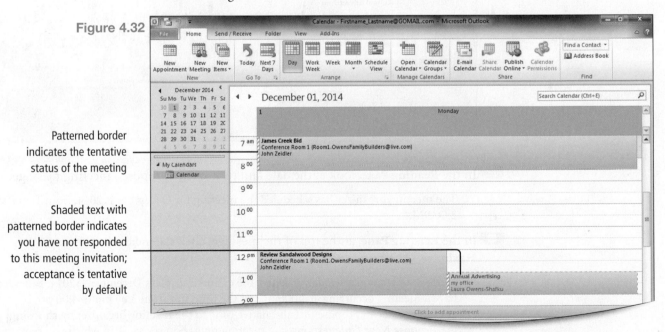

**6** Display the **Start** menu 🌐, and open the **Snipping Tool**. Click the **New arrow**, and then click **Window Snip**. Click in the window to capture it, and then click the **Save Snip** button 🖫. Navigate to your storage device. Click in the **File name** box, and then using your own name, type **Lastname_Firstname_4A_December_2014** Click the **Save as type arrow**, and then click **JPEG file**. Click **Save**. **Close** ☒ the **Snipping Tool**. Submit the end result to your instructor as directed.

## Activity 4.12 | Proposing a New Meeting Time

It is likely that you will, from time to time, receive meeting invitations that conflict with other activities. Outlook enables you to respond to a meeting invitation by proposing a different time. In this activity, you will propose a different meeting time for a meeting invitation that Warren Owens received.

**1** In the **Navigation Pane**, click the **Mail** button, and then select the **Laura Owens-Shafku – Annual Advertising** message. Compare your screen with Figure 4.33.

When displayed on the bottom, the Reading Pane shows the Calendar command at the top of the meeting invitation. This command is especially useful if you want to see the calendar date for a meeting. Depending on the size and resolution of your screen, the Calendar command is not always visible when the Reading Pane is displayed on the right.

Figure 4.33

Calendar command in Reading Pane

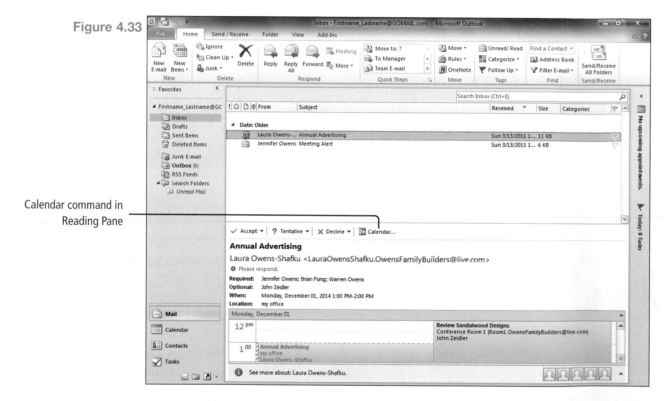

**2** In the **Reading Pane**, look at the date and time of the proposed meeting message.

The meeting organizer has scheduled the meeting for December 1, 2014, from 1:00 PM to 2:00 PM.

**3** In the **Reading Pane**, at the top of the message, click **Calendar**. If necessary, **Maximize** ☐ the window.

Outlook opens *a new window* in which the calendar displays December 1, 2014. You already have a meeting occurring at 1:00 pm, but the time slot from 3:00 pm to 4:00 pm is available. You can propose this alternative time to the meeting organizer by choosing the *Propose New Time* response—a meeting invitation response in which you request that the meeting organizer change the meeting to a time at which you can attend.

**4** Click the *Annual Advertising* meeting to select it. On the **Calendar Tools Meeting tab**, in the **Respond group**, click the **Propose New Time** button. From the displayed menu, select **Tentative and Propose New Time**.

Two options are displayed for proposing a new meeting time. *Tentative and Propose New Time* is used when the initial meeting request is tentatively accepted, but a new time is proposed as a replacement. Clicking *Decline and Propose New Time* declines the initial meeting request and proposes a new meeting time in its place.

**5** In the **Propose New Time: Annual Advertising** dialog box, position the pointer on the red border of the column and drag it to **4:00**, scrolling as necessary. Position the pointer on the green border, and drag it to **3:00**, and then compare your screen with Figure 4.34.

Recall that free/busy time will not display if the date of the meeting is more than 10 months from the current date.

**Figure 4.34**

Propose New Time dialog box

Your calendar may display free/busy time if the current date is within 10 months of 12/01/2014

Yellow column indicates current meeting time

Drag borders to set different start and end times

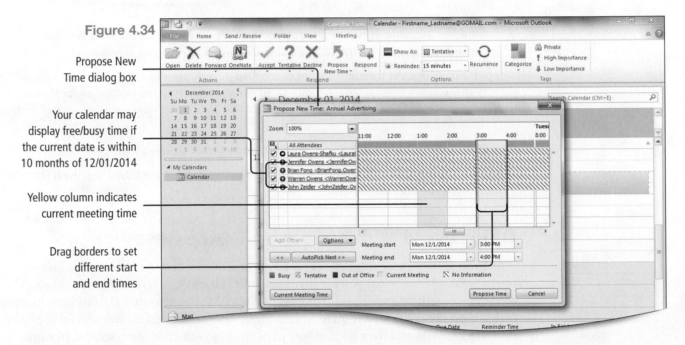

**6** In the lower right corner of the **Propose New Time: Annual Advertising** dialog box, click **Propose Time**.

A Meeting Response form displays. The banner indicates the current and proposed times for this meeting, and the prefix New Time Proposed is placed at the beginning of the Subject text.

**7** Using techniques you have previously practiced, create the following message in the comments area: **Laura, I'm already in a meeting at your proposed time. Can we move it to 3:00 on the same date? I really want to see the Web site! Warren** Compare your screen with Figure 4.35.

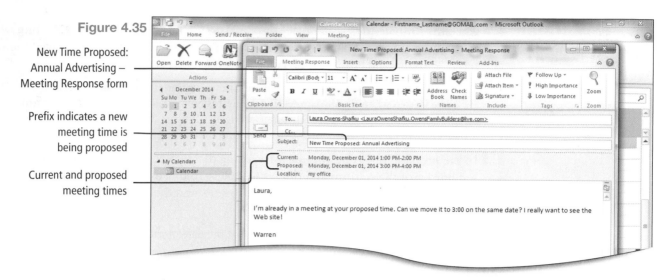

**Figure 4.35**

New Time Proposed:
Annual Advertising –
Meeting Response form

Prefix indicates a new
meeting time is
being proposed

Current and proposed
meeting times

---

**8** **Send** the message. If necessary, display the **Calendar** and use the **Date Navigator** or the **Go To Date** dialog box menu to display **December 1, 2014**.

> Notice that the meeting time for the *Annual Advertising* meeting is still at the original time proposed by the meeting organizer and that it occurs at the same time as the *Review Sandalwood Designs* meeting. It has a *Tentative* status while you try to arrange a different meeting time.

**9** **Close** ☒ the **Calendar** window and return to your Outlook window.

> The message for the Annual Advertising meeting is still in the Inbox because it has not been accepted or declined.

## Objective 4 | Schedule an Office Resource

If you work in an Exchange Server environment, you may be able to schedule—reserve—a resource when you are planning your meetings. A **resource** might be a conference room or audiovisual equipment. To schedule a resource, it must have its own mailbox on the server—an e-mail address. Your network administrator sets up the resource mailbox and then gives others permission to schedule the resource. In some organizations, only managers have permission to schedule a resource.

### Activity 4.13 | Setting Up an Office Resource

To reserve a resource such as a conference room, it must appear as a contact in your Contacts list. A resource must have an e-mail address, and you must have permission to reserve it. In this activity, you will add a resource to Warren's Contacts list.

**1** In the **Navigation Pane**, click the **Contacts** button, and then open a new contact form.

**2** In the **Contact** form, in the **File as** box, type **Conference Room 1**

> When creating a contact that is a resource, type in the *File as* box rather than the *Full Name* box. Otherwise, Outlook will reformat the name in a *Lastname, Firstname* format and then will alphabetize the conference room name as *1, Conference Room*.

**3** In the **E-mail** box, type **Room1.OwensFamilyBuilders@live.com** Click in the **Display as** box, and then compare your screen with Figure 4.36.

> A resource must have an e-mail address. Your network administrator sets up the mailbox for the resource and assigns permission for specific individuals to schedule it.

Figure 4.36

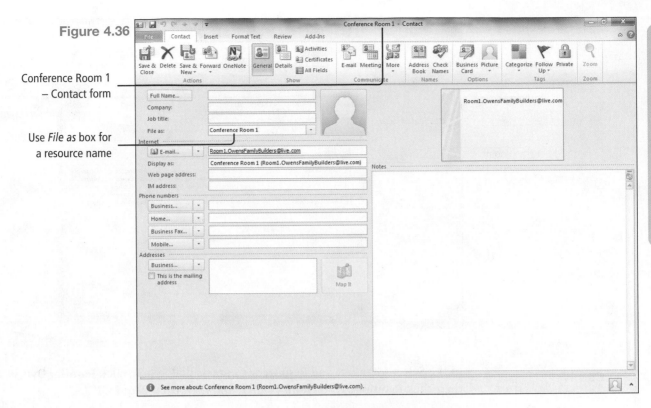

Conference Room 1
– Contact form

Use *File as* box for
a resource name

**4** **Save & Close** the contact.

## Activity 4.14 | Reserving a Resource for a Meeting

After your resource has been set up with an e-mail address by your network administrator and you have added it to your Contacts list, you can schedule it for meetings as necessary. In this activity, you will plan a meeting for Warren Owens and two of his colleagues, using the Conference Room 1 resource.

**1** In the **Navigation Pane**, click the **Calendar** button. On the **Home tab**, in the **Go To group**, click the **Today** button.

Clicking the *Today* button will ensure that the current date is selected.

**2** In the **Navigation Pane**, in the **Date Navigator**, click the **right arrow**, and advance the calendar to next June or December, whichever month is closest to the current month. Click the **first Monday**, a day for which you have already scheduled appointments.

**3** Click the **11:30 am** time slot. On the **Home tab**, in the **New group**, click **New Meeting** to display the Meeting form. In the **Meeting form**, on the **Meeting tab**, in the **Show group**, click the **Scheduling** button.

The Meeting form displays, and the free/busy information reflects the appointments in your calendar for that day.

**4** In the lower portion of the **Untitled – Meeting** window, click the **Add Others** button, and then click **Add from Address Book**. Compare your screen with Figure 4.37.

The Select Attendees and Resources: Contacts dialog box displays. The list includes the *Conference Room 1* contact you just added.

Figure 4.37

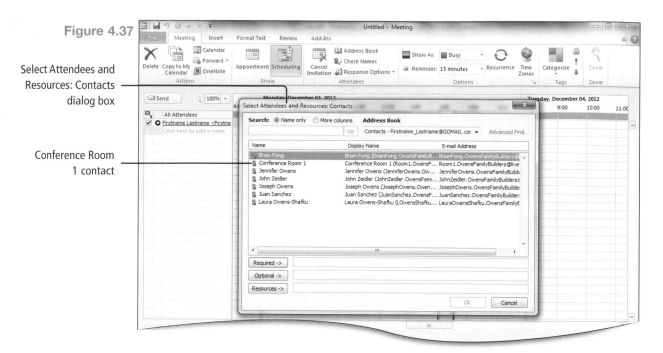

Select Attendees and
Resources: Contacts
dialog box

Conference Room
1 contact

**Another Way**

To select multiple
contacts, click the first
contact, hold down `Ctrl`
and then click each
additional contact that
you want to invite to
the meeting.

**5** In the **Select Attendees and Resources: Contacts** dialog box, click **Jennifer Owens**, and
then click **Required**. Click **John Zeidler**, and then click **Required**.

The required attendees display in the Required box.

**6** Click **Conference Room 1**, and then click **Resources**. Click **OK**. Compare your screen
with Figure 4.38.

The Untitled - Meeting window redisplays and shows the free/busy information for the
meeting attendees. No schedule information is available for the conference room resource.
Under All Attendees, the icon for the conference room indicates that it is a resource.
Notice that Jennifer Owens is not free at the desired meeting time.

Figure 4.38

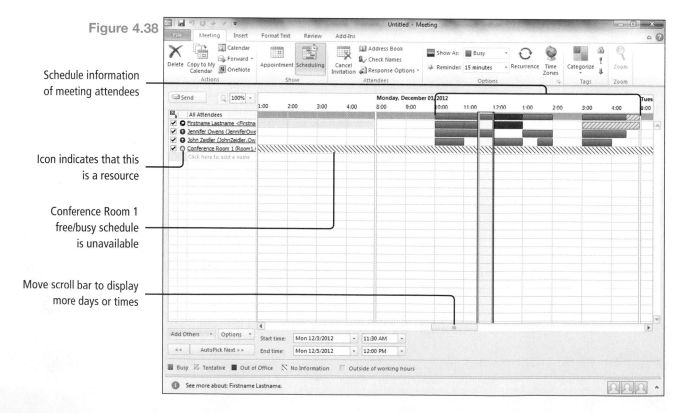

Schedule information
of meeting attendees

Icon indicates that this
is a resource

Conference Room 1
free/busy schedule
is unavailable

Move scroll bar to display
more days or times

**7** Use the **right scroll arrow** and **left scroll arrow** to see the rest of the work day.

Although 2 PM to 3 PM is available for all attendees, Warren Owens does not want Jennifer and John to have a full afternoon of meetings without a break. You decide to schedule the meeting outside of regular working hours—8 AM to 5 PM. Recall that you can display the entire day.

**8** In the lower portion of the **Untitled – Meeting** window, click the **Options** button, and then click **Show Only My Working Hours** to clear the check mark.

**9** Click the **right scroll arrow**, and then click the column under **6:00** so that the meeting time is 6:00 PM to 6:30 PM. On the **Meeting tab**, in the **Show group**, click the **Appointment** button.

In the Meeting form, the To box contains the e-mail addresses of all the invited meeting attendees. The *Location* box displays *Conference Room 1*.

**10** In the **Subject** box, type **Cost Overruns on the Greenwood Development** Click the **Reminder arrow**, and then click **None**. Using techniques you have previously practiced, type the following message in the comments area: **Jennifer and John, Sorry this is so late in the day, but it is important. We need to address the cost overruns right away. Warren** Compare your screen with Figure 4.39.

Figure 4.39

Cost Overruns on the Greenwood Development-Meeting form

Banner indicates invitations have not been sent for this meeting yet and Warren has an adjacent appointment

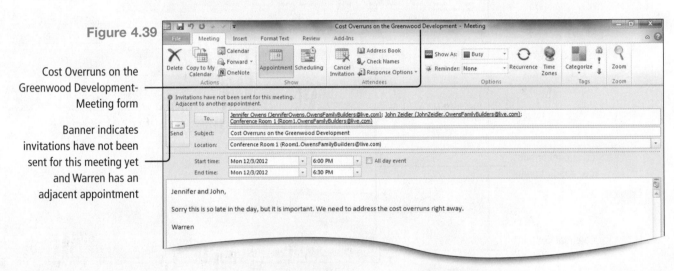

---

**Alert! | Are you using an Exchange Server?**

If you are working in an Exchange Server environment, you should remove Conference Room 1 as a recipient of your meeting invitation. You must be granted permission from your network administrator to use resources in Outlook when using Exchange Server accounts. Outlook may not send the meeting invitation if you include a resource as a meeting attendee.

---

**11** **Send** the meeting invitation.

Outlook adds the meeting to your calendar. The resource will accept the invitation if it is free and decline it if it is already busy. If it accepts the invitation, the time is automatically scheduled in the resource's calendar. Depending on the size and resolution of your screen, a small, gray arrow may display at the bottom right of the Appointment area. Recall that this indicates an appointment that does not appear in the viewing area.

**12** If necessary, in the **Calendar**, scroll down to **6:00 pm** to view the *Cost Overruns on the Greenwood Development* meeting.

# Objective 5 | Manage Meeting Information

If your schedule includes many meetings, you may find it helpful to print meeting invitations and calendar information. Printing meeting information is similar to printing other items in Outlook. Deleting meetings in your calendar must be handled somewhat differently because they may be linked to sent invitations.

### Activity 4.15 | Printing Meeting Information

In this activity, you will print Warren's calendar for the day of the meetings he has planned, as well as one of his invitations.

**1** Display the same Monday in June or December in which you have been working, which now shows six meetings and appointments. Compare your screen with Figure 4.40.

> Depending on your screen resolution, all six meetings may not be visible.

**Figure 4.40**

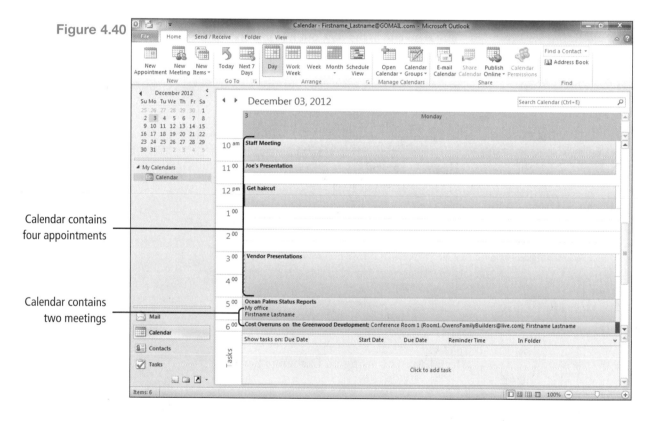

Calendar contains four appointments

Calendar contains two meetings

**2** From **Backstage** view, click **Print**. Under **Settings**, click the choices to view the available print styles, and then click **Daily Style**. Under **Printer**, click **Print Options**. In the **Print** dialog box, click the **Page Setup** button.

**3** In the **Page Setup: Daily Style** dialog box, click the **Header/Footer tab**, and delete any existing header or footer information, including dates and page numbers. In the left footer box, using your own name, type **Lastname_Firstname_4A_Warren's_Calendar** Click **OK** to redisplay the **Print** dialog box. Preview the calendar, and then print it or create a PDF document. Submit the end result to your instructor as directed.

**4** In the calendar, click the **Cost Overruns on the Greenwood Development** meeting to select the meeting.

**5** From **Backstage** view, click **Print**. Under **Settings**, scroll down and click **Memo Style**. Under **Printer**, click the **Print Options**. In the **Print** dialog box, click the **Page Setup** button to display the **Page Setup: Memo Style** dialog box. On the **Header/Footer tab**, delete any existing header or footer information, including dates and page numbers. In the left **Footer** box, using your own name, type **Lastname_Firstname_4A_Overruns_Meeting** and click **OK**. Preview the meeting, and then print it or create a PDF document. Submit the end result to your instructor as directed.

### Activity 4.16 | Deleting Meetings

When you delete meetings from your calendar, you may need to update meeting attendees to let them know the meeting has been cancelled. In this activity, you will delete Warren's meetings and other Outlook information.

**1** With the same **Monday** in June or December still displayed, click the **Cost Overruns on the Greenwood Development** meeting.

**2** On the **Meeting tab**, in the **Actions group**, click the **Cancel Meeting** button. Compare your screen with Figure 4.41.

The Meeting form opens and a banner indicates that the meeting attendees have not been notified that the meeting is cancelled. As the meeting organizer, you should notify meeting attendees when a meeting is cancelled.

**Figure 4.41**

Banner indicates cancellation for this meeting has not been sent

Send Cancellation button

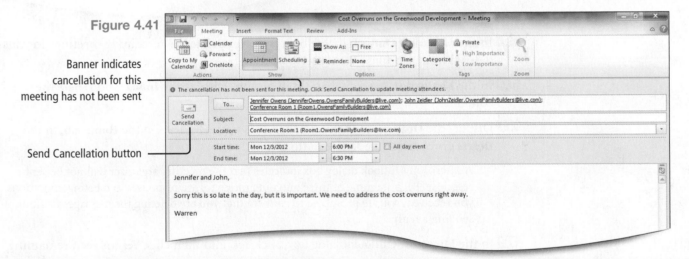

**3** Click the **Send Cancellation** button to send an update to all attendees and remove the meeting from your calendar.

**4** Click the **Ocean Palms Status Reports** meeting. On the **Meeting tab**, in the **Actions group**, click the **Cancel Meeting** button.

**5** In the **Meeting** form, click the **Send Cancellation** button.

**6** Hold down (Shift) while selecting the four remaining appointments in the calendar for this day. Right-click any of the selected appointments to display the shortcut menu, and then click **Delete**.

**7** On the **Home tab**, in the **Go To group**, click the **Go To** dialog box launcher. In the **Go To Date** dialog box, type **12/01/14** and then click **OK**.

The calendar displays December 1, 2014. This date contains the meeting invitations that you accepted and tentatively accepted or for which you proposed a new time.

**8** Click the **Review Sandalwood Designs** meeting. On the **Meeting tab**, in the **Actions group**, click **Delete**, and then compare your screen with Figure 4.42.

The Microsoft Outlook dialog box asks whether or not you want to send a response to the organizer of the meeting. It is good manners to inform the meeting organizer when you are unable to attend a meeting for which you have already accepted an invitation; however, for purposes of this instruction, it is not necessary to do so.

Figure 4.42

Microsoft Outlook dialog box

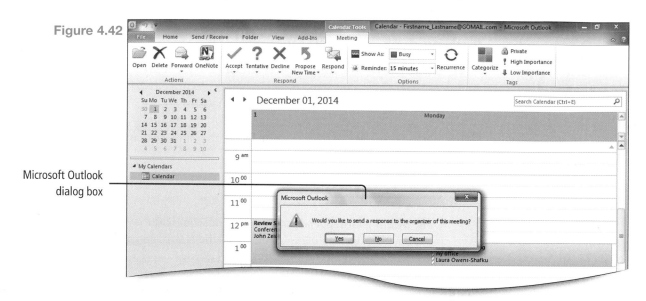

**9** In the **Microsoft Outlook** dialog box, click **No**. Delete the remaining meetings for this date without sending a response.

**10** In the **Navigation Pane**, click the **Mail** button. Display the **Inbox**, and **Delete** the contents.

**11** Display the **Outbox**, and select all the items in the folder. On the **Home tab**, in the **Delete group**, click the **Delete** button.

A Microsoft Outlook dialog box indicates that the meeting organizer will not be sent a response. Because some of these outgoing messages are responses to meeting invitations you received, you are prompted to confirm that you are deleting the messages without sending a reply.

**12** In the **Microsoft Outlook** dialog box, click **Yes**, and then click **Yes** for each remaining meeting response that is deleted.

**13** Display the **Contacts** folder, and delete its contents. Display the **Folder List** 📁, and then empty the **Deleted Items** folder.

**14** From **Backstage** view, click **Options**. In the **Outlook Options** dialog box, on the left, click **Advanced**. Under **Send and receive**, select the **Send immediately when connected** check box.

**15** Click the **Send/Receive** button. In the **Send/Receive Groups** dialog box, under **Setting for group "All Accounts"**, restore the default settings by selecting the appropriate check boxes. Click **Close**.

**16** In the **Outlook Options** dialog box, on the left, click **Calendar**. Under **Calendar options**, click the **Free/Busy Options** button. In the **Free/Busy Options** dialog box, delete the text in the **Publish at my location** box, and then clear the **Publish at my location** check box. Click **OK**. If you changed your time zone, under **Time zone**, click the **Time zone arrow**, and then locate and click your time zone. Click **OK** to close the dialog boxes.

**17** In the **Folder List**, click **Calendar** to display the Calendar folder. In **Backstage** view, on the **Print tab**, under **Printer**, click **Print Options**. In the **Print** dialog box, under **Print style**, click **Define Styles** to display the **Define Print Styles** dialog box.

> Outlook remembers header and footer information. You can restore the print styles you used to their default setting.

**18** In the **Define Print Styles** dialog box, click **Daily Style**, click **Reset**, and then click **OK**. In the **Define Print Styles** dialog box, click **Memo Style**, click **Reset**, and then click **OK**. **Close** the dialog box. In the **Print** dialog box, click **Cancel**.

**19** In the **Navigation Pane**, click **Mail**. On the **View tab**, in the **Layout group**, click the **Reading Pane** button, and then click **Right**.

**20** **Close** ☒ Outlook.

**End** **You have completed Project 4A**

# Content-Based Assessments

## Summary

Use Outlook to schedule meetings and coordinate your schedule with others. In this chapter, you created appointments and examined how Outlook stores your free/busy information. You practiced publishing your free/busy schedule on a file server and accessed the free/busy schedule of others. You organized a meeting, planned a meeting, and invited meeting participants. You practiced accepting and declining meetings and responding to meetings with a Tentative reply. You practiced responding to a meeting invitation by proposing a different meeting time when the original invitation conflicted with another appointment in your calendar. You also set up and scheduled a meeting using a resource. Finally, you practiced printing meeting information and deleting meetings from your calendar.

## Key Terms

## Matching

Match each term in the second column with its correct definition in the first column. Write the letter of the term on the blank line in front of the correct definition.

_____ 1. A group of four indicators displayed by Outlook, which can be viewed by others who have the ability to view your calendar, and that indicate your availability for a date and time in your calendar.

_____ 2. The Outlook calendar stored on the hard drive of your computer.

_____ 3. Special server software that provides a system for sharing Outlook information among members on a network.

_____ 4. The default free/busy setting that Outlook assigns to all new appointments.

_____ 5. A free/busy setting that indicates you are away from your office and not available for other meetings or appointments and that is indicated by an appointment with a purple bar.

_____ 6. A meeting response in which the meeting organizer is notified that you might attend the meeting and that places the text *Yes, I might attend this meeting* in a banner at the top of the sent reply.

_____ 7. A calendar activity that requires inviting other people and/or scheduling a room or equipment.

_____ 8. A term used to refer to a meeting attendee without whom, because of special knowledge or input, a meeting cannot take place.

_____ 9. The individual who plans a meeting and issues the meeting invitations.

_____ 10. A person whose attendance at a meeting is not critical and without whom the meeting can still take place.

**A** Accept

**B** Busy

**C** Decline

**D** Exchange Server

**E** Free/busy information

**F** Local calendar

**G** Meeting

**H** Meeting organizer

**I** Optional attendee

**J** Out of Office

**K** Propose New Time

**L** Required attendee

**M** Resource

**N** Tentative

**O** Working hours

_____ 11.  A meeting invitation response in which you agree to attend a meeting and that notifies the meeting organizer, by sending an e-mail message, that you will attend.

_____ 12.  A meeting invitation response in which you do not agree to attend a meeting and that notifies the meeting organizer, by sending an e-mail message, that you will not attend.

_____ 13.  A meeting invitation response in which you request that the meeting organizer change the meeting to a time at which you can attend.

_____ 14.  A facility, such as a conference room, or a piece of equipment, such as a projector, whose availability and use you can schedule within Outlook.

_____ 15.  The weekday hours between 8:00 a.m. and 5:00 p.m.

## Multiple Choice

Choose the correct answer.

1.  Meetings are displayed in the calendar in a manner similar to this Outlook feature.
    A. Notes  B. Email messages  C. Appointments

2.  The status used to indicate that you are away from your office and are not available for other appointments or meetings.
    A. Out of Office  B. Busy  C. Tentative

3.  The people who participate in a meeting.
    A. Attendees  B. Participants  C. Contacts

4.  The button on the Meeting form that you can click to display a list of each meeting attendee, his or her status as required or optional, and the attendee's response status.
    A. Scheduling  B. Tracking  C. Appointments

5.  The button you can click to instruct Outlook to scan the free/busy information of meeting attendees in order to find the first time that every attendee is available.
    A. AutoMeet Next  B. AutoSchedule Next  C. AutoPick Next

6.  The type of access assigned to those who have the ability to both view and store information on a server.
    A. Read/write  B. Administrative  C. Log in

7.  The folder in which a meeting invitation that you receive displays in Outlook.
    A. Inbox  B. Outbox  C. Sent Items

8.  In the Untitled - Meeting window, the color assigned to the shaded column that indicates the meeting start time.
    A. Blue  B. Red  C. Green

9.  In the Untitled - Meeting window, the color assigned to the shaded column that indicates the meeting end time.
    A. Blue  B. Red  C. Green

10.  The number of possible response options with which you can respond to a meeting invitation.
    A. Two  B. Three  C. Four

# Content-Based Assessments

1. Publish Free/Busy Information
2. Schedule a Meeting
3. Schedule an Office Resource
4. Manage Meeting Information

## Mastering Outlook | Project **4B** Construction Calendar

In the following Mastering Outlook project, you will schedule appointments and meetings for Warren Owens. The company is managing an important Town Center construction project and you will use the free/busy information of company personnel to schedule a meeting and resources. Your completed documents will look similar to the ones shown in Figure 4.43.

### Project Files

For Project 4B, you will need the following files:

o04B_Construction_Contacts
JenniferOwens.vfb
JohnZeidler.vfb
JenniferOwens2014.vfb
JohnZeidler2014.vfb

You will print or create a PDF for two files with the following footers:

Lastname_Firstname_4B_Meeting
Lastname_Firstname_4B_Construction_Calendar

### Project Results

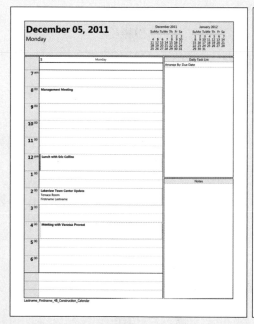

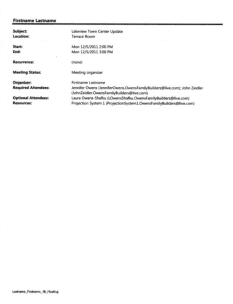

**Figure 4.43**

(Project 4B Construction Calendar continues on the next page)

# Content-Based Assessments

**1** Click the **Start** button, and then point to the **Shut down button arrow**. On the **Shut down** menu, click **Switch user** to display the Windows 7 desktop. Click the user account you created in Chapter 1. If the account does not exist, refer to Chapter 1, Activities 1.01 and 1.02 to setup the Windows 7 user account and to configure Microsoft Outlook. **Start** Outlook, display the **Inbox** and delete any existing messages. Display the **Contacts** and delete any existing contacts.

**2** From **Backstage** view, click **Options**. In the **Outlook Options** dialog box, on the left, click **Advanced**. Under **Send and receive**, clear the **Send immediately when connected** check box if necessary. To the immediate right, click the **Send/Receive** button. In the **Send/Receive Groups** dialog box, under **Setting for group "All Accounts"** clear all five check boxes. Click **Close**.

**3** If your computer clock is not set to display time in the *Eastern Time (US & Canada)* zone, in the **Outlook Options** dialog box, click **Calendar**. Under **Time zones**, click the **Time zone arrow** and then select (**UTC-05:00**) **Eastern Time (US & Canada)**. Click **OK**.

**4** Display the **Calendar**. In the **Date Navigator**, advance the calendar to next **June** or **December**, *whichever month is closest to the current month*. Click the **first Monday** in the month, and then, if necessary, delete any existing calendar items for that day. Create an appointment for a **Management Meeting** from **8:00 am** to **9:00 am** with no reminders. Create another appointment with no reminders for a **Lunch with Eric Collins** from **12:00 pm** to **1:00 pm**, and then change the **Show As** setting to **Out of Office**. Create an appointment for a **Meeting with Vanessa Provost** from **4:00 pm** to **5:00 pm** with no reminders and then change the **Show As** setting to **Tentative**.

**5** Display the **Contacts** folder, and then add a resource as a **New Contact**. In the **File as box**, type **Projection System 1** and then click in the **E-mail box**. Type **ProjectionSystem1.OwensFamilyBuilders@live.com** and then **Save & Close** the contact.

**6** With the **Contacts** folder displayed, from **Backstage** view, click the **Open tab**, and then click **Import**. Click **Import from another program or file**, and then click **Next**. Click **Outlook Data File (.pst)**, and then click **Next**. In the **Import Outlook Data File** dialog box, click the **Browse** button. In the **Open Outlook Data Files** dialog box, navigate to the location where the student files for

this textbook are stored. Click in a blank area of the **address bar** at the top of the dialog box to select the entire pathname (the pathname may seem to extend beyond the border of the dialog box).

**7** Right-click the selected pathname, and then click **Copy**. In the displayed **Open Outlook Data Files** dialog box **Open** the file **o04B_Construction_Contacts**. In the **Import Outlook Data File** dialog box, click **Next**. Under **Select the folder to import from**, click **Contacts**, and then click **Import items into the current folder**. In the **Import Outlook Data File** dialog box, click **Finish**.

**8** Open the **John Zeidler** contact, and then display the **Details**. Under **Internet Free-Busy**, in the **Address** box, delete any existing text, and then type **file:\\** With the insertion point still located in the **Address** box, right-click after the text you just typed, and from the displayed shortcut menu, click **Paste**. With the insertion point still located in the **Address** box, after the pathname information, type **\JohnZeidler.vfb** to complete the address information for this contact's free/busy file. **Save & Close** the contact. (Note: If the current year is 2014 or later, type \JohnZeidler2014.vfb to use the correct free/busy file.)

**9** Open the **Jennifer Owens** contact, and then using the technique you practiced, add her **Internet Free-Busy Address**. In the **Address** box, type **file:\\** and then **Paste** the location information. At the end of the pathname, type **\JenniferOwens.vfb** and then **Save & Close** the contact. (Note: If the current year is 2014 or later, type \JenniferOwens2014.vfb to use the correct free/busy file.)

**10** Display the **Calendar**, and then use the **Date Navigator** to advance the calendar to the date in which you created the appointments in Step 4. Click the **10:00 am** time slot. On the **Home tab**, in the **New group**, click **New Meeting** to display the Meeting form. In the **Subject** box, type **Lakeview Town Center Update** and in the **Location** box type **Terrace Room**

**11** On the **Meeting tab**, in the **Show group**, click the **Scheduling** button, and then drag the red border to schedule the meeting until **11:00 am**. In the lower left, click the **Add Others** button, and then click **Add from Address Book**. Select **John Zeidler**, and then click **Required** to add his name to the Required box. Select **Jennifer Owens**, and then click **Required**. Click **OK**.

**12** Notice that John and Jennifer are not available at the selected meeting time. Click **AutoPick Next** to instruct

(Project 4B Construction Calendar continues on the next page)

Outlook to locate the first available time when all three participants are available, and notice that *2:00* is selected. Click **Add Others**, and then from the address book, add **Brian Fong** and **Laura Owens-Shafku** as **Optional**. Add the **Projection System 1** as a **Resource**, and then click **OK**. If a message box displays asking if you would like to update the current location, click No. **Send** the meeting.

**13** Open the **Lakeview Town Center Update** meeting. On the **Meeting tab**, in the **Show group**, click the **Tracking** button. Under **Response**, change the response for **John Zeidler** and **Laura Owens-Shafku** to **Accepted** and for **Jennifer Owens** to **Tentative**. **Close** the **Meeting form**, select the **Save changes but don't send** option, and then click **OK**.

**14** With the **Lakeview Town Center Update** meeting selected, on the **Meeting tab**, in the **Attendees group**, click the **Add or Remove Attendees** button. In the **Optional** box, select and delete **Brian Fong**. Click **OK**. **Close** the **Meeting form**, select the **Save changes and send update** option, and then click **OK**. Select the **Send updates only to added or deleted attendees** option, and then click **OK**.

**15** **Print** or use **OneNote** to create a PDF of the **Lakeview Town Center Update** meeting in **Memo Style** with the footer **Lastname_Firstname_4B_ Meeting Print** or use **OneNote** to create a PDF of the calendar in **Daily Style** with the footer **Lastname_Firstname_4B_Construction_Calendar** and then submit the end results to your instructor as directed.

**16** Cancel the meeting, delete all appointments, contacts, and e-mails in both the Outbox and Inbox, and then empty the **Deleted Items** folder. Reset the Outlook **Calendar, Time zone,** and **Send and receive** options to their default settings. Reset the **Memo Style** and **Daily Style** Calendar print styles, and then **Close** Outlook.

**End** **You have completed Project 4B** —————————————————————

# Content-Based Assessments

Apply **4A** skills from
these Objectives:

- Respond to Meeting
  Requests
- Manage Meeting
  Information

## Mastering Outlook | Project **4C** New Projects

In the following Mastering Outlook project, you will manage an Inbox by responding to meeting requests regarding new construction projects. Your completed documents will look similar to the ones shown in Figure 4.44.

### Project Files

For Project 4C, you will need the following file:

> o04C_New_Projects

You will print or create a PDF for three files with the following footers:

> Lastname_Firstname_4C_New_Projects
> Lastname_Firstname_4C_Projects_Tentative
> Lastname_Firstname_4C_Projects_Decline

### Project Results

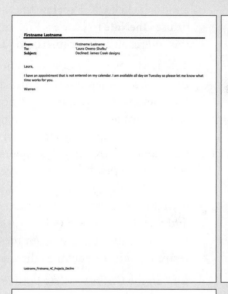

**Figure 4.44**

(Project 4C New Projects continues on the next page)

# Content-Based Assessments

**1** Switch to the Windows 7 user account you created in Chapter 1. If the account does not exist, refer to Chapter 1, Activities 1.01 and 1.02 to setup the Windows 7 user account and to configure Microsoft Outlook. Start **Outlook**, display the **Inbox** and delete any existing messages. Display the **Contacts** and delete any existing contacts.

**2** From **Backstage view** display the **Outlook Options** dialog box, and then on the left, click **Advanced**. Under **Send and receive**, clear the **Send immediately when connected** check box if necessary. To the immediate right, click the **Send/Receive** button. In the **Send/Receive Groups** dialog box, under **Setting for group "All Accounts"**, *clear* all five check boxes. Click **Close**.

**3** If your computer clock is not set to display time in the *Eastern Time (US & Canada)* zone, in the **Outlook Options** dialog box, click **Calendar**. Under **Time zones**, click the **Time zone arrow** and then select (**UTC-05:00**) **Eastern Time (US & Canada)**. Click **OK**.

**4** Display the **Inbox**. In **Backstage** view, click **Open** and then click **Import**. Use the **Import and Export Wizard** to import an **Outlook Data File** from your student data files—**o04C_New_Projects.pst**. Import the **Inbox** into your Inbox.

**5** In the **Inbox**, click the **Summerset Development** message from *Brian Fong*, and then mark the meeting as **Tentative**. Choose **Edit the Response before Sending**, and then in the comments area of the **Meeting Response form**, using the message format you've practiced, type **Brian, This is definitely a priority. Please be sure that both of our project managers can attend. We can set another time if they are not available. Warren** and then **Send** the reply.

**6** Select the **Bike Path** message from *Laura Owens-Shafku*, and then **Accept** the message to schedule the meeting.

**7** Select the **James Creek designs** message from *Laura Owens-Shafku*, and then **Decline** the message. Choose **Edit the Response before Sending**, and create the following message in the comments area using appropriate spacing: **Laura, I have an appointment that is not entered on my calendar. I am available all day on Tuesday so please let me know what time works for you. Warren Send** the reply.

**8** Display the **Calendar**, and then use the **Go To Date** dialog box to display the meetings that you scheduled on **12/03/14** In **Backstage** view, click the **Print** tab, display the **Page Setup: Daily Style** dialog box, and then delete any existing header or footer information. In the left **Footer** box, type **Lastname_Firstname_4C_New_Projects** and then click **OK**. **Preview** the calendar, and then **Print** or use **OneNote** to create a PDF of the document. Submit the end result to your instructor as directed.

**9** In the **Navigation Pane**, click **Mail** and display the **Outbox** folder. For both messages, display the **Page Setup: Memo Style** dialog box, and then delete existing header or footer information. In the *Laura Owens-Shafku* message, create a left **Footer** with the text **Lastname_Firstname_4C_Projects_Decline** and then **Preview** and **Print** or use **OneNote** to create a PDF of the message. In the *Brian Fong* message, create a left **Footer** with the text **Lastname_Firstname_4C_Projects_Tentative** and then **Preview** and **Print** or use **OneNote** to create a PDF of the message. For both messages, submit the end result to your instructor as directed.

**10** In the **Outbox**, delete both items without sending any type of messages. Display the **Calendar** date **12/03/14** and delete the meetings that you scheduled without sending messages. Empty the **Deleted Items** folder.

**11** In **Backstage** view, reset the **Send and receive** and **Time zone** options to their defaults, and then reset the print styles that you used. **Close** Outlook.

**End You have completed Project 4C** ———————————

# Outcomes-Based Assessments

## Rubric

The following outcomes-based assessments are *open-ended* assessments. That is, there is no specific correct result; your result will depend on your approach to the information provided. Make *Professional Quality* your goal. Use the following scoring rubric to guide you in *how* to approach the problem and then to evaluate *how well* your approach solves the problem.

The *criteria*—Software Mastery, Content, Format and Layout, and Process—represent the knowledge and skills you have gained that you can apply to solving the problem. The *levels of performance*—Professional Quality, Approaching Professional Quality, or Needs Quality Improvement—help you and your instructor evaluate your result.

|  | Your completed project is of Professional Quality if you: | Your completed project is Approaching Professional Quality if you: | Your completed project Needs Quality Improvements if you: |
|---|---|---|---|
| **1-Software Mastery** | Choose and apply the most appropriate skills, tools, and features and identify efficient methods to solve the problem. | Choose and apply some appropriate skills, tools, and features, but not in the most efficient manner. | Choose inappropriate skills, tools, or features, or are inefficient in solving the problem. |
| **2-Content** | Construct a solution that is clear and well organized, contains content that is accurate, appropriate to the audience and purpose, and is complete. Provide a solution that contains no errors in spelling, grammar, or style. | Construct a solution in which some components are unclear, poorly organized, inconsistent, or incomplete. Misjudge the needs of the audience. Have some errors in spelling, grammar, or style, but the errors do not detract from comprehension. | Construct a solution that is unclear, incomplete, or poorly organized; contains some inaccurate or inappropriate content; and contains many errors in spelling, grammar, or style. Do not solve the problem. |
| **3-Format and Layout** | Format and arrange all elements to communicate information and ideas, clarify function, illustrate relationships, and indicate relative importance. | Apply appropriate format and layout features to some elements, but not others. Overuse features, causing minor distraction. | Apply format and layout that does not communicate information or ideas clearly. Do not use format and layout features to clarify function, illustrate relationships, or indicate relative importance. Use available features excessively, causing distraction. |
| **4-Process** | Use an organized approach that integrates planning, development, self-assessment, revision, and reflection. | Demonstrate an organized approach in some areas, but not others; or, use an insufficient process of organization throughout. | Do not use an organized approach to solve the problem. |

# Outcomes-Based Assessments

**Apply a combination
of the 4A skills.**

## GO! Think | Project **4D** Race

### Project Files

For Project 4D, you will need the following file:

    o04D_Race_Contacts

You will print or create a PDF for one file with the following footer:

    Lastname_Firstname_4D_Race

Owens Family Builders is a principal sponsor of a local 10K race. Volunteers from the company will work the race course on the day of the race. Warren Owens is organizing the company volunteers and is calling for a meeting of the team leaders to discuss the preparations. You will schedule the meeting for Mr. Owens.

Start Outlook. Using the techniques you have practiced, set the Send and receive options to place your sent e-mail messages in the Outbox. Import the file o04D_Race_Contacts into your Contacts list, and then create a new contact for Room 3 at Owens Family Builders, using the e-mail address Room3.OwensFamilyBuilders@live.com.

Plan a 1-hour, morning meeting for the first Monday in June or December, whichever month is closest to the current date. Jennifer Owens and Brian Fong are required attendees for the meeting to take place. Laura Owens-Shafku is optional. The meeting should take place in the conference room you added to your contacts list. Type a subject of the meeting that relates to the 10K race. Type several lines of comments that describe the purpose of the meeting, which is to go over each team member's responsibilities and assignments on the day of the race. Send the meeting invitation.

Print or create a PDF of the meeting in Memo Style using the footer **Lastname_Firstname_4D_Race** Submit the end results to your instructor as directed. Delete the meeting from the calendar without sending the cancellation, and then delete the contents of the Contacts folder, the Outbox folder, and the Deleted Items folder. Restore the Send and receive options to the default settings on your computer. Reset any print styles you used. Close Outlook.

**End** You have completed Project 4D —————————————

# Outcomes-Based Assessments

Apply a combination of the **4A** skills.

## GO! Think | Project **4E** Daily Calendar

### Project Files

For Project 4E, you will need the following file:

o04E_Daily_Calendar

You will print or create a PDF for two files with the following footers:

Lastname_Firstname_4E_Daily_Calendar
Lastname_Firstname_4E_Calendar_Decline

Owens Family Builders has several project bids that are due in December. Several employees have sent Warren Owens meeting requests regarding these topics to which you will reply.

Start Outlook. Using the techniques you have practiced, set the Send and receive options to place your sent e-mail messages in the Outbox. If your time zone is not Eastern Time (US & Canada), change the Outlook Time zone to (UTC-5:00) Eastern Time (US & Canada). From your student files, import the Inbox from the o04E_Daily_Calendar into your Inbox.

Decline the meeting invitation from Brian Fong without editing the response. Decline the meeting invitation from John Zeidler regarding Sandalwood Designs, and ask him to schedule the meeting for the next day so that Mara Kenzie can attend. Accept the meeting from Laura Owens-Shafku and choose the Send the Response Now option. Mark the James Creek Bid meeting with John Zeidler as Tentative and choose the Send the Response Now option. Display the calendar for the day of the meetings, and print it or create a PDF in an appropriate print style using the left footer **Lastname_Firstname_4E_Daily_Calendar** Submit the end result to your instructor as directed.

Print or create a PDF of the Outbox message to John Zeidler regarding Sandalwood Designs in Memo Style using the left footer **Lastname_Firstname_4E_Calendar_Decline** Submit the end result to your instructor as directed. Delete the Inbox and Outbox items, and do not send responses. Display the calendar date on which the meetings were scheduled, and then delete the meetings without sending responses. Empty the Deleted Items folder.

Restore your Send and receive options to the default setting on your computer. If you changed the Outlook Time zone, restore the Outlook Time zone setting to its default setting. Reset any print styles you used. Close Outlook.

**End** You have completed Project 4E ————————————————

# Organizing and Managing Outlook Information and Notes

## OUTCOMES
At the end of this chapter you will be able to:

### PROJECT 5A
Manage Outlook information and notes.

## OBJECTIVES
Mastering these objectives will enable you to:

**1.** Manage Mail Folders (p. 319)
**2.** Modify the Master Category List (p. 337)
**3.** Use Notes (p. 341)
**4.** Archive Outlook Information (p. 345)
**5.** Recover and Export Outlook Information (p. 350)

©candyboxphoto, shutterstock.com

## In This Chapter

Outlook has several tools that help you keep your information organized. You can create folders for specific types of e-mail and have messages placed in those folders. If you use categories to organize your information, you can create your own category names to add to Outlook's preset list of categories. Outlook's Notes component is also a convenient way to keep track of pieces of information you might need later. For long-term storage, Outlook enables you to store older information either manually or automatically. You can also export and recover Outlook information.

With gardening booming as a hobby, **Southland Media**, a TV production company headquartered in Irvine, California, saw a need for practical and entertaining information on the subject. *Southland Gardens* was developed especially for the year-round gardener in southern California. The show features experts on vegetable and flower gardening, landscape design, projects for children, and tours of historical and notable gardens. The company also offers a companion Web site where viewers can get more information about show segments, purchase supplies, and e-mail guests of the show.

# Project 5A Outlook Organization

## Project Activities

In Activities 5.01 through 5.19, you will create e-mail folders and use various tools to organize the e-mail received by Elizabeth Robinson, who is the cohost of Southland Media's television program, *Southland Gardens*. You will create new categories to assign to Outlook items and use Outlook's Notes feature to store information for a short time. You will snip notes and e-mail folders and print notes, which will look similar to the ones shown in Figure 5.1.

## Project Files

For Project 5A, you will need the following file:

> o05A_Robinson_Inbox

You will save your files as:

> Lastname_Firstname_5A_Rules.jpg
> Lastname_Firstname_5A_Junk_Mail.jpg
> Lastname_Firstname_5A_Comments_Filter.jpg
> Lastname_Firstname_5A_Master_Categories.jpg
> Lastname_Firstname_5A_Southland_Archive.jpg

You will print or create a PDF for one file with the following footer:

> Lastname_Firstname_5A_Robinson_Notes

## Project Results

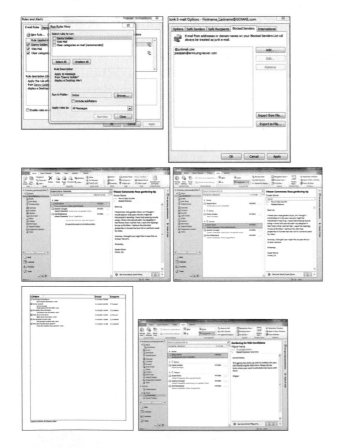

**Figure 5.1**
Project 5A Outlook Organization

# Objective 1 | Manage Mail Folders

To organize e-mail information within Outlook, you can create e-mail folders, rename existing folders, and then move messages from one folder to another. You can move incoming e-mail into specific folders using *rules*, which are one or more actions taken on e-mail messages that meet certain conditions, along with any exceptions to those conditions. For example, you might use a rule to move all messages you receive from your supervisor into a specific folder.

Outlook also enables you to screen your e-mail messages, sorting legitimate messages from unwanted and junk e-mail. Additionally, you can control which messages you want to display in an e-mail folder.

---

**Alert! | Starting Project 5A**

It is recommended that you schedule enough time to complete this project in one working session using your Windows 7 user name account. If possible, use the same computer that you used when you created the Windows 7 user account in Chapter 1. If you cannot use the same computer or if the Windows 7 user account that you created in Chapter 1 was deleted, refer to Chapter 1, Activities 1.01 and 1.02 to set up the Windows 7 user account and to configure Microsoft Outlook 2010. Allow approximately one hour to complete Project 5A.

---

## Activity 5.01 | Creating a Mail Folder

When you create a mail folder, the folder is typically a subfolder of the Inbox folder. You can view its contents like any other Outlook folder. In this activity, you will create a mail folder to hold messages for Elizabeth Robinson, co-host of Southland Media's *Southland Gardens* television program.

**1** Click the **Start** button, and then point to the **Shut down button arrow**. On the **Shut down menu**, click **Switch user** to display the **Windows 7** desktop. Click the user account that you created in Chapter 1. If the account does not exist, refer to the Alert at the beginning of this Activity to set up the account.

**2** **Start** Outlook. From the **Navigation Pane**, display the **Folder List** ▭, and then display the **Inbox** folder. If necessary, delete any existing messages in the **Inbox**.

**3** Right-click the **Inbox**, and then click **New Folder** from the displayed shortcut menu. In the **Create New Folder** dialog box, in the **Name** box, type **Southland Gardens**

**4** Under **Select where to place the folder**, click **Inbox** if necessary. Be sure the **Folder contains** box displays *Mail and Post Items*. Compare your screen with Figure 5.2.

> You must specify the type of information a new folder will contain. Because the Inbox was selected when you opened the Create New Folder dialog box, Outlook sets the new folder to contain *Mail and Post Items*.

Figure 5.2

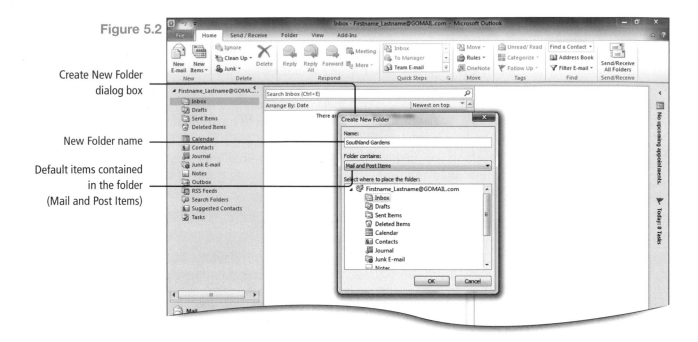

Create New Folder
dialog box

New Folder name

Default items contained
in the folder
(Mail and Post Items)

**5** In the **Create New Folder** dialog box, click **OK** to create the new folder.

> The Southland Gardens folder is a subfolder of the Inbox. A collapse or expand button displays next to the Inbox, indicating that the Inbox folder contains a subfolder. Recall that clicking these buttons shows or hides information in the folder.

**6** Be sure the **Inbox** folder is expanded; if necessary, click the **Expand** button ▷ to display the **Southland Gardens** folder. Compare your screen with Figure 5.3.

Figure 5.3

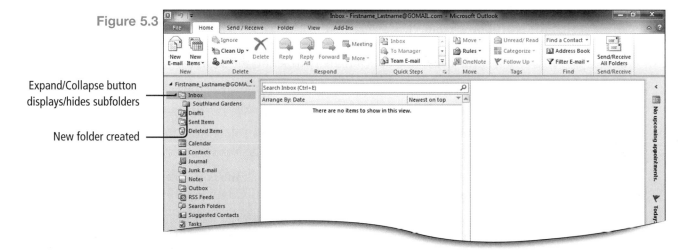

Expand/Collapse button
displays/hides subfolders

New folder created

## Activity 5.02 | Renaming a Folder and Importing Messages

You can rename a folder in the same manner as you rename a file. Renaming a folder is useful when the contents or purpose of the folder changes and you want the folder name to reflect the kinds of items stored in the folder. In this activity, you will edit the Southland Gardens folder name and then import messages into your Inbox for Elizabeth Robinson.

**1** In the **Navigation Pane**, click the **Southland Gardens** folder to select and open it. Right-click the **Southland Gardens** folder to display the shortcut menu, and then click **Rename Folder**. Compare your screen with Figure 5.4.

> The folder name—*Southland Gardens*—is highlighted in blue, indicating that the name can be edited.

Figure 5.4

Outline indicates the folder name can be edited

Southland Gardens folder selected

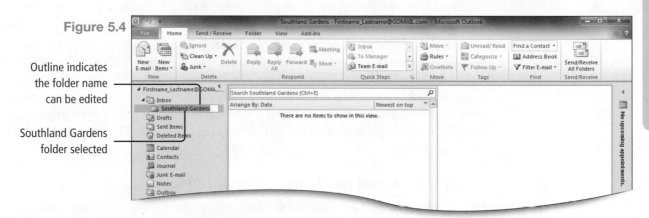

**2** Type **Southland** and then press Enter to rename the folder. In the **Navigation Pane**, display the **Inbox** folder.

**3** From **Backstage** view, click **Open**, and then click **Import**. In the displayed **Import and Export Wizard** dialog box, under **Choose an action to perform**, click **Import from another program or file**, and then click **Next**. In the **Import a File** dialog box, under **Select file type to import from**, click **Outlook Data File (.pst)**. Click **Next**.

**4** In the **Import Outlook Data File** dialog box, click the **Browse** button and navigate to your student files, locate and click **o05A_Robinson_Inbox**, and then click **Open**. Click **Next**.

**5** In the **Import Outlook Data File** dialog box, click **Import items into the same folder in** your user name account. Click **Finish**, and then compare your screen with Figure 5.5.

Figure 5.5

Group indicates the date of messages (yours may differ)

Six new messages

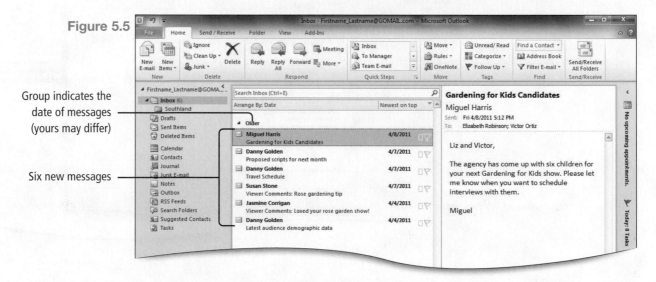

**6** Click the first message to display that message in the **Reading Pane**, and then click each subsequent message to read its content.

## Activity 5.03 | Creating Rules to Process Incoming Mail

Receiving a large volume of e-mail messages can be difficult to manage, so Outlook lets you create rules that will organize your messages before you read them. A *message rule* defines the actions that Outlook takes for sent or received messages that meet certain conditions. Rules are based on *conditions*—criteria that determine how incoming e-mail messages will be handled. For example, conditions might include the sender's e-mail address, the size of the message, or certain words found in the subject of the message.

You can create a rule using Outlook's ***Rules Wizard***, which is a program that guides you through the process of creating a message rule. Elizabeth Robinson receives e-mail from viewers of her television program. They send e-mail to the show's hosts using the program's Web site, which adds the phrase Viewer Comments to all the subjects of the messages. In this activity, you will create a rule that places all the e-mail messages that Elizabeth Robinson receives from viewers regarding her TV program into her Southland folder.

**1** In the **Navigation Pane**, be sure the **Inbox** is the current folder.

In the Folder List, recall that the number in parentheses next to *Inbox* indicates the number of new, unread messages. When you create a rule, that rule applies to the currently selected folder. This rule will apply to *all* Inbox messages, read or unread.

**2** On the **Home tab**, in the **Move group**, click **Rules**, and then click **Manage Rules & Alerts**. Compare your screen with Figure 5.6.

The Rules and Alerts dialog box displays. Outlook enables you to create rules based on selected conditions. Any existing rules that have been defined may display in the dialog box.

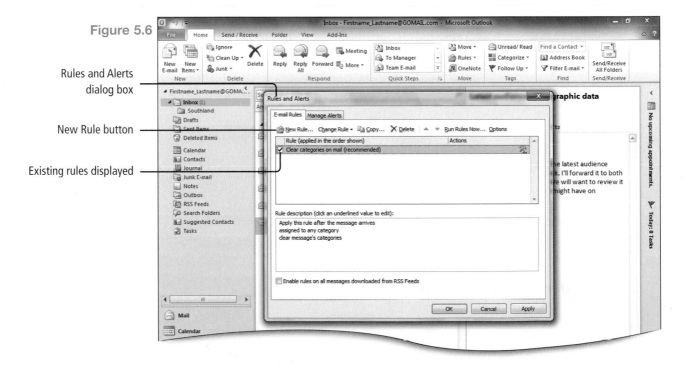

Figure 5.6

Rules and Alerts dialog box

New Rule button

Existing rules displayed

**3** In the **Rules and Alerts** dialog box, click **New Rule**. Compare your screen with Figure 5.7.

The Rules Wizard dialog box displays. Outlook enables you to create rules from a *template*, which is a set of predefined conditions and actions used for common processing tasks. You can also create a rule from scratch by using a *blank rule*—you define your rule by specifying your own conditions and actions. Templates are a good way to get started with rules when your processing needs are simple. The default setting is to create the rule using a template.

Figure 5.7

Rules Wizard dialog box

Select a template

Start from a blank rule

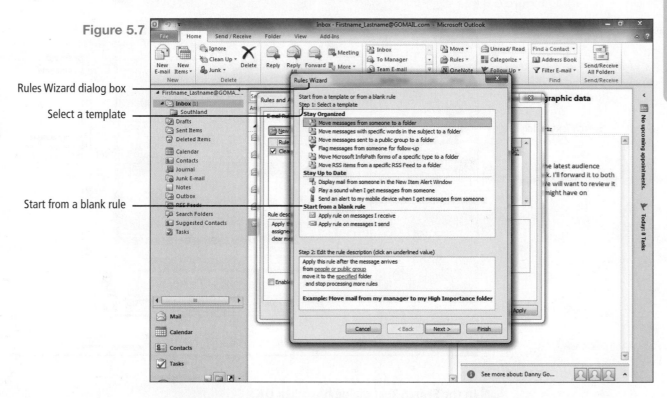

**4** In the **Rules Wizard** dialog box, under **Step 1: Select a template**, click **Move messages with specific words in the subject to a folder**, and then read the information under **Step 2** that describes what the selected template does.

Step 2 in the Rules Wizard contains the *rule description*—an explanation of the actions a rule performs on a message. The description changes as you add conditions and exceptions to the rule.

At this point in the instruction, the description for this rule is that Outlook will move incoming messages to a designated folder, based on specific words in the subject of the message. Recall that Elizabeth Robinson's goal is to have Outlook automatically move incoming e-mail from viewers of the television show into her Southland folder.

**5** In the **Rules Wizard** dialog box, under **Step 2: Edit the rule description (click an underlined value)**, click **specific words**.

A Search Text dialog box displays. Use this dialog box to specify the words Outlook should search for in the Subject field of incoming messages.

**6** In the **Search Text** dialog box, in the **Specify words or phrases to search for in the subject box**, type **Viewer Comments** and then click **Add**. Compare your screen with Figure 5.8.

> The phrase "*Viewer Comments*" is added to a list of words for which Outlook will search in the Subject field of incoming messages. You can add as many words or phrases as needed.

Figure 5.8

Search Text dialog box ⎯⎯⎯⎯⎯

"Viewer Comments"
specified ⎯⎯⎯⎯⎯

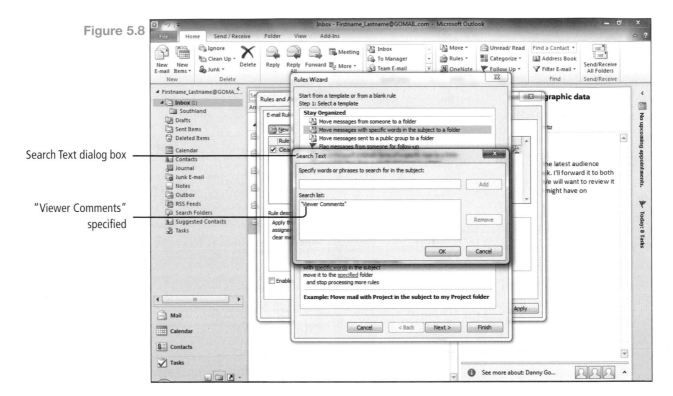

**7** In the **Search Text** dialog box, click **OK**.

> Under Step 2, the rule description indicates the rule will be applied to messages with *Viewer Comments* in the subject.

**8** In the **Rules Wizard** dialog box, under **Step 2: Edit the rule description (click an underlined value)**, click **specified**. Compare your screen with Figure 5.9.

> A Rules and Alerts dialog box displays, showing your Folder List. Here you specify the folder where Outlook should move messages that contain the phrase *Viewer Comments* in the subject.

Figure 5.9

Rules and Alerts
dialog box

Click to expand

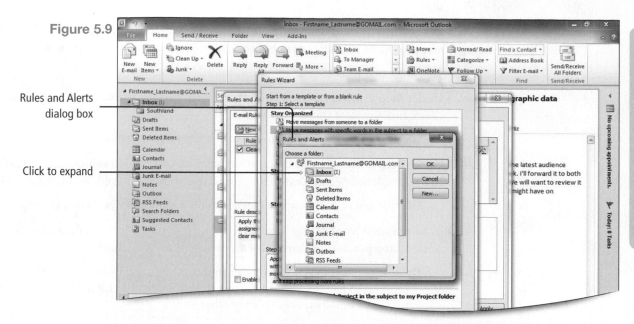

**9** In the **Rules and Alerts** dialog box, to the left of **Inbox**, click the **Expand** button ▷, and then click **Southland**. Click **OK**.

Under Step 2, the rule description indicates that the message will be moved to the *Southland* folder. If you were done writing the rule, you could click Finish; but, in this activity, you will continue to modify the rule.

**10** In the **Rules Wizard** dialog box, click **Next**, and then compare your screen with Figure 5.10.

Step 1 indicates with check marks the conditions you have already specified. One condition is selected—*with specific words in the subject*. Step 2 displays the current description of the rule, which moves messages with *Viewer Comments* in the subject to the *Southland* folder.

Figure 5.10

Rules Wizard dialog box

Add more conditions to a rule

Condition specified

Current rule description

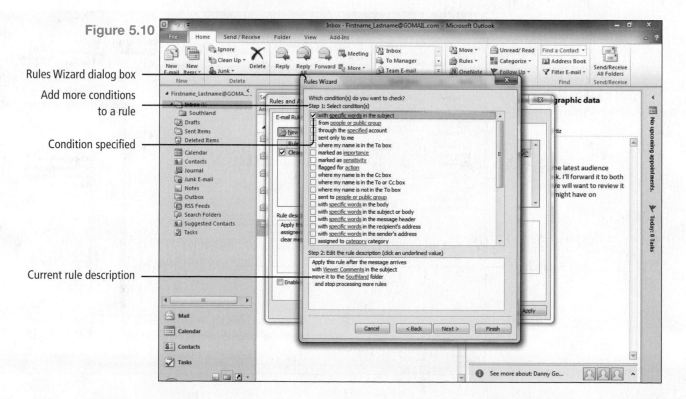

**11** In the **Rules Wizard** dialog box, under **Step 1: Select condition(s)**, click the **down scroll arrow** to view the other possible conditions you can add to your rule.

Notice that there are numerous conditions you can add.

**12** Under **Step 1: Select conditions(s)**, locate **with specific words in the body**, and click its check box to select this condition.

The new condition is added to the rule description under Step 2.

**13** Under **Step 2: Edit the rule description (click an underlined value)**, click **specific words**. In the displayed **Search Text** dialog box, type **show** click **Add**, and then click **OK**.

The rule description now includes a search for *show* in the body of a message.

**14** In the **Rules Wizard** dialog box, click **Next**. Under **Step 1: Select action(s)**, click the box next to **stop processing more rules** to remove the check mark.

There are numerous actions you can apply to a message if you want to do so. For example, in addition to moving the message to a specific folder, you could also play a sound and move a copy of the message to some other folder.

**15** In the **Rules Wizard** dialog box, click **Next** to display the list of exceptions.

When a message meets the conditions you have specified, *exceptions* are instances when you want to exclude the message from the specified action. For example, you could exclude a message that has *Viewer Comments* in the subject and body of the message but is sent from an e-mail account other than the company's Web site. In this rule, there are no exceptions.

**16** In the **Rules Wizard** dialog box, click **Next** to finish the rule setup, and then compare your screen with Figure 5.11.

The Rules Wizard dialog box displays a summary of the rule and asks you to name the rule. The wizard uses the phrase you specified in the first condition of the rule as the default name. The default is to turn on the rule. Notice also that you can run a rule on the existing contents of the Inbox. If you decide you want to make changes to the rule, you can use the Back button to return to a previous Rules Wizard page.

Figure 5.11

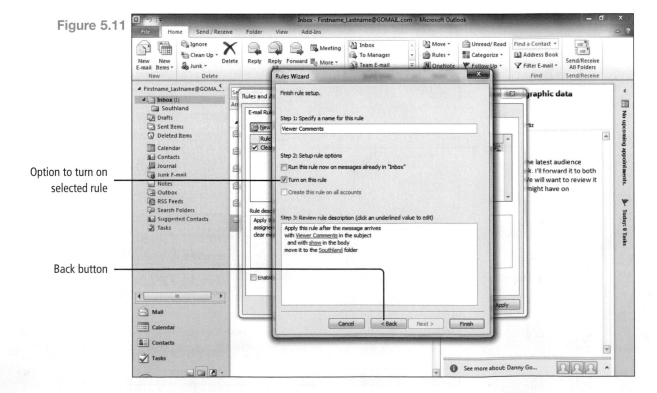

Option to turn on selected rule

Back button

**17** In the **Rules Wizard** dialog box, in the **Step 1: Specify a name for this rule box**, delete the existing text, type **Web Mail** and then click **Finish**.

> The Rules and Alerts dialog box redisplays and lists the *Web Mail* rule. The check mark next to the rule name indicates that the rule is active and will be applied to all new incoming e-mail. Clearing the check mark gives you the option of turning the rule on and off as needed. For example, you might turn on this rule only when the volume of e-mail from the Web site is particularly heavy.

---

**Alert!** | **Are additional rules displayed?**

Other rules and alerts may be listed in the Rules and Alerts dialog box. One rule that may be displayed is "Clear categories on mail (recommended)." This is a default rule for Outlook 2010.

---

**18** In the **Rules and Alerts** dialog box, click **OK**.

---

**More Knowledge** | **Creating Automatic Replies Using the Out of Office Assistant**

In addition to creating rules, if you have an Exchange Server e-mail account, you can use the Out of Office Assistant to create automatic replies to incoming messages when you are not in your office. For example, when you are on vacation, you might want to use this feature to let message senders know that you will respond to their messages when you return. To use the Out of Office Assistant, click the Exchange Server Mailbox in the Navigation Pane, and then from Backstage view, click Automatic Replies, and select Send automatic replies. Select a time range in which to send the automatic replies, and then add messages for people in and out of your organization.

---

## Activity 5.04 | Applying a Rule

In this activity, you will apply the rule to Elizabeth Robinson's existing Inbox messages. Recall that viewers of the TV show can visit the show's Web site to send e-mail messages with their comments.

**1** In the **Navigation Pane**, be sure the **Inbox** is displayed. Locate the messages with the phrase **Viewer Comments** in the subject or body of the message. Compare your screen with Figure 5.12.

> Two messages contain the phrase *Viewer Comments* in the subject. The rule was not applied to any messages because they were already in your Inbox when you created the rule. However, you can apply a rule to existing Inbox messages.

Figure 5.12

Subjects include
*Viewer Comments*

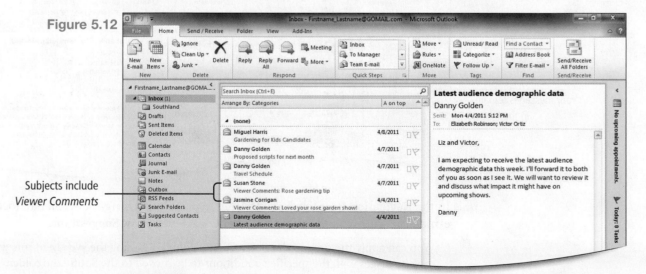

**2** On the **Home tab**, in the **Move group**, click **Rules**, and then click **Manage Rules & Alerts**. In the displayed **Rules and Alerts** dialog box, click **Run Rules Now.**

> The Run Rules Now dialog box displays.

**3** In the **Run Rules Now** dialog box, under **Select rules to run:**, click to select the **Web Mail** check box. Compare your screen with Figure 5.13.

> You have created one rule you can run—the Web Mail rule. You can apply the rule to All Messages, Read Messages, or Unread Messages. The default setting is to apply the rule to All Messages.

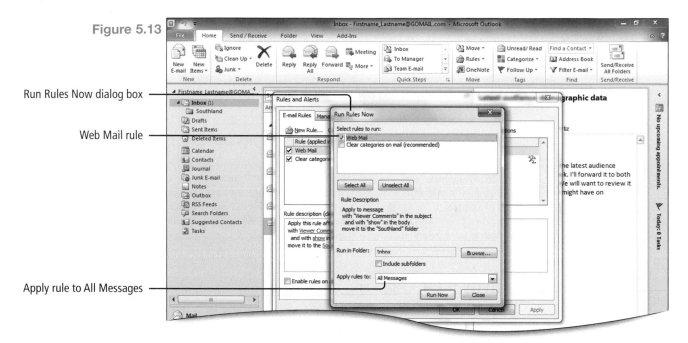

Figure 5.13

Run Rules Now dialog box

Web Mail rule

Apply rule to All Messages

**4** In the **Run Rules Now** dialog box, click **Run Now**. Click **Close**. In the **Rules and Alerts** dialog box, click **OK**, and then compare your screen with Figure 5.14.

> The Inbox redisplays. There are only four messages in the Inbox. The two messages with the phrase *Viewer Comments* in their subjects have been moved to the Southland folder.

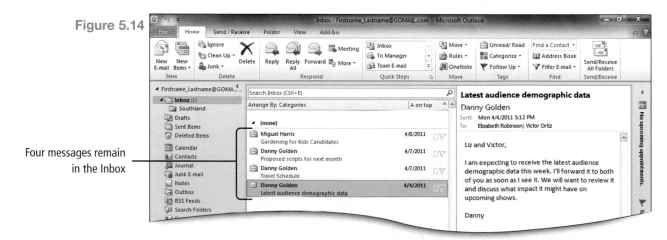

Figure 5.14

Four messages remain in the Inbox

**5** In the **Navigation Pane**, click the **Deleted Items** folder. Using the scroll bar, locate the e-mail message with the subject **Viewer Comments: Show Suggestions**.

> You can apply the rules to the Deleted Items folder. Running the Web Mail rule will cause any messages with the specified conditions to be moved to the Southland folder.

**6** On the **Home tab**, in the **Move group**, click **Rules**, and then click **Manage Rules &
Alerts**. In the displayed **Rules and Alerts** dialog box, click **Run Rules Now.**

**7** In the **Run Rules Now** dialog box, select the **Web Mail** check box; and then, in the
lower right corner, click **Run Now**. Click **Close**. In the **Rules and Alerts** dialog box,
click **OK**.

**8** In the **Navigation Pane**, click the **Southland** folder. To arrange the messages by date, if
necessary, click the **Arrange By** column heading, and then click **Date**.

> The folder contains three messages with the phrase *Viewer Comments* in the subject.

---

**More Knowledge** | Performing Actions Using Quick Steps

You can apply Quick Steps to perform actions without specifying conditions. To use Quick Steps, select the message or messages to which you want to apply the Quick Step. On the Home tab, in the Quick Steps group, choose the Quick Step you want to apply. The first time you use a Quick Step you may need to define settings related to your account. The default Quick Step options allow you to move selected messages to a specified folder, forward or create messages to managers or team members, mark messages as complete, and reply to a message while deleting the original.

---

### Activity 5.05 | Creating a Rule That Uses a Desktop Alert

When new items arrive in your Inbox, by default Outlook plays a sound, briefly
changes the mouse pointer, and displays an envelope icon in the *notification area*—the
rightmost portion of the Windows taskbar, next to the system time. Outlook can be set to
display a New Mail Desktop Alert when new items arrive in your Inbox. A *Desktop Alert* is
a notification that displays on your desktop when you receive an e-mail message, meeting
request, or task request. This notification presents itself as a small window that displays
for a short duration. You can control the duration, location, and appearance of Desktop
Alerts. You can also create Desktop Alerts that display for specific messages you receive in
your Inbox. In this activity, you will create a Desktop Alert for Elizabeth Robinson's Inbox
that notifies her whenever she receives a message from her boss, Danny Golden—the
president of Southland Media.

**1** In the **Navigation Pane**, display the **Inbox** folder. Click the **Travel Schedule** message
from *Danny Golden*.

**2** Right-click the **Travel Schedule** message, point to **Rules**, and then click **Create Rule**.
Alternatively, on the Home tab, in the Move group, click the Rules button, and then
click Create Rule. Compare your screen with Figure 5.15.

> The Create Rule dialog box displays. This is an alternative method for creating a rule that
> is especially useful when you are basing the rule on a specific e-mail message. The dialog
> box contains optional conditions using the name of the sender, the recipient, and the
> subject of the selected message. The dialog box also has an option to move the message
> to a specified folder.

Figure 5.15

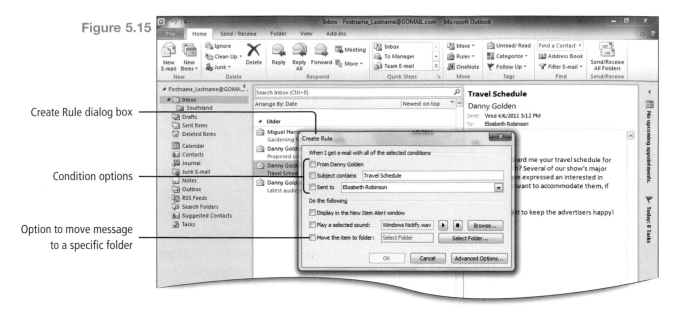

Create Rule dialog box

Condition options

Option to move message to a specific folder

**3** In the **Create Rule** dialog box, select the **From Danny Golden** check box, and then click **Advanced Options**.

The Rules Wizard dialog box displays. The condition *from Danny Golden* is already selected.

**4** In the **Rules Wizard** dialog box, using the **scroll bar**, locate and, if necessary, *clear* the **on this computer only** check box. Click **Next** to display the possible actions you can take on messages from Danny Golden.

**5** In the **Rules Wizard** dialog box, under **Step 1**, using the **scroll bar**, locate and click to select the **display a Desktop Alert** check box, and then compare your screen with Figure 5.16.

Under Step 2, the rule description adds the selected action, which is to display a Desktop Alert.

Figure 5.16

display a *Desktop Alert* action selected

Description includes *Danny Golden* and *display a Desktop Alert*

Scroll down

**6** In the **Rules Wizard** dialog box, click **Next** to display the list of exceptions. Click **Next** to skip the list of exceptions and finish the rule setup.

The Rules Wizard displays the default name for the rule—Danny Golden. This is a good name for this rule, so it does not have to be modified.

**7** If any extra characters appear after *Danny Golden*, delete them. In the **Rules Wizard** dialog box, in **Step 2**, select the **Turn on this rule** check box. Click **Finish** to close the dialog box.

Outlook will display a Desktop Alert for any message arriving in the Inbox from Danny Golden. You can apply the rule to existing Inbox messages.

**8** On the **Home tab**, in the **Move group**, click **Rules**, and then click **Manage Rules & Alerts**. In the displayed **Rules and Alerts** dialog box, click **Run Rules Now.**

The Run Rules Now dialog box lists the two rules you have created—the Web Mail rule and the Danny Golden rule—as well as any other rules that exist.

**9** Display the **Start** menu 🏁, and then click **All Programs**. Locate and then click the **Accessories** folder. Click the **Snipping Tool**. In the **Snipping Tool** dialog box, click the **New arrow**, and then click **Window Snip**. Click anywhere in the **Rules and Alerts** window to capture it, and then click the **Save Snip** button 💾. Navigate to the location where you are storing your files. Click in the **File name** box, and then using your own name, type **Lastname_Firstname_5A_Rules** Click the **Save as type arrow**, and then click **JPEG file**. Click **Save**. **Close** ❌ the **Snipping Tool**, and then submit the end result to your instructor as directed.

**10** In the **Run Rules Now** dialog box, select the **Danny Golden** check box.

**11** At the bottom of the **Run Rules Now** dialog box, click **Run Now**. Click **Close**, and then click **OK** to close the dialog box. Compare your screen with Figure 5.17.

Outlook displays a Desktop Alert three times, one time for each of the three messages in the Inbox for Danny Golden. By default, alerts display in the lower right portion of the screen for only a few moments, and the image is transparent. The first two alerts display in quick succession; the third alert remains on the screen the longest. Each alert contains the subject and the first line of the message.

**Figure 5.17**

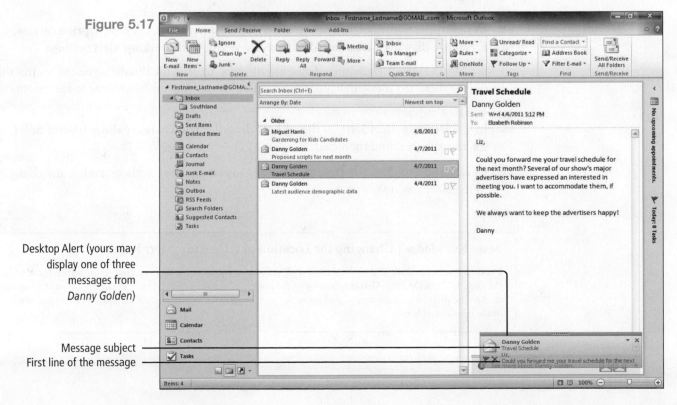

Desktop Alert (yours may display one of three messages from *Danny Golden*)

Message subject
First line of the message

**12** Display the **Run Rules Now** dialog box again, and then select the **Danny Golden** check box. Click **Run Now.** Click **Close,** and then click **OK.** Quickly point to one of the alerts before the alert fades from view. Compare your screen with Figure 5.18.

> An alert remains visible as long as the mouse pointer is located in the alert. A ScreenTip indicates that you can open the item by clicking it. Two buttons in the lower left portion of the Alert window enable you to flag or delete the item. A small arrow in the upper right corner of the alert displays an Options menu.

Figure 5.18

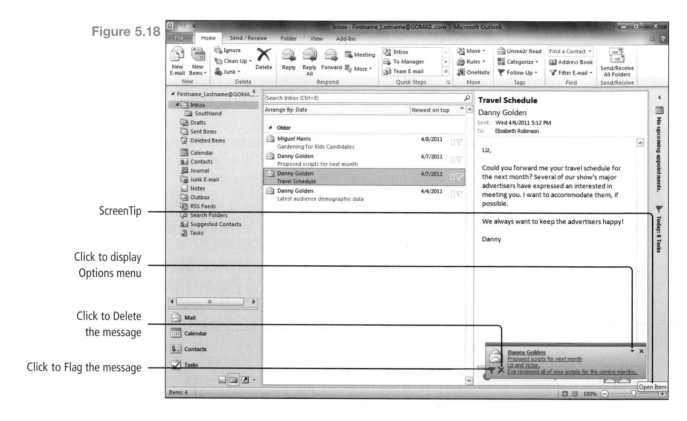

ScreenTip

Click to display
Options menu

Click to Delete
the message

Click to Flag the message

**13** In the upper right portion of the displayed **Desktop Alert,** click the **Options arrow.** From the displayed **Desktop Alert Options** menu, click **Desktop Alert Settings.**

> The Desktop Alert Settings dialog box displays. You can use this dialog box to control the duration and transparency of the alert. The Preview button enables you to see the effects of your changes.

**14** In the **Desktop Alert Settings** dialog box, drag the **Transparency slider** toward *Solid,* to **0% transparent,** and then click **Preview** to view the results.

**15** Click **Cancel** to close the **Desktop Alert Settings** dialog box without saving any changes to the alert settings.

---

**More Knowledge | Changing the Location of a Desktop Alert Rule**

Desktop Alerts normally display in the lower right corner of the screen. You can change the screen location of the alert. When a Desktop Alert displays, move the pointer to the alert before the alert fades from view. Drag the alert to the desired screen location, and move the pointer away from the alert. All subsequent alerts will display in the new screen location.

---

## Activity 5.06 | Disabling and Removing Rules

You might want to apply rules only at certain times. For example, you might have rules that perform cleanup operations on your e-mail folders, but you do not necessarily want these rules to run every time you receive e-mail. For example, you might want to periodically run a rule that deletes all messages from a specific sender. You might also have rules that are no longer needed. You can disable rules and delete rules. In this activity, you will disable and remove the rules you created for Elizabeth Robinson's messages.

**1** On the **Home tab**, in the **Move group**, click the **Rules** button, and then click **Manage Rules & Alerts**. In the **Rules and Alerts** dialog box, click the **Danny Golden** rule, and then click **Delete**. Compare your screen with Figure 5.19.

Figure 5.19

Highlight indicates Danny Golden rule is selected

Confirm Delete

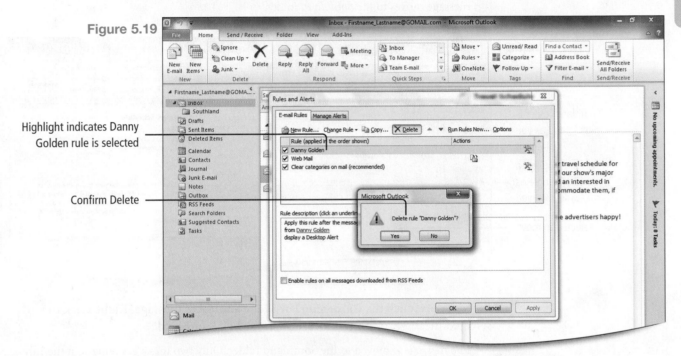

**2** In the **Microsoft Outlook** dialog box, click **Yes**.

**3** Use the same technique to delete the **Web Mail** rule. Click **OK** to close the **Rules and Alerts** dialog box.

---

**More Knowledge | Changing a Rule**

You can add and delete conditions, actions, and exceptions to any existing rule. In the Rules and Alerts dialog box, click the rule you want to edit, click Change Rule, and then click Edit Rule Settings. Use the Rules Wizard to edit the rule. In the Rules and Alerts dialog box, you can also click the arrow next to the Change Rule command button to display a menu of other changes you can make to a rule, including changing the name of the rule or applying the rule to a different folder.

---

## Activity 5.07 | Moving Messages to Another Folder

When you have a large volume of e-mail, another way to organize your messages is to manually move them to different e-mail folders. There are several ways to move messages. For example, you can drag them from one folder to another. Dragging is the action of pointing to an object, holding down the left mouse button, moving the object to another location on the screen, and then releasing the left mouse button. You can also use commands on the Ribbon or the shortcut menu. In this activity, you will move several of Elizabeth Robinson's messages from her Inbox to her Southland folder.

**1** In the **Navigation Pane**, click the **Folder List** button 📁 to display the Folder List. If necessary, expand the **Inbox** to display the **Southland** folder in the **Folder List**. Display the **Inbox**, and then click the **Travel Schedule** message from *Danny Golden*.

**2** Point to the **Travel Schedule** message, hold down the left mouse button, and then drag the message to the **Southland** folder, as shown in Figure 5.20. Release the mouse button.

As you drag the message into the Folder List, a small rectangle is attached to the pointer, and the Southland folder is highlighted when you point to the folder. The *Travel Schedule* message moves to the *Southland* folder.

Figure 5.20

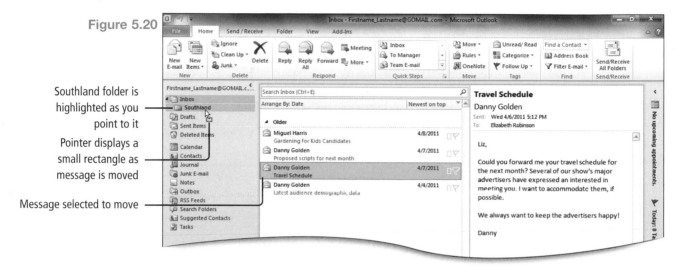

Southland folder is highlighted as you point to it

Pointer displays a small rectangle as message is moved

Message selected to move

**3** In the **Inbox**, click the **Gardening For Kids Candidates** message. Right-click the selected message, point to **Move**, and then click **Southland**.

The message is moved to the Southland folder. Only two messages remain in the Inbox folder.

### Activity 5.08 | Using Outlook's Junk Mail Filter

Almost everyone with an active e-mail account receives unsolicited junk e-mail. You can use Outlook's junk e-mail filter to screen out a number of these unwanted messages. Recall that a *filter* is a set of instructions to screen a folder, based on conditions you define. In this activity, you will modify Elizabeth Robinson's junk e-mail filter to screen out messages from specific sources.

**1** On the **Home tab**, in the **Delete group**, click the **Junk** button, and then click **Junk E-mail Options**.

The Junk E-mail Options dialog box displays. Outlook's default setting for junk e-mail is the Low setting, which filters out most obvious junk e-mail. You can set the filter to High, but doing so risks filtering out some of your regular e-mail.

**2** In the **Junk E-mail Options** dialog box, click the **Blocked Senders tab**. Click **Add**, and then compare your screen with Figure 5.21.

In the Add address or domain dialog box, you can enter specific e-mail addresses you always want treated as junk e-mail. The addresses you specify do not have to be junk e-mail. You can block the messages of anyone from whom you do not want to receive e-mail.

Figure 5.21

Junk button

Add address or domain
dialog box

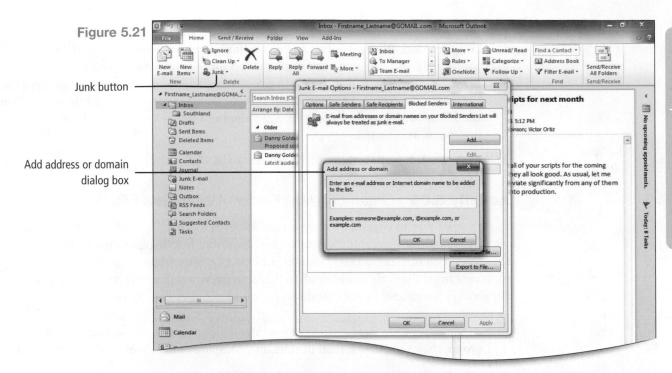

**3** In the **Add address or domain** dialog box, type **joespam@annoyingviewer.com** and then click **OK**. Compare your screen with Figure 5.22.

The address is added to your list of blocked senders.

Figure 5.22

Junk E-mail Options
dialog box

Source of unwanted
mail specified

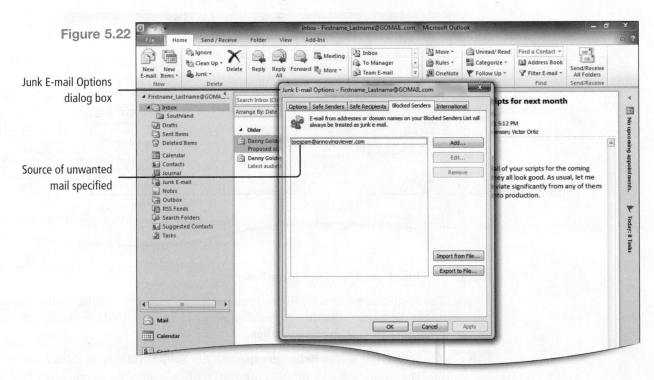

**4** In the **Junk E-mail Options** dialog box, click **Add**. In the **Add address or domain** dialog box, type **@junkmail.com** and then click **OK**.

You can also block an entire domain name. Recall that a domain name is the portion of an e-mail address that defines the e-mail system or Internet Service Provider. Use this option only when you are certain all messages from the domain name are unwanted, because blocking a domain means that messages from anyone with that domain name will be blocked. All mail received from these senders will be placed in the Junk E-mail folder.

**5** Display the **Start** menu ⊕, and open the **Snipping Tool**. Click the **New arrow**, and then click **Window Snip**. Click in the **Junk E-mail Options** dialog box to capture the window, and then click the **Save Snip** button 🔲. Navigate to your storage device. Click in the **File name** box, and then using your own name, type **Lastname_Firstname_5A_Junk_Mail** Click the **Save as type arrow**, and then click **JPEG file**. Click **Save**, and then **Close** 🗙 the **Snipping Tool**. Submit the end result to your instructor as directed.

**6** In the **Junk E-mail Options** dialog box, click **OK**.

## Activity 5.09 | Organizing Mail Folders Using View Filters

Another way to organize a large e-mail folder is to create a filter that screens the folder view. A *view filter* leaves all the messages in the folder but displays only those you want to see—based on instructions you define. For example, you might want to see only those messages from a specific individual. In this activity, you will create a view of Elizabeth Robinson's Southland folder that displays only the *Viewer Comments* messages.

**1** In the **Navigation Pane**, select the **Southland** folder. On the **Home tab**, in the **Find group**, click the **Filter E-mail** button, and compare your screen with Figure 5.23.

You can create filters with different conditions. You can filter messages based on message characteristics, such as read status, attachments, received date, categories, flags, message importance, or to whom the message was sent. Additional filter options are available when you click More Filters.

Figure 5.23

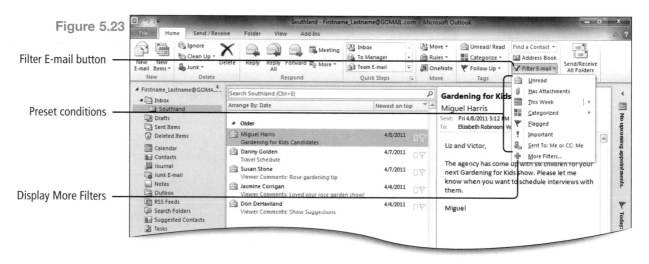

Filter E-mail button

Preset conditions

Display More Filters

**2** In the **Filter E-mail** list, click **More Filters**.

The Southland folder is highlighted and the Search Tools are available on the Ribbon. Above the message list, the *Type words to search for* box is outlined in orange and the insertion point is blinking in the box.

**3** On the **Search tab**, in the **Refine group**, click the **Subject** button, and then notice that in the *Type words to search for* box, the search filter—*subject*—displays with the word *keywords* selected and enclosed in parentheses. In the **Type words to search for** box, with *keywords* selected, type **Viewer Comments** to replace the selected text. Compare your screen with Figure 5.24.

The *Southland* folder displays only three messages, all containing the phrase *Viewer Comments* in their subjects.

Figure 5.24

Subject keyword search

Three messages display
Viewer Comments in
the subject

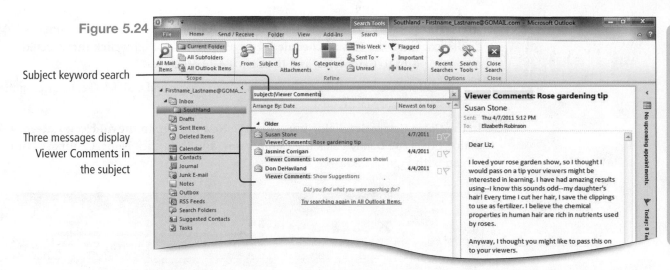

**4** Display the **Start** menu ⊕, and open the **Snipping Tool**. Click the **New arrow**, and then click **Window Snip**. Click in the window to capture it, and then click the **Save Snip** button 🔲. Navigate to your storage device. Click in the **File name** box, and then using your own name, type **Lastname_Firstname_5A_Comments_Filter** Click the **Save as type arrow**, and then click **JPEG file**. Click **Save. Close** ⊠ the **Snipping Tool.** Submit the end result to your instructor as directed.

**5** On the **Search tab**, in the **Close group**, click the **Close Search** button to clear the search and redisplay the entire Southland folder.

---

**More Knowledge | Managing Mailbox Size by Using Mailbox Cleanup**

Another way to manage mailbox information is by using Outlook's Mailbox Cleanup feature. You can use this tool to view total mailbox size and the size of individual folders within the mailbox. You can also locate and delete messages larger than a certain size. This is a useful feature when you have storage limitations on your e-mail server. To use the Mail Cleanup tool, from Backstage view, click Cleanup Tools.

---

## Objective 2 | Modify the Master Category List

When you assign Outlook items to categories, you select from the *Master Category List*, which is the Outlook-supplied list of color categories used for grouping, filtering, and sorting Outlook information. You have used categories to organize your calendar items, tasks, and messages. In addition, you have renamed the categories used in the Master Category List to include descriptive terms such as *Personal* and *Supplier*.

Outlook enables you to create your own categories, which you can add to the Master Category List. The advantage of creating your own categories is that you can organize your Outlook information in a way that is most meaningful to you. For example, you might be assigned to a special project that will last for several months. You can create a category named specifically for that project. As the project progresses, you can assign all the relevant tasks, calendar entries, and messages to the category.

### Activity 5.10 | Adding New Categories to the Master Category List

In this activity, you will create new categories in the Master Category List that Southland Media's Elizabeth Robinson will use to assign all her company-related messages.

**1** In the **Navigation Pane**, be sure the **Southland** folder is selected and its contents displayed. Click the **Travel Schedule** message to select it. Right-click the selected message, point to **Categorize**, and then click **All Categories**.

> The Color Categories dialog box displays. Here you can add and delete categories in the Master Category List.

**2** In the **Color Categories** dialog box, click the **New** button. In the **Add New Category** dialog box, type **Danny** Click the **Color arrow**, and then click **None**. Compare your screen with Figure 5.25.

Figure 5.25

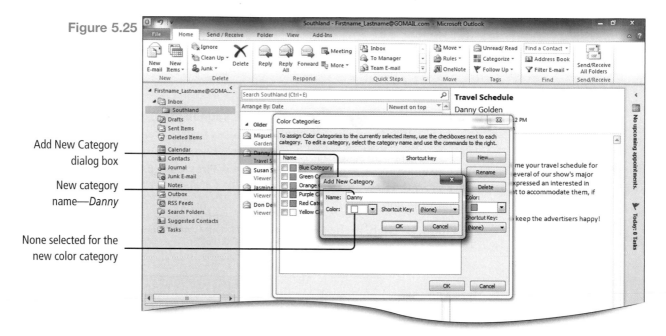

Add New Category dialog box

New category name—*Danny*

None selected for the new color category

**3** In the **Add New Category** dialog box, click **OK**. Click **OK** to close the **Color Categories** dialog box.

> The *Danny* category is applied to the Danny Golden message and displays at the top of the message in the Reading Pane.

**4** Click one of the messages with the phrase **Viewer Comments** in the subject. Then, hold down Ctrl and click each of the other two messages whose subject begins with the phrase **Viewer Comments**. Right-click one of the selected messages to display the shortcut menu, point to **Categorize**, and then click **All Categories**.

> In the Color Categories dialog box, notice that the Danny category displays in the list in alphabetical order.

---

**Note** | Viewing New Categories

Immediately after a new category is created, that category will display at the bottom of the Master Category List—before closing the Color Category dialog box. When the Color Categories dialog box is reopened, all categories will display in alphabetical order.

---

**5** In the **Color Categories** dialog box, click the **New** button. In the **Add New Category** dialog box, type **Viewers** Click the **Color arrow**, and click **None**. Click **OK**, and then compare your screen with Figure 5.26.

> The new category is added to the bottom of the Master Category List, and is selected.

Figure 5.26

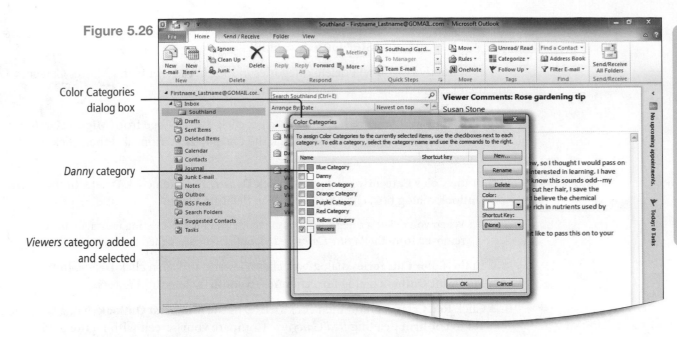

Color Categories dialog box

*Danny* category

*Viewers* category added and selected

**6** In the **Color Categories** dialog box, click **OK**.

The three selected messages are assigned to the *Viewers* category, and the category displays at the top of the current message in the Reading Pane. You can view the contents of the folder by category. In a folder with a large volume of mail, this can be a useful way to organize your messages.

**7** On the **View tab**, in the **Arrangement group**, click the **Categories** button. If necessary, expand each category to display all the folder items. Compare your screen with Figure 5.27.

Three groups display: the two new categories—*Danny* and *Viewers*—and one group for unassigned messages—*(none)*.

Figure 5.27

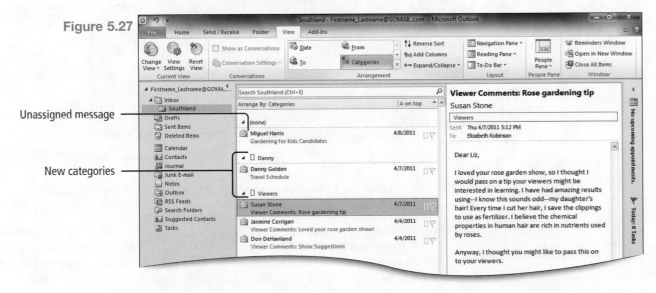

Unassigned message

New categories

**8** Start the **Snipping Tool**, create a **Window Snip**, and then using your name, save the JPEG image as **Lastname_Firstname_5A_Master_Categories.jpg** Close [X] the **Snipping Tool** window. Submit the end result to your instructor as directed.

**9** On the **View tab**, in the **Arrangement group**, click the **Date** button to redisplay the folder in its default arrangement—arranged by date.

## Activity 5.11 | Deleting Categories and Restoring the Master Category List

In this activity, you will delete categories in Elizabeth Robinson's Master Category List and then restore the list to the Outlook default.

**1** With the **Southland** folder still displayed, click the message from **Miguel Harris**. On the **Home tab**, in the **Tags group**, click the **Categorize** button, and then click **All Categories**.

**2** In the **Color Categories** dialog box, click **Danny**, and then click **Delete**. In the **Microsoft Outlook** dialog box, click **Yes** to confirm deleting *Danny*.

> When you delete a category that is currently assigned to existing messages, the category is removed from the *Master Category List*, but remains assigned to those messages.

**3** In the **Color Categories** dialog box, click **Viewers**, and then click **Delete**. In the **Microsoft Outlook** dialog box, click **Yes** to confirm deleting *Viewers*.

**4** Click **Red Category**, and then click **Delete**. In the **Microsoft Outlook** dialog box, click **Yes** to confirm deleting *Red Category*. Compare your screen with Figure 5.28.

> All three categories are removed from the *Master Category List*. You can delete any category on the list, including Outlook's preset categories.

**Figure 5.28**

Color Categories dialog box

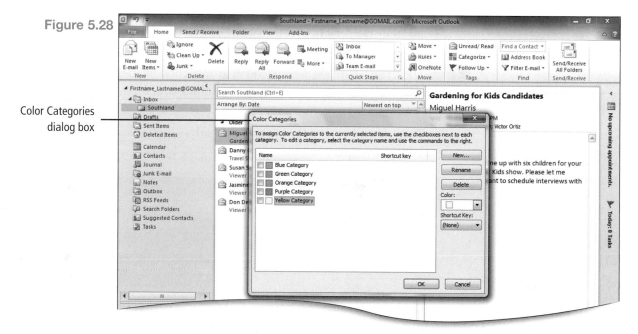

**5** Click **OK** to close the **Color Categories** dialog box. On the **View tab**, in the **Arrangement group**, click the **Categories** button.

> The *Danny* and *Viewers* categories still display. An item retains its category assignment even if the category is deleted from the Master Category List. This enables you to create a custom category, assign items to the category, and then delete the category when you no longer need it. If you display the Color Categories dialog box for an unassigned item, the deleted categories will not be listed.

**6** On the **Home tab**, in the **Tags group**, click the **Categorize** button, and then click **All Categories**.

> If you delete a preset category, it cannot be recovered because the Master Category List is stored in your Outlook data file (.pst). You must create a new category to replace any deleted category.

**7** In the **Color Categories** dialog box, click **New**. In the **Add New Category** dialog box, type **Red Category** Click the **Color arrow** and then make certain **Red** is selected. If necessary, click Red—the first color in the first row. Click **OK**, and then compare your screen with Figure 5.29.

*Red Category* is restored to the Master Category List.

Figure 5.29

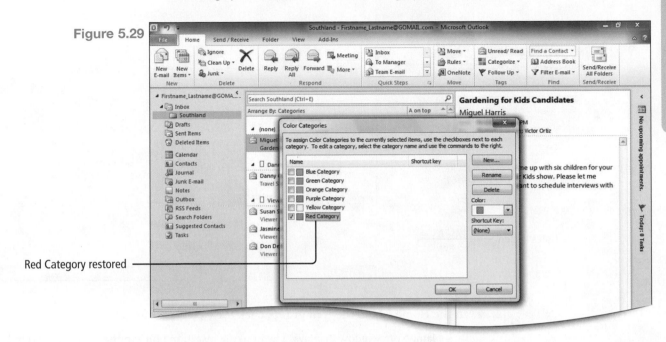

Red Category restored

**8** Click to remove the check mark from the **Red Category** check box. Click **OK** to close the **Color Categories** dialog box.

The Southland folder displays. The contents are still displayed in Category view.

# Objective 3 | Use Notes

Outlook *Notes* are the electronic equivalent of sticky paper notes. Notes are a convenient way to organize and keep track of bits of information you might want to use later. You can use notes to write down directions, phone numbers, reminders, or ideas—anything you might write on a paper note. You can leave notes open on the screen while you work. Any change you make to a note is saved. You can print notes and display them in different ways.

## Activity 5.12 | Creating and Editing Notes

You can access the Notes component of Outlook using the Navigation Pane. In this activity, you will create some notes for Elizabeth Robinson.

**1** In the **Navigation Pane**, at the bottom of the pane, click the **Notes** button ☐. **Delete** any existing notes if necessary. Compare your screen with Figure 5.30.

The Notes folder displays. As with other Outlook components, the Notes folder has its own commands on the Ribbon.

Figure 5.30

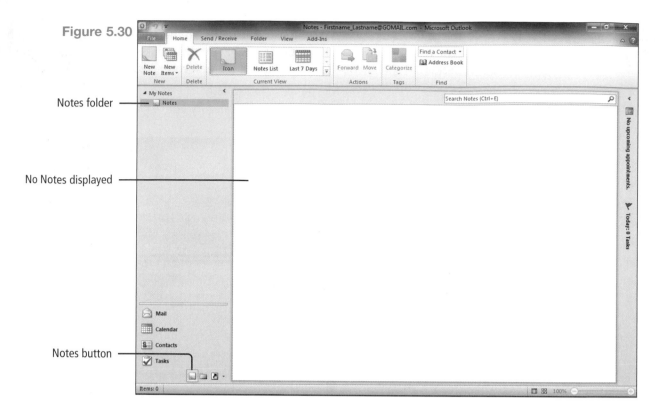

Notes folder

No Notes displayed

Notes button

**2** On the **Home tab**, in the **New group**, click the **New Note** button.

A blank Note window displays. The blinking insertion point in the Note window indicates that you can begin entering the text of the note.

**3** In the **Note** window, type **Get car serviced!** and then compare your screen with Figure 5.31.

Figure 5.31

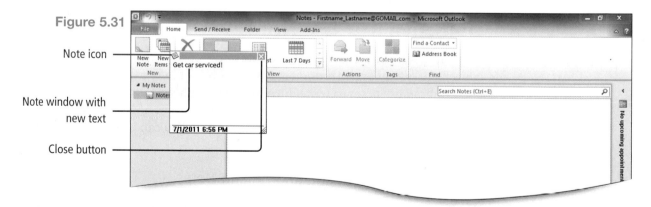

Note icon

Note window with
new text

Close button

**4** In the upper left corner of the **Note**, click the **Note** icon , and then click **Save & Close**. Alternatively, in the Note window, click the Close button .

The note closes, and a new note icon displays in the Notes folder.

**5** Right-click any blank area of the Notes folder, and then click **New Note**. Type **Show idea: Vacation home gardens?** and then close the note.

**6** Double-click a blank area of the Notes folder to create a new note. Type **Pick up Bryan's revised script** and then close the note. Create another new note with the text **Get Danny's new cell number** and then close the note.

**7** Create a new note with the text **Make dinner reservations** and then close the note. Create another new note with the text **Don't forget to feed Bosco** and then close the note. If necessary, on the Home tab, in the **Current View group**, click **Icon**. Compare your screen with Figure 5.32.

> The Notes folder displays six notes, all of which can be edited.

Figure 5.32

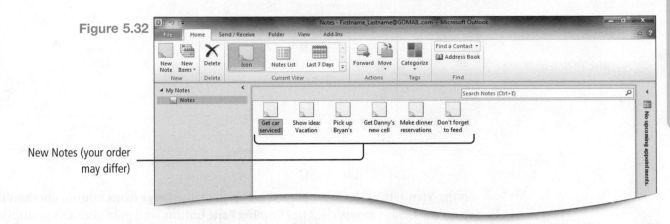

New Notes (your order may differ)

**8** Double-click the **Get car serviced!** note to open it. In the **Note** window, click to place the insertion point at the end of the existing text, press [Enter], type **Dealer phone: 619-555-0400** and then close the note.

> The note you just modified has been moved from the first position to the last in the Notes folder.

### Activity 5.13 | Viewing, Organizing, and Printing Notes

Outlook has several viewing options for notes, just as it does for messages, contacts, calendar items, and tasks. You can also organize your notes by assigning them to categories. Printing notes is similar to printing other Outlook items. In this activity, you will work with the notes you created for Elizabeth Robinson.

**1** Display the **Notes** folder, if necessary. On the **View tab**, in the **Arrangement group**, click the **List** button.

> The notes are reduced in size and arranged in a list.

**2** On the **View tab**, in the **Layout group**, click the **Reading Pane** button, and then click **Bottom**. Click to select the **Get car serviced!** note. Compare your screen with Figure 5.33.

> The full content of the selected note displays in the Reading Pane.

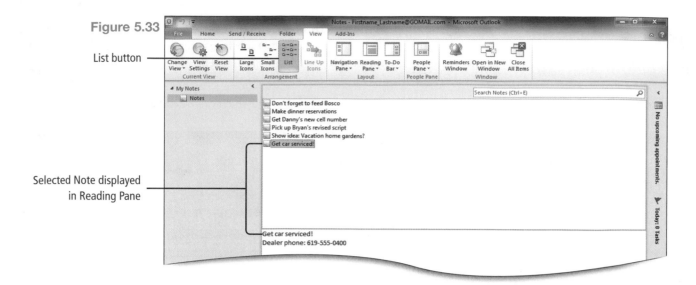

**Figure 5.33**

List button

Selected Note displayed in Reading Pane

---

**3** On the **View tab**, in the **Arrangement group**, click the **Large Icons** button. On the **View tab**, in the **Layout group**, click the **Reading Pane** button, and then click **Off** to display the **Notes** folder in its default view.

**4** On the **Home tab**, in the **Tags group**, click the **Categorize** button, and then click **All Categories**.

**5** In the **Color Categories** dialog box, select **Blue Category** and then click **Rename**. With **Bluc Category** selected, type **Personal** and then press Enter.

**6** Using the technique you just practiced, rename the **Green Category** as **Southland** and then press Enter. **Close** ☒ the **Color Categories** dialog box.

**7** Click the **Get car serviced!** note. On the **Home tab**, in the **Tags group**, click the **Categorize** button, and then click **Personal**.

In the Notes folder, the icon for the Get car serviced! note displays in blue—the category color.

**8** Right-click the **Make dinner reservations** note, point to **Categorize**, and then click **Personal**.

**9** Click the **Get Danny's new cell number** note to select it. Hold down Ctrl, and then click the **Pick up Bryan's revised script** and **Show idea: Vacation home gardens?** notes. Right-click any of the selected notes, point to **Categorize**, and then click **Southland**.

The three notes are assigned to the new Southland category.

**10** On the **Home tab**, in the **Current View group**, click the **Notes List** button in the gallery. In the **Notes** folder, click the **Categories** column heading to sort the folder by Category, and then compare your screen with Figure 5.34.

The Notes folder shows three groups: the *Personal* and *Southland* categories, and one unassigned note.

**Figure 5.34**

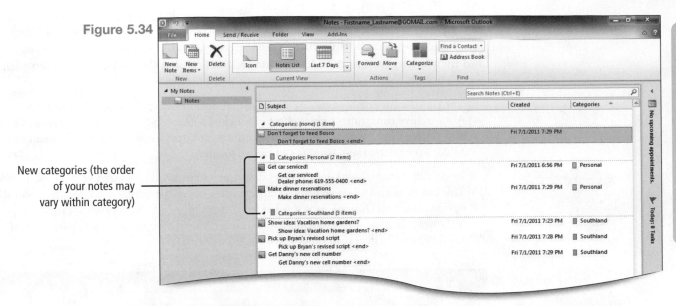

New categories (the order
of your notes may
vary within category)

**11** In the **Notes** folder, click the **Subject** column heading to sort the folder by Subject.

**12** From **Backstage** view, click the **Print** tab. Under **Settings**, click **Table Style**. Under **Printer**, click **Print Options**. In the **Print** dialog box, click the **Page Setup** button.

**13** In the **Page Setup: Table Style** dialog box, on the **Header/Footer tab**, delete any existing header or footer information, including page numbers and dates. In the left **Footer** box, type **Lastname_Firstname_5A_Robinson_Notes** and then **Preview** the notes. **Print** or use **OneNote** to create a PDF of the notes list as described in Activity 1.24. Submit the assignment to your instructor as directed.

> As in other components of Outlook, use the Table Style to print the entire contents of the folder. Use the Memo Style to print individual notes.

**14** On the **Home tab**, in the **Current View group**, click the **Icon** button to display the **Notes** folder in its default view.

## Objective 4 | Archive Outlook Information

As you accumulate information in your Outlook folders, you will find it helpful to *archive* information you want to keep. When you archive an item, you move that item to a location for storage and future access. Outlook has a feature called *AutoArchive* that performs this task.

AutoArchive automates the process of moving Outlook items to a storage location for possible future access. AutoArchive also discards expired items that are no longer valid, such as a meeting request that occurred months in the past but still displays in your Inbox. You can also archive older information manually. Archived information can be stored in a separate folder on your computer or in an external location, such as a network drive.

### Activity 5.14 | Configuring AutoArchive

Outlook is configured to perform an AutoArchive on all Outlook folders except the Contacts folder. In this activity, you will change the default settings.

**1** Display the **Folder List** 📁, and then display the contents of the **Southland** folder. From **Backstage** view, display the **Options** dialog box. On the left, click **Advanced**, and then, under **AutoArchive**, click **AutoArchive Settings**. Compare your screen with Figure 5.35.

> The AutoArchive dialog box displays. The first option determines how frequently AutoArchive runs. AutoArchive checks for expired items such as old meeting requests and deletes them. AutoArchive checks for the age of items, copies older items to an archive folder, and deletes them from their original location.
>
> By default AutoArchive runs every 14 days, but you can run AutoArchive more frequently. This can be useful when you have a large volume of daily e-mail. Notice also the second option, in which Outlook prompts before AutoArchive runs. This prompt displays a Microsoft Outlook dialog box, similar to a Reminder window, asking you whether you would like to archive your older items.

Figure 5.35

Default setting is to Run AutoArchive every 14 days

AutoArchive dialog box

Default is to prompt before AutoArchive runs

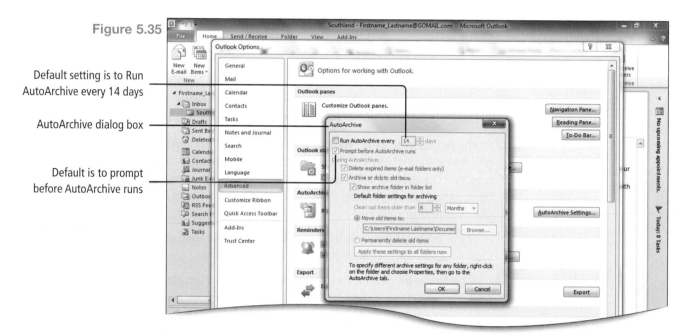

**2** In the **AutoArchive** dialog box, click the **Run AutoArchive every** check box, and then click the **spin box down arrow** until **7** displays.

> AutoArchive is set to run every seven days. You can also change the age of items Outlook archives. Outlook has different aging periods for different folders. The Inbox, Calendar, Notes, Journal, and Drafts folders have a default period of six months. The Outbox default is three months, and the Sent Items and Deleted Items folders defaults are two months. The aging period you set in this dialog box is a *global* setting—that is, the setting applies to all of Outlook's folders. If you prefer, you can apply aging periods to individual folders.

**3** In the **AutoArchive** dialog box, click **OK**, and then click **OK** to close the **Outlook Options** dialog box. In the **Navigation Pane**, right-click the **Southland** folder, and then click **Properties** to display the **Southland Properties** dialog box.

**4** In the **Southland Properties** dialog box, click the **AutoArchive tab**. Click **Archive this folder using these settings**. Use the arrows to set **Clean out items older than** to **2 Weeks**, and then compare your screen with Figure 5.36.

> Messages in this folder are set to be archived when they are older than two weeks.

**Figure 5.36**
AutoArchive tab selected

Southland Properties
dialog box

Setting indicates items
older than 2 weeks
are archived

**5** In the **Southland Properties** dialog box, click **OK**.

AutoArchive is set to run every seven days, and messages in the Southland folder that are more than two weeks old will be archived.

---

**Alert! | Does an AutoArchive prompt display?**

When you change the AutoArchive settings to archive your folders, during this instruction Outlook may display the Microsoft Outlook dialog box that asks you if you want to AutoArchive your old items now. Recall that this prompt is an option in the AutoArchive dialog box, and this option is selected by default. Normally you would allow Outlook to archive your older items. If this dialog box displays during this instruction, click No.

---

## Activity 5.15 | Manually Archiving Mail Messages

Outlook also enables you to archive your data manually. This can be useful when you want to archive a specific folder that is not currently scheduled for archiving with AutoArchive. For example, you might want to archive your Inbox before you go on vacation. In this activity, you will manually archive Elizabeth Robinson's Southland folder.

**1** In the **Navigation Pane**, be sure the **Southland** folder displays. From **Backstage** view, click the **Cleanup Tools** button, and then click **Archive** to display the **Archive** dialog box. Under **Archive this folder and all subfolders**, expand the **Inbox** folder, and click **Southland**.

The Southland folder is selected as the folder that will be archived.

**2** In the **Archive items older than:** box, type **04/10/11** and then compare your screen with Figure 5.37.

This specifies the date for Outlook to use in determining which items in the Southland folder to archive. All the items in the Southland folder are older than the date you typed, so all messages in the folder will be archived.

Figure 5.37

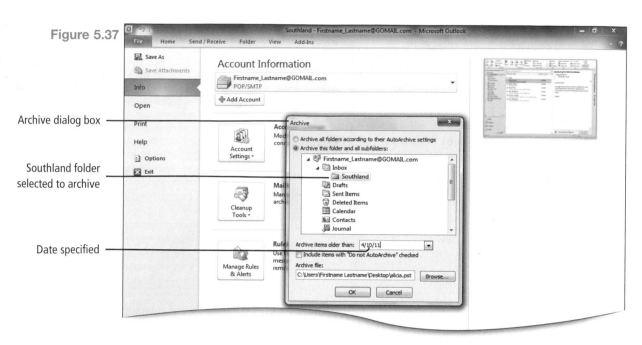

Archive dialog box

Southland folder selected to archive

Date specified

**3** Under **Archive file**, click **Browse**, navigate to the location where you are storing your files, and then click the **New Folder** button. In the displayed new folder, with **New Folder** selected, type **Chapter 5** and then compare your screen with Figure 5.38.

Figure 5.38

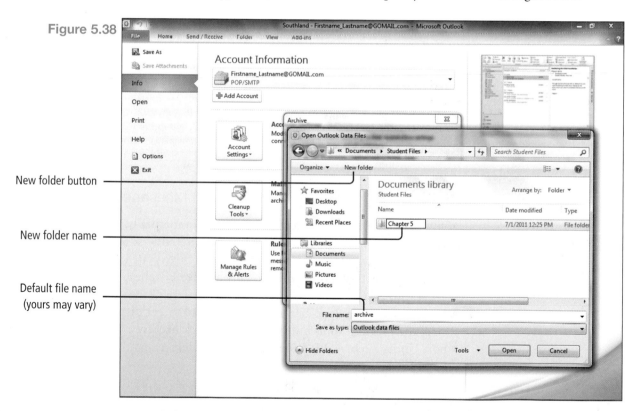

New folder button

New folder name

Default file name (yours may vary)

**4** With the insertion point located to the right of **Chapter 5**, press Enter. Double click the **Chapter 5** folder to open it.

The new folder name displays in the Address box, indicating that the folder is open and ready for you to store your files. The File name box may show the name of a previous user's file name or the default file name. Outlook uses *archive* as the default file name for all archived information. You will specify a different file name using the location of your stored files.

**5** In the **Open Outlook Data Files** dialog box, in the **File name** box, delete any existing file name, and then type **Lastname_Firstname_5A_Southland_Gardens** using your own name. Click **OK**. If a **Microsoft Outlook** dialog box displays a warning that all items in the folder will be archived, click **Yes** to continue.

**6** In the redisplayed **Archive** dialog box, click **OK**, and then click the **Home tab**.

The Archive dialog box closes, and Outlook archives the Southland folder. The Folder List now includes a set of file folders named *Archives*, which is Outlook's default name for the location of files stored for future use.

**7** In the **Navigation Pane**, if necessary, use the **scroll bar** to display the **Archives** folder in the **Folder List**.

> **Note** | Do you have more than one folder labeled Archives?
>
> Your Folder List may show more than one Archives folder. When Outlook performs an AutoArchive of your Outlook folders, Outlook normally adds Archives to the Folder List. This folder remains open and displayed in your Folder List. Outlook identifies all archive folders in the Folder List as Archives, even if the additional archive files have different file names. If you have more than one Archives folder displayed in your Folder List, the Archives folder at the bottom of the Folder List will contain your Southland folder archive data. You should open this Archives folder.

**8** In the **Folder List**, to the left of Archives, click the **Expand** button ▷ to display the Archives subfolders. In the **Archives subfolders**, to the left of the **Inbox**, click the **Expand** button ▷. Compare your screen with Figure 5.39.

The Inbox subfolder contains another subfolder—the Southland folder. This is the folder that contains your archived messages.

Figure 5.39

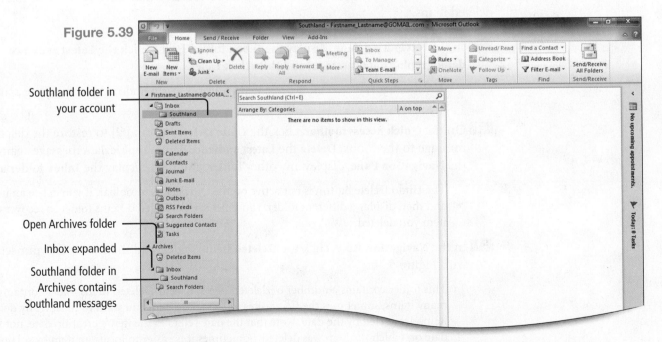

Southland folder in your account

Open Archives folder

Inbox expanded

Southland folder in Archives contains Southland messages

**9** In the **Folder List**, under **Archives**, click the **Southland** folder. To arrange messages by category, if necessary, on the **View** tab, in the **Arrangement group**, click the **Categories** button in the gallery.

The archived messages from the Southland folder display.

**10** Start the **Snipping Tool**, create a **Window Snip**, and then save the **JPEG** image as Lastname_Firstname_5A_Southland_Archive.jpg using your own name. **Close** ❎ the **Snipping Tool** window. Submit the end result to your instructor as directed.

**11** With Outlook displayed, in the **Folder List**, right-click **Archives**, and then click **Close "Archives"** to close the Archives folder. **Close** any additional Archives folders that may display in the Folder List.

> Recall that you saved your archived file earlier in this activity with the file name Lastname_Firstname_5A_Southland_Gardens. Closing the Archives folder removes the Archives folder from Outlook, but does not delete the data file.

## Objective 5 | Recover and Export Outlook Information

There will be times when you must recover information you have deleted or archived. Deleted items can be recovered as long as they still reside in the Deleted Items folder. Archived items can be restored to their original locations by accessing the Archives folders.

You can also export Outlook information. You might want to export Outlook information to provide folder information to someone else or to place your Outlook information on a different computer, for example, when you acquire a new computer.

### Activity 5.16 | Retrieving Items from the Deleted Items Folder

You can locate and retrieve items from the Deleted Items folder in several ways. If you have a large number of items in the folder, you might want to sort the folder to locate the specific item. In this activity, you will delete a message in Elizabeth Robinson's Inbox and then retrieve the message from the Deleted Items folder, which already contains many deleted items.

**1** In the **Navigation Pane**, display the **Inbox** folder. Right-click the **Latest audience demographic data** message, and then click **Delete**.

> The message is sent to the Deleted Items folder. You can undo a deletion as long as the folder is still displayed.

**2** On the **Quick Access toolbar**, click the **Undo Delete** button 🔄 to restore the deleted message to the Inbox. **Delete** the **Latest audience demographic data** message again. In the **Navigation Pane**, display any other folder, and then display the **Inbox** folder again.

> The Undo Delete button is not active on the Quick Access toolbar. If you delete an item and then display a different folder, you must use the Deleted Items folder to recover the item you deleted.

**3** In the **Navigation Pane**, click the **Deleted Items** folder, and then compare your screen with Figure 5.40.

> This folder contains a number of deleted items. If your Deleted Items folder contains many items, sometimes the first task is to locate the item you want to retrieve. By default, items are sorted by the date. Note that the date refers to the item's creation date, not the date on which the item was deleted. Sometimes it is easier to locate an item by sorting the folder contents by type. The icons next to each item indicate whether the item is a calendar, task, note, contact, or mail item.

Figure 5.40

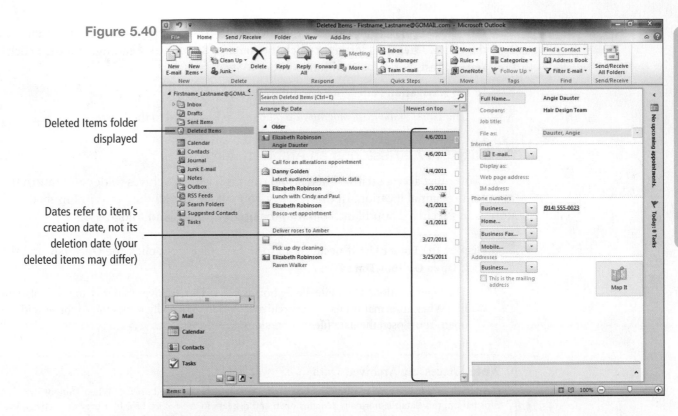

Deleted Items folder displayed

Dates refer to item's creation date, not its deletion date (your deleted items may differ)

**4** In the **Deleted Items** folder, click the **Arrange By** column heading, and then click **Type** to sort the folder by type.

**5** Locate and select the **Latest audience demographic data** e-mail message from *Danny Golden*. Right-click the message, and then point to **Move**. Compare your screen with Figure 5.41.

A shortcut displays a list of folders to which the message can be moved.

Figure 5.41

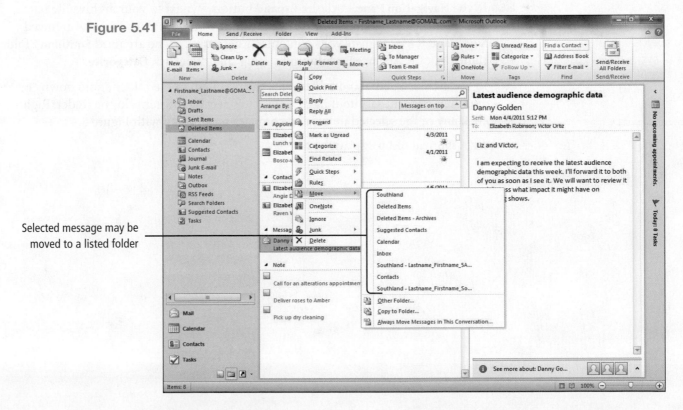

Selected message may be moved to a listed folder

**6** From the displayed shortcut menu, click **Inbox** to move the message to the Inbox. In the **Deleted Items** folder, right-click the **Arrange By** column heading, and then click **Date** to restore the Deleted Items folder to its default sort order.

**7** In the **Navigation Pane**, click the **Inbox** folder.

The *Latest audience demographic data* message is restored to the Inbox.

## Activity 5.17 | Restoring an Archived Item

If you must access archived items, you can display the Archives folder and return the item to its original location. In this activity, you will restore all the items in Elizabeth Robinson's archived Southland folder to the original Southland folder.

**1** Display the **Folder List** if necessary. From **Backstage** view, click the **Open tab**, and then click **Open Outlook Data File**.

The Open Outlook Data File dialog box displays. The Archives folder is an Outlook data file. When information has been archived, Outlook normally leaves the Archives folder open. You closed the data file in a previous activity.

---

**Note | Accessing Archived Data**

The default location for archived information is an Outlook data file called *archive*. When Outlook archives information, this data file normally remains open and displays in the Folder List. In a previous activity, you created your own data file when you manually archived the Southland folder data. Unless you have created a separate data file for your archived information, you will find the information in the *archive* data file.

---

**2** Navigate to the location where you are storing files for this chapter, and then double-click your **Lastname_Firstname_5A_Southland_Gardens** file to open it.

The archive file name displays in the Folder List.

**3** In the **Navigation Pane**, click the **Expand** button ▷ next to your archive file name, and then click the **Expand** button ▷ next to the **Inbox** folder. Click the archived **Southland** folder to display its contents. If necessary, in the archived **Southland** folder, right-click the **Arrange By** column heading, and then click **Categories**.

**4** In the archived **Southland** folder, click the first item in the folder , hold down [Shift] and then click the last item in the folder to select all the items in the folder. Right-click any of the selected items, and compare your screen with Figure 5.42.

A shortcut menu displays.

Figure 5.42

Shortcut menu

Archive file name

**5** On the displayed shortcut menu, point to **Move**, and then click **Southland**.

> Notice there are two Southland folders—Southland and Southland – Archives. The items in the archived Southland folder are moved to their original location. The archived Southland folder is now empty.

**6** In the **Navigation Pane**, right-click your archive folder name, and then click **Close "Lastname_Firstname_5A_Southland_Gardens"** to close the Archives folder. In the **Navigation Pane**, click the **Southland** folder. On the **View tab**, in the **Arrangement group**, click the **Date** button in the gallery.

> The messages have been restored to their original location and are displayed in the default view.

## Activity 5.18 | Exporting Outlook Information

From Outlook, you can export data to other programs. When you *export* information, you copy data into a file that can be used by another program. You can export Outlook information to Microsoft Access, Microsoft Word, Microsoft Excel, and Microsoft PowerPoint, among other programs.

Exporting Outlook information can be very useful. For example, you may want to use the names and addresses in your Contacts list in an Excel spreadsheet. By exporting the information from Outlook, you do not have to retype the information. You can also export Outlook information to an Outlook data file, which can then be copied to a different computer. In this activity, you will export Elizabeth Robinson's Southland folder.

**1** In the **Navigation Pane**, be sure the **Southland** folder is displayed.

**2** From **Backstage** view, click the **Open tab**, and then click **Import**. In the **Import and Export Wizard** dialog box, under **Choose an action to perform**, click **Export to a file**, and then click **Next**.

**3** In the **Export to a File** dialog box, under **Create a file of type**, click **Outlook Data File (.pst)**, and then click **Next**. Compare your screen with Figure 5.43.

> The Export Outlook Data File dialog box displays.

Figure 5.43

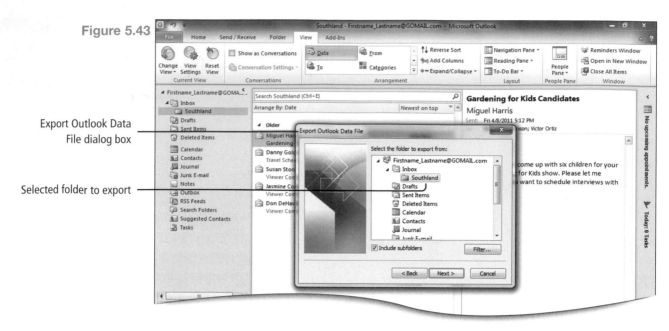

Export Outlook Data
File dialog box

Selected folder to export

**4** In the **Export Outlook Data File** dialog box, click the **Southland** folder if necessary, and then click **Next**.

**5** In the **Export Outlook Data File** dialog box, click **Browse**, and then navigate to the location where you are storing your files for this chapter. In the **Open Outlook Data Files** dialog box, in the **File name** box, delete any existing file name, and type **Lastname_Firstname_5A_Southland_Exported** Click **OK**.

> The Export Outlook Data File dialog box redisplays.

**6** In the **Export Outlook Data File** dialog box, click **Finish**.

> The Create Outlook Data File dialog box displays.

**7** In the **Create Outlook Data File** dialog box, click **OK**.

> The Southland folder is exported to the location of your stored files without adding an optional password.

## Activity 5.19 | Restoring Outlook's Default Settings

In this activity, you will restore Outlook to its default settings.

**1** In the **Navigation Pane**, right-click the **Southland** folder, click **Delete Folder**, and then click **Yes**. Delete the contents of the **Inbox**.

**2** In the **Navigation Pane**, click the **Notes** folder. Right-click the **Make dinner reservations** note, point to **Categorize**, and then click **All Categories**.

> Recall that you modified the Master Category List. To restore the default categories, you must do so before permanently deleting all items—messages, notes, tasks, contacts, or calendar items.

**3** In the **Color Categories** dialog box, click the **Personal** category, and then click **Rename**. With **Personal** selected, type **Blue Category** and then press [Enter]. Using the technique you just practiced, rename the **Southland** category as **Green Category** Click **OK** to close the **Color Categories** dialog box.

**4** In the **Notes** folder, select and delete all the notes. Display the **Folder List**, and then empty the contents of the **Deleted Items** folder, including the **Southland** subfolder.

**5** From **Backstage** view, click **Options**. In the **Outlook Options dialog box**, on the left, click **Advanced**, and then click **AutoArchive Settings**. In the **AutoArchive** dialog box, in the **Run AutoArchive every** box, set the number to **14** Be sure that **Clean out items older than** displays **6 Months**. Click the check box for **Run AutoArchive every** to deselect the check box if this was the default setting. Click **OK**, and then click **OK** to close the Outlook Options dialog box.

**6** In the **Navigation Pane**, click **Mail**. On the **Home tab**, in the **Delete group**, click the **Junk button**, and then click **Junk E-mail Options**. Click the **Blocked Senders tab**.

**7** In the **Junk E-mail Options** dialog box, click **@junkmail.com**, and then click **Remove**. Click **joespam@annoyingviewer.com**, and then click **Remove**. Click **OK**.

**8** In **Backstage** view, on the **Print tab**, under **Printer**, click **Print Options**. In the **Print** dialog box, under **Print Style**, click **Define Styles** to display the **Define Print Styles** dialog box.

> Recall that Outlook remembers header and footer information. You can restore the print style you used to its default setting.

**9** In the **Define Print Styles** dialog box, click **Table Style**, click **Reset**, and then click **OK**. Click **Close**. Click **Cancel** to close the **Print** dialog box. **Close** ☒ Outlook.

**End** **You have completed Project 5A** ─────────────────────

---

**More Knowledge | Removing Your E-Mail Account from Outlook**

When you are finished with all activities for this chapter, remove the fictitious e-mail account from Outlook. From Backstage view, click the Account Settings button, and then click Account Settings. In the Account Settings dialog box, under E-mail Accounts, click your GOMAIL.com account, and click Remove. In the displayed Account Settings dialog box, click Yes. and then click Close to close the Account Settings dialog box.

# Content-Based Assessments

## Summary

Outlook has a number of tools that help you organize and manage information. In this chapter, you created and renamed e-mail folders. You created rules to have Outlook place incoming e-mail messages into specific e-mail folders. You organized your e-mail messages by moving messages from one folder to another. You worked with Outlook's junk e-mail filter to screen out unwanted and unsolicited e-mail. You organized your e-mail messages by using different view filters. You modified the Master Category List by adding new categories and deleting existing ones. You created, edited, and printed various notes and viewed them in different ways. You also archived Outlook information. Finally, you recovered and exported Outlook information.

## Key Terms

## Matching

Match each term in the second column with its correct definition in the first column. Write the letter of the term on the blank line in front of the correct definition.

_____ 1. Actions taken on messages that meet certain conditions, along with any exceptions to those conditions.

_____ 2. In a rule, the criteria that determine how incoming e-mail messages will be handled.

_____ 3. A feature that defines the actions that Outlook takes for sent or received messages that meet certain conditions.

_____ 4. A program that guides you through the process of creating a message rule.

_____ 5. A set of predefined conditions and actions in rule creation used for common processing tasks.

_____ 6. In a message rule, the criteria that excludes a message from the specified action when all other conditions of the rule are satisfied.

_____ 7. The rightmost portion of the Windows taskbar, next to the system time, in which Outlook displays information such as alerts.

_____ 8. A notification that displays on your desktop briefly when you receive an e-mail message, meeting request, or task request.

_____ 9. A set of instructions to screen a folder, based on conditions you define.

_____ 10. The Outlook-supplied list of color categories used for grouping, filtering, and sorting Outlook information.

_____ 11. The Outlook component that is the electronic equivalent of sticky paper notes used to keep track of bits of information you want to use later.

_____ 12. To move Outlook information that you want to keep to a location for storage and future access.

**A** Archive

**B** Archives

**C** AutoArchive

**D** Conditions

**E** Desktop Alert

**F** Exceptions

**G** Filter

**H** Global

**I** Master Category List

**J** Message rule

**K** Notes

**L** Notification area

**M** Rules

**N** Rules Wizard

**O** Template

_____ 13. The term used to refer to Outlook settings that apply to all, not just some, of Outlook's folders.

_____ 14. Outlook's default name in the Folder List for the location of files stored for future access.

_____ 15. The Outlook feature that automatically moves information that you want to keep to a location for storage and future access.

## Multiple Choice

Choose the correct answer.

1. The folder under which a new mail subfolder is typically created.
   - **A.** Inbox
   - **B.** Outbox
   - **C.** Deleted Items

2. An explanation of the actions a rule performs on a message.
   - **A.** Message rule
   - **B.** Rule Wizard
   - **C.** Rule description

3. A notification that displays when you receive an e-mail message, meeting request, or task request.
   - **A.** Desktop Alert
   - **B.** Message Alert
   - **C.** Rule Alert

4. The default location on the screen where Desktop Alerts display.
   - **A.** Lower right corner
   - **B.** Lower left corner
   - **C.** Upper left corner

5. A message rule defined by specifying your own conditions and actions.
   - **A.** Conditional rule
   - **B.** Template rule
   - **C.** Blank rule

6. The filter used to screen incoming e-mail for unwanted, unsolicited messages.
   - **A.** Junk e-mail filter
   - **B.** Spam e-mail filter
   - **C.** View filter

7. The type of filter used to display specific messages in an e-mail folder.
   - **A.** Criteria filter
   - **B.** Advanced filter
   - **C.** View filter

8. The view in the Notes folder that displays notes in a table and shows the text of the notes.
   - **A.** Icon
   - **B.** Notes List
   - **C.** Last 7 Days

9. The default view in the Notes folder.
   - **A.** Icon
   - **B.** Notes List
   - **C.** Last 7 Days

10. The folder that is not archived when AutoArchive is performed.
    - **A.** Calendar
    - **B.** Notes
    - **C.** Contacts

# Content-Based Assessments

## Mastering Outlook | Project **5B** Show

In the following Mastering Outlook project, you will organize Elizabeth Robinson's e-mail folders and create notes for her about an upcoming show on roses. Ms. Robinson's *Southland Gardens* program is planning a show devoted exclusively to rose gardening. She has received several messages related to the show. Your completed documents will look similar to the ones shown in Figure 5.44.

### Project Files

For Project 5B, you will need the following file:

o05B_Show_Inbox

You will save your files as:

Lastname_Firstname_5B_Show_Rules.jpg
Lastname_Firstname_5B_Show_Categories.jpg

You will print or create a PDF for one file with the following footer:

Lastname_Firstname_5B_Show_Notes

### Project Results

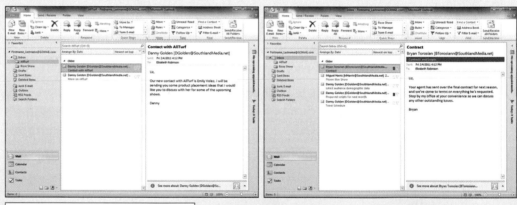

**Figure 5.44**

(Project 5B Show continues on the next page)

**1** Click the **Start** button, and then point to the **Shut down button arrow**. On the **Shut down menu**, click **Switch user** to display the **Windows 7** desktop. Click the Windows 7 user account you created in Chapter 1. If the account does not exist, refer to Chapter 1, Activities 1.01 and 1.02 to set up the account. Start **Outlook**, display the **Inbox**, and then delete any messages in the Inbox. With the Inbox selected, display **Backstage** view, click the **Open tab**, and then **Import** from your student files the **Outlook Data File (.pst) o05B_Show_Inbox**. Import only the **Inbox**, and select the option to **Import items into the same folder in** your **Firstname Lastname** account. View each message.

**2** Right-click the **Inbox**, and then click **New Folder**. In the **Create New Folder** dialog box, in the **Name** box, type **AllTurf** and then place the folder in the **Inbox** and verify that only *Mail and Post Items* are included. Click **OK**. With the **Inbox** displayed, create another **New Folder** and name it **Rose Show** using the same options that you used to create the *AllTurf* folder.

**3** In the **Navigation Pane**, be sure the **Inbox** is the current folder, and then display the **Rules and Alerts** dialog box. Click **New Rule**, and then under **Step 1: Select a template**, click **Move messages with specific words in the subject to a folder**, under **Step 2: Edit the rule description (click an underlined value)**, click **specific words**, and then in the **Search Text** dialog box, in the **Specify words or phrases to search for in the subject box**, type **AllTurf** and then click **Add**. In the **Search Text** dialog box, click **OK**.

**4** In the **Rules Wizard** dialog box, under **Step 2: Edit the rule description (click an underlined value)**, click **specified**. In the **Rules and Alerts** dialog box, expand the **Inbox**, and then click **AllTurf**. Click **OK**, and then click **Next** until the Rules Wizard dialog box displays the **Step 1: Specify a name for this rule** box. For the rule name, type **AllTurf Mail** and then click **Finish**. Run the **AllTurf Mail** rule. Click **Close**, click **OK** to close all dialog boxes.

**5** Display the **AllTurf** folder, and then use the **Snipping Tool** to create a **Window Snip** that displays the contents of the AllTurf folder. **Save** the snip as **Lastname_Firstname_5B_Show_Rules.jpg** and then submit to your instructor as directed. **Delete** the **AllTurf** rule.

**6** Display the **Inbox**, and then click the **Rose Quotes** message from *Miguel Harris*. Point to the **Rose Quotes** message, hold down the left mouse button, and then drag the message to the **Rose Show** folder. Release the mouse button. In the **Inbox**, right-click the **A rose is a rose** message, point to **Move**, and then click **Rose Show**.

**7** In the **Inbox**, select the **Contract** message from *Bryan Torosian*. Display the **Color Categories** dialog box, and then create a **New** category with the name **Contracts and Scripts** Change the color of the new category to the last color block—**Dark Maroon**. Click **OK**. Assign the category to the **Contract** message from *Bryan Torosian* and to the **Proposed scripts for next month** message from *Danny Golden*.

**8** Select the **Contract** message from *Brian Torosian*. Start the **Snipping Tool**, create a **Window Snip**, and then using your name, save the **JPEG** image as **Lastname_Firstname_5B_Show_Categories.jpg**

**9** In the **Navigation Pane**, click the **Notes** button, and then **Delete** any existing notes. On the **Home tab**, in the **New group**, click the **New Note** button. Type **Get new garden gloves** and then close the note. Using the same techniques, create two new notes with the following text:

> **Call Sylvia about her rose pendant**
>
> **Get some rose-colored sunglasses?**

**10** Display the **Color Categories** dialog box, and then **Rename** the **Red** category to **Rose Show**. Assign the **Rose Show** category to the last two notes that you created. Change the **Current View** to **Notes List**, and then sort the notes by **Categories**.

**11** From **Backstage** view, click the **Print** tab. Under **Settings**, click **Table Style**. Display the **Page Setup: Table Style** dialog box and then delete any existing header or footer information. In the left **Footer** box, type **Lastname_Firstname_5B_Show_Notes** and then **Print** or use **OneNote** to create a PDF of the document. Submit your work to your instructor as directed.

**12** In the **Navigation Pane**, display the **AllTurf** folder. From **Backstage** view, click the **Open tab**, and then click **Import**. In the **Import and Export Wizard** dialog box, under **Choose an action to perform**, click **Export to a file**. Export the **AllTurf** folder as an **Outlook Data File (.pst)** and store it with your student files with the file name **Lastname_Firstname_5B_Show_Exported**

**13** Delete and rename categories as necessary to return the Master Category List to its default. Delete the contents of the **Inbox**, including the subfolders that you created. Display and delete the three notes that you created, and then empty the **Deleted Items** folder. **Close** Outlook.

**End** **You have completed Project 5B**

# Content-Based Assessments

**Apply 5A skills from these Objectives:**

- **1** Manage Mail Folders
- **4** Archive Outlook Information

## Mastering Outlook | Project **5C** Inbox

In the following Mastering Outlook project, you will organize Elizabeth Robinson's Inbox. Ms. Robinson works closely with Danny Golden and she would like to separate and save for future reference all correspondence between them. She would also like to create an archive of their correspondence. Your completed files will look similar to the ones shown in Figure 5.45.

### Project Files

For Project 5C, you will need the following file:

o05C_Inbox

You will save your file as:

Lastname_Firstname_5C_Inbox_Archive.jpg

You will print or create a PDF for one file with the following footer:

Lastname_Firstname_5C_Inbox_Subfolder

### Project Results

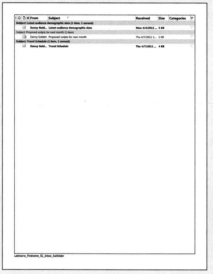
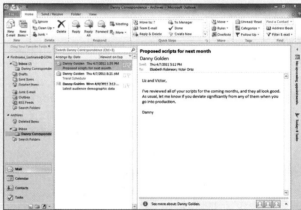

Figure 5.45

(Project 5C Inbox continues on the next page)

# Content-Based Assessments

## Mastering Outlook | Project **5C** Inbox (continued)

**1** Display the Windows 7 user account you created in Chapter 1. If the account does not exist, refer to Chapter 1, Activities 1.01 and 1.02 to set up the account. Start **Outlook**, display the **Inbox**, and then delete any messages.

**2** With the Inbox selected, display **Backstage** view, click the **Open tab**, and then **Import** from your student files the **Outlook Data File (.pst) o05C_Inbox**. Import the **Inbox**, and select the option to **Import items into the same folder in** your user name account.

**3** Create a subfolder in the **Inbox**, and then type **Danny Correspondence** as the folder name; be sure the folder contains *Mail and Post Items*. Move all messages from **Danny Golden** to the **Danny Correspondence** folder.

**4** Display the **Danny Correspondence** folder, and then sort the messages so that they are arranged by **Subject**. From **Backstage** view, on the **Print tab**, display the list in **Table Style**, and then display the **Page Setup: Table Style** dialog box. Delete all header and footer information. In the left footer, using your own name, type **Lastname_Firstname_5C_Inbox_Subfolder** and then **Print** or use **OneNote** to create a PDF of the document. Submit your work to your instructor as directed.

**5** From **Backstage** view, click the **Cleanup Tools** button, and then click **Archive**. Select **Archive this folder**

**and all subfolders**, and then expand the **Inbox** and select **Danny Correspondence**. In the **Archive items older than:** box, type **04/10/11** click **Browse**, and then navigate to the **Chapter 5** folder that you created earlier in this chapter. If the folder does not exist, navigate to the location where you are storing your files, click the New folder button, and create the Chapter 5 folder.

**6** Open the **Chapter 5** folder. In the **Open Outlook Data Files** dialog box, using your own name, in the **File name** box type **Lastname_Firstname_5C_Archive** and then click **OK** as necessary to close all dialog boxes.

**7** Display the **Folder List**, and use the scroll bar to display the **Archives** folder. Expand the **Archives** folder, and then expand the **Inbox**. Select the **Danny Correspondence** folder. Start the **Snipping Tool**, create a **Window Snip**, and then, using your own name, save the image as **Lastname_Firstname_5C_Inbox_Archive.jpg** Submit to your instructor as directed.

**8** In the **Navigation Pane**, close the **Archives** folder. Expand the **Inbox** folder if necessary and delete the **Danny Correspondence** folder, delete the contents of the **Inbox** folder, and empty the **Deleted Items** folder. Reset the **Table Style** print style, and then **Close** Outlook.

**End** **You have completed Project 5C**

# Outcomes-Based Assessments

## Rubric

The following outcomes-based assessments are *open-ended* assessments. That is, there is no specific correct result; your result will depend on your approach to the information provided. Make *Professional Quality* your goal. Use the following scoring rubric to guide you in *how* to approach the problem and then to evaluate *how well* your approach solves the problem.

The *criteria*—Software Mastery, Content, Format and Layout, and Process—represent the knowledge and skills you have gained that you can apply to solving the problem. The *levels of performance*—Professional Quality, Approaching Professional Quality, or Needs Quality Improvement—help you and your instructor evaluate your result.

|  | **Your completed project is of Professional Quality if you:** | **Your completed project is Approaching Professional Quality if you:** | **Your completed project Needs Quality Improvements if you:** |
|---|---|---|---|
| **1-Software Mastery** | Choose and apply the most appropriate skills, tools, and features and identify efficient methods to solve the problem. | Choose and apply some appropriate skills, tools, and features, but not in the most efficient manner. | Choose inappropriate skills, tools, or features, or are inefficient in solving the problem. |
| **2-Content** | Construct a solution that is clear and well organized, contains content that is accurate, appropriate to the audience and purpose, and is complete. Provide a solution that contains no errors in spelling, grammar, or style. | Construct a solution in which some components are unclear, poorly organized, inconsistent, or incomplete. Misjudge the needs of the audience. Have some errors in spelling, grammar, or style, but the errors do not detract from comprehension. | Construct a solution that is unclear, incomplete, or poorly organized; contains some inaccurate or inappropriate content; and contains many errors in spelling, grammar, or style. Do not solve the problem. |
| **3-Format and Layout** | Format and arrange all elements to communicate information and ideas, clarify function, illustrate relationships, and indicate relative importance. | Apply appropriate format and layout features to some elements, but not others. Overuse features, causing minor distraction. | Apply format and layout that does not communicate information or ideas clearly. Do not use format and layout features to clarify function, illustrate relationships, or indicate relative importance. Use available features excessively, causing distraction. |
| **4-Process** | Use an organized approach that integrates planning, development, self-assessment, revision, and reflection. | Demonstrate an organized approach in some areas, but not others; or, use an insufficient process of organization throughout. | Do not use an organized approach to solve the problem. |

# Outcomes-Based Assessments

Apply a combination of the **5A** skills.

## GO! Think | Project **5D** Contract Information

### Project Files

For Project 5D, you will need the following file:

o05D_Contract_Information

You will print or create a PDF for two files with the following footers:

Lastname_Firstname_5D_Contract_Subfolder
Lastname_Firstname_5D_Expense_Notes

Elizabeth Robinson receives many messages that relate to her contract and expenses. She would like to separate these emails from those that relate to the show. In this project, you will organize Ms. Robinson's Inbox.

Start Outlook, and import o05D_Contract_Information. Create a category for Contract Items in the Master Category List and assign the category to all messages that contain the word Contract in the subject. Create a subfolder in the Inbox for messages that have the word Contract in the subject. Print the folder in Table Style with the footer **Lastname_Firstname_5D_Contract_Subfolder** and then submit to your instructor as directed.

Display the Notes folder, and create at least three notes related to Ms. Robinson's expenses. Display the Notes folder in a view that shows the text of the notes, and print the folder in an appropriate Table Style using the footer **Lastname_Firstname_5D_Expense_Notes** Submit to your instructor as directed. Restore the folder to its default view, and delete the notes you created. Restore the Master Category List to its default categories, delete the contents of the Inbox and the Deleted Items folder, and reset any print style you used. Close Outlook.

**End** **You have completed Project 5D**

# Outcomes-Based Assessments

## GO! Think | Project **5E** Messages

### Project Files

For Project 5E, you will need the following file:

o05E_Messages

You will save your file as:

Lastname_Firstname_5E_Folders.jpg

You will print two files with the following footers:

Lastname_Firstname_5E_Travel_Messages
Lastname_Firstname_5E_Notes

Elizabeth Robinson has noticed that she receives three basic types of messages—those related to her contract and expenses, those related to vendors with whom she works, and those related to her show. She would like to organize her inbox according to these three types of messages.

Start Outlook, and import o05E_Messages into your Inbox folder. Create three folders based on the three types of messages that Elizabeth receives, and move each of her messages into one of the folders. With the Inbox selected and expanded, create a Window Snip that shows that you have created the three folders and that each folder contains messages. Save the snip as **Lastname_Firstname_5E_Folders.jpg**

Create a new category with the name Travel and the Dark Maroon color and assign it to any messages with Travel in the subject. (Hint: These messages should be in the folder that holds contract messages.) Print or create a PDF of the folder containing the travel messages in Table Style with a footer **Lastname_Firstname_5E_Travel_Messages**

Display the Notes folder, and create one note that relates to travel, one note that relates to the shows, and one note that relates to vendors. Create and assign a category for each note. Display the folder in a view that shows the text of your notes and the category assignments. Print or create a PDF of the folder in Table Style using the footer **Lastname_Firstname_5E_Notes** Submit the end results to your instructor as directed.

Restore the Master Category List to its default categories. Delete the notes you created, and display the folder in its default view. Delete the folders you created, the contents of the Inbox, and the Deleted Items folder. Reset any print styles you used. Close Outlook.

**End** **You have completed Project 5E** _____

# Glossary

**Accept** A meeting invitation response in which you notify the meeting organizer by an e-mail message indicating that you will attend.

**Annual event** A recurring event that happens once each year.

**Appointment** A calendar activity occurring at a specific time and day that does not require inviting people or reservations.

**Appointment area** A one-day view of the day's calendar entries.

**Archive** The action of moving Outlook items to a location for storage and future access.

**Archives** Outlook's default folder name for the location of files stored for future use.

**At sign @** A symbol used to separate the two parts of an e-mail address.

**Attachment** A separate file that is included with an e-mail message, such as a Word file, a spreadsheet file, or an image file.

**Attendees** Meeting participants.

**AutoArchive** The Outlook feature that automatically moves information to a location for storage and future access.

**AutoComplete** The Outlook feature that assists you in typing addresses by suggesting previously typed addresses based on the first character you type.

**Backstage tabs** Tabs that display in Backstage View, including Info, Open, Print, and Help.

**Backstage view** A centralized space for tasks related to file management.

**Bcc** An abbreviation for blind courtesy copy or blind carbon copy.

**Black border** An outline around an appointment, which is an indication that the appointment is selected.

**Blank form** A lined page added to the Card Style printout that you can use to manually list new contacts.

**Blank rule** A message rule that you define by specifying your own conditions and actions.

**Blind carbon copy (bcc)** A copy of a message in which the recipient's name is not visible to other recipients of the message.

**Blind courtesy copy (bcc)** A copy of a message in which the recipient's name is not visible to other recipients of the message.

**Business days** Days that are not Saturday, Sunday, or a holiday.

**Busy** The default free/busy setting that Outlook assigns to all new appointments that indicates that you have an appointment or meeting scheduled for that time.

**Calendar** The Outlook folder that stores your schedule and calendar-related information.

**Carbon copy** The term formerly referring to a paper copy made with carbon paper, now used to denote an electronic copy of an e-mail communication.

**Categories** Colors, with optional words or phrases, applied to Outlook items for the purpose of finding, sorting, filtering, or grouping.

**Client** A program that runs on a personal computer and relies on the server to perform some of its operations.

**Collapse** The action of hiding information by clicking a symbol.

**Column heading** Text that identifies message fields.

**Command** An instruction in a computer program that causes an action to be carried out.

**Comments area** The lower half of a form in which you enter information not otherwise specified in the form.

**Conditions** In a rule, criteria that determine how incoming e-mail messages will be handled.

**Contact** A person or organization about whom you can save information such as street and e-mail addresses, telephone and fax numbers, birthdays, and pictures.

**Contact group** A collection of contacts to whom you send e-mail messages.

**Contact Index** A set of lettered buttons used to move through contact items displayed in Business Card view.

**Contacts** A component of Outlook used as your e-mail address book for storing information about people, organizations, and businesses with whom you communicate.

**Contacts folder** The default location for Outlook's Contacts information.

**Conversation** A chain of e-mail messages that all have the same subject.

**Courtesy copy** Represented by the letters Cc, a copy of an e-mail message that is sent to a recipient who needs to view the message.

**Date Navigator** A monthly view of the calendar used to display specific days in a month.

**Decline** A meeting invitation response in which you do not agree to attend a meeting and that notifies the meeting organizer by an e-mail message that you will not attend.

**Desktop Alert** A notification that displays on your desktop when you receive an e-mail message, meeting request, or task request.

**Domain name** The second part of an e-mail address which identifies the host name of the recipient's mail server.

**Editors** Programs with which you can create or make changes to existing files.

**Event** A calendar activity that lasts 24 hours or longer.

**Exceptions** In a message rule, criteria that exclude a message from the specified action, when all other conditions of the rule are satisfied.

**Exchange Server** Server software that provides a system for sharing Outlook information among members on a network.

**Exchange Server environment** A shared environment for Outlook that requires a special server and that is set up by your system administrator.

**Expand** The action of showing information by clicking a symbol.

**Export** An Outlook feature in which data is copied into a file that can be used by another program.

**Field** A category of information within an Outlook item, such as the subject of a message, the date and time received, or a company name or address.

**Filter** A set of instructions that causes only some items in a folder to display, based on conditions you define.

**Flagging** Marking a message with a flag to draw attention to the message.

**Form** A window in Outlook used to display and collect information.

**Formatting text** The process of changing the appearance of the text in a message.

**Forwarding** Sending an e-mail message you have received to someone who did not originally receive it.

**Free/busy information** One of four indicators displayed by Outlook associated with your availability for a date and time in your calendar: Busy, Free, Tentative, or Out of Office.

**Full week view** The calendar view that displays a weekly, seven-day view in frames.

**Global** The term used to refer to Outlook settings that apply to all, not just some, of Outlook's folders.

**Group** Related commands on a displayed tab.

**HTML** A format for text that can include numbering, bullets, lines, backgrounds, and multimedia features that can be viewed in a Web browser.

**Icons** Graphic representations of objects you can select and open.

**Import** The action of bringing information into Outlook from another program in which the information already exists.

**Importance** Marks that are applied to messages based on the urgency of the message—for example, information that should be read immediately or information that can be read later.

**Inbox** A folder in which e-mail is stored.

**Info tab** A page in Backstage view that displays information about the current account.

**Item** An element of information in Outlook, such as a message, a contact, an appointment, or a task.

**Journal** A folder that provides a timeline of your activities and interactions, including a record of your day-to-day events.

**Local calendar** The Outlook calendar stored on the hard drive of your computer.

**Master Category List** The Outlook-supplied list of color categories used for grouping, filtering, and sorting Outlook information.

**Meeting** A calendar activity that requires inviting other people, reserving a room, or ordering equipment.

**Meeting form** Similar to an Appointment form, this form includes a To: box, a Send button, and a Cancel Invitation button.

**Meeting organizer** The individual who issues a meeting invitation.

**Memo Style** A style that prints the text of the selected items one at a time.

**Message delivery options** Optional settings for an e-mail message that can include the time a message should be sent or the address that should be used for replies.

**Message header** The basic information about an e-mail message such as the sender's name, the date sent, and the subject.

**Message rule** A feature that defines the actions that Outlook takes for sent or received messages that meet certain conditions.

**Natural language** A language spoken or written by humans, as opposed to a computer programming language.

**Navigation Pane** A column on the left side of the Outlook window that provides quick access to Outlook's components and folders.

**Notes** The Outlook component that is the electronic equivalent of sticky paper notes used to keep track of bits of information you want to use later.

**Notes area** A blank area of a contact form that can be used for any information about the contact that is not otherwise specified in the form.

**Notification area** The rightmost portion of the Windows taskbar, next to the system time, in which Outlook displays information such as alerts.

**Offline** A computer connection status in which the computer is not connected to a network or to the public Internet.

**Online** A computer connection status in which the computer is connected to your organization's network or to the public Internet.

**Optional attendees** People whose attendance is not considered critical for a meeting; if they cannot attend, the meeting can still take place.

**Out of Office** A free/busy setting that indicates you are away from your office and not available for other meetings or appointments.

**Overlay mode** A view that displays multiple calendars in an overlapping view.

**Pathname** The sequence of the drive letter and folder names that identifies the location of a file.

**Personal information manager** A program that enables you to store information about your contacts and tasks in electronic form.

**Plain Text** A format for text that allows no special formatting.

**POP3** A protocol that provides a simple, standardized way for users to access mailboxes and download messages to their computers.

**Print Preview** A view of a screen or message as it will appear on the paper when you print it.

**Print style** A combination of paper and page settings that determines the way Outlook items print.

**Profile** The Outlook feature that identifies which e-mail account you use and where the related data is stored.

**Propose New Time** A meeting invitation response in which you request that the meeting organizer change the meeting to a time at which you can attend.

**Quick Commands** A set of icons located above the File tab which provide access to commonly used commands.

**Range of recurrence** The date of the final occurrence of an appointment based on its end date or the number of times an appointment occurs.

**RE:** A prefix added to a reply that is commonly used to mean in regard to or regarding.

**Reading pane** An Outlook window in which you can preview an e-mail message without opening it.

**Read/write access** A type of access to a server that provides you with the ability to view and store information on that server.

**Recurrence pattern** The frequency of an appointment, which may be daily, weekly, monthly, or yearly.

**Recurring appointments** Appointments that occur regularly on specific dates and times at specific intervals and have associated reminders.

**Recurring task** A task that occurs repeatedly, for example, a weekly staff meeting or a monthly haircut.

**Reminder** An Outlook window accompanied by a tone that automatically displays at a designated date and time before appointments or tasks.

**Required attendees** People who must attend a meeting for the meeting to take place.

**Resource** A conference room or piece of equipment whose availability and use can be scheduled by Outlook.

**Ribbon** An area above an Outlook form that displays commands, organized by groups and tabs.

**Rich Text** A format for text that can include character and paragraph formatting and embedded graphics.

**Rule description** An explanation of the actions a rule performs on a message.

**Rules**   One or more actions taken on e-mail messages that meet certain conditions, along with any exceptions to those conditions.

**Rules Wizard**   A program that guides you through the process of creating a message rule.

**Schedule View**   A calendar arrangement option in which the current day displays horizontally on a time line.

**Scheduling button**   The button that changes the view to display available free/busy information for all meeting attendees.

**ScreenTip**   A small box that displays the name of a screen element.

**Scrolling**   The action of moving a pane or window vertically (up or down) or horizontally (side to side) to bring unseen areas into view.

**Selecting text**   Highlighting areas of text by dragging with the mouse.

**Sensitivity**   A security label applied to messages that should not be read by others because of the message content.

**Server**   A computer or device on a network that handles shared network resources.

**Signature**   A block of text that is added at the end of a message and that commonly includes a name, title, address, and phone number.

**Snip**   An item captured with the Snipping Tool.

**Snipping Tool**   A Windows 7 application with which you can capture all or part of a screen.

**Suggested Contacts folder**   A folder that displays e-mail addresses for people who have emailed you or whom you have e-mailed that are not in your Contacts list.

**Syntax**   The way in which the parts of an e-mail address are put together.

**Table Style**   A style that prints multiple items in a list with the visible columns displayed, such as the contents of the Inbox.

**Tabs**   Part of the user interface in Outlook that provide access to different commands based on particular activities.

**Task**   A personal or work-related activity that you want to keep track of until it is complete.

**Task body**   The blank area in the lower half of the task form in which you can add information not otherwise specified in the form.

**TBA**   A common acronym for To Be Arranged or To Be Announced.

**Template**   In rule creation, a set of predefined conditions and actions used for common processing tasks.

**Tentative**   A free/busy setting that indicates an appointment is scheduled but not confirmed. Also a setting that indicates that the specified time might be available or that your attendance at an appointment or meeting is uncertain.

**Third party**   Someone to whom you forward a message who was not included in the original e-mail message exchange.

**Time Bar**   The times next to the appointment area of the calendar, displayed in one-hour time increments.

**To-Do Bar**   An Outlook feature that provides a consolidated view of appointments, tasks, and e-mail that have been flagged for follow-up.

**Toggle**   A button that is used to turn a feature both on and off.

**Tracking button**   The button that changes the view to display a list of each meeting attendee, his or her status as a required or optional attendee, and the attendee's response status.

**Tri-fold Style**   A calendar print style that includes three sections.

**User account**   A collection of information that tells Windows 7 what files and folders the account holder can access, what changes the account holder can make to the computer system, and what the account holder's personal preferences are.

**vCard**   An Internet standard file format for creating and sharing virtual business cards.

**.vfb**   The file extension and abbreviation for a virtual free/busy Outlook file.

**View filter**   A feature that leaves all the messages in the folder but displays only those you want to see based on criteria you define.

**Views**   Ways to look at similar information in different formats and arrangements.

**VIP**   An abbreviation for Very Important Person.

**Virtual free/busy file**   A file that stores an individual's Outlook calendar information.

**Week view**   A view that displays a full seven-day week.

**Weekly Agenda Style**   A calendar print style that arranges the appointments in a table style, one cell per day, with the weekend day cells smaller than the work week.

**Weekly Calendar Style**   A calendar print style that arranges the appointment frames one column per day, similar to the Week view in the calendar.

**Wizard**   A tool that walks you through a process in a step-by-step manner.

**Wordwrap**   The Outlook feature in which text typed in the Message form is moved from the end of one line to the beginning of the next line to fit within the established margins.

**Work Week view**   A calendar arrangement view that shows only the weekdays, Monday through Friday.

**Working hours**   The workday hours between 8:00 a.m. and 5:00 p.m.

# Basic Computer Concepts

## OBJECTIVES

Mastering these objectives will enable you to:

## In This Chapter

Computers are an integral part of our lives. They are found in homes, offices, stores, hospitals, libraries, and many other places. Computers are part of cars and phones, and they enable you to access bank accounts from home, shop online, and quickly communicate with people around the world by means of e-mail and the Internet. It is difficult to find a business or occupation that doesn't rely on computers. Whether it's a truck driver who keeps an electronic travel log or a high-powered stockbroker who needs up-to-the-second market information, computers can make these tasks faster, easier, more efficient, and more accurate.

Computers are all around us, which makes it important to learn basic computing skills and gain the knowledge to be a responsible computer user. Knowing how to use a computer makes you ***computer fluent***.

This chapter looks at different types of computers and their functions. It discusses computer hardware and software and the benefits of networking. In addition, this chapter also discusses the importance of safe computing practices and the ways that you can protect your computer from various threats.

# Objective 1 | Define Computer and Identify the Four Basic Computing Functions

***What are the benefits of becoming computer fluent?*** Becoming computer fluent can benefit you in several ways. The advantage of being computer fluent is that it makes employees more attractive to potential employers. Many employers expect employees to have basic computer skills when they are hired. Computers have certainly changed the way we work. The traditional memo has given way to e-mail messages. Business reports can now be shared on a network, enabling a group of individuals to collaborate by adding their own notes and comments before the final report is finalized. Presentations are seldom delivered via overhead transparencies; presentation graphic software is widely used to share information with an audience in a conference room or via the company's intranet. Spreadsheet software is a key tool in presenting financial information and developing sound business plans.

On the other hand, if you are knowledgeable about computers and their uses, it also makes you a better consumer. You feel more comfortable when it comes to purchasing the right computer hardware and software for your needs, adding a peripheral for a specific use, or detecting basic problems when a system does not work properly. Also, if you have a basic understanding of today's technology, you can better understand and use *new* technologies.

***What are the basic functions of a computer?*** A ***computer*** is a programmable electronic device that can input, process, output, and store data. The term ***programmable*** signifies that a device can be instructed to perform a task or a function when fed with a program or software. A computer takes data and converts it into information. ***Data*** represents text, numbers, graphics, sounds, and videos entered into the computer's memory during input operations.

***Information*** is data that has been processed so that it can be presented in an organized and meaningful way. Think of data as the pieces of a jigsaw puzzle and information as the finished puzzle. Putting the pieces of the puzzle together gives you the overall picture. For example, CIS1100, the letter B, and the name Amy Stevens are pieces of data. Individually, these pieces of data seem meaningless. However, when processed, this data becomes the information on a grade report that indicates Amy Stevens received a grade of B in her CIS 1100 class.

These four basic computer functions work in a cycle known as the ***information processing cycle***. See Figure 1.1.

The functions of this cycle are:

- ***Input***—The computer gathers data or enables a user to enter data.
- ***Process***—Data is manipulated and converted into information.
- ***Output***—Information is displayed or shown to the user in a way that is understandable.
- ***Storage***—Data and/or information is stored for future use.

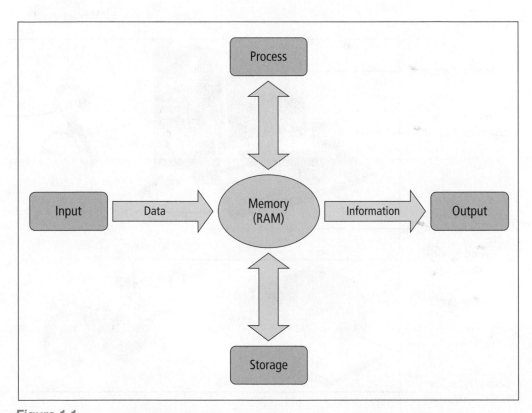

**Figure 1.1**

These are the four computer functions within the information processing cycle. Memory is not considered a function, but it is the center of flow of data and information within this cycle.

In the grade report, the instructor used a computer to enter, or input, the students' grades into the school's computerized grading system. A computer then processed this data along with data for other classes the students might have taken. In the example, the student Amy then received a written record of her grade or she accessed her grades online. The grade report was output by the computer. In addition, her grades remain stored in the system so they can be used to generate her transcript or to determine her future grade point average as she continues to take classes. See Figure 1.2.

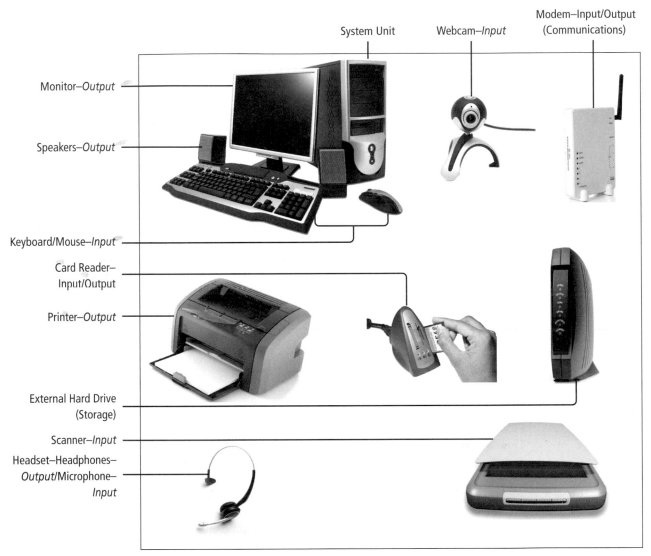

**Figure 1.2**

The components of a typical computer system and the appropriate step in the information processing cycle.

## Objective 2 | Identify the Different Types of Computers

***What are the different types of computers and what are their uses?*** Although computers come in a variety of sizes and shapes, the basic components required to complete the information processing cycle must be present in them. In addition to ***microcomputers***, the desktop and notebook computers and mobile devices that many of us are familiar with, there are also specialty computers, including servers, mainframes, supercomputers, and embedded computers. See Figure 1.3.

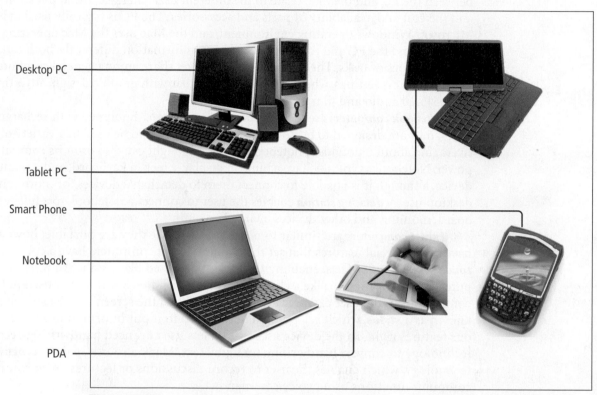

Desktop PC

Tablet PC

Smart Phone

Notebook

PDA

**Figure 1.3**
Types of microcomputers

## Microcomputers

***What are microcomputers?*** The term microcomputer means that the main component of a computer is a microprocessor, a tiny but powerful chip that is very small in size compared to a mainframe or a supercomputer. Microcomputers are classified as small, inexpensive, and designed for personal use or as part of a network of computers in a business environment. Computers in this category range in size from a desktop size system that is ideal when portability is not required to handheld devices that fit in your pocket. Some of the most common types of microcomputers include the following:

- ***Desktop computers*** are computers that sit on the desk, floor, or table, and typically have a detachable keyboard, mouse, monitor, and possibly other peripheral devices, such as digital cameras, scanners, and music players. Desktop computers are used in most homes and in business applications where portability is not needed. They can be configured in a multitude of arrangements depending on the specific needs and budget constraints. To ***configure*** means to put together by selecting a specific combination of components, features, and options.

- ***Gaming computers*** are mostly used by video game enthusiasts. They are usually configured with a fast CPU, large amount of memory, a special video card, joystick or game pad, and sound card with surround sound speaker system.

Desktop computers generally fall into two main categories: PCs or Macs. The PC, or personal computer, originally referred to as the IBM personal computer when it was released in the early 1980s, is now manufactured by a variety of companies including Hewlett-Packard, Dell, and Gateway. Today the term *PC* applies to any personal computer based on an Intel microprocessor, or on an Intel-compatible microprocessor. The Apple Macintosh computer, now known as Mac, is manufactured exclusively by Apple Inc. with an Intel microprocessor and can perform the same functions as the PC.

There are pros and cons to both types of computers, but in reality, both are good systems and the choice usually comes down to personal preference. The primary differences between the PC and the Mac relate to the different user interface, the application software, and the cost and availability of parts and accessories. The PC is typically used in a Microsoft Windows operating environment, and the Mac uses the Mac operating system. Although and the PC and the Mac each process information differently, both can perform the same types of tasks. The PC has a larger market share among general computer users and in business settings, whereas the Mac is popular with graphic design, advertising, and professional audio and film industries.

***Notebook computers*** are ideal for people "on-the-go." Equipped with rechargeable batteries, they are designed to be portable, permitting them to be used in a variety of places. Averaging about 6 pounds, a notebook's size and weight can also limit its computing power. Notebooks typically have a built-in display screen, a keyboard, and a pointing device, although it is possible to connect them to detachable devices for more comfortable desktop use. A ***docking station*** enables the user to connect a notebook to a full-size keyboard, monitor, and other devices in an office setting.

***Tablet computers*** are similar to notebooks because they are portable; however, they have some special features that set them apart. Tablet computers have a convertible ***touch screen*** that swivels, enabling the tablet to be used like a standard notebook computer in one position or like a clipboard in the second position. When used in the tablet configuration, the user can actually write directly on the screen using a special pen known as a ***stylus***, which is a pointed device used to input information and access various features right on the device's screen. Tablets use advanced handwriting-recognition technology to convert handwriting to digital text. Many also use ***speech-recognition*** technology, which enables the user to record discussions or lectures, or to control the computer functions using voice commands.

***Mobile devices*** include items such as ***personal digital assistants (PDAs)***, ***handheld computers*** (Pocket PCs), and ***smartphones***. These devices vary in size and purpose, but they are all ultra-lightweight and portable. PDAs were initially designed to provide a convenient resource for maintaining an organized calendar and list of business and personal associates. Handheld computers enable users to access personal productivity software and send e-mail over the Internet, while smartphones add Internet capability to the wireless communication aspects of cell phones.

The newest mobile devices are often referred to simply as "handhelds." Many handheld devices now include personal productivity software and enable the user to play music, take photos and video, make phone calls, and access the Internet. PDAs and Pocket PCs often use a stylus. It is not uncommon for these devices to use a small detachable keyboard for text and data entry. As the features of mobile devices continue to converge, permitting them to perform similar tasks, it becomes more difficult to differentiate between them. If you are in the process of buying one of these handhelds, you need to do some research and make sure that you get the features and functions you want.

## Servers

***What are servers?*** When computers are connected together in a ***network*** environment, ***servers*** are specialized computers that manage network resources through the use of administrative software (see Figure 1.4). They provide other computers with access to the network and can handle a variety of functions or may be assigned to just one particular type of task. Thus, within the same company, you might find a Web server that holds and delivers the organization's Web pages, a file server that handles the storage and retrieval tasks for all of the company's files, and a printer server that handles all print requests. Also, virtual servers (not real, but an abstraction) can manage other specialized servers without the added cost of additional hardware.

**Figure 1.4**
Network server

***What are mainframe computers?  Mainframe computers*** are large computers often found in large businesses, organizations, and government agencies where thousands of users need to simultaneously use the data and resources of their institution (see Figure 1.5). Mainframe computers ***multitask***; that is, they can perform more than one task at a time. Mainframes can store vast amounts of data using a variety of storage. Mainframes are often used for high-security applications, bulk data processing such as data surveys and census, and statistics. Early mainframe computers were very large and required separate rooms to house them, while today's mainframes are significantly smaller, faster, and more powerful than their predecessors.

**Figure 1.5**
Mainframe computer

## Supercomputers

***What are supercomputers?  Supercomputers*** are large, powerful, and ultrafast computers that perform specialized tasks. Some of these are used for research, processing intensive scientific calculations, and multi-scale simulations. Since June 2008, the IBM nicknamed "Roadrunner," at the Department of Energy's Los Alamos National Laboratory in New Mexico, holds top spot as the world's fastest supercomputer. (See http://www.top500.org/ for more information about Roadrunner.)

Supercomputers (see Figure 1.6) are the fastest and most expensive computers. Unlike a mainframe computer that can handle a number of programs simultaneously, the supercomputer is designed to run fewer programs at one time, but to do so as quickly as possible. They perform sophisticated mathematical calculations, track weather patterns, monitor satellites, and perform other complex, dedicated tasks.

**Figure 1.6**
Supercomputer

## Embedded Computers

***What are embedded computers?*** **Embedded computers** are small specialized computers built into larger components such as automobiles and appliances. Functions such as emission control systems, antilock braking systems (ABS), airbags, and stability control systems are common in today's vehicles. These computers use a specially programmed microprocessor to perform a set of predefined tasks, and may require little or no input from the user. Other examples include electronic appliances, microwave ovens, digital cameras, programmable thermostats, medical devices, and diagnostic equipment.

## Objective 3 | Describe Hardware Devices and Their Uses

***What is computer hardware?*** **Hardware** is the computer and any equipment connected to it. Hardware devices are the physical components of the computer. Items such as the monitor, keyboard, mouse, and printer are also known as **peripherals** because they attach to the computer. In Figure 1.3, the computer and different peripherals are matched with the individual steps of the information processing cycle.

The computer itself is known as the **system unit**, and it contains many of the critical hardware and electrical components. The system unit is sometimes referred to as the tower, box, or console. When the system unit is combined with the appropriate peripheral devices, the system can perform the four basic computer functions: input, process, output, and storage. Peripheral devices are used to input and output data and information, and the system unit processes and stores the data.

## System Unit

***What is inside the system unit?*** If you remove the cover from the system unit, you will find several key components inside. One of the most essential components is the ***motherboard***, a large printed circuit board to which all the other components are connected (see Figure 1.7). The ***microprocessor chip***, also known as the ***central processing unit (CPU)*** and RAM, the computer's main memory, are connected to the motherboard (see the table in Figure 1.8). The motherboard also provides some of the ports used to connect peripheral devices to the system. Ports are explained and illustrated later in this chapter.

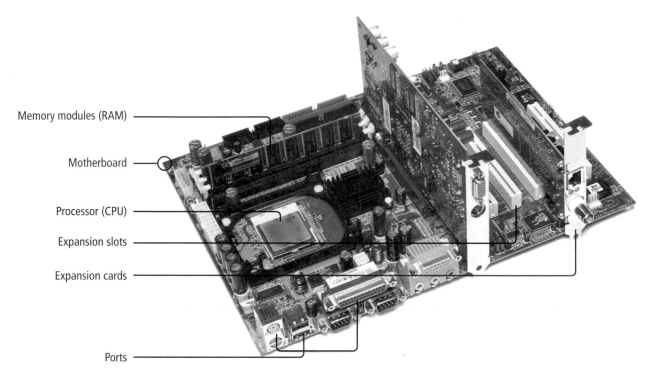

Memory modules (RAM)
Motherboard
Processor (CPU)
Expansion slots
Expansion cards
Ports

**Figure 1.7**
The motherboard and some of its components

## Motherboard Features

| Component | Description |
|---|---|
| Motherboard / System board | The main computer circuit board into which all components are plugged. It is installed safely inside the box or case called the system unit. |
| CPU | The central processing unit is responsible for getting data from memory, performing arithmetic and logical operations, and converting data to information. |
| Memory modules (RAM) | Temporary storage area where data is stored before processing, output, or storage. RAM is the center of flow of data and information within the information processing cycle. |
| Expansion slots | Slots or connectors on the motherboard that allow you to connect expansion cards. |
| Expansion cards | Removable circuit boards used to add new peripherals or increase the computer's capabilities. If the motherboard does not have a specific port to connect a peripheral device, the appropriate expansion card will allow you to do so. |
| Ports | Connecting points used as an interface between peripherals and the motherboard. |

**Figure 1.8**
Motherboard features

## Input Devices

*Input devices* are used to enter data into memory (RAM). The two most familiar input devices are the keyboard and the mouse, but they are not the only ones. See Figure 1.9.

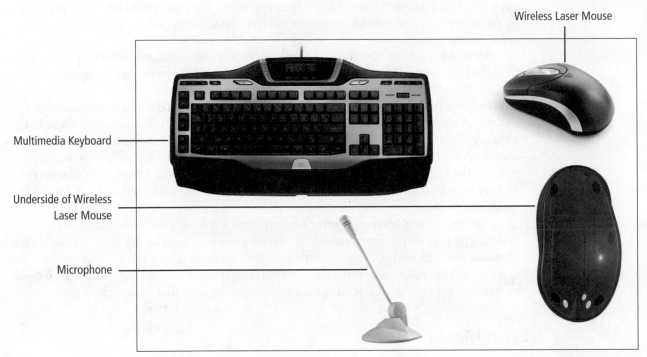

Wireless Laser Mouse

Multimedia Keyboard

Underside of Wireless Laser Mouse

Microphone

**Figure 1.9**
Input devices

## Keyboards

*Are there different types of keyboards?* The **keyboard** is the primary input device for computers. There are actually several different kinds of keyboards. The QWERTY keyboard is the one most common. It is based on the original typewriter keyboard and is named for the arrangement of the letters on the upper left alphabetic row of keys. Another style is the Dvorak keyboard, which arranges the letters and numbers in a different pattern for increased typing speed. Some ergonomic keyboards use a split keyboard arrangement, offsetting each half at an angle to reduce the incidence of repetitive stress injuries such as carpal tunnel syndrome.

Keyboard size and layout on notebook and tablet computers can differ slightly from a standard keyboard due to space constraints. Keyboards usually send information to the computer through a cable connected to a USB port; however, **wireless** or remote keyboards are gaining in popularity. A wireless keyboard communicates with the computer by infrared or radio frequency technology. These wireless devices require batteries.

*What are all these other keys used for?* In addition to the standard alphanumeric keys originally found on typewriters, computer keyboards have a variety of keys that provide additional functionality.

*Control keys*, such as the Ctrl, Alt, and Windows keys, often provide shortcuts or increased functionality to the keyboard when used in combination with another key. If you press the Shift key and a letter, the result is an uppercase, rather than a lowercase, letter. In the same way, using one of the control keys enables the standard keys to be used for additional purposes. For example, pressing Ctrl and the letter P opens the Print dialog box. Another example of a control key is the Esc key, which can often be used to stop, or *escape*, from a currently running task. A unique control key that is found only on Windows-based keyboards is the Windows key.

The **numeric keypad**, located at the right of the keyboard, provides an alternative method of quickly entering numbers. This is useful for individuals who are accustomed to using an adding machine or calculator.

**Function keys** are located above the standard row of number keys. Numbered F1 through F12, these keys are generally associated with certain software-specific commands. Pressing the F1 key will usually open the Help menu for a program; however, pressing one of the other function keys can produce different results, depending on the software program running.

**Arrow keys** are the keys located at the bottom of the keyboard between the standard keys and the numeric keypad. These keys enable the user to move the insertion point around the window one space at a time.

Toggle and other keys, which are located just above the arrow keys, are used for various purposes, including navigation and editing. The Insert, Num Lock, and Caps Lock keys are all examples of toggle keys. A **toggle key** works just like a light switch; press it once and the feature is turned on, press it again and it is turned off. If you've ever accidentally pressed the Caps Lock key and typed a long string of all capital letters, you've seen this feature in action. Pressing the Caps Lock key again allows you to return to normal keyboarding mode.

**Multimedia and Internet control keys** are typically found at the top edge of the keyboard. The precise placement and function of these keys usually depends on the keyboard manufacturer. However, most modern keyboards have at least a few keys or buttons that can be used for such tasks as muting or adjusting speaker volume, opening a **Web browser**, and sending an e-mail. Generally, each button has an icon that indicates its function.

## The Mouse

***Is there an easier way to control the action on the computer screen?*** Yes, the **mouse** is an input device (also called a pointing device) that, together with the keyboard, enables the user to control the operations of the computer. The mouse became popular with the introduction of graphical user interfaces, such as Microsoft Windows. This point-and-click device is useful for positioning the **insertion point** by translating hand movements into corresponding actions on the screen. The mouse is represented on the screen by a symbol called the **mouse pointer**. The user can move the mouse and position this pointer anywhere on the screen to move objects or make selections from available program icons or menus.

Some mice have a roller ball on the bottom that, as you move it, translates your movement into electrical impulses. Others use laser technology (optical) to control the pointer movement. Because the bottom of an optical mouse is sealed, dirt and debris are less likely to get inside and interfere with the mouse's internal mechanisms. This laser beam can be harmful if pointed to your eyes; do not look at it directly or point it at anybody else's eyes. See Figure 1.4. Just like a keyboard, the mouse can be wired or wireless. Notebook and tablet computers can use a mouse, but most of them have a built-in touchpad, a trackball, or track point to move the insertion point and mouse pointer. Most mice today are equipped with two buttons and a wheel button in the center that provides easy zoom and scroll functions.

***How can the mouse be used more efficiently?*** Although there are different kinds of mice, the traditional mouse has two buttons and a scroll wheel. The palm of your hand should rest comfortably over the mouse in such a way that your index finger rests on the left mouse button and the middle finger on the right mouse button. The following provides a brief description of some of the ways the mouse can be used:

- **Click**—By default, the left mouse button is considered the primary button. When instructed to click, it is understood that the mouse pointer is moved to a certain location on the screen and the left mouse button is be pressed and released one time.

- **Double-click**—When instructed to double-click, it is understood that the mouse pointer is moved to a certain location on the screen and the left mouse button is pressed and released twice in rapid succession. It is important that the mouse does not move while double-clicking or the command will not produce the expected results.

- **Drag**—This means to press the left mouse button and continue to hold it while dragging, or moving, the mouse then releasing it. This action can be used to select large blocks of text, to move objects, or to resize other objects.

- **Right-click**—Pressing and releasing the right mouse button one time will open a **shortcut menu**. Shortcut menus are usually context-sensitive, which means they will vary depending on what or where you have clicked and what program you are using. The right mouse button is also known as the secondary button and is not typically pressed more than one time; no double-clicking for the right button. After the shortcut menu has been opened, you select the appropriate choice by clicking it with the left mouse button.

- **Right-drag**—This is done by pressing the right mouse button and continuing to hold it while dragging, or moving, the mouse. This action is used when copying or moving files or folders within different storage devices.

- **Scroll wheel**—If your mouse is equipped with a scroll wheel, it can be used to quickly move a page up or down in a window, thus the name of the action to **scroll**. It is an easy way to navigate through lengthy documents or websites.

**Are there other input devices?** Although the keyboard and mouse are the two most common input devices, there are many other input devices. **Scanners** are similar to copy machines, but instead of producing a paper copy, they convert documents or photos to digital files that can then be saved on your computer. **Microphones** are used to digitally capture and record sounds. Game controls such as **joysticks** are used to control movement within video games. **Digital cameras** and **digital video recorders** enable you to capture digital images and movies and transfer them directly to your computer.

## The Processor

***What does the CPU do?*** The CPU (see Figure 1.10) is the brain of the computer and is responsible for executing program instructions and manipulating data to convert to information. It has two main parts—the ***control unit*** and the ***arithmetic logic unit (ALU).*** The control unit is responsible for obtaining and executing instructions from the computer's memory. Example: The user wants to print a document and selects the "Print" command from an icon on the screen. The CPU gets the command from memory (RAM), interprets the command, and sends the document as output to a selected printer. In other words, the CPU coordinates the internal activities and the activities of all the other computer components. The arithmetic logic unit (ALU) performs the arithmetic and logic functions for the computer. The ALU handles addition, subtraction, multiplication, and division, and also makes logical and comparison decisions. This enables the CPU to perform tasks such as sorting data alphabetically or numerically and filtering data to locate specific criteria.

**Figure 1.10**
Two sides of a CPU

## Different CPUs

As important as the CPU is to your computer, you might expect it to take up a large amount of space in the console. However, the CPU is actually rather small, thus the term *microchip*. Over the years, manufacturers have successfully reduced the size of microprocessor chips while continuing to increase their computing power. In fact, Moore's law (formulated in 1965 by Gordon Moore, cofounder of Intel) addresses this increase in computing power, observing that current production methods enable CPU capacity to double about every 24 months or so!

***Are there different brands of CPUs?*** Yes, the most well-known chip manufacturers include Intel and Advanced Micro Devices (AMD). Chip manufacturers often produce several different models of chips. Some of the chips that Intel makes include the *Intel® Core™ i7 processor Extreme Edition*, the *Intel® Core™2 Quad Processor* for desktops, and the *Intel® Centrino® 2 Processor Technology* for portable computers. AMD manufactures chips such as the *AMD Phenom™ II X4* for desktops, and the *AMD Turion™ X2 Ultra Dual-Core Mobile Processor* for portable computers. Intel and AMD chips are the mainstays for PCs. Using multiple processors (dual core or quad core) has several advantages over a single-processor CPU, including improved multitasking capabilities and system performance, lower power consumption, reduced usage of system resources, and lower heat emissions.

***How is a CPU's processing power measured?*** One indicator of a CPU's processing power is its ***clock speed.*** Clock speed measures the speed at which a CPU processes data (number of instructions per second) and is measured in ***megahertz (MHz)*** or ***gigahertz***

*(GHz)*, depending on the age of the CPU. Early computers had CPUs that processed at speeds of less than 5 MHz, whereas modern processors can operate at over 3 GHz (the equivalent of 3,000 MHz) and newer processors continue to surpass these numbers.

**What types of memory does a computer have?** Memory is another critical computer component of a computer system. The term *memory* signifies storage. There are two basic types of memory: temporary or **volatile** and permanent or **nonvolatile**.

**Permanent memory** includes **Read-Only Memory (ROM),** which is prerecorded on a chip. The information on a ROM chip cannot be changed, removed, or rewritten, and is generally inaccessible to the computer user. ROM is nonvolatile memory because it retains its contents even if the computer is turned off. ROM contains critical information, such as the program used to start up or boot—start— the computer.

Storage devices such as hard disks and flash drives and storage media such as CDs and DVDs are considered permanent or nonvolatile memory. These are presented later in this chapter.

**Temporary memory**, the computer's temporary or volatile memory, is **Random Access Memory (RAM)**. RAM (see Figure 1.11) acts as the computer's short-term memory and stores data and program instructions waiting to be processed. RAM is considered volatile because its contents are erased when the computer is turned off.

**Figure 1.11**
Random Access Memory (RAM) / RAM chips

**Why is it important to have enough RAM?** The more tasks your computer performs at the same time, or the more programs you have open, the more RAM it uses. We described RAM earlier as the center of the flow of data and information in the information processing cycle (see Figure 1.1). That flow slows down when there is not enough RAM. Your computer's RAM is like the top of your desk. The size of the desk that you need is determined by the work you do at a given moment. You may need to use a notebook computer, several books, a clipboard with notes, a holder for pens and pencils, and a telephone. If your desk is not big enough to fit these items, you cannot work with all of them at the same time. If you do not have a sufficient amount of RAM in your system, you might notice your computer slows down or even stops responding when you try to perform tasks.

Computer users often think this means they have too much information saved on their computers' hard drives. What it actually means is that they are running out of memory, not permanent storage space. To fix this problem, you can reduce the number of programs running at the same time, disable some features of the Operating System, or simply add more RAM to your system. Installing additional memory is one of the most inexpensive and easiest upgrades for your computer and often results in noticeable performance improvements.

Memory is measured in several units such as **_megabytes (MB)_**, which is approximately one million bytes, **_gigabytes (GB)_**, which is approximately one billion bytes, or **_terabytes (TR)_**, which is one trillion bytes. Study the table in Figure 1.12.

## Units to Measure Memory

| Name | Abbreviation | Number of Bytes | Relative Size |
| --- | --- | --- | --- |
| Byte | **B** | 1 byte | Holds one character of data |
| Kilobyte | **KB** | 1,024 bytes | Holds about a half page of double-spaced text |
| Megabyte | **MB** | 1,048,576 bytes | Holds about 768 pages of typed text |
| Gigabyte | **GB** | 1,073,741,824 bytes | Holds approximately 786,432 pages of text |
| Terabyte | **TB** | 1,099,511,627,776 bytes | This represents a stack of typewritten pages almost 51 miles high |
| Petabyte | **PB** | 1,125,899,906,842,624 bytes | This represents a stack of typewritten pages almost 52,000 miles high |

**Figure 1.12**
Measuring memory—these units are used to measure the size and capacity of RAM and also of storage devices/media

RAM size requirements vary depending on the operating system in use. Older computers that run Windows XP should have between 512 MB to 1 GB of RAM. For newer computers, a minimum of 2GB possibly more is recommended.

## Output Devices

**_Output devices_** display information after data has been processed in a useful format. This format can be text, graphics, audio, or video. Monitors and printers are the two most common output devices.

## Monitors

**_What are monitors? Monitors_** are display devices that show images of text, graphics, and video once data has been processed. The image on a monitor is called **_soft copy_**; you can view it, but you cannot touch it. See Figure 1.13.

Touch screen display                    LCD Wide monitor

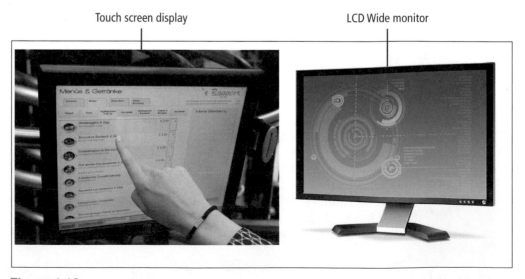

**Figure 1.13**
Output devices—monitors

**What is an LCD monitor?** Monitors come in a variety of sizes and styles, but the standard today is the **LCD (liquid crystal display)**. **Flat-panel** LCD monitors use a liquid crystal display and are thin and energy efficient.

**What factors determine a monitor's display quality?** The number of **pixels**, a monitor's display, is made up of millions of tiny dots known as pixels or picture element. Each pixel represents a single point on a display screen or in a graphic image. The number of pixels on the screen determines a monitor's sharpness and clarity, also known as its **resolution**. A higher number of pixels results in a clearer and sharper monitor resolution. A standard screen resolution might be expressed as 1024 x 768, which means there are 1,024 columns, each containing 768 pixels, for a total of more than 786,000 pixels on the screen. Monitor sizes are determined by measuring their screens diagonally.

**Dot pitch** is another display characteristic and refers to the diagonal distance between two pixels of the same color. Dot pitch is measured in millimeters with smaller measurements resulting in a crisper viewing image because there is less blank space between the pixels. For best viewing, monitors should have a dot pitch measurement of .28 mm or less. LCD monitors use an electric current to illuminate the pixels.

**Refresh rate** is the speed at which the pixels are reilluminated and it's measured in cycles per second, expressed as hertz (Hz). Refresh rates generally average between 75 and 85 Hz, which means the screen image is redrawn 75 to 85 times per second. Higher refresh rates result in less screen flicker and less eye strain.

**What are touch screen monitors?** Touch screen monitors are both input and output devices. They display images just like regular monitors but also enable users to touch their surfaces and make selections directly from the screen. These monitors are widely used in retail stores at checkout counters, in airports for passengers' fast check-ins, and HP has released a personal computer in which the monitor is also the system unit and uses touch screen technology.

**Which monitor is best?** Choosing the right monitor is always a combination of what you like, want, and can afford. A higher resolution, small dot pitch, fast refresh rate, and large monitor size are desirable, but all come with a higher price tag.

## Printers

Using a monitor is a good way to view the information on your computer, but sometimes a soft copy isn't sufficient for your needs. ***Printers*** generate a ***hard copies*** or ***printouts***, which are a permanent record of your work on paper. See Figure 1.14.

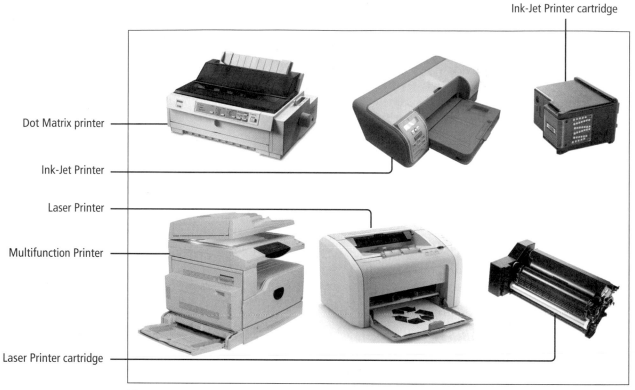

**Figure 1.14**
Output devices—printers

***What types of printers are available?*** There are two categories of printers: impact and nonimpact. ***Impact*** printers have small hammers, similar to a typewriter's, that strike an ink ribbon against paper, leaving behind the image of the character or symbol. The ***dot matrix*** printer is an impact printer. Once very popular because of their low cost, dot matrix printers are still in use today, limited only to certain applications that require continuous forms or multipart forms (an original and several copies), such as invoices or purchase orders.

***How does a nonimpact printer work?*** ***Nonimpact*** printers do not actually touch the paper when printing. There are a variety of nonimpact printers, but the two most commonly used with home computers are the ink-jet printer and the laser printer. The ***ink-jet*** printer uses a special nozzle and ink cartridges to spray ink in small droplets onto the surface of the paper. Ink-jet printers easily print in color, in black, and in grayscale to produce good quality printouts. They are relatively inexpensive to buy and maintain. ***Laser printers*** use the same process as photocopiers to produce their output. They use a special cylinder known as a drum, dry ink or toner, and a laser. Static electricity attracts toner to the surface of the drum, and the laser distributes the toner in the correct pattern. The drum transfers the toner to the paper and heat is used to permanently fuse the toner to the paper. Laser printers are generally more expensive to purchase than ink-jet printers, although they often print more quickly and are more cost effective. Lower-end laser printers print only in black and white; however, more expensive printers can produce color copies.

**How do you assess a printer's capabilities?** When you select a printer, there are some key characteristics to consider.

Print speed is often expressed as **pages per minute (ppm)**. Print speed can vary depending on the manufacturer and model, and is also affected by whether the page is text-only, if it includes graphics, and if the printout is in color or in black and grayscale.

Just as with monitors, resolution is also important to print quality. For printing purposes, resolution is expressed as **dots per inch** or **dpi**. The higher the dpi, the better the print quality. Print qualities of 300 to 600 dpi are typical of most printers, although special photo printers can offer resolutions up to 1,200 dpi. Professional printers can reach even higher values.

Color output and its related cost is another important consideration. Ink-jet printers offer four- or six-color options. Many ink-jet printers use one cartridge for black ink and one or more cartridges for color. When available, printers that offer a separate cartridge for each color are a practical choice because you need to replace only one color at a time as the cartridges run out. Laser printers use separate toner cartridges for each color.

**What are all-in-one printers?** All-in-one printers bundle multiple capabilities in one device. All-in-one devices usually include:

- A printer, either ink-jet (color or black and grayscale) or laser (output)

- A scanner to convert text or images into files that can be stored and further manipulated by the computer (input)

- A facsimile (fax) function to send and receive documents via the telephone (communications)

- A copier function to duplicate documents (output)

- Network capabilities to enable this **multifunction device (MFD)** to work as part of a network environment both wired or wireless (communications)

## Speakers and Multimedia Projectors

**Are there other output devices?** **Speakers** and **multimedia projectors** are also examples of output devices. Many computers include small speakers to enable the user to listen to CDs or DVDs and hear any auditory signals the computer sends. However, if you're serious about multimedia, you will probably want to invest in a better set of speakers for improved performance. Multimedia projectors are used to conduct presentations and training sessions. These projectors enable information to be displayed on a big screen so it can be easily viewed by a large group of attendees.

**Under what category do digital cameras fall?** A digital camera is a device that stores pictures digitally rather than using conventional film. After images are captured, they are stored in the camera's internal memory. Some cameras use removable flash memory cards as storage media. These cards can be read by a computer, which can then edit them and save them as files. So, the camera itself is a form of "hand-held" computer, which, if connected to a computer, serves as an input/output device. The same thing can be said to describe camcorders.

## Storage Devices

**What are storage devices?** *Storage devices* are used to store the data, information, and programs for future use. This storage is often referred to as permanent memory because, unlike data that is in RAM, data saved to a storage device remains there until the user deletes or overwrites it. Data can be stored using internal hardware devices located in the system unit or in removable units that enable portability. See Figure 1.15.

**Figure 1.15**
Storage devices

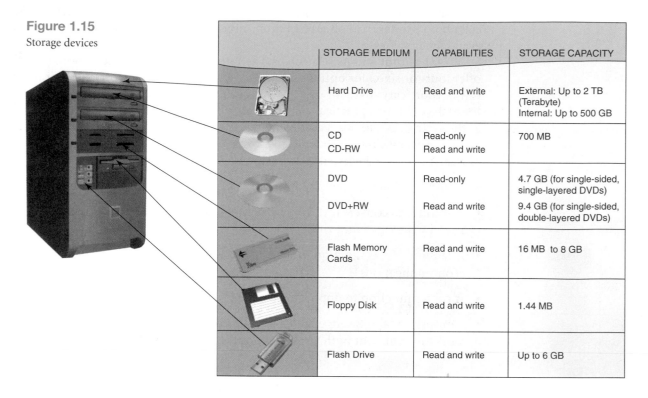

| STORAGE MEDIUM | CAPABILITIES | STORAGE CAPACITY |
|---|---|---|
| Hard Drive | Read and write | External: Up to 2 TB (Terabyte)<br>Internal: Up to 500 GB |
| CD<br>CD-RW | Read-only<br>Read and write | 700 MB |
| DVD | Read-only | 4.7 GB (for single-sided, single-layered DVDs) |
| DVD+RW | Read and write | 9.4 GB (for single-sided, double-layered DVDs) |
| Flash Memory Cards | Read and write | 16 MB  to 8 GB |
| Floppy Disk | Read and write | 1.44 MB |
| Flash Drive | Read and write | Up to 6 GB |

**How is a storage device different than storage media?** A *device* is a piece of hardware such as a hard drive or a DVD drive. Media is the removable part that actually contains the stored data. Media requires a device to *read* and *write* on it. Read is the action of retrieving or opening existing data and write is the action of saving or storing data. Following is a list of devices and their media:

• CD and DVD optical drives read and write on CDs and DVDs, which are the media.

• Card readers read and write on flash memory cards, which are the media.

• Flash drives or thumb drives are media that require a connection to a USB port for read/write operations.

• Tape backup drives read and write onto tape cartridges, which are the media.

• The exception to this is the hard drive, in which the hardware and the media are all contained in a sealed unit that cannot be taken apart.

**How is data stored?** Data is generally stored using one of three forms of storage: magnetic, optical, or flash memory:

• *Magnetic* storage uses tape or film covered in a thin, magnetic coating that enables data to be saved as magnetic impulses. It works in much the same fashion as an audiocassette or videotape works. Hard drives and backup tape drives are both forms of magnetic storage. Before magnetic storage can occur, media has to be formatted. This is the process in which media is divided into *tracks* and *sectors*. Tracks are magnetic concentric circles and sectors are segments within those circles Data is stored magnetically within the spaces created by these tracks sectors. Magnetic media has read/write capability, which means it is possible to use it over and over again, enabling you to delete or revise existing data and save new data.

- *Optical* storage uses flat plastic discs coated in a special reflective material. Data is saved by using a laser beam to burn tiny pits into the storage medium. A less intensive laser is used to read the saved data. The saved data is organized using tracks and sectors, similar to those used in magnetic media. ***Compact discs (CDs)*** and ***digital video discs (DVDs)*** are examples of optical media. Unlike magnetic media, not all optical storage is read/write capable. ***CD-ROMs***—CD media that was burned once and from that moment on can only be read—and ***DVD-ROMs***—DVD media that is burned once and from that moment on can only be read—are considered read-only media (ROM). The information contained on them can be read, but not changed or deleted, and it is not possible to save new data to them. If you purchase new software, music, or a movie, it is most likely on a CD-ROM or DVD-ROM. A record-only disc (CD-R) enables you to record, or ***burn***, information to the disc one time only; information saved this way cannot be deleted or rewritten. A rewritable disc (CD-RW) enables information to be recorded, revised, or deleted, and new data can also be written to the disc, similar to magnetic media. The same possibilities are available in DVDs. However, there are currently two competing formats DVD-R/RW, known as "DVD dash," and DVD+R/RW, known as "DVD plus." The R/RW suffix indicates the DVD can be used to record and can also be rewritten. Although most DVD players can play either format, if you want to record to a DVD, you need to know which format the DVD recorder requires.

**What is LightScribe?** **LightScribe** is a disc-labeling technology that burns text and graphics onto the surface of a specially coated LightScribe CD or DVD. This is an alternative to printing a conventional sticker label and attaching it to a regular CD or DVD but it does require that you purchase LightScribe media. See Figure 1.16.

**Figure 1.16**
LightScribe direct disc labeling

- **Flash memory** uses solid-state technology. It is completely electronic and has no moving mechanical parts. Flash memory is a quick and easy form of rewritable storage and is often used in mobile devices such as PDAs, digital cameras, and MP3 players. Depending on the manufacturer, flash memory cards may be called Memory Stick, CompactFlash, Secure Digital, or MultiMediaCard. Typically, a device can use only one style of memory card; however, a computer equipped with the appropriate card reader can read any of them. Small, removable storage devices known as flash drives or thumb drives also use flash technology, require a USB port to connect to the system unit, and are very popular to transport data.

**What are the main types of storage devices?** Depending on the age and type of computer you have, you might find some or all of the following internal storage options:

- **Hard disk drive**—A hard disk drive is the computer's main internal storage device. Also referred to as a hard drive, its storage space is usually measured in gigabytes (GB), with newer computers ranging in size from 80 GB to 750 GB, although it is possible to find some specialized, high-end computers with storage space measuring up to 2 terabytes (TB). As with everything else in computing, these numbers tend to increase with each new model. Hard drives are traditionally permanent storage devices fixed inside the system unit.

- **Floppy disk drive**—This is a device that reads/writes floppy diskettes that have a maximum storage capacity of 1,450 MB. Because of this limited storage capacity compared to other media, you will seldom see floppy disks used by computer users today.

- **CD and/or DVD drives**—Your computer may have one or two of these optical drives in the system unit. It's important to know whether these drives are simple CD-ROM drives, which can only read CDs, or if it is a **CD-RW** drive, also known as a CD burner. A **CD burner** gives you the ability to save, or burn, files to a CD-R (compact disk recordable). You might also have a separate drive that can read and/or write DVDs.

Although CDs and DVDs look alike, DVDs are capable of holding much more information than CDs. A CD can hold up to 700 MB of data, but a DVD can store almost 10 GB! Because of their differences, a CD drive is unable to read DVDs, although a DVD drive can read CDs.

***Is it possible to add a storage device to a system?*** If you are running out of hard disk space or your system doesn't have a particular storage device, it may be possible to add a storage device, provided your system has enough room for it. You would need an available drive bay, which is the physical location within the system unit, or you might consider removing an existing device and replacing it with another. For instance, if you only have a CD-ROM drive, you could remove that and replace it with a CD-RW/DVD drive, thereby giving you the ability to read and burn CDs and play DVDs too. It is also possible to purchase many of these units as external storage devices. An external storage device is a peripheral that attaches to the computer via a port and performs the same tasks as its corresponding internal device. One of the most popular of these today is the external hard drive, which can greatly increase a computer's storage capacity and make your data fully portable.

***Are there other types of storage devices?*** Other storage devices you might be familiar with include flash drives, a currently popular form of data storage, and older but still reliable backup tape drives.

***Flash drives*** are removable storage devices that use flash memory and connect to the computer by a USB port. Flash drives are also known as thumb drives, universal serial bus (USB) drives, and jump drives. The flash drive is typically a device small enough to fit on a keychain or in a pocket and, because of its solid-state circuitry and lack of moving parts, it is extremely durable. Available in several storage sizes ranging from 16 MB to 64 GB, a flash drive is a quick and easy way to save and transport files. As an example, a 64-MB flash drive, which is relatively small, holds the equivalent of almost 45 floppy disks! To use one of these devices, you simply plug it into a computer's USB port. The computer recognizes the new device and enables the user to save or retrieve files from the flash drive.

***Backup tape drives*** are storage devices that resemble audiocassette tape recorders and save data to magnetic tape media. Although they are rarely used for home computers anymore, many businesses and organizations still rely on tape backup systems to safeguard their data on a daily basis. See Figure 1.17.

The capacity of the components found in your system unit is measured in terms of storage size or speed. Computer systems continue to increase in storage capacity and

**Figure 1.17**
Tape backup drive and media

computing speed, while decreasing in size. Generally, higher measurements indicate a system that is quicker and more powerful than a system with lower measurements. However, it is important to balance size and speed with financial considerations too. Although it is tempting to consider buying a computer with the most power possible, a lesser computer may be more reasonably priced and still be sufficient for the typical user's needs. Recall that CPU speed is measured in megahertz (MHz) or gigahertz (GHz). The amount of RAM in a computer is generally measured in megabytes (MB), while storage space is usually measured in megabytes or gigabytes (GB), depending on the device.

## Ports

**What are ports?** A **port** acts as an interface or connector between a system's peripheral devices and the computer, enabling data to be exchanged easily. Ports (see Figure 1.18) have different shapes and sizes. The same ports are typically found on a desktop too, although they might be arranged in a different order. Various input and output devices use different data exchange methods, requiring different types of ports and connectors (or plugs). If your computer does not have a particular port, you can buy an expansion card that connects to the motherboard and provides the needed connection.

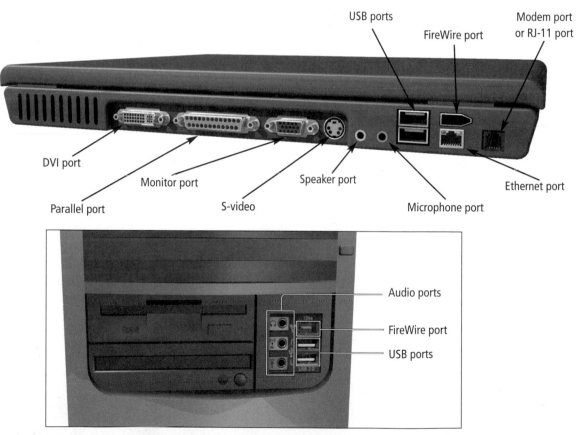

**Figure 1.18**
Ports

**How do you determine which port a peripheral device needs?** Manufacturers have attempted to make the process of connecting peripheral devices less complicated on newer computers. Rather than trying to match the size and shape of a connector to its port, many manufacturers now use a color-coding system that coordinates the colors of the connectors with their corresponding ports. Additionally, many newer desktop computers include ports, such as USB and audio ports, on the front panel of the system unit to provide easier access to them. Locating these ports on the front or back panels makes it a simple process to connect and disconnect devices that are used only occasionally, such as digital cameras, external hard drives, or MP3 players. Peripherals that are rarely disconnected, such as a keyboard or printer, are generally plugged into the ports on the back of the computer.

**What are the different ports used for?** Serial and parallel ports are two of the oldest types of ports found on a computer. **Serial ports** are ports that can send data only one bit at a time, so the data exchange rate is slow compared to newer technology. The maximum rate at which a standard serial port can transfer data is 115 **kilobits** or one thousand bits per second (Kbps). The mouse and modem are examples of devices that might use a serial port. A **parallel port** is a port that sends data in groups of bits, at transfer rates of up to 500 Kbps, so it is a considerably faster method of transferring data than the serial port. Older printers were often connected to a computer through a parallel port.

**Are there faster ports?** Over the years, newer ports have come into existence. One of these is the **universal serial bus (USB) port**. This type of port is able to interface with several different peripheral devices, which reduces the need for individual, dedicated ports. USB ports are also able to transfer data at extremely high rates of speed. Original USB ports, known as USB 1.1, are capable of speeds of 12 **megabits** or one million bits per second (Mbps). The newest version, USB 2.0, can attain a rate of 480 Mbps, 40 times faster than USB 1.1 technology and over 400 times faster than a serial port! USB 2.0 ports are backwards compatible, which means that older USB devices work with them; however, data will transfer only at the slower USB 1.1 speed. The higher data transfer capabilities of USB ports, coupled with their capability to work with multiple devices, have made the older serial and parallel ports obsolete. Because of the USB port's speedy data transfer rate and its capability to be used with numerous devices, new computers often include six or more USB ports. Devices using USB ports include keyboards, mice, printers, scanners, digital cameras, MP3 players, and PDAs. In general, it's a good idea to get a computer with as many USB ports as possible. See the table in Figure 1.19.

## Ports and Their Uses

| Port Name | Data Transfer Speed | Typical Use |
|---|---|---|
| Serial | 115 Kbps | Mice / External modems |
| Parallel | 500 Kbps | Printers / External Zip drives |
| USB 1.1 | 12 Mbps | Mice / Keyboards / Printers / Scanners / Game controllers |
| USB 2.0 | 400 Mbps | Same as USB 1.1 but at faster transfer rates. Also, camcorders, digital cameras, and MP3 players. It maintains compatibility with USB 1.1. |
| FireWire / FireWire 800 | 400 Mbps / 800 Mbps | Digital video camcorders / Digital cameras |
| Ethernet / Gigabit Ethernet | Up to 100 Mbps / Up to 1,000 Mbps | Network connections / Cable modems |

**Figure 1.19**
Port speeds and uses

The **FireWire port**, developed by Apple and also known as IEEE 1394, is another means of transferring data quickly. The FireWire 400 has a data transfer rate of 400 Mbps, while the newer FireWire 800 transfers data at a blazing 800 Mbps! This port is typically used to connect devices that need to transfer huge amounts of data to a computer quickly, such as digital cameras or digital video recorders, or external hard drives. FireWire ports are standard on many Apple products, but are usually found only on higher-end Windows PCs and peripheral devices. Some peripheral devices offer users a choice of connecting using a USB port or a FireWire port.

***What kind of port is used to connect to another computer? Connectivity ports***, such as Ethernet and modem ports, are used to connect a computer to a local network or to the Internet. An ***Ethernet port***, also known as an RJ-45 jack, resembles a standard phone jack, but is slightly larger. The Ethernet port is used for network access and can also be used to connect a cable modem or router for Internet access. A ***modem port*** is the same size and shape as a phone jack and is used to connect the modem to a phone system, enabling ***digital subscriber line (DSL)*** or dial-up Internet access. DSL is a type of communications line in which signals travel through copper wires between a telephone switching station and a home or business. The maximum data transfer rate for a modem is 56 Kbps, whereas the most common Ethernet standard, Fast Ethernet, transfers data at the rate of 100 Mbps. However, Gigabit Ethernet, with a potential transfer rate of 1,000 Mbps, is becoming an option on higher-end systems and is standard on many Mac systems.

Even faster Ethernet technologies, such as 10 Gigabit Ethernet or 10 GbE exist, but they are currently used for network backbones and enterprise network infrastructures rather than home users.

***Are there special purpose ports?*** Despite the prevalence of USB ports, which can be used for a variety of peripherals, there are still some devices that require special ports. These ports include Musical Instrument Digital Interface (MIDI), IrDA, Bluetooth, video, and audio ports.

***MIDI ports*** are used to connect electronic musical devices, such as keyboards and synthesizers, to a computer, enabling musicians to create digital music files.

The ***IrDA port*** is used to enable devices such as PDAs, keyboards, mice, and printers to transmit data wirelessly to another device by using infrared light waves. In order to transmit information, each of the devices must have an IrDA port, and a clear line of sight, with no other objects blocking the transmission.

***Bluetooth*** is another type of wireless technology that relies on radio wave transmission and doesn't require a clear line of sight. Bluetooth-enabled devices such as PDAs or other mobile devices can communicate only with each other over short distances, typically less than 30 feet.

Video ports include standard monitor ports, DVI ports, and S-video ports. A ***monitor port*** is used to connect the monitor to the graphics processing unit, which is usually located on the motherboard or on a video card. However, to get the best results from a flat-panel (LCD) monitor, the ***Digital Video Interface (DVI) port*** should be used instead. The DVI port transmits a pure digital signal, eliminating the need for digital-to-analog conversion and resulting in a higher quality transmission and a clearer picture on the monitor. The ***S-video port*** is typically used to connect other video sources, such as a television, projector, or digital recorder, to the computer.

Similar to video ports, ***audio ports*** connect audio devices, such as speakers, headphones, and microphones, to the computer's sound card. These jacks will be familiar to anyone who is used to using standard stereo components.

## Evaluating Your System

Each computer might have a different configuration. The way a computer system is set up or the combination of components that make up the system is called its ***configuration***. This is important when buying a computer, expanding an existing system, or when connecting computers together in a network environment.

Now that you have learned most of the hardware components of a typical personal computer, you are ready to explore the computer's configuration, specifications, and features. If you didn't buy your computer brand new, you might not know all the details about your computer. If you did buy a new computer, the easiest way is to check your paperwork; all the basic information should be there. However, if your computer isn't new or you didn't keep the paperwork, there are some ways to determine exactly what is in your system. Also if you start a new job or a new position and are given a computer system, you can do a number of things again to determine exactly what is in your system.

***What kind of computer do you have?*** This is one of the easiest questions to answer. Like almost every other appliance you've used, you can probably find the manufacturer's name and a brand name or model number on the case of the computer. If not, check the back of the unit; there should be a metal tag that includes the manufacturer's name, model number, and serial number. This information might be necessary if you have to have service performed under warranty. Use the following steps to see your system properties, which will answer some questions.

If you are a Windows XP user and you have the My Computer icon on the desktop:

**1** Right-click My Computer.

**2** Select Properties and read the contents of the General tab.

If you do not have the My Computer icon on the desktop, follow these steps:

**1** Click the **Start** menu, select **Settings**, and then click **Control Panel**.

**2** From the next window, click **Performance** and **Maintenance**.

**3** Then click **System** and read the contents of the **General** tab.

Windows Vista users can follow these steps:

**1** Right-click the **My Computer** icon on the desktop and select **Properties**.

**2** If the icon is not on the desktop, open the **Start** menu and then right-click the **Computer** button and select **Properties**. See Figure 1.20.

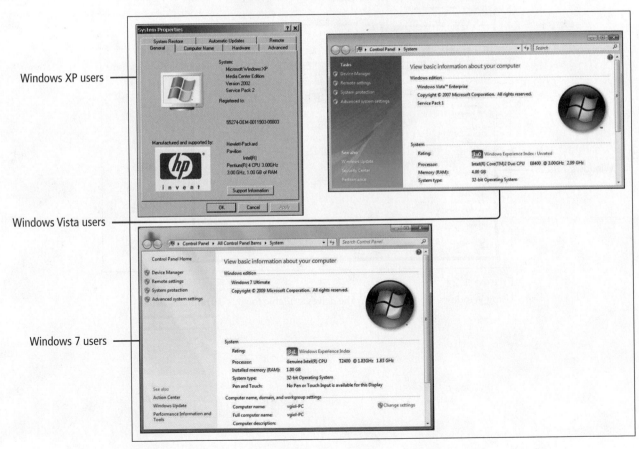

**Figure 1.20**

Evaluating your system—General Properties

***What operating system does the computer use?*** If you watch carefully as a computer boots up, you can often determine the operating system. You will usually see a ***splash screen*** showing the version of Windows that runs—for example, Windows ME, Windows XP, Windows Vista, or Windows 7, which is the working name for a new version of Windows to be released sometime in 2010.

***How much memory is in the computer? What is the type and speed of the CPU?*** Figure 1.21 displays (for several versions of Windows) a window with information on the computer's operating system, the type and speed of the CPU, and the storage capacity of RAM.

***How do you determine what drives are on the system and how much storage space is available?*** It's important to know how much information you can store on your computer, what disk drives are available, and how much room you have left on each drive. Is there enough storage space or are the storage devices getting full? Use My Computer (or Computer) to find the answers. If the desktop does not have a My Computer (or Computer) icon, you can access it through the Start menu.

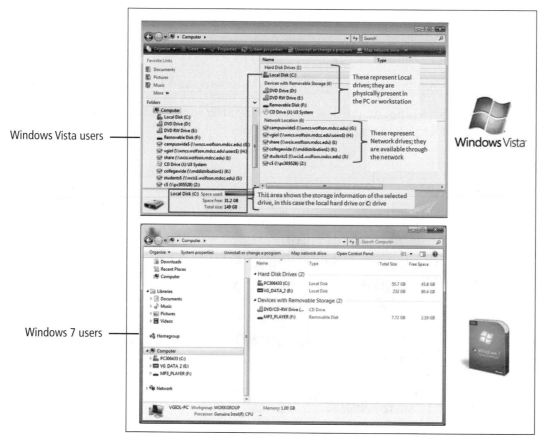

Windows Vista users

Windows 7 users

**Figure 1.21**

Using Windows Explorer to view the drives available to your computer

Figure 1.22 shows the Computer (or Windows Explorer) window in which the user can see all available local drives (devices within the system unit or peripherals to that unit) and network drives (devices available through a network). Also, right-click on any drive symbol, and select Properties from the shortcut menu. A new dialog box displays the drive's information similar to the one shown in Figure 1.22. The pie chart displayed on the General tab is a good visual tool that shows the size of your storage device and how much space is free.

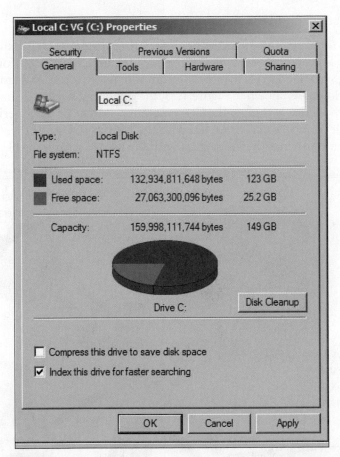

**Figure 1.22**

The properties of one of the storage drives (the hard drive)

## Objective 4 | Identify Types of Software and Their Uses

So far we have described computer hardware, the physical components of the system. However, without software, the computer would just be a collection of useless electronic and mechanical parts. Software provides the instructions or commands that tell the computer what to do. To perform various tasks, the computer requires a set of instructions called ***programs***. These programs enable individuals to use the computer without the need for special programming skills. There are two categories of computer software—***system software*** and ***application software***. Both types of software are required to work effectively with your computer.

## System Software

System software provides the instructions that the computer needs to run. It contains the directions needed to start up the computer (known as the **boot process**), checks to ensure everything is in good working order, and enables you to interface or interact with the computer and its peripheral devices so that you can use them. System software consists of two main programs: the **operating system** and **utility programs**.

## Operating Systems

**What is the operating system?** The **operating system (OS)** is a special computer program that is present on every desktop computer, notebook, PDAs, or mainframes. The operating system controls the way the computer works from the time it is turned on until it is shut down. As shown in Figure 1.23, the operating system manages the various hardware components, including the CPU, memory, storage devices, peripheral devices, and network devices. It also coordinates with the various software applications presently running and provides the interaction with the user (user interface).

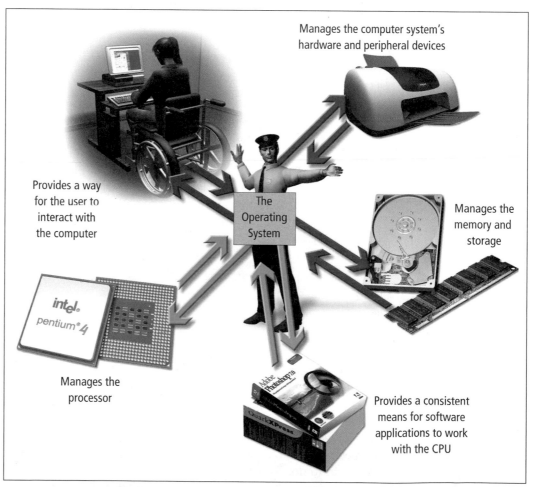

Manages the computer system's hardware and peripheral devices

Provides a way for the user to interact with the computer

The Operating System

Manages the memory and storage

Manages the processor

Provides a consistent means for software applications to work with the CPU

**Figure 1.23**
The operating system

**Is it possible to communicate with the operating system?** Although the operating system communicates with the computer and its peripherals, it also includes a **user interface** that you can use to interact and communicate with the computer. Early operating systems used a text-based or keyboard-driven interface. The early **Disk Operating System (DOS)** required knowledge of special commands that had to be typed accurately to achieve the desired results. This type of system was not very "**user friendly.**" Most current operating systems use a point-and-click format known as a ***graphical user interface (GUI)***. GUIs are more user friendly and intuitive than DOS systems. Rather than typing specific commands, you can use a mouse to select from on screen objects such as ***icons*** (a graphical depiction of an object such as a file or program), ***menus*** (lists of available commands), or ***dialog boxes*** (windows used to make choices or give the system specific instructions as to the action you want to take or task to perform). GUI operating systems display information on the monitor in the form of rectangular boxes called ***windows***. Although you interact with system software every time you use the computer, in some ways you don't notice it.

***Do all computers need an operating system?*** Yes, the operating system is a critical part of a computer system. Without an OS to provide specific instructions, the computer would be unable to fulfill its four main functions. However, different computers require different types of operating systems. There are several popular operating systems available for home computers. They include Microsoft Windows, Mac OS, and Linux.

***Microsoft Windows*** has the largest market share of the three main operating systems and is found on most of today's desktop and notebook computers. There have been many versions of Microsoft Windows, including Windows 3.0, Windows 95, Windows 98, Windows Me, Windows Vista, and Windows 7 to be released in 2010. Although a previous version of Windows might be found on an older computer, Windows Vista is the current version installed on most computers. A sample Windows Vista desktop is displayed in Figure 1.24.

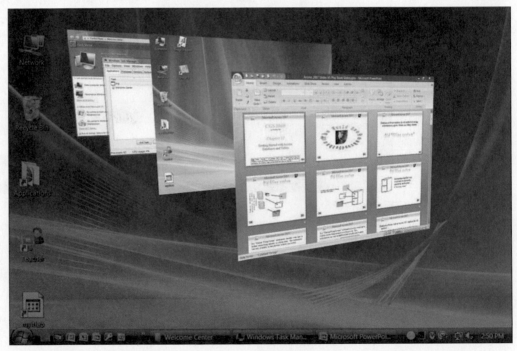

**Figure 1.24**
A sample of the Windows VISTA desktop

***Why are there so many versions of Windows?*** Software developers are always updating and refining their software to adapt to new technology, respond to vulnerabilities, and improve their product. Because Microsoft also manufactures application software, some of its products have similar names and users can become confused. It's important to note that even though your computer might use Microsoft Windows for its operating system, it might not have Microsoft Office (an application software suite) installed.

**Mac OS** is an operating system designed specifically for Apple's Macintosh computers. Figure 1.25 shows the Mac OS desktop that is similar to Windows because it also uses a GUI. In fact, Apple was the first company to introduce a commercially successful GUI operating system for the consumer market. But, because of the popularity of the Windows-based PCs, Mac OS has a much smaller market share. If you are looking to purchase a PC or a peripheral for a PC, you have a variety of choices among different manufacturers. Only Apple manufactures Apple products and peripherals for its computers and they tend to be a bit pricier.

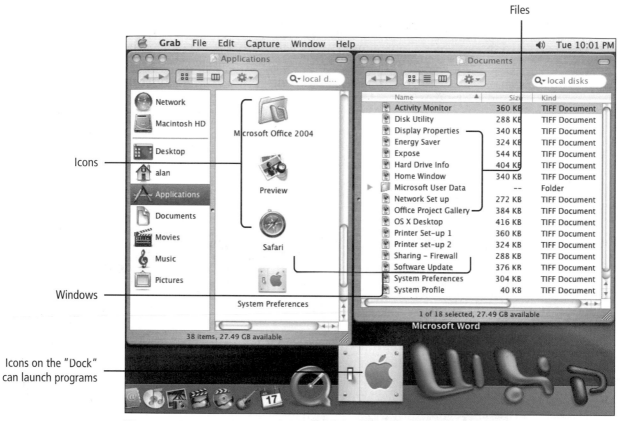

**Figure 1.25**
Mac OS desktop

**Can Windows run on an Apple computer?** Until recently, the Mac OS could not run on a PC, and the Windows OS could not run on a Mac. Software is available to start a Mac that will run Windows applications. Microsoft's Virtual PC for Mac features specifications such as:

- Access PC-only software, files, networks, and devices with your Mac

- Zero-configuration printing; better graphics handling; expanded preferences

- Cut and paste between platforms; share folders and other media between platforms

- Easily shut down virtual PC and relaunch right where it left off

- Use PC and Mac peripherals

**Linux** is an alternative operating system. Based on the UNIX operating system developed for mainframe computers, it also has a dedicated group of users. Linux is an **open-source** operating system, which means it is not owned by a single company and some versions are available at no cost.

**How is open-source software different from other types of software?** Open-source software makes its source code, essentially the program instructions, available to anyone who would like to see it. Programmers are encouraged to work with and change the code as they see fit, in the hope that having many "eyes" looking at the code will streamline and improve it. Proprietary software, such as Microsoft Windows, keeps this code secret and inaccessible to programmers who are not authorized by the software development company.

**Why is Linux used?** Linux is rarely used by novice computer users, although it is popular among developers and other technologically advanced individuals who prefer to use an alternative operating system. Some people appreciate the opportunity to work in this more "open" programming environment. However, one of the disadvantages of Linux is that, because no single company is responsible for it, technical support is not easily found. Users might find help from various resources such as user groups and Internet communities. Alternatively, some software companies have chosen to develop and sell a version of Linux that includes a warranty and technical support as a way of alleviating user concerns. Figure 1.26 shows an example of one version of the Linux operating system.

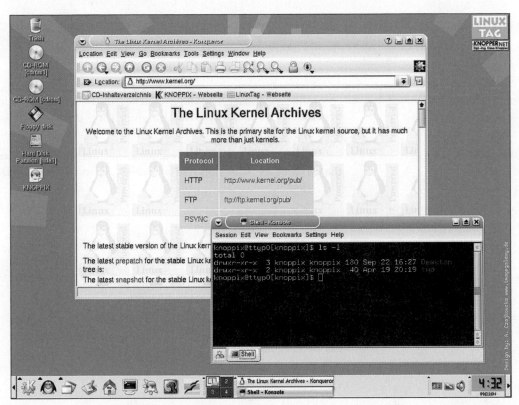

**Figure 1.26**

Example of one of the versions of the Linux operating system

## Utility Programs

**What are utility programs?** Operating system software is the most critical software on the computer, because nothing can run without it. However, utility programs are another important component of system software. These small applications handle many important tasks involved with the management and maintenance of your system. Utility programs can be used to help back up important files, remove unwanted files or programs from your system, and schedule various tasks to keep your system running smoothly. Some of these utilities are included with the operating system, whereas others are stand-alone versions that you can purchase or download for free. The table in Figure 1.27 displays a variety of utility programs that ship with the Windows operating system and compares them with similar stand-alone products, describing the function of each utility.

## Windows Utility Programs

| Program | Function |
|---|---|
| Windows Explorer | Create folders, manage files, and compress/extract files. Read disk drive's properties including view storage capacity and free disk space, check drive for errors, defragment utility, and back up/restore utility |
| Windows Task Manager (Ctrl + Alt+ Delete) | Lets the user view the list of active applications, and switch or end any of them. Also, check the performance of the computer including CPU usage, RAM availability, and network utilization |
| Control Panel | |
| • System and Security | Review your computer's status<br>Back up your computer<br>Find and fix problems |
| • Network and Internet | View network status and tasks<br>Choose home group and sharing options |
| • Hardware and sound | View devices and printers<br>Add a device<br>Connect to a projector<br>Adjust commonly used mobility settings |
| • Programs | Install/uninstall programs<br>Add desktop gadgets |
| • User Accounts and Family Safety | Add or remove user accounts<br>Set up parental controls for any user |
| • Appearance and Personalization | Change the theme<br>Change desktop background<br>Adjust screen resolution |
| • Clock, Language, and Region | Change keyboards or other input methods<br>Change display language<br>Let Windows suggest settings |
| • Ease of Access | Optimize visual display |
| Administrative Tools | Schedule tasks |
| Security | |
| • Security Configuration Manager | Set account policies, local policies, network list manager policies, software restriction policies, and application control policies |
| • Firewall and Advanced Security | Set firewall and advanced security on local computer |

**Figure 1.27**
Windows utility programs

## Application Software

Application software or applications are comprised of programs that enable you to accomplish tasks and use the computer in a productive manner. Applications are programs created to perform a specific task, solve a specific problem, or address a specific need.

***How do system software and application software work together?*** System software is like the breathing you need to do to live; however, you don't usually think much about it unless something goes wrong. Application software might be compared to a musical instrument like a flute. When a musician combines each of these breaths and her flute, the result may be a beautiful melody (if she has practiced, of course!). Computer software works together similarly; the system software acts as the "breath," while the application software provides the "instrument," enabling you to create something.

There are many different kinds of application software, although they often fall into one of several general categories, each of which has a different purpose. These categories include financial and business-related software, graphics and multimedia software, educational and reference software, entertainment software, and communication software. You might be most familiar with productivity software, which includes the following applications.

- ***Word processing software*** is used to create, edit, format, print, and save documents and other text-based files. Word processing software enables you to create or edit letters, reports, memos, and many other types of written documents that you can print or attach to an e-mail message. Revisions to existing documents can be made quickly and easily, without having to re-create the entire document. Documents created with this type of software can also include pictures, charts, ***hyperlinks,*** and other graphic elements. A hyperlink is a connection to another area of a document or a connection to an Internet URL. Microsoft Word, Lotus Word Pro, and Corel WordPerfect are all examples of word processing programs. A document created using Microsoft Word 2007 is shown in Figure 1.28. Notice that the document

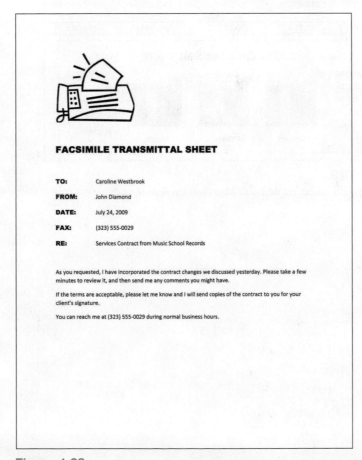

**Figure 1.28**

Sample document created with Microsoft Word 2007

contains a graphic element as well as text. Using word processing software replaces the use of conventional typewriters, on which editing was virtually impossible once the document was finished.

- *Spreadsheet software* enables the user to enter data in rows and columns format and:
  - Perform calculations on numeric data with user-defined formulas.
  - Convert part of the data into one or more charts, such as a column chart, a pie chart, or a line chart.
  - Work with lists to organize data and sort it in alphabetic or numeric order.
  - Create different scenarios and perform "what-if" analyses, the basis for sound decision making.

A key advantage of spreadsheet software is its capability to recalculate spreadsheets without user intervention. When data used in a calculation or a formula is changed, the spreadsheet software automatically updates the worksheet with the correct result. Microsoft Excel, Lotus 1-2-3, and Corel Quattro Pro are examples of spreadsheet programs. Figure 1.29 shows a worksheet and a chart created with Microsoft Excel 2007. The use of spreadsheet software replaces the old manual method of entering data in ledgers or journals and using a desktop calculator to do the math computations.

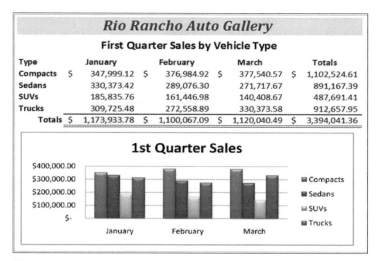

**Figure 1.29**

Example spreadsheet created with Microsoft Excel 2007

A database is a collection of data or unorganized facts. **Database software** is used to store, organize, update, and retrieve large amounts of data. **Relational database software (RDBMS)** stores information in tables, which enable users quick access to the data by connecting tables with common fields. **Data mining** is a function in some databases that looks for hidden patterns in the data to anticipate future patterns. This is commonly used in scientific applications and as a marketing tool to predict future consumer trends. Typically, database software can be used to manage various types of information, such as that found in large mailing lists, inventories, students' records, order histories, and invoicing. Databases help you to enter, store, sort, filter, retrieve, and summarize the information they contain and then generate meaningful reports. Common database programs include Microsoft Access, Lotus Approach, and Corel Paradox. Figure 1.30 shows a database object created in Microsoft Access 2007. Database software replaces an old manual filing system where information is stored in filing cabinets in a single location.

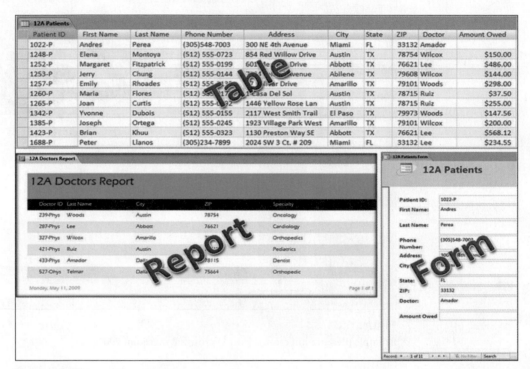

**Figure 1.30**

Examples of database software objects

*Presentation software* has become a standard in replacing flip charts, slide projectors, or overhead transparencies used by speakers and lecturers. This software is used to create electronic slides and project slide shows to visually present materials and ideas to large groups in a conference room or on the Web. Presentation software is also used to create audience handouts, speaker notes, and other materials that can be used during an oral presentation or for distribution to a group of participants. Microsoft PowerPoint, Lotus Freelance Graphics, and Corel Presentations are examples of presentation software programs. Figure 1.31 shows a presentation created with Microsoft PowerPoint 2007.

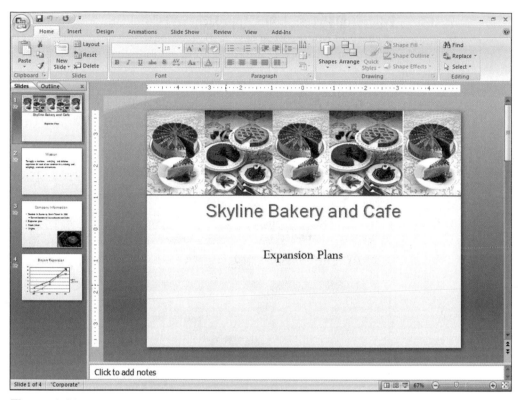

**Figure 1.31**

Example presentation created with Microsoft PowerPoint 2007

*Communication and organizational software*—Communication software can cover a broad range of tasks including videoconferencing and telephony. However, applications in the productivity category are most often used to send and receive e-mail. These applications typically include an address book (contacts list), a scheduler, a calendar, and task functions, which help users organize their personal and professional responsibilities. Microsoft Outlook, Lotus Notes, and Corel WordPerfect Mail are examples of communication and organizational software. Figure 1.32 shows an example of a calendar in Microsoft Outlook 2007.

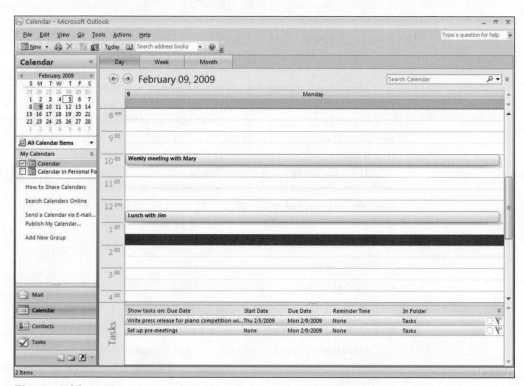

**Figure 1.32**
Example of a calendar in Microsoft Outlook 2007

*What is a software suite?* Although it is possible to buy any of the previous applications separately, most software manufacturers, including Microsoft, Corel, and Lotus, also group applications together into a package called a *suite*. There is an alternative suite called OpenOffice and it's free. It is designed as an open source software in such a way that users can report bugs, request new features, or change and improve the software.

Another advantage of using a suite is that because products from the same company have many common elements, such as basic window design and layout, toolbars containing similar tools, dictionaries, and media galleries, many users find this familiarity makes it easier to switch between the programs in a suite. Examples of suites include Microsoft Office, Corel WordPerfect Office, and Lotus SmartSuite.

*What are some other common software applications?* As mentioned earlier, there are many different types of application software besides productivity software, each one with a specific function. Some of these are the following:

- You might use Microsoft Publisher or QuarkXPress to create newsletters or brochures.

- Bookkeepers rely on special accounting packages such as Peachtree Accounting or QuickBooks to balance the books and handle other accounting functions.

- Graphic designers turn to packages such as Adobe Photoshop or Adobe Illustrator to develop creative artwork.

- You might use Microsoft Expression Web or Macromedia Dreamweaver to create your own Web site.

- **IM** (instant messaging) software enables users to communicate in real time like a phone conversation but using text only. The software can alert you if a member of your group is online at that moment.

- Web browsers are software used to locate and display Web pages and navigate through them. They also enable users to store their frequently used sites for quick access.

    If you have a specific need, chances are there is software that will address those needs. Today the best way to find software is to do a Web search using a search engine.

## Objective 5 | Describe Networks and Define Network Terms

*What are the components of a network?* Connecting one computer to another creates a network. Recall that computers and the various peripherals that are connected to them are called hardware. Networks consist of two or more connected computers plus the various peripheral devices that are attached to them. Each object connected to a network, whether it is a computer or a peripheral device, is known as a *node*.

*Why are computers connected to networks?* Some of the benefits of computer networks include the capability to share data, software, and resources such as printers, scanners, Internet access, video conferencing, and VoIP. Computers can be connected to a network using several media, the conductors of the network signals:

- Existing telephone wires
- Power lines
- Coaxial cables
- Unshielded twisted pair (UTP) cables
- Fiber optic

    *Wireless networks* use radio waves instead of wires or cables to connect. Most networks use a combination of media and wireless communications (see Figure 1.33).

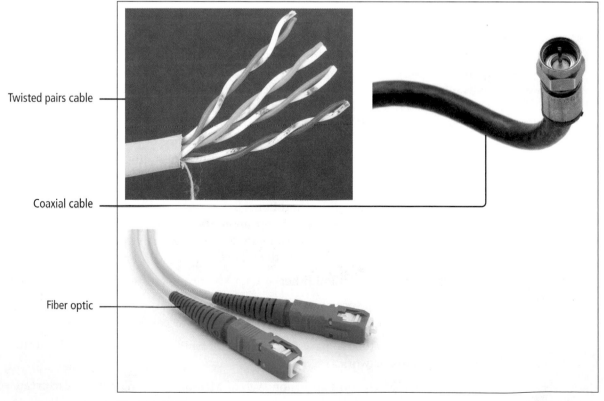

Twisted pairs cable

Coaxial cable

Fiber optic

**Figure 1.33**
Network media, the conductor of network signals

Today, using computer networks, institutions are able to ***video conference***, that is, communicate audio and/or video between two or more individuals in different locations, optimizing communications, information sharing, and decision making.

***Voice over Internet Protocol*** (***VoIP***) enables voice, facsimile, and voice-messaging communications over networks and the Internet.

***Can networks be different sizes?*** A network that connects computers reasonably close together, say within a few city blocks in adjacent buildings, is called a ***local area network (LAN).*** See Figure 1.34.

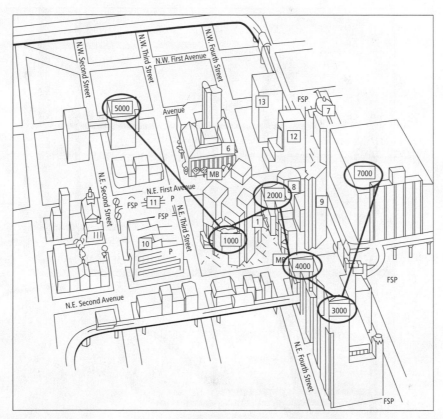

**Figure 1.34**

Example of a local area network, a college campus network that covers several buildings within a few city blocks

If the network grows to cover a larger geographic area or begins to include other networks, it becomes a **wide area network (WAN)**. An example is a state college campus that connects its computers with a LAN while all of its campuses connected together form a WAN. Because the different campuses are connected through WANs, students, faculty, staff, and administrators can easily and seamlessly use the resources of the entire network. Both LANs and WANs can be wired, wireless, or a combination of both. See Figure 1.35. The Internet is actually the largest WAN because it connects computer networks all around the world.

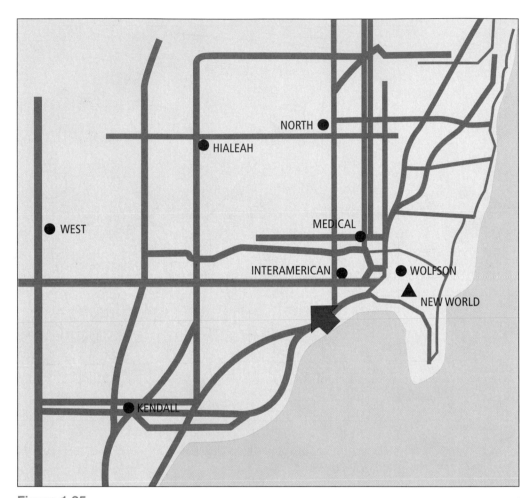

**Figure 1.35**
Example of a wide area network, which is a college network that links campus LANs in several cities within a county

**Are networks public or private?** They can be either. If you want to post information and make it available to any user, you post it on a website with no restrictions. If you want to protect certain information, you create an **intranet** in which access is restricted to authorized users only. Within an intranet, network administrators can limit the specific rights and privileges of different users.

**How are networks configured?** Networks can be configured in several ways. There are two main categories: peer-to-peer and client/server. **Peer-to-peer** or **P2P networks** are most commonly found in homes and small businesses. In a peer-to-peer network, each node can communicate with every other node without a dedicated server or hierarchy among computers. Peer-to-peer networks are relatively easy to set up, but tend to be rather small. This makes them ideal for home use, although not as desirable in the workplace. If a network grows to more than, say, ten to fifteen nodes, it is generally best to use the **client/server network**. In a client/server network, the server manages and controls all network resources. A node can be a computer, printer, scanner, modem, an external hard disk, or any other peripheral device connected to a computer. Therefore, it isn't difficult to find more than ten nodes in an office or business setting.

**How is a client/server network different from a P2P network?** Client/server networks typically have two different types of computers. The **client** is the computer used at your desk or workstation to write letters, send e-mail, produce invoices, or perform any of the many tasks that can be accomplished with a computer. The client computer is the one most people directly interact with. In contrast, the server computer is typically kept in a secure location and is used by network technicians and administrators to manage network resources. If a server is assigned to handle only specific tasks, it is known as a **dedicated server.** For instance, a Web server is used to store and deliver Web pages, a file server is used to store and archive files, and a print server manages the printing resources for the network. Each of these is a dedicated server.

As a client/server network grows in number of nodes and geographical distance covered, servers are assisted by distance-spanning devices such as switches and routers to optimize data traffic.

**Network topology** describes the different types of network architecture used for client/server networks (see Figure 1.36). Just as there are different sizes and styles of buildings that are designed for different purposes, networks are designed to be physically configured and connected in different ways.

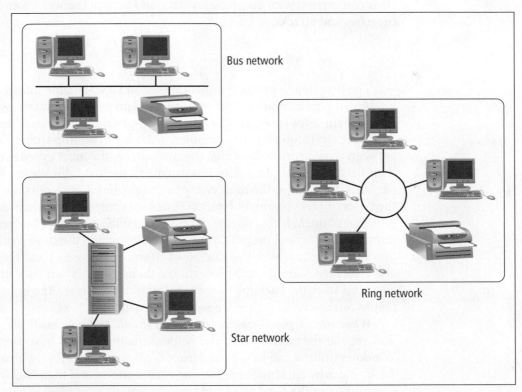

**Figure 1.36**
Common network topologies

**Which topologies are used most often?** The three most common layouts are explained in the following list:

- **Bus topology** connects each node to a single, central high-speed line known as a bus. No server is used, and although it is possible for each node to communicate with all the others, they can only do so one at a time. If one computer or device is sending over the network, all the others must wait until the transmission is complete before they can begin. Because this is an inexpensive and easy way to connect, this topology is often found in peer-to-peer networks.

- *Ring topology*, sometimes known as ***token-ring topology***, connects each node to the next, forming a loop or a circle. The data that's sent is passed from node to node, traveling around the circle in only one direction. A token travels around the ring until one of the nodes is ready to send a transmission. The node then holds the token until the transmission is finished, preventing any of the other devices from sending until the token is released to make its way around the circle again. This type of topology gives each device an equal chance of being able to send data and prevents one node from doing all the communicating. This topology is being retired in favor of star topology.

- *Star topology* is the most frequent networking style used for businesses and homes. It offers a high degree of flexibility. Each node is connected to a special device known as a switch, which is centrally located. Each node must go through the switch to communicate with the others. If something happens to one node, the others are still able to communicate.

## Objective 6 | Identify Safe Computing Practices

Being computer fluent implies you are a responsible computer user. This means more than just understanding the key components of a computer or the differences between hardware and software. Responsible computer users also know how to properly maintain their computers, back up necessary data, and protect themselves and others from security breaches and attacks.

### Computer Maintenance

The first step to protect your computer and the valuable information it contains is to establish a regular maintenance routine. Backup utility programs, which may be part of your system software or purchased separately, enable you to back up your files. You can back up everything on your computer, just one or two important files, or anything in between. People often think that the computer is the most expensive item to replace if their hard drive fails. In reality, it is usually all the lost information that was contained on the hard drive that is the most costly to replace, if it is even possible to do so. Think about the types of files you might have on your own computer like financial records, your personal phone/address directory, resumes, scanned images of important documents, homework or school projects, your CD collection and purchased music files, and family photos and videos. Now imagine how you would re-create these files if they were irretrievably damaged. Would you be able to find them again? If you back up files on a regular basis and store the backups in a secure location, you lessen the impact that a mechanical failure or security breach will have on your data.

***What other types of maintenance tasks should be performed?*** In addition to backing up files, regular file maintenance also helps to maintain order in your system. Several useful Windows utilities can be accessed from the System Tools folder. You can access the System Tools folder by clicking Start, clicking All Programs, and then clicking Accessories. Disk Cleanup scans the hard drive and removes unnecessary files such as those found in the Recycle Bin, in addition to temporary Internet files and other temporary files created by various programs. It is possible to adjust the settings and select which files to delete and which files to retain.

Similarly, the Disk Defragmenter scans the hard drive. However, rather than removing files, it attempts to reallocate files so they use the available hard drive space more efficiently. Recall that data is stored on hard drives in sectors and tracks. As file sizes change, they can outgrow their original location. When that happens, the remaining portion of the file may be stored elsewhere. If a file size decreases, or a file is deleted, this can create a blank area on the hard drive. Defragmenting a hard drive enables scattered portions of files to be regrouped and open spaces to be rearranged. This results in faster and more efficient file access, which improves the response time of the hard drive.

*Is there a way to automate these maintenance tasks?* Running these programs can be time-consuming, especially when you want to use your computer for other tasks. It is also easy to forget to do these things on a regular basis. That is why newer versions of Windows include a Task Scheduler. This utility enables you to create a task and select the best time for each task to run, in addition to how often, which makes the whole process automatic. Figures 1.37 and 1.38 show the steps to follow to reach the Task Scheduler dialog box for Windows Vista users and Windows 7 users, respectively.

Steps to go to the Task Scheduler

The Task Scheduler window

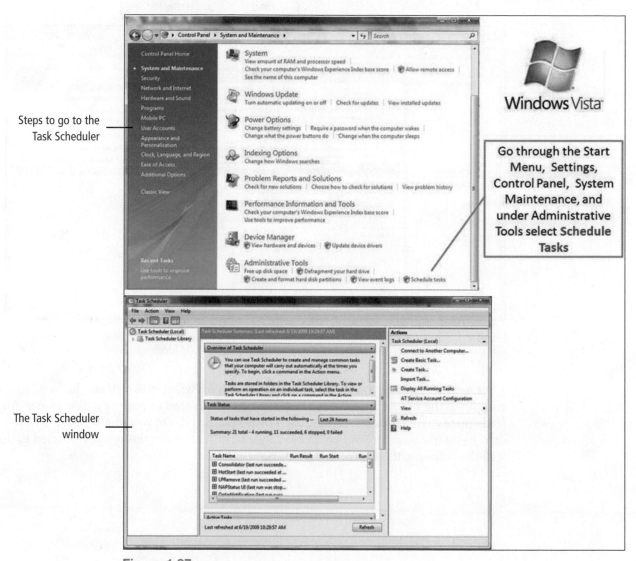

**Figure 1.37**
Computer maintenance—Task Scheduler (Windows Vista users)

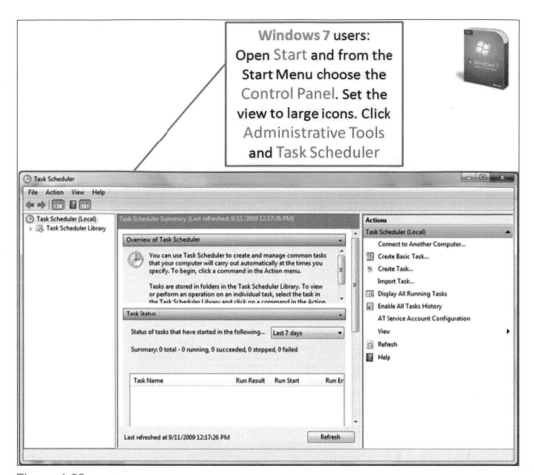

**Figure 1.38**

Computer maintenance—steps to set a task in the Task Scheduler (Windows 7 users)

***Can changes to my system be undone?*** Sometimes when new software is installed on a computer, the results are not what you anticipated. Instead of playing a new game, you find your system stops responding each time you start it. Or, you might find the new driver you installed for your printer is causing conflicts. Even though you've tried to uninstall the software, the system is still not right.

Fortunately, if you are running a newer version of Windows, the System Restore utility come to the rescue. Periodically, Windows creates a ***restore point***, which records all the settings for your system. It's similar to taking a picture of how everything is currently set up. Figures 1.39 and 1.40 show steps to create a restore point for Windows Vista and Windows 7 users, respectively.

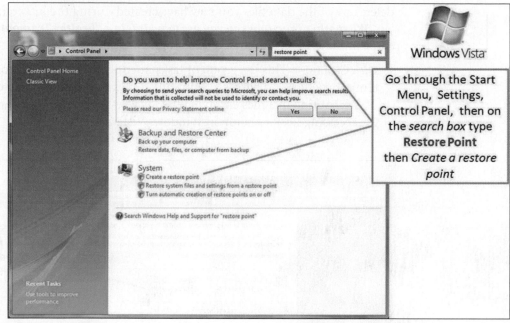

**Figure 1.39**

Computer maintenance—steps to create a Restore Point (Windows Vista users)

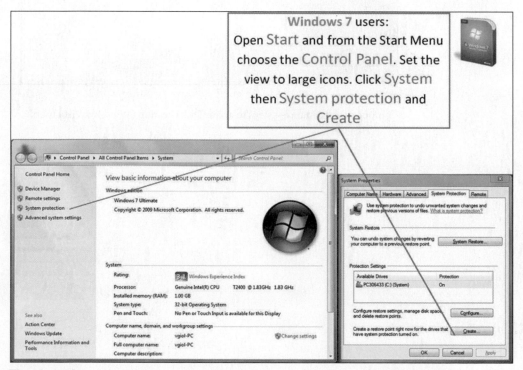

**Figure 1.40**

Computer maintenance—steps to create a Restore Point (Windows 7 users)

It is also possible to set manual restore points, and it is highly recommended that you set one before installing new software or hardware, or when making any major changes to your system. If you experience a problem with your system after the new software is installed, you can roll your system back to an earlier restore point when the system was working correctly. Think of it as an Undo button for your operating system. The good news is, returning to an earlier restore point affects only your system settings. It does not delete any of the data files you may have created during the interval.

***What other functions can you use to maintain a "healthy" computer?*** Following are some of the other things that keep computers healthy:

- **Disk Cleanup**—This is a group of tasks intended to free disk space cause by Internet temporary files and hard drive unwanted files that accumulate from time to time. Part of this routine includes emptying the Recycle Bin. Figures 1.41 and 1.42 show the steps for accessing Disk Cleanup in Windows Vista and Windows 7.

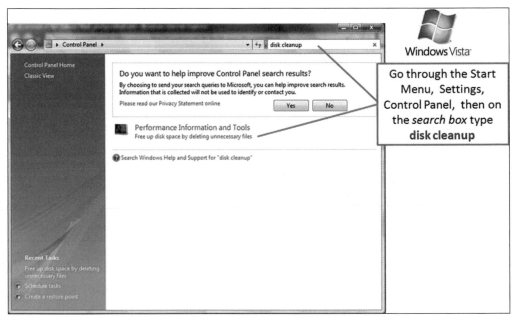

**Figure 1.41**
Computer maintenance—steps to access Disk Cleanup (Windows Vista users)

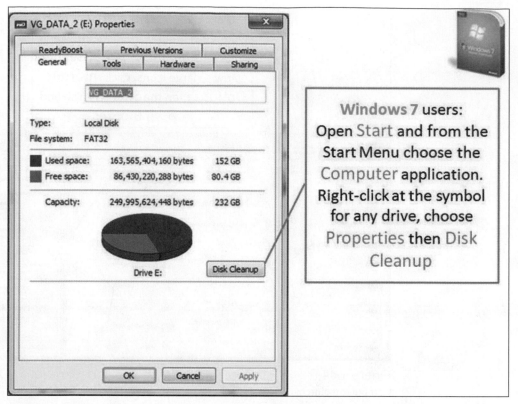

**Figure 1.42**

Computer maintenance—steps to access Disk Cleanup (Windows 7 users)

- **Activate and set up the Internet Pop-up Blocker**—This lets the user the select options to allow or to block advertising and other pop-up windows while surfing the Net. Figures 1.43 and 1.44 show the steps for accessing Pop-up Blocker in Windows Vista and Windows 7.

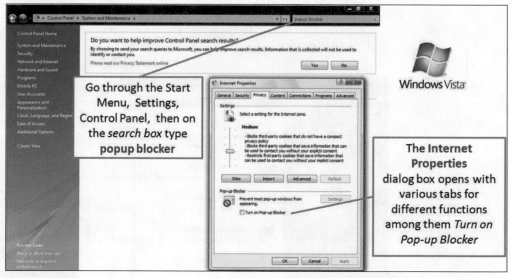

**Figure 1.43**

Computer maintenance—steps to access the Pop-up Blocker (Windows Vista users)

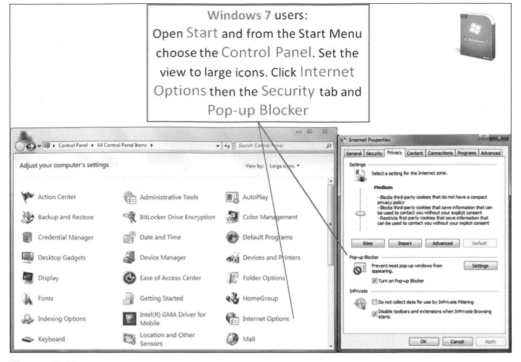

**Figure 1.44**

Computer maintenance—steps to access the Pop-up Blocker (Windows 7 users)

- **Access and set up Security settings**—You can set security settings, such as:

  - Check for security updates

  - Select the settings for the Windows Firewall

  - Check for Windows software updates

  - Scan for spyware and other potentially unwanted software

  - Change Internet security options

    Figures 1.45 and 1.46 show the steps for accessing security settings in Windows Vista and Windows 7.

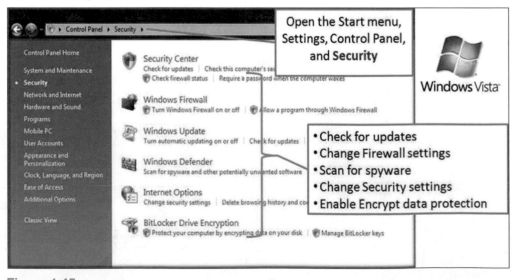

**Figure 1.45**

Computer maintenance—steps to access the Security settings (Windows Vista users)

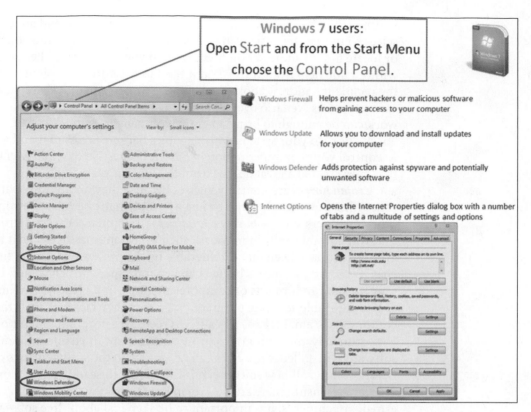

**Figure 1.46**
Computer maintenance—steps to access the Security settings and other functions (Windows 7 users)

## Viruses

Establishing the habit of performing regular maintenance on your computer is one way to protect it, and yourself, from data loss. But there are many other dangers you need to be aware of too. Viruses, spyware, and **hackers** are all out there waiting to pounce on the unwary computer user. The term *hacker*, as used here, signifies an expert in computers and programming languages who uses his/her expertise to obtain unauthorized access to computer systems with the purpose corrupting data and/or stealing information.

**What are viruses and how do they get on the computer?** Computer **viruses** are malicious codes or software designed to invade your computer system and alter or destroy data without your knowledge and against your wishes. The severity of a virus can vary. Some viruses merely seem to be nuisances or might not even be obvious to the user; some cause files to be corrupted or erased; and others are capable of shutting down a computer and erasing the entire hard drive. Viruses infect a system and then attach themselves to a program or file to spread to other users.

Viruses can be distributed in several ways. In the early days of computers, viruses were spread by sharing infected floppy disks. Now, due to the ease in which files can be shared over the Internet, viruses are able to spread much more quickly. One of the most common ways to send a virus is through e-mail attachments. Security experts recommend that you never open an e-mail attachment unless you have first scanned it with antivirus software to determine that it is virus-free. Experts also recommend that unless you know the sender and have been expecting the e-mail attachment, it is best to delete the attachment without ever opening it. File-sharing services are another source for these types of problems.

**Are viruses and worms the same thing? Worms** are similar to viruses because they are also malicious programs that spread from computer to computer; however, unlike viruses, worms are able to do this without any human interaction and are able to replicate themselves so numerous copies can be sent. Worms can burrow into your e-mail address book, or locate e-mail addresses on files saved on your hard drive, then send themselves out without any help from you. When it reaches the e-mail recipient, it does the same thing to the recipient's address book. Also, because worms can quickly replicate themselves, they can repeat this scenario over and over. Just the sheer amount of traffic they cause on a network can be enough to bring an entire company to a grinding halt. Worms can also open a "back door" to your system, which enables hackers access to it and gives them the ability to control your computer remotely. Sasser, Blaster, NetSky, and MyDoom are all worms that have created a great deal of trouble in recent years.

*Trojan horses* are not truly viruses because they do not duplicate themselves or infect other files; however, they can be just as problematic because they open your system for other intruders such as *botnets*. A *botnet* is a popular term for a group of software robots that run automatically in networks such as instant massagers, chat rooms, and discussion groups that have been made vulnerable by the presence of Trojan horses. Once inside a chat room, for instance, a botnet can generate *spam,* which is bulk unsolicited e-mail messages to random lists of computer users. At first glance, a Trojan horse often appears to be a desirable software program but in fact they facilitate unauthorized access to a computer system. Perhaps it is a free screensaver program or a set of animated cursors. Unfortunately, these programs come with an unwanted and hidden agenda. After the software is installed, the effects can be similar to those that viruses or worms cause. Before you install new software, it is important to scan the program files with antivirus software to ensure there are no Trojan horses lurking there. And, as with unknown e-mail attachments, it is important to be skeptical about free software; it's not often that you really get something for nothing!

## Spyware

*How is spyware different from viruses?* *Spyware* is software designed to capture personal and confidential information that resides on your system and send it elsewhere. It has quickly become as large a problem as viruses. Spyware's primary threat is to your privacy and confidentiality. Although spyware is not usually intended to harm your system, it can sometimes have that effect on it. *Adware* is spyware that tracks your Internet browsing and can install malicious cookies on your computer. A *cookie* is a small text file that contains information that can identify you to a website. Cookies are not necessarily bad. They are useful when they are used to help personalize your Web browsing experience, but cookies can threaten your privacy if they are used to reveal too much information.

*How can you tell if spyware is on a computer?* One symptom that indicates adware is on a computer is an increase in the number of pop-up ads the user receives, some of which might even address the user by name! Adware can generate pop-up ads even when you're not online. Some types of adware can also reset a Web browser's home page to a page of its choosing and take control of the search engine, directing you to websites that have been predetermined by the adware.

*Are there other privacy threats?* *Key loggers* are another type of spyware. In this case, a software program records every keystroke made on the computer. Key loggers can capture all sorts of confidential information this way—passwords, credit card numbers, bank account numbers, and so on—and then relay this information elsewhere. Entire e-mail messages and instant messaging conversations can be recorded this way too. Some key loggers are hardware, rather than software, although they perform the same devious function. Such hardware devices can be attached between the keyboard and the computer. The information stolen through the use of key loggers can easily make you a victim of identity theft. Trojan horses can be used to distribute key loggers and other types of spyware just as easily as they deliver viruses.

***How can you avoid being a victim?*** To minimize the risk of having spyware installed on your computer, there are some practical precautions you can take. One of the most prevalent methods of spreading spyware is through file-sharing services, such as Morpheus or Kazaa. Not only can the file-sharing software include spyware, but often the files you think you are downloading for free are infected too. Although it's tempting to get the newest song or video for free from such a site, don't risk it!

This problem can be avoided if you use one of the legitimate, pay-as-you-go file-sharing services such as iTunes or the reincarnated Napster. Do not trust files or software sent by friends or acquaintances. Additionally, be cautious when you download and install freeware or shareware software. Make sure you deal with a reputable software publisher, scan the downloaded software for viruses and spyware, and read the licensing agreement. Some licensing agreements actually include information about additional software that will be automatically installed if you accept it.

Another way to prevent spyware is to avoid pop-up and banner ads whenever possible. You should never click on them. Often the "No Thanks" button is just a ruse to get you to click it and enable the spyware installation. Close pop-up ads by clicking the Close button in the top right corner. Installing pop-up blocking software can help to eliminate this risk almost entirely.

If you are running the most recent version of Windows, you already have a pop-up blocker available to you. You can view the pop-up blocker settings for Windows Vista in Figure 1.43 and access this dialog box through Internet Explorer's Tools menu. Many popular search engines, such as Google and Yahoo!, also include pop-up blocking features in their toolbars, which you can download at no charge. It is also wise to avoid questionable websites, because some of them can install spyware on your system just by visiting the site.

## Protecting Yourself and Your Computer

In addition to being cautious in your Internet travels, there are some proactive measures you can take to protect yourself and your computer from viruses and spyware. These include:

- ***Software updates*** and ***patches***—Keeping your operating system and software up to date is critical. Software manufacturers are constantly on the lookout for security threats, and they issue updates and patches to help protect your system. Check for these and install them regularly. Software manufacturers have begun to implement automated procedures to check and install such updates. If your computer has this capability, it's a good idea to use this feature.

- ***Antivirus and antispyware software***—*Antivirus software* is a utility program used to search your hard drive and files for viruses, and remove those that are found. ***Antispyware software*** works in a similar fashion, but searches for spyware rather than viruses. No computer should be without this protection. Many users erroneously think that because they aren't regularly online or use only a slow dial-up connection, they aren't a target. Nothing could be further from the truth! Recent studies show more than two-thirds of all computer users have some form of virus or spyware on their system.

There are a variety of antivirus and antispyware products available. Unfortunately, there are also a lot of dishonest companies purporting to offer these products. Too often, these are really scams that will actually install spyware or viruses on your system! To avoid being scammed or downloading something malicious, you should never respond to offers that are received in a pop-up ad or unsolicited e-mail. To obtain legitimate products, it is best to purchase them from the manufacturer's website or from a local retailer. Additionally, some internet service providers are beginning to provide some of these products as part of their services.

Some well-known antivirus products include Norton AntiVirus (*www.symantec.com*), McAfee VirusScan (*www.mcafee.com*), and AVG Anti-Virus (*www.grisoft.com*).

Antispyware products include eTrust PestPatrol (*www.pestpatrol.com*), Ad-Aware (*www.lavasoft.com*), and Spybot Search & Destroy (*www.safer-networking.org*). You can search for other products at popular download sites such as Download.com (*www.download.com*) or Tucows (*www.tucows.com*) but you should be sure to read the software reviews and evaluate their usefulness before downloading or installing them.

It is best to use only one antivirus product, because running more than one can cause conflicts between the programs. However, because there are so many different types of spyware, antispyware products may address these problems in different ways. Experts recommend running at least two different antispyware applications in order to catch as many spyware programs as possible. It's not enough to install antivirus and antispyware software on your system; you need to update it frequently, at least once a week. Doing so will protect you against any new viruses or spyware created since the last time you checked. Software should be set to scan incoming data files, e-mail, and so on but regular full-system scans should be conducted on a weekly basis as well.

***Personal firewalls—Firewalls*** may be software programs or hardware devices, although their purpose is the same to prevent unauthorized access to your computer. When a firewall is installed properly, it can make your computer invisible to hackers and other invaders. Not only can a good firewall help prevent infections and identity theft; it can also prevent hackers from accessing your computer and turning it into a ***zombie***. A zombie computer is one that can be controlled remotely and can be used to help spread viruses, spyware, or junk e-mail known as spam. Zombie computers can also be used in ***denial of service (DoS)*** attacks. DoS attacks occur when a large number of computers try to access a website at the same time, effectively overloading it and causing it to shut down. If you are using Windows XP or Windows Vista, you already have a firewall available to you.

You can access the firewall settings by clicking the Start button, settings, Control Panel, Security, and Windows Firewall.

***What else should I look for?*** It might sound simple, but when online, do not give out personal information unless it is for legitimate purposes. It is important to avoid spam e-mail and ***phishing*** attacks e-mails that masquerade as authentic entities, such as banks and credit card companies, and ask for confidential information. Legitimate organizations will not ask for passwords, bank account numbers, or credit card details through e-mail. It is also possible to check for hoaxes and scams at a variety of websites, including many of the antivirus and antispyware sites. When in doubt, do some research to see if the request you've received is legitimate. If necessary, make a telephone call to the agency in question. Viewing such requests with a critical eye can help you avoid online scams and hoaxes.

## Summary

In this chapter, you examined the benefits of computer fluency and identified the four basic functions of computing. You explored the various types of computers and their components, including CPUs, RAM, and storage devices. This chapter also discussed how to evaluate a computer system and understand the terminology used to measure storage capacity, memory, and microprocessor speed. Various hardware and peripheral devices were reviewed, including input and output devices, and different types of storage devices and media. You explored the basic types of computer software system software and application software and the different uses for each type. You identified various types of networks and the different ways networks can be configured. You also reviewed ways to maintain your computer and keep it safe from various threats, including viruses and spyware.

## Key Terms

# Content-Based Assessments

# Content-Based Assessments

## Matching

A  Application software

B  Computer

C  Computer network

D  Console/system unit

E  CPU

F  Hardware

G  DVDs or CDs

H  Memory (RAM)

I  Motherboard/ system board

J  Peripherals

K  Port

L  Server

M  Software

N  Spyware

O  Topology

Match each term in the second column with its correct definition in the first column. Write the letter of the term on the blank line in front of the correct definition.

___M___ 1.  Computer programs.

___A___ 2.  Programs that enable you to accomplish a specific tasks or solve a specific need.

___C___ 3.  Two or more computers connected together to enable resource sharing.

___L___ 4.  Used to manage network resources, this type of computer can be dedicated to a specific task.

___G___ 5.  Optical disk drives use this type of storage media.

___O___ 6.  The layout or design/arrangement of computers connected to a network.

___K___ 7.  A peripheral device uses this to attach to the computer.

___B___ 8.  A programmable electronic device that can input, process, output, and store data.

___F___ 9.  The physical components of a computer system.

___K___ 10.  Hardware connected outside the computer's system unit.

___D___ 11.  The hardware unit that typically contains the CPU, RAM, a hard disk, and a power supply.

___I___ 12.  A large printed circuit board to which all the other components are connected.

___H___ 13.  The temporary storage that holds data and instructions waiting to be processed.

___E___ 14.  The processing unit.

___N___ 15.  This type of program threatens a user's privacy.

# Content-Based Assessments

## Multiple Choice

Circle the correct response.

1. Which of the following requires one byte of storage?
   a. Page   b. Paragraph   c. Sentence   **d. Character**

2. Which of the following units represents the fastest CPU clock speed?
   a. 733 MHz   b. 286 MHz   **c. 2 GHz**   d. 2 GB

3. Which of the following is not an input device?
   a. Keyboard   **b. Speaker**   c. Mouse   d. Stylus

4. Which of the following is an example of optical storage media?
   a. Disk drive   b. Flash card   c. RAM   **d. Compact disc**

5. Which of the following is not a type of computer?
   a. Mainframe   **b. Multitask**   c. Server   d. Supercomputer

6. Before a computer can process data, where must data be stored?
   **a. In RAM**   b. On a disk   c. In the control unit   d. On the monitor

7. What term, related to computers, means billions?
   a. Byte   b. Mega   **c. Giga**   d. Hertz

8. Which of the following is not a type of microcomputer?
   a. Desktop   b. Notebook   c. Personal digital assistant   **d. Microprocessor**

9. Which of the following can prevent the easy and casual connection to your computer by a nonauthorized user?
   a. Disk defragmenter   b. Antivirus software   **c. Firewall**   d. Key logger

10. Which of the following is capable of opening a "back door" on a computer and is able to spread without human interaction?
    a. Trojan horse   **b. Worm**   c. Adware   d. Zombie

# Glossary

**Adware**  Spyware that tracks your Internet browsing and can install malicious cookies on your computer.

**Antispyware software**  A utility program used to search your hard drive for spyware, and remove those that are found.

**Antivirus software**  A utility program used to search your hard drive for viruses, and remove those that are found.

**Application software**  Programs that accomplish specific tasks, such as word processing, photo editing, or sending e-mail, and using the computer in a productive manner.

**Arithmetic logic unit (ALU)**  Handles addition, subtraction, multiplication, and division, and also makes logical and comparison decisions.

**Arrow keys**  Keys located at the bottom right of the keyboard between the standard keys and the numeric keypad that enable the user to move the insertion point around the active window.

**Audio port**  Similar to video ports, these ports connect audio devices, such as speakers, headphones, and microphones to the computer's sound card.

**Backup tape drive**  A storage device used to save data to tape media resembling audiocassettes.

**Bluetooth**  A type of wireless technology that relies on radio wave transmission and doesn't require a clear line of sight. It is typically limited to less than 30 feet.

**Boot**  The process of starting up a computer; the computer begins when power is turned on.

**Botnet**  Term associated with malicious software or software *robots*.

**Browser**  See Web browser.

**Burn**  The process that saves data by using a laser beam that burns tiny pits into the storage medium.

**Bus topology**  In a computer network, it connects each node to a single, central high-speed line known as a bus.

**CD**  Acronym for compact disk; a polycarbonate material with one or more metal layers capable of optically storing digital information.

**CD burner**  Type of optical drive capable of reading and writing data from and to a CD (provided the media is recordable, like CD-Rs and CD-RWs).

**CD drive**  Type of optical drive that can read CDs (compact disks).

**CD-ROM**  CD media that was burned once and from that moment on can only be read.

**CD-R**  Also known as CD-Recordable, a type of compact disk that can be recorded using a CD burner (drive).

**CD-RW**  A rewritable disc that enables data to be recorded, revised, or deleted, and new data written to the disc, similar to magnetic media.

**Central processing unit (CPU)**  The part of the computer responsible for controlling all the commands and tasks the computer performs, acting as the brain of the computer.

**Click**  A mouse function in which you point at an object, press and release the left (or primary) mouse button once.

**Client**  In a client/server network, the computer used at a desk or workstation to write letters, send e-mail, produce invoices, or perform any of the many tasks that can be accomplished with a computer.

**Client/server network**  A network in which two different types of computers have different functions. See also Client and Server.

**Clock speed**  A measure of the speed at which a CPU processes data (number of instructions per second).

**Communication and organizational software**  A program such as Microsoft Outlook 2007, used to send and retrieve e-mail, manage day-to-day tasks such as appointments and contacts.

**Compact disk**  See CD

**Computer**  A programmable electronic device that can input, process, output, and store data.

**Computer fluent**  Describes a person who understands the capabilities and limitations of computers and knows how to use computer technology to accomplish tasks.

**Configure**  To put together by selecting a combination of components, features, and options.

**Connectivity port**  Ports such as Ethernet and modem that are used to connect a computer to a local network or to the Internet.

**Control keys**  Keys such as the Ctrl, Alt, and the Windows key that provide shortcuts or increased functionality to the keyboard when used in combination with other keys.

**Control unit**  In the CPU, the component responsible for obtaining and executing instructions from the computer's memory.

**Cookie**  A small text file that contains information that can identify you to a website.

**CPU**  See Central processing unit

**Data**  Represents text, numbers, graphics, sounds, and videos entered to the computer's memory during input operations.

**Database software**  Programs, such as Microsoft Access 2007, used to store and organize large amounts of data and perform complex tasks such as sorting and querying to generate specialized reports.

**Data mining**  A function is some database software that looks for hidden patterns in the data to anticipate future trends.

**Dedicated server**  A server in a network that is assigned to handle only specific tasks.

**Denial of service (DoS)**  Attacks that occur when a large number of computers try to access a website at the same time, effectively overloading it and causing it to shut down.

**Desktop computer**  A class of microcomputer, such as a PC or a Mac, that typically occupies a working area around a desk.

**Device**  A hardware component that attaches to a computer. Includes disk drives, printers, mice, keyboards, and modems.

**Dialog box**  A frame or window that shows the presets or defaults for a specific function and enables the user to make changes before moving ahead.

**Digital camera**  A device that stores pictures digitally rather than using conventional film.

**Digital video recorder**  Devices that let you capture digital images and movies and transfer them directly to your computer.

**Digital Video Interface (DVI) port**  Ports that transmit a pure digital signal, eliminating the need for digital-to-analog conversion and resulting in a higher quality picture on an LCD monitor.

**Docking station** Device that enables the user to connect a notebook to a full-size keyboard, monitor, and other devices in an office setting.

**DOS** The original OS for personal computers in the early 1980s. This was a text-based or keyboard-driven operating system.

**Dot matrix** Printers that have small hammers, similar to a typewriter's, that strike a ribbon against paper, leaving behind the image of a character or symbol.

**Dot pitch** A display characteristic in monitors that refers to the diagonal distance between two pixels of the same color. The smaller the dot pitch results in a crisper viewing image because there is less blank space between the pixels.

**Dots per inch (dpi)** How resolution is expressed. The higher the dpi, the better the print quality.

**Double-click** The action of clicking and releasing the left mouse button twice in rapid succession while keeping the mouse still.

**Drag** The action of moving something from one location on the screen to another; the action includes pointing and clicking (releasing the mouse button at the desired time or location).

**DSL** Acronym for digital subscriber line. Type of communications line in which signals travel through copper wires between a telephone switching station and a home or business.

**Dual-boot** A computer that can run more than one operating system.

**Dual-core** Processors that have several advantages over a single processor CPU, including improved multitasking capabilities, system performance, and lower power consumption.

**DVD** Acronym for Digital Video Disk or Diversified Video Disk; media that holds data written by an optical device.

**DVD drive** Digital Video Disk drive capable of reading and writing DVD media.

**DVD-ROM** DVD media that was burned once and from that moment on can only be read.

**DVI port** See Digital Video Interface.

**Embedded computers** Small specialized computers built into larger components such as automobiles and appliances.

**Ethernet port** A port, slightly larger than a telephone jack, that can transmit data at speeds up to 1,000 megabits per second (Mbps) and is usually used to connect to a cable modem or a network.

**Firewall** A combination of hardware and software used to prevent unauthorized access to your computer.

**FireWire port** A port used to send data at rates up to 800 megabits per second (Mbps), frequently used for digital cameras or digital video recorders.

**Flash drive** A small, portable, digital storage device that connects to a computer's USB port (Universal Serial Bus); also called a thumb drive, jump drive, or USB drive.

**Flash memory** Portable, nonvolatile memory that uses electronic, solid-state circuitry.

**Flat-panel displays** Flat-panel displays or LCD monitors that use a liquid crystal display and are thin and energy efficient.

**Floppy diskette** Magnetic media used for data storage.

**Floppy disk drive** Device used to read and write to floppy diskettes media.

**Function keys** Keys that are located above the standard row of number keys and numbered F1 through F12. These keys are generally associated with certain software-specific commands.

**Gaming computers** Computers that are mostly used by video game enthusiasts. They are usually configured with a fast CPU, large size memory, a special video card, sound card, and surround sound speaker system.

**Gigabyte (GB)** Approximately one billion bytes; a unit used to measure memory size and storage space.

**Gigahertz (GHz)** One billion hertz; a hertz is one of the units used to measure processor speed. One hertz is one cycle (instruction read) per second.

**Graphical user interface (GUI)** Today's operating systems provide a *user-friendly* way to operate a computer with their graphical user interface. The user controls the action using the keyboard, a mouse, or a touch screen to make selections from onscreen objects such as icons, menus, or dialog boxes.

**GUI** See Graphical user interface.

**Hackers** Derogatory term to describe individuals who gain unauthorized access to computer systems for the purpose of corrupting or stealing data.

**Handheld computers** Small portable computers that might include personal productivity software and enable the user to play music, take photos and video, make phone calls, and access the Internet. PDAs, Pocket PCs, and smart phones fall in this category.

**Hard copy** The output of a printer (synonymous with printout).

**Hard disk drive** A combination of a device and media used as the main storage in most computers.

**Hardware** The physical or tangible components of the computer and any equipment connected to it.

**Hyperlink** A connection to another area of a document or a connection to an Internet URL.

**Icon** A graphic representation of an object on the screen. Icons can be selected with the mouse or using your fingers on a touch screen.

**IM** Acronym for instant messaging, software that enables users to communicate in real time like a phone conversation but using text only.

**Impact** A type of printer that resembles a typewriter; a key punches an inked ribbon to imprint a characters on paper.

**Information** Data that has been organized in a useful manner.

**Information processing cycle** The cycle composed of the four basic computer functions: input, process, output, and storage.

**Ink-jet** A nonimpact printer that uses a special nozzle and ink cartridges to distribute liquid ink on the surface of the paper.

**Input** During this step of the information processing cycle, the computer gathers data or allows a user to enter data onto memory.

**Input devices** Computer hardware used to enter data and instructions into a computer; examples include the keyboard, mouse, stylus, scanner, microphone, and digital camera.

**Insertion point** A blinking vertical line on the screen that shows where the next typed character will appear.

**Internet control key** Typically located at the top of certain keyboards, these keys enable the user to assign to each key a unique Web browser functions such as sending e-mail, browsing a specific site, or accessing their online bank account.

**Intranet** A network or part of a network in which access is restricted to authorized users only.

**IrDA port** A port that is used to allow devices such as PDAs, keyboards, mice, and printers to transmit data wirelessly to another device by using infrared light waves.

**Joysticks**  Game controls that are input devices used to control movement within video games.

**Key logger**  A type of spyware that records every keystroke made on the computer and can capture all sorts of confidential information this way such as passwords, credit card numbers, bank account numbers, and so on.

**Keyboard**  The primary input device for computers.

**Kilobit**  One thousand bits. It takes eight bits to make one byte.

**Kilobyte**  Approximately one thousand bytes.

**LAN**  Acronym for local area network. A network that connects computers that are reasonably close together.

**Laser printer**  A type of nonimpact printer that uses a drum, static electricity, and a laser to distribute dry ink or toner on the surface of the paper.

**LightScribe**  A disc-labeling technology that burns text and graphics onto the surface of a specially coated LightScribe CD or DVD.

**Linux**  An alternative operating system. It is open source software, which means it is not owned by a single company and some versions are available at no cost.

**Liquid crystal display (LCD)**  Technology used in flat panel monitors, resulting in thinner, lighter monitors that consume less energy.

**Local area network (LAN)**  A network in which the nodes are located within a small geographic area.

**Mac OS**  An operating system designed specifically for Apple's Macintosh computers.

**Magnetic**  A type of storage process using magnetized film to store data; used by devices such as hard disks, or media such as tape cartridges.

**Mainframe computers**  Computers often found in large businesses, organizations, and government agencies where thousands of users need to simultaneously use the data and resources for their everyday operations.

**Megabit (Mb)**  Approximately one million bits. It takes eight bits to make a byte.

**Megabyte (MB)**  Approximately one million bytes; a unit of measure for memory and storage space.

**Megahertz (MHz)**  One million hertz; a hertz is one of the units used to measure processor speed. One hertz is one cycle (instruction read) per second.

**Memory**  A generic term that signifies storage.

**Menu**  A list of commands that perform specific tasks within a program.

**MFD**  Acronym for Multi-Function Devices.

**Microcomputer**  The computer most users are familiar with and that ranges in size from large desktop systems to handheld devices. The name comes from its main component or brain called the "microchip" or microprocessor.

**Microphones**  Input devices used to capture and record sounds.

**Microprocessor chip**  A microcomputer's main component; it is a tiny but powerful chip compared to a mainframe or a supercomputer.

**Microsoft Windows**  The operating system that runs most microcomputers today and provides a graphical user interface to make the computer "user friendly."

**MIDI port**  Ports used to connect electronic musical devices, such as keyboards and synthesizers, to a computer.

**Mobile devices**  These devices fall into the category of handheld computers; they are small enough to fit in the palm of your hand and enable users to access personal productivity software, send and read e-mail, navigate the Internet, and some are capable of wireless communications.

**Modem port**  Ports used to connect a computer to a local network or to the Internet.

**Monitor (or display screen)**  Display devices that show images of text, graphics, and video once data has been processed.

**Monitor port**  A port that is used to connect the monitor to the graphics-processing unit, which is usually located on the motherboard or on a video card.

**Motherboard**  A large printed circuit board located in the system unit to which all other boards are connected; the motherboard contains the central processing unit (CPU), the memory (RAM) chips, expansion card slots, and ports.

**Mouse**  An input device (pointing device) used to enter commands and user responses into a computer. This device controls a symbol on the screen (mouse pointer) used to manipulate objects and select commands.

**Mouse pointer**  In a graphical user interface environment, a pointer is a small arrow or other symbol on the screen that moves as you move the mouse. This lets the user make selections from objects on the screen such as icons, menus, or dialog boxes.

**Multifunction device (MFD)**  Hardware devices such as All-in-One printers that provide a number of functions in one unit.

**Multimedia control key**  Some modern keyboards have at least a few keys or buttons that can be used for such tasks as muting or adjusting speaker volume, opening a Web browser, and sending e-mail.

**Multimedia projectors**  Output devices used to display information on a screen for viewing by a large audience.

**Multitask**  To perform more than one task simultaneously.

**Network**  A group of two or more computers (or nodes) connected together via cables or wirelessly, to share information and resources.

**Network topology**  The layout and structure of a computer network.

**Node**  Any object connected to a network that is a computer or a peripheral device.

**Nonimpact**  Printers that generate hard copies by means other than striking elements on to a ribbon and paper. They do not touch the paper when printing.

**Nonvolatile**  Permanent storage; type of storage that holds its contents even when power is shut down. "Read Only Memory" (ROM) is a type of permanent storage.

**Notebook computer**  Also known as a laptop, this microcomputer is smaller than a desktop and designed to be portable.

**Numeric keypad**  A cluster of keys located at the right of the keyboard. This provides an alternative method of quickly entering numbers.

**Open-source**  An operating system not owned by any company and that can be changed by people with the appropriate programming knowledge.

**Operating system (OS)**  The software that controls the way the computer works from the time it is turned on until it is shut down.

**Optical**  A type of storage process that uses a laser to read and write data; used to burn media such as CDs and DVDs.

**OS**  See Operating system.

**Output**  Data that has been processed and converted into information.

**Output device**  Computer hardware components used to display information (show it) to the user; examples include the monitor, printer, and speakers.

**P2P network (Peer-to-peer)**  A type of network in which each node can communicate with every other node. No PC has control over the network.

**Parallel port** A port that sends data in groups of bits as opposed to one bit at a time.

**PDA** See Personal digital assistant.

**Peripheral** A hardware device connected to a computer but not inside the system unit, such as a monitor, printer, a scanner, or mouse.

**Permanent memory** Type of memory that retains data and information even if the computer's power is turned off.

**Personal digital assistant (PDA)** These handheld devices vary in size and purpose, but they are all ultra-lightweight and portable. Initially designed to maintain and organize calendar appointments and business contacts, they enable users to access personal productivity software, send and read e-mail, and navigate the Internet.

**Personal firewall** Software or hardware that, when installed properly, can make your computer invisible to hackers and other invaders.

**Phishing** The process of attempting to acquire sensitive information such as usernames, passwords, and credit card details by pretending to be as a reputable entity.

**Pixel** An abbreviated name for "picture element." Tiny dots that make up images on computer monitors.

**Port** An interface or a connecting point by which peripherals are connected to the computer's system unit.

**Ppm** Acronym for "pages per minute." A measure of the speed of a printer.

**Presentation software** A program, such as PowerPoint 2007, used to create dynamic slideshows and generate speaker notes and audience handouts.

**Printer** An output device used to generate hard copy or printout.

**Printout** The output of a printer (synonymous with hard copy).

**Process** A CPU function in which data is converted into information.

**Program** Also known as software, sets of instructions or commands that tell the computer what to do and are used by the computer to perform certain tasks.

**Programmable** A device that can be programmed or instructed to perform a specific task guided by commands or instructions.

**RAM** Acronym for Random Access Memory.

**Random Access Memory (RAM)** The computer's temporary storage space (short-term memory). It stores data on chips connected to the motherboard. This data is held just before processing by the CPU.

**RDBMS** Acronym for Relational Database Management System and is database software that stores information in tables, which enable users quick access to the data by connecting tables with common fields.

**Read Only Memory (ROM)** See ROM.

**Read/write** Read is the action of retrieving or opening existing data and write is the action of saving or storing data.

**Refresh rate** The speed at which the screen's (monitor) image is redrawn.

**Resolution** The measurement used to assess the clarity and sharpness of an image on a monitor; determined by pixel density.

**Restore point** A file in which all your computer system settings are stored. It's similar to taking a picture of how everything is currently set up. If there is a system failure, Windows can come to the rescue.

**Right-click** The action of pressing and releasing the right mouse button.

**Right-drag** A mouse function done by pressing the right mouse button and continuing to hold it while dragging, or moving, the mouse pointer to another location.

**Ring (or token-ring) topology** A network layout that connects each node to the next, forming a loop or a circle.

**ROM** Acronym for Read Only Memory. A type of memory prerecorded on a chip that the computer can only "read," not write or change its contents.

**S-video port** Short for Super-Video, a technology for transmitting video signals over a cable by dividing the video information into two separate signals, color and brightness.

**Scanners** Input devices used to convert hard copy documents or images into digital files.

**Scroll** The action of moving up or down within a window to access any part of that window.

**Scroll wheel** A button on some mice, useful when scrolling within a document; rolling the wheel enables you to quicky move up or down within a window. Also, holding the Ctrl (Control) key while moving the wheel button lets you zoom in or out for closer or more distant viewing.

**Sectors** Wedge-shaped sections of a hard disk drive on a hard disk drive or any magnetic storage media (ZIP disks and floppy disks), each measured from the center point to the outer edge.

**Serial port** Ports that can send data only one bit at a time.

**Server** In a client/server network, a server is the computer that manages shared network resources and provides access to the client computer when requested.

**Shortcut menu** A type of menu that is displayed when the user right-clicks at an onscreen object. These menus are "*context sensitive.*" That means they display commands and options specifically related to the object that is being pointed at.

**Smartphones** Handheld devices that combine mobile phone capabilities with other features typically associated with pocket PCs and PDAs.

**Soft copy** The image generated by a display monitor as the result of output.

**Software patches or Software updates** Software manufacturers are constantly on the lookout for security threats, and they issue updates and patches to help protect your system. Check for these and install them regularly.

**Spam** Unwanted or unsolicited bulk e-mail messages.

**Speech recognition** Technology that enables the user to record discussions or lectures, or to control the computer functions using voice commands.

**Speakers** Output devices that enable the user to hear any auditory signals the computer sends.

**Splash screen** A window used to inform the user of what kind of software is necessary in order to view a specific website. Also a window shown before a user is given the option to continue to the content of a website.

**Spreadsheet software** A program such as Microsoft Excel 2007 used to organize data in rows and columns, perform calculations, create charts, and perform numerical analyses.

**Spyware** Software designed to capture personal and confidential information that resides on your system and send it elsewhere.

**Star topology** Each node in this type of network is connected to a special device known as a switch, which is centrally located. Each node must go through the switch to communicate with the other nodes.

**Storage** To retain data or information for future use.

**Storage devices** Hardware components that retain data and information to be used in the future.

**Stylus** A "pen-like" input device used to write on a tablet computer or PDA.

**Suite**  A collection of application software programs developed by the same manufacturer, bundled together and sold at a price that is usually less than the cost of purchasing each program individually. One example is Office 2007.

**Supercomputer**  A large, powerful computer typically devoted to specialized tasks.

**System software**  The set of programs that enables a computer's hardware devices and program to work together; it includes the operating system and utility.

**System unit**  The tower, box, or console that contains the critical hardware and electrical components of a computer. Typically, the motherboard, the CPU, RAM, and the hard drive are contained within the system unit.

**Tablet computer**  A portable computer that features a screen that swivels and can be written on using advanced handwriting recognition software.

**Temporary memory**  Short-term memory that stores data and program instructions that are waiting to be processed.

**Toggle key**  Keystroke combinations that activate a function or, if pressed again, de-activate that function.

**Terabyte**  One trillion bytes; a unit of measure for memory and storage space.

**Token-ring topology**  A network topology that connects each node to the next, forming a loop or a circle.

**Touch screen**  A part of tablet computers that swivel and enable the tablet to be used like a standard notebook computer in one position or like a clipboard in the second position. These screens are considered input/output devices.

**Touch screen technology**  A type of display screen that has a touch-sensitive panel, which enables the user to touch and make selections from onscreen objects using the tip of the finger.

**Tracks**  Concentric circles on a hard disk drive or any magnetic storage media that together with sectors provide the storage space for data and information.

**Trojan horse**  A destructive program that presents itself as a genuine application.

**Universal serial bus (USB) port**  A type of port able to interface with several different peripheral devices, which reduces the need for individual, dedicated ports.

**User friendly**  A user interface that can be used easily with minimum training because it provides visual aids and onscreen help for novice users.

**User interface**  The feature of a computer's operating system that enables you to interact with the computer. Also see GUI (graphical user interface) and DOS (disk operating system text-based interface).

**Utility program**  A component of system software, typically small programs used to perform routine maintenance and housekeeping tasks for the computer.

**Video conferencing**  The use of networks to communicate audio and/or video between two or more individuals in different locations, optimizing communications, information sharing, and decision making.

**Virus**  Malicious programs that are usually installed on your computer without your knowledge. Viruses can cause files to be corrupted or erased, are capable of shutting down a computer, or erasing the entire hard drive.

**VoIP**  Acronym for Voice over Internet Protocol. Allows voice, facsimile, and voice-messaging communications over networks and the Internet.

**Volatile**  Nonpermanent memory; type of storage that is lost when the computer is turned off.

**WAN**  Acronym for Wide area network.

**Web browser**  Software used to locate and display Web pages and navigate through them.

**Wide area network (WAN)**  A network composed of local area networks connected over long distances.

**Window**  A frame on the computer screen that holds a program, a dialog box, or an object.

**Wireless**  Technology that transmits and receives data without a physical cable connection.

**Wireless network**  A network that connects using radio waves instead of wires or cables.

**Word processing software**  A program such as Microsoft Word 2007 used to create, edit, print, and save documents such as term papers, letters, forms, posters, and resumes.

**Worm**  Similar to viruses, malicious programs that spread from computer to computer; however, unlike viruses, worms are able to do this without any human interaction and are able to replicate themselves.

**Zombie**  A computer that can be controlled remotely by a hacker and can be used to spread viruses, spyware, or spam.

# Getting Started with Internet Explorer 8

## OBJECTIVES
At the end of this chapter you will be able to:

## OUTCOMES
Mastering these objectives will enable you to:

### PROJECT 1A
Use Internet Explorer 8 to Navigate and Search the Internet, Create and Manage Favorite Internet Sites, and Save and Print Web Pages.

1. Start Internet Explorer 8 and Identify Screen Elements (p. 437)
2. Navigate the Internet (p. 440)
3. Create and Manage Favorites (p. 450)
4. Search the Internet (p. 453)
5. Save and Print Web Pages (p. 455)

Monkey Business Images/Shutterstock

## In This Chapter

Lake Michigan City College is located along the lakefront of Chicago—one of the nation's most exciting cities. The college serves its large and diverse student body and makes positive contributions to the community through relevant curricula, partnerships with businesses and nonprofit organizations, and learning experiences that enable students to be full participants in the global community. The college offers three associate degrees in 20 academic areas, adult education programs, and continuing education classes on campus, at satellite locations, and online.

The Internet got its start in the 1960s as an experiment by the Department of Defense as a way for large computers to communicate with other large computers. The Internet has evolved into the largest online computer network in the world—one accessed by hundreds of millions of people every day.

Today, using the Internet, you are able to locate old classmates, communicate with friends by using email or chat, or find phone numbers, directions, and maps so you can arrange visits. The Internet enables you to explore the museums of the world or shop for items that are unavailable at your local mall, all with the click of a button. You can control your finances or improve your mind with educational opportunities any time of day and from any location. The Internet gives you a greater connection to the world.

This introduction to Internet Explorer 8 provides a basic overview of Internet Explorer 8 features and how to use them to explore the Internet. You will practice accessing Web sites, navigating the Internet, saving your favorite Web sites, searching for information, and saving and printing Web pages.

# Project 1A College and Career Information

## Project Activities

In Activities 1.1 through 1.15, you and the students in Mr. Tony Adair's CIS 101 course will use Internet Explorer 8 to find information about opportunities after graduating from Lake Michigan City College. Some students are interested in transferring to a four-year college and others want to begin a job and work before thinking about more college. Your completed projects will look similar to those shown in Figure 1.1.

## Project Files

For Project 1A, you will need the following file:

New blank Word document

You will save your documents as

Lastname_Firstname_1A_College_Money
Lastname_Firstname_1A_Career_Info

## Project Results

**Figure 1.1**
Project 1A College and Career Information

## Objective 1 | Start Internet Explorer 8 and Identify Screen Elements

*Internet Explorer 8* is a software program that enables you to view the contents of the World Wide Web. Software of this type is called a *Web browser*. By using Internet Explorer as your Web browser, you can connect to the Internet to search for information, display Web pages, and receive email. Internet Explorer also assists with downloading and transferring files from the Internet, displaying the graphics on a Web site, playing audio and video files associated with a Web site, and executing small programs found in Web sites.

### Activity 1.1 | Starting Internet Explorer 8

In the following activity, you will start Internet Explorer 8 and identify features of the Internet Explorer program window. The way you start Internet Explorer 8 will vary depending on the version of Windows you are using and the way your system has been set up by you, your college, or your organization. The standard installation of Windows places Internet Explorer at the top of the Start menu.

**1** On the Windows taskbar, click the **Start** button 🔵, and then using Figure 1.2 as a guide, locate Internet Explorer on your system.

Organizations can customize the arrangement of programs on the Start menu. If Internet Explorer is used as the standard browser program on your computer, it displays at the top of the Start menu. In other cases, Internet Explorer will display in the All Programs list. If the Internet Explorer logo displays as an icon on your desktop, you can double-click the desktop icon to start the program. The Internet Explorer logo might also display on the Quick Launch toolbar.

**Figure 1.2**

Internet Explorer icon on the desktop

Internet Explorer on the Start menu

Internet Explorer on the Quick Launch toolbar

---

**Alert! | Are you sure that you have an Internet connection?**

To complete the activities in this chapter, your system must be connected to the Internet. This connection might be through your college or organization's network or your personal *Internet Service Provider (ISP)*. An Internet Service Provider is a company that provides an Internet connection through a regular telephone line, a special high-speed telephone line, or a cable. These services are provided by companies such as AT&T, Yahoo!, Verizon, or Comcast, or by local cable and telephone companies.

**2** On your system, click **Internet Explorer**. In the upper right corner, **Maximize** ⬜ the window if it is not already maximized.

Each time you start Internet Explorer 8 when your system is connected to the Internet, the home page that has been set on your system displays. Your *home page* is the Web page that displays every time you start Internet Explorer 8 and can be any Web page. In a college environment, the home page is usually set to the college's Web page. On your own system, you can choose any Web page.

A *Web page* is a document on the World Wide Web that displays as a screen with associated links, frames, pictures, and other features of interest. A *Web site* is a group of related Web pages published to a specific location on the World Wide Web; for example, all the various screens—pages—that comprise your college's Web site. Each Web site has its own unique address, called a *Uniform Resource Locator* or *URL*.

**3** In the **Address bar**, type **microsoft.com**, and then press ⏎. As you type the first few characters in the Address bar, Internet Explorer 8 recalls sites that you have visited in past browsing sessions. These sites are displayed as a drop-down list directly beneath the Address bar. Matching characters are highlighted in blue. Compare your screen with Figure 1.3.

Because Web sites are regularly updated, your screen might look slightly different than Figure 1.3. The Windows Live toolbar is an optional toolbar to make searching easier. It is not a default feature of Internet Explorer 8.

**Figure 1.3**

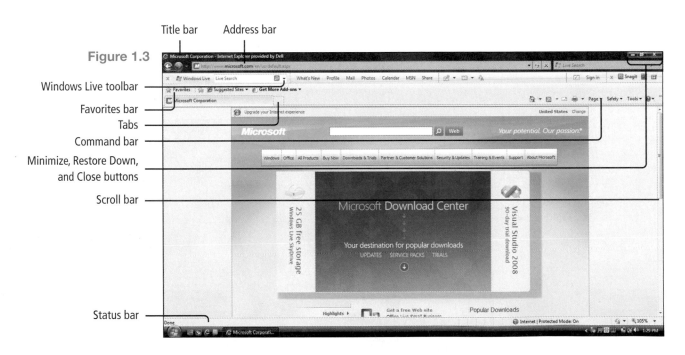

Title bar
Address bar
Windows Live toolbar
Favorites bar
Tabs
Command bar
Minimize, Restore Down, and Close buttons
Scroll bar
Status bar

**4** Click the **Favorites** button ⭐, and then click **Add to Favorites** ⭐ to display the **Add a Favorite** dialog box. Compare your screen with Figure 1.4.

Figure 1.4

Favorites button —

Add a Favorite dialog box —

Web site name to be
added to Favorites Center —

Add button —

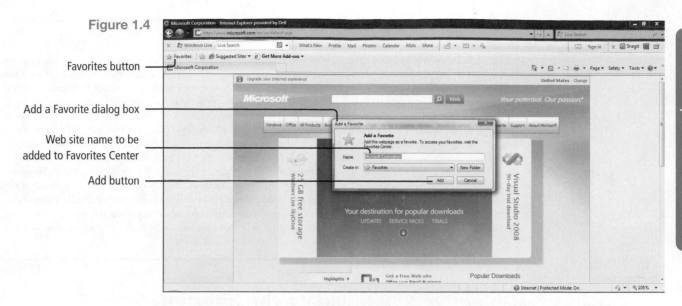

**5** In the **Add a Favorite** dialog box, click the **Add** button. Take a moment to review the
Microsoft Internet Explorer 8 screen elements shown in the table in Figure 1.5.

The Web page has been added to your Favorites Center.

## Internet Explorer 8 Screen Elements

| Screen Element | Description |
| --- | --- |
| Title bar | Identifies the program as Windows Internet Explorer and also displays the name of the active Web page. |
| Minimize, Restore Down, and Close buttons | Provide a way to vary the size of the window you are viewing. |
| Command bar | The toolbar located immediately above the right side of the browser window that can provide quick access to commands such as Home, Page, Safety, and Tools. |
| Address bar | Displays the address of the active Web page. |
| Favorites bar | The toolbar located immediately above the left side of the browser window that can provide quick access to a favorite Web site. |
| Mouse pointer | Displays as a pointing hand when you point to a link (Link Select pointer). |
| Hyperlinks | When clicked, display other Web pages in this site, or other Web sites. Links can also take you to a document, email address, picture, or sound clip. |
| Scroll bar | Allows vertical or horizontal navigation of a Web page. |
| Status bar | Provides information about the security of a site and information about a link's destination as you point to a link. |
| Tabs | Allow multiple Web sites to be open at the same time. |

Figure 1.5

## Objective 2 | Navigate the Internet

Most Web pages contain links that you can use to navigate to other sites on the Internet. Internet Explorer 8 also provides commands that are accessible on the toolbars, a History list, and the Address bar, all of which you can use to navigate the Web. Internet Explorer 8 has tabs that enable you to have multiple Web sites open at the same time. In Activities 1.2 through 1.6, you will use each of these tools to access different Web sites.

### Activity 1.2 | Navigating the Internet

**1** Click the **Back** button to return to your home page, and then notice that the **Forward** button becomes available.

**2** On the **Address bar**, point to, but do not click, the **Forward** button, and then compare your screen with Figure 1.6.

A ScreenTip identifies the Web page that will display when you click the button. A *ScreenTip* is a small note that displays information about a screen element and is activated by pointing to a button or other screen object.

Figure 1.6

Back button
Forward button
ScreenTip
Home button
Refresh button
Stop button

**3** On the **Address bar**, click the **Forward** button 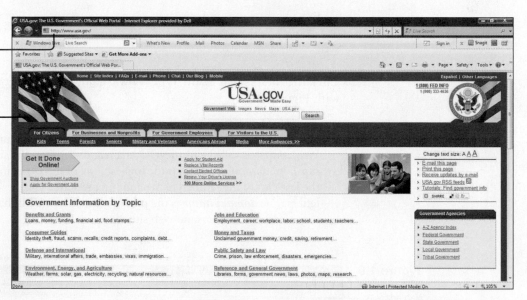 to redisplay the **Microsoft.com** home page.

**4** On the Command bar, click the **Home** button.

Regardless of how many Web pages you view or Web sites you visit, clicking the Home button returns you to the site that is set as the home page on the system at which you are working.

### Activity 1.3 | Accessing Web Sites from the Address Bar

**1** Near the top of the **Internet Explorer** window, click anywhere in the **Address bar**.

The existing Web address is highlighted indicating that it is selected.

**2** With the current Web address selected, type **www.usa.gov** Press Enter, and then compare your screen with Figure 1.7.

The USA.gov site's home page displays. When an existing Web address is selected, typing a new address replaces the selected text. As you type, a history list might display. Internet Explorer displays a list of all the sites you have accessed recently that begin with the characters you type. If you see the site you are typing in the history list, you can click the site name in the list rather than type the complete address.

**Figure 1.7**

Web site address in
Address bar

Home page of USA.gov
Web site (your screen will
likely differ)

**3** Take a moment to study the table in Figure 1.8 that describes how Web addresses are formed.

## Parts of the Web Address

| Parts of the Web Address | Description |
| --- | --- |
| http | The abbreviation of Hypertext Transfer Protocol—the standard *protocol* for retrieving Web sites. A protocol is a set of rules for transferring data over the Internet. Another protocol is *ftp*, or *File Transfer Protocol*. FTP is a protocol that enables individuals to copy files from one computer to another on a network. |
| :// | Three characters identified by Internet creators for separating the protocol from the rest of the Web address. These three characters were identified because they had never appeared together in computer programs and other computer-related contexts. |
| www.USA.gov | The domain name. In this case, the domain name includes the abbreviation for World Wide Web *(www)*, the name of the organization, and top-level domain—*.gov* stands for government. Not all domain names start with www, but many do. Other domain types include *.com* (commercial), *.edu* (education), *.org* (organization), *.net* (network), and *.mil* (military). Most countries have their own domain types such as *.ca* for Canada and *.fr* for France. |

Figure 1.8

**4** Click the **Address bar** again, type **www.bls.gov** and press Enter. Compare your screen with Figure 1.9.

> The U.S. Department of Labor, Bureau of Labor Statistics Web site displays. Because sites are regularly updated, your screen will likely not match Figure 1.9 exactly. The *.gov* in the Web address is called a top-level domain and identifies the site as a government site. A *top-level domain*, or *TLD*, is the highest level of the Domain Name System expressed as the last part of the domain name and is represented by a period followed by three or four letters. The *domain name* is the part of a text-based URL that identifies the company or organization that owns the Web site.

Figure 1.9

Web address

U.S. Department of Labor, Bureau of Labor Statistics Web site

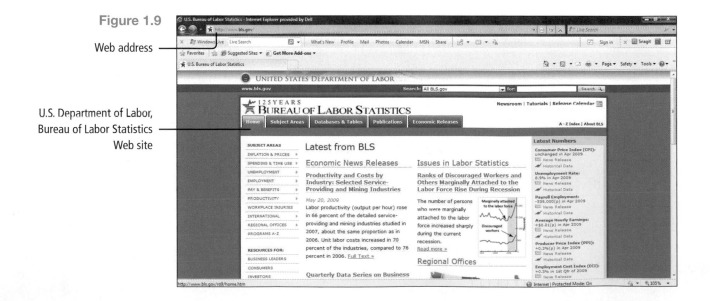

**5** At the right end of the **Address bar**, click the **Address bar down arrow** ⌄ and point to but do not click the **http://www.usa.gov** Web address. Compare your screen with Figure 1.10.

The list of recently accessed Web sites on your computer will differ from those shown in Figure 1.10. The sites listed represent those most frequently visited on your system.

Figure 1.10

Site to select

Address Bar down arrow

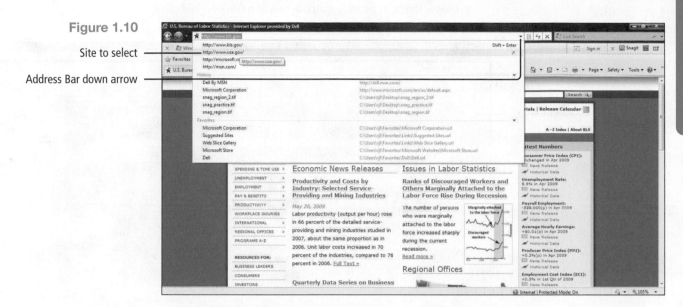

**6** In the displayed list, click the **http://www.usa.gov** Web address to display that Web site. Then, in the **Address bar**, type **www.ed.gov** and press Enter.

The U.S. Department of Education Web site displays.

**7** On the **Address bar**, locate the **Recent Pages button down arrow** ▼ to the right of the Forward button, and then click the arrow to display the most recently visited Web sites. Click the listing for the **USA.gov** Web site. Then, click the **Forward** button ⬅ to return to the **U.S. Department of Education** Web site. Compare your screen with Figure 1.11.

The U.S. Department of Education Web site displays, and the Forward button is unavailable because you have used it to return to this Web site.

Figure 1.11

Forward button (which is unavailable because you used it to get to this site)

Recent Pages button down arrow

**8** On the Favorites bar, if necessary, click the **Favorites Center** button  to display the task pane. Click **Microsoft Corporation**. Compare your screen with Figure 1.12.

> The *Favorites Center* enables you to view the Favorites, Feeds, and History lists. With Internet Explorer 8, you can add Web pages directly to the Favorites bar for easy access. The *Favorites bar* is the toolbar located immediately above the left side of the browser window that can provide quick access to a favorite Web site.

Figure 1.12

Web address ⎯

Favorites bar ⎯

**9** In the **Address bar**, click and type **www.psu.edu** and press [Enter]. Compare your screen with Figure 1.13.

> Internet Explorer displays the Penn State Web site. The top-level domain *.edu,* is the domain type reserved for colleges and universities.

Figure 1.13

## Activity 1.4 | Opening a Second Web Site

**1** Near the right of the **Welcome to Penn State's Home on the Web tab**, position your mouse pointer over the **New Tab** button , but do not click. Compare your screen with Figure 1.14.

A ScreenTip displays, indicating a new tab will be opened.

*Tabs* in Internet Explorer 8 enable you to have multiple Web pages open at the same time without having to open multiple instances of the browser.

Figure 1.14

New Tab

ScreenTip

**2** Click **New Tab** .

A new tab displays that enables you to view another Web site while keeping the Penn State Web site open.

**3** In the **Address bar**, type the URL for the Web site of your school, and then press Enter. Compare your screen with Figure 1.15.

Your school's Web site displays and the name of the Web page displays on the New Tab along with a Close Tab button.

Figure 1.15

Your school's Web site in a new tab

Close Tab button

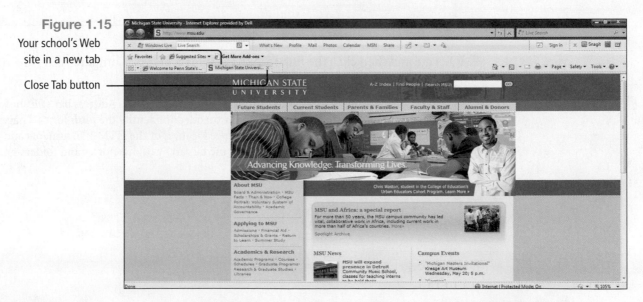

**4** Use the **Close Tab** button ⊠ to close the tab displaying your school's Web page.

**5** On the Command bar, click the **Home** button 🏠 to return to the home page that is set on your computer.

### Activity 1.5 | Displaying Web Pages with Hyperlinks

Most Web sites contain *hyperlinks,* which provide another navigation tool for browsing Web pages. Hyperlinks are text, buttons, pictures, or other objects displayed on Web pages that, when clicked, access other Web pages or display other sections of the active page. Linked Web pages can be pages within the same Web site or Web pages on sites of other companies, schools, or organizations. In this activity, you will use hyperlinks to display Web pages about college financial aid.

**1** In the **Address bar**, type **www.students.gov** and then press ⏎. Move the mouse pointer to various parts of the screen to locate areas where the **Link Select pointer** 🖑 displays, as shown in Figure 1.16.

Internet Explorer displays the students.gov home page. As you review Figure 1.16, notice that the mouse pointer displays as a pointing hand—the *Link Select pointer*—when you point to an item that links to another Web page. Web sites contain Web pages with links that connect to other pages on the site. These other pages contain links that lead to still other pages and also link back to the home page of the Web site.

Figure 1.16

Scholarships & grants link

Link Select pointer

**2** Locate and then click the link for **Scholarships & grants**. Compare your screen with Figure 1.17.

The Scholarships & grants page displays. The address in the Address bar still shows the *students.gov* Web site, but the URL has expanded to identify the *path* for this page. A path is the sequential description of the storage location of the HTML documents and files making up the Web page and stored in the hierarchy of directories and folders on the Web server.

**Figure 1.17**

Expanded URL path

students.gov Home link

Scholarships & grants page title

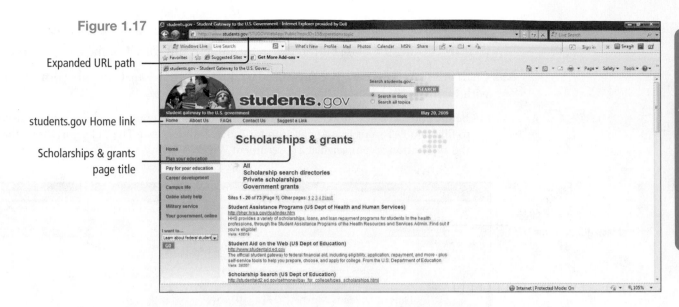

---

**Alert!** | **Is the Web page available?**

Because Web sites are updated frequently, the links on the Web sites also change. If the Scholarships & grants link on the *students.gov* Web site does not display, choose another link to follow.

---

**3** On the **Address bar**, click the **Back** button .

The *students.gov* home page displays.

**4** Scroll down as necessary to locate the link for **State financial aid** and click it. Compare your screen with Figure 1.18. Click on your state to try to find information about your state's financial aid. One or more links to information about financial aid in your state will display below the list of states. Click any one of these links.

Internet Explorer opens the individual state's financial aid links in a new window. Each Web page contains settings that control whether linked pages open in a separate window or in the same window. In addition, settings that are active on your computer control the linked page's display.

The new Web page opens in a separate window on top of the State financial aid window.

**Figure 1.18**

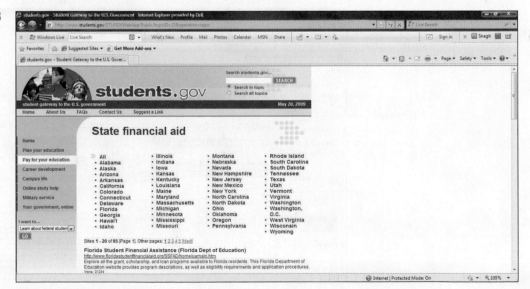

**5** When you are finished viewing the information, return to the State financial aid Web page by clicking the **Close** button ☒ in the upper right corner of the new window.

**6** Click in the **Address bar**, type **www.fafsa.ed.gov** and press Enter. Compare your screen with Figure 1.19.

> Before you can apply for financial aid such as scholarships, grants, or loans, you will need to fill out a FAFSA or Free Application for Federal Student Aid. The TLD, *.gov*, shows that the application is completed at a government Web site.

**Figure 1.19**

Web address showing *.gov* as the TLD ⎯

FAFSA Web site ⎯

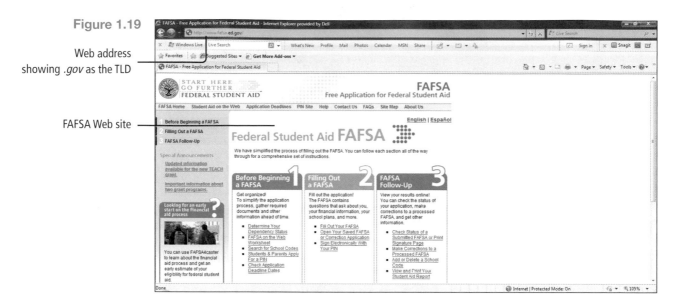

**7** At the top of the FAFSA Web page, locate and then click the link for **PIN Site**. Compare your screen with Figure 1.20. The PIN Federal Student Aid Web site displays in a new window. You can see that the new Web page opens in a separate window on top of the FAFSA window.

> Notice that the top-level domain name (*.gov*) in the Address bar shows that this is a government Web site. Both you and your parents can apply for a Federal Student Aid PIN at this site. Your PIN, or Personal Identification Number, serves as an electronic signature for your FAFSA.

**Figure 1.20**

PIN Web site ⎯

PIN Site link ⎯

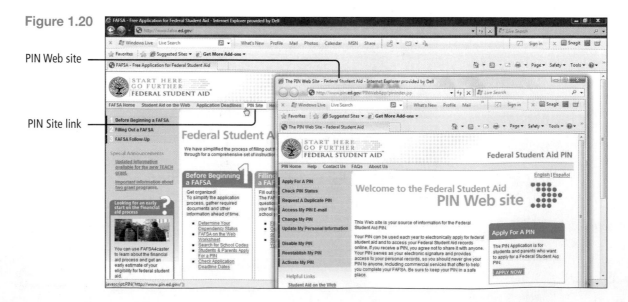

**8** On the displayed Web site's title bar, click the **Close** button ⊠ to close the new window. Then click the **Home** button 🏠 to return to your home page.

### Activity 1.6 | Using Internet Explorer 8 History

The Internet Explorer 8 *History* feature tracks recently visited Web sites. You can display the History list by using the Favorites Center button, and then clicking the History tab to view a site that you recently visited. You can view the History list by Date, Site, Most Visited, and by Order Visited Today. You can also use the Search History option to locate sites. In this activity, you will use the History list to display recently visited sites.

**1** On the Favorites bar, click the **Favorites** button ⭐ , and then if necessary, click the **History** tab. The History list displays on the left side of the Internet Explorer window. If necessary, click the down arrow to locate and click **View By Date**, and then click **Today**. Compare your screen with Figure 1.21.

The listings of items on your computer may differ from those shown in the figure. However, many of the listings shown for Today should be the same. Notice that the sites accessed today display in alphabetical order.

**Figure 1.21**

Favorites button —

Pages visited Today —

**2** In the **History** list, click **bls** (**www.bls.gov**), and then compare your screen with Figure 1.22.

The Web site name associated with the URL displays as a link below the URL. If you click the link, the Web site will open. This is another way to open a Web site. You can also locate and open a Web site by clicking the **View By Date down arrow** and choosing the Search History option. Then type keywords into the Search for box.

Figure 1.22

URL of a recently visited site

Associated Web site name

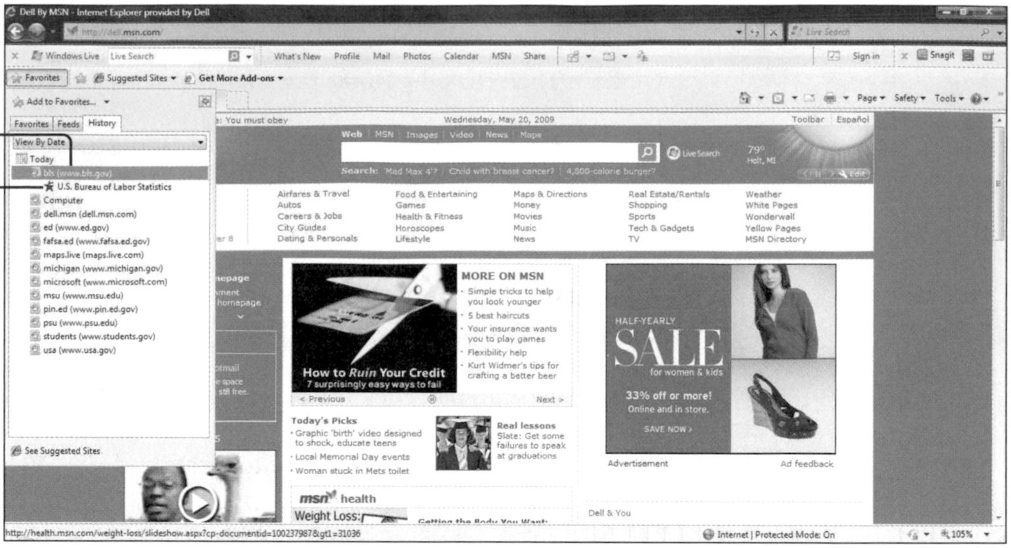

**3** Scroll down the **History** list as necessary, and then click **usa** (**www.usa.gov**) to display the associated Web site name for the USA.gov Web site. Click on the Web site name link to open the **USA.gov** Web site.

---

**More Knowledge | Setting History Options**

By default, Internet Explorer 8 tracks sites visited in the last 20 days. To reduce the amount of disk storage space required to maintain the History list, you can customize the settings to change the number of days tracked and to clear the list. You can change the options that control and clear the History list by setting Internet Options under the Tools command. You can choose to delete temporary files, history, cookies, saved passwords, and Web form information. You can also choose to set the amount of disk space to use.

---

## Objective 3 | Create and Manage Favorites

The History list automatically tracks sites that you visit each time you start Internet Explorer 8—many of which you may never visit again. The Favorites list works differently. The Favorites list contains Web addresses for sites you plan to visit frequently. You intentionally add addresses to the Favorites list and Internet Explorer 8 keeps the list for you. When you install Internet Explorer 8, a short list of Microsoft sites is added to the Favorites list. You can delete these addresses, add new addresses, and organize favorite site addresses into folders. For example, you may have a folder for Travel Sites, for College Sites, and so on. In Activities 1.7 through 1.9, you will add a new favorite, create a new folder, navigate to a site listed in the favorites, and delete a favorite.

### Activity 1.7 | Adding an Address to the Favorites List

In this activity, you will display a Web page and add it to the Favorites list, using the Add to Favorites button.

**1** In the **Address bar**, type **www.prenhall.com/go** and then press [Enter].

**2** On the Favorites bar, click the **Favorites** button [⭐], and the Favorites tab, if necessary. Then click **Add to Favorites** to display the **Add a Favorite** dialog box. Compare your screen with Figure 1.23.

The Add a Favorite dialog box displays with the title of the Web site indicated in the Name box.

Figure 1.23

Favorites button

Name of Web page

Add button

**3** In the **Add a Favorite** dialog box, click **Add.**

You can also add a shortcut to a favorite directly to the Favorites bar by clicking the Add to Favorites Bar button.

**4** On the Favorites bar, click the **Favorites** button ⭐. Click the **Favorites** tab, if necessary, to display the Favorites. Click the **Add to Favorites down arrow**, and then click **Organize Favorites**. Near the bottom of the **Organize Favorites** dialog box, click the **New Folder** button. In the new folder that was added to the list, type **Textbook Sites** and then press Enter.

The folder is created and displays in the listing of all folders and Web site favorites that is already established. When you have a number of sites that are related to a specific topic, you can create a new folder and use it to store related site addresses. The Organize Favorites dialog box displays a list of folders and links contained in the Favorites list and command buttons for creating folders, renaming folders and links, moving links to folders, and deleting folders and links from Favorites.

**5** In the **Organize Favorites** dialog box, click the **GO! Web page**, and then click the **Move** button. In the **Browse For Folder** dialog box, click the **Textbook Sites** folder, and then click **OK**. In the **Organize Favorites** dialog box, click the **Close** button ❌.

> **Another Way**
>
> To move a Web site after the folder is created, in the Organize Favorites dialog box, drag the Web site to the desired folder.

Internet Explorer 8 adds the GO! Web page address to the Textbook Sites folder in the Favorites list.

**6** Click the **Home** button 🏠 to display your home page.

## Activity 1.8 | Displaying a Favorite Web Site

In this activity, you will use the Favorites list to display a Web site.

**1** If necessary, on the Favorites bar, click the **Favorites** button ⭐. Click the **Favorites** tab, click the **Textbook Sites** folder, and then notice that the link to the GO! Web site displays, as shown in Figure 1.24.

Figure 1.24

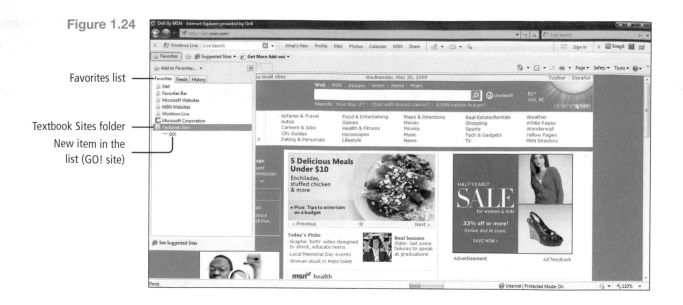

Favorites list

Textbook Sites folder

New item in the
list (GO! site)

**2** Click the link to the **GO! Web site.**

The GO! Web site displays.

## Activity 1.9 | Deleting a Web Address from Favorites

In this activity, you will remove an address from the Favorites list.

**1** On the Favorites bar, click the **Favorites** button ⭐, click the **Add to Favorites down arrow**, and then click **Organize Favorites**. Compare your screen with Figure 1.25.

Figure 1.25

List of folders and links
in the Favorites list

Command buttons

**2** In the **Organize Favorites** dialog box, scroll down if necessary and click the **Textbook Sites** folder to list its contents. Click the **GO! Web page** link one time to select it.

**3** In the **Organize Favorites** dialog box, click the **Delete** button, and then compare your screen with Figure 1.26.

Figure 1.26

Delete File dialog box

**4** In the **Delete File** dialog box, click **Yes**, and then in the **Organize Favorites** dialog box, click the **Close** button ⊠ .

> Internet Explorer 8 removes the GO! Web site from the Favorites list and closes the Organize Favorites dialog box.

**5** On the Command bar, click the **Home** button 🏠 to display your home page.

## Objective 4 | Search the Internet

When you know the name of an organization or the Web address you want to locate, accessing the site is easy and straightforward. When you want to locate information about topics from a variety of sources or find sites for businesses, journals, and other sources, it presents a greater challenge because of the large number of sites available on the Internet. There are several Web sites with search capabilities called *search engines*, programs that search for keywords in files and documents or other Web sites found on the Internet.

Internet Explorer 8 includes an Instant Search box that connects to a default search engine (such as Live Search or Bing) and easily allows you to add additional search engines. With Internet Explorer 8, Instant Search makes it easier to search for keywords within the text of the current Web page. In this activity, you will search the Internet for topics related to student financial aid.

### Activity 1.10 | Adding a Search Engine and Searching the Internet

**1** On right side of the **Address bar**, click the **Search down arrow**, and then click **Find More Providers**.

> The Add-ons Gallery: Search Providers Web page opens. It enables you to add additional search providers to Internet Explorer.

**2** In the **Add-ons Gallery: Search Providers** list, scroll down or go to page 2 to locate **Google Search Suggestions**. Then click the **Add to Internet Explorer button.** In the **Add Search Provider** dialog box, click the **Make this my default search provider** check box. Compare your screen with Figure 1.27.

**Figure 1.27**

Google added as a
search provider

Make Google the
default search provider

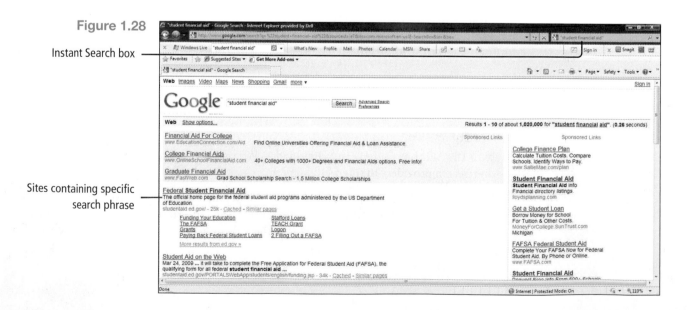

**3** Click the **Add** button.

Google now displays as the default search provider in the Instant Search box.

**4** On the **Address bar** in the **Instant Search** box, type **"student financial aid"** including the quotation marks, and then press Enter. Compare your screen with Figure 1.28.

You can begin a search by typing a single word, a phrase, a question, or a statement. You can easily change the size of the Instant Search textbox by dragging the edge. This makes it easier to see all of the characters in a long search string. Typing *student financial aid* without the quotation marks directs the search engine to look for three different terms. Placing the text in quotation marks ensures that the search engine looks for sites that contain the entire phrase. You can see that the number of sites found during this particular search that contain the phrase *"student financial aid"* is quite large. Internet Explorer 8 displays links to the Web sites in a ranked order based on the quality and quantity of the content at the Web sites it returns. Several factors are considered, such as how closely the site matches the search phrase, the number of references to the search text contained in the site, the number of other links to that site, and how recently the site has been updated.

**Figure 1.28**

Instant Search box

Sites containing specific
search phrase

**5** On the right side of the screen, under **Sponsored Links**, click the first link. Compare your screen with Figure 1.29.

> *Sponsored links* are sites that pay to be displayed with results on a search engine site. Sponsored links are frequently placed near the top or on the right side of the search engine results page so they are easily seen and clicked. Sponsored links generally are commercial sites, so they stand to gain from increasing traffic to their Web site. The top-level domain is *.com* for commercial sites.

**Figure 1.29**

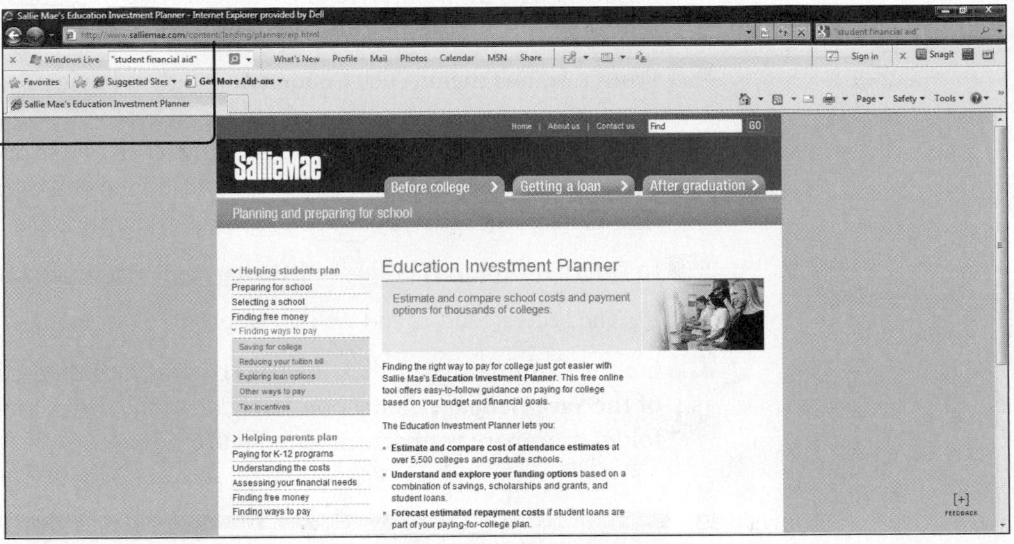

Web address of first sponsored site (yours will vary)

**6** Click the **Back** button to return to your search results. Scroll as necessary, and then locate and click the link for **Federal Student Financial Aid**.

> The home page for student aid programs administered by the U.S. Department of Education displays. If you are interested in this information, you can print it or put it on your Favorites list to examine at a later time. Financial aid information found at a sponsored Web site (*.com*) is likely to be a loan opportunity, whereas a government financial aid Web site (*.gov*) is more likely to offer information on grant and scholarship opportunities.

**7** On the Command bar, click the **Home** button to display your home page.

## Objective 5 | Save and Print Web Pages

Saving a copy of a Web page on your system or storage device is referred to as *downloading*. Downloading means that you request a copy of a file or program from a remote server, such as a Web server, and save it on your local system or storage device. You can also download other types of Web files, such as graphics, and save them on your computer or disk so that you can review them later. When you download a Web page displayed in Internet Explorer 8, Internet Explorer 8 creates a new folder at the location you indicate to save all associated graphics, pictures, and other features of the Web page so that when you view the file offline, it resembles the entire page as it was displayed on the Web. Other techniques for accessing Web pages include setting a desktop shortcut to the Web page and sending a link to a Web page to someone through email. Setting a desktop shortcut creates an icon on your desktop for the Web page so that it opens very quickly. Both techniques are accomplished from the Page button on the Command bar.

Because of the widespread threat of system viruses, as a general precaution, avoid downloading or saving files from unknown Web sites, and be sure your virus protection program is up-to-date before downloading Web files on your system. You must also be careful not to violate copyright-protected Web materials.

### Activity 1.11 | Downloading and Saving a Web Page

In this activity, you will download and save a Web page.

**1** Determine where you will be storing your files for this chapter, for example, on your own disk or USB flash drive or on a network drive, and be sure that storage location is available. If necessary, check with your instructor or lab coordinator.

**2** From the **Start** menu, click **Computer**, and then navigate to the drive—USB flash drive, computer hard drive, or network drive—where you will be storing your files. In the right pane of the **Computer** window, right-click an empty space. In the context-sensitive menu that displays, click **New**, and then roll over and click **Folder.** With **New Folder** selected, type **IE8 Chapter** and then press Enter. **Close** ☒ the window.

**3** In **Internet Explorer**, in the **Address bar**, type **studentaid.ed.gov** and then press Enter.

The Federal Student Aid Web site displays.

**4** On the Command bar, click the **Page** button, and then click **Save As**. In the left pane of the **Save Webpage** dialog box, navigate to the drive, and then to your **IE8 Chapter** folder. Compare your screen with Figure 1.30.

Figure 1.30

Selected storage location (yours may vary)

Default file name

Default file type

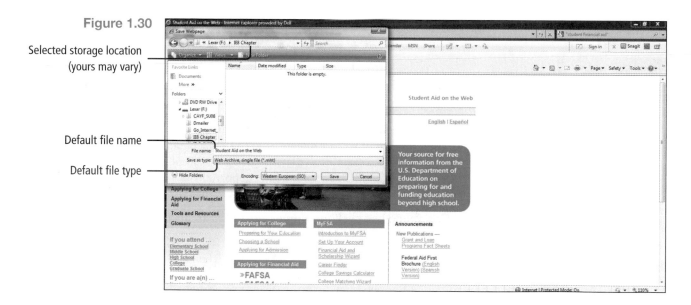

**5** At the bottom of the **Save Webpage** dialog box, click the **Save as type arrow** and if necessary, click **Web Archive, single file (*.mht)**. Click in the **File name** box to select the existing text, and then replace the selected text by typing **Lastname_Firstname_1A_ College_Money** substituting your own names for Lastname and Firstname, and instead of spaces between words, use the underscore key, which is Shift + - . Then, in the lower right corner, click the **Save** button.

An *MHTML* file— which has a file extension of *.mht*—is a format used to save Web pages into a single archive, including all the page elements such as text and graphics.

**6** Click the **Home** button 🏠. In the **Address bar**, type the drive, such as **f:\** or the location where you saved the file, and the most recent files in that location will display. Compare your screen with Figure 1.31.

**Figure 1.31**

Location in Address bar

Files recently saved to the drive and directory

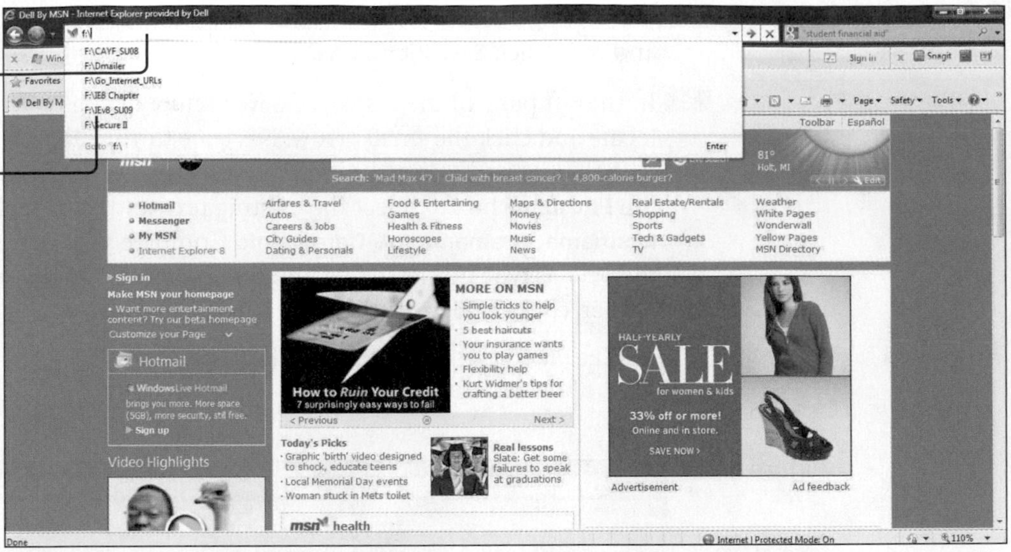

**7** Scroll down as necessary, and click the **IE8 Chapter folder**. In the **Computer** window, if necessary, double-click the IE8 Chapter folder. Then double-click the **Lastname_Firstname_1A_College_Money** MHTML document.

> The Web page opens in a new tab. Notice the Address bar shows the Web page address as the location where you saved the Web page as a MHTML file. If you were looking at the actual Web page, the Address bar would display the URL as *http://studentaid.ed.gov/PORTALSWebApp/students/english/index.jsp*.

> Even though a Web page may look as if it is one single file, it is actually made up of several objects and files. Each graphic is its own file and the text content is another file. In addition, the Web page may be divided into *frames*. Frames are used to divide a Web page into separate panes that still display as one complete Web page. Navigation is controlled by one of the panes while viewing several different pages of content displayed within a single browser window. The MHTML format saves all of the objects, files, and frames together as one Web archive for viewing offline.

**8** **Close** ⊠ the new tab displaying the Federal Student Aid MHTML file.

**9** If necessary, on the Command bar, click the **Home** button 🏠 to display your home page.

---

**More Knowledge | Downloading New Programs**

Downloading, as you used it in Activity 1.11, saves a Web page and associated files in the folder you specify. You can also download entire software programs and other items from the Internet. For example, if you display the Microsoft.com Web site, you can download free trial programs, install them on your system, and try them before you purchase them. When sites offer free downloads, a **Download** link usually displays on the page. When you click the link, Internet Explorer 8 prompts you to save the file on your system. The prompt message also provides an option to open or run the program from the server.

   It is generally recommended that you download and save the file on your system before trying to install it. After it is saved to your system, run the program file through your virus protection software before installing the new program. A good rule to follow is to be careful what you download, and download only from well-known and trusted sites.

---

## Activity 1.12 | Downloading and Saving Graphics from a Web Page

**1** In the **Address bar**, type **www.bls.gov** and then press Enter. On the **Bureau of Labor Statistics Web site home page**, scroll toward the bottom of the page, and then locate and click the **Career Information for Kids** link. Point anywhere in the displayed picture, right-click the mouse button to display a context-sensitive shortcut menu, and then click **Save Picture As**.

**2** In the left pane of the displayed **Save Picture** dialog box, to the left of **Computer**, locate and click the small arrow. Navigate to your **IE8 Chapter** folder and double-click it so that its name displays in the **Save in** box. At the bottom of the dialog box, click in the **File name** box to select the existing text, and then replace it by typing **Lastname_Firstname_1A_Career_Info** Compare your screen with Figure 1.32. Leave the **Save as type** box as the default type—JPEG (*.jpg)—and then in the lower right corner, click the **Save** button.

> The file is saved as a JPEG file. The Save Picture dialog box closes and you are returned to the browser window.

Figure 1.32

Save in box

File name box

Save as type box

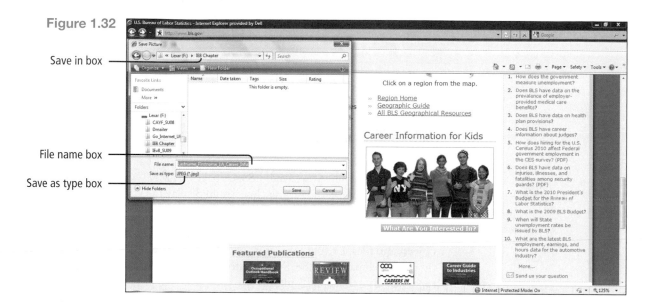

**3** On the Command bar, click the **Home** button to display your home page.

## Activity 1.13 | Printing Web Pages

Web pages are constructed to contain a variety of different elements—pictures, navigation panes, links, text, and so on. When you print Web pages, all the elements displayed on the Web page print unless you select the specific text, picture, or frame you want to print. Most of the options contained in the Print dialog box in Internet Explorer 8 are the same as those seen in the Print dialog box for other programs. However, the Print dialog box in Internet Explorer 8 contains options that enable you to print pages, frames within a Web page, or a table of pages that are linked to the active Web page.

Because frames and objects are placed so closely together on the Web page, selecting just the information you want to print can be a challenge without activating a hyperlink or selecting additional information as well. In this activity, you will review options in the Print dialog box and print a Web page.

**1** From the **Start** menu, click **Computer**, and then navigate to the drive—USB flash drive, computer hard drive, or network drive—where you stored your files for this chapter. Locate and then double-click your MHTML file **Lastname_Firstname_1A_College_Money**. Compare your screen with Figure 1.33.

**Figure 1.33**

The Web site has been opened from a storage location

**2** On the Command bar, click the **Print button down arrow** [icon], and then click **Page Setup** to display the Page Setup dialog box. Locate the three **Header: down arrows** and click **Empty** for each. Locate the section labeled **Footer**: Using the first down arrow, click **URL**. Using the second down arrow, click **Title.** In the third down arrow, click **Date in Short Format.** Compare your screen with Figure 1.34.

**Figure 1.34**

Page Setup dialog box

Footer section

Header section

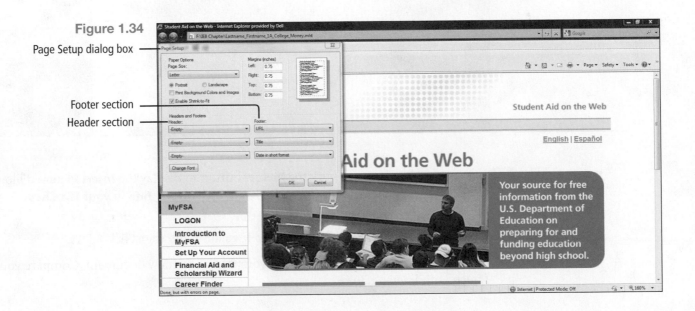

**3** In the **Page Setup** dialog box, click **OK**. On the Command bar, click the **Print button down arrow** [icon], click **Print**, and then at the bottom of the displayed **Print** dialog box, click the **Print** button.

> The saved Web page print. It is likely that two or more pages will print. At the bottom of each page, the footer you created displays.

**4** On the Command bar, click the **Home** button [icon] to display your home page. Submit it as directed by your instructor.

## Activity 1.14 | Printing Web Graphics

When you print a Web page, you print all of the elements that make up that Web page, both the graphics and text. It is possible to print only the graphics that are part of the Web page. In this activity you will create a document with a graphic that you have saved from a Web page and print the document.

**1** From the **Start** menu, point to **All Programs**, click **Microsoft Office**, and then click **Microsoft Office Word 2007**.

> Microsoft Office Word, a word processing program, will open a new document. You will add text and graphics to this new document.

**2** In the new **Word** document, type **Lastname_Firstname_1A_Career_Info** and then press [Enter]. On the **Insert tab**, in the **Illustrations group**, point to **Picture** (but do not click). Compare your screen with Figure 1.35.

Figure 1.35

Insert tab

Picture button

Text that has been added

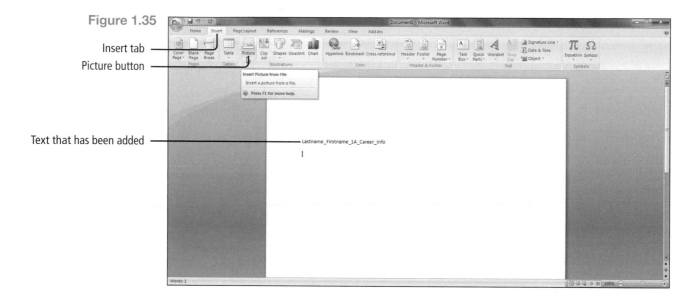

**3** In the **Illustrations group**, click the **Picture** button to display the **Insert Picture** dialog box. Navigate to the file **Lastname_Firstname_1A_Career_Info** in your **IE8 Chapter** folder. This graphic was downloaded in Activity 1.12.

**4** In the **Insert Picture** dialog box, click the file name, and then click **Insert**.

**5** The Web graphic displays underneath your text in the new document. Compare your screen with Figure 1.36.

**Figure 1.36**

Internet Explorer 8 | Chapter 1

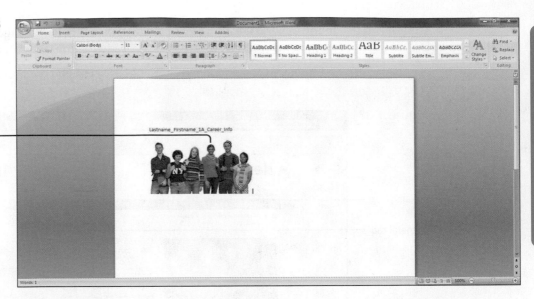

Web graphic that has been inserted

**6** From the **Office** button , click **Save As** and then navigate to your **IE8 Chapter** folder so that its name displays in the **Save in** box. At the bottom of the dialog box, click in the **File name** box to select the existing text, and then replace it by typing **Lastname_Firstname_1A_Career_Info** Leave the **Save as type** box as the default type, and then in the lower right corner, click the **Save** button.

> **More Knowledge | Be Aware of Copyright Issues**
>
> Almost everything you find on the Web is protected by copyright law, which protects authors of original works, including text, art, photographs, and music. If you want to use text or graphics that you find online, you will need to get permission. One of the exceptions to this law is the use of small amounts of information for educational purposes, which falls under Fair Use Guidelines. Another exception is to use work that is considered in the *public domain*. These works are created with the intention of letting anyone use them for any reason; also a work becomes public domain when the copyright has expired.
>
> Copyright laws in the United States are open to different interpretations, and copyright laws can be very different in other countries. As a general rule, if you want to use someone else's material, get permission first.

**7** From the **Office** button , click **Print**, and then at the bottom of the displayed **Print** dialog box, click the **OK** button. Submit as directed by your instructor.

The document containing the saved Web graphic prints.

**8** **Close** Word to return to the **Internet Explorer** window.

## Activity 1.15 | Printing Selected Text from Web Pages

**1** In the **Address bar**, type **www.denverpost.com** and press Enter.

The Denver Post Web site displays current information and news items.

**2** On the Web page, drag your mouse over the first paragraph under the article heading in the left column to select it.

The paragraph will display as light text on a dark background.

**3** On the Command bar, click the **Print button down arrow** , and then click **Print** to display the **Print** dialog box.

**4** On the **General tab** of the **Print** dialog box, under **Page Range,** click the **Selection** option. Compare your screen with Figure 1.37. After comparing your screen, click **Print**.

Internet Explorer 8 prints only the selected text and not the entire Web page.

Figure 1.37

Print dialog box ────

General tab ────

Page Range area ────

Selection option ────

**5** On the Internet Explorer title bar, click the program's **Close** button ⊠ .

**End** **You have completed Project 1A** ───────────────

## Summary

In this project, you explored basic Internet Explorer 8 features such as starting the browser, navigating among Web pages, and working with Favorites. You learned how to search for Web sites containing information about topics you specify and how to download and save Web pages and graphics. You learned how to print a Web page, a graphic saved from a Web page, and selected text on a Web page.

## Key Terms

## Matching

Match each term in the second column with its correct definition in the first column. Write the letter of the term on the blank line in front of the correct definition.

_____ 1. A protocol that enables individuals to copy files from one computer to another on a network.

_____ 2. A Microsoft software program that enables you to view the contents of the World Wide Web.

_____ 3. A company that provides an Internet connection through a regular telephone line, a special high-speed telephone line, or a cable.

_____ 4. Software that enables you to use the World Wide Web and navigate from page to page and site to site.

_____ 5. The unique address used to locate a Web page or Web site.

_____ 6. A small note that displays information about a screen element and is activated by pointing to a button or other screen object.

_____ 7. An Internet Explorer 8 feature that enables you to view the Favorites, Feeds, and History lists.

_____ 8. The toolbar located immediately above the right side of the browser window that can provide quick access to commands such as Home, Page, Safety, and Tools.

_____ 9. A browser feature that enables you to have multiple Web pages open at the same time without having to open multiple browsers.

_____ 10. The sequential description of the storage location of the HTML documents and files making up the Web page and stored in the hierarchy of directories and folders on the Web server.

**A** Command bar

**B** Downloading

**C** Favorites Center

**D** File Transfer Protocol (FTP)

**E** History

**F** Internet Explorer 8

**G** Internet Service Provider (ISP)

**H** MHTML

**I** Path

**J** ScreenTip

**K** Sponsored link

**L** Tabs

**M** Uniform Resource Locator (URL)

**N** Web browser

**O** Web page

_____ 11. An Internet Explorer 8 feature that tracks recently visited Web pages and sites.

_____ 12. A site that pays to be displayed with results at a search engine site.

_____ 13. To request a copy of a file or program from a remote server, such as a Web server, and then to save it on your local system or storage device.

_____ 14. A format used to save Web pages into a single archive, including all the page elements such as text and graphics.

_____ 15. A document on the World Wide Web that displays as a screen with associated links, frames, pictures, and other features of interest.

## Multiple Choice

Circle the correct response.

1. The part of a text-based URL that identifies the company or organization that owns the Web site is called a:
   a. Top-level domain       b. Public domain       c. Domain name

2. The Web page that displays when you start Internet Explorer 8 is called a:
   a. Portal                 b. Home page           c. Sponsored link

3. A group of related Web pages published to a specific location on the World Wide Web is called a:
   a. Favorites bar          b. Home page           c. Web site

4. A home page that contain links to frequently visited sites, up-to-the-minute news, weather reports, maps, and directories is called a:
   a. Portal                 b. Favorites Center    c. Public domain

5. The highest level of the Domain Name System expressed as the last part of the domain name and represented by a period followed by three or four letters is called the:
   a. FTP                    b. TLD                 c. ISP

6. The toolbar located above the left side of the browser window that provides immediate access to a favorite Web site is called the:
   a. History                b. Command bar         c. Favorites bar

7. Text, buttons, pictures, or other objects displayed on Web pages that, when clicked, access other Web pages or display other sections of the active page are called:
   a. Hyperlinks             b. Link Select pointers  c. ScreenTips

8. The method used to divide a Web page into separate panes that appear to be one complete Web page is called:
   a. Tabs                   b. Portals             c. Frames

9. A program that searches for keywords in files and documents or other Web sites found on the Internet is called a:
   a. Search engine          b. Portal              c. File Transfer Protocol

10. The set of rules for transferring data over the Internet is called a:
    a. Path                  b. Protocol            c. Public domain

# Content-Based Assessments

Apply **1A** skills from these Objectives:

1. Start Internet Explorer 8 and Identify Screen Elements
2. Navigate the Internet
3. Create and Manage Favorites
4. Search the Internet
5. Save and Print Web Pages

## Skills Review | Project **1B** Playing Music from a Favorite Link

In the following Skills Review project, you will open a Web site, save it in Favorites, and locate and listen to a radio station that is near Lake Michigan City College. You can use the radio tuner to locate radio stations in your area and, if you have a sound card, you can listen to the radio as you work. Your screen will look similar to Figure 1.38.

### Project Files

For Project 1B, you will save your file as:

Lastname_Firstname_1B_Radio

### Project Results

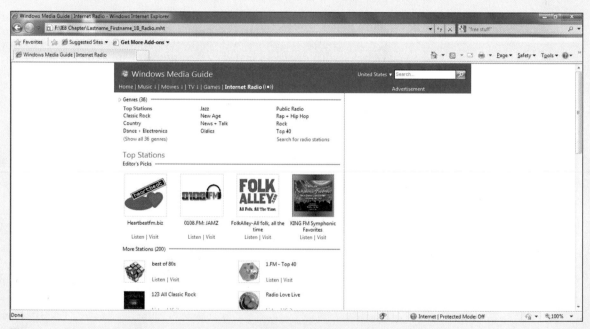

**Figure 1.38**

(Project 1B Playing Music from a Favorite Link continues on the next page)

# Content-Based Assessments

## Skills Review | Project **1B** Playing Music from a Favorite Link (continued)

**1** On the Windows taskbar, click the **Start** button, and then locate **Internet Explorer 8** on your system. On your system, click **Internet Explorer**. In the **Address bar**, type http://windowsmedia.com/radiotuner Press Enter.

**2** On the Favorites bar, click the **Favorites** button, and if necessary, click the Favorites tab. Then click **Add to Favorites** to display the **Add a Favorite** dialog box.

**3** In the **Add a Favorite** dialog box, change the name to **Radio Station Guide** and then click the **Add** button.

Each category under Genres can be clicked to display additional stations. You can use links to visit a radio station or listen to the station. You can locate more stations by looking in the More Stations section or by using the Search box.

**4** In the **Top Stations** list, click the first station to open the Windows Media Player.

**5** In the Windows Media Player that displays, notice the buttons to pause the music and to close the Windows Media Player when you are finished listening.

The Windows Media Player opens and the station plays. This may take a few seconds as the streaming process occurs. Depending on the active settings on your system, Internet Explorer 8 may present a message box asking if you want to play the station in Internet Explorer. If you are prompted, click Yes to play the station.

**6** On the Command bar, click **Page** and then click **Save As** to display the **Save Webpage** dialog box. In the **File name** box, type **Lastname_Firstname_1B_Radio** Change the **Save as type** to **Web Archive, single file (\*.mht)**. In the **Save in** box, navigate to the **IE8 Chapter** folder that you created earlier in this chapter.

**7** In the **Save Webpage** dialog box, click **Save**.

**8** In the **Address bar**, type the drive—for example **f:\**— and the location where you saved the file, and the most recent files in that location will display. Scroll down as necessary, and click the file name that you saved in Step 6.

**9** On the Command bar, click the **Print down arrow** to open the **Print** dialog box. Click the **Print** button to print the saved Web page. Submit it as directed by your instructor.

**10** In the **Windows Media Player** window, click the **Stop** button to stop the live broadcast, and then click the Media Player's **Close** button to close the pane.

**11** Click the **Close** button to close Internet Explorer.

**End** You have completed Project 1B

# Content-Based Assessments

Apply **1A** skills from these Objectives:

1. Start Internet Explorer 8 and Identify Screen Elements
2. Navigate the Internet
5. Save and Print Web Pages

## Skills Review | Project **1C** Searching for Multimedia

In the following Skills Review, you will search for free downloads of multimedia for your music appreciation class at Lake Michigan City College.

The Internet provides opportunities to locate and download several types of multimedia, such as animated graphics and sound or video files. However, the ease with which it is possible to copy these files does not always make it legally acceptable. The Fair Use Guidelines for Educational Multimedia allow for the use of copyrighted materials for educational purposes under certain circumstances. These circumstances address the purpose of use and the quantity of materials to be used. In addition, consideration must be given to whether the work has been put into the public domain, and there must be no effect on any potential market. Follow these instructions to perform a search for copyright-free sound files. Your screen will look similar to Figure 1.39.

## Project Files

For Project 1C, you will save your file as:

Lastname_Firstname_1C_Multimedia

## Project Results

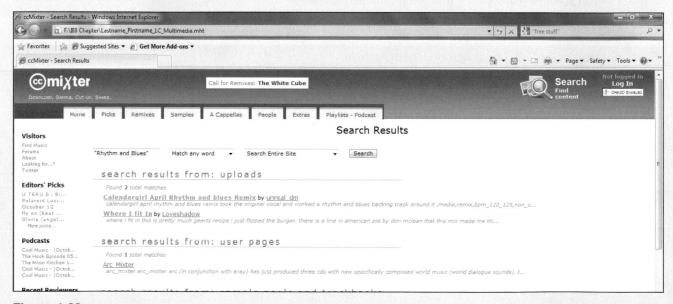

**Figure 1.39**

(Project 1C Searching for Multimedia continues on the next page)

# Content-Based Assessments

## Skills Review | Project **1C** Searching for Multimedia (continued)

**1** On the Windows taskbar, click the **Start** button, and then locate **Internet Explorer 8** on your Start menu. On your system, click **Internet Explorer**.

**2** In the **Address bar**, type **ccmixter.org** and then press Enter.

The ccMixter Web site displays. This site offers copyright-free and royalty-free sound files that are available for listening, downloading, remixing, and sharing through a Creative Commons license.

**3** In the upper right corner, click the **Search Find Content** link.

**4** In the **SearchFind content** pop-up that displays, in the **Search Text** box, type **"Rhythm and Blues"** including the quotation marks. Leave the default Match and What choices selected. Click the **Search** button.

**5** On the Command bar, click **Page** and then click **Save As** to display the **Save Webpage** dialog box. In the

**File name** box, type **Lastname_Firstname_1C_Multimedia** Change the **Save as type** to **Web Archive, single file (*.mht)**. In the **Save in** box, navigate to the **IE8 Chapter** folder that you created earlier in this chapter.

**6** In the **Save Webpage** dialog box, click **Save**.

**7** In the **Address bar**, type the drive—for example **f:\**—and the location where you saved the file, and the most recent files in that location will display. Scroll down as necessary, and click the file name that you saved in Step 5.

**8** On the Command bar, click **Print down arrow** to open the **Print** dialog box. Click the **Print** button to print the saved Web page. Submit it as directed by your instructor. **Close** Internet Explorer.

 **You have completed Project 1C** ——————————

# Content-Based Assessments

1 Start Internet Explorer 8 and Identify Screen Elements

4 Search the Internet

5 Save and Print Web Pages

## Mastering | Project **1D** Searching for Picture Space

In this project, you will search for free photographic services for the Alumni Club at Lake Michigan City College. The festivities on Homecoming Weekend were a great success and brought in alumni from around the state. Many sites on the Internet offer free space for storing and sharing pictures. From these sites, friends and family can view pictures and order copies of those pictures they want to keep. You can locate these services by searching the Internet. Follow these steps to locate and explore sites to determine which one best meets your needs. Your screens will look similar to Figure 1.40.

### Project Files

For Project 1D, you will save your files as:

Lastname_Firstname_1D_Photo_1
Lastname_Firstname_1D_Photo_2

### Project Results

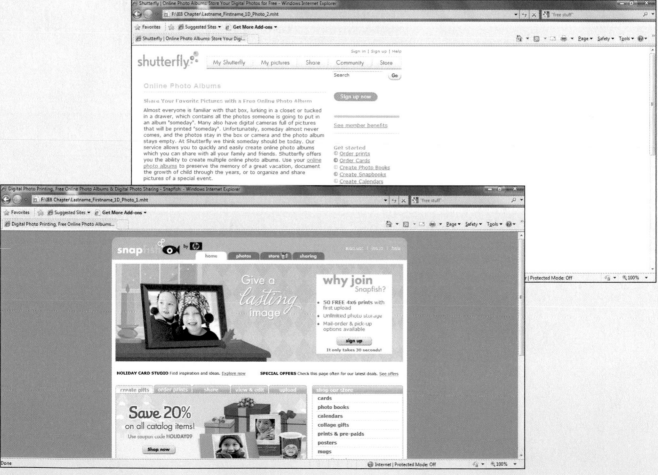

Figure 1.40

(Project 1D Searching for Picture Space continues on the next page)

# Content-Based Assessments

## Mastering | Project **1D** Searching for Picture Space (continued)

**1** Open **Internet Explorer 8**.

**2** On the **Address bar**, in the **Search** box, type **"free online photo albums"** and then press Enter. Several Web sites that offer free photographic services, such as storage and online photo albums, display.

**3** In the list of **Web Results**, click the first link to display a Web site providing a free online photo album that is not a sponsored site. Scroll down the Web page until you locate information about how that online photo album works.

**4** On the Command bar, click the **Page** button, and then click **Save As** to display the **Save Webpage** dialog box. In the **File name** box, type **Lastname_Firstname_1D_Photo_1** Change the **Save as type** to **Web Archive, single file (*.mht)**, and then in the **Save in** box, navigate to the **IE8 Chapter** folder that you created earlier in the chapter.

**5** In the **Save Webpage** dialog box, click **Save**. Click the **Back** button to return to the search results.

**6** Click another link in the list of Web Results to display another Web site providing a free online photo album. Scroll down that Web page until you locate information about how that online photo album works.

**7** On the Command bar, click the **Page** button, and then click **Save As** to display the **Save Webpage** dialog box. In the **File name** box, type **Lastname_Firstname_1D_Photo_2** Change the **Save as type** to **Web Archive, single file (*.mht)**, and then in the **Save in** box, navigate to the **IE8 Chapter** folder that you created earlier in the chapter.

**8** In the **Save Webpage** dialog box, click **Save**.

**9** Use the **Address bar** to open each of the two saved files and then on the Command bar, click the **Print** button to print each of the saved files. Submit them as directed by your instructor.

**10** **Close** Internet Explorer.

 **You have completed Project 1D** ——————————

# Content-Based Assessments

Apply **1A** skills from these Objectives:

■1 Start Internet Explorer 8 and Identify Screen Elements

■3 Create and Manage Favorites

■4 Search the Internet

■5 Save and Print Web Pages

## Mastering | Project **1E** Locating Free Items

In the following project, you will search for free coupons, offers, and programs available on the Internet as marketing giveaway items for a club at Lake Michigan City College. As you become more familiar with the Internet, you will find free items such as software programs, computer equipment, computer services, and so on—available from Web sites. Not all of these offers are legitimate. Search the Internet for free items and review some of the offers. As you explore and evaluate the sites, remember that you should download programs and information only from sites you know and trust. Determine which sites make legitimate offers and which do not. Several criteria will help you with this determination. The following set of questions will be helpful as you perform an evaluation of a Web site:

- Is the site attractive and professional looking?

- When was the last time that the Web site was updated? Are there broken links or misspelled words?

- Who owns or sponsors the site? Do they seem qualified to make this type of offer?

- Are you required to provide personal data such as name, location, age, or credit or financial information in order to receive "free" items?

Your screens will look similar to Figure 1.41.

### Project Files

For Project 1E, you will save your files as:

    Lastname_Firstname_1E_Free_1
    Lastname_Firstname_1E_Free_2

### Project Results

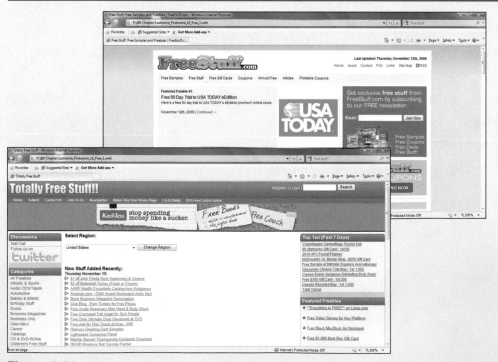

**Figure 1.41**

(Project 1E Locating Free Items continues on the next page)

# Content-Based Assessments

## Mastering | Project **1E** Locating Free Items (continued)

**1** Open **Internet Explorer 8**.

**2** On the Address bar, in the **Search** box, type **"free stuff"** and then press Enter.

**3** In the list of **Web Results**, click on the first link to display a Web site providing free stuff that is not a sponsored site. Scroll down the Web page until you locate the answers to the set of questions in the previous list to help you determine the legitimacy of the free offers.

**4** On the Favorites bar, click the **Favorites** button, and then click **Add to Favorites** to open the **Add a Favorite** dialog box.

**5** In the **Add a Favorite** dialog box, click the **New Folder** button. In the **Folder Name** box, type **Free Stuff** Click **Create**, and then click **Add** to add the Web site to the folder. A new folder named Free Stuff displays in the list of Favorites and the current Web site has been added to it.

**6** On the Command bar, click the **Page** button, and then click **Save As** to display the **Save Webpage** dialog box. In the **File name** box, type **Lastname_Firstname_1E_Free_1** If necessary, change the Save as type to Web Archive, single file (*.mht), and then navigate to the **IE8 Chapter** folder that you created earlier in the chapter. Click **Save**.

**7** Use the **Address bar** to open the saved file and then on the Command bar, use the **Print** button to print the saved file. Submit it as directed by your instructor.

**8** On the **Address bar**, click **Back** to return to the Web Results. Scroll down the list to choose another Web site offering free stuff. Click the link to that Web site and answer the same set of questions to determine the legitimacy of the free offers.

**9** On the Favorites bar, click the **Favorites** button, and then if necessary, click Add to Favorites to display the Add a Favorite dialog box. Be sure the **Free Stuff** folder is displayed in the **Create in** box, and then click the **Add** button.

**10** On the Command bar, click the **Page** button, and then click **Save As** to display the **Save Webpage** dialog box. In the **File name** box, type **Lastname_Firstname_1E_Free_2** If necessary, change the Save as type to Web Archive, single file (*.mht), and then navigate to the **IE8 Chapter** folder that you created earlier in the chapter. Click **Save**.

**11** Use the **Address bar** to open the saved file and then on the Command bar, use the **Print** button to print the saved file. Submit it as directed by your instructor.

**12** On the Favorites bar, click the **Favorites** button if necessary, scroll down, and then click on the **Free Stuff** folder to display the two Web sites that you added to the folder.

**13** Click anywhere outside the **Favorites** list to close it. **Close** Internet Explorer.

**End** You have completed Project 1E

# Content-Based Assessments

## Mastering | Project 1F Protecting Your Privacy

In this project, you will search the Internet for information about yourself or other members of your family as part of your sociology project at Lake Michigan City College. The World Wide Web stores information about individuals in addition to companies. Many businesses store data about their clients and customers in databases on the Web so that they can place orders online. Families often store family trees on Web sites so that others can track their family history. Search the Internet for information about yourself to see what information is stored about you and others with your name. You might prefer to search for information about your family name to see if family tree data is available. The World Wide Web provides a means to easily gather personal information about you and your family. One of the best ways to learn about protecting your family and yourself is to look at the privacy policies of Web sites that you visit. Locate and review the privacy policy at any Web site you find that contains information about you or your family. Answer these questions:

- How does the Web site collect information about you?
- How is the information used?
- Are there options for you to prevent the collection and sharing of your personal data?

Your screen will look similar to Figure 1.42.

### Project Files

For Project 1F, you will save your file as:

Lastname_Firstname_1F_Privacy

### Project Results

**Figure 1.42**

(Project 1F Protecting Your Privacy continues on the next page)

# Content-Based Assessments

## Mastering | Project **1F** Protecting Your Privacy (continued)

**1** Open **Internet Explorer 8**.

**2** In the **Address bar**, type **www.whitepages.com** and then press Enter to display the **WhitePages** home page.

**3** Under **Find People**, type your first name, last name, your city, and your state in the appropriate boxes. Click the **Find** button. A number of results are displayed. Take a moment to review them.

**4** Scroll down to the bottom of the results page. Click the **Privacy** link. Read the privacy policy to determine the answers to the questions listed at the beginning of this project.

**5** On the Command bar, click the **Page** button, and then click **Save As** to display the **Save Webpage** dialog box. In the **File name** box, type **Lastname_Firstname_1F_Privacy** If necessary, change the Save as type to Web Archive, single file (*.mht), and then navigate to the **IE8 Chapter** folder that you created earlier in the chapter. Click **Save**.

**6** Use the **Address bar** to open the saved file and then on the Command bar, use the **Print** button to print the saved file. Submit it as directed by your instructor.

**7** **Close** Internet Explorer.

 **You have completed Project 1F** ————————————————————

# Outcomes-Based Assessments

## Rubric

The following Outcomes-Based Assessment is an open-ended assessment. That is, there is no specific correct result; your result will depend on your approach to the information provided. Make Professional Quality your goal. Use the following scoring rubric to guide you in how to approach the problem and then to evaluate how well your approach solves the problem.

The *criteria*—Software Mastery, Content, Format and Layout, and Process—represent the knowledge and skills you have gained that you can apply to solving the problem. The *levels of performance*—Professional Quality, Approaching Professional Quality, or Needs Quality Improvements—help you and your instructor evaluate your result.

| | Your completed project is of Professional Quality if you: | Your completed project is Approaching Professional Quality if you: | Your completed project Needs Quality Improvements if you: |
|---|---|---|---|
| 1-Software Mastery | Choose and apply the most appropriate skills, tools, and features and identify efficient methods to solve the problem. | Choose and apply some appropriate skills, tools, and features, but not in the most efficient manner. | Choose inappropriate skills, tools, or features, or are inefficient in solving the problem. |
| 2-Content | Construct a solution that is clear and well organized, contains content that is accurate, appropriate to the audience and purpose, and is complete. Provide a solution that contains no errors of spelling, grammar, or style. | Construct a solution in which some components are unclear, poorly organized, inconsistent, or incomplete. Misjudge the needs of the audience. Have some errors in spelling, grammar, or style, but the errors do not detract from comprehension. | Construct a solution that is unclear, incomplete, or poorly organized, contains some inaccurate or inappropriate content; and contains many errors of spelling, grammar, or style. Do not solve the problem. |
| 3-Format and Layout | Format and arrange all elements to communicate information and ideas, clarify function, illustrate relationships, and indicate relative importance. | Apply appropriate format and layout features to some elements, but not others. Overuse features, causing minor distraction. | Apply format and layout that does not communicate information or ideas clearly. Do not use format and layout features to clarify function, illustrate relationships, or indicate relative importance. Use available features excessively, causing distraction. |
| 4-Process | Use an organized approach that integrates planning, development, self-assessment, revision, and reflection. | Demonstrate an organized approach in some areas, but not others; or, use an insufficient process of organization throughout. | Do not use an organized approach to solve the problem. |

# Outcomes-Based Assessments

Apply a combination of the **1A** skills.

## GO! Think | Project **1G** Exploring Copyright Laws

Use the skills you practiced in this chapter to locate information on copyright laws and the appropriate use of copyrighted information for educational purposes. The major focus of legislation in this area includes findings on Fair Use.

### Project Files

For Project 1G, you will save your files as:

Lastname_Firstname_1G_Copyright
Lastname_Firstname_1G_Fair_Use

Conduct a search to locate the Web site of the government organization that oversees copyright law and a Web site of an educational institution that pertains to Fair Use. Explore these Web sites to locate information on copyright and Fair Use. Save the government Web page as **Lastname_Firstname_1G_Copyright** Save the educational institution Web page as **Lastname_Firstname_1G_Fair_Use** Print each Web page and submit the documents as directed.

 **You have completed Project 1G** —————————————

# Glossary

**Command bar**  The toolbar located immediately above the right side of the browser window that can provide quick access to commands such as Home, Page, Safety, and Tools.

**Domain name**  The part of a text-based URL that identifies the company or organization that owns the Web site.

**Downloading**  To request a copy of a file or program from a remote server, such as a Web server, and then to save it on your local system or storage device.

**Favorites bar**  The toolbar located immediately above the left side of the browser window that provides quick access to favorite Web sites.

**Favorites Center**  An Internet Explorer feature that enables you to view the Favorites, Feeds, and History lists.

**File Transfer Protocol (FTP)**  A protocol that enables individuals to copy files from one computer to another on a network.

**Frames**  The method used to divide a Web page into separate panes that appear to be one complete Web page. Navigation is controlled by one of the panes while viewing several different pages of content displayed within a single browser window.

**FTP**  *See* File Transfer Protocol.

**History**  An Internet Explorer feature that tracks recently visited Web pages and sites.

**Home page**  The Web page that displays every time you start Internet Explorer—it can be any Web page.

**Hyperlinks**  Text, buttons, pictures, or other objects displayed on Web pages that, when clicked, access other Web pages or display other sections of the active page.

**Internet Explorer 8**  A Microsoft software program that enables you to view the contents of the World Wide Web.

**Internet Service Provider (ISP)**  A company that provides an Internet connection through a regular telephone line, a special high-speed telephone line, or a cable.

**Link Select pointer**  The mouse pointer view that displays as a pointing hand when you point to an item that links to another Web page.

**MHTML**  A format used to save Web pages into a single archive, including all the page elements such as text and graphics.

**Path**  The sequential description of the storage location of the HTML documents and files making up the Web page and stored in the hierarchy of directories and folders on the Web server.

**Portal**  Home pages that contain links to frequently visited sites, up-to-the-minute news, weather reports, maps, and directories.

**Protocol**  A set of rules for transferring data over the Internet.

**Public domain**  Works that are created with the intention of letting anyone use them for any reason; also a work becomes public domain when the copyright has expired.

**ScreenTip**  A small note that displays information about a screen element and is activated by pointing to a button or other screen object.

**Search engine**  A program that searches for keywords in files and documents or other Web sites found on the Internet.

**Sponsored link**  A site that pays to be displayed with results at a search engine site.

**Tabs**  A browser feature that enables you to have multiple Web pages open at the same time without having to open multiple browsers.

**Top-level domain (TLD)**  The highest level of the Domain Name System expressed as the last part of the domain name and represented by a period followed by three or four letters.

**Uniform Resource Locator (URL)**  The unique address used to locate a Web page or Web site.

**Web browser**  Software that enables you to use the World Wide Web and navigate from page to page and site to site.

**Web page**  A document on the World Wide Web that displays as a screen with associated links, frames, pictures, and other features of interest.

**Web site**  A group of related Web pages published to a specific location on the World Wide Web.